# THE UNRULY QUEEN

ALSO BY FLORA FRASER

*Emma, Lady Hamilton*

FLORA FRASER

# THE UNRULY
# QUEEN

*The Life of Queen Caroline*

UNIVERSITY OF CALIFORNIA PRESS
Berkeley · Los Angeles

University of California Press
Berkeley and Los Angeles, California

First Paperback Printing 1997
Published by arrangement with Alfred A. Knopf, Inc.

Library of Congress Cataloging-in-Publication Data

Fraser, Flora.
    The unruly queen : the life of Queen Caroline / Flora Fraser.
      p.  cm.
    Originally published: New York : Knopf, 1996.
    Includes bibliographical references and index.
    ISBN 0-520-21275-4 (pbk. : alk. paper)
    1. Caroline, Queen, consort of George IV, King of Great Britain,
1768–1821.  2. Great Britain—History—George IV, 1820–1830.
3. Queens—Great Britain—Biography.  I. Title.
DA538.A2F73  1997
941.07′4′092—dc21
[B]                                      97-11950
                                        CIP

Manufactured in the United States of America
1   2   3   4   5   6   7   8   9

The paper used in this publication meets the minimum requirements
of American National Standard for Information Sciences—
Permanence of Paper for Printed Library Materials,
ANSI Z39.48-1984. ∞

FOR STELLA ANTONIA ELIZABETH

# CONTENTS

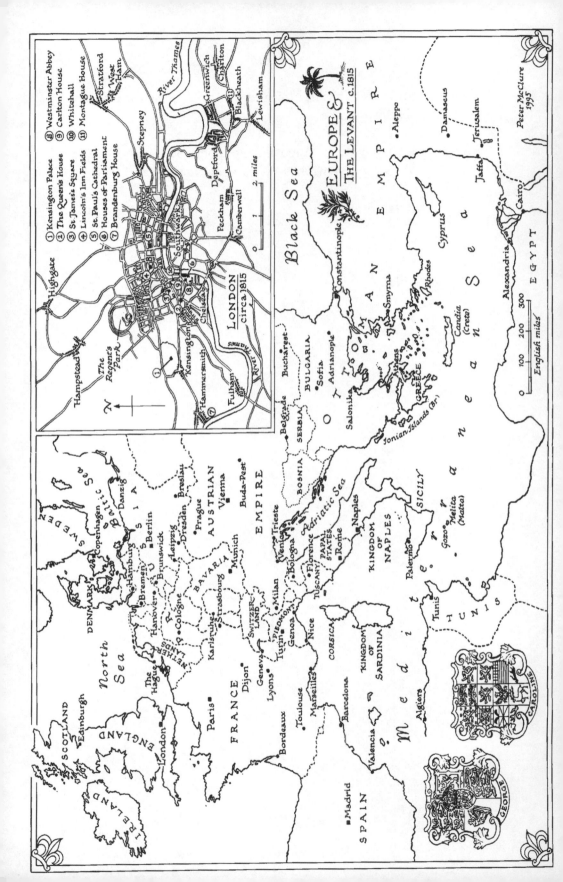

EUROPE & THE LEVANT c.1815

Peter McClure 1995

### LONDON circa 1815

① Kensington Palace
② The Queen's House
③ St James's Square
④ Lincoln's Inn Fields
⑤ St Paul's Cathedral
⑥ Houses of Parliament
⑦ Brandenburg House
⑧ Westminster Abbey
⑨ Carlton House
⑩ Whitehall
⑪ Montague House

*River Thames*

Hampstead · Highgate · Stepney · Stratford · West Ham · Greenwich · Charlton · Blackheath · Lewisham · Deptford · Peckham · Camberwell · Southwark · Chelsea · Kensington · Hammersmith · Fulham · The Regent's Park

0   1   2 miles

*North Sea*   *Baltic Sea*

IRELAND · SCOTLAND · Edinburgh · ENGLAND · London · SWEDEN · DENMARK · Copenhagen · Danzig · PRUSSIA · Hamburg · Bremen · Berlin · Breslau · Hanover · Brunswick · Leipzig · Dresden · Prague · Cologne · NETHERLANDS · The Hague · Karlsruhe · Strasbourg · Munich · BAVARIA · AUSTRIAN EMPIRE · Vienna · Buda-Pest

FRANCE · Paris · Dijon · SWITZERLAND · Geneva · Lyons · PIEDMONT · Turin · Milan · Genoa · Nice · Bordeaux · Toulouse · Marseilles · Barcelona · Valencia · SPAIN · Madrid

CORSICA · KINGDOM OF SARDINIA · TUSCANY · Florence · Bologna · PAPAL STATES · Rome · Venice · Trieste · *Adriatic Sea* · KINGDOM OF NAPLES · Naples · Palermo · SICILY · Gozo · Melita (Malta) · TUNIS · Tunis · Algiers

*Mediterranean Sea*

*Black Sea* · Bucharest · Belgrade · SERBIA · BOSNIA · BULGARIA · Sofia · Adrianople · Salonika · GREECE · Athens · Ionian Islands (Br.) · OTTOMAN EMPIRE · Constantinople · Smyrna · Rhodes · Candia (Crete) · Cyprus · Aleppo · Damascus · Jerusalem · Jaffa · Alexandria · Cairo · EGYPT

0   100   200   300
English miles

GEORGE · CAROLINE

# ILLUSTRATIONS

## MAPS

Europe and the Levant *c.* 1815, with London *c.* 1815 inset
(page x, opposite)
The principal journeys of Queen Caroline, 1794–1820
(page xvi)

## SECTION ONE

1. Philip Jean, *Caroline [of Brunswick], Princess of Wales*. Water-colour on ivory, miniature. Royal Collection.
2. R. Houston after Sir Joshua Reynolds, *Augusta, Duchess of Brunswick*. Mezzotint. British Museum.
3. Pompeo Batoni, *Charles William Ferdinand, Duke of Brunswick*. Oil on canvas. Herzog Anton-Ulrich Museum, Brunswick.
4. John Hoppner, *George IV as Prince of Wales*. Oil on canvas. Wallace Collection.
5. After Richard Cosway, *Portrait of Mrs Fitzherbert*. Cameo. Usher Gallery, Lincoln.
6. British School, *Caroline, Princess of Wales*. Mezzotint. Museum of London.
7. After John Russell, *Queen Caroline and Princess Charlotte*. Stipple. British Museum.
8. Watson after Gardner, *Frances, Countess of Jersey*. Mezzotint. British Museum.

PHOTOGRAPHIC CREDITS

1, 27, Royal Collection © Her Majesty the Queen; 2, 7, 8, 10, British Museum; 3, Herzog Anton-Ulrich Museum; 4, 9, Wallace Collection; 12, 20, 21, National Portrait Gallery; 6, Museum of London; 11, Greenwich Local History Library; 13, Pitkin Pictorial, by kind permission of the Dean and Chapter, St George's Chapel, Windsor; 14, 15, 16, 17, 18, 22, Andrew Edmunds; 5, 19, 23, 25, Bridgeman Art Library; 24, 26, Mansell Collection.

# THE FAMILY OF GEORGE IV

```
Georges I  =  Sophia Dorothea
1660–1727      of Zell
               1666–1726
                    |
         George II  =  Caroline
         1683–1760     of Ansbach
                       1683–1737
                            |
                       and other issue
```

```
Augusta          =  Frederick Lewis
of Saxe-Gotha       Prince of Wales
1719–1772           1707–1751
```

```
Charles William Ferdinand  =  Augusta
Duke of Brunswick             1737–1813
1735–1806
```

```
George III  =  Charlotte Sophia
1738–1820      of Mecklenburg-Strelitz
               1744–1818
```

```
Henry Frederick  =  Lady Anne Horton
Duke of Cumberland
1745–1790
```

```
William Henry
Duke of Gloucester
1743–1805
```

```
Caroline Matilda  =  Christian VII
1751–1775            of Denmark
                     1749–1808

and other issue
```

```
Caroline  =  George IV          Frederick          William IV          Edward  =  Mary Louisa      Augusta      Elizabeth          Ernest              Augustus          Adolphus          Mary  =  William          Sophia      Amelia
1768–1821    1762–1830          Duke of York       1765–1837          Duke of    Victoria         1768–1840    Landgravine        Duke of             Duke of Sussex    Duke of Cambridge  1776–1857    Frederick        1777–1848   1783–181
                                1763–1827          Charlotte          Kent       of Saxe-Coburg-                of Hesse-          Cumberland          1773–1843         1774–1850                   Duke of
and                                                Queen of           1767–1820   Saalfeld                      Homburg            King of                                                           Gloucester
other                                              Wurtemberg                                                  1770–1840          Hanover                                                           1776–1834
issue                                              1766–1828                      Queen                                            1771–1851
(see                                                                              Victoria
separate                                                                          1818–1901
table)
```

```
Charlotte  =  Leopold of Saxe-Coburg-Saalfeld
1796–1817     later King of the Belgians
              1790–1865
```

# THE FAMILY OF QUEEN CAROLINE

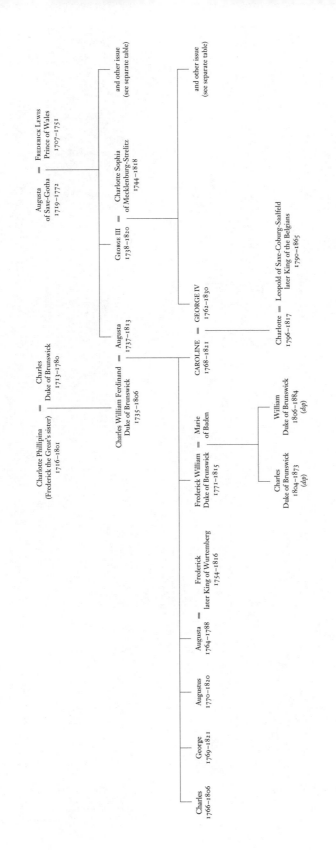

Charlotte Phillipina
(Frederick the Great's sister)
1716–1801
=
Charles
Duke of Brunswick
1713–1780

Augusta
of Saxe-Gotha
1719–1772
=
FREDERICK LEWIS
Prince of Wales
1707–1751

and other issue
(see separate table)

Charles William Ferdinand
Duke of Brunswick
1735–1806
=
Augusta
1737–1813

GEORGE III
1738–1820
=
Charlotte Sophia
of Mecklenburg-Strelitz
1744–1818

and other issue
(see separate table)

Charles
1766–1806

George
1769–1821

Augustus
1770–1820

Augusta
1764–1788
=
Frederick
later King of Wurtemberg
1754–1816

Frederick William
Duke of Brunswick
1771–1815
=
Marie
of Baden

CAROLINE
1768–1821
=
GEORGE IV
1762–1830

Charles
Duke of Brunswick
1804–1873
(dsp)

William
Duke of Brunswick
1806–1884
(dsp)

Charlotte
1796–1817
=
Leopold of Saxe-Coburg-Saalfeld
later King of the Belgians
1790–1865

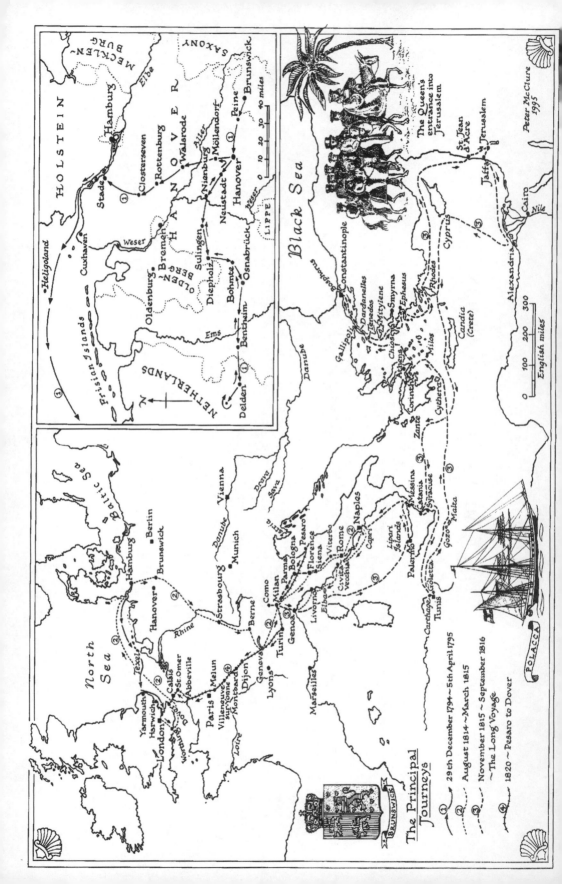

**The Principal Journeys**

① 29th December 1794 ~ 5th April 1795
② August 1814 ~ March 1815
③ November 1815 ~ September 1816 ~ The Long Voyage
④ 1820 ~ Pesaro to Dover

Peter McClure
1995

*Inset map (Hanover region):*

HOLSTEIN · MECKLEN~BURG · SAXONY · HANOVER · OLDEN~BERG · LIPPE · NETHERLANDS

Heligoland · Frisian Islands · Cuxhaven · Hamburg · Stade · Closterseven · Rottenburg · Walsrode · Nienburg · Möllendorf · Neustadt · Hanover · Peine · Brunswick · Weser · Bremen · Oldenburg · Sulingen · Diepholz · Bohmte · Osnabrück · Bentheim · Delden · Ems · Weser · Aller · Elbe

0 10 20 30 40 miles

N

*Main map:*

North Sea · Baltic Sea · Berlin · Brunswick · Hamburg · Hanover · Texel · Yarmouth · Harwich · Worthing · London · Dover · Calais · St Omer · Abbeville · Paris · Melun · Villeneuve~sur~Yonne · Montbard · Dijon · Geneva · Berne · Lyons · Marseilles · Strasbourg · Munich · Vienna · Rhine · Loire · Drava · Sava · Danube · Turin · Genoa · Como · Milan · Parma · Bologna · Pesaro · Florence · Siena · Livorno · Elba · Civita vecchia · Viterbo · Rome · Naples · Capri · Lipari Islands · Palermo · Messina · Catania · Syracuse · Carthage · Goletta · Tunis · Gozo · Malta

Black Sea · Constantinople · Bosphorus · Gallipoli · Dardanelles · Tenedos · Mitylene · Chios · Smyrna · Ephesus · Samos · Corinth · Milos · Zante · Cythera · Candia (Crete) · Rhodes · Cyprus · Alexandria · Nile · Cairo · Jaffa · St Jean d'Acre · Jerusalem

The Queen's entrance into Jerusalem

0 100 200 300
English miles

POLACCA

BRUNSWICK

# PREFACE

I wish to thank Her Majesty the Queen for graciously permitting me to make full use of the records in the Royal Archives, on which this biography is based. I would also like to thank Mr Oliver Everett, Librarian and Assistant Keeper of the Archives, and Lady de Bellaigue, Registrar of the Royal Archives, for their generous help and advice since October 1988, when I first ventured into the Round Tower at Windsor Castle, where the Archives are housed. The papers relating to Queen Caroline are multitudinous and include both defence and Crown lawyers' documents concerning the Queen's 'trial' in the House of Lords in 1820. I am consequently very grateful to all the staff of the Royal Archives, including Miss Pamela Clark, Miss Allison Derrett, Miss Maud Eburne, Mrs Jill Kelsey and Mrs Pat West, for their expert guidance and unstinting patience while I ferreted among the crammed boxes of papers in their care.

The Queen Caroline papers, unlike other collections of manuscripts in the Archives, are not catalogued in detail. A fascinating hotchpotch, the documents include letters in French, depositions in Italian and Austrian police reports. I have translated into English all documents which I have quoted. I have moreover modernized the capitalization, the spelling and, occasionally, the punctuation in these extracts, a policy which I have followed with quotations from other archival sources. I have not updated sterling figures. The value of the pound halved over the lifetime of Queen Caroline and of course has continued to fall. Until the last decade of the eighteenth century the pound was worth fifty times its present day value. During the war years 1793–1815 it decreased in value to twenty-five times today's pound, recovering to thirty times by 1820.

Most of the later correspondence of King George III and the correspondence of King George IV has been published, edited in masterly style by the late Professor Arthur Aspinall. I have made extensive use of these invaluable volumes. I am also indebted to Mr Christopher Hibbert's two-volume life of King George IV, which draws on the Queen Caroline papers. I would also like to thank Mr Martin Clayton of the Print Room, Royal Library, for his iconographical advice. Although the Royal Archives have been the primary archival source for this biography, I have consulted numerous other manuscript collections, private and public, elsewhere in the United Kingdom and abroad. I am most grateful accordingly to the Hon. Jane Dormer for permission to study and quote from the journals of Lady Elizabeth Foster, Duchess of Devonshire. I wish to thank the Duke of Hamilton for letting me consult the papers of Lady Anne Hamilton, lady-in-waiting to Queen Caroline. I am also grateful to the Duke of Argyll for permission to study the papers of another of the Queen's ladies, Lady Charlotte Bury. Miss Lavinia Davies kindly gave me access to the papers of Henry Brougham in her possession. I wish to record my thanks to Mr Brian Horsfield for allowing me to study and quote from the family papers in his possession. I am also grateful to Mr R. S. S. Hownam-Meek for showing me Queen Caroline's sketch-book. I am grateful too to the Directors of Coutts and Co. for permission to consult and quote from the archives of the bank, and I wish to thank additionally the Trustees of Sir John Soane's Museum Library and Archives for permission to study the documents relating to the preparations in the House of Lords for Queen Caroline's 'trial'.

I have consulted the Lord Great Chamberlain's Records in the House of Lords Record Office and manuscripts relating to King George IV's coronation in the Muniments Room, Westminster Abbey. The National Portrait Gallery Registry and the Gallery's Heinz Archive and Library have interesting material about Sir George Hayter's painting, *The Queen's Trial*, and other iconographical matters. Mr Richard Walker's catalogue of Regency portraits in the National Portrait Gallery was of outstanding value. I have also consulted the Brougham manuscripts in the Manuscripts and Rare Books Room, University College Library, London, and the manuscripts of the first Earl of Minto in the Department of Manuscripts, National

Library of Scotland. The Department of Manuscripts, British Library, and the Public Record Office, Kew, have been rich sources of additional manuscripts. Lieutenant-Colonel Harold E. Scott has kindly given me permission to quote from copies of the papers of the first Lord Eldon held in the Royal Archives. Mr Anthony Gell has likewise permitted me to quote from copies of Queen Caroline's letters to Sir William Gell, also in the Royal Archives. I have made use too of the Hyett of Painswick papers in the Gloucestershire Record Office.

Venturing abroad, I have consulted in Milan the Archivio di Stato, where papers exist relating to Queen Caroline's residence in Lombardy when she was Princess of Wales. I have also studied and quoted from manuscripts in the Archivio Storico di Commune, Como, and in the Archivio di Commune, Pesaro. I am most grateful to Prince Ernst August of Hanover for permission to consult the papers of the Brunswick-Wolfenbüttel ducal family lodged in the Niedersachsisches Staatsarchiv in Wolfenbüttel.

For their help in locating papers and answering my queries, I would like to thank all the archivists and staffs of the above institutions, especially Mrs Barbara Peters and Miss Tracey Earl, Coutts and Co.; Miss Susan Palmer, Archivist, Sir John Soane's Museum Library; Mr Colin Johnston, Curatorial Assistant, Register House, Scottish Records Office; Dr Anthony R. Smith of the Royal Commission on Historical Manuscripts; Dr Tony Trowles, Assistant Librarian of the Westminster Abbey Muniments; Mr Kai Kin Yung, Registrar of the National Portrait Gallery; Dr Frances Harris, Department of Manuscripts, British Library.

The 'Queen Caroline affair' of 1820 generated a mass of political satire, pamphlets, fairings and even printed handkerchiefs. My guide throughout has been the British Museum *Catalogue of Personal and Political Satires*. I am grateful to Mr. Michael Codron for allowing me to study his unique collection of Carolingiana; to Mr Andrew Edmunds, printseller, for showing me his stock; to Mr John May for an illuminating discussion about commemorative china; to Mrs Edwina Ehrman of the Museum of London; to the directors of the Mansell Collection for kindly lending me a rare book of caricatures for study purposes; and to Miss Miranda Dewar and her colleagues at the

Bridgeman Art Library for their patience with my queries. I would also like to thank Mr Robert Powell-Jones, the Hon. Mrs Henry Keswick, Mr Edward Fitzgerald and Mr Andrew Roberts for gifts which form the nucleus of my own collection of Carolingiana.

For his help with questions of parliamentary procedure I am most grateful to Mr David L. Jones, Librarian of the House of Lords, to whom I was introduced by my grandfather Frank Longford. For their help with problems of canon law I wish to thank His Honour Judge Bursell, QC; the Bishop of Chichester, the Right Reverend Eric Kemp; the late Monsignor Francis Bartlett; Monsignor Ralph Brown; Father Huw Chiplin and Canon Vincent Strudwick. For translation from German I am grateful to Mr Franz Calice. For advice on matters of German and specifically Hanoverian history I am most grateful to Professor Ernst Grefe of Frankfurt University, and also to Mr Giles MacDonogh. I would like to thank M. Jean-Marc Droulers and Mrs Jean Salvadore of the Grand Hotel Villa d'Este, Como, for their kindness and hospitality. I am also grateful to Signorina Roberta Martufi, architectural historian, and Signor Celio Francioni, architect of Pesaro, for guiding me round Queen Caroline's former homes there.

In the course of researching and writing this biography, I have been advised and encouraged by a great many people. I would like to record my gratitude to all of them, and I only hope that any I do not name will forgive the oversight: Dr Tanya Alfillé, Mr Christopher Bower-bank, Miss Edith Clay, Sir Geoffrey de Bellaigue, M. Guy de Selliers, His Honour Lord Dunboyne, Mr Julian Fellowes, the Hon. Mrs Virginia Fraser and the late Master of Lovat, Mr Christopher Golden, the late Lord Goodman, Miss Emma Hart, Miss Chrysta G. Hogg, Mrs Kim Jones, Miss Ann Joussiffe, Miss Henrietta Koenig, Mrs Julie Lynn-Evans, Miss Janet Maclennan, Mr Michael Nash, Mrs Hazel Orme, Dr Margaret O'Sullivan, Mr Stephen Patterson, Mr Harold Pinter, Mr Francis Russell, Miss Judy Slinn, Mrs Claire Tomalin, Professor J. A. H. Wass, Lord Weidenfeld, Mr John Wells, Mr A. N. Wilson and Mrs Susan Wood.

I am indebted to Mr Christopher Hibbert, Dr Rana Kabbani, Mr John Boxall and Mrs Penelope Hughes-Hallett for reading the manuscript at different stages and offering valuable suggestions.

I am especially grateful to my former agent Miss Anne McDermid of Curtis Brown, who over many years sustained, advised and listened to me. Her successor Mr Jonathan Lloyd has responded energetically to my continuing demands. As always, Mrs Leonora Clarke has typed my successive drafts with swiftness and imagination, despite their haphazard arrival. Mr Peter McClure's cartographical skills likewise triumphed. I am grateful to Mr Douglas Matthews, who compiled the index with his usual thoroughness.

I would like to thank Mr Robert Gottlieb of Alfred A. Knopf, for proposing in 1986 that I write the life of Queen Caroline, and for his encouragement and supervision of the enterprise ever since. I am also grateful to Mr Sonny Mehta of Knopf for his unfailing support. Bob Gottlieb has been joined in his editing by a most distinguished team. Mr Roland Philipps and Miss Tanya Stobbs of Macmillan inherited the manuscript from Miss Linden Lawson and the late Mr Christopher Falkus of Weidenfeld & Nicolson. I am grateful to Mr Jon Riley for helping to bring this unruly project to an ordered conclusion. The *capo dei capi*, however, has been Mr Peter James, who has for the past two years by the kindness of Macmillan applied his fertile mind to honing this biography. Our conferences have been at once comradely and an education.

I am in addition grateful for the steadfast support of my publisher, the Hon. David Macmillan. His father and mine were friends and fellow MPs for over thirty years, and I hope my friendship and professional association with David will last as long.

To my mother Antonia Fraser and my grandmother Elizabeth Longford, who read the book in an early form, I am grateful for historical and literary advice. My cousin William Stirling accelerated publication by his vigilant assistance with the references. Throughout her eight years, my daughter Stella has been hemmed in by a circumvallation of Carolingian books and papers. Its dismantlement now leaves her free to discover that Caroline was delightful as well as distracting.

FLORA FRASER
London
*July 1995*

# CORONATION DAY

## 19 July 1821

*'Let me pass; I am your Queen'*

*At length the day came when the heads of the nation*
*Assembled to see George the Fourth's Coronation,*
*When the Queen and her suite to the Abbey repair'd*
*For surely in justice she should have been there.*
*But, how shall I tell it, a footlicker base*
*Did there shut the door in his mistress's face:*
*She said not one word, tho' her proud heart it bled,*
*And from that same hour she ne'er held up her head.*

(From James Catnach, *An Attempt to Exhibit the*
*Leading Events in the Queen's Life in Cuts and Verse*,
VIII, 1821)[1]

F ROM THE WARREN of slum dwellings around Tothill Street to the wharves and alehouses on the river, east of Bridge Street up Parliament Street and Whitehall as far as Charing Cross, the roads converging on the great palace and abbey of Westminster were packed at first light on Thursday, 19 July 1821. As more people struggled over Westminster Bridge or gathered in St James's Park, the congestion increased. The order of the day's ceremonial had already been published. The coronation procession would assemble in Westminster Hall that morning at ten o'clock and depart at eleven along the 'Route', a canopied wooden platform.

Under the watchful eye of Lord Edward Somerset and his staff, officers of the Royal Horse Guards and the Life Guards were already in position, facing each other across the width of the platform. Raised some 3 feet from the ground, 25 feet wide and 1500 feet in length, the Route snaked from the north door of the arched Hall round the gardens and churchyard of St Margaret's Church – where trees obstructing its progress had been cut down and stands raised all around – to the great west door of the Abbey.[2]

Among the 900-odd persons bidden to assemble in the Hall (which forms part of the Palace of Westminster) before processing to the Abbey were all the lords spiritual and temporal with attendants, the Honourable Band of Gentlemen Pensioners, and those Privy Councillors who were not peers. The 'habiliments' of the latter consisted of doublet, trunks and mantle of blue satin edged with gold. Meanwhile, the Duke of St Albans was kitted out as the Hereditary Grand Falconer of England, complete with falconer's glove.[3] 'The dresses of the Pursuivants, Gentlemen Pensioners, the attendants of the Lords spiritual ... were formed after the model of the earliest times,' observed the *Annual Register*'s correspondent, who failed to do justice to the rich mixture of Van Dyck, Henri IV and medieval apparel which the new King had conceived to be appropriate to the solemnity of the occasion. 'Splendid and in some instances grotesque' was the correspondent's opinion of the different costumes.[4] William Webb, the royal robemaker, submitted a bill for £2044 4s 0d for dressing members and officers of orders of chivalry, kings of arms and heralds alone.[5] A royal herbwoman, Miss Fellowes, and her six maids were more conventionally attired in white satin and gauze. They were to strew flowers before his Majesty's gouty, slippered feet *en route* to the Abbey.[6]

Given that the Queen would not be at the King's side, there had been some confusion whether the peeresses were to accompany their husbands in the procession. 'Lord —— is in alternate paroxysms of delight that he and his wife may walk at it, and of terror at the expense,' Mrs Richard Trench, mother of a future Dean of Westminster, had recorded a few days earlier. She had gleefully informed the worried peer that each costume would cost £800. In the event, peeresses did not walk in the procession, but – with the female members of the royal family, ambassadors and ladies of lesser degree – proceeded along a shorter platform constructed between the House of Lords entrance and Poets' Corner in the Abbey, and thence to their seats.

Mrs Trench described her early rising on the day: 'I opened my eyes on a hairdresser at a quarter before four, was *en route* in a white satin dress gown and court plume at five, and seated in the Hall by six.'[7] As a perquisite, peers were allowed several tickets, the number depending on their rank. The full complement of tickets issued by the Earl Marshal and Lord Great Chamberlain – the former had jurisdiction over the Abbey, the latter over the Hall, where the Banquet would follow the Coronation – was 4000 for the Abbey, 3000 for the Hall.[8]

Those of the middling and industrious classes who had no influence to secure tickets had paid as much as ten guineas for seats in the makeshift booths, stands and galleries which bordered the canopied Route. If the constructions hardly deserved their imposing names – the Royal Sovereign and the Regalia Galleries, the Ladies' Fancy, the Garden Pavilion – they housed nonetheless this early morning a fluttering, writhing mass of respectable humanity. And they proved a considerable source of income for the Dean, Dr Ireland, and the Chapter Clerk, Mr Vincent. The Chapter Clerk rented out the space before his house to two Pimlico builders for the erection of a stand, with the proviso that the view from his drawing-room should not be obscured. He was good enough to allow ladies on the stand access through his house to the privy beyond.[9]

The Dean, for his part, let out to Mr Jeremiah Glanville and Mr Jeffrey Wyatt the whole of the western end of the interior of the Abbey for £300; these two entrepreneurs subsequently sold places on the stands they erected and in the nunneries or upper vaultings west of the choir for £60 a head. They also paid the Dean and Chapter £750 18s to erect scaffolding and stands on the ground between the Jerusalem Chamber and St Margaret's.[10] From here a panoramic view of the procession would be enjoyed, which accounts for the vast sum paid. Others had paid for advantageous places at the windows or on the roofs of the conglomeration of taverns, chop houses and residences which adjoined the precinct.

Mr Henty, an enterprising confectioner, advertised an opportunity to purchase through his premises in Bridge Street 'egress and regress' to numbers 5 and 6 The Terrace, New Palace Yard. Successful applicants would command 'a view of the [King's] Champion's stable'.[11] Custom immemorial dictated that a mounted knight, traditionally one of the Dymoke family, should interrupt the Coronation Banquet by riding into Westminster Hall and challenging anyone to dispute the King's claim to the throne. The horse for this occasion had been hired from Astley's Circus. Mr Henty's clients this morning also had ample opportunity to cheer or hiss public characters as they passed by on their way to the Hall. 'For the Attorney- and Solicitor-General an unmixed hissing of the loudest kind,' reported the lawyer MP Henry Brougham. In the previous year Brougham had pitted his wits on behalf of the Queen of England against the Attorney and the Solicitor and had won a great victory.

Brougham had remarked earlier: 'This town is in a state of general lunacy, beginning most certainly with the illustrious person on the throne.'[12] The King had spent the eve of his Coronation in the Speaker's House behind Westminster Hall, savouring the complicated and expensive arrangements of the day to come. His regalia of sceptre, crown and orb, supplementary to Edward the Confessor's symbols of power, had cost £33,000. Mr Webb, the robemaker, was even now on his way upriver with twenty assistants to help robe the peers and his Majesty. The Lord Mayor and his aldermen, including the Queen's former champion Alderman Wood, were also proceeding upriver from Blackfriars Bridge to take their places in the procession. Meanwhile, the celebrated cook Jean Baptiste Watier was overseeing preparations for the banquet in twenty-three kitchens behind the Hall.[13]

These and other details had been pored over and committed to memory by thousands of King George IV's subjects in an excess of nationalist, royalist pride. It was to be a day to remember, a day on which the arcane dignity of the English Crown, so recently in doubt, would reassert itself. Throughout the nine years of his Regency, and earlier, when his father King George III had exhibited signs of mental incapacity, the then Prince had fretted in anticipation of this day.

In the tumultuous months which followed his accession to the throne in January 1820, as the sacred Coronation billed for that July was postponed, the new King had bombarded his ministers with minutes on trivial points connected with it. Meanwhile, England stood on the brink of revolution. Now that the day of his apotheosis had dawned, he had only one fear. Queen Caroline, his estranged consort, had made known her intention to defy his injunction and attend his Coronation. Further, she had declared that she would be crowned herself, despite a Privy Council ruling that her crowning lay in the sovereign's gift – and it was not a gift he intended to proffer.

The King had taken precautions. Rumours circulated that he had a carriage at the ready to return to Carlton House, his London residence, and that a boat was waiting to take the Queen to the Tower, if she made good her boast. More soberly, no ticket had been issued to the Queen by the Lord Great Chamberlain or Earl Marshal. The Home Secretary Lord Sidmouth had instructed the doorkeepers at the Hall to allow in no one without a valid ticket, while Jackson, the famous pugilist, was commander-in-chief to other practitioners of his art standing in readiness at the various doors to the Palace of Westminster. In addition, four Gold Staff officers had been detailed by the Earl Marshal to 'receive' and turn away the Queen if she should attempt to gain entrance to the Abbey.[14]

The Gold Staffs were assembled in the lobby of the House of Lords awaiting their final orders from the Earl Marshal when, shortly before 6 a.m., 'a shout outside' and sounds of commotion caused them some anxiety. Their forebodings were not misplaced. Soon after five, Queen Caroline had set out for Westminster from her town residence, Cambridge House in Mayfair, determined to attend her husband's Coronation. Her 'walks and calls' in the Abbey and Palace precincts were to give rise to one of the most dramatic incidents in royal history. Three gentlemen – her Chamberlain, Lord Hood, a German officer, Captain Hesse, and her adoptive son, Willy Austin – preceded her in one carriage. The Queen, accompanied by her ladies-in-waiting Lady Anne Hamilton and Lady Hood, occupied the state carriage, a yellow-bodied mulberry with brown facings.

Though he was determined to form no part of her assault on the Abbey, curiosity drew Mr Henry Brougham early to the Queen's house. Arriving half an hour too late, he followed on foot through Green Park down Constitution Hill and found 'she had swept the crowd after her'. Brougham, a dark and nervous figure, followed in the Queen's wake as far as he dared. Most of the account he gave his friend Mr Thomas Creevey MP was hearsay, because he had 'been obliged to leave [the scene] speedily, being recognized and threatened with honours'.[15]

Those who occupied the booths and stands close to the great west door of Westminster Abbey and to Dean's Yard had tantalizing glimpses of what happened next. From the ranks at Storey's Gate the Queen's emergence from St James's Park aroused shouts in her support, and hats and handkerchiefs were waved in token of respect. The carriages deposited the Queen and her suite in Dean's Yard south of the Abbey. With her sharp, sunken features and startlingly black eyebrows, she was immediately recognizable from a hundred caricatures. Her dress was of muslin, with a silver-brocade petticoat. 'She wore a small purple scarf, and had a splendid diamond bandeau on her head, with feathers.'[16] The other ladies were also sumptuously attired, and Lord Hood wore Court dress.

The Queen took Lord Hood's arm, the other two couples formed up behind, and they advanced to the door giving on to the West Cloister. Hood waved a document, but the doorkeeper stood firm. The royal party paused, disconcerted, then advanced to the next door, which gave on to the East Cloister. Meeting with no greater success here, the Queen ordered her carriages to be brought up. The doorkeepers explained, as Brougham put it, that they were not 'at liberty to recognize her or anyone, except as ticket-bearers'. Hood afterwards showed Brougham a ticket 'which they said would pass any one of the party [the Duke of Wellington had, from compassion, sent a ticket the day before] but she refused to go in except as Queen and without a ticket'.[17]

Wrote Brougham: 'She flinched – I verily believe – for the first time in her life; and instead of insisting on admission at the great [west] gate, she drew back on the refusal ... and she was entirely defeated.'[18] It seems, rather, that she had been informed at one of the doors that members of the royal family were to enter the Abbey by the entrance at Poets' Corner, and she now determined so to do herself. After some delay, the carriages reappeared, and the Queen and her suite then drove round the great cathedral towards Poets' Corner at the north-east, following the line of the platform. The cries in her favour from the booths and stands were mostly encouraging, even though their occupants had paid good money to see a different show, which these antics might cancel.

From others, however, who had appeared on the roof of the committee rooms of the House of Commons in grotesque processional dress, came cries of 'Shame!' The Queen's next step was determined on the spur of the moment: she would try to join the procession assembling in Westminster Hall. Accordingly, she descended from her carriage before she reached Poets' Corner. One of the ladies with a seat in the Hall, Miss Elizabeth Robertson, later recounted with relish Caroline's attempt to storm the Hall:

> We had to amuse ourselves the best way we could from six to eight, and Queen Caroline did her best to amuse us. There came a sough to the Hall that the Queen was come down, and that she had got into the Abbey alone. Just as the crowded boxes and galleries were all murmuring about this news, we were electrified by a thundering knock at the Hall door, and a voice from without loudly said 'The Queen – open!' A hundred red pages ran to the door, which the porter opened a little, and from where I sat I got a glimpse of her, leaning on Lord —— [Hood], followed by Lady —— [Hood] and Lady Anne Hamilton, standing behind the door on her own ten toes, with the crossed bayonets of the sentry under her chin.
>
> She was raging and storming and vociferating, 'Let me pass; I am your Queen, I am Queen of Britain.' The Lord High Chamberlain was with the King, but he sent his deputy who, with a voice that made all the Hall ring, cried, 'Do your duty, shut the Hall door,' and immediately the red pages slapped it in her face![19]

Even then the Queen was not discouraged, and she trudged onwards with her party to Poets' Corner, her original objective. Sir Robert Harry Inglis, Gold Staff, recorded in a memorandum, 'I learnt by a shout that the Queen was approaching, an hour at least before she was expected. I ran down through Old Palace Yard and reached Poets' Corner as the Queen was parleying at that gate of the Abbey.' Squeezing between Lady Anne Hamilton and the wall, Inglis managed to get in front of the Queen's party. He then turned and stood in the doorway. 'I found her Majesty, accompanied by Lord Hood, presenting herself for admission ... I said to her, respectfully, I hope,

Madam, it is my duty to inform your Majesty that there is no place for your Majesty in the royal box, or with the royal family. (I forget which.) The Queen replied, I am sorry for it.' After some further conversation, the Queen asked how she could get her carriage. 'I answered that I would give directions that her Majesty's carriage should be brought up as near as possible: and accordingly ... I accompanied her Majesty from Poets' Corner across New Palace Yard to Bridge Street.'[20]

As the carriage retreated with difficulty from Abbey and Hall, the Queen sat stony-faced, with the carriage-hood thrown open. The crowd had turned ugly, impatient now with her 'walks and calls', but she made no response to the repeated cry, 'Go back to Pergami!' Only when she passed through the Horse Guards and the soldiers presented arms did she react. Alarmed by their sudden movement, she cried, 'I am the Queen; you dare not stop me!'[21] But she had been defeated, and not even her exotic lover Baron Pergami could save her from the fate that now awaited her.

CHAPTER ONE

# Princess Caroline

## 1768–1794

*'She will be unhappy for all her life'*

PRINCESS CAROLINE Amelia Elizabeth of Brunswick-Wolfenbüttel was born on 17 May 1768 in the small duchy of Brunswick,
a vassal state of Prussia in northern Germany. The birth of this little
princess, granddaughter to the reigning Duke, was unimportant in
itself. Her grandmother Duchess Charlotte had remarked after the
birth of Caroline's elder sister Augusta in 1765, 'It's only a girl. . . . it
was hardly worth waiting so long, as there are quite enough princesses
in the world, and we are often most useless beings.'[1] But then the
Duchess was a sister to Frederick the Great of Prussia and had high
standards. The birth of a Brunswicker prince, which happened to take
place in England the following year, placated Charlotte, although on
first seeing him she declared that he was quite a little English savage.

However, Princess Caroline's father, Charles William Ferdinand,
was a man of consequence in European affairs. As Hereditary Prince
– this was the German style for an heir apparent – he would inherit
his father's duchy. A flurry of imposing addresses from emperors,
kings and other sovereign princes of Europe duly greeted Princess
Caroline's birth.[2] But Charles was eminent for more than his ducal
pedigree. Indeed, he came from a long line of warriors. 'Nature
destined him for a hero,' wrote his maternal uncle, Frederick the
Great.[3] At Hastenbeck in 1757, during the Seven Years' War, Charles
showed Brunswicker courage in recapturing, sword in hand, a central
battery. In the course of this war, which devastated Europe from 1756
to 1763, the Hereditary Prince was attached to the staff of his paternal
uncle, Duke Ferdinand of Brunswick-Oels, who was given the British
command abroad. After the war's close in 1763 he rejoined the
Prussian service and modelled himself on his distinguished uncle, like

him clothing his slim and elegant figure on all possible occasions in
the Prussian uniform and boots.

Duke Ferdinand was also something of a military hero, as the
victor of Minden in 1759. William Pitt the Elder had Ferdinand in
mind when he wrote in 1760 of 'the most sincere, but unimportant
homage, which my heart pays to the virtues and genius of the
Hereditary Prince. Admiration, and devoted attachment, to the two
great Princes, uncle and nephew, are terms synonymous with zeal for
the common cause of Europe, of which they are the glorious
instrument.'[4]

Charles's mother, Duchess Charlotte, was a tiny woman whose
ethereal looks belied a steely ambition on behalf of her children. She
encouraged her eldest son in his reverence for her brother Frederick.
Like him a dedicated child of the Enlightenment, she had arranged
for Charles a prodigious course of instruction in the humanities under
tutors who included the Abbé Jerusalem, before sending him on a
Grand Tour of Europe with the archaeologist Winckelmann as bear-
leader. The Hereditary Prince more than met her expectations. He
was equally happy at his uncle's palace at Potsdam, near Berlin,
drilling with Frederick at the camp, listening to him play the flute or
discourse on European literature. At home in Brunswick life was
more fractious. His father the Duke had nearly bankrupted the
country through incompetence and prodigality. In the year of Princess
Caroline's birth, the Hereditary Prince was forced to negotiate on
behalf of his unpopular father with the Provincial Diet, or parliament.

Caroline's mother Augusta, Hereditary Princess of Brunswick, was
the elder sister of George III, King of England and Elector of
Hanover. Despite being wholly German by blood, she was a foolish
English patriot in her hostility to all things east of the Rhine. On her
marriage in 1764 she wrote to her brother the King, giving her first
impressions of Germany and recounting 'the odd figures and manners
of these people, as for instance the brother in law of Barg [Berg?]
holds his glass between his legs, and a lady today put her fan while
she dines in the same place.'[5] Time did not alter her opinions, and
twenty-four years later the statesman Mirabeau described her as still
'wholly English, in her tastes, her principles and her manners, to the
point that her almost cynical independence makes, with the etiquette

of the German courts, the most singular contrast that I know'.[6] Her more formal mother-in-law could at least reflect that the English Princess had brought a *dot*, or dowry, of £80,000.[7]

The Duke and Duchess, the Duke's brother Ferdinand, the Hereditary Prince and Princess and their different households all lodged at the Grauer Hof, a sprawling stone palace with wooden wings added piecemeal around a central courtyard. Tree-lined allées at the back led past pavilions and flower gardens down to the River Oker, which ringed the city of Brunswick. Across the Bohlweg, the main street at the front, lay the houses of the wool and silk merchants and the cathedral of St Blasius, which Caroline's Guelph ancestor, Henry the Lion, had founded to mark his 1172 pilgrimage to Jerusalem. Here also stood a military academy, the Collegium Carolinum, which attracted students from all parts of Germany, and from England too. The Hôtel d'Angleterre hosted a weekly club where professors, nobility and burghers met under the presidency of Duke Ferdinand to discuss matters philosophical, literary, intellectual – and Masonic. Brunswick was the centre of German Freemasonry, and Ferdinand a grand master of the Order.

West and south of this prosperous quarter, confined within the loop of the river, lay a hinterland of medieval timbered houses and dark narrow streets, inhabited by more than 20,000 shopkeepers and others. The townspeople and Court mingled at the Fair, a traditionally merry event which twice a year drew merchants from all over northern Germany to buy and sell wares and where the Court stocked up on provisions, coffee and chocolate. 'The coffee is better here than with us,' the Hereditary Princess informed her brother, 'and the chocolate, but the tea is abominable so that I don't hurt my nerves with drinking it.'[8] The Court also attended occasional performances at the opera house and a few prescribed public balls and masquerades. But the Court's straitened finances, as well as distinction of birth, prevented further intercourse with the general public.

At the Grauer Hof, the ducal households dined in each other's apartments by rote, with an array of foreign visitors, ladies and gentlemen and officials of the Court. In Duchess Charlotte's apartments the greatest state was kept, and the better food and wine. Formal conversation in a circle was the rule before and after dinner, which was held around four in the afternoon. At her own table, her daughter-in-law observed the German habit, ladies ranged on one side facing the gentlemen on the other. However, Augusta chose to ignore the finer points of etiquette and would advance patriotically on any English visitor, before he had finished his bow, with hands outstretched. After dinner, she sometimes gave what she dubbed a concert, at which music was performed while the company played cards for hours at a time, or a *casino* (an undress ball followed by a supper).

The Hereditary Princess was a true Hanoverian, with protuberant eyes, loose mouth and long face. In the early years of her marriage she considered herself blessed in her handsome husband. 'There is both confidence and amity between the Prince and me,' she wrote, shortly after her daughter Augusta's birth. 'No two people live better together than we do, and I would go through fire and water for him.'[9]

She continued in this happy frame of mind, despite the Prince's public flirtation with her friends in London while she was pregnant with their son Charles. 'Even when he is grave, it's never with me,' she wrote.[10] She endured the winter months in the Grauer Hof with him at her side. The summer months, however, when the Prince went to camp, were dreary. Augusta was not entertained by the scholars and men of letters – Lessing, the German dramatist, among them – whom the Duchess attracted to Brunswick with positions at Court. The Prince, understanding his wife's reluctance to be left with the 'old people',[11] built her a retreat from the rigours of Court life, a pavilion above the River Oker a mile from Brunswick, and named it Little Richmond, after the fashionable clutch of villas on the banks of the Thames. Princess Caroline, later in life, painted a watercolour of this haven, showing the pavilion and wooded hill, and a herdsman pasturing cows and sheep by the river beneath, with a windmill and the towers and spires of Brunswick in the background.[12]

There was also Antoinettensruh, a pleasant country mansion ringed by beechwoods near Wolfenbüttel, the fine medieval city seven miles from Brunswick and anciently the capital of the Duchy. Here, in the summer after Princess Caroline's birth, the Hereditary Princess took the baby, an English wet-nurse, Mrs Ward, and the two elder children. Augusta amused herself by eating heavy luncheons and dinners, playing cards and gossiping in undress and slippers with her Brunswick ladies.

Three more children were born – George, Augustus and Frederick William (known as William) in 1769, 1770 and 1771. But the pattern of Augusta's days, her dissatisfaction with Court life and her satisfaction with her husband did not alter, nor did her husband's forbearance. The six children in their youth were a source more of anxiety than of pleasure to their parents. When Prince Charles (the eldest boy) was afflicted with cramps at the age of three, his mother wrote: 'It's really frightful to see what he endures . . . I cannot stay in the room when he crimes [screams]. . . .'[13]

When Augusta was called to England in 1771, to the deathbed of her mother the Dowager Princess of Wales, the Hereditary Prince refused to allow the children, some of whom were still convalescing from smallpox, to follow. 'My second daughter [Caroline], who has only begun to emerge from a critical state, might suffer a relapse,' he wrote.[14] When the Hereditary Princess returned the following year, she extended her period of mourning. 'I believe I have at least the satisfaction of enraging their Highnesses by the life I lead, which is *very* retired,' she informed her brother the King.[15] A seventh child, Amelia, was born that year, but not even the ministrations of Mrs Ward could save her. Augusta continued to delight in entertaining English visitors. She wrote of Lord Beauchamp to her brother, 'my younger daughter [Caroline, then four years old] think it's you who's here and she always calls him the King of England'.[16]

The Hereditary Princess had taken some pleasure in 1769 in the misdemeanours of her husband's sister, Elizabeth, Princess of Prussia, as confirming her poor opinion of the German royal houses. Frederick the Great had locked Elizabeth up after she refused to live with 'that stinking man', her husband.[17] But Augusta's pride in her English heritage was dented when her own siblings proved a scandalous lot. Her sister Queen Caroline Matilda of Denmark was sent into exile and her marriage dissolved in 1772. Caroline Matilda had conducted a flagrant affair with the revolutionary Count Johann Francis Struensee, a Minister at the Danish Court. In the same year, their brother William Henry, Duke of Gloucester, revealed that in 1766 he had secretly married Maria, Countess of Waldegrave, who was illegitimate.

This revelation followed the June 1772 Royal Marriages Act, an unpopular measure which the King pushed through Parliament after his youngest brother, the Duke of Cumberland, had married Mrs Anne Horton without notifying him in advance. The new Duchess's father was a well-known reprobate. Still more lamentable, her sister Miss Elizabeth Luttrell, who took up residence with the Cumberlands, was described somewhat unusually as a 'roué', who 'governed the family with a high hand, marshalled the gaming table, gathered round her the men, and led the way in ridiculing the King and Queen'. Worse, she cheated at cards, gave a hairdresser £50 to marry her and was convicted of pickpocketing in Augsburg, for which she was condemned to clean the streets chained to a wheelbarrow. Eventually she brought her strange life to an end by swallowing poison.[18]

In an attempt to avoid further such connections, the Act provided that future marriages of descendants of King George II which had not received the sovereign's consent would be void. Although the Act expressly excluded the issue of princesses who married into foreign families, Augusta highly approved of it, going so far as to treat her children as subject to it. In addition she refused to stand godmother to the Gloucesters' child, Princess Sophia Matilda.

Augusta was more charitable to her sister Caroline Matilda, who was given sanctuary by their brother King George III first at Goerde, then at the moated castle of Celle in his Electorate of Hanover, close to Brunswick. He hoped that 'by mildness, she will be brought back to the amiable character she had before being perverted by a wicked and contemptible Court'.[19] Against the wishes of her husband and his parents, the Hereditary Princess visited her sister at Celle for weeks at a time, leaving her children to her husband's care. The Prince bore his wife's allegiance to her disgraced sister with patience. But he was not so sanguine about her increasing disinclination, even when he was at Brunswick, to appear at Court. Had the Hereditary Princess been a less foolish wife, she might have envisaged the consequences when she turned to religion as a consolation for her lot and as an excuse to live a still more retired life. In a conversation with the writer Massenbach, the Hereditary Prince opined:

> Only private persons can live happily married, because they can choose their mates. Royalty must make marriages of convenience, which seldom result in happiness. Love does not prompt these alliances, and these marriages not only embitter the lives of the parties to them, but all too frequently have a disastrous effect upon the children, who often are unhealthy in mind or body.[20]

(It seems inconceivable that the Prince did not have in mind his own children. Three of his sons were to be found unfit for military service.)

While the Princess turned to religion, the Prince persuaded Mlle Luise von Hertefeld, beautiful and highly educated, to abandon the Berlin Court for Brunswick. The Prince dined with her on a given day in the week and found in her all the qualities the Princess lacked, including a readiness to appear at Court, where she soon occupied an honoured place. The Princess was incensed by what she termed the immoral example her husband was setting his children, though as the eldest of them, Princess Augusta, was only twelve the effect on the children was not as yet apparent. An acrimonious correspondence developed, nevertheless, between their parents in 1777 after the Princess announced her determination to appear no more at Court and to devote herself to God and to her children. 'I hope that by living more retired', she wrote,

> I can attend to the duties which are dear to my heart. I cannot hide from myself that my children need great attention on my part, and that I am responsible for them to God. I know I make you angry by speaking, but in time you would be more angry if I had let weakness keep me silent, when it is a question of my children's well-being. In short, we could avoid a scandal if I lived less in public. The children will see nothing, and will not consort with people who could do them harm. Your sisters' example makes me tremble.[21]

The Hereditary Prince's other sister, although she went under the title of Abbess of Gandersheim, was extremely 'coming'.[22]

The Prince agreed to his wife's wish to pursue a course of religious studies with the Bishop at Fürstenberg. 'You know anyway that complete freedom . . . had always been the basis of my actions in your regard,' he wrote. Then, numbering her phrases, he replied to each of the other points in her letter:

> As long as you wish to live as my wife, it is necessary to live according to your rank, state, and according to received custom. . . . The children belong to us in common, and your responsibility to God does not exceed my own. I do not ask of you complaisance or weakness or silence. I would not know what to do with it. Only a little more calm in your conduct. You would then give a very useful example to my daughters, and save their future husbands much trouble.
>
> Since you are married, I advise you to live as custom dictates. If you execute one day your plan [of separation], you may do as you like. . . . Where I think fit to admit my children, have no fear that they will see anything reprehensible. There is never anyone admitted whose conduct is suspect. You know that as well as I.

He ended by hoping, like her, for the regeneration of her soul, but observed that, as long as she came armed for offence like the Biblical Judith, it seemed in doubt.[23]

It was plainly now an unhappy marriage, and consequently an unhappy home. Princess Caroline, by this time nine years old, later supposedly confided to a lady-in-waiting her recollection of the pain that the situation at home had caused her. Lady Charlotte Campbell, in her *Diary of a Lady in Waiting*, purported to recreate Caroline's German accent:

> Dere were some unlucky tings in our court, which made my position difficult. My fader was most entirely attached to a lady for thirty years, who in fact was his mistress; she was the beautifullest creature, and the cleverest; but, though my fader continued to pay my moder all possible respect, my poor moder could not suffer this attachment; and de consequence was, I did not know what to do between them; when I was civil to the one, I was scolded by the other, and was very tired of being shuttlecock between them.[24]

Later that year, 1777, the Prince meditated joining the Russian service, to escape his wife's complaints and animadversions on his conduct. The Princess told her brother in England that if her husband were to do so, 'I will be left without a sou.' It was hard when, 'as it is, he spends all my money outside the kingdom'[25] – on military manoeuvres and horses. 'My children and ladies complain' of his economy, she wrote.[26] Princess Caroline later described her father as 'a man of inordinate ambition ... [who] was not at all pleased with only reigning over so small a principality as Brunswick. Frederick William II [who succeeded Frederick the Great of Prussia in 1786] was a very weak prince, and my father always determined to have the whole management of Prussia.'[27]

Nothing came of the Prince's plan, and he was still in the Prussian service three years later when his father died, in 1780, and he inherited the dukedom. The new Duke set about the work he had begun as prince, to free the Duchy from debt, and instituted liberal reforms that his father had long contested. The children were growing up. Duchess Augusta later described her elder daughter, Princess Augusta, as 'wanting a husband with all her might' at this time (she was fifteen). The Duchess noted, in explanation, that her daughter had been 'the victim of scenes which she saw here', and had 'a fear of having a similar fate to mine'.[28] The Hereditary Prince of Württemberg offered for her hand, and was accepted. With her departure in this same year, 1780, the Duke and Duchess turned their attention at last to their younger daughter, Princess Caroline, who the Duchess said was very good and biddable – another way of dealing with home discomforts.

The Duke was a stern if loving father, who expected his sons to follow him into the Prussian service, in accordance with the hallowed military traditions of the family. To his profound disappointment, three of the four were to prove themselves physically and mentally unfit for military service, even as junior officers. The eldest, Charles, was indolent in body and passive in intellect, and a spell in Geneva at a military academy was no cure. Augustus, although eager for a military career, was so short-sighted that he had to resign from the Hanoverian army, and George, judged fit for nothing, remained at home under the care of a tutor (or warder, as one observer believed). Only William was to become a soldier of merit. In compensation, and adding to the chagrin of the new Duchess, a former mistress had produced a son, Forstenburg, who was the delight of Duke Charles's life and, as fate would have it, was to become an outstanding soldier.

The two girls were better favoured physically than their brothers, of similar slim build and fair good looks, with curly hair and graceful manners. It was unfortunate in the Duchess's view that, during the visit to Brunswick of her English nephew Prince Frederick in June 1781, Princess Caroline, just turned thirteen, could appear only occasionally. The Duchess dreamt of an alliance between one of her children and a child of her brother, the English King. (King George III, on the other hand, did not favour marriages between first cousins, 'german cousins'.)

Caroline had only recently recovered from a mysterious sickness, whose symptoms included cramps, nervous debility and hysteria. 'These are ills which I have feared all my life without knowing them,' her mother wrote to King George III, who in his twenties had suffered similar disorders. 'These are hysterics, cramps, nerves, which make me despair, and believe she will be unhappy for all her life, by the care one must take. All that excites her arouses the disorder. So for a time she cannot appear [at Court], which gives her pain, and that can do her no harm.' The Duke, from camp, wrote, 'I am very anxious about the health of little Caroline.' He hoped the summer heat was primarily responsible.[29]

The malady lingered on, but by the end of the year Caroline had recovered, and her mother confided to her brother in England that a suitor was in the offing. Although the identity of this suitor has not emerged, Caroline in later life declared that she had had proposals from the Dutch heir apparent the Prince of Orange, Prince George of Hesse-Darmstadt and Queen Charlotte's brother Prince Charles, later Duke of Mecklenburg-Strelitz. Her father wished her to marry the future Prince of Prussia, but she favoured his cousin Prince Louis Ferdinand and many years later pronounced it a love-match.[30] 'I hope that her fate will soon be decided,' the Duchess wrote to King George III in 1781. 'You will be the first to know.'[31] But the planned match foundered.

A young Englishman, Sir John Stanley, who spent a year in Brunswick from 1781 to 1782, wrote down much later his impression of the Court. The Anglophile Duchess invited him to Little Richmond to sail on the river, and he walked often in the *allées* of the palace garden. His recollection of Brunswick was 'one of green and leaves and flowers and birds, as well as of a Court and operas'. His fondest memory was of Princess Caroline, whom he described as 'a beautiful girl of about fourteen ... lively, pretty ... with light and powdered hair hanging in curls on her neck ... with looks animated, and always simply and modestly dressed'. She was present at Court functions 'three or four times a week, but as a star out of my reach'. The Princess made a strong impression on the young Stanley. He wrote, 'I did think and dream of her day and night at Brunswick, and for a year afterwards. . . .'[32]

The Duchess continued to hanker after intermarriage between the House of Brunswick and that of England, and in November 1782 suggested her eldest son Charles as a suitable bridegroom for one of her brother's elder daughters.[33] A month later she dropped a heavy hint about Prince Frederick, later Duke of York, who was still in Germany pursuing military studies. 'If he were a Prince Epouseur, I would suggest him for my Caroline,' she wrote to the King.[34]

The Duchess was indefatigable. The following year she suggested that her daughter might visit England. An unenthusiastic answer from her brother did not shake her. 'I would die content if Caroline was established,' she sighed. 'You warn against the dissipation of London, and you have good reason. And I too have good reason to condemn – a plague on them – the morals of Germany,'[35] She had confided earlier to her brother:

> The Queen [Queen Charlotte of England] is quite right to be difficult about the females admitted to Court. When one has daughters, one cannot be too much on one's guard. In Germany, where all the women are coquettes and their husbands without any delicacy, it is impossible to refuse to receive them. And when one receives one, how can one shut the door on another?[36]

Caroline, as a result of this philosophy, led a sequestered life in the palace, dining apart with her governess, rarely appearing in public, forbidden to dance when she did. Her father later averred, 'She is no fool, but she lacks judgment; she was brought up strictly, and necessarily so.'[37] He referred more to the moral climate of the Court than to any real sin beyond impulsiveness in his daughter. The

Princess Royal of England, who had herself endured a restricted upbringing, later condemned Caroline's parents:

> she is to be pitied for her bad education; indeed her relations are unpardonable for allowing those about her to treat her with such cruel severity. Will you believe it, at thirteen years old she had a governess who would not allow her to go to the window; she was seldom or never permitted to dine at table, or even to come downstairs when there was any company; if she did, her eyes were always full of tears, and her mother, instead of either speaking kindly to her or leaving her alone, always bid her go on crying, for it was only her naughtiness that made her so passionate.[38]

Aged sixteen Caroline so indulged her rebellious nature as to convince one of her father's Guards officers that she was showing 'strong symptoms of insanity': a great ball was given, to which the Duchess would not let her go in spite of her pleadings. The ball had only just begun when a messenger came post-haste to the Duke and Duchess to say that the Princess had been taken seriously ill. The assembly at once broke up and the Duke and Duchess returned without delay to the apartment of their daughter, whom they found in bed screaming. Pressed by her mother to say what was the matter with her, the girl said that it was impossible to conceal the cause of her agony. 'I am in labour,' she declared, 'and entreat you, Madam, to send for an *accoucheur* immediately.' When at length the *accoucheur* arrived the Princess wiped off the livid colouring from her face, and jumped out of bed, saying with a hearty laugh, 'Now, Madam, will you keep me another time from a ball?'[39] She later informed a friend that at night she used to climb out of the window she was forbidden to approach in order to attend the meetings of a society of *illuminés* to which she belonged. The accounts which her governesses kept, and which M. de Feronce, the Minister of State, signed, reveal none of this appetite for mischief. They suggest that Princess Caroline led a blameless schoolroom existence, on 200 thalers a year, while she waited for a bridegroom.[40] The seasons of the year were marked by such items as a Twelfth Night cake, or firewood for the Dutch chimney. The Princess found her friends among the servants of the palace. On one occasion she sent coffee and sugar, and bread and milk, to some guards who were ill. Her grandmother's maid received numerous gifts.[41]

Princess Caroline's education was a curious affair. Although her governesses, and mother, were so watchful and critical of her conduct, she had little formal education, except in the sphere of music. She spent sixteen hours a week with M. Fleischer, her harpsichord master, considerably more time than with any other professors. In consequence, she became an extremely proficient performer and was sometimes allowed to give a 'concert' after dinner – to her mother and father only. The Princess's staple evening occupation appears in the words 'perte au jeu', or lost at cards, which feature regularly in the accounts. Other indulgences are sugared bread, face cream, and Pyrmont and Fribourg water.[42]

Another consequence was that when Countess Eleonore von Münster arrived from Hanover in 1783 to superintend the fifteen-year-old Princess's education, she found that her charge made no effort to spell correctly. Her punctuation was also slapdash at best, wild at worst. (The Duchess chaperoned her daughter at all her lessons, and might have raised a protest. But the Duchess wrote appalling French – and English – herself.) Countess Münster, a gifted poet with a wide circle of literary friends, attempted to redress this negligence over the next six years. Inks, paper and writing books are regular items in the accounts she kept, and M. Boutny came from the august Collegium Carolinum to teach the Princess grammar and history, which she enjoyed. In some respects, Countess Münster made little headway with her pupil. Although the Duke blushed for his daughter, Caroline continued to omit or scatter full stops, capital letters and apostrophes where she wished. Eventually the Princess won her strange vendetta against orthography and acquired a secretary, to whom she dictated.[43]

Caroline's letters, however, are always vivid when read aloud, for the Princess wrote or dictated as impulsively as she spoke. Furthermore, Countess Münster successfully encouraged the novice Caroline in an ardent love affair with literature. She read widely from now on, in French and German – classical literature, Shakespeare, poetry, novels, memoirs, history. Her reading list informs one tempestuous letter which she wrote to M. de Feronce, during a quarrel with Countess Münster:

> This Tisiphone Monster burst into my gryphon's lair, where I was busy with my own affairs. This Westphalian Minotaur in the costume of Goliath complains of revisions of her accounts, she attacks me and has written me letter no. 4 [presumably enclosed]. There she exhales her wrath, which is so violent and not half so fragrant as forget-me-not or jasmine as to pierce the triple envelope. I prudently turned my nose away, and returned her a very moderate reply, no. 5.[44]

The satirical style of this letter, the over-complicated and faintly offensive imagery are characteristically Carolingian, as is the stubborn disdain for the rules of writing. Princess Caroline was in general extremely fond of Eleonore, and remained grateful for her tutelage many years after they had parted ways.

The Duchess was ecstatic when another prospective bridegroom for her daughter appeared in the winter of 1783, in the shape of the Margrave of Baden's second son. 'He has 60,000 florins a year,' she informed her brother, and was, besides, very intelligent. To cap it all, he would very likely inherit the Duchy of Baden in due course, as his elder brother, the Hereditary Prince, had no sons. In December she wrote to the King, 'My daughter is so pretty that I am sure she will please him as a wife.... [I was] so afraid that our style of life would be prejudicial to my children, and that no one would want them. Thank God, all has finished better than I dared hope, and Augusta [Caroline's elder sister] not being at all a coquette, which is a general failing in Germany, has, I think, decided the Margrave of Baden to take my daughter.'

The Duchess asked her brother to tell no one but his wife, Queen Charlotte, of the intended match. 'When there is so much to arrange, the least thing can upset it. If this does not come off, I know of no more husbands for her.'[45] The negotiations continued. 'Caroline's portrait has gone, and we must wait the outcome with patience,' the Duchess wrote in February 1784.[46] There are two portraits of Princess Caroline of approximately this date, in one of which her fair curls are roped with pearls. Even allowing for the flattery of Court painters, both show a remarkably attractive girl, with sharp eyes, a long nose and a pretty mouth.[47]

Mysteriously, this match also foundered. Caroline's sixteenth birthday in May 1784 came and went, then her seventeenth, then her eighteenth, and Countess Münster's schoolroom accounts for her pupil continue undisturbed by nuptial announcements. When Caroline was eighteen, her governess successfully petitioned M. de Feronce for a pianoforte, which the Princess had longed for. Odd items appear in the accounts – for tickets to the comedy or for trinkets suitable for Court appearances. Some of Caroline's teeth were pulled; she was blooded by the Court physician.[48]

Occasionally, visitors to the Court of Brunswick remark on Princess Caroline, generally in flattering terms. Comte Mirabeau, politicking between Berlin and Brunswick, described her in 1786 as 'most amiable, lively, playful, witty and handsome'. He records the Princess interrupting his conversation with her father, who was asking for a definition of time and space. 'Time', observed the Princess, looking round at an elderly lady of the Court, 'is in Madame de Bode's face, and space in her mouth.'[49] Even in a natural history lesson, when she was supposed to answer by rote, she answered her governess's question 'Where is the lion to be found?' with the pert reply, 'In the heart of a Brunswicker.'[50]

Princess Caroline was still unmarried when news reached Brunswick in 1787 that her elder sister Augusta had been cruelly abandoned in St Petersburg by the Hereditary Prince of Württemberg. In a frosty interview with Augusta's father in Berlin, Prince Frederick, who had returned to Germany with their two young sons, attempted to exculpate himself. Princess Augusta had behaved so licentiously, he declared, that he would have had no honour left to him had he condoned her conduct. He had left her in the care of her kinswoman, the Empress Catherine of Russia, who had handsomely promised Augusta her protection.

The Duchess of Brunswick had a different version of the story from Augusta herself, which she reported to her brother the King. 'There is nothing so terrible as a Prince of the Holy Roman Empire,' she wrote.[51] Her daughter Augusta had discovered in St Petersburg that her husband – a profligate, the Princess herself said – was planning to blacken her name for his own nefarious purposes and had engaged an aide-de-camp to press his attentions on her in the night. Augusta had taken the precaution of having her maid sleep in her room, so that the aide, when he burst in, was obliged to retire. Princess Augusta then threw herself on the mercy of the Empress Catherine, who ordered the scheming husband from her service and gave Augusta sanctuary.[52]

Augusta's parents were shocked by their daughter's separation from her husband and children, but they had taken no action when new reports reached Brunswick. The Empress had become disenchanted with Princess Augusta, whom she had formerly made a favourite, and had imprisoned her, it was later suggested, in the remote Castle Lode, near Revel on the Baltic. The Duke of Brunswick asked the Empress for an explanation. None was forthcoming. Augusta's crime remained, like her whereabouts, a mystery. Then in 1789 her father was baldly informed that she was dead, and the Gothic tale of this Brunswick Princess appeared to have reached its end. But all attempts to learn the cause of her death, and to recover her body for burial at Brunswick, met with silence. Some believed that Augusta had escaped her prison and was still living elsewhere in Europe. Subsequent 'sightings' of the Princess encouraged this belief. Augusta's sister Caroline took a ghoulish pleasure till late in life in recounting this tale and declaring that she too believed her sister to be still alive. On one occasion she added that Augusta had recently been seen in a box at the Genoa Opera.

It is puzzling that the Duke of Brunswick did not make stronger representations to the Empress of Russia. But then he was prone to vacillation when confronted by power. The Duchess might have been expected to call on her brother in England to send his envoys to rescue her daughter, but in the winter of 1788 the King succumbed to a nervous excitement which gave way to mania, and for nearly five months he was not well enough to conduct the business of his own country, let alone pursue the interests of another state. The Duchess meanwhile redoubled her guard over her younger daughter Caroline in Brunswick.

While King George III lay ill, no longer able to impose his authority, the Dean and Chapter of Westminster Abbey offered a fervent prayer: 'Restore, we implore Thee, cur beloved sovereign to his family and to his kingdom.'[53] They further begged that 'it shall seem fit to Thine unerring wisdom presently to remove from us this great calamity with which we are afflicted'. No sooner had the King recovered than, across the Channel, King Louis XVI and the French royal family were beset by a very different threat to order. When the people of Paris rose up and stormed the Bastile on 14 July 1789, they liberated more than the few prisoners inside. The caged ambitions of the commons, the Third Estate, took wing, seeking the destruction of the monarchy and two other estates – the nobility and the clergy. The French Revolution, which was to lead to the execution of the King and his Queen, Marie Antoinette, had begun. It was to convulse France, and later the Continent, bringing both thrilling liberty and authoritarian repression.

The Court of Brunswick became congested, as did many of the German courts, when noblemen and clerics followed the lead of the Comte d'Artois, brother of Louis XVI, and fled France. One prelate, the Abbé Baron, spent that winter in Brunswick, and noted how restricted was the freedom of the twenty-one-year-old Caroline. 'She is supervised with the greatest severity, as they claim that she is already aware of what she is missing. She is naively convinced that she would willingly change her lot with that of the daughter of a simple shopkeeper. I doubt if the torches of hymen will illuminate for her. Although always attired with style and elegance, she is never allowed to dance.' After she had seen the first dance begin, Caroline had to seat herself at a whist table, with three old ladies. She was, he noted, 'not tall, but well proportioned, with a striking, richly tinted complexion, and brilliant, lively eyes, suggesting great spirit. Without having a beautiful countenance, she is very pretty.'[54]

For all the Abbé's prognostications, this October the Duchess wrote exultantly to an old friend in England the Duchess of Argyll (who distinguished herself by marrying two dukes and begetting four):

My spirits are up again with the hope of marrying my daughter; she was the only thing that used to hurt me, as example is catching, and also I feared that our manner of life would frighten young men from wishing a nearer connection with us. . . . All my wishes have been for these twenty years that they might turn out well, for I looked on myself as a widow, for the Duke does not care about them, nor do the children love him as a parent; those that are handsome he flatters, which has vexed me, as it cost me much more trouble to keep them in order; and Caroline knew exactly how to humour him, which would have been her ruin if she had remained longer with us.[55]

Unfortunately the Duchess's hopes were dashed once more, and the match in question, with a prince of Hesse-Darmstadt, came to nothing. Furthermore, in 1790, for all the Duchess's plans, Prince Frederick of England, now titled Duke of York, married Caroline's cousin Princess Frederica of Prussia. The Duchess of Brunswick had to content herself with arranging the marriage of her son Prince Charles – Hereditary Prince since 1780 – to Frederica, Princess of Orange. On the new Hereditary Princess's arrival in Brunswick in 1791, Princess Caroline was allowed to dance twice, once with her brother Charles – 'as wide and fat as a barrel of oil', according to the Abbé Baron – and once with the Prince of Orange, the bride's brother (the man who, Caroline later claimed, had courted her). 'One could not be more hemmed about, more watched, more guarded,' wrote the Abbé of Caroline. When her parents were absent, Caroline was not even allowed to dine with her brother George. That may not have been so great a disappointment, as George was 'a complete imbecile', according to the Abbé.[56]

The Abbé declared that Princess Caroline had more spirit than her four brothers put together, but she seemed destined to languish all her days at her parents' Court, playing cards, knotting, netting and embroidering with her ladies. As the Princess approached her twenty-third birthday in May 1791, Countess Münster had signed her accounts for the last time. The Princess's prolonged education was complete, and still no bridegroom was in prospect.

Caroline herself explained her continuing spinsterhood with the observation that her father preferred her to remain in Brunswick rather than marry on the Continent. But she also wrote of having been prevented from marrying the man of her choice, a man whose station was not equal to hers, so perhaps she was not eager to wed another. It is not clear who this suitor was, but a contemporary biographer referred to 'a young officer who was a constant visitor at her father's court . . . a native of Ireland . . . usually denominated "the handsome Irishman".' In one martial engagement, in hussar dress and with a white plume floating from his cap, he was in the thick of the fray. 'Careless of life, and bent on victory, his arm scattered death and destruction around him', and he succeeded in killing the opposing commander and snatching the enemy standard. On his return to Brunswick 'her Serene Highness exhibited a peculiar share of regard and solicitude. . . .'[57]

Caroline, as the daughter of an acclaimed hero, was always susceptible to military men. Miss Mary Frampton, an English diarist, knew a Major Töbingen, who claimed to have been given an amethyst stud or pin by the Princess.[58] And Prince Louis Ferdinand of Prussia, whom Caroline described later as 'the cleverest and first man in the world', was a military man himself.[59] But it was not enough that they be soldiers alone; they had to be handsome. One German warrior prince came strutting oafishly through her father's halls, 'with his great jackboots, his long queue, his clinging spurs, his harlequin habiliments, and his meerschaum pipe'.[60] Caroline refused, in no uncertain terms, his formal offer for her hand.

There were other stories to account for Princess Caroline's unmarried state. Lord St Helens, a British diplomat, spoke of a 'stain' on her character.[61] Mr Robert Huish, another contemporary biographer, emphatically denied that, when she was fifteen, she had become pregnant and had had to retire to the country.

> In her rides and walks, she never saw a rustic, chubby boy, but she immediately stopped and questioned it. . . . It was certainly a very uncommon circumstance for a high-born princess, with the blood of the Guelphs and the Brunswicks flowing in her veins, to take delight in chatting with dirty peasant children, and often to visit the hovels in which the children resided. . . . Calumny followed her to the cottage . . . and in her visits, nothing was discerned but . . . a secret desire to escape from the prying eye of her family and the Court, to enjoy the society of one to whom . . . her affections were engaged.[62]

Queen Charlotte in England was more frank. When her brother, Prince Charles of Mecklenburg-Strelitz, contemplated offering for Caroline, she told him: 'They say that her passions are so strong that the Duke himself said that she was not to be allowed even to go from one room to another without her governess, and that when she dances, this lady is obliged to follow her for the whole of the dance to prevent her making an exhibition of herself by indecent conversations with men.' She added that the Duke and Duchess had forbidden her to speak to anyone except her governess and that 'all her amusements have been forbidden her because of her indecent conduct. . . . There, dear brother, is a woman I do not recommend at all.'[63]

As we have seen, Queen Charlotte's daughter, the Princess Royal, put a gloss sympathetic to Caroline on her enforced chaperonage. But Caroline, all her life, took a childish delight in flouting convention, even if this meant exposing her decidedly lustful nature. No less naively, she probably believed her indelicate speech to be the summit of sophistication. 'Possessing the je ne sais quoi in an eminent degree', in Huish's words,[64] she responded with relish to the attentions of the dashing courtiers around her. In sum, the young Caroline had only flirted, but she behaved impetuously enough to convince Queen Charlotte that she had nymphomaniac tendencies.

The Duke was more than ever an absentee father; even when he was at Brunswick, he was occupied with envoys, delegations and refugees from revolutionary France. Their numbers grew as, following the Revolution, the French expelled all the German bishops and landowners from the Rhineland. In April 1792 France had declared war on Austria. Since the preceding year Austria and Prussia, traditionally enemies, had been in alliance, and under their treaty Prussia was bound to come to its ally's aid. The French, however, were confident that neither army would trouble them. When news came in June that both armies were marshalling east of the Rhine, the confusion in Paris was considerable. The Duke, with that other liberal German prince, his cousin the Duke of Saxe-Weimar, had sympathized with the original intention in 1789 to moderate Louis XVI's inflated powers. Then, as the Fürstenbund, or League of German Princes, contemplated war on France, the French National Assembly begged the Duke of Brunswick to take command of its army. At the same time the Prussian King Frederick Wilhelm II urged him to commit his Brunswick forces to the Fürstenbund army.

The Duke's loyalty to Prussia knew no bounds. Although he distrusted and despised Frederick Wilhelm, his sister's 'stinking' husband, he threw in his lot with the Fürstenbund and crossed the Rhine. At Coblenz on 25 July, he was persuaded by other belligerent princes to issue in his name a manifesto addressed to 'the inhabitants of France'. This began by stating that the Prussian King and his ally, the Emperor of Austria, proposed to enter France:

> to bring the anarchy inside France to an end, to stop the assaults on throne and altar, to re-establish the King's legal authority, restoring to him the security and freedom of which he has been deprived, and to enable him to exercise his legitimate powers.
>
> Any inhabitants of cities, towns or villages who dare take arms against the imperial and royal troops or shoot in open country or from windows, doors and apertures will be dealt summary justice according to the rules of combat, and their houses demolished or burnt.

The manifesto reserved its strongest language and threats for the city of Paris. 'Their imperial and royal Majesties will hold responsible for any suffering the King might undergo all the members of the National Assembly, officials of the *départements*, the district authorities. . . . If there is any violence [inflicted on the royal family] at the Tuileries they will exact a vengeance of a hitherto unmatched severity.'[65] Despite these threats, the people of Paris on 10 August stormed the Tuileries Palace and incarcerated their King in the Temple Prison.

Indeed, the Duke of Brunswick's manifesto served only to unite the disparate French communities against the enemy Prussians and Austrians. After some initial Austrian and Prussian victories, the ferocity of the irregular French troops began to take its toll on the German forces and their commanders, including Brunswick, who had honed their skills in well-drilled formation on the parade ground. After the muddy skirmish of Valmy on 20 September, where Marshal Kellermann's artillery had alarmed Brunswick into withdrawing his troops, the Germans suffered grievous casualties in the confusion of retreat back across the Rhine. The poet Goethe, bivouacking with the Duke of Weimar the night after the battle, both men lying wrapped in their cloaks on a sea of mud, declared to the troops: 'From this place and day begins a new epoch in history, and you can say that you were there.'[66]

Goethe was a true prophet. The day after Valmy the newly elected National Convention met in Paris for the first time and abolished the monarchy, declaring the following day to be the first of the revolutionary calendar, which commenced with the month Vendémaire. Furthermore, the Brunswick manifesto was midwife to the Compulsory Liberty Decree, which the National Convention issued in November 1792. This offered military assistance to all peoples wishing, on the French model, to overthrow their kings and proclaim a republic. 'The French nation', ran this provocative document, 'declares that it will treat as an enemy of the people everyone who, refusing liberty or renouncing it, wishes to keep, recall or negotiate with the prince [or] privileged classes.'[67] The Convention showed the way by executing King Louis XVI two months later.

Meanwhile, another French army had moved into Austria's Belgic provinces, also known as the Austrian Netherlands (The Netherlands proper, or Holland, remained independent). This gave France access to Antwerp and what is now Belgium's Flanders coastline and aroused Britain's fears for its naval supremacy. French warships then violated Dutch neutrality by entering the mouth of the Scheldt. Finally, resenting Prime Minister Pitt's refusal to recognize their republic and his objection to their activities in the Scheldt, the French in February 1793 declared war on Britain, Holland and Spain, while still facing Austrian and Prussian armies in the Rhineland. In this way commenced a struggle for power in Europe which was to rage for twenty-two years, consuming the lives of Caroline's father, her half-brother Forstenburg, her brother William and Prince Louis Ferdinand of Prussia, among countless others.

In September 1793 an English expeditionary force was sent to the Austrian Netherlands at the request of the Prince of Orange and under the command of Frederick, Duke of York, to repel the French. After initial successes, this allied army suffered reverses. York himself proved such an incompetent and unpopular Commander-in-Chief that Pitt had the painful duty of explaining to King George III in October 1794 that his son had to go. The King was not less affronted and ashamed than York himself when the news was broken to him in

Flanders. In a desperate attempt to save face, he announced that he
was prepared to cede his place only to his maternal uncle the veteran
Duke of Brunswick. Sir Brooke Boothby and William Eliot, experienced diplomats, were dispatched to Brunswick to beg the Duke to
take up arms for England. (He had sent troops to fight on Britain's
side in the American War of Independence of 1776–83.) The Duke
enraged the envoys by the caution with which he responded to their
entreaties. 'He seemed struggling between an inclination to accept an
offer which gratified his ambition, and the fear of Prussia – the last
prevailed,' wrote Lord Malmesbury, who arrived subsequently.[68]

But dynastic rather than military interests absorbed the attention
of the Brunswick Court. While the Duke hesitated to commit himself
to England, his daughter Caroline felt no such qualms. William Eliot,
on his arrival at Brunswick in October 1794, found the Court in
commotion and the Duchess in high glee. She said that he must speak
only English to Caroline, for she had been learning it for six weeks,
ever since the King of England had asked her hand in marriage for
his son George, Prince of Wales. As soon as her mother's attention
was diverted, Princess Caroline addressed Eliot in French. 'When do
you think Lord Southampton' – the envoy expected with the formal
proposals and marriage treaty – 'will leave?'[69] With the intoxicating
prospect of freedom before her, her excitement was great – but then
she knew nothing of her future bridegroom's character and tastes.
This knowledge she was to acquire only too soon.

## CHAPTER TWO

# THE BRUNSWICK BRIDE

## 1794–1795

*'Caught by the first impression, led by the first impulse'*

GEORGE, PRINCE OF WALES, born in 1762 and now aged thirty-two, was blessed with a fine intelligence, abundant fair hair, florid good looks – although he was inclined to fat – and great charm of manner. He had, however, fought with disastrous consequences against his father's creed of domestic virtue and economy ever since he had acquired his own establishment – Carlton House in Pall Mall – and income in 1781.

He was a man of artistic vision, who created at Carlton House exquisite interiors, rich in gold and sumptuous textiles, the better to show off the furniture, paintings, ornaments, armour and plate which he had collected – without thought for their expense. In the midst of the gilded showcase, the Prince himself shone. He was as fastidious in his toilet as in his choice of furniture, and the tailors, hairdressers, jewellers and apothecaries of London enjoyed his lavish patronage.

The Prince of Wales's extravagance was hard enough for his father to bear. But he went further. Since 1770 Britain had been governed almost without a break by Tory ministries favoured by the King, and early on the Prince had made his friends among the Whig Opposition whom the King abhorred. (During the eighteenth century all the Hanoverian sovereigns quarrelled with their heirs, so the Opposition party of the day clustered about the Prince of Wales in the hope of future patronage. This mutual attraction between Opposition and heir became known as the reversionary interest.) Chief among the Whig friends of Caroline's future husband were the politicians Mr Charles James Fox and Mr Richard Brinsley Sheridan. With them and a group of Whig ladies including Georgiana, Duchess of Devonshire, her sister Lady Bessborough and the Duchess of Rutland, the Prince indulged himself in a ceaseless round of womanizing, gaming, drinking deep and vituperating his father and his father's Tory ministers. In 1783 the Prince's friends, briefly in power, infuriated the King by proposing a grant to the Prince of £100,000. They were succeeded by William Pitt the Younger, aged only twenty-four, whose first and lengthy Premiership was to be bedevilled by the Prince of Wales. Although nominally a Whig, Pitt had the backing of the King and was supported in the House of Commons by Tories as well as members of his own party. In time, his became a purely Tory administration.

When the Prince was twenty-three, he succumbed to a passion which was to have a lasting effect on his later marriage to the Brunswick Princess. Already prone to infatuations, he fell madly in love with Maria Fitzherbert, a beautiful Catholic six years older than the Prince and twice widowed. Thomas Fitzherbert, Maria's second husband, had died abroad as a result of wounds inflicted in London during the anti-Catholic Gordon Riots in 1780. When Mrs Fitzherbert returned to London in 1783, she became a general favourite. With fair curls and blue eyes, she resembled a lovely shepherdess, and the artist Richard Cosway depicted her in that mode. She became particularly popular among the Prince's Whig friends, who were anyway in favour of repealing the laws which kept Catholics out of public life. In the throes of his grand passion, the Prince made advances. Mrs Fitzherbert, her virtue shored up by her religion, resisted. Flinging himself on his bed, the Prince of Wales stabbed himself, declared himself at death's door and prevailed on four members of his Household to bring Maria to him – she insisted on a chaperone in the person of the Duchess of Devonshire – whereupon he begged her to marry him before he expired. Greatly alarmed, Mrs Fitzherbert consented to have a ring put on her finger, and a document was drawn up.[1]

It was a mockery of a marriage ceremony, but it was an affair with potentially dangerous consequences should it become public. Feeling in the country still ran high against Catholics, and the Prince's liaison would attract little but hostility. As the Catholic, Mrs Fitzherbert would be still more calumniated than the Prince, as well as losing her reputation. The day after the ceremony she left for France, and for a year travelled abroad. The Prince, forbidden by his father to leave the country, pursued her with an emotional correspondence, now promising marriage in earnest. Mrs Fitzherbert gave way at last, returning to London in December 1785.

The Prince of course was aware, more than anyone, of the forbidding provisions of the 1689 Bill of Rights. These provisions, restated in the Act of Settlement of 1700, excluded from the throne not only Catholics – Bonnie Prince Charlie was still alive in Rome in 1785 – but also anyone who 'shall marry a papist'. In the event of such exclusion, the crown would pass to whoever would have inherited it if 'the said person ... marrying as aforesaid were naturally dead'. As if that were not enough, the Royal Marriages Act of 1772 required the Prince to obtain from King George III his prior consent to any marriage.

Fox, on hearing reports that the Prince intended to go through a second 'mock marriage, for it can be no other', advised strongly against his taking:

> The very desperate step (pardon the expression).... Consider the circumstances in which you stand: the King not feeling for you as a father ought; the Duke of York professedly his favourite, and likely to be married to the King's wishes; the nation full of its old prejudices against Catholics, and justly dreading all disputes about succession. In all these circumstances your enemies might take such advantages of any doubt of this nature as I shudder to think of. ...

If the Prince did ascend the throne, and if he meant then to repeal all Acts against his marriage and marry his bride anew, 'it will be said that a woman who has lived with you as your wife without being so is not fit to be Queen of England and thus everything that is done for the sake of her reputation will be used against it ...'. The Prince returned an easy letter: 'believe me, the world will soon be convinced that there not only is not, but never was, any ground for these reports which of late have been so malevolently circulated ...'.[2]

Despite these assurances, on 15 December the Prince of Wales and Mrs Fitzherbert went through a ceremony of marriage, in the drawing-room of her house in Park Street, Mayfair, conducted by an

Anglican clergyman, the Reverend Robert Burt, and in the presence of two witnesses, Maria's uncle Henry Errington and her brother Jack Smythe.

Whether the pair were successfully joined in holy matrimony was a question shrouded in confusion. By Anglican canon law, in the absence of Parliamentary intervention, the marriage was valid. The imperatives of secrecy prevented the publication of banns and its appropriate alternative, the obtaining of a special licence from the Archbishop of Canterbury, which was needed if the ceremony was to be held in a private residence. But this omission rendered the marriage merely irregular: it did not invalidate it.

Anglican canon law, however, must always yield to Act of Parliament. No matter how closely the forms of canon law had been followed in Park Street, Mayfair, that day, King George III had not given his prior consent under the Royal Marriages Act. The marriage was therefore 'null and void' for all purposes, the civil courts being empowered to enforce the will of Parliament within the jurisdiction of the ecclesiastical courts by the issue of a writ of prohibition.[3] Indeed, it was not long before the civil courts upheld the primacy of the 1772 Act.[4]

The Glorious Revolution measures of 1689 and 1700, some thought, faced the Prince with constitutional extinction if he married a Catholic. In fact this anxiety was misplaced, for they did not come into operation if, under the provisions of the Royal Marriages Act, there had been no marriage.

What complicated the issue was that, according to the Catholic Church, there had been a marriage – by virtue simply of the mutual promise, no priest or witnesses being necessary. And fifteen years later Rome was to declare that the Catholic Mrs Fitzherbert was indeed the wife of the Prince of Wales. That the ceremony was valid according to her faith was what persuaded the devout Mrs Fitzherbert to proceed with it, whatever its status in English law. She could thus grant the Prince the conjugal rights he sought, and he could declare it a marriage 'in the eyes of God'[5] – though he knew that he would escape from its practical and constitutional effects thanks to the Act of 1772. So he blithely ignored the warning read from Cranmer's

Prayer Book on that December day in Park Street – that marriage is 'not by any to be enterprised ... unadvisedly, lightly or wantonly, to satisfy men's carnal lusts and appetites'.

The Prince and Mrs Fitzherbert continued to inhabit separate houses, but rumours of a secret marriage soon circulated, its alleged consequences often enough determined by partisan fervour or by ignorance of the competing jurisdictions. James Gillray, the cartoonist, published a satirical picture (there were many others) entitled 'The Morning After Marriage', with the Prince of Wales's feathers featuring prominently, of a couple drowsily emerging from bed. Caroline's mother – the Prince's aunt – wrote to her friend the Duchess of Argyll that she had heard Mrs Fitzherbert was pregnant, 'and that there is to be a clandestine marriage. How can that be with a Roman Catholic? What a piece of work! Overturning the constitution. ...'[6] In London, Lady Jerningham, a Catholic, wrote three months after the ceremony, 'Mrs Fitzherbert is generally believed to have been married to the Prince. But it is a very hazardous proceedings, as there are two Acts of Parliament against the validity of such an Alliance. ... The Prince is very assiduous in attending her in all publick places, but she lives at her own house, and he at his.'[7] However, nobody, except those few in the Park Street drawing-room on 15 December 1785, knew for certain what truth there was in the report.

The Prince admitted the marriage to no one, but refused all invitations which did not include Mrs Fitzherbert. They appeared often at the opera, where she rented a box at a hundred guineas a year, and she bought a house in St James's Square, close to Carlton House. Curiously enough, the King and Queen were quite favourably inclined towards Mrs Fitzherbert, under whose domestic influence the Prince indulged in less wild a style of life. It was even rumoured that the King welcomed reports of his eldest son's marriage, in the belief that public opinion would effectively disbar the Prince from inheriting the throne. It would then fall to the King's favourite son, the Duke of York.

A year after his invalid marriage, the Prince's domestic bliss was blighted by the pressing need to pay debts which had again escalated, this time to a sum of £269,878 6s 7¼d.[8] He shut up Carlton House and, hoping to impress his father and Parliament with his economy, went with Mrs Fitzherbert to live at the seaside town of Brighton, where they lived in a modest way, inhabiting separate houses. By 1787, the Prince was in occupation of a newly built Marine Pavilion. One MP at least, Mr Horne Tooke, was impressed by Mrs Fitzherbert's rectitudinous influence, and he printed an ironical pamphlet entitled *The Reported Marriage of the Prince of Wales*, in which he suggested that Mrs Fitzherbert be recognized as Princess of Wales.[9]

Not all in Parliament felt the same way. When, on 27 April 1787, Alderman Newnham proposed in the Commons that the state should relieve the Prince of his debts, there was an angry response. One MP rose to say that the question 'went immediately to affect our constitution in Church and state'.[10] If the rumours of the Prince of Wales's marriage, and to a Catholic, were true, the Prince appeared to be disbarred from inheriting the crown. Many MPs saw no reason, in that case, to grant the Prince the relief from his debts that he sought. Mr Charles James Fox rose on 30 April to declare, on the 'immediate authority' of the Prince, that 'as a peer of Parliament, he was ready in the other House to submit to any of the most pointed questions which could be put to him'. Fox roundly denied 'that miserable calumny' – this was the euphemism used by MPs for the marriage – going so far as to state, 'The fact in question ... never had, and common sense must see, never could have happened.'[11] The House of Commons voted the Prince the relief he sought, and Mrs Fitzherbert, publicly humiliated, said that Fox had 'rolled her in the kennel like a street-walker; that he knew every word was a lie'. She was able, nonetheless, to take comfort from the support of her friends: 'the knocker of her door was never still during the whole day'.[12] She was persuaded not to break with the Prince only after he swore to her that he had never authorized Fox to make his statement. Nevertheless, she never spoke to Fox again.

In October 1788, as we have noted, King George III fell victim to a malady which afflicted him until the following February. One of his ministers described its beginnings as 'a humour which was beginning to show itself [in swellings] in the legs when the King's imprudence [he neglected to change his wet stockings] drove it from thence to the bowels [causing terrible stomach cramps]; and the medicines which they [the doctors] were then obliged to use for the preservation of his life have repelled it on the brain'.[13] The Prince of Wales's physician told Lady Spencer on 12 November, 'Rex noster insanit.'[14] The King, who had suffered similarly in his twenties, exhibited the symptoms of a rare metabolic disorder called porphyria that was unknown to the doctors of the period.* While the King was frothing at the mouth, ennobling his pages and declaring his love for Lady Pembroke, the King's doctor Sir George Baker had no idea, beyond administering senna pods, how to cure the ailment. The King called for an embargo on the import of senna into the country. Sir Lucas Pepys, who had cured insanity in Lady Harcourt's family, was called in. In all, nine doctors saw the royal patient, who vilified them singly and in a body.

While the King lay sick at Windsor, the Prince of Wales and his brother York at first behaved uncommonly well. However, as more and more doctors pronounced – though never publicly – their belief that the King's illness was chronic, the Prince of Wales, not unreasonably, looked forward to becoming regent. Dr Richard Warren, a Whig doctor, confirmed this diagnosis of chronicity, and the Prince became perfunctory in his attentions to his mother. She anyway clung to the opinion of Dr Willis, a 'madhouse keeper' lately brought in to treat her husband, that the King would recover under a strict regime that allowed the doctor to 'control' his patient's excesses. The King, removed to Kew, was confined to a strait-waistcoat or to a restraining-chair, tied to his bed and even gagged at one point when he spoke lustfully of Lady Pembroke. Meanwhile, the Prince and his brothers amused themselves by publicly mimicking their father's lunacy.[15]

With little information from the doctors, whose bulletins were cautious in the extreme, the Cabinet agreed that a Regency Bill must be tabled. Mr William Pitt, resigned to losing office to the Whigs when the Prince became regent, endeavoured to enact a limited Regency. The Bill had passed the House of Commons and was on its

* Porphyria is a disease which produces a greatly increased formation and excretion of the purple-red pigments in the blood; their excess causes 'widespread intoxication of all parts of the nervous system, peripheral and central' (Ida Macalpine and Richard Hunter, *George III and the Mad-Business* (1969), p. 173). This diagnosis of porphyria is supported by Ian R. Christie (*History*, lxxxi, no. 232 (1986), pp. 205–21) and by Vivian Green, *The Madness of Kings: Personal Trauma and the Fate of Nations* (1993).

way to the Lords when the unthinkable occurred and the King recovered, apparently vindicating Dr Willis.

The Bill was thus abandoned, and the King resumed his duties as sovereign. His first act on 26 February was to discontinue the 'physicians' report'.[16] His relations with his eldest son, never good, worsened considerably when he learnt of the Prince's treacherous part during the Regency crisis. The King refused to receive him, although the Queen forgave her favourite son readily. In the hope that his heir would never succeed him, the King urged his second son, the Duke of York, to marry, and in 1790, as we have seen, the Duke took as his bride Princess Frederica of Prussia. Eventually, in 1791, after Mrs Fitzherbert had calmed the Prince, and the Prince's eldest sister, Charlotte, the Princess Royal, had placated her father, a reconciliation between father and son was effected, although it was more of an uneasy truce.

The Prince and Mrs Fitzherbert lived for the next three years between London and Brighton, in something of an uneasy truce themselves. The Prince wrote later of 'all the commérage, chit-chat, tracasseries which the various disagreements and misunderstandings between Mrs Fitzherbert and me naturally occasioned'.[17] Many of the disagreements were about finance. Mrs Fitzherbert later reported that she had often had to lend – effectively give – the Prince money to pay his mounting debts. This she did from her relatively modest annuity of £2000. Her uncertain status further heightened the tension between them. The problem was that the Prince's expenditure still exceeded his income. At Brighton he employed the architect Mr Henry Holland to remodel his house as a marine villa, and the decorating firm of Mr Frederick Crace to embellish its interior. Pleased with the work of the Crace brothers at Brighton, he gave them a further commission to rehang some of the rooms at Carlton House, where he continued to collect paintings and furniture. The opportunities for acquiring French furniture after the Revolution were too tempting to resist, and the Prince sent a succession of agents, including Louis Weltje, his cook, over to France to purchase on his behalf.

The Prince also rented a house near Kempshott, and now drew his friends from a fraternity of gentlemen who enjoyed hunting, shooting, racing and other country sports. The carriages, horses and guns purchased for these pursuits were naturally of the finest. In addition, the Prince kept a racing stud, till his jockey was warned off New-market Heath and that item was struck off his accounts. He was less constantly with his Whig friends, not least because they denounced the expedition sent to oust the French from the Austrian Netherlands in 1793; he, on the other hand, hoped to play a part in that war. His interest in politics perforce abated, and Mrs Fitzherbert's dislike for Fox pushed the Prince and Whigs further apart.

His rural activities did nothing to lessen the Prince's expenditure. He owed Leader, his coachmaker, £32,777 and Choppin, the horse dealer, £7200; his racing establishment cost £30,000 a year.[18] By the summer of 1794 he had accumulated £550,000 worth of debts. The London bankers refused to come to his aid, and Parliament, faced with having to pay for the costly campaign against the French, was in no mood to pay his debts. The Prince wrote to his brother York in August that year of 'the very uncomfortable situation I have been in for some months, and indeed for some years, but particularly for the latter three or four months, which occasioned me so much chagrin and pain . . .'. York's own situation was hardly more comfortable. He had proved such an ineffective commander in the Austrian Nether-lands that, as we have seen, he was soon sacked (and offered to cede his position to the Duke of Brunswick). The Prince's letter referred not only to his debts, but also to his relationship with Mrs Fitzherbert: 'In short we are finally parted, but parted amicably, and I believe from what you know of my temper, disposition and the unvaried attention and affection I have ever treated her with, you will not lay the fault, whatever it may be, at my door.'[19] Almost everyone did blame him, except York himself, who pointed his finger at the mistress: 'I have been grieved to see how very miserable Mrs Fitzherbert's unfortunate temper made you, and once, if you remember, some years ago, advised you not to bear with it any longer. I am rejoiced to hear that you are now out of her shackles.'[20]

In July a decision by the Court of Privileges had helped to annul the Prince of Wales's residual feelings of loyalty to Mrs Fitzherbert. His brother Prince Augustus had the previous year secretly married Lady Augusta Murray, first in Rome and then in London. King

George III, acting through his Proctor, Mr James Heseltine, had sought a declaration under the 1772 Royal Marriages Act that 'both the marriages were void, for want of the royal consent, by virtue of the statute aforesaid'. The judge, Sir William Wynne, Dean of Arches, duly obliged, declaring the marriage 'null and void to all intents and purposes in law, whatsoever'.[21] If the Prince had ever entertained fears that he might pay the price for his supposed marriage to Mrs Fitzherbert, they could now be laid to rest.

To complicate the Prince's troubled life further, he had recently fallen under the spell of Frances, Lady Jersey, a bewitching and ambitious creature of forty-one, who had her own plans for the Prince. She was described by a contemporary as a 'bitch', a regrettable epithet for a bishop's daughter to attract. She was, according to another, 'clever, unprincipled, but beautiful and fascinating'. A mother to nine children, and a grandmother, she was nearly ten years older than the Prince, but her 'irresistible seduction' proved too much for him.[22] In Hoppner's portrait her tumble of thick dark hair, doe eyes and creamy bosom indeed seem seductive. Mrs Fitzherbert later told her friend and relative Lord Stourton that:

> Her first separation from the Prince was preceded by no quarrel or even coolness, and came upon her quite unexpectedly. She received when sitting down to dinner [in the last week of June] at the table of ... the Duke of Clarence, the first intimation of the loss of the affections of the Prince; having only the preceding day received a note from his Royal Highness written in his usual strain of friendship, and speaking of their appointed engagement to dine at the house of the Duke of Clarence. The Prince's letter was written from Brighton, where he had met Lady Jersey. From that time she never saw the Prince.[23]

Captain Jack Payne, naval officer and a mutual friend of both, was dispatched to the Clarence household with the message from the Prince that (in Mrs Fitzherbert's words) 'he would never enter my house again'. The Prince next sat down to compose a long epistle, which Payne was instructed to take to Mrs Fitzherbert. On 8 July the Prince wrote to Payne of his composition: 'To tell you what it has cost me to write it and to rip up every and the most distressing feelings of my heart and which have so long lodged there is impossible to express.'[24] The letter, he judged, concluded everything on his part, and within the month Lady Jersey was established as the Prince's constant and influential companion. A new staircase was installed at Brighton, 'made to lead to Lady Jersey's apartments'. These rooms were reserved for her use when she came to stay, with or without her husband. (Lord Jersey received his reward for this complaisance the following year, when he became the Prince's Master of the Horse.) Queen Charlotte, always pathetically eager to please her son, quickly made a favourite of Lady Jersey, and invited her and her eldest daughter to a grand ball at Windsor on the Prince's birthday, 12 August 1794. The King raised no objection. Meanwhile, Mrs Fitzherbert retired with dignity to Marble Hill, a villa at Richmond-on-Thames. Her Whig friends, especially those who were Catholic, were disgusted by the Prince's behaviour, and made a public display of their support for her.

In late August the King and Queen, summering at Weymouth in Dorset with their son Prince Ernest and their six daughters, received a visit from the Prince of Wales. With him came a band of gentlemen who had been his shooting companions at Kempshott. The King's equerry, Mr Robert Fulke Greville, observed the calibre of the Prince's party on one occasion during their stay when they accompanied the royal party on a sailing excursion to Portland Island. At an inn there, the Portland Arms, the Prince of Wales 'resolved to be merry for half an hour' after the King left the dinner table. His friends Lord Walsingham and Lord Clermont, 'ere he parted with them, began to feel the powerful effects of conviviality'. Sailing back to Weymouth, the Prince and his friends were moved to take a second dinner and a liberal 'potation' on board the *Minotaur*. Lord Walsingham was 'totally overcome by it' and had to be left, 'stripped and laid out on a couch on board'. The Prince, his brother Prince Ernest and Lord Clermont meanwhile were 'much animated' at cards in the King's apartment at Gloucester Lodge.[25]

The Prince's 'excess of conviviality' was only natural, considering that he had earlier in the course of his visit embarked on a momentous discussion with his father. At the beginning of September, he returned to Weymouth and told Mr Robert Fulke Greville, while out riding, that he was going to be married, and that 'the Princess of Brunswick was the object of his choice. He then informed me that he had opened this intention to his Majesty on his last visit here and that he had the happiness to find that his choice and intention had most entirely met with his Majesty's approbation.'[26] His father had said that 'it was the only proper alliance, and indeed the one in all respects he should have wished for himself, and the one he should have wished to have pointed out to me'.[27] The subject of Mrs Fitzherbert had occupied them only briefly, the Prince of Wales informing his father of his irreparable breach with her.

There had been discussions with the Government, or at least with Pitt, some time earlier. The King, writing in September to his Prime Minister, reported, 'Agreeable to what I mentioned to Mr Pitt before I came here I have this morning seen the Prince of Wales, who has acquainted me with his having broken off all connection with Mrs Fitzherbert, and his desire to entering into a more creditable line by marrying; expressing at the same time that my niece, the Princess of Brunswick, may be the person.'[28]

'Lady Jersey made the marriage,' the Duke of Wellington much later told Lady Salisbury, 'simply because she wished to put Mrs Fitzherbert on the same footing as herself, and deprive her of the claim to the title of lawful wife.' (Mrs Fitzherbert, as we have noted, had no such claim, but the legend lingered on.) Lady Jersey made her choice of a bride, said Wellington, with 'indelicate manners, indifferent character, and not very inviting appearance, from the hope that disgust for the wife would secure constancy to the mistress'.[29] Moreover, in the Prince's enlarged married establishment, Lady Jersey could play a leading role.

The Prince's reasons for this sudden decision to marry and to desert his putative wife of eight years were not hard to seek. On his marriage, Parliament would agree to settle his debts and, furthermore, increase his income from the Civil List to that of a married man. Whether or not Lady Jersey encouraged the Prince cynically to discard Mrs Fitzherbert in July in order to make way for a bride with a Parliamentary dowry in August, she undoubtedly fostered the choice of Princess Caroline of Brunswick. (The Prince of Wales later told Caroline that she ought to feel grateful to Lady Jersey for this favour.)[30]

Although the King had agreed to the marriage and had summoned a Council of Ministers to announce his son's intentions, he wished to defer the wedding till the following spring. 'That neither meets my wishes nor those of his Majesty's ministers,' the hard-up Prince wrote on 29 August to the Duke of York. 'We are all working and moving heaven and earth to immediately send for her over.'[31] The other fly in the ointment for the Prince was his mother's sullen response to his choice of bride, against whom she had already warned her brother. Queen Charlotte told her son Prince Ernest, who told his brother the Prince of Wales, that 'she had resolved never to talk, no never to open her lips about your marriage, so that no one should say she had any hand in anything; though she never liked the Duchess of Brunswick, yet she should treat the Princess very well. . . . all this she said with tears in her eyes'. Dutifully she set about preparing Caroline's trousseau and was soon noting in her diary the growing family interest: 'After coffee we all, even the King, went upstairs to see Mrs Spilsbury, just arrived from Hampshire, who is to make the robes for the Princess of Wales's wedding. . . . She made my robes when I married.'[32]

The Prince of Wales, being the Prince of Wales, overreached himself in his enthusiasm for his coming nuptials. He wrote to his father to nominate candidates for his intended wife's household and received the following dampening reply on 20 September:

> Your wanting thus early to fix on her intended servants seems highly premature: you should first know what income you are to have and what number of servants are thought necessary, otherwise you will run into a terrible scene of expense, and to regain the opinion of the public you must set out with a most rigid plan of economy. . . .[33]

Still concerned with the Prince's failure to economize, the King wrote (probably in September 1794) to his sister in Brunswick: 'I should not have acted fairly towards her whose interest will become entrusted to my care if I had not insisted that his debts should be put into some kind of form not to lay a dead weight upon him. The impatience of the young man makes him think all this an unnecessary delay. . . .'[34]

The Prince, overjoyed by the prospect that Pitt held out in September of a married man's income from Parliament of £100,000 a year (increased from £60,000), had paid little attention to his father. Even before an envoy had been appointed to go to Brunswick to seek Princess Caroline's hand formally in marriage, the Prince had commissioned Mr Henry Holland, the architect, to oversee the appointment of rooms, with furnishings supplied by M. Daguerre, on the principal or ground floor of Carlton House as 'the Princess of Wales's bedchamber, ante-room etc.', at a cost of £5000.[35]

Furthermore, quite contrary to etiquette, 'the impatience of the young man' had prompted the Prince of Wales on 8 October to send his own envoy, Major Hislop, to Brunswick with a graceful letter for his bride and his personal assurances to her parents that he wished her to depart as soon as possible. Caroline, in Brunswick, did not give a hang for etiquette either, and sent Hislop back with her portrait for the Prince, charging him to tell her future husband: 'she is in hourly and anxious expectation of being immediately sent for, so much so that she said if the carriage was ready at the door she would not wait for anybody to hand her into it'.[36] And, as we have seen, she pestered Mr William Eliot to know when the envoy would arrive. If the Prince could not wait to get clear of his debts, the Princess could not wait to be shot of Brunswick.

In the event, Lord Malmesbury, and not the expected envoy Lord Southampton, arrived in Brunswick at the end of November. He recorded in his diary on 20 November his first impressions of the future Princess of Wales. She was:

> Much embarrassed on my first being presented to her – pretty face – not expressive of softness – her figure not graceful – fine eyes – good hand – tolerable teeth, but going – fair hair and light eyebrows, good bust – short, with what the French call 'des épaules impertinentes'. Vastly happy with her future expectations. The Duchess full of nothing else – talks incessantly.[37]

Malmesbury resumed an acquaintance with the Dowager Duchess, who talked to him of Berlin in the old days, when her brother

Frederick had been king, and with Mlle Hertefeld, whom he had also known at the splendid Berlin Court. She was at first 'rather ashamed to see me, but soon got over it'. The Duchess Augusta meanwhile abused her sister-in-law Queen Charlotte and said she was 'an envious and intriguing spirit'. Malmesbury found, at the opera, that Princess Caroline 'improves on acquaintance, is gay and cheerful with good sense'. Of all those he met, he most admired Caroline's sister-in-law, the Hereditary Princess, who was bearing her family's misfortunes in Holland with dignity and strength.

On 3 December, two days after the arrival of the full instructions and credentials for which Malmesbury had been waiting, the Duke and Duchess formally consented to 'the demand which I had it in command to make', Malmesbury recorded. He was then conducted to Princess Caroline, who in turn replied 'in the most graceful and dignified manner to what I said, although not without some confusion'.[38] By a happy chance, Major Hislop had returned that same day to present a miniature of the Prince to his bride. The future Princess of Wales 'invested herself with it, as with an Order', wrote Hislop to the donor of the miniature, 'in presence of the fullest Court that perhaps Brunswick ever saw'.[39] Malmesbury was less delighted with the letter Hislop brought him from the Prince, urging him to set out with the Princess immediately, instructions which ran contrary to those he had received from the King. Malmesbury replied the following day that they would 'set out on the 11th, if before that day I receive intelligence here of the fleet which is to escort us having sailed'.[40]

Further gifts and letters were exchanged. The Prince received a box which had been given to Malmesbury by the Princess's old nurse, containing 'a shoe she [Princess Caroline] wore in her infancy'. The nurse had cherished it these twenty-six years in the hope, now realized, of bestowing it on her charge's bridegroom, 'in conformity to an old custom in this country'.[41] The Duchess sent her future son-in-law 'a set of China with the views of all the Duke's houses and my picture on the cups'. The Princess on the other hand received a box of English dresses, which became her very well in the opinion of duenna Malmesbury. Her mother the Duchess had written in October, advising Queen Charlotte that white suited her daughter best, and yellow and pink not at all.[42] This suggests that Caroline's complexion was sallow. When she reached England, if not before, she disguised this with liberal application of rouge.

The marriage treaty duly signed by Malmesbury and de Feronce, the Brunswick Minister, Malmesbury received a series of unsolicited confidences about Princess Caroline from her mother, her father and Mlle Hertefeld. One evening after dinner the Duke held 'a very long and very sensible discourse' with Malmesbury about his daughter. The Duke begged him to recommend to the Princess 'not to ask questions, and, above all, not to be free in giving opinions of persons and things aloud'. He hinted delicately at the free and unreserved manners of his wife the Duchess, 'who at times is certainly apt to forget her audience', noted Malmesbury.[43]

At a Court ball the following day, Mlle Hertefeld repeated the substance of the Duke's words of warning. Princess Caroline was 'not clever, or ill-disposed, but of a temper easily wrought on, and had no tact'. Mlle Hertefeld said that advice from Lord Malmesbury would be more welcome to the Princess than instruction from her father, whom she feared, although she respected him: 'she had no respect for her mother, and was inattentive to her when she dared'.

The Duke continued anxious. He was with his daughter two hours one morning, attempting to inculcate in her a sense that 'the high situation in which she was going to be placed was not simply one of amusement and enjoyment; that it had its duties, and those perhaps difficult and hard to fulfil'. He begged Malmesbury 'not to forsake her when in England', explaining that 'he dreaded the Prince's habits'. Malmesbury in his turn counselled Princess Caroline at supper that evening to 'avoid familiarity . . . have no confidantes . . . be perfectly silent on politics and party . . . be very attentive and respectful of the Queen . . . endeavour, at all events, to be well with her'. The Princess 'takes all this well', Malmesbury noted; 'she was at times in tears, but on account of having taken leave of some of her old acquaintance'.[44]

Malmesbury took every opportunity, till the signal should come to set out for England, to prepare the Princess for her future. Although she asked his advice constantly herself and appeared to be a docile pupil, he was secretly worried. He took advantage of a promenade with his fellow diplomat Sir Brooke Boothby (still in Brunswick on that very different mission to persuade the Duke to take command of the allied army in the Austrian Netherlands) to discuss her shortcomings. Both men regretted 'the apparent facility of Princess Caroline's character – her want of reflection and substance – [we] agree that with a steady man she would do vastly well, but with one of a different description, there are great risks'.[45] Rumours of the Princess's susceptibility to dashing officers had plainly reached the circumspect Malmesbury.

Malmesbury was disheartened to hear that 'Lady —— [Jersey] was very well with the Queen; that she went frequently to Windsor, and appeared as a sort of favourite. This, if true, [is] most strange, and bodes no good,' he wrote,[46] and he was disconcerted when Princess Caroline asked him about Lady Jersey. Having no more than scanty information, she seemed to think her 'an intrigante, but not to know of any partiality or connection between her and the Prince'. Malmesbury took the opportunity, however, to say that Princess Caroline should never be too familiar or too easy to her ladies, of whom Lady Jersey was to be one. When she said 'she wished to be popular', Malmesbury told her that popularity never was attained by familiarity, and that she should take the Queen as a model. But the Princess was afraid of her future mother-in-law. 'She was sure she would be jealous of her and do her harm.' After Malmesbury had reassured her, the Princess asked him to be her mentor in England. 'She said of her own accord, "I am determined never to appear jealous. I know the Prince is léger [flighty], and am prepared on this point."' Malmesbury recommended her to abjure 'reproaches and sourness', should she see 'any symptoms of a goût in the Prince', in favour of 'softness, endearments and caresses'. Malmesbury 'knew enough of the Prince to be quite sure he could not withstand such a conduct, while a contrary one would probably make him disagreeable and peevish . . .'.[47]

Unfortunately, the day before departure towards the end of December an anonymous letter from England arrived, castigating Lady Jersey as 'the worst and most dangerous of profligate women', who would try to lead the Princess into gallantry herself. The Duchess foolishly – in Malmesbury's view – showed this letter to her daughter. Malmesbury told the Princess that 'anybody who presumed to love her was guilty of high treason, and punished with death, if she was weak enough to listen to him; so also would she. This startled her,' wrote Malmesbury.[48] Despite his coy rendition of the provisions of the 1351 Treason Act, he had evidently made her aware that, were she to take a lover, the consequences might be fatal.

The Duchess compounded her foolishness by next showing her daughter a letter from the King, wherein he expressed his hopes that his niece would not show too much vivacity and that she was prepared to lead a sedentary and retired life. On this warning note, the Princess took leave of her father, who was much affected by his loss, begging Malmesbury to be a second father to her. The party at last set out from Brunswick on 29 December, as cannons fired a salute from the ramparts. Three days earlier, with Lord Malmesbury's orders from the King to depart for England had come a letter from the Prince forbidding the Princess to bring with her a secretary, Mlle Rosenzweit, whom her father had wished to accompany her. The Duke, on this refusal, admitted to Malmesbury that his anxiety had been that the Princess wrote very ill and spelled very ill, and he did not wish this to be apparent. In the event, the Princess took to England only two maids, one of whom, Charlotte Sander, remained with her for over twenty years.

The Duchess, much against her will, had been persuaded to accompany her daughter on the route west to Hellevoetsluis, where the English squadron was to meet them. The later stages of their journey would take them along the Waal river close to the French lines. 'If I am taken,' said the Duchess, 'I am sure the King will be very angry.'[49] The Princess was in high spirits, blithe in the face of potential danger – more so than Malmesbury, who, extremely anxious on her behalf, had instructed Major Hislop to 'keep before us and give notice in case of danger from the enemy'. The state of the country to the west this severe winter was parlous, and cartloads of refugees packed the roads. After they had passed through Peine, Hanover and Diepholz, Lord Malmesbury received at Osnabrück on 1 January 1795 couriers with news first of French victories over the Dutch, then of an English assault on the French. He refused to proceed further without better information about the French position and without confirmation that the fleet had got into Hellevoetsluis.

Malmesbury's fears on both counts were well founded. The squadron had in fact had to turn back for England, prevented by ice and
fog from getting in to Hellevoetsluis. While waiting for further
intelligence, Malmesbury continued his education of the Princess,
and reproved her, after an evening of cards, for calling ladies she had
never seen before 'Mon coeur, ma chère, ma petite'.[50] When he at
last yielded to pressure and set out from Osnabrück, he received
letters on 9 January to say that the French had moved north across
the Waal, blocking their passage to Hellevoetsluis. General Harcourt,
the commander in Holland in lieu of York, advised them to turn
back. Princess Caroline bore this with good humour and patience,
and only said next morning that she was sorry not to go on.
Malmesbury mentioned the sounds of heavy cannonade in the night.
'That doesn't matter,' she replied. 'I am not afraid of cannons.'

As the party retraced their steps to Osnabrück, Malmesbury,
impressed by Caroline's spirit, reflected:

> if her education had been what it ought she might have turned out
> excellent, but it was that very nonsensical one that most women receive
> – one of privation, injunction and menace. . . . she has quick parts,
> without a sound or distinguishing understanding . . . a ready concep-
> tion, but no judgment; caught by the first impression, led by the first
> impulse . . . loving to talk, and prone to confide and make missish
> friendships that last twenty-four hours. Some natural, but no acquired
> morality, and no strong innate notions of its value and necessity; warm
> feelings and nothing to counterbalance them; great good humour and
> much good nature – no appearance of caprice – rather quick and vive,
> but not a grain of rancour. . . . She has no governing powers, although
> her mind is physically strong. She has her father's courage, but it is to
> her (as to him) of no avail. *He* wants mental decision; *she* character and
> tact.[51]

This last point was proved indubitably when during the eleven days
they now stayed at Osnabrück, Princess Caroline had a tooth drawn
and sent it down to him by a page. He was absolutely revolted, having
weeks before observed her dental decay. Her mother's view was that
'her [Caroline's] courage surpasses every thing, at Osnabrück she had
a tooth pulled out, by a man she had never seen before'.[52]

The party set out back to Hanover ('Cold intense – 17 degrees below zero, Réaumur's scale') on 22 January. Malmesbury made a last effort on the eve of their arrival there to help his impulsive charge to some 'acquired morality'. Her conduct in Hanover, where the King of England was Elector, had to be beyond reproach. Princess Caroline, 'prone to confide' as ever, confessed her unease about the Prince's character, to which Malmesbury replied that she must 'domesticate him – give him a relish for all the private and home virtues; that he would then be happier than ever; that the nation expected this at her hands'.[53]

Princess Caroline, her mother and Lord Malmesbury were forced to remain at Hanover for two long months, from the end of January till late in March, while the war raged over the frozen spaces of The Netherlands. 'She supports herself with great courage in this trying conflict between the parting with her friends and the great prospect of grandeur that waits for her,' the Duchess wrote to her brother the King on 24 March.[54] In a private letter to the Duke of Portland, Secretary of State for the Home Department, Lord Malmesbury considered the delay not without merit. He had been reluctant to return with Caroline to Brunswick, where her situation was 'a subordinate one, and of great restraint, where her mind had not fair play; where it never could act for itself, where it was governed severely, not guided gently . . . and where the ladies . . . had allowed themselves towards her habits of familiarity and easy intimacy always pernicious in their effects from the gossiping to which they lead . . .'.

In Hanover the manners of the Court were 'uncommonly proper and decorous', by contrast; 'those who compose it are of a most respectable character. . . . The Princess Caroline is here received and treated exactly as a Princess of Wales Elect should be treated. . . .'[55] Malmesbury was confident that their time at Hanover would 'form and shape the Princess's mind and manners to her situation'. Queen Charlotte's brother, Prince Ernest of Mecklenburg-Strelitz, wrote from Hanover to his nephew, the Prince of Wales, to declare that his bride gained all the world by her politeness and affability.[56]

Malmesbury, during the enforced wait at Hanover, felt himself impelled to give the Princess some very frank instructions about her washing habits. He confessed himself amazed how much 'on this point her education has been neglected, and how much her mother,

although an Englishwoman, was inattentive to it'. Malmesbury had
two separate conversations with the Princess about her toilette. At a
time when hair and feet were seldom washed, Princess Caroline's lack
of personal hygiene must have been offensive to a degree for
Malmesbury to feel bound to instruct her in this way. Of the first
exchange he wrote, 'She piques herself on dressing quick; I disapprove
this,' and he asked Mme Bussche, the Duchess's lady, to explain to
the Princess that 'the Prince is very delicate, and that he expects a
long and very careful *toilette de propreté*, of which she has no idea. On
the contrary, she neglects it sadly, and is offensive from this neglect.
Madame Busche executes her commission well, and the Princess
comes out the next day well washed all over.'[57]

When news came that the squadron would be at Stade on 9 March,
Malmesbury made a final bid to persuade the Princess of the need for
'great and nice attention to every part of dress, as well as to what was
hid, as to what was seen. (I knew she wore coarse petticoats, coarse
shifts, and thread stockings, and these never well washed, or changed
often enough.)'[58] He had done what he could to shape Princess
Caroline into a fitting Princess of Wales. Her father recognized this,
when he came from Brunswick to take leave on the road at Walsrode,
forty miles north of Hanover, on 24 March. 'All his domestic
happiness depended on her doing well,' he told Malmesbury. He was
infinitely obliged to him for what he had done, and entreated him not
to forsake her when in England.[59] The English squadron was nearing
the Elbe river, down which it would sail to Stade, where the Princess
of Wales Elect – and the distracted Malmesbury – would embark for
England.

General Harcourt's wife had been pressed into service as a lady
companion for the voyage, and had joined them at Hanover on 16
March, reluctant to leave the army suffering in the north, and no less
anxious that she had no dresses suitable for this unexpected duty. The
Princess, who had to share her cabin with Mrs Harcourt on the
*Jupiter*, the fifty-gun frigate which they boarded on the 28th,
remained good humoured, even when Lord Malmesbury, in a last
lesson of etiquette, instructed her that she must not, in English, speak
of 'being sick, etc'. The English, he told her, were more nice in their
language than foreigners.[60]

Captain Jack Payne, who had fallen from favour with the Prince since he had delivered Mrs Fitzherbert her royal congé (he had too openly shown himself still her friend), was, as luck would have it, the captain appointed to bring the Princess Caroline, Mrs Fitzherbert's substitute, to England on the *Jupiter*. He discussed privately with Malmesbury the Prince's relations with Lady Jersey: 'her behaviour, by his account, very far from proper', and the Prince weak.[61] The Princess of Wales Elect had her first sight of England on Good Friday, 3 April 1795, after being held up off Great Yarmouth for two days, and on Easter Sunday, after sailing south to Gravesend, the party transferred to the Royal yacht *Augusta*. They disembarked at Greenwich to shouts from crowds on either riverbank – to find that the Princess's lady-in-waiting, Lady Jersey, had kept the carriages waiting in London.

When she did condescend to arrive, Lady Jersey objected to Princess Caroline's flippancy. On seeing the maimed pensioners at the Hospital, Caroline enquired, 'Do all Englishmen have only one arm or one leg?' 'No persiflage, Madame, if you please,' was Lady Jersey's tart reply.[62] The presumptuous lady-in-waiting then criticized the Princess's dress, before declaring that she could not possibly sit facing backwards in a coach – the motion made her unwell – and that she hoped that she might sit forward. Malmesbury said sharply: 'as she must have known that riding backward in a coach disagreed with her, she ought never to have accepted the situation of a lady of the Bedchamber'.[63] Lady Jersey yielded, the Princess sat facing forward alone, with Mrs Harcourt and the disgruntled Lady Jersey opposite, as the carriages drove into London and up to St James's Palace.

It was in the St James's apartments of Prince Ernest, her future brother-in-law, where the Princess was to lodge till her wedding, that that famous and farcical first meeting between the two cousins, bride and groom, took place, on 5 April. In comes the Prince of Wales to greet his bride. There being no one else to do it, Lord Malmesbury makes the introductions.

She very properly, in consequence of my saying to her it was the right mode of proceeding, attempted to kneel to him. He raised her (gracefully enough), and embraced her, said barely one word, turned round, retired to a distant part of the apartment, and calling me to him, said, 'Harris, I am not well; pray get me a glass of brandy.'

Malmesbury suggested instead a glass of water.

Upon which he, much out of humour, said, with an oath, 'No; I will go directly to the Queen,' and away he went. The Princess, left during this short moment alone, was in a state of astonishment; and, on my joining her, said, 'Mon Dieu! est-ce que le Prince est toujours comme cela? Je le trouve très gros, et nullement aussi beau que son portrait.'

Malmesbury was saved her further comments, as he was that moment ordered to attend the King.[64]

# MATRIMONY

## 1795

*'I never saw such children, nor such tricks'*

AFTER THIS humiliating and uncouth reception from her fiancé, all Princess Caroline's good intentions, her determination to follow the course of conduct Lord Malmesbury had so carefully prescribed, deserted her. She took refuge in her Brunswick manners, and the Prince's initial distaste for his bride was compounded by a disastrous show she gave, at dinner that night, of 'flippant, rattling' behaviour, 'affecting raillery and wit, and throwing out coarse vulgar hints about Lady Jersey, who was present, and, though mute, le diable n'en perdait rien', wrote Malmesbury. The Prince was disgusted, and 'this unfortunate dinner fixed his dislike,' continued Malmesbury, 'which, when left to herself, the Princess had not the talent to remove; but, by still observing the same giddy manners and attempts at cleverness and coarse sarcasm, increased it till it became positive hatred.'[1]

On the following day, Princess Caroline outraged the Prince, as he later declared, by 'reciting the particulars of the anonymous letters', which had been received in Brunswick, regarding 'the intimacy of my friendship with Lady Jersey, under all the false colour which slander has given it'. According to the Prince, at this interview the Princess gave herself credit 'for having suppressed all mention of their purport but to myself'. The Prince then took the opportunity to explain: 'Lady Jersey was one of the oldest acquaintances I had in this country and that the confidence resulting from so long a friendship had enabled her to offer advice which contributed not a little to decide me to marriage.'[2]

Nothing that the Princess did pleased the Prince. When she showed herself at a window at St James's and 'bowed exceedingly' to the people gathered below, 'the Prince shut the window and made excuses of her being fatigued', Horace Walpole, Lord Orford, informed his protégée Miss Mary Berry. 'Everybody speaks most favourably of her face as most pleasing,' he added, 'though with too much rouge. She is plump and by no means tall.'[3]

The Prince of Wales's gross conduct to his bride on her arrival may have been an instinctive reaction of disappointment, in traditional royal fashion, that the original was less physically attractive than the portrait he had in his possession. (The Princess, as we have seen, felt the same way.) Yet the Princess was generally acknowledged by those who saw her at this time to be a good-looking young woman with a fine complexion. Mr Charles Greville, cousin of the diarist and vice-chamberlain to the King, wrote to Sir William Hamilton in Naples, 'she was announced as fair and fat; we found her fair . . . and in private life [she] would be thought a pretty woman'. When Emma, Lady Hamilton, replied, she asked 'Is the Princess of Wales handsome? How can red hair be handsome?' Her hair in fact was straw-coloured.[4] Lady Charlotte Campbell, daughter of the Duchess's old friend the Duchess of Argyll, recorded her 'quick, glancing, penetrating eyes, long cut and rather sunk in the head, which gave them much expression – and a remarkably delicately formed mouth'. On the deficit side, the Princess had white eyelashes, and, as Walpole remarked, her figure was dumpy. 'Her head', noted Lady Charlotte, 'was too large for her body and her neck too short.'[5]

Probably – and this is the reason most often adduced for the Prince's demand for brandy – Caroline had forgotten the advice of her preceptor, Lord Malmesbury, and was not on this occasion 'well washed all over'. Certainly the Prince complained to his mother almost a year later of his wife's 'personal nastiness' – he meant that she smelt. Even so, given that no later observers or intimates record such an objection, it is fair to conclude that the Princess became better acquainted with soap. Slatternly, however, she remained all her life. As one of her ladies-in-waiting later reported:

> it is no wonder [the Prince] was disgusted with the Princess of Wales, who was a sloven, and did not know how to put on her own clothes. These kind of people should let themselves be dressed as you dress a

doll. She did sometimes; but then she was sure to spoil it all again by putting on her stockings with the seam before, or one of them wrong side outwards: and then her manner of finishing [gartering] them – it was shocking!⁶

Whatever her personal charms, or lack of them, the Prince had, in his view, good reason to dislike the Princess. The self-evident truth was that Princess Caroline was not Maria Fitzherbert, and the Prince of Wales blamed her for that. He was in a highly nervous state when he met his bride. It was now eight months since he had formed the idea of a public marriage, so as simultaneously to rid himself of his debts and to increase his income, and he had perhaps broken his secret ties of marriage with Mrs Fitzherbert to that end. In the interval he had come to think of this abandoned wife with passionate and nostalgic longing. (The Prince did not acknowledge feelings of guilt or remorse.) It would have been quite in keeping with his distorted view of the world if he saw the apparition of Princess Caroline as something approaching an instrument of the devil, rather than a vision which his own Aladdin's lamp had conjured up.

This point had been well made in a prophetic Gillray cartoon in January 1795, entitled 'The Lover's Dream', and quoting Milton's lines:

> A thousand virtues seem to lackey her,
> Driving far off each thing of sin and guilt.

A late companion piece to his 1785 cartoon 'The Morning After Marriage', which celebrated the rumoured nuptials of the Prince and Mrs Fitzherbert, 'The Lover's Dream' showed the Prince in a bedroom once more – but alone, asleep and clutching a pillow.⁷ The impression is one of turbulence, even shipwreck, as figures from his past and future hover about him. A vision of Princess Caroline floats towards him, attended by a cherub and illuminated by a seraph bearing a torch of Hymen, from the side dexter. Her image is based on the portrait then appearing in ladies' magazines and public prints to 'satisfy the public curiosity'. Her right hand touches the Prince of Wales's feathers above the bedhead, while from the side sinister his parents leer in approval. King George III shakes at his son a bulging money bag inscribed '£150,000 pr. Annm', and Queen Charlotte holds up with a smile a book entitled *The Art of Getting Pretty Children*. Further off to the left, a Bacchanalian cherub falls off a barrel of port in alarm at this newfound righteousness, Mr Charles James Fox stares aghast and the dice fall from his shaker. In the distance two racehorses and their jockeys take flight. And Mrs Fitzherbert, the figure on the extreme left of the cartoon, distinguished by burnt and tattered Prince of Wales's feathers, slinks away with an alarmed backward glance. Gillray completes the satire with an extra twist of the knife. A bottle sticking out of a chamber-pot at the Prince's side, on the side of righteousness, bears a label, 'Velno', or quack remedy for venereal disease.

The Prince, moreover, was extremely vexed with the world in general, and with his father in particular. The war against France continued, three of his brothers were playing their part in the army, while he was a mere 'cypher'. In March 1795, he had told Mr Henry Dundas, the Secretary for War, that if he was not granted the military rank of major-general, after which he hankered and which his father was withholding from him, 'it must lead to a total separation between the King and the Prince of Wales'. The Prince later put his case to his father: 'I have no option but to lead a life which must to the public eye wear the colour of an idleness depending on my choice, and which, from the sense of its so appearing, must sit irksomely upon me.'[8]

Dundas replied at length: 'The extent of your Royal Highness's debts will undoubtedly attract attention. . . . the circumstances will produce some disagreeable sensations in the public mind. . . . nothing could render the measure palatable either to Parliament or the public but the anxiety they entertain for the happiness of the royal family.' Dundas reiterated his advice: 'If it were for a moment supposed that the first fruits of your Royal Highness's establishment were to be a disunion in the royal family', Parliament would not come to the aid of the Prince in the summer session.

The Prince bowed to this threat, if he ignored Dundas's other remarks. 'The times are awful and momentous beyond any former period,' Dundas continued, 'and in the cause which agitates every corner of Europe . . . the personal character and conduct of the royal

family in every country forms an essential ingredient in the contest.'
Lord Moira, a devoted friend to the Prince, echoed Dundas: 'cultivate
the King and ... be well with him. The double right of a sovereign
and a father makes his Majesty's claim upon your attachment so
powerful that no ordinary reasons would satisfy the world as to the
justice of a dissatisfaction proclaimed on your part. . . .'[9]

As a result of these warnings, in March the Prince wrote in a more
conciliatory manner to his father than he had originally intended,
although his sense of injury was still apparent. 'The heroic Edward
gave to the inexperienced Prince of Wales', he wrote, 'the command
of the vanguard at Crécy, and the services of the son, not on that day
alone but through life, repaid the confidence of the father.'[10] To this
the Prince received no reply for a full month. He knew, however,
from his mother that the King had no intention of indulging his
eldest son's longing to emulate the Black Prince.

All the Prince's earlier haste to be married had thus evaporated
when he encountered his bride in April. He was disbarred from
honourable occupation. Furthermore, he was made anxious by the
repeated claims that Pitt would have great difficulty, even without a
rupture between King and Prince, in getting through Parliament the
increase of £40,000 a year to the Prince's income which he had
promised in September 1794. As Lord Moira had pointed out, 'The
public mind is much soured.' The Government, rendered uneasy by
the French Revolutionary War, had suspended the Habeas Corpus
Act and was vigorously repressing all impetus towards Parliamentary
reform. In March 1795 the war had taken a turn for the worse: the
Flanders expeditionary force had been evacuated from Bremen; and
Prussia made peace with France, leaving Britain with only two allies
(Austria and Spain). The extravagance of the Prince, who had
promised to burden the country no more with his debts in 1787 and
now asked for an increase in income as well as relief from creditors to
whom he owed the remarkable sum of £630,000, was unlikely to
command much sympathy. In short, Caroline, far from proving the
golden goose of 'The Lover's Dream', now seemed to the Prince a
very ugly duckling.

The marriage of the Prince of Wales and Princess Caroline of
Brunswick, despite all the Prince's reservations, took place in the

Chapel Royal at St James's Palace on the evening of Wednesday, 8 April 1795. The Prince, who was usually fascinated by ritual, ceremony and show, left all the arrangements to his conscientious, if unimaginative, mother. She modelled all the arrangements for the wedding – including Princess Caroline's robe of ermine-lined velvet and dress of silver tissue and lace festooned with bows and ribbons – on those which had obtained at the wedding of George's and Caroline's common grandparents Frederick and Augusta, Prince and Princess of Wales, in 1736. The King later in the year had Mr Gainsborough Dupont paint Caroline in this dress; two other artists, Mr John Singleton Copley and Mr William Hamilton, were commissioned to paint the wedding.[11]

King George III characteristically chose the Prince's wedding day to dampen any spirits he might have left, and to inform him that he had no intention of granting him a commission. His younger brothers, the King informed the Prince, could have no other situations in the state or occupation

> but what arise from the military lines they have been placed in. You are born to a more difficult one, and which I shall be most happy if I find you seriously turn your thoughts to; the happiness of millions depend on it as well as your own. May the Princess Caroline's character prove so pleasing to you that your mind may be engrossed with domestic felicity, which may establish in you that composure of mind perhaps the most essential qualification in the station you are born to fill, and that a numerous progeny may be the result of this union.[12]

Despite this paternal advice, the Prince, on the very morning of his wedding to Caroline, said to his brother the Duke of Clarence, 'William, tell Mrs Fitzherbert she is the only woman I shall ever love.' In the coach on the way to the Chapel Royal he repeated his sentiments to Lord Moira. 'It's no use, Moira, I shall never love any woman but Fitzherbert.'[13] As he walked up the aisle, Lord Melbourne wrote, 'the Prince was like a man doing a thing in desperation; it was like Macheath going to execution; and he was quite drunk'. Lord Malmesbury concurred that the Prince, who was – literally – supported by the bachelor dukes of Bedford and Roxburghe, had 'manifestly had recourse to wine or spirits'.[14]

Ignorant of her bridegroom's torment, Princess Caroline was 'in the greatest joy possible going to the Chapel', according to an observer, 'and did nothing but chatter with Prince William, Duke of Clarence, while she was waiting with him at the altar for the arrival of the Prince'.[15] During the ceremony, all agreed, she behaved 'gravely and decently', while the Prince appeared very agitated. He stood up in the middle of a prayer for no apparent reason, as if to flee the service.

The Archbishop of Canterbury, the Most Reverend John Moore, caused something of a sensation when, after asking whether there were any just impediment to this lawful matrimony, he boldly 'laid down the book and looked earnestly at the King, as well as the bridegroom, giving unequivocal proof of his apprehension that some previous marriage had taken place. . . .' Sir Nathaniel Wraxall continued, 'Not content with this tacit allusion, the Archbishop twice repeated the passage in which the Prince engages to live from that time in nuptial fidelity with his consort. . . . The Prince was much affected, and shed tears. . . .'[16] Even so, he had been reassured, thanks to the King's Proctor Mr James Heseltine, that he was no bigamist. But despite the Prince's preoccupation with Mrs Fitzherbert, it was not she who threatened his nuptial fidelity: when he looked up at all during the service, he stared fixedly, another observer remarked, at Lady Jersey.

The Duke of Leeds walked immediately in front of the Prince and Princess of Wales as they processed from the Chapel to the drawing-room in St James's Palace. 'I could not help remarking how little conversation passed between them during the procession,' he noted, 'and the coolness and indifference apparent in the manner of the Prince to his amiable bride.'[17] One of the equerries told Lady Maria Stuart that, when the Prince did speak to the Princess, he 'twice spoke crossly'. Lady Maria herself, crushed against the door of an inner drawing-room in the palace, remarked that the bride still seemed 'in the highest spirits . . . smiling and nodding to everyone'. The Prince, on the other hand, 'looked like death and full of confusion, as if he wished to hide himself from the looks of the whole world'.[18] The Dowager Countess Spencer reported that the Princess said to her new husband more than once in French, 'What is the matter, my Prince? You have such a sad face on.'[19]

The bridal night which followed at Carlton House was a disaster, even by the traditionally low standards of such occasions. In her *Diary of a Lady in Waiting*, Lady Charlotte Campbell reported Caroline's later confidence: 'Judge what it was to have a drunken husband on one's wedding day, and one who passed the greatest part of his bridal night under the grate, where he fell, and where I left him.'[20] The Princess of Wales was also to hint most indelicately to the politician and diplomat Lord Minto that the Prince was impotent. He wrote to his wife, 'If I can spell her hums and haws, I take it that the ground of his antipathy was his own incapacity, and the distaste which a man feels for a woman who knows his defects and humiliations.'[21] After a quarter of a century had passed, Caroline's memory of her first days at Carlton House had still not faded: 'Within the short space of a few hours after marriage the King was in such a state that he was obliged to be put to bed by himself.'[22] Nevertheless, a child of this marriage was born early in the following year, and extrapolating from the date of birth and assuming an average period of gestation, was probably conceived around 16 April. Caroline further disclosed to Minto that she and the Prince ceased to live 'as man and wife' after two or three weeks of marriage.[23]

The Princess saw her husband, according to this statement which she gave to legal counsel drafted in 1820, only for a short time the day after the wedding, when the Queen, the King and all the royal family breakfasted at Carlton House. Thereafter the Princess was left to take stock of her new home by herself, while the Prince went out on a solitary ride, slices of wedding cake were boxed up and dispatched to the households of the royal servants, and those who had been invited to the nuptial drawing-room called to enquire after the health of the bride. 'What an odd marriage,' commented one among them, an innocent young girl.

The Princess of Wales's new home, Carlton House, was situated close to St James's Palace on the south side of Pall Mall, the busy thoroughfare which lay south of Piccadilly and north of St James's Park. The house was set back and shielded from the street front by a screen of Ionic pillars which ran across the principal courtyard. The stables and carriage-house were disposed around a secondary yard to the east. Here the tradesmen made their deliveries or besieged Lord

Cholmondeley, the Prince's chamberlain, for payment in his office in Warwick House, an adjacent building, which acted as grace-and-favour apartments for the Prince's Household.

Sentries at the gates to the principal courtyard prevented creditors gaining access to the massive Corinthian portico across the way, which fronted Carlton House and afforded privacy to the Prince's visitors descending from and entering their carriages. Within this porte-cochère, two halls, painted granite green and splendidly appointed, led past a Grand Staircase to the principal apartments. On turning right one entered the state apartments – antechambers, drawing-rooms and dining-rooms. Left past the Grand Staircase lay the Princess's apartments, all with views of the park, and glimpses of the Mall beyond, to the south.

The Princess of Wales's apartments had been decorated, as we have seen, when the Prince was contemplating his marriage with misconceived joy. Her bedchamber, with toilette and dressing-room, occupied the south-east corner of the palace, and a private salon was hung with green brocade and matching fringe, tassels and gimp. In her private drawing-room, known as the Tapestry Room, crimson damask curtains and seat covers complemented the crimson ground to the Don Quixote Gobelin tapestries that hung on the walls. An antechamber completed the superb enfilade of rooms.[24] Unfortunately, amid this splendour, there was no room to house any of the Princess of Wales's ladies or women of the bedchamber. The whole of the rest of the mansion had long been appropriated to the Prince's bachelor needs.

All the rooms in the house were decorated and furnished in the most harmonious and magnificent style, reflecting the Prince's taste, tantamount to genius, as well as the £600,000-odd which he now owed as a result of indulging that taste. The Prince and his architect Holland had a special fondness for the Chinese style. 'The walls and overdoors' of one room in the basement floor 'were decorated with Chinese figure scenes on a white ground and the doors and window embrasures with arabesques on a yellow ground' – at a cost in 1792 of £700.[25] Owing to the slope on which the house stood, the basement floor appeared from the garden front to be the ground floor. The rest of the basement was a warren of kitchens, servants' quarters and other offices, including silver sculleries, wine cellars and a large confection-ery room.

The Prince's private apartments, with the Armoury and a library, were directly above the Princess's on the inappropriately named Attic Storey and, indeed, were connected to those of his bride by a private staircase. One may assume that this private staircase was little used. Public access from principal to attic floor was by way of the celebrated Grand Staircase, with a winding balustrade of wrought iron and brass and, at mezzanine level, colossal statues of Time holding a clock and Atlas bearing the weight of a gilded wind dial on his shoulders. Illuminated by domes of painted glass overhead, the Prince, his gentlemen and the Carlton House servants passed up and down like figures in a stage-set between the hall below and the octagonal Grand Vestibule above. The Princess of Wales was not encouraged by her husband to venture upstairs.

On the third day after their marriage, she stated in 1820, 'he actually called for his carriage with an intent of going to Mrs Fitzherbert.... the Honourable Mr Keppel, who was in attendance on the occasion ... placed himself before the door to prevent the [Prince] from going out and told him he should not go, upon which the [Prince] put himself into such a passion that he struck the Honourable Mr Keppel a blow on the chest; but being so intoxicated the recoil of his own blow brought him to the ground from whence he was taken up. . . .'[26]

The marriage was hardly likely to prosper, given not only that the Prince still carried a torch for Mrs Fitzherbert but that he also continued in thrall to Lady Jersey. As Lady Spencer wrote, 'Lady Jersey is in everything, and by everybody most thoroughly disap-proved.' Mrs Howe received a card from the despotic Lady Jersey, ten days after the wedding, bidding her to Carlton House at nine in the evening. 'She found only several men who had dined there.' The Princess spent most of her time playing rubbers of casino in another room with the octogenarian Lady Holdernesse, then played 'vastly well' on the pianoforte, 'the Prince accompanying her on the violon-cello, crying out *Brava* several times and seeming really pleased'.[27]

Music was not the food of love, unfortunately, in this marriage, and this was one of the few harmonious evenings where M. Fleischer's star pupil pleased her husband at Carlton House. On the whole she had little idea of how to please her husband. Lady Charlotte Campbell quoted her as remembering, 'One of the civil things his Royal Highness did just at first was to find fault with my shoes; and, as I was very young and lively in those days, I told him to make me a better pair, and bring them to me.'[28] In some cases it was impossible to avoid his wrath: during these early days he was offended by her complimentary language about Mrs Fitzherbert. After another dinner at which she had behaved 'very lightly and even improperly' with the Prince of Orange, the Prince of Wales railed against Lord Malmesbury in the privacy of his closet. How did Malmesbury like these manners? The diplomat took the opportunity of reporting to the Prince the substance of the Duke of Brunswick's advice regarding his daughter: 'that it was expedient *de la tenir serrée* [to keep her under lock and key]; that she had been brought up very strictly, and if she was not strictly kept, would, from high spirits and little thought, certainly emancipate too much'.

The Prince said, 'I see it but too plainly.' Malmesbury defended himself against the Prince's charge that he should have written of this from Brunswick. The Duke was a severe father, he protested, and he did not consider what he had been told 'any real slur or aspersion' on the Princess. Had there been any 'notorious or glaring defects, or such as were of a nature to make the union unseemly', Malmesbury continued, he would have felt it his duty to state them – but to the King, at whose command he had sought the Princess's hand in marriage. 'To this the Prince appeared to acquiesce,' Malmesbury concluded, 'but I saw it did not please, and left a rankle in his mind. . . . It is impossible to conceive or foresee any comfort from this connection, in which I lament very much having taken any share, purely passive as it was.'[29]

The Princess derived some comfort from her uncle the King's warmth of manner towards her. The press informed their readers: 'The manners of the Princess of Wales are very different from what might have been expected . . . – are easy, affable and playful, free from austere restraint. She chats with natural and becoming freedom, familiarizes as much with his Majesty as if . . . born and bred his favourite child; and with this gaiety the King is highly pleased.'[30]

The King, desperately anxious that the marriage should succeed for the good of the royal family and of the country, took a sanguine view of his son's fidgets. Given time, he believed that the couple would prosper together, and he ordered a series of Court celebrations. On 13 April 1795 the Theatre Royal put on a new drama entitled *Windsor Castle*, with a grand masque, *The Marriage of Peleus and Thetis*, in graceful allusion to the recent nuptials. Meanwhile, a few days after their wedding, the Prince and Princess of Wales visited the King and Queen at Windsor. It was the King's innocent pleasure after church on Sunday to walk in procession with his family on the Terrace. The display of domestic piety and harmony this particular Sunday was somewhat injured by the Prince of Wales, who chose neither to attend church nor to walk upon the Terrace. The King made good the omission by offering the Princess his own arm.

While the King ignored his son's sulks, the Queen had made no effort to afford either welcome or advice – which might not have been agreeable, but would have been useful – to her new daughter-in-law. The Princess was thus left dependent on her husband and on Lady Jersey for instructions in all aspects of ceremonial and domestic life at this foreign Court. A period of some weeks spent in May with both of them at the Prince's house at Kempshott was especially mortifying, and long rankled with the Princess.

A letter the Princess wrote to her sister-in-law Princess Elizabeth on 23 May from Kempshott argues a modicum of harmony. 'I am well content and happy in the country ... I do not ride any more, but the Prince takes me out in an open carriage ...'.[31] (The Princess, it was suspected, was a few weeks pregnant.) However, the letter was dictated by the Prince. Lord George Seymour recounted how punch and pipes had been produced after one dinner and the Prince had drunk from Lady Jersey's glass, whereupon the Princess had snatched a guest's pipe and puffed it contemptuously at her husband.[32] Caroline, showing some wit and a knowledge of Shakespeare, later told Lord Minto that she could have fancied herself at Eastcheap. Lady Jersey was the only woman present, and the 'blackguard companions of the prince ... were constantly drunk and filthy, sleeping and snoring in boots on the sofas'.[33]

In Brunswick both Duke and Duchess were disturbed by reports they received of their daughter's married life. The Duke wrote to the

King in August 1795, 'I hope, and I think I may dare to count on it, that nothing will ever distance her from the principles of religion and morality which have been the base of her conduct, and that she will make all efforts possible to render herself worthy of your protection.'[34] He had written no less anxiously to his daughter in England on 20 May, 'Several people complain that they see you seldom, and only in public.' Lady Stafford, as a very old friend, once a lady of the bedchamber to the Duchess of Brunswick, was especially concerned. 'Another correspondent says – would she be not too giddy,' the Duke informed his daughter severely, 'while saying much good of you.'[35] Later that month the Duchess wrote to the King, 'I hope and trust that the dear Princess of Wales follows yours and the Queen's example in attending church. The Prince has made himself very unpopular among the lower order of people by the neglect of public worship and for her own sake I hope she will do every thing that is right both in public and private. She is very sensible of your partiality for her,' the Duchess concluded kindly.[36]

The Prince was, in fact, deeply unpopular with almost all classes, not just the 'lower order of people', in England. This became evident in the plain speaking that ensued in the House of Commons on all sides, when Pitt introduced on 14 May two equally troublesome and connected questions. The Prince's debts were now in excess of £630,000. Should Parliament afford him any relief and, if so, on what terms? Furthermore, the Prince was now a married man, with a married establishment to support. What, if any, increase should Parliament vote to his Civil List income?

Pitt's own proposal was to provide £125,000 Civil List annual income for the Prince, on the condition that £25,000 per annum of that sum go towards payment of his debts. It was admitted on all hands, the Prime Minister declared, that the debts ought never to have been contracted. Still, now that the Prince was 'impressed with a just sense of the line of conduct which a regard to his character and situation required him to pursue', he hoped that the House would not refuse to adopt a measure 'so necessary for the character and credit of his Royal Highness, and so intimately connected with his personal comfort and the splendour of his rank'. On 1 June the Prince's Solicitor-General, Mr Anstruther, informed the House that the

Prince was eager to establish 'order and regularity in the expenditure of his income and to prevent the incurring of debt in future.'[37]

The House was not to be so easily led. Mr Charles Grey said, with bitter reference to the Prince's broken promises of economy in 1786, 'no reliance could be had that those provisions which might be made with respect to future conduct would be of any avail'. Fox suggested a novel solution: 'It appeared a little unseemly that at a time of such general calamity his Majesty should be the only person in the kingdom who did not contribute a single farthing to the discharge of the incumbrances of the Prince of Wales.' He recommended that the Duchy of Cornwall be sold, to supply the Prince's creditors.

Sheridan, admittedly, spoke up for the Prince, declaring that the debts ought to be paid 'for the dignity of the country and the situation of the Prince'. However, his infelicitous argument – 'He ought not to be seen rolling about the streets in his state-coach as an insolvent prodigal'[38] – pleased no one, least of all the outraged Prince. Pitt had to shift his ground dramatically to prevent a wholesale revolt among his supporters. When he moved on 5 June that a committee of the whole House decide how much was to go to liquidate the Prince's debts, it was on the understanding that a total of £78,000 be put aside every year for the next nine years for this purpose. This comprised £65,000 from the Civil List annuity of £125,000, and the whole revenues of the Duchy of Cornwall, roughly £13,000.

The Prince referred bitterly to 'the infamous deceit of Pitt'.[39] As a bachelor Prince of Wales, he had received the Duchy of Cornwall revenues and £60,000 from the Civil List, totalling £73,000 per annum. Under this new proposal, the total was reduced to £60,000 a year and now he had a wife and her establishment – and a nursery in prospect – to support. In short, the Prince of Wales felt himself very much the poorer, if his creditors were the richer, for his marriage. In the Lords, before the Annuity Bill was passed, the Duke of Clarence defended his brother clumsily, if valiantly. It was 'a notorious fact', he declared, that when the Prince of Wales's marriage had first been mooted there had been a stipulation that he should, in the event of that union, be exonerated from his debts. The Prince had now been forced, said Clarence, to express his consent to whatever Parliament offered, in order that something might be done. 'He was in the situation of a man who, if he could not get a haunch of venison, would rather take any other haunch than go without.'[40]

As a result of all the Parliamentary criticism, the Prince was thoroughly disgruntled – and was forced to make economies where he could. Towards the end of June he retired to Brighton for the summer with the Princess of Wales and a small retinue, including Lady Jersey and Miss Gertrude Vanneck, the Princess's keeper of the privy purse. After a short stay in a rented house, the party moved into the Marine Pavilion, which had been undergoing rebuilding and decoration. The Princess was 'extremely delighted with this place', the Prince informed the Queen, 'which seems to agree with her most perfectly, as she is in the best health and spirits possible, excepting at moments a little degree of sickness which is the necessary attendant upon her situation'. The Princess's pregnancy – which she considered something of a miracle – had been confirmed, and the baby was expected in January. The Prince was meanwhile making economies to accord with 'the reduced income to which the liberal arrangement of the ministers and the Parliament have condemned me'.[41] He had dismissed all his own gentlemen, except Lords Cholmondeley and Jersey, Generals Hulse and Lake.

Parliament had specified that £5000 of the sum voted him annually was intended for the Princess of Wales, and the Prince had very properly appointed Lord Cholmondeley and Lord Jersey as trustees for this sum. (In addition, Parliament had agreed a jointure of £50,000 for the Princess, in the event that the Prince predeceased her.) This 'pin-money', as the Queen described the £5000, would pay for the Princess's 'clothing, menu plaisir, charities, and many unavoidable expenses in her present situation'.[42] The Prince, he himself reported, had further given her 'between seven and eight thousand pounds more to pay the rest of the establishment, which I think she ought to retain to support her rank'. He had dismissed only his wife's maids of honour, and the Princess retained, as well as her privy purse, her four ladies and her four women of the bedchamber.[43] But these eight attendants did not all serve at the same time. One lady and one woman did their duty together for three months, before being replaced by a second pair.

Of all this, he was pleased to hear, his father heartily approved. It seemed possible that, in the new line of 'retirement' which the Prince had been forced to adopt, he would find domestic happiness with his wife and, in due course, his child. Unfortunately such happiness still eluded the Prince and Princess of Wales at Brighton, as it had in London and Kempshott. 'Here is a letter from the Prince that I do not comprehend,' the Duchess of Brunswick informed her brother the King in July, 'having not wrote a word to my daughter either of you or the Queen, nor ever mentioned the Prince one way or other.' The Prince had complained, in his letter to Brunswick, that the Princess had first burnt a letter from her mother which criticized him, and then made 'a noise' about it to him. 'I never saw such children, nor such tricks. I am glad I am so far from them,' the Duchess wrote angrily. 'I told her at parting that I should never write any particulars for all my advice would come too late, so that from beginning to end it's a lie. Therefore you know best if the Prince is given to lying, or if it is Caroline.'[44]

It seems probable that Caroline was the liar in this instance: perhaps, having hurled some accusations at the Prince, she took fright and attributed them to her mother. If so, she was found out, for the Duchess, writing to the Prince to congratulate him on Caroline being 'a-breeding', denied absolutely his charges against herself. The Prince never let Caroline forget that she was 'a liar'.

Lord and Lady Sheffield spent an evening at the Pavilion with the Prince and Princess towards the end of July. 'She, poor little creature, is, I am afraid, a most unhappy woman; her lively spirits, which she brought over with her, are all gone,' Lady Sheffeld wrote, 'and . . . the melancholy and anxiety in her countenance is quite affecting.'[45] The Princess's feelings this summer, as she grew large with child, may be summed up in a letter she wrote to a friend in Germany: 'I do not know how I shall bear the loneliness, the Queen seldom visits me, and my sisters-in-law show me the same sympathy. . . . The Countess [Jersey] is still here. I hate her, and I know she feels the same towards me. My husband is wholly given up to her, so you can easily imagine the rest. . . .'[46]

Horace Walpole heard that Mr Thomas Tyrwhitt, the Prince's private secretary, had 'roundly lectured Lady Jersey on her want of reverence to the . . . Princess'. Thereupon Lady Jersey swooned, at which point the Prince came in and, on hearing the cause, dismissed Tyrwhitt – temporarily – from his service. Lady Jersey's high-handed ways enraged all the establishment at Brighton. 'Miss Vanneck is come away furious also,' Walpole noted later in August, 'on never being asked to play cards; nay, she was desired for her amusement to bring her spinning wheel into the [card] play room.'[47] The Prince, for his part, wrote to tell his mother in September that the Princess was 'as wicked, as slanderous and as lying as ever'.[48] The following month, the Duchess of Devonshire wrote that a friend was just back from Brighton, 'full of stories, which I always discourage. . . . But I fear it is very bad, and the poor little Princess really very ill used, as he certainly made her cry during all the last ball, which was a stupid thing in him to do, whatever the reason, as it only exposed him. . . .'[49]

The Duchess of Brunswick wrote in great agitation to her brother on 7 October, after hearing a tale of woe from her daughter in Brighton: 'I fear some black design, Lady Jersey turns every word the poor Princess says, and her whole thrust is to hurt her in your opinion and the Queen's. . . . You know, dear brother, that the innocenter one is the easier one falls into scrapes, the Prince has told her . . . that he will not constrain her in nothing; that she may live with who she pleases. . . .' The Duchess added, 'she is frightened out of her senses. . . . the Prince made it a point that she should treat her [Lady Jersey] with distinction, and indeed she has till now obeyed blindly all his whims. . . .' Her mother no doubt prayed that Caroline would not be foolish enough to obey this latest directive. The Duchess concluded her litany of her nephew's sins: 'HRH left her in the country without ever taking leave of her, or saying that he was going.'[50] The Prince had visited his parents in Weymouth, before joining friends to shoot.

The public came to know of the private disagreements at Brighton, and of Lady Jersey's part in them, following newspaper accusations that the Countess had intercepted, opened and shown to members of the English royal family private letters which the Princess had written to her family in Germany. The Princess had apparently referred to her husband in these letters in uncomplimentary terms, and to the Queen as 'the old Bégune', an allusion to the long cloak and hood as of a religious order which her Majesty often adopted. The newspapers glossed over this discourtesy and concentrated their attacks on Lady Jersey's dishonourable conduct.

It was a storm in a teacup. One Dr Randolph had undertaken at Brighton in August to carry a packet of letters for the Princess of Wales to Brunswick, where he was returning after many years' absence. Finding that his journey was delayed – Mrs Randolph was ill in Bath – the doctor, according to his own narrative, called at Carlton House to enquire how he should best return to the Princess her correspondence. Send it to the Princess, he was informed, care of Lady Jersey, by the Brighton post-coach. It leaves daily from Charing Cross.

Randolph acted on those instructions next morning and was consequently surprised at Bath a fortnight later to receive from Lady Jersey on the Princess's behalf an enquiry about the packet: her Royal Highness was uneasy about the whereabouts of her letters. A week later, on 8 September, Lady Jersey wrote again, to say that the Princess was not, after all, uneasy about her letters. It was one of the Princess's German women who had thought her letters valuable. Greatly distressed by the implication that he had withheld the Princess's letters, Dr Randolph published a vindication of his conduct. The newspapers added their cudgels to his, whereupon Lord Jersey entered the fray on his wife's behalf and published a pamphlet of his own, declaring his wife's innocence.[51]

The sum of it was this: the Princess had written unwisely but had thought herself safe in her messenger; Lady Jersey had meddled where she ought not; Queen Charlotte and the Prince of Wales grew no fonder of the Princess of Wales. More important, it was clear where public sympathy lay. The Prince had intended that the Jerseys should go, on return to London, into Warwick House, the building adjoining the secondary courtyard of Carlton House. This plan foundered after Lord Thurlow's remonstrance that it would be very unwise in the present disturbed state of public opinion. The Jerseys took up residence instead in another house on Pall Mall – 'still harping on Carlton House', as Walpole put it.[52]

## CHAPTER FOUR

# THE CARLTON HOUSE SYSTEM

## 1795–1796

*'Nature has not made us suitable to each other'*

TOWARDS THE END OF NOVEMBER 1795 the Prince and Princess of Wales took up residence again in Carlton House, although not before what he called an 'explanation' had been given to her in the garden of the Pavilion by 'mutual friends'. During this encounter the 'mutual friends' admitted to his wife, now seven and a half months pregnant, the Prince's attachment to a lady of rank – better so, they said, than an attachment to a 'low woman'.[1] Dr Underwood, the *accoucheur* selected for the Princess's confinement, had been anxious, with the Queen, that the Princess should return to London well in advance of the child's birth.

The Queen put aside her personal feelings towards the Princess to assemble the necessary attendants for the royal confinement and for the nursery thereafter. She reminded her son also about the 'childbed linen', which should be ordered as soon as possible. Since August she had been interviewing doctors, wet-nurses, monthly nurses. Lady Dashwood, one of Princess Elizabeth's ladies, was to bear the stern title of Governess to the infant.

There were no grand dinners or entertainments in the state rooms at Carlton House this winter. Those rooms were shut up under the new system of economy, their furniture encased in holland covers. The Prince was anyway rarely at Carlton House in the weeks before his wife's accouchement, preferring The Grange, a house with a shoot in Northington, Hampshire, which he had rented in October; and the Queen and the princesses seldom visited Caroline at Carlton House. Far from criticizing them for this inattention, the Prince later complained to his father of his wife's own 'private conduct in the family' and wrote of 'The cruel calumnies with which she has loaded the Duke and Duchess of York, especially the Duchess ... her attempts to sow the seeds of discord between every branch of us: her odious endeavours to vitiate the principles of my innocent sisters ...'.[2] The Princess of Wales objected once that she did not see how the Prince could be so well informed of all her faults as he had seen no more of her than she had seen of Mr Pitt, a dozen times at Court.[3] She made a few new friends in his absence and held occasional evening parties in her private apartments, composed of ladies and gentlemen on the list supplied by the Queen.

Her uncle, the Duke of Gloucester, who had returned to favour with his brother the King since his disreputable marriage, and Princess Sophia Matilda, his pretty daughter, were favourites with the Princess of Wales, as were the Cholmondeleys, who steered a difficult course between their royal master and mistress. (Lady Cholmondeley was one of the Princess's ladies.) One of her women of the bed-chamber, Mrs Fitzroy, became a friend, but another, Mrs Pelham, was Lady Jersey's intimate, and therefore a thorn, with the Countess herself, in the Princess's side.

The royal birth was eagerly awaited. Early in January 1796 Lady Dashwood, who was at Nerot's Hotel in Leicester Fields awaiting the commencement of her duties, wrote to Princess Elizabeth that she thought the Princess's time was not far off. 'You may easily imagine what a constant state of anxiety we have been in ...', wrote Princess Elizabeth on 4 January to her brother, the Prince of Wales:

> whenever the door opens we are in expectation of good news and when at Frogmore the house bell makes me jump and fly to the window in hopes of being the person to bring the news of this happy event to mama who thinks much of you, for we are sure you are upon the high fidgets walking about the room, pulling your fingers and very anxious.[4]

The Princess of Wales began 'a terrible hard labour' in the evening of 6 January. At nine in the morning of the 7th, twelve hours later, in the presence of a throng including the Archbishop of Canterbury, her uncle the Duke of Gloucester, the Lord Chancellor and the Lord President of the Council, she gave birth to 'an immense girl', as the Prince informed his mother. 'And I assure you notwithstanding we might have wished for a boy, I receive her with all the affection possible, and bow with due deference and resignation to the decrees of providence. . . .'[5] The King greeted the news with enthusiasm, 'drank her health at dinner, and went into the equerries' room and made them drink it in a bumper'. He had hoped that the child would be a girl, he wrote to his son. 'You are both young, and I trust will have many children, and this newcomer will equally call for the protection of its parents and consequently be a bond of additional union.'[6]

The child, who on 11 February was christened Charlotte Augusta after her two grandmothers, proved nothing of the kind. While mother and child did well, the Prince of Wales succumbed, a few days after Princess Charlotte's birth, to a fit of rage and self-indulgence, possibly exacerbated by spirits, during which he came to think himself close to the grave. He ventilated his feelings, in consequence, in a last will and testament which ran to 3000 words. In this extraordinary document, the Prince unexpectedly afforded sentimental recognition to his union with Mrs Fitzherbert. 'To her who is called the Princess of Wales I leave one shilling', and 'All my worldly property of every description to my Maria Fitzherbert', was the burden of the Prince's plaintive will. He left his infant daughter Charlotte expressly to the care of his father and mother, thereafter to his brothers and sisters and Lord Moira:

> The mother of this child, called the Princess of Wales, should in no way either be concerned in the education or care of the child, or have possession of her person, for though I forgive her the falsehood and treachery of her conduct towards me, still the convincing and repeated proofs I have received of her entire want of judgment and feeling make me deem it incumbent upon me and a duty, both as a parent and a man, to prevent by all means possible the child's falling into such improper and bad hands as hers. . . .

Furthermore, the Prince commanded that the contents of one box among his papers, marked 'Private', should be published, 'in order that if any objection is made from any quarter . . . to the strict arrangement I have marked out for the trust respecting my daughter, the world may then know why I have so justly and continuously attended to her education, and therefore why I have nominated my brothers and sisters, together with the Earl of Moira, for the sole care of both her person and education'. The papers in this box were presumably correspondence between the Prince and the Princess, or perhaps the letters the Princess wrote to Brunswick. Any letter handwritten by Caroline, of course, would have cast grave doubts on her fitness to superintend a child's writing and grammar lessons, but that was hardly the Prince's point.

The Prince left no personal property in his will to that child, Charlotte, to whose interests he professed himself devoted. All his property was to pass to Mrs Fitzherbert, 'the wife of my heart and soul, and though by the laws of this country she could not avail herself publicly of that name, still such it is in the eyes of Heaven, was, is and ever will be such in mine ...'. He declared that only 'the most infamous ... calumnies' against her had brought 'my too credulous and perceptible heart' to think of separating from her. 'Nor was such a separation, Oh my God!, as thou well knowest, voluntarily sought by me,' the Prince asserted in his hysteria.

Despite his all-embracing bequest of 'All my worldly property', the Prince stated that he was leaving to Maria all the furniture in Carlton House, as well as a prodigious list of all the items which might not be included under that description, including chimneypieces, hangings, cabinets, consoles, chairs, tables. He willed her his clocks, mirrors, lustres, candelabras, plate, china, wine, liquor. She was to receive all his books, plans, maps, prints and drawings, jewels, rings, watches, boxes. His possessions in the country and at Brighton, including his horses and carriages there, were to be hers. 'In short, every article of property that is mine ... I will, bequeathe and leave to my Maria Fitzherbert, my beloved and adored wife.'

With the injunction that the jewels he had given 'her who is called the Princess of Wales' should be removed and given to his infant daughter – theft, rather than legacy – the Prince closed this bizarre testament.[7] He then recovered with speed from the illness which he had thought fatal. With a mind to the funeral arrangements which he fancied were imminent, the Prince had directed in the will that his 'constant companion', a miniature of Maria, should be placed in the grave with him, around his neck on a ribbon 'as I used to wear it when I lived and placed right upon my heart'. Apparently as swiftly, the Prince of Wales forgot Mrs Fitzherbert's charms, and the will was left unwitnessed among his papers (no more valid than the marriage of which he wrote). A few weeks later, the MP Mr Charles Abbott recorded that Lady Jersey was invited with the Prince's party to the Queen's House

> and put to a card table with the Princess Augusta and Lady Holdernesse. The Prince of Wales in the course of the evening repeatedly came up to her table, and publicly squeezed her hand. The King sees and disapproves of the Carlton House system. The Queen is won over to the Prince's wishes by his attentions and presents in jewels, etc; the Princess says, her father told her to observe everything, but say nothing.[8]

The 'Carlton House system' had become something of an open scandal when Lady Jersey came once more into waiting shortly after Princess Charlotte's birth. The Princess was, as she put it, 'shut up all long day' with the Countess till after dinner, at which the Prince might or might not be present. The Princess then retired, while the Prince and Lady Jersey attended parties of pleasure together. The Prince considered that he was merely following the Princess's own father's advice, to keep her confined, and paid no heed to cries in the public prints that the Princess of Wales was a 'state prisoner'.

The nursery quarters at Carlton House were fashioned out of rooms on the attic floor, overlooking Pall Mall, and included the nursery itself, a room for Lady Dashwood's convenience and a bedchamber for Miss Garth. Miss Frances Garth, a niece of the King's equerry General Garth, was appointed sub-governess at the end of January, when Lady Dashwood's health gave cause for concern. The Princess of Wales spent many hours in the nursery with her child, Miss Garth and the other attendants – Mrs Bower, the nurse, the nursery maid and two rockers.[9] Caroline also often joined the nursery party when her daughter was carried down to the garden for her morning airings, with the page, Robert Hownam, in attendance.

The Princess's free association with her daughter, the exercise of her maternal feelings, was a source of grave discontent to the Prince. He had laid down rules for the governess and sub-governess, which allowed only for a morning visit from the child, before or after her airing, to her mother. The Prince, however, in the very month his daughter was born, told the Queen that Lady Dashwood had 'let me into her ideas . . . that everything was not quite as she or I could wish'. He begged his mother to see Miss Garth, who was just appointed, 'to give her her lecture, and to put her on her guard, before ever she sets foot in the house, and to let her know that she is responsible to Lady Dashwood and to me'.[10]

But the Princess of Wales unexpectedly made a friend of sensible, quiet Miss Garth, who had been brought up 'in a very plain and solid way' by her grandmother. Miss Garth, aged twenty-three, was of course a good deal closer in age to the Princess, now aged twenty-seven, than any of her ladies. Caroline was sympathetic to the sub-governess's restricted life, and a note survives urging her to go out for the evening as the Princess was downstairs and could hear if Charlotte cried. Lady Dashwood took the baby on weekly visits to her grandmother at the Queen's House (Buckingham House). Because the governess's health was not good, on several occasions Miss Garth had to perform this duty. Lady Dashwood sent a note, instructing the sub-governess to wrap the child up well, as 'the wind on the staircase at the Queen's House is very great'.[11]

The Princess of Wales accompanied her child on these visits to the Queen, but, as an account of one of them shows, she was not accorded a warm welcome. Princess Sophia, who for want of any other beaux was amorously entangled with General Garth, wrote to his niece, Miss Garth, in some distress:

> The idea only of doing any thing unkind myself by any soul breaks my heart. In short last Wednesday when I had the comfort of seeing my amiable Miss Garth and of sitting and conversing with her in the drawing Room at the Queen's House I left you abruptly in order to take leave of the dear Princess of Wales. She took hold of my hand in the most affectionate manner and asked me to follow her as she wanted to speak to me. . . . I did not dare as the Queen called me back – I thought I saw my dear sister was hurt, which . . . smote my heart most deeply.

Happily, when Princess Sophia next saw the Princess, all was resolved. The Princess of Wales said, 'I perceived you withdrew from me but I saw your motive, and approved greatly.'[12] As Lord Malmesbury had said, Caroline had not a grain of rancour in her body.

To add to the troubles at Carlton House, the Prince was still 'deeply in debt', for all Parliament's aid, as he told his father in February. Pitt would do nothing unless the King so directed, and the Prince's creditors were about to descend. The jeweller Nathaniel Jeffries, who the previous year had supplied him with £60,000 worth of diamonds and other nuptial jewels – including all those the Prince wished to remove from his wife – published a pamphlet outlining his grievances. Another creditor, it was reported, lay in wait at the gate to tell the Prince, 'You will soon be in your Papa's Bench.' There were rumours that bailiffs had sat in the splendid hall of Carlton House.

Yet still the Prince continued the 'Carlton House system' with Lady Jersey. Mr Charles Abbott reported in the spring, 'The Princess of Wales dines always alone [that is, without the Prince]; and sees no company but old people put on her list by the Queen, Lady Jersey, etc. She goes nowhere but airings in Hyde Park. The Prince uses her unpardonably.'[13] He had reported in mid-March: 'The Queen openly patronizes Lady Jersey. The Prince and Princess of Wales within these three days have had an open difference, but at the opera last night affected an extraordinary cordiality.'[14]

According to the Princess, the Prince said to her during this 'open difference' that she ought to be pleased that he was attached to 'an inclination of ancient date rather than to a young and beautiful woman'.[15] Perhaps the Prince had forgotten that the day after their marriage he had claimed mere friendship with Lady Jersey. The public cordiality was a sham, and the Prince, deeply sensitive to his public standing, suspected the Princess of attempts to 'give false impressions of me to the public and to raise herself at my expense'. He did not consider that his own neglect of the Princess stirred up public sympathy in her favour, but instead summoned Lord Malmesbury to him on Friday, 18 March. After speaking intemperately of the Princess, 'how I have been deceived, how I have been treated', the Prince of Wales ended by announcing his wish to part from her. Malmesbury wrote to the Prince a week later, expressing his earnest hope that 'your Royal Highness has, on more mature consideration, entirely dismissed from your thoughts the idea of carrying into effect a step which you then appeared to have nearly resolved upon'. He counselled the Prince: 'in your exalted situation, it is not your private feelings alone ... that you have to consult ... your interests and happiness are so closely united with those of the country at large that it is impossible for you to take any material step on which the public will not claim a right to form a judgment. ...'[16]

These arguments convinced the Prince and he replied disingenuously that Malmesbury had misunderstood him (Malmesbury firmly replied that every word of their conversation would 'ever remain deeply impressed on my memory'): 'I never can wish, as long as the Princess and myself dwell under the same roof, to state to the world her real character but which I may hereafter be obliged to do in justification of my own, should she either be so ill-advised as to force it, or unconquerable circumstances require it.' The Prince was presumably considering publication of the contents of that 'Private' box to which he had referred in his will. In his eyes, the rumours that the Princess was a 'state prisoner', that he treated her brutally, emanated directly from the Princess herself. It did not occur to him that she had, in her restricted life, little opportunity to disseminate these opinions. He mentioned the 'explanation' which he had had with the Princess at Brighton. If she insisted upon 'further explanations before anybody but before my own family ... the immediate consequence ... must be our immediate separation'.

The Prince's resolution was put to the test only a month after he had written to Lord Malmesbury, when a heated correspondence developed between him and his wife. (While this domestic dispute engulfed the royal family, the French general Napoleon Bonaparte, on the orders of the Directory, France's new government, was embarking on his campaign to drive the Austrians from Italy.) The Princess later told the Duke of Leeds that 'the correspondence which had passed between them was of a most extraordinary nature, and ... if her grandchildren were to see them they would scarcely believe possible. The letters were dated from the Green or Yellow Room according to the parties who wrote them, and some of his letters in such a style as she scarcely conceived any man would have written to any woman.'[17] It is fair to say that the Princess's own letters displayed little delicacy.

The Prince had been 'led for some time into a course of dinners abroad' in London, as he put it, and the Princess had perforce dined alone with Lady Jersey. Furthermore, the Princess averred in May, she had not even seen him for three months except in public or at the Queen's House. In the third week of April, her patience gave way. She first charged Lord Cholmondeley with a message for her husband, then, receiving no answer, wrote the Prince a letter herself, 'as I never have the pleasure to see you alone'. The Princess plainly saw, she declared, that the Prince could not bring himself to dine with her. She begged that he would cease to exact a similar sacrifice from her – 'to dine alone with a person whom I can neither like nor respect, and who is your mistress, and to be shut up with her all the long day'. She asked him to reflect on her 'extremely disagreeable and embarrassing' situation, and alter it, thus displaying the generosity of spirit for which the English nation was famed. If her expressions were too strong, her heart was 'torn by the most lively pain and mortal chagrin'.[18] She appealed to him as the mother of the child who was so dear to him.

The Prince sent Lady Cholmondeley to his wife's apartments with a written response the same day. He was outraged by the 'indelicate expressions' his wife used about his trusted friend Lady Jersey, and whom he had declared, on the Princess's arrival in England, 'not to be my mistress as you indecorously term her'. As we have noted, the Prince was not as consistent on this point as he now claimed. But veering round to the attack he argued that, in any case, the Princess's declared repugnance at the idea of his taking a mistress sat oddly with her 'praises of another woman ... the only drift of which could be to reconcile me to a person whose conduct I always must resent with just indignation'. He was referring, with characteristic ambivalence, to Mrs Fitzherbert.

The Prince objected to the Princess's complaint that he obliged her to dine 'tête-à-tête' with the Countess. She had seven other ladies in her family, 'any or every one of whom it is in your power to summon either for dinner or for company at any hour of the day'.

Although there were indeed seven other ladies, in practice Caroline was restricted to the two currently serving their three months. Even so, the Prince expressed the fear that her complaint was 'not meant for me, who must know the total want of foundation for such a representation'. He believed that the 'forced and invidious compliment paid to the English nation' in her letter betokened her intention to appeal to a wider audience. He warned her against 'your attempting – and in which you must fail – to establish an interest . . . irreconcilable to my own' with 'unfair and insidious attacks'. He counselled moderation:

> We have unfortunately been obliged to acknowledge to each other that we cannot find happiness in our union. Circumstances of character and education . . . render that impossible. It then only remains that we should make the situation as little uncomfortable to each other as its nature will allow . . . which is only to be done by not wantonly creating or magnifying uncomfortable circumstances. . . .[19]

The Princess wrote back in distress. It was the Prince who had brought up the subject of Mrs Fitzherbert on her arrival in the country, and she, Caroline, had only expressed an interest in the lady, in that she had formerly 'had the good fortune to possess your heart'. She would have believed the Prince's assurances that he gave his heart to her on marriage, and that Lady Jersey was not his mistress, if he had not, by his coldness and ill-treatment towards her, shown the real state of affairs. Moreover, at Brighton and in March of this year, she wrote, he had explicitly acknowledged his attachment to Lady Jersey. The Princess was most distressed at the insinuation that she sought to 'form a party in the Kingdom. I am not more offended than I am astonished. I am nothing here but through you. I have hardly seen the country, and I know almost none of the inhabitants. You must see in me a lofty spirit, or an unmeasured ambition, to believe me capable of imagining such a ridiculous project.' She admired the Queen for the distance she kept from politics, and took her as her model.[20]

The correspondence at Carlton House rumbled on in the last week of April, with recrimination and counter-recrimination conducted by Lord and Lady Cholmondeley between the combatants in their separate apartments. If the Princess revered the Queen, the Prince of

Wales informed her, then she should 'take example from the amiable solicitude with which she has always studied the King's disposition and promoted his comfort'. This was not to be accomplished by 'irritating insinuation or fretful complaints', or by showing the correspondence to her uncle, the Duke of Gloucester.[21]

The Princess replied, why did the Prince not copy his father's conjugal example towards his wife? The appeal she had made to the Duke of Gloucester was only natural; she had no one else to turn to 'in this immense country'. She was astonished by the Prince's own appeal to Lord Malmesbury, and by the false accusations he had made to him against her.[22] The Prince replied with a somewhat obscurely phrased proposal for their continued existence together.[23] The Princess begged him to explain himself in person to her, whether before mutual friends or even before the King.[24]

The Prince was reluctant to explain himself, had had difficulty in 'indicating even distinctly' to Lady Cholmondeley 'circumstances which can with decorum hardly be mentioned between woman and woman'. He believed, however, that Lady Cholmondeley understood him fully, and he begged her 'to be perfectly explicit' with the Princess, as the 'hints' so far delivered on the subject had not answered. Lady Cholmondeley declared herself 'totally unequal to a conversation of such an unpleasant nature this morning',[25] and it was not till the following day that the Princess understood the nature of the Prince's proposal. She asked for it to be put in writing, and the Prince, who had retreated to Windsor, wrote on 30 April:

> As Lord Cholmondeley informs me that you wish I would define, in writing, the terms upon which we are to live. I shall endeavour to explain myself upon that head with as much clearness and with as much propriety as the nature of the subject will admit. Our inclinations are not in our power, nor should either of us be held answerable to the other because nature has not made us suitable to each other. Tranquil and comfortable society is, however, in our power; let our intercourse therefore be restricted to that, and I will distinctly subscribe to the condition which you required through Lady Cholmondeley, that even in the event of any accident happening to my daughter ... I shall not infringe the terms of the restriction by proposing, at any period, a connection of a more particular nature.[26]

The Prince received no reply to this letter for a week. He was then horrified to receive at Petworth, in Sussex, a letter from the Princess informing him that she had sent a copy of his letter, and of this one to him, to the King, as to her sovereign and her father. 'The knowledge of your conversation with Lady Cholmondeley does not offend or astonish me,' she wrote. 'It only confirmed what you have tacitly insinuated for over a year. . . . I would not have replied, had your letter not been so constructed as to leave doubt whether the arrangement originated from me or from you, and you know that yours is the sole honour.'[27]

The Prince told his mother he did not know whether he was not dreaming. 'Who the advisers of this step can be, I cannot imagine.' The Princess did indeed now have a counsellor, in the shape of Lord Thurlow, who was her husband's own legal adviser and, in addition, was on her 'list'. So she could summon him with propriety. Thurlow declared that he was with the Princess when she wrote to the King, but that the letter 'was written by the Princess of her own accord, and though in his [Thurlow's] presence, without any assistance from him'. He further affirmed that 'nothing could be more judicious than her conversation, and that in many instances he preferred her mode of arguing the subject to his own'.[28]

The Princess's letter to the King began, 'Allow me in the embarrassing position in which I am placed, your Majesty, to implore your intervention in a matter which has infinite importance for the happiness of your family, and of which you are consequently the sole judge.' And she implored her uncle to 'accord your royal protection to a mother and daughter on an occasion which affects the safety of both'.[29] Four days after the Duke of Gloucester took the letters to his brother at Windsor, Lord Jersey made an ill-judged appeal to the King regarding his and his wife's posts in the Prince's Household, which 'no invidious malice or the most designing artifices will induce us to resign'.[30]

While all around him raged and begged, the King counselled moderation. He returned the Princess's packet of letters to her, with a kindly meant note: 'a disunion between the parents is the ruin of the little one which should be an essential object to both. . . . In place of reopening your complaints, do your best to make your home agreeable.'[31] To the Duke of Gloucester he wrote, 'As [for] the dispute that led to this unhappy correspondence, too much heat appears from both sides, which tends only to further acrimony. It is high time to put a stop to it. . . . My son seems willing to live on terms of civility and good humour. You have told me she is willing to do so also.' The King suggested that the Duke, as related to both, might listen to both sides and 'get materials for such an explanation as may prevent further altercation. . . . The Princess seems to think no former etiquette [of previous Princesses of Wales] necessary that frustrates her idea of amusement. Learn from my son what he expects and bring the Princess to acquiesce to his ideas. Believe me, submission in a woman always secures esteem, she must obtain that before more can be expected.'[32]

The Prince, quite distracted, hardly knowing what to do, even sent his brother Prince Ernest to Mrs Fitzherbert to propose a reconciliation. 'She is frightened to death,' reported Prince Ernest on 17 May, 'knows not what to say, as is natural to be assumed as you have come upon her so unexpectedly. . . . She always owns to this, that if she did make it up, you would not agree a fortnight.'[33] The following day, notwithstanding these overtures to his supposed first wife, the Prince, who still remained away, wrote to the Princess. 'From sincere anxiety to prevent a rupture', he once more proposed conditions of 'future domestic intercourse'. It would be her own fault, he then wrote aggressively, if by revolting him with indecorous behaviour she did not receive from him every due mark of attention. He must go about still, where he was called. The Princess had a list of suitable people whom she might invite. 'That a greater latitude of society is not permitted to the Princess, she must know to be solely due to the etiquette attached to her rank.'[34]

Unfortunately, the Princess did not submit to the Prince's ideas. She decided to insist that Lady Jersey be removed from her family or household. But this the Prince refused to concede. The matter was now one of public knowledge. On 24 May *The Times* printed a 'rumour of a separation in high life'. The Margravine of Anspach even offered the Princess the use of Brandenburg House at Hammersmith, 'in case the Princess thought proper to remove from Carlton House'.[35] The Duke of Leeds was in his box at the opera when the

Princess arrived on the Saturday, with Lady Carnarvon, Mrs Fitzroy and Colonel Thomas, the Prince's vice-chamberlain. 'The pit and some of the boxes began to applaud and the whole house almost instantly rose and joined in the applause.' The Duke went down to her and, according to Walpole, who was also present, persuaded her not to retire, but to curtsey to the house. The Princess asked Leeds, as the applause and the huzzas continued, 'My God! what does this mean?' He answered that he did not dare say what he thought.

When the Princess finally sat down, the audience called for 'God Save the King', which the orchestra immediately played, to universal acclamation – 'One person with great emphasis calling out, God save the Princess, say I.'[36] Walpole noted that 'their Majesties were not there, or a third person [the Queen] might have heard something unpleasant, as the town has got a notion of too much favouring Lady Jersey, at least'.[37] (The beleaguered Lady Jersey was meanwhile mourning her infant son, who had died this same day.) The Princess told Leeds 'she supposed she should be guillotined . . . for what had passed this evening' when the Prince returned to town on the Monday.

Three days later, Walpole reported again. 'The crisis ripens, the universal applause was repeated on Tuesday at the opera, but nothing offensive heard. I think her appearance was well advised; her absence would have fallen on her husband, and been imputed to him; to suppose that she sought popularity would have offended nobody but him.'[38] The Princess lamented the situation to the Duke of Leeds, 'and the effect which might be produced by the public applause she met with as perhaps offending still more the Prince. She did not attribute his cruel treatment of her to himself but to Lady Jersey.'

The Duke expressed his astonishment that Lady Jersey 'had not common sense enough to resign on pretext of ill-health or mourning, rather than venture actual danger from the mob; she said it was otherwise ordered, and the Prince would not hear of her resignation'. The Princess spoke of the Prince's allegations against herself of 'among other crimes . . . immoderate ambition, and intending to create a party against him. God knows,' she continued, 'I had no other ambition than to make him and of course myself happy; what was I independent of him had I been ambitious? nobody, my only consequence was derived from being his wife. . . .'[39]

The Prince was, as his wife foretold, hysterical with rage at the declarations of support for her and took pains to discover who were the most active at the opera. As he had suspected, they were 'the primitive agents of Mrs Fitzherbert'. Lord Darnley and Lord Henry Fitzgerald were among many friends of Mrs Fitzherbert who deplored the Prince's behaviour to her. It was certainly curious that they should cheer the Princess who had supplanted her. In the Prince's view, they had been trying for months past to form a party 'by every species of lie through the channel of the unsuspecting part of their acquaintance as well as through every scurrilous newspaper'.

He believed, he told the Queen, that the 'machinations' of Lord Thurlow, whom the Prince had now forbidden to visit Carlton House, and of Lady Stafford were unconnected with the supposed party, although Lady Stafford visited Mrs Fitzherbert:

> Their end is evidently the same, to answer their own interested views by the most unjustifiable and malignant means, the blackening to the world of my reputation, and by it striking at that of most of the royal family. Think for a moment, my dearest mother, of the dangerous consequences of the Princess having thrown herself into such hands. . . .

He expressed his 'thorough conviction that not only my humiliation but my total destruction is aimed at . . .'.[40] Lord Thurlow agreed with the Duke of Leeds that 'the Prince's strange conduct could alone be imputed to madness'.[41]

In a further letter that day the Prince said, 'I neither will give myself up, nor those who are solely injured on my account' – that is, Lady Jersey. He refused to humiliate himself before 'the vilest wretch this world was ever cursed with, who I cannot feel more disgust for from her personal nastiness than I do from her entire want of principle', and called the Princess 'a very monster of iniquity'.[42] He was now determined on a separation from her and wrote to the King, confident that it would be granted now that the Princess was, in his opinion, evidently an instrument of party.

The King replied on 2 June, forbidding a separation in terms which the Lord Chancellor, Lord Loughborough, believed 'cannot fail to make a just impression on the Prince of Wales'.[43] But the Prince felt unable to obey his father. 'I am serving my family in the most essential manner,' he wrote to his mother, 'by ridding them of a fiend under whose influence otherwise, not only I, but you and all the rest of us must make up our minds to submit to for the rest of our lives.'[44] His sister Princess Elizabeth wrote to him to insist that 'a resignation [that of Lady Jersey] must take place for the sake of the country and the whole royal family'.[45] The Prince took no notice.

Meanwhile, the King was consulting with the Chancellor to halt the lunacy. Moira told the Prince 'of this extraordinary ferment. . . . Things, indeed, are very bad. . . . how violently the tide of prejudice runs.'[46] The King believed that 'some person or other worked on the Princess and whoever they are they are acting exceedingly wrong'.[47] Yet he saw the justice of her request to have Lady Jersey replaced. The Chancellor and Moira consulted together, and Moira was empowered to offer terms to the Princess.

At the ensuing conference, the Princess accepted that the Prince could not be seen to submit to her, and she spoke happily of 'an honourable accommodation' after she had been assured that Lady Jersey would resign. However, the Princess had not understood that she would be expected to receive Lady Jersey, not in private, but at larger gatherings, should the Prince's finances permit them, at Carlton House. When she realized this, she became as violent in her way as the Prince. 'She never would suffer Lady Jersey to set foot in any house in which she was,' she told Cholmondeley, 'as long as she lived, and . . . if she came to dinner she would get up from the table and go and dine in her own room.'[48] When this was reported to the Prince, he spoke again of a separation by mutual consent and employed the same image of the dining-table – with reference to Caroline herself. 'My abhorrence of her is such,' he confessed, 'and the rooted aversion and detestation that I feel towards her, that I shudder at the very thoughts of sitting at the same table with her, or even of being under the same roof with her.'[49]

The Princess of Wales, whose 'rooted aversion' was to Lady Jersey and not to her husband, recanted. She wrote to the King on 12 June:

My sole and true happiness cannot but consist in a perfect reconciliation with the Prince of Wales. . . . However, I declare at the same time
that I can see no other true means of permanent reconciliation than
the absolute retreat of Lady Jersey from my service and private society.
If the pecuniary affairs of the Prince of Wales alter, and I hold
drawing-rooms or grand assemblies and balls, Lady Jersey shall be
admitted as any other indifferent person, as long as the Queen consents
to receive her also.[50]

The Prince, when given a copy of this barbed proposal, returned
no answer but wrote in despair to Moira: 'A reconciliation is only
desirable from the view of keeping up appearances and thereby
standing well in the public opinion.'[51] Matters were at a standstill.
The Prince remained in the country, shuttling gloomily between
Oatlands, the home of his brother the Duke of York, and Richmond,
that of his brother Clarence. He was not cheered by reports of the
Princess's behaviour at the Westminster election. Not content with
holding her daughter up to the crowds who cheered Mr Charles James
Fox in Pall Mall on his way to the hustings, she then drove to Fox's
house, according to the Prince, to congratulate him on his victory.

Lady Jersey's resignation and the formal reconciliation of the
Prince and Princess of Wales were now eagerly sought by all but the
Prince. Mr Charles Abbott commented, 'The conduct of the Princess
of Wales seems to have been the most discreet and amiable which in
her peculiar situation could be expected. She has addressed herself to
those whom the Prince has pointed out to her as his friends and
friends of the royal family, viz. Lord Thurlow, Duke of Leeds, etc.'[52]
But still the Prince returned no answer to the Princess's paper of 12
June.

After the drawing-room on 16 June, the Princess had a conference
with both the Duke of Leeds and Lord Cholmondeley, at which it
was agreed that Cholmondeley should go to the Prince at Richmond
and require an answer. The Princess was not sanguine, and lamented
'the unceasing misery she had experienced ever since her marriage'.
Lord Cholmondeley regretted privately to the Duke 'the cruel
situation of the unfortunate Princess, and the strange infatuation of
the Prince, who seemed equally insensible both to his reputation in
the world and his own comfort, as to the situation in which his

conduct might place him eventually whether as heir apparent or actually entitled to the crown.'[53]

At Richmond Lord Cholmondeley found the Prince 'more violent than ever, his chief wish seemed to be a total separation from the Princess. . . . he declared in the strongest terms his antipathy towards her, adding that he had rather see toads and vipers crawling over his victuals than sit at the same table with her!!!' The Prince did not raise 'any very strong objection' to Lady Jersey's dismissal, 'but would not be dictated to, and was determined to see what company he pleased at any time at Carlton House'.[54]

With this concession the Princess had to be content, and in the course of the next few days the Prince wrote to his father, assenting to Lady Jersey's resignation. The King was eager that all should be settled, and refused to see the Prince, who begged a hearing, on the ground that any conversation would retard matters. On receiving a letter from the Princess complaining that the public believed that she was opposed to a reconciliation, the King, according to Prince Ernest, said he would avail himself of the opportunity to reply that 'He had heard so.'[55] He did write – and firmly – to the Princess on 25 June: 'I will not hide from you that this opinion begins to take root. There is only one way to destroy it.' As the Prince had consented to her desire that the Countess should leave her service, 'you must make witness to your desire that he comes back to you'.[56]

Lady Stafford told her son, Lord Granville Leveson Gower, on 29 June that Princess Caroline 'wrote [to her husband] in consequence one of the prettiest letters you ever saw, to which she had a most cold, stupid answer, to say that he should be at Carlton House in the course of Monday [27 June]. At what time he arrived I know not, but at eight o'clock he called for dinner, and desired to let the Princess know.' Lord Moira had counselled the Prince in vain: 'It would not become your Royal Highness to enter into a war of peevishness . . . not to give her any plausible pretext, so that the breach, if a new one . . . may be distinctly her fault.'[57] As Lady Stafford reported:

> His behaviour was like his letter, insomuch that had he behaved so to any other lady the husband must have thought that he meant to let her know he never desired to see her again. As soon as dinner was over he

went to Lady Jersey. He protests he will never go to the opera with the Princess, and is entirely directed by Lady Jersey. This is called a reconciliation! How great a curse is he to the poor King, and to these nations![58]

The exhausting quarrels that led to this 'reconciliation' ended with Lady Jersey's letter of resignation to the Princess,[59] which *The Times* called 'one of the most disrespectful we ever recollect to have read'. The Princess had won her object, but the cost was high. She had increased by her battle her husband's enmity. Moreover, by asserting herself against the Prince, she had alienated the Queen still further, shocked the princesses and set doubts in her uncle the King's mind about her conduct. The Princess, however, was for the moment triumphant. At the Opera House, the Duke of Leeds 'thought it right to prepare her Royal Highness for the firing of the robber' (for a pistol-shot) during a ballet, *The Scottish Sorceresses*. She answered, 'When the daughter of a hero marries a zero, she does not fear gunfire.'[60]

The Prince summered at Crichel in Dorset and at Brighton. She remained in London with her daughter, although Walpole heard in August that one of her bedchamber women, Mrs Lisle, was commissioned to search for a villa.[61] The season proved too advanced, but the indications were clear: the Prince and Princess, although formally reconciled, would in future live separate lives.

## CHAPTER FIVE

# UNOFFICIAL SEPARATION

## 1796–1798

*'Under no further obligations and rules'*

IN THE AUTUMN OF 1796 the Prince of Wales returned to Carlton House to discover that the Princess had taken advantage of his absence during the summer, on two occasions, to invite 'company to dinner composed of others besides her Household' and had 'increased her evening parties beyond the list' which the Prince had furnished to Lord Cholmondeley. 'Any infringement of these rules', the Prince told Cholmondeley in October, 'I never can nor will admit of whilst the Princess remains under my roof as it would lead to consequences subversive of all order and arrangement.'[1] The Duke of Leeds had been present in September at one of these 'subversive' dinners, together with the Prince of Orange. The Prince of Wales was determined that his wife should not deviate from the arrangements he had prescribed. He wrote to the Queen, 'she still persists in the line of conduct she so artfully and maliciously has adopted of endeavouring to draw popularity to herself at my expense and at the expense of the whole family . . .'.[2]

The Prince was still infatuated by Lady Jersey. Apparently forgetful of the cause of his summer purgatorial unpopularity, he revived his plan that his friends the Jerseys should inhabit Warwick House. Even the Queen remonstrated with the Prince: 'The world in general will make it a new instrument against you. . . . the effect of such a public insult makes me shudder.'[3] The Prince justified himself to his mother at length. 'After having been so grossly insulted, traduced and belied by the Princess and her emissaries as I have been, I cannot say that I ever through life can feel the smallest temptation to be particularly attentive to her.'[4] The Princess of Wales told the Duke of Leeds 'that the situation of the House [Warwick House] was well calculated for a spy', as the windows looked directly into hers. 'She added how strange it seemed for Lady Jersey to take possession of her new house just before the meeting of Parliament, as if to remind the public of all that had passed.'[5] As a result of this move, Lord Cholmondeley shifted his office to nearby Chudleigh Court.

The Princess of Wales came to view the Prince's letter of 30 April as according her greater freedom than she had previously enjoyed. She evidently inferred this licence from her husband's words, 'Our inclinations are not in our power, nor should either of us be held answerable to the other because nature has not made us suitable to each other.' It is unlikely that the Prince felt himself to have issued any such licence, at any rate to the Princess. He even continued to act in concert with his mother, rather than his wife, in directing the nursery at Carlton House. Lady Dashwood, a 'treasure' on whom the Prince and the Queen had relied, died, to their consternation, in early October. The Queen hunted through the 'Red Book', or Court Calendar, in which all the ladies and gentlemen in royal employment were listed, to find a fit successor – 'independent, unconnected with party, and whose principles are such as to be depended upon'.[6] The Prince by no means liked the friendship which had developed between the Princess of Wales and the sub-governess, Miss Garth.

The Queen had great difficulty in finding a new governess who would fulfil her duty 'without interfering into any other concerns but the Nursery'. She hoped that one candidate, Lady Templetown, was 'no politician, for the Prince has an aversion to women politicians, and a particular dislike to make the nursery an assembly'. Unfortunately, Lady Templetown proved unsuitable, having, according to Lady Bath, 'a most active mind and a rage for politics'.[7]

The Prince, meanwhile, continued to be outraged by the Princess's conduct. In October he wrote to his mother of a new 'emergency' that had arisen. Lord and Lady Cholmondeley were staying at Houghton, their magnificent house in Norfolk, when Lady Cholmondeley received a letter from her sister Lady Willoughby, who had replaced Lady Jersey as lady-in-waiting to the Princess of Wales. The Princess, wrote Lady Willoughby, had 'expressed a desire of visiting Houghton next week, for two or three days'. Lord Cholmondeley's

letter requesting the Prince's permission for this impromptu visit was
the 'emergency' in question.[8]

The innocent proposal of a country visit became in the Prince's
mind a revolutionary enterprise, designed to whip up the rustic
populace against him. He complained to his mother that 'The idea of
a Princess of Wales travelling all over England ... thus having an
opportunity by showing herself in the country of repeating her tricks'
was one of alarming novelty. He begged the Queen to consult the
King.

> I never heard of the late Princess Dowager [of Wales, his grandmother]
> scampering over England in this kind of way, attended only by her
> lady.... I really am quite astonished at Cholmondeley.... You must
> see that the Princess will never rest quiet, and that as she has already
> encroached in other instances so l'appétit vient en mangeant....[9]

The Prince, relieved to find that the King entered into all his
feelings on the matter, wrote to his wife to tell her that 'upon enquiry,
not finding any precedent for a Princess of Wales making any such
visit', he could not comply with her request.[10] The Princess, however,
pursued the matter:

> I should not have proposed [the visit] ... had I thought it against
> Court etiquette, but as the Queen has been to stay a day or two with
> Lord and Lady Harcourt I did not imagine it would be deemed
> improper for me to do the same with Lord and Lady Cholmondeley,
> particularly as they are your friends. I am the more disappointed as you
> had promised that I should enjoy uninterrupted those innocent
> pleasures consistent with my rank....[11]

She was mistaken, came the joyous reply. The Queen had visited the
Harcourts only in attendance upon the King and at his wish. As for
her 'innocent pleasures', the Prince wrote stiffly, 'those pleasures can
never be admitted or thought of at the expense either of etiquette or
precedent.... any innovation is opening the door to endless inconvenience and impropriety'.[12]

The Prince still suspected the Princess of fomenting, in private and
in public, his unpopularity. 'Hostile paragraphs' still appeared in the
press, notably the Whig newspaper the *Morning Herald*. Colonel

McMahon, whom the Prince often employed in underhand activities with newspaper editors and others, combated these with his own insertions in the *Morning Post*. He believed in November, that it would be 'highly indeed worth doing' to secure the *Herald*, through payments to the proprietor, in the Prince's interest: 'As an enemy, it has been formidable. As an ally, it would be invaluable.' McMahon was convinced, in December, that 'Some invisible agent is certainly kept at work, Sir, by some quarter in the interest of the —— [Princess]; but I trust in God, Sir, that Stuart [the proprietor of the *Morning Post*] will worm him out.'[13]

McMahon was also instructed to observe the Princess's visits to the opera, and reported, also in December, that an appearance, advertised in *The Times*, had not taken place. 'After traversing the house in every part' – McMahon was of diminutive stature, with a red and spotty face – 'I could not discover her Royal Highness's absence to create any particular disappointment, nor discover the smallest disposition to mark her presence by any particular or unusual tokens whatever.'[14] *The Times*, on the other hand, reported, 'The disappointment seemed to be severely felt by the audience.' The Prince's suspicions of the Princess had no discernible foundation. Her former advisers, the Duke of Leeds and Lord Thurlow, were no longer on her 'list'. Those who inserted paragraphs in her praise were more likely enemies of the Prince than agents of hers. McMahon, however, encouraged the Prince in his view and continued to search for the Princess's 'invisible agent'.

The Queen, meanwhile, begged the King to allow her not only to 'shut up shop' or hold no drawing-rooms, as he had suggested, till the town filled, but 'to shut up shop entirely as far as relates to assemblies'. She explained, 'Since the unpleasant affairs of the Prince and Princess of Wales began ... my dislike to everything public is greatly increased.' When she had appeared in public, on the Terrace at Windsor or on the Esplanade at Weymouth, 'I found every word I spoke in the papers and thereby was convinced that spies were sent to watch me. ... I have been so thoroughly wounded at that time that nothing can make it up to me. ...'[15]

Princess Charlotte celebrated her first birthday at Carlton House on 7 January 1797. Her aunts at Windsor sent gifts: a necklace from the sensible Princess Royal, a pair of bracelets from shadowy Princess Augusta, a doll from fashion-plate Princess Mary, a fan from young Princess Amelia, a silver rattle from nervy Princess Sophia and a china toy from the artist in the family, Princess Elizabeth. The Queen sent a cross, with the mournful wish that Charlotte's 'crosses may never be heavier' than this one, when tied around the child's neck.[16]

The Prince drew up new regulations to accompany the appointment of Charlotte's new governess, Lady Elgin, an elderly lady with a strong Scottish accent and a reverence for the royal family, who took up her duties that January. The child, who was taking her first steps, now had a midday sleep, then dinner, an airing and supper before going to bed at eight o'clock. 'Order and regularity' were the great points for the ladies in the nursery to observe. Miss Garth was to continue to have two evenings a week at her disposal, when Lady Elgin would attend the whole evening.[17] Regrettably, less 'order and regularity' were observed by the Prince in the payment of the ladies' salaries, and Miss Garth, whose salary was nine months in arrears in June, was becoming restive to quit her post.

Lord Cholmondeley had found a suitable country residence for the Princess of Wales in the house next to his at Charlton, close to the airy expanses of Blackheath and the river at Greenwich. While the chamberlain disputed a rental of £700 a year with the owner's agent, the Princess took part in April and May in the family celebrations accompanying the Princess Royal's marriage. The bridegroom was none other than the Hereditary Prince of Württemberg, the widower of Caroline's sister Princess Augusta of Brunswick, who had perished so mysteriously. The Princess Royal was the eldest of the 'Sisterhood', as the six princesses were known, and – at thirty years old – the first to dare to make her wish for matrimony known to her father. On seeing her bridegroom, who was now enormously fat, she almost repented.

The Prince of Wales had hoped that he might be spared his wife's presence at his sister's wedding, but the King decreed otherwise: in public, if not in private, the Prince and Princess of Wales were to appear as man and wife. The Prince, obliged to appear at the weekly drawing-rooms in his wife's company, ignored her; when he could, he excused himself from attending them. The artist Copley, who was still working on his painting of the Waleses' wedding, now felt unable to ask for the loan of the Prince's nuptial coat as he had long planned. In Carlton House the Prince avoided his wife, and had Princess Charlotte brought to him at his breakfast, so as to run no risk of meeting the Princess of Wales in the nursery. The Princess declared in August that she had not seen him since March.

The Queen continued to pay all public marks of respect to her daughter-in-law, and begged the Prince to pardon her for not doing more, in the fatigue of the wedding preparations, than coming to breakfast on his wife's twenty-ninth birthday, 17 May. In private the Queen continued to treat the Princess of Wales with coldness, and encouraged her daughters in the same behaviour. Princess Sophia alone of the Sisterhood had a 'partiality for the amiable princess', as she confided to Miss Garth, but this had led her into trouble at Windsor. 'I grieve that it is not in my power to do any good,' she had written earlier. '. . . You know I must be silent, and God knows in silence I feel most deeply attached to her. . . .'[18] This year in April, she wrote to Miss Garth: 'I have and still I fear shall pass many an unhappy moment on that subject for I cannot say what I don't think; therefore I hold my tongue, but it breaks my heart. . . . I try all in my power to keep out of disputes, for which reason I am chiefly alone. . . .'[19]

Miss Garth finally won her wish to resign from her nursery duties at Carlton House when she was appointed bedchamber woman to the Princess of Wales on 5 April 1797. (The salaries of these ladies were paid more regularly.) The Prince objected, however, and Miss Garth was still in residence in the nursery at Carlton House when the new sub-governess, Miss Ann Hayman, came to town at the end of May. 'Miss Garth protested against staying another hour,' Miss Hayman recorded as she took up the nursery baton.[20]

Miss Ann Hayman was a very lively and intelligent young woman from Wrexham in Wales, who moved in the best circles there and became on her arrival in London a pet of, among others, Mrs Crewe, Lady Carysfort and the politician Mr George Canning. She was wholly unacquainted with Courts and etiquette, and the witty and irreverent letters she wrote to her mother from Carlton House give a vivid picture of the domestic battles in that mansion in the summer of 1797. Princess Charlotte was 'the merriest little thing I ever saw', and with a great resemblance to her father, Miss Hayman wrote on first making her charge's acquaintance. 'Pepper hot too, if contradicted she kicks her little feet about in great rage, but the cry ends in a laugh before you well know which it is.' Miss Hayman played with Charlotte before the child's supper of bread and milk at six. The little Princess was greatly taken with her new companion and showed her all her treasures. The next night, quite at ease, the toddler directed her sub-governess on which chair she should sit to watch her being washed. 'She had a coffee pot just before lying down,' Miss Hayman wrote to her mother, 'but in the midst of it said "ta" and went to sleep.'[21]

The Princess of Wales came into the nursery on Miss Hayman's first night in Carlton House and spoke 'very affably' to her several times. She asked, the new sub-governess informed her mother in Wales, if Charlotte was not 'wonderfully like the Prince of Wales, whether I was fond of children, etcetera, and told me hers was very hot [tempered] but very soon pacified – that she had been naughty, but was now by Lady Elgin's care quite a good child'. The Princess of Wales had now obtained her house, the Old Rectory, at Charlton and was busily engaged in going to and fro between London and her new dwelling. She appeared in the nursery constantly, however, when in town. On this occasion, Miss Hayman's first day, she 'chose some lace for frocks, and was very kind in her manner to Lady Elgin', noted the sub-governess. Miss Hayman's own opinion of Lady Elgin was that she was a 'very good old soul ... and though not *very* accomplished seems to have good natural sense enough – by no means the goose she was represented'.[22]

Next morning Miss Hayman had a first meeting, by chance, with the Prince. 'Never had any one such captivating manners. I could have sat down and cried that he is not all he ought to be – sometimes it is impossible to think his heart not naturally good.' Her own good sense reasserted itself, and she described how, the evening before, the Prince had sat at home till midnight, 'meaning every instant to go' and bid farewell to his sister, the Princess Royal, who was leaving for Württemberg next morning. (Their departure had been delayed by the naval mutiny at the Nore, where sailors demanding better conditions briefly threatened Britain's command of the sea in the midst of war.) It was too painful to contemplate, and he deferred the farewell till the morning. He rose at five o'clock with every intention of going, but 'his heart again failed him'. He ended by writing his sister a letter instead. 'This I dare say is characteristic, it shows great feeling, and as great want of fortitude. . . .'

Miss Hayman recorded Lady Elgin's attempt to present her formally to her royal mistress that same morning. 'She [Caroline] laughed, rose up and said "Oh we will shake hands." I took off my glove, she then took off hers, and when she shook hands with me, I begged permission to kiss it.' These formalities over, the Princess had a long conversation with Miss Hayman about books – 'from sermons to novels'. She praised *The Children of the Abbey*, and promised to send it to the sub-governess, which she duly did. On another occasion, hearing that Miss Hayman never had sight of a newspaper – the Prince's papers were 'swallowed up' by his gentlemen – the Princess arranged to send her own up to the nursery.[23]

She called Miss Hayman down to her apartments to play Handel on her 'very delightful' pianoforte for Princess Sophia Matilda of Gloucester, and in every way loaded the governess with attentions. Miss Hayman described in detail how that most ceremonious day of the year, the King's Birthday, 4 June, passed at Carlton House. In the morning, the Princess of Wales took Miss Hayman and Princess Charlotte into her apartment to show them her Court dress, which she was to wear that evening. She played the pianoforte and offered the sub-governess 'camphor julep if I felt alarmed'. Miss Hayman was to go that morning to the Queen's House with Princess Charlotte, who, she had already informed her mother in Wales, was to wear 'a silver muslin frock trimmed with silver net'.

Miss Hayman was directed, on her return, to tell the Princess how the visit to the Queen's House had passed. 'I shall never be a good courtier,' she confessed to her mother. 'I never can feel as much impressed with awe and their grandeur, or as much gratified by their condescension as my poor Lady Elgin and others seem to do.' However, Miss Hayman enjoyed Princess Charlotte's performance on this day of celebration, when the coach drove twice up and down the park. 'She huzzaed and kissed her hand the whole time, the people looked extremely delighted, running with the coach all the way.'

The Princess of Wales ordered up her jewels, and freely praised the Prince's taste in choosing them. Miss Hayman thought them 'more light and elegant than I conceived it possible for diamonds to be'. The Queen's, which she had seen that morning, were 'not near so beautiful though she had many in her head above an inch long and almost square'. The Princess came up and sat in the nursery while Princess Charlotte ate her dinner, then, 'when she was dressed, sent for us down to see her', before she departed for Court with Lady Cholmondeley. Princess Charlotte ended her day huzzaing out of the nursery window 'to a great mob, and all the procession of mail coaches'.[24]

A week after her arrival, Miss Hayman told her mother, 'it is no longer remarkable that I talk and walk with the Princess of Wales for two or three hours a day'.[25] A few days earlier, she had written, 'no hour after twelve is secure from the Princess'. Caroline sat with her in the garden, while Princess Charlotte was drawn about in a little chaise by Hownam, the page. She flitted into Miss Hayman's room, with Princess Charlotte or without.

One evening Miss Hayman was playing with Princess Charlotte on the sofa there, when 'in walked a man covered over with gold and in a jockey cap'. He was a messenger from the Queen, come to enquire why she was still waiting for her granddaughter, whom she had expected at five o'clock. The Princess of Wales walked in upon this scene and laughed at Miss Hayman's consternation. 'Oh my dear, don't ask me,' she said, then proposed sending for Lady Elgin.[26] The Princess showed Miss Hayman some of the magnificent disused state-rooms, 'throwing up the covers of the chairs and turning them down again, as she said, "like an old housekeeper"'. She described the rest of the house, which Miss Hayman had not seen, as equally fine and 'quite useless, she says, for the bedrooms are too fine for anyone to sleep in, and so much is for show that it is fortunate she has no more children, as they could not be accommodated'.[27]

That summer the Prince, who had uncharacteristically made no decorative changes in the house since his marriage, exchanged his bedchamber above the Princess's, overlooking the garden, for that of his daughter, overlooking the stables and park. The convenience for the Princess of Wales, who could now communicate by the private staircase with the nursery above, was probably less in his mind than the wish to reside with her, if reside he must, at the greatest possible distance. His child's attendants were the losers, as the Prince kept all his previous rooms except his bedchamber when he commandeered the nursery apartments. Miss Hayman was disappointed in her new rooms, adjacent to her charge's. They were small and narrow and dark, and looked into the back court.[28]

Miss Hayman's hopes of a fine bedroom and of obtaining promotion for her brother Watkin via her prestigious employment both proved vain. 'I do not see the least probability of it,' she wrote to Watkin. 'He [the Prince of Wales] has no establishment of his own worth speaking of nor the least interest I believe anywhere else. The Princess and Gloucesters . . . can do nothing at all, you know – even in the nursery I scarce think Lady Elgin has the power of change. . . .' The Queen had settled all at the beginning.[29]

Miss Hayman, though full of affection for Princess Charlotte, was anxious, as Miss Garth had been, about her salary and was not keen to remain after the end of August. 'The truth is that the Prince spends all his money on himself. . . ,' Miss Hayman told her mother, 'the nursery department is an extra expense.' The Prince wished 'Pitt and the nation' to pay for it; Pitt and the nation would not. The result was that Miss Garth was still owed three-quarters of her salary as sub-governess and was in debt to her brother Lieutenant Thomas Garth and to tradesmen. Miss Hayman herself had to pay out 'a good many guineas' to servants and messengers: 'The suspense and perplexity are very unpleasant.'[30]

The Prince and Princess of Wales had a passage of arms towards the end of June, when the Princess begged to have Charlotte to stay at the Old Rectory, where she had now taken up residence for the summer, while the Prince was at Brighton. Miss Hayman had escorted Princess Charlotte on a visit to the Princess there earlier that month. The house stood 'a little to the left of Black Heath. . . . the Princess showed me all her house even to the kitchen, laundry and coal hole, and afterwards took me through her garden to Lord Cholmondeley's with whom she is connected by a wicket [gate] in the true genteel style'. Miss Hayman wondered at the Princess's enthusiasm for her new house, without considering that it represented independence and liberty and was, besides, the first house of which she had ever been mistress. 'The situations are beautiful of course as they command the river,' Miss Hayman wrote, 'but Essex as usual looks flat and ugly.'[31]

The Princess wrote to her husband on 25 June, 'This summer as I wished to be in the country for my health you was so good as to allow me to have this place and I had no doubt of being permitted to have the child with me, when the weather was fine enough.' While the Prince had continued in town, she had not requested her child's presence at Charlton. 'As you are now going in to the country and there seems to be some hesitation about her coming to remain at Charlton I shall be much obliged if you would give the order for her removal ... and allow me the pleasure of having my child as she is my greatest comfort in this world.'[32] There was plenty of room for her daughter, the sub-governess and under-attendants in the house. A small house could be taken for Lady Elgin close by.

Two days later, on 27 June, Lord Cholmondeley informed the Princess that the Prince refused her request, whereupon the Princess took her wrongs to the King. 'It is as a mother with a sorrowful heart that I ask for your sage counsel,' the Princess wrote. 'As I am obliged for my health to be in the country' – the Princess was ill several times this summer – 'I wish to have my child with me here.' The Princess enclosed a copy of the letter she had written to the Prince of Wales, so that the King could judge that it could not have offended him or injured his 'amour propre'. And now he refused her 'this great consolation, to have my child with me, as all my happiness and so my consolation is in ... this dear child ...'.[33] She went on to ask the King to guide her in her conduct.

The Princess came from Charlton to London three or four days a week to see Princess Charlotte while the matter remained undecided. Before he left for Brighton, the Prince meanwhile saw his daughter most days. 'She is getting to an age that amuses him, and he grows very fond of her,' Miss Hayman wrote. 'The nurses take her to him, without me' – the Prince disliked his wife's friendship with the sub-governess – 'generally when he breakfasts, and he spoils her dinner with a great piece of bread.'[34]

Princess Charlotte, aged one and a half, was agreed by all to be a 'delightful' child in appearance and character, although subject to great 'passions', or tantrums. With a mop of fair curls, big blue eyes, fair complexion and rosebud mouth, she was considered to have a great resemblance to her father. She was high-spirited. Miss Hayman told how she 'tears her caps with showing me how Mr Canning [who lived on Pall Mall] takes off his hat to her as he rides in the park and I hold up her Royal Highness to the Summer House window'.[35] Charlotte was appropriately solemn when she said her prayers at night: 'Bless Papa, bless Mama, Charlotte and friends' – although on one occasion she blessed 'fleas' instead of 'friends', having been bitten by one the day before.

Old Lady Elgin wrote of all her hopes and fears for the Princess to the child's aunt, the Princess Royal, now Hereditary Princess of Württemberg, who wrote back from Germany in February 1798:

> God grant that you may be enabled to keep her in perfect ignorance of the unfortunate differences between her parents! ... It gives me great pleasure to know that my dear little Charlotte is equally kind to both her parents; maybe, in the end, that little creature may itself serve as a sort of magnet to make them a little better. ...[36]

The Prince of Wales refused to entertain the idea that Princess Charlotte should live anywhere under the same roof as her mother except at Carlton House. The benefit of country air or sea breezes in the summer months, however, could not be ignored. The Prince had no intention of having Princess Charlotte at Brighton. But the Princess of Wales's appeal to the King had an effect, and in August she won a partial victory. The Prince rented Montague House, which occupied a corner of Greenwich Park facing Blackheath, from the Duchess of Buccleuch for Princess Charlotte and her attendants. The Duchess wrote, 'I am afraid it is not in very good order, having been very long uninhabited. The situation, however, I flatter myself will make it agreeable to the Princess of Wales.'[37]

Miss Hayman thought the house 'rather melancholy ... so sur-rounded with trees that it will be dark in autumn'. The Princess of Wales, however, was delighted to have Charlotte with her. Charlotte enjoyed herself, too, at a concert her mother gave for the Prince's birthday in August, 'dancing and amusing herself *by herself* for a full hour in the midst of the circle'. Miss Hayman had to prevent her exuberant charge from playing on the harpsichords and violoncellos. The Stadholder (William V of Orange) – 'like a pig (very)' – and the Princess of Orange, the Duchess of York and the Duke and Duchess of Dorset were among the company. Mrs Lisle, Lady Cholmondeley's sister, was in waiting.[38]

Although the Princess rarely entertained on so lavish a scale, she spread her wings at Charlton, on the understanding that here she was not subject to the restrictions of the 'list' enforced at Carlton House. One of her chief delights at Charlton was that there was room for her ladies to live in the house with her, and she was taking steps, as she slowly increased her acquaintance, to surround herself with congenial companions. The Princess was an affectionate employer, although, when in waiting, her ladies and women of the bedchamber were kept busy: in addition to attending her when company came to visit, or when she went to town, they were expected by the Princess to read to her from the latest publications and to act as her secretary.

Caroline derived great enjoyment from the genteel diversions to be had in the neighbourhood of Blackheath. Her ladies walked out on the heath or in Greenwich Park with her daily, and down to church at Greenwich on Sundays. They drove out with her on airings, or on morning visits to neighbours she had discovered – Lord Dartmouth on Blackheath and Mr John Julius Angerstein at Lee. They breakfasted, dined and supped with her, while she kept up a stream of conversation. In Carlton House, when no lady was with her, Miss Hayman was the recipient of the royal conversation. Wrote the sub-governess drolly, after the Princess had spent several hours in her room talking, 'she is now just like Mrs Turner to me, only that I cannot *yet* turn her out by the shoulders when I find her troublesome . . . .'.[39]

The Princess's ladies also took luncheon with her, which the Princess once invited Miss Hayman to attend in London. 'Of the chicken (a *large* one) her Royal Highness picked every bone of except one leg – I then helped her to a bone of mutton, and after that to another – all which she ate.' In mitigation Miss Hayman added, 'I find the German ladies do eat immoderately – the Queen has such a luncheon every day, yet she dines at four o'clock. Today – at one or after her luncheon is roast beef and plum pudding.'[40] Luncheon tended to be a light meal, if it was taken at all. The most substantial meal of the day was dinner, usually taken around six o'clock; supper at nine ended the evening.

The Princess had won her struggle to secure Miss Garth as a bedchamber woman. And she liked Mrs Lisle. In the autumn, however, a battle developed with the Prince when Miss Hayman's employment as sub-governess proved unsatisfactory to him. He objected to the Princess sending for Miss Hayman, as she did when in town – 'the sub-governess is a person whose constant attendance must be such as will entirely preclude every other avocation'[41] – and had as an ally Lady Elgin, whom he instructed in September to sound out Lady Charlotte Belasyse as a replacement sub-governess.

'No one can have her [Princess Charlotte's] interest more at heart than me,' the Prince wrote to Lady Elgin on 9 October, 'which I shall prove by the care I shall take of her education, and of her manners and temper, by those I shall suffer to approach her little person.' He explained his position further on the 17th. His strained relations with his wife precluded him from 'frequently visiting the nursery of my child'. He had not seen enough of Miss Hayman to judge her, but, although he heard she was of a 'lively and convivial turn', she was 'not exactly the person I want to have about my child, particularly at her present tender age'.[42]

Lord Minto, a friend of Miss Hayman's, reported on 7 November, 'Miss Hayman ... has just been dismissed by the Prince, because being uncommonly agreeable and sensible, the Princess liked her company. This is in part Lady Elgin's manoeuvre, partly the Prince's own brutality.'[43] The Princess of Wales wrote to Miss Hayman on 21 October, directly she heard from Lady Elgin of her dismissal. Caroline proposed that Miss Hayman join her establishment instead, as a woman of the bedchamber, and offered 'the same salary ... by it you will see my daughter most days'.[44] The Princess had already written, by Miss Garth, to Lord Cholmondeley to propose the plan. Miss Hayman, who was now staying with friends in London – a Miss Gale had taken her place in the Carlton House nursery – accepted gratefully the same day. Unfortunately Cholmondeley, at the Prince of Wales's behest, forbade the appointment on the ground that it had been ordained before she came over from Brunswick that the Princess of Wales should have no person in her establishment 'inferior in rank to the other bedchamber women and superior to a mere domestic'.

The Princess replied angrily that she had not objected when she came from Brunswick to bringing no German ladies with her. It was 'a very small sacrifice to me as I expected to have enjoyed so much of his [the Prince's] society'. She wrote of the 'solitary hours' she spent instead at Carlton House, 'especially as the Prince himself separated from me having never dined with or spoke to me from the month of March, which your Lordship too well knows'. She added that, although the Prince had 'lately disapproved of my having the sub-governess in my private society', Miss Hayman was the only person she could occasionally send for, as no other lady lived in the house.[45]

The Prince found this letter, 'like the rest of her conduct, dictated by wilful misapprehension and calculated for the purpose of artful misrepresentation'. Lord Thurlow, whose exclusion from Carlton House was no obstacle to his attendance at Charlton, was very probably the Princess's adviser for this and other letters she wrote this autumn. The Prince declared that he had the King's approval for his decision not to allow Miss Hayman in his wife's family. As for the Princess's solitary hours at Carlton House, she had two ladies on whom she might call at any time. 'In the country the lady of the bedchamber and the bedchamber woman should always be in the house with the Princess; in London it never has been the custom, as they are so near at hand that it could not reasonably be required.' The Prince ended by writing, 'With respect to the disappointments which the Princess says she has met with since she came into this country ... you will remember that they cannot have exceeded mine, yet I continued to live in her society till she pursued every method to render it quite impossible for me to do so any longer.'[46]

The Princess of Wales replied to Lord Cholmondeley on 10 November that she now had to live at Carlton House and not in the country with her two ladies, 'the Prince having expressed his disapprobation of my dear child's residing with me *except* in Carlton House'. Her proposal for Miss Hayman was a plan to get 'more comfortable'. She corrected the Prince: the Dowager Princess of Wales, their grandmother, had had a bedchamber woman in residence when she lived at Carlton House; so had Queen Charlotte when she lived at St James's. She ended: 'after the Prince's arrangement I must look upon myself as quite separated from him, and therefore I should suppose I was under no further obligations and rules, to sacrifice everything to the Prince of Wales . . .'.[47]

The Prince made no reply to this assertion of independence, being for some weeks out of town. The Princess of Wales then suggested that Miss Hayman should be appointed her keeper of the privy purse. With this the Prince concurred, and agreed to ask Miss Vanneck himself for her resignation, hoping for an end to 'so absurd a correspondence upon a subject upon which enough and more than enough has already been said, and concerning which I neither can nor shall alter my determination'. He warned Lord Cholmondeley, however, that Miss Hayman's keeping the Princess's accounts 'will not make her in the least nearer the living in the house, for that is quite out of the question and never can or shall be in any house of mine . . .'.[48] In the event, Miss Hayman succeeded as privy purse only on the death of Miss Vanneck the following year.

The Princess was by no means content with this end to her claims to autonomy in the choice of her attendants and their living arrangements. The Prince regarded her 'pretensions' as 'only the indication of a deeper system of general resistance'. He told the King on 30 November that his wife 'received into her society persons he did not approve of'. Whether these 'persons' were Miss Hayman, Lord Thurlow or whoever – it was suggested that the Princess had invited gentlemen not the husbands of her ladies to dine – the King took no pains to discover. It was enough for him that a wife had not submitted to her husband. He authorized his son to speak to Lord Cholmondeley, who then waited on the Princess on Saturday, 2 December, and informed her 'That it was his Majesty's opinion that she could not receive any society but such as the Prince approved of'.[49]

The Princess of Wales then unwisely declared that, when the King sent his commands in writing, or spoke them to her, she would readily obey them. The Prince happily asked the King to correct the impression that he had 'taken an unwarrantable liberty with his Majesty's name and of having advanced a gross falsehood, of both which he hardly thinks it necessary to add he is wholly incapable'. The King sent his commands to Lord Cholmondeley the same day: 'lest they should not have been clearly explained I now have put these words on paper'.[50]

In the meantime, the Prince and Princess had had a further disagreement. On 11 October a British fleet under Admiral Duncan had smashed the Dutch fleet at Camperdown. This victory, following that in February of Admirals Jervis and Nelson over a Spanish fleet at Cape St Vincent (the previous year Spain had abandoned the British and joined the French side in the Revolutionary War), was thought to secure Britain from invasion.* A thanksgiving service for these naval victories, and for Ushant in 1794, was to be held at St Paul's Cathedral later in December. The Princess wished to attend, but the Prince, anxious that she should not go, commissioned his sister Princess Augusta to discuss the matter with the King. His Majesty agreed with the Prince that he was perfectly right not to go himself, because, following his economies, he lacked the requisite attendants, carriages, liveries and sets of horses for the procession. Equally, said the King, the Princess of Wales 'must go in state or not at all'. 'Now my dear!' wrote Princess Augusta to her brother, 'how can she do that without attendants, carriages, horses, etcetera ... ? I shall be very happy indeed if this letter brings you any comfort. ...'[51]

When Lord Cholmondeley delivered his message from the King, to the effect that the Princess was to receive only those of whom the Prince approved, the Princess was already smarting under her husband's refusal to allow her, as she saw it, to attend church. To Cholmondeley she 'made no reply except that she would immediately go up to the Prince's apartment, and have an explanation.' Cholmondeley suggested, and the Princess agreed, that he should instead tell the Prince, when he was disengaged, of the Princess's wish to see him – and alone. 'This the Prince chose to decline from prudential motives,' the Prince informed the King.[52] In the afternoon of the following day, 4 December, the Prince was at the stables and about to mount his horse when a page came hurrying over to him with the

* On 17 October, however, Britain had lost its one remaining ally, when by the Treaty of Campo-Formio Austria had recognized Napoleon's conquests in Italy.

oral message: 'That the Princess must and would see the Prince either immediately or in the course of the day, that she had only a few words to say, and no explanation was to take place on the occasion, and that the Prince might bring whatever gentleman or lady he thought proper to be present at the conversation'.

The Prince had to bow, under this public pressure, to the Princess's demand. With Lord Cholmondeley he accordingly proceeded to the Princess's apartments at five o'clock. He had warned Cholmondeley beforehand that he meant to 'preserve under all circumstances the strictest silence during the interview'. The Princess of Wales made the following speech in French immediately upon her husband's entry:

> Monsieur, Monsieur, there is no point in any explanation, I have only two words to say to you. I have been two and a half years in this house. You have treated me neither as your wife, nor as the mother of your child, nor as the Princess of Wales. I advise you that from this moment I have nothing more to say to you, and that I regard myself as being no longer subject to your orders, or your – rules.

She spoke this last word in English.

The Prince asked if that was all that she had to say to him. The Princess replied in the affirmative, and the Prince bowed and withdrew. He immediately sat down and wrote to the King an account of 'this most extraordinary conduct on the part of the Princess',[53] while the Princess also wrote to the King to request his permission to attend the thanksgiving service.

To the Princess the King returned a friendly but firm answer – the Prince's straitened finances did not permit either of them to attend. He ignored the Prince's letter entirely, but his son was now determined that his wife's 'pretensions' should be stopped. He was equally determined that there was no other route open to him but to part with her. Following her speech to him, he initiated a series of interviews between his Solicitor-General, Mr Vicary Gibbs, and the Princess.

Gibbs first asked the Princess if she stood by what she had said to the Prince. She did, and confirmed it to him in writing. The Prince then 'found himself', as he told his father, 'under the necessity of desiring to know more precisely the Princess's meaning' and sent her a written message to this effect on Sunday, 10 December, by Cholmondeley. In fact, his letter stated that, as the Princess no longer felt bound to obey him, 'an insurmountable difficulty consequently arises with regard to any arrangement in the Prince's house'.[54]

The Princess told Cholmondeley that 'it was not a specific proposal, and she wanted one'. The Prince was much put out by this, for he wished the proposal for a separation to originate with the Princess. He sent back Cholmondeley on the Monday to say, 'it had not been in the Prince's contemplation to make any specific proposal, but that he could not help inferring from her conduct that she could not have any other plan than to live in a separate house'.[55] (When Lord Loughborough, the Lord Chancellor, was shown this account by the Prince of his negotiations with the Princess, he declared, 'That inference does not seem very obvious.')[56] The Prince desired 'to be exactly informed of her wishes, in order that he might weigh his own capacity of concurring in her object, before he should take his Majesty's pleasure upon it'. According to the Prince, 'the terms which would render a separate residence agreeable to the Princess' were then fully discussed by her and Cholmondeley. On the Tuesday the Prince 'was happy to find it within his power to make such a provision as was deemed requisite', and a separation seemed in immediate prospect.[57]

On the Friday, 15 December, Cholmondeley carried the Prince's proposal to the Princess. She was to have 'a house in town, twenty thousand pounds a year to be paid by the Prince in addition to the five thousand pounds already in trust'. Princess Charlotte would remain with her mother until she was seven years old, and her governess and sub-governess would be appointed by her father.[58] The Princess thanked the Prince for his liberality, according to the Prince, and afterwards asked Lord Thurlow to declare to the Prince her 'satisfaction at the fairness of the Prince's conduct'.

The Prince wrote to the King on 24 December, 'On both sides these preliminaries were fully considered and agreed upon.' He explained to his father that any other husband, in a private situation, would have put an end 'of his own power' and much earlier to the behaviour which he had suffered from the Princess. But he, the

Prince, could not 'exert such an authority without ... entailing upon himself infinite obloquy. He is therefore placed in the painful dilemma of either exciting an outcry, which would not be the less mischievous for being unjust, or of submitting to a pretension which no man whatever could tolerate in his own house.' He then appealed to the King to approve the proposed separation: 'An agreement of this sort, if sanctioned by his Majesty, would pass with little observation from the public as there was no necessity for recurrence [recourse] to Parliament.'[59]

The Prince was unaware that the Lord Chancellor, Lord Loughborough, was conferring with two members of the royal family, probably the Duke of Gloucester and the Duke of York, and probably at the King's suggestion. They communicated this advice, through Lord Thurlow, to the Princess on 26 December: 'It is best for the Princess to remain in a state of absolute inaction; and to write no more on the subject, nor answer without advice....' She should 'continue to let it be seen that you merely submit to the Prince's pleasure, by acquiescing in any arrangement which his Majesty should think fit to make upon the Prince's proposition.... This will not derogate from the just anxiety, repeatedly expressed, to have the care of the Princess Charlotte.'

The Princess had selected learned counsel, and Thurlow told her that he had thanked the Chancellor and the other advisers for favouring the Princess with their advice, 'in which you implicitly acquiesced'.[60] The Princess wrote to Miss Garth on 6 January 1798, begging her to come into waiting in February: 'every thing is in the same confusion as when you left me, and therefore my friends advise me to stay at Charlton till every thing is settled ...'. Although the prospect of an independent life, with her own house in town and custody of her child, was now in view on extremely generous terms, the Princess did not appear elated. She was more concerned with her daughter's second birthday, which fell on the following day: 'My dear little Charlotte is very well and improved every day in beauty....'[61]

The weight of the King's disapproval came down upon his son on 9 January and, with it, cold water for the Prince's hopes of a formal separation from the Princess of Wales. The King had taken

Loughborough's opinion of the Prince's letter, which was hardly flattering:

> The terms of the separation are not disclosed ... neither does it [the Prince's paper] profess to have been presented with the concurrence of the Princess. ... No causes of separation are alleged which could warrant such a step between persons of any condition whatever. For a separation on mere disagreement of temper is repugnant to all the laws that govern any state which professes a reverence for religion and morality. ...

Furthermore, in Loughborough's opinion the Prince was deceived if he thought the separation would be 'imputed to any impropriety in the temper or behaviour of her Royal Highness, or that her consent would be deemed to be more than an acquiescence in his pleasure'. The Princess's sentiments as expressed to Thurlow, the Lord Chancellor noted, were 'not those of a woman desirous of a separation for her own personal satisfaction, but as submitting with much grief and concern at her own unhappiness for his displeasure to conform in all respects to the Prince's wish ...'. In the Chancellor's opinion, the cause of the dispute between husband and wife was 'extremely slight' – the Princess's wish to employ Miss Hayman as woman of the bedchamber. The Prince's suggestion that it was 'an indication of a deeper system of general resistance' on the part of the Princess was effectively rebutted, in Loughborough's view, by the 'submissive language' the Princess had authorized Thurlow to use.

In short, the Chancellor remarked, 'no serious misunderstanding could have arisen ... had it not been for that unhappy distaste the Prince has been too apt to explain, and upon which it is impossible to reason'. He ended with a 'gloomy ... forecast of the mischief to be apprehended from the general indisposition towards the Prince, which ... cannot, consistently with the public safety, admit at this time of any increase ...'.[62]

The King praised Loughborough's skill in 'so ably' condensing 'the unhappy subject of the Prince of Wales's dislike of the Princess of Wales, and his mode of putting forced constructions on ill-advised expressions she may have used, to ground the supposition that she is desirous of a separation'. He so approved the Chancellor's comments that he authorized him to express to the Prince of Wales the impossibility of my consenting to any public separation between him and the Princess of Wales, as incompatible with the religion, laws and government of my kingdom; secondly, to effect a reconciliation of the present difference between the Prince and Princess and persuade them to live on terms at least of reciprocal respect, however their intercourse may be unhappily limited; and thirdly, to establish rules which may prevent mutual irritation in future, and prevent the repetition of appeals to me.[63]

The Prince had to bow to his father's authority. He saved face by saying that the Princess had 'at length come forward and expressed her sense of the impropriety' of her behaviour in receiving those of whom her husband could not approve. 'Accommodation' on that point was now easy, although 'the reconciliation cannot go further'. The Prince remained firmly convinced that 'the respective comfort of the Princess as well as his own depended on a separation according to the proposed plan', but 'with all duty and submission' he sacrificed his own sentiments to his father's wishes.

It was his 'earnest desire (in concurrence it is to be hoped with the Princess) to study that their future residence under the same roof may be as little embarrassing to each other as the nature of the case will admit of . . .'. He was willing, as he always had been, to have the Princess add any person she chose 'to the list of those who are to be occasionally invited', on the understanding that he might also veto anyone he chose. 'The difference is incalculable', the Prince burst out, 'between the indulgence having its source in the Prince's own liberality towards the Princess and its being assumed by her in professed defiance of his control. The dereliction of such an authority would render a man in any class despicable in the eyes of his Household and of the world. . . .'[64]

So yet again the Prince was baulked of the opportunity he so eagerly sought, to rid himself of his troublesome wife. Furthermore, he had so alienated his father, with the 'falsehoods' of which he professed himself 'wholly incapable', that the King now favoured the Princess of Wales more strongly than ever before.

In public the Prince and Princess submitted to the King. However, privately this winter's quarrel ended with various bargains suggested to the couple by their advisers. Loughborough put forward a plan of economic tyranny, whereby the Princess of Wales's 'expenses should be so governed by the Prince, that not a candle should be lighted, or a dish of tea drunk without his approbation' – let alone guests invited. Wily Thurlow advised the Prince to make a 'private compact' with the Princess, as the King would not hear of an official separation. 'Upon the first occasion [that offered] they should part,' Thurlow suggested. Till then, the Princess of Wales should 'remain always in the country, excepting when she came to Carlton House to dress for Court ... sacrifice all society and give up going to the opera'. Lady Jersey counselled the Prince against this 'compact', which Thurlow would have made known to the ministers and which would have appeared tyranny to the world. 'You know the reasons I have to abhor her,' Lady Jersey wrote to McMahon, 'and you must be convinced that I can have no motive for wishing the Prince to be gentle and indulgent to her, but that he may appear in a true light. . . .'[65]

Although no bargain or compact was struck, the Prince and Princess of Wales, already unofficially leading separate lives, also made sure that they were rarely under the same roof. The Princess stayed at Carlton House less and less as 1798 wore on. She continued to visit in the daytime to see Princess Charlotte if the child did not come to her at Charlton. She attended with Lady Elgin and stayed at Carlton House when Princess Charlotte was inoculated against smallpox in April. In May she gave an 'elegant breakfast' and a 'select dinner' there on the occasion of her thirtieth birthday. She dressed there for the opera, which she attended rarely, and for Court. (At a June drawing-room the Prince and she skirted each other warily.) When the Princess was not enjoying 'the splendid gratifications of her own rank' in London, she was to be found at Blackheath. In the summer of this year, she exchanged the house at Charlton for Montague House, by Greenwich Park, which the Prince had formerly rented for Princess Charlotte.

Montague House was a curious home, not very large, and with only the park wall shutting it off from the constant traffic on Blackheath. A conservatory or greenhouse stood outside the principal or Blue Room, which lay below the Princess's apartments. Connected to the main house by a passage was a small building known as the Round Tower, set in the corner of the park wall, and containing a set of rooms for a lady-in-waiting, her spouse and their servant. Here at Montague House, as at Charlton, she lived the life of a 'private gentlewoman', exempt from the 'great vexations' to which she had been subjected and enjoying the 'simple pleasures of a private life'.

The personable politician Lord Minto, who was invited to an 'extremely agreeable' and unusual breakfast party at Blackheath by the Princess in June, told his wife that 'the Princess seemed delighted herself, and contrived to satisfy all her guests. These little indulgences seem to be the consequence of some late interposition of her family, who desired formally to know the cause of the extraordinary treatment she received.' Tables were laid in the little strip of garden that separated the house from Greenwich Park, and 'a slight shower, which drove the white muslins for a few minutes into the house', was only an incident enlivening the feast. Princess Charlotte was there, 'led about by Lady Elgin on a leading string, though she seems stout and able to trot without help'.[66]

The war, meanwhile, had moved to a new theatre with the Directory's dispatch of an expedition under Bonaparte, fresh from his successes in Italy, to capture Egypt from the Turks and to disrupt British trade in the eastern Mediterranean. The Turks were duly crushed at the Battle of the Pyramids on 21 July, but on 1 August a British fleet under Admiral Nelson, which had been searching for the expedition fleet, found it anchored off Aboukir Bay. Here, in the Battle of the Nile, the French lost eleven of their thirteen ships of the line, a defeat which left Bonaparte's troops stranded in Egypt.

In London, however, the news of this great victory had to compete with a rumour that the Whig Opposition, with whom the Prince was now on friendly terms again, thought to foster a reconciliation between Prince and Princess 'in order to diminish the Prince's unpopularity'. This alarmed the Princess, and Minto was dispatched, on his arrival at Blackheath one day, to 'Miss Hayman's round tower in the garden' – where the Princess's new keeper of the privy purse now resided. Here Minto was shown 'part of the correspondence between the Prince and Princess, Lord Malmesbury, Lady Elgin, etcetera, relative to their separation, the child, and other similar matters'.[67] The Princess wished him to see that 'she should not be to blame if she refused such offers'. Minto, although he did not necessarily believe the rumour, strongly urged Caroline to accept a reconciliation should the Prince offer it.

When the rumour that the Prince wished a reconciliation grew stronger, Minto wrote to his wife:

A reconciliation is a thing which so much affects the general security and happiness of this kingdom as to require the sacrifice of some portion of private and personal comfort. But the moment you come to consider the matter on the footing of duty ... the question of substantial interest and happiness is also decided. Nothing can be more certain than that the Princess has no other chance, even for a tolerable share of comfort, than by keeping not only in the right, but so much on the right side of right as to be completely out of reach of that left-handed wisdom which generally accompanies malice, and which is sure not to miss a blot.[68]

The Princess of Wales's fears that the Prince meant to suggest a reconciliation were borne out in December 1798 when she received a letter from him, 'desiring her to dine at Carlton House and settle there for the winter'.[69] The Princess declined, on the reasonable ground that he had asked her only because he wished to stand well with her while he negotiated a large loan from the Landgrave of Hesse, one of her relations. She was aware of the Prince's duplicity: while thus propositioning his wife, he was simultaneously seeking a reconciliation with Mrs Fitzherbert.

## CHAPTER SIX

# MONTAGUE HOUSE

## 1798–1804

### 'That wicked Princess on the heath'

THE PRINCE OF WALES had thought of Mrs Fitzherbert on his
wedding day. He wrote her that impassioned love letter, mas-
querading as a will and testament, on the birth of his child in January
1796. When he thought of separating from the Princess that spring,
he sent his brother to Mrs Fitzherbert with the proposal that they
'make it up'.

When the Prince and Princess began – privately – to live separately
in 1798, the Prince's thoughts turned again to Maria. He was
invariably led to think of the domestic, and apparently illicit, charms
of Mrs Fitzherbert when suffering from chagrin after the King had
refused one of his applications for military preferment, as he did in
1795 and again in 1798. What he wished for was simple promotion
to higher rank and a more resplendent uniform to match those of his
brothers York and Prince Augustus, respectively field marshal and
general. He often complained that he had no useful role in the
country, but one can be sure that the burdens of an actual command
were far from his mind. The frustration which prompted these
complaints aroused in him particular antagonism against the Princess
of Wales – who represented, as the King never failed to remind him,
his chief official duty. Just as Blackheath and the life of a 'private
gentlewoman' appealed to the Princess of Wales after her experiences
at Carlton House, so the Prince of Wales yearned in 1798 to be
reconciled with Mrs Fitzherbert and live 'retired' with her.

To this end the Prince of Wales dispatched McMahon in August
1798 to Cheltenham, where Mrs Fitzherbert had taken rooms at the
Plough Inn, with instructions to spy out the land. Unfortunately, Mrs
Fitzherbert regarded McMahon as a 'strong partisan' of Lady Jersey,

so that 'no material conversation has happened'. Moreover, paragraphs had appeared in the London papers linking the Prince's name
with that of the actress Mrs Crouch. 'Mrs Fitzherbert has had
particular letters from town respecting this affair,' McMahon
lamented. 'I have taken care to do your Royal Highness ample justice
by a side wind through one or two ladies with whom she associates
chiefly here. . . . I have reason to think . . . that your Royal Highness
occupies her thoughts a vast deal. . . .'[1]

The Prince also let his sisters Princess Mary and Princess Augusta
into his secret hopes. In October, Princess Mary wrote to him of
'your amiable left hand (as you call her)'.[2] In a morganatic, or unequal,
marriage, in German – but not in English – law, where a person of
exalted rank married a social inferior, the bridegroom gave the bride
his left hand. Since his marriage to Princess Caroline, the Prince had
apparently come to think of his marriage to Mrs Fitzherbert as in this
morganatic style. (After all, he would in due course become Elector
of Hanover!) Princess Mary corresponded with Mrs Fitzherbert and
conveyed at least one message from the Prince to his former
companion.

Princess Augusta wrote, probably in autumn 1798, to tell her
brother of the very great concern all the Sisterhood felt at 'the
dejected appearance you made'. She asserted that Mrs Fitzherbert
would be

> highly respected for her conduct and affection were she to act as would
> become the respectability she has ever borne on your account. After
> such real affection, not to say adoration on your side, and I am
> confident from all I have heard pretty near the same on hers, I am
> certain it is nothing less serious than a reconciliation, which would
> surely make both of you happy.

Princess Augusta added, 'If what the world says of the Princess is
true, that she declares she hopes to hear of her [Mrs Fitzherbert]
being with you, why then should she [Mrs Fitzherbert] not wish to
make her happy situation known to all the world . . . ?'[3] The Princess
had apparently said 'she hoped her husband would not feel her any
impediment to the reconciliation he was so desirous for'. The Prince,
on being given this message, replied, 'Did she say so? Indeed, she is

very good-natured.'[4] The Princess always spoke without rancour of Mrs Fitzherbert and was later reported to have said, 'That is the Prince's true wife; she is an excellent woman; it is a great pity for him he ever broke vid her.'[5]

Mrs Fitzherbert resisted the Prince's overtures, as well she might. Besides the gossip about Mrs Crouch, rumour continued – and correctly – to link Lady Jersey's name with the Prince. The dangers of a reconciliation were not limited to the Prince's flighty ways. The relationship between Mrs Fitzherbert and the Prince would once again be the subject of speculation. If a general belief in their earlier marriage revived, Mrs Fitzherbert's 'respectability' might blossom. The Prince, on the other hand, exposed himself to all manner of evils, from a public which was never backward in criticizing him on the ground that it supported him financially, and whose sympathy was all for the Princess of Wales. The most dangerous question of all was whether an earlier marriage affected his, and especially Princess Charlotte's, succession to the throne of England.

If the Prince romantically thought of his marriage to Mrs Fitzherbert as something approaching a morganatic marriage, a matter of domestic comfort, which could coexist happily with an official marriage, contracted for reasons of state – the offspring of a morganatic marriage had no claim to succeed their father – no such thing existed in English law. His marriage to Mrs Fitzherbert, however, was valid in the eyes of the Catholic Church, even though it was both invalid and illegal in that same English law. If the Prince resumed his ties with Mrs Fitzherbert, in time to come anti-Catholic feeling might prevent him from acceding to the throne. Furthermore, account had to be taken of the potent rumour that the Prince's marriage to the Princess of Wales was bigamous and Princess Charlotte illegitimate. ('I never did commit adultery but once, and I have repented of it ever since,' Caroline later said. 'It was with the husband of Mrs Fitzherbert.')[6]

When Mrs Fitzherbert and the Prince had separated in 1795, the rumours about their marriage, and doubts about the Prince's eventual succession, had faded away. If the Prince revived his relations with Mrs Fitzherbert now, not only would the public revile the insult to the Princess, but all those rumours and doubts would resurface and,

with them, would arise doubts about Princess Charlotte's succession
to the throne.

The Prince, like the Princess, was intent on his private comfort to
the exclusion of considerations of state or of his child's future. When
he proposed in December 1798 the reconciliation with the Princess
of Wales, and showed himself willing to put aside his feelings for Mrs
Fitzherbert, his private comfort depended on raising money from the
Princess's cousin, the Landgrave. After the Prince had obtained the
loan, he forgot the idea of a reconciliation and concentrated on
wooing back Mrs Fitzherbert. In February 1799 he asked one of his
confidantes, the Duchess of Rutland, to convey to Mrs Fitzherbert
the news that 'everything is finally at an end IN ANOTHER QUARTER,
so far that I think there is but little probability of my even visiting
there in a common way much more'.[7] He referred to his liaison with
Lady Jersey. (By June 1799, the Countess and her husband had
vacated Warwick House. In the New Year, Lord Jersey was relieved
of his position as Master of the Horse.)

Ten days later the Prince heard that Mrs Fitzherbert was on her
deathbed, then he heard she had died, at Bath (Mrs Fitzherbert had
caught a bad cold in December 1798 when she had visited Portsmouth
to discuss taking care of a baby, Mary (or Minnie) Seymour, whose
mother, Lady Hugh Seymour, had had to go to Madeira for her
health). He was utterly distraught. 'To describe my feelings, to talk
even of the subject,' he wrote to the Duchess of Rutland, 'is totally
impossible; for I could neither feel, think, speak. . . . Indeed, it was a
mercy of providence that I was thus bereft of all sense, for had I not,
I am convinced . . . I should have put an end to my existence
myself. . . .'[8] When the reports proved unfounded, the Prince pressed
his suit. Prince Edward, newly created Duke of Kent, informed his
brother in July that, after 'a very long tête-à-tête' with Mrs Fitzherbert, he believed 'your wishes will ere long be accomplished'. Mrs
Fitzherbert's only stipulation was that there were 'some points . . .
you must give up to her . . . a reconciliation with a woman who
possesses that attachment. . . . which . . . she does for you, is worth
any sacrifice . . .'.

The sacrifice in question, as it transpired, was that the Prince and
Mrs Fitzherbert should inhabit separate houses, that she should not

live as his 'mistress or wife', but that they should live as 'brother and sister'.[9] In his frenzy, the Prince agreed to this, as he did – though prospective head of the established and Protestant Church of England – to Mrs Fitzherbert's request that they should seek a Papal blessing for their marriage.

The Prince's animosity to his titular wife, Caroline, was as great as ever. He was enraged that the King insisted on marking the Princess's birthday in May 1799 with a dress ball – the Queen told the Prince his father meant no 'personal offence towards you'. He was no better pleased when the Duke and Duchess of York refused to exclude his wife from a fête at Oatlands a few weeks later. In June he bewailed his fate to Lady Elgin: 'the continual provocation and insult I am exposed to from the most unprincipled and unfeeling person of her sex . . . who, though I do not interfere with, still will not let me alone, drives me almost out of my senses; there is no end to her wickedness, her falsity, and her designs . . . .'

In July the Prince thought to make Lord Thurlow an emissary, to carry to the Princess of Wales a plan that she occupy a 'separate residence' in town. This Thurlow refused to do on the ground that 'was I . . . to be the bearer of any message that had respect to any other house than that lately occupied by the Master of the Horse [Warwick House] . . . I should be negotiating for a direct separation'.[10] The King, wrote Lord Thurlow, had declared his 'disapprobation' of any such plan, and it might 'draw down much public observation upon the separation of the Princess from the child'. Thurlow suggested instead that the Prince should agree to the Princess's own suggestion, that she inhabit Warwick House and have her daughter's 'society' without interrupting her education. As this house was the Prince's own, Thurlow conceived, 'a separation might ensue nearly as efficient as if it had received the stamp of legal authority'.[11] The Prince instead thought of settling Princess Charlotte and her establishment in Warwick House.

The Princess of Wales was by no means averse to a separate residence in town, given the Prince's hostility towards her. In August 1799 the newly promoted Rear Admiral Jack Payne – now restored to favour, together with all Mrs Fitzherbert's friends – and Lord Cholmondeley were negotiating with the Princess a financial arrangement whereby she would vacate Carlton House and give up Montague House in return for £12,000 from the Prince per year, a substantial increase on the sum she had been receiving from him. The £5000 Civil List pin-money she received would not alter, as the separation would be extremely private. The Princess told Payne, 'It is very much my wish to be as little expensive as possible while the Prince's affairs are embarrassed.'

Cholmondeley, however, felt it his duty to advise the Princess that £12,000 would not cover the expenses of a separate establishment for her, as the Prince had been funding her ladies, pages and servants out of his own resources. He told her that she 'had better not leave Carlton House ... that it is proposed as a trap to get me into some embarrassment...'. Furthermore, the Prince had asked her to 'give in writing my idea to leave Carlton House'. Cholmondeley advised her not to write, 'for fear it should appear to be all my wish only ...'.[12] The matter was not resolved; the Princess continued to inhabit Montague House and make occasional forays to Carlton House.

Cholmondeley told the Princess that the Prince 'got spies to watch me' at Blackheath, including a Mr Clarke, whom Cholmondeley met 'coming to watch who came in and out of my house'. The company the Princess invited this summer of 1799 must have disappointed Clarke. It included Mr Pitt, the Premier, and Lord Loughborough, the Lord Chancellor. (Princess Charlotte had gone with Lady Elgin to summer at Weymouth with her grandparents for the first time.) While the Prince of Wales pursued his hopes of domestic retirement in 1799, the Princess of Wales was flirting – quite literally – with his father's ministers and Tory gentlemen at Blackheath.

Lord Minto continued to visit the Princess of Wales till he went to Vienna in June 1799. He noticed that the company included, by contrast with the previous year, several prominent Tories – Mr William Windham (Secretary at War), Mr John Hookham Frere (Under-Secretary at the Foreign Office) and Mr George Canning (at the Board of Control). Moreover, for all their respectability, the guests now had to indulge the Princess in a taste for boisterous games after dinner. One Sunday in August they played at 'musical magic', during which Mr Dundas, the Treasurer of the Navy, had to kneel and kiss a Miss Crewe's hand. Lady Charlotte North, daughter of the former Prime Minister Lord North, presented Pitt with the Queen of Prussia's bust, which he, in turn, had to salute. 'The Princess was to tie Mr [Charles] Long [a Secretary to the Treasury] and Mr Frere together, and make each nurse a bolster as a baby.' Pitt drew the line only at blindman's buff and said, 'I will endeavour to shut my eyes all I can, but I cannot promise the rest of the world will do the same.'[13]

The energetic displays of friendship for the Princess that these 'knights of the Round Tower' made – Dundas 'squeezed the Princess's hand in the tenderest manner possible, called her angel repeatedly and said he hoped no one but himself would know how much he loved her' – were not wholly disinterested. The question of the royal succession continued to exercise the King and his ministers. It was a possibility at least that the Princess of Wales, if her husband's own accession were barred, might in due course be appointed regent to her daughter Princess Charlotte. It could do no harm to cultivate the Princess of Wales and show an avuncular interest in her daughter. And the Princess's confidences about her relations with her husband – if sometimes alarmingly frank – had their own appeal.

The Princess took particular pleasure in singling out a 'favourite' gentleman among the company and adjourning with him to another room to make her confidences. Miss Hayman, her privy purse, felt obliged to remonstrate when she led Frere off to the Blue Room, which gave on to the greenhouse and garden. The Princess took no notice. On another occasion she carried off two guests from a large assembly, Windham and Mr Tom Grenville, for a wet walk in Greenwich Park and was so long away that she returned to find an empty house. 'She has a great contempt for the common observation of what is called the world,' wrote Minto, 'that is of strangers, on the particulars of her conduct and manners. It has required a constant exertion to enforce these observances....'[14]

While the Princess's tête-à-têtes were mostly innocent, this was not necessarily the case with the junior minister Mr George Canning. In the late spring and early summer of 1799, he was a constant visitor to Blackheath. Then, quite suddenly on a country visit, he fell in love with, and subsequently married in 1800, a Miss Joan Scott. He wrote to Lord Granville Leveson Gower this autumn of 1799 of 'those [sentiments] which I know-not-what feelings – vanity, perhaps, and romance, and a certain sort of lively and grateful interest (but not love) had created in me and consecrated to a very different object'. He did not name the Princess. If he had not met Miss Scott, he continued, 'I know not how I should have resisted, as I ought to do, the abundant and overpowering temptation to the indulgence of a passion ... which must have been dangerous, perhaps ruinous, to her who was the cause of it, and to myself.'

Canning confessed that, with all his good resolutions, 'the day of the last dinner was not quite so blameless as I promised you it should be'. He had one other interview, in which he told the Princess he could not call again for some time, 'for the Keeper [of the privy purse, Miss Hayman] is going on a visit to her friends in the country, and during her absence I have said I cannot possibly call at the r.T. [the Round Tower, where Miss Hayman lodged] or elsewhere'. Canning reflected, 'Marriage will be the most effectual remedy to all the danger, and ... there is quite mind enough in her to meet all my sentiments, and even to rejoice with me upon reflection at our escape.'[15]

Canning prophesied correctly. He remained on good terms, after his marriage, with the Princess of Wales, who never bore grudges, and she stood godmother to his eldest child in 1801. Canning later said that the Princess showed him the Prince's April 1796 letter of licence – which she had also shown to Minto.* He declared it to free her entirely, and 'they took advantage of it on the spot'.[16] In fact, Canning's autumn letter indicates that they were more cautious; the likelihood is that they indulged in the prophylactic sport of heavy petting, as her contemporaries so often did. His declaration, therefore, if he made it, was a qualified one, and anyway related only to her being freed from some of the constraints of marriage. As we have seen, Princess Caroline in Brunswick had been much struck, Lord Malmesbury thought, by the warning he gave her that adultery for her was high treason – and, by Edward III's original statute, the 1351 Treason Act, punishable by death. No letter of licence could possibly

---

* In fact Canning claimed to have been present when Princess Caroline received the letter. His own letters indicate, however, that their relationship was at its most intense in 1799 rather than 1796. The letter shows the day and month of composition, but not the year: perhaps Caroline misled her eager suitor about its date.

save an English subject who became lover of the Princess of Wales –
or save the Princess of Wales herself, as accessory to the fact – from
the penalties for committing high treason. At all costs, a woman
whose legitimate children would be in line to the throne had to
avoid impregnation by a lover. Charlotte would have to remain the
Princess's only child.

The Princess of Wales's flirtation with Canning is the first docu-
mented example of her reacting with a show of sexual independence
to her rejection by her husband, to his relationship with Lady Jersey
and to his return to Mrs Fitzherbert. By someone, if not by Canning,
the Princess of Wales was from now on convinced that that April
letter gave her a considerable measure of freedom. It is hardly
surprising that Caroline, aged thirty-one, was so exercised by this
point – and canvassed, as she plainly did, several opinions on the
subject. Her future was bleak. The King forbade a separation. So, till
the Prince's death or hers, she was tightly shackled to him, while he,
apparently, was very loosely chained to her.

The Princess of Wales continued to give dinners and to visit
friends at their houses in the neighbourhood of Blackheath, often
creating mayhem by arriving unexpectedly. At the Bennets' in Beck-
enham, she rode up one day with Miss Hayman, and, 'meaning
apparently to stay half an hour . . . ended in . . . staying to dinner and
till suppertime. . . . When the carriage drove off, Bennet took off his
coat and flew about the room, huzzaing and capering for joy. . . .' The
three daughters of Lord North became particular friends of the
Princess. Charlotte, the cleverest of this agreeable family, was a lively
participant at her dinner parties, as we have seen. Catherine, who had
married Lord Glenbervie, often entertained her at the Pheasantry, a
shooting box in Bushey Park near Roehampton. And Anne, who had
become Lord Sheffield's third wife in 1798, was appointed her lady-
in-waiting. On one of her visits to Sheffield Park, the Princess drove
in a little chaise at full gallop with Lord Sheffield beside her, while
Mr Tom Pelham drove Lady Charlotte North and two other ladies
in 'a kind of tandem'. Lady Sheffield, mounted on a little pony, cried
out 'in expectation of seeing them all scattered over the road with
broken arms and legs'.[17]

The Princess was not always so noisy. When she was with her

ladies alone at Blackheath, she was content to have them read to her in the evenings. Earlier, at Carlton House, she had taken lessons on the harp from Mrs Elwes and in music from Mr Thomas Attwood. From September 1800, she took singing lessons at Blackheath from the Neapolitan opera conductor Ferrari, and, unusually, lessons in clay modelling from the sculptor Turnerelli. She produced a bust of her father, among a number of artefacts.

Other examples of the Princess's taste for handiwork were littered about Montague House. She marbled paper, painted in water colours and made ornamental table-tops by arranging dried flowers under glass. 'I am making flower lamps again,' Miss Hayman wrote to her mother from Blackheath in a letter detailing the entertainments provided, 'and learning a very good imitation of paper.'[18]

The news from abroad was no less diverting. Trapped with his army in Egypt after the Battle of the Nile, Bonaparte had sought to extricate himself by invading Syria and marching home through Asia Minor. But in February 1799 he had been thwarted at Acre, where Sir Sidney Smith landed forces to support the local garrison. Napoleon was obliged to return to Egypt where he learnt that the Austrians and Russians had driven the French from Italy. Seizing his opportunity, he abandoned his troops and sailed for France in late August and by November had overthrown the unpopular Directory and installed himself as First Consul. He was thirty years old.

A less dramatic move that autumn was Princess Charlotte's to Shrewsbury House, on Shooter's Hill, when she returned from Weymouth. She continued to constitute a chief delight of her mother's life, and Caroline visited and was visited by her regularly. The Prince, however, remained sole director of their daughter's upbringing. He warned Lady Elgin in October, 'my child is not to be made the partaker or the puppet at her early age of any large company or society'. In particular she was always to dine separately by herself at Montague House.[19] Lady Elgin informed Miss Hayman in January 1800 that the Princess of Wales could not visit Princess Charlotte on her fourth birthday, as she had to take the child to the Prince at Carlton House. It would be 'a great fatigue to us all going to town and coming back'. She suggested the Princess come the day before or after, when 'I am sure the Love will divert the Princess with her evening gambols.'[20]

The Prince continued to press Mrs Fitzherbert to return to him. In December 1799, he sent her a copy of his last will and testament of 1796, so that she could know him 'better than ever you did'. Mrs Fitzherbert then retired to Wales, with her protégée Minnie Seymour, to consider her position. In June 1800 she at last consented to return to the Prince – although continuing to live separately – and gave a great breakfast for him in her house in Tilney Street, by way of advertising the fact. Father Nassau, a priest she had sent to the Pope in Rome, returned in August with a Papal brief which supported her in her belief that by the 1785 marriage ceremony she was the Prince's 'canonical wife'.

While Mrs Fitzherbert and the Prince were constantly in each other's company but inhabited separate houses, the Prince and Princess of Wales did not speak but continued both to occupy apartments in Carlton House when in town. There was no more discussion of a separate town residence for the Princess. Following the Prince's resumed relations with Mrs Fitzherbert, however, he agreed that June to pay the £12,000 she had previously hoped for, to meet the expenses of her establishment at Montague House.

The Princess of Wales's life continued quietly at Blackheath. She did, however, have a very inflammatory painting, laden with symbolism, painted by Mr Richard Cosway's daughter Maria in 1800, of herself with Princess Charlotte. Mother, looking sweetly pensive, and child – sturdy – lean against a colossal statue group of Britannia and her lion. One of Charlotte's hands grasps Britannia's protecting shield, while Caroline holds the other.[21] At the end of this year, 1800, Caroline commissioned Mr Thomas Lawrence, who was a good friend of Mr John Julius Angerstein, her neighbour at Woodlands, a mansion on the other side of Blackheath, to paint her with her daughter again. The finished work shows Caroline looking sugary at her harp, with a curly-haired Princess Charlotte at her feet.[22] (A later portrait by Lawrence of the Princess of Wales alone in 1804 is altogether more vigorous. In a ruffed red velvet dress and feathered top hat, Caroline sits foursquare on a sofa, wielding a modelling tool

– like a weapon – with a set and possibly menacing expression. The bust she sculpted of her father watches over her in the background.)[23]

As the painter Mr William Beechey had apparently done before him, Lawrence stayed several nights at Montague House in the winter of 1800, so as to lose no time when Princess Charlotte came from Shrewsbury House in the morning. 'After dinner he came down to the room where I and my ladies generally sat in an evening,' the Princess later recorded; 'sometimes there was music, in which he joined, and sometimes he read poetry. Parts of Shakespeare's plays I particularly remember, from his reading them very well; and sometimes he played chess with me.'[24] The games may not have ended there. Five years later, she was accused by a former page, whose evidence seems reliable, of adultery with the painter. Lawrence was a young man on the make, and one may fairly conclude that his flirtatious hostess, who never cared to be discreet, was receptive to his advances.

The Locks at Norbury Park, Surrey, and the Angersteins at Woodlands had been close friends of both Lawrence and Caroline since her move to Blackheath. The two families were also interlinked by marriage. Amelia, daughter of Mr John Julius Angerstein, Lawrence's patron and an 'opulent merchant' of Russian extraction, married old Mr William Lock's son George. In addition the two families were linked by a love of art – Angerstein's collection later formed the nucleus of the National Gallery – and by a fondness for the Princess of Wales, whose exuberant company they and their families bore with fortitude.

The Princess was not unaware of the state of exhaustion to which she reduced her friends. She wrote to Miss Hayman, after detailing a visit she had paid to Norbury Park, of herself as 'that wicked Princess on the heath, she is such a rake, she is such a rioter, and such an irregular person, that she makes rebellions, and mutinies, in every well-regulated house – but she comes from abroad, and so she is good for nothing, as you remember my old hobbling ever-green Greenwich Park beaux used to say.'[25] Caroline presumably referred to pensioners at the Royal Naval Hospital who, ignorant of her identity, engaged her in conversation about the Princess on the heath.

The Angersteins and the Locks appreciated the Princess of Wales's regular religious observances – Mr George Lock, William's son, was the rector at Lee and she often went with her ladies to hear him preach. One of his sermons, she wrote, 'dissolved our three hearts'. On another occasion she had a cleric come to the house to hold divine service. The Princess also endeared herself to her neighbours by her charitable ventures. She interested herself in the education of 'eight or nine poor children', who were 'boarded by her with honest people in the neighbourhood', according to the writer Abbé Joachim Heinrich Campe from Brunswick. He visited the Princess at Montague House in 1802 and wrote that the Princess 'directed everything relative to their education and instruction', and visited them every day 'to converse with them'.

Campe was introduced to these 'little foster-children', who appeared 'clothed in the cleanest but at the same time in the simplest manner, just as the children of country people are in general dressed', when he was sitting with the Princess and her ladies at breakfast. The Princess called the children to her, one at a time, 'and among the rest a little boy, five or six years old, who had a sore upon his face. . . . She . . . gave him a biscuit, looked at his face to see whether it had got any better, and manifested no repugnance when the grateful infant pressed her hand to his bosom.' She told Campe, 'those who are acquainted with the splendour of the higher classes will be well aware of the danger of taking children from the more happy condition of inferior rank for the purpose of raising them into the former'. She had unambitious aims for her protégés: 'The boys are destined to become expert seamen; and the girls skilful, sensible, industrious housewives – nothing more.'[26]

In fact, the Princess had one of these children baptized Edwardine Kent, after the Duke of Kent, who stood godfather in the autumn of 1801, and gave her to her gardener's wife, Mrs Gosden, to nurse. At ten months the baby came to Montague House and lived there for a time before being sent to reside with the Sicards. Edwardine had been found as a baby on the heath and the Princess believed her mother to have been a French refugee of superior birth. For this reason she later paid for the child to attend Mrs Twiss's academy in Bath.[27]

The Princess rented from the Duchess of Buccleuch the Pagoda, a Chinese pavilion across the heath from Montague House, where she installed a family and set them to growing vegetables in the garden, 'which she had principally laid out herself'. Campe was charmed with 'the neat borders of flowers between which we passed, and was doubly rejoiced to find them so small ... the Princess remarked, too much room ought not to be taken from the useful vegetables, merely for pleasing the eye'.[28]

The Princess herself confirmed to Miss Hayman that she was now unrecognizably sober: 'To disappoint the whole world, to put them all in astonishment she is changed.' She breakfasted at ten, dined (like the Queen) at four, 'takes a very quiet evening drive or walk, and at eleven she flies to Morpheus' arms'.[29] This came no doubt as a relief to her ladies and her friends. On one occasion, a dinner guest – they were still at table – ventured the remark that morning was at hand. The Princess's reply was unnerving: 'Ah, God, he knows when we may all meet again – to tell you God's truth, when I am happy, I could sit on for ever.'[30]

It appeared to the outside world a reasonable compromise, if the Prince and Princess of Wales could not live comfortably together, that they should live in comfort apart. And Mrs Fitzherbert's conduct was so respectable, her manner so dignified, that the Prince's relations with her were hardly censured. The Princess of Wales made no ripples in the world with her quiet life at Blackheath. Princess Charlotte, aged five in 1801, seemed likely to be the chief sufferer, in her lonely life at Shrewsbury House with old Lady Elgin and her nurse Mrs Gagarin.

In the spring of 1801 the Princess of Wales was plagued by ill-health. Dr Mills from Greenwich was a constant visitor to Montague House, where he blooded the Princess, and she took laudanum. She also consulted her London doctor, Dr Baillie, and sent him Dr Mills's assessment of her blood – as she had once sent Lord Malmesbury her tooth for inspection at Osnabrück. To her relief, she had five nights without laudanum, entirely due to 'Dr Baillie's incomparable pills ... she don't wish to forsake her old friends, the pills, too soon', and requested another box. But the Princess's ill-health lingered on. Even the Queen was concerned, and advised the Princess to call in Sir Francis Millman, which Miss Garth persuaded her to do at the end of March. Canning wrote at the beginning of June, distressed that the Princess had been so indisposed when he and Mrs Canning had dined at Blackheath.[31]

The health of King George III gave cause for still greater concern. This spring, after Pitt, his trusted Prime Minister, was forced to resign when the King refused the Catholic emancipation which Pitt had promised to Ireland, the symptoms of the illness which had given rise to the Regency crisis in 1788 reappeared, especially that worrying 'hurry' or agitation in his conversation. The doctors were called in. Although Mr Henry Addington, the former Speaker of the House of Commons and now Prime Minister, attempted to keep the King's illness secret, the Prince was openly jubilant at the renewed prospect of a Regency. 'Are you aware, my father is as mad as ever?' he enquired of M. de Calonne, the French Finance Minister, at a dinner.[32] The Prince even fell out with his greatest supporter, the Queen, after he called repeatedly to see his father at times when he was resting. He countered with protests that he was not allowed to see the doctors' reports on his father's health, though it so nearly affected his own future.

The King was not so incapacitated as he had been in the winter of 1788, but equally he did not recover so quickly. Although he was officially ready to do business by June 1801, symptoms of the malady lingered on for a further three and a half years, with occasional acute attacks. The King was not wholly better till January 1805. During this difficult time, the Queen and most members of the royal family attempted to keep his mind free from anxiety. Unfortunately, he displayed the most violent animosity to his wife and spoke of living separately from her – on occasion, he fantasized about living with the elderly Lady Pembroke. At the same time he behaved with great fondness towards the Princess of Wales.

> The first time he rode out after his illness he rode over Westminster Bridge to Blackheath, never telling anyone where he was going, till he turned up at the Princess's door. She was not up, but jumped out of bed and went to receive him in her bed-gown and night-cap. He told Lord Uxbridge that the Princess had run in his head during his illness perpetually, and he had made a resolution to go and see her the first time he went out without telling anybody.[33]

The King was eager for the Princess to play a larger part in her daughter's upbringing, and projected that the two of them should live at Windsor, or perhaps together – in the same house – at Blackheath.

Princess Elizabeth wrote to Dr Willis, the King's 'mad-doctor', on 6 June 1801 to report that the subject of the Princess was still in the King's mind, 'to a degree that is distressing, from the unfortunate situation of the family'. The Queen thought the Lord Chancellor should be informed, and wished 'with a most fervent wish that the dear King may do nothing to form a breach between him and the Prince – for she really lives in dread of it . . .'. Princess Elizabeth confided to Willis, 'his [the King's] ideas concerning the child [are] so extraordinary that to own to you the truth I am not astonished at Mama's uneasiness'.

Princess Elizabeth referred to one plan of the King's for Mr Wyatt, the architect, to build a new wing to Montague House – presumably to accommodate Charlotte. 'You know full well how speedily every-thing is now ordered and done,' she wrote. (She believed that her brother Ernest, created Duke of Cumberland in 1799, was 'underhand the grand friend of the Princess and . . . we much fear his doing mischief'.) The Princess of Wales herself had spoken, it seemed, to Princess Elizabeth of a conversation she had had with the King. She 'expressed her distress, and I told her how right she was in not answering, as I feared the King's intentions, though most kindly meant, might serve to hurt and injure her in the world. . . . I am always afraid when she speaks to me on such unfortunate subjects.'[34]

The King had conceived, among other notions, the idea of making the Princess of Wales Ranger of Greenwich Park. With this honour came the occupancy of the Ranger's or Queen's House in the park – which could certainly accommodate both mother's and child's estab-lishments. The Duke of Kent and Prince Adolphus, who accompanied the King to Blackheath on 17 June, were told to go and see the Ranger's House and the Observatory in the park. The King mean-while had a very satisfactory conversation with the Princess. He told the Duke of Kent, on their return to London, that the Princess had 'declined on the Queen's account the offer of the Rangership'. (The Rangership was traditionally in the Queen's gift.)[35]

Although the King's overtures to the Princess had no tangible results at present, his feelings for her remained extremely warm. He told Princess Sophia, the only one of his daughters sympathetic to the Princess, that he wished all his daughter-in-law's friends were as sincere as Miss Garth. Kent told his brother the Prince of Wales that the King seemed to hope 'for the sake of the appearance to the world that you and her some day or other should again be upon a footing of exterior civility'.[36] The Duchess wrote to the King from Brunswick, 'My daughter has made me very happy by assuring me that you approve of her conduct; if there had been any fault on her side, a word from you or the Queen would have put things right in a moment, for I never knew a more obedient creature. . . .'[37] (The Duchess wrote again in August to say that her brother, on enquiry, would find that all the tales of the Princess when living in town were shocking falsehoods.)[38]

The Prince of Wales responded to his father's championing of the Princess by sending the Duke of Kent on 23 July to Montague House to discuss the 'excess' in the Princess's expenditure, especially 'the expenses incurred by alteration and repair to the buildings and . . . the great number of company invited to her house'. The Princess promised to be more 'guarded in future', Kent told the Prince, and she agreed 'she could not expect a larger allowance than that she had while yours continued so reduced'. The Prince recommended that she reduce her establishment.[39]

Besides her mistress of the robes, two ladies of the bedchamber (reduced from four), four women of the bedchamber and the keeper of the privy purse, the establishment at Montague House included two pages of the backstairs, two pages of the presence, a man cook, a coffee-room woman and three housemaids, two kitchen maids, a watchman and a stewards-room man. In the stables were two coachmen, two postillions, a coachman for the bedchamber women, three footmen and two chairmen.[40]

The Princess agreed to reduce her bedchamber ladies' salaries from £500 to £400 a year, and appeared at first resigned to dismissing her women of the bedchamber altogether. She asked, in return, if her neighbour Lord Lewisham might regulate her household in place of the Prince's appointee, his vice-chamberlain Colonel Thomas. Her affairs required, in her opinion, 'a more minute attendance and labour than might be compatible with the distance at which he [Thomas] lived from Blackheath, and the sort of indolent life she conceives him habituated to'.[41] ('Her great fault . . . is imprudence,' lamented

Princess Sophia, 'and sometimes rather too much spirit. . . . surely giving way a little might make essentials easier to be obtained. . . . of course all my remarks I keep to myself, for God knows the poor creature is black enough in this house without making things worse.')[42]

The Princess of Wales had no intention of giving way. She countered the Prince's accusations of extravagance, and wrote to the King in November of her 'uncomfortable situation'. In June 1800, she said, the Prince had added £12,000 to her £5000 'pin-money' appointed by Parliament in 1795. However, when her establishment in town had been paid for by Lord Cholmondeley on the Prince's behalf, it had cost £17,000, including payments direct to the Princess, but excluding the Parliamentary allowance. This brought the total running costs to some £22,000. 'I have endeavoured . . . to reduce the expenses of my Household to this sum [£17,000],' the Princess informed the King, 'but I find it will be totally impossible unless I part with my ladies, which I am very unwilling to do.'[43]

This was a masterstroke. It was quite improper that the Princess should have no ladies resident in her country house. (The bedchamber ladies, as opposed to the women, attended daily and resided in town.) When she appeared meekly to accept this economy, she had suggested that she should appoint a 'Dame de Compagnie', Mrs Fitzgerald, who could lodge with her daughter in the Round Tower on a modest stipend.

The Princess had had debts of £4000 in June 1800, she told the King, when the new arrangement began. 'Even if my allowance were regularly paid', she could not discharge these debts. As her allowance was now 'three-quarters in arrear I find myself in debt and difficulty without the possibility of extricating myself'. She begged that 'whatever income is to be allowed to me may be paid regularly'.

The King replied on 23 November 1801, praising 'the propriety of your conduct in a very difficult and unpleasant situation'.[44] He advised her to consult with Lord Eldon, successor as Lord Chancellor to Lord Loughborough (now Earl of Rosslyn). The Princess won her point, all but the dismissal of Colonel Thomas. The arrears of her allowance and her debts were all paid in July 1802. Furthermore, she kept her bedchamber women, while appointing Mrs Fitzgerald and her daughter to join the Montague House establishment. Her dinner parties did not diminish either in size or in frequency, and her outlay on building and furnishing alterations continued. Between 1801 and 1803 she was invoiced by carpenters and bricklayers, painters and glaziers, paper hangers, carpet manufacturers, linen drapers and upholsterers for sums totalling £4427 13s 8d. She was not, after all, living within her means.[45]

The Prince's opinion of his wife at this time is apparent from a correspondence between him and the Queen. In June 1802, the Queen invited all the royal family, including the Princess, to a fête at Frogmore to celebrate the King's Birthday. This occasioned a furious response from the Prince of Wales. 'Hitherto the King has always been esteemed to set his face against any woman disobeying the lawful commands of the man supposed to be her husband. . . . After this, what must I think, and how must I feel, at this marked support for the Princess?'[46] The Queen responded, 'though I am far above wishing to gain popularity by improper means, I should likewise not choose to lose the good opinion of the world by glaring incivility to anybody'.[47] She had always invited the Princess to events where custom demanded her attendance. The Prince stood firm. 'The Princess had not thrown off as completely the mask, or gone the very great lengths she has since', when he had appeared in public with her at the last fête the Queen gave, for his sister's wedding in 1797.[48]

The Princess of Wales obtained a longer lease on Montague House in 1801, and among her building projects were a Gothic dining-room and a new library overlooking the park. She wrote to Miss Hayman of an economical 'ten thousand workmen smelling of the humble humanity and stupid as posts and slow as snails'.[49] She had another project for 'fitting up one of the rooms in my house after the fashion of a turkish tent'. In the winter of 1801, or early in 1802, she seems to have found a new lover in Sir Sidney Smith, the Hero of Acre, who was living on Blackheath with a naval colleague, Sir John Douglas, and his wife. Sir Sidney 'furnished me with a pattern for [the room], in a drawing of the tent of Murat Bey, which he had brought over with him from Egypt. And he taught me how to draw Egyptian arabesques, which were necessary for the ornament of the ceiling.'[50]

The Princess had Lady Elgin invite Sir Sidney, in all innocence, to dine at Shrewsbury House at this time. Another gentleman was unable to attend, and Lady Elgin cancelled Sir Sidney, 'feeling the propriety of her Royal Highness's observation, that it would be unpleasant not to have two gentlemen of the party'.[51] The Princess was later to explain defensively that 'Sir Sidney Smith's conversation, his account of the various and extraordinary events and heroic achievements in which he had been concerned, amused and interested me; and the circumstances of his living so much with his friends, Sir John and Lady Douglas, in my neighbourhood on Blackheath, gave the opportunity of his increasing his acquaintance with me'.[52]

The thirty-seven-year-old Sir Sidney had travelled the world in his naval career from North America to Morocco, from Finland to Guadeloupe, and after service in the navy of Gustavus III he had been awarded a Swedish knighthood. For two years, 1796–8, he had been incarcerated in the Temple in Paris, where the French royal family had been imprisoned in 1792. In 1799 at St Jean d'Acre, after Bonaparte had stormed Jaffa, Smith captured at sea all the French siege artillery and eighty gunboats, then went on land to hold the breach till Turkish ships arrived. Here, as so often, he overreached his authority and rashly concluded a treaty which had to be repudiated by the British Government. He was, according to Colonel Bunbury, 'an enthusiast ... restlessly active ... extravagantly vain', and with 'no fixity of purpose save that of persuading mankind that Sidney Smith was the most brilliant of chevaliers. He was kind hearted, generous, and as agreeable as any man can be supposed to be who is always talking of himself.'

Few of the Princess's political friends, whom she continued to entertain, make mention of Sir Sidney or of the Douglases, with whom he lodged, being at Montague House. Lord Minto, however, informed his wife in March 1802, 'She is at present entirely wrapped up in Sir Sidney Smith, who is just the sort of thing that suits her.... Lady Douglas is now the prima female favourite, and lives entirely with the Princess. She attends her to town without any of her own ladies.... Lady Douglas is a handsome showy woman and seems clever.'[53] Throughout 1802 all three were constant visitors to the house, and the Princess often dined at the Douglases', and the following facts are not in doubt. In the spring of 1802 Charlotte, Lady Douglas, dark and attractive, occupied the Round Tower and acted as the Princess's bedchamber woman when Miss Garth was ill.

In gratitude Caroline asked the Earl of St Vincent, First Lord of the Admiralty, to find a post for her husband, though nothing ever came of it. Sir John was an officer in the Marines, and he, like many another officer on half-pay, found the environs of Greenwich agreeable, with cheaper accommodation than was available in town. The Douglases had one daughter when they took up residence at Montpellier Row, on Blackheath, and in the summer of 1802 Lady Douglas gave birth there to another daughter. This baby was christened Caroline Sidney at Lewisham Church on 22 August, and the Princess of Wales and Sir Sidney, with the Duchess of Atholl, stood godparents.[54]

Princess Charlotte meanwhile was at Weymouth with Lady Elgin, bathing every other day and picking up shells on the sands at Portland. 'By the time she leaves this I dare say she will be well qualified', Lady Elgin wrote to the Princess of Wales, 'to run races and jump over little mounds.'[55] The Princess's maternal feelings were not satisfied with her weekly visits to and from Princess Charlotte, nor with the orphans she boarded out around Blackheath. In the autumn of 1802 she asked her servants to look out for a baby, as she would like to take one to live in the house. Providentially, a baby of three months old, named William (Willy or Billy) Austin, was produced from nearby Deptford in October, when he accompanied his mother, Sophia Austin, to Montague House. Her purpose was to beg the Princess to exert her influence, as she had for others, on behalf of her husband Samuel, who had been dismissed from the Dockyard following the Treaty of Amiens, which the previous March had brought the war between England and France to an end. Stikeman, the page who interviewed her, said that nothing could be done at the Dockyard, but he offered Samuel Austin work turning the mangle at his wife's laundry in Pimlico. He added that the Princess might like to adopt Willy and relieve the family of one burden at least. Mrs Austin could visit the boy as she liked, but the Princess would bring him up and educate him.[56]

The wife of the Princess's gardener, Mrs Gosden – who had earlier nursed the child Edwardine Kent – came to live at Montague House to act as nurse to Willy, a nursery was fitted out and the Princess's curious action was clothed in as much respectability as possible. 'To be sure,' Lord Thurlow later observed, 'it was a strange thing to take a beggar's child but a few days old' – in fact, Willy had been born at the Brownlow Hospital in Deptford in July 1802 – 'and adopt it as her own ... however, princesses had sometimes strange whims which nobody could account for ... in some respects her situation was deserving of great compassion.'[57]

The Princess of Wales, consciously or unconsciously, often modelled her life and her interests on those of her husband – witness her attempt to emulate his decorative schemes at Carlton House and Brighton with her 'Gothic' dining-room and 'turkish tent'. The Prince was showing a great interest in Minnie Seymour, now three years old, the child whom Mrs Fitzherbert had promised to take care of while her mother and father, Lord and Lady Hugh Seymour, were abroad. Both parents died tragically in 1801, and Lord Hertford, Minnie's paternal uncle, was appointed guardian to their six children.

Mrs Fitzherbert, on the other hand, was allowed to keep Minnie till 1803, when, it was decreed, the child should join her brothers and sisters. It is possible that the Princess looked out for a baby in some strange spirit of competition with her husband and Mrs Fitzherbert. She seems not to have thought of the effect her new acquisition would have on Princess Charlotte, now aged six, who was deeply affronted by Willy's presence in the house. Caroline considered only the joy of having a baby near her and expected Princess Charlotte to play with the infant on her visits.

In the autumn of 1802, when Caroline set up Willy's nursery, a Norfolk acquaintance of Lady Townshend, Captain Thomas Manby, was fitting out a frigate at Deptford. He dined at Montague House and entertained the Princess with stories of surveying the north-west coast of America. The Douglases departed for Plymouth at Christmas 1802, and the Princess welcomed this new neighbour. Lady Douglas later reported Sir Sidney Smith's mortifying experience one evening at the Princess's house: 'he observed her seek Captain Manby's foot under the table, and, when she had succeeded, put her foot upon Captain Manby's and sat in that manner the whole evening dealing out equal attention and politeness above board to them both'. Sir Sidney was then obliged to watch her lead Manby from the room, whereupon the young Captain none too discreetly 'saluted' her on the lips.[58] Sir Sidney at once departed, vowing never to see the

Princess Caroline of Brunswick. A contemporary commented
on her 'penetrating eyes, long cut and rather sunk in the head.'

The elaborate monument to Princess Charlotte erected in St George's Chapel, Windsor, following her death shortly after childbirth.

Princess again. Whatever the truth of those allegations, Manby evidently supplanted Sir Sidney as Caroline's lover, and soon she was deliberately quarrelling with the Douglases, no doubt to keep their inquisitive eyes from her new liaison.

Caroline was now at her most reckless. Lady Hester Stanhope, who sometimes acted as lady-in-waiting, recalled the pattern of her mistress's behaviour at this time: 'She had a Chinese figure in one of her rooms at Blackheath that was wound up like a clock, and used to perform the most extraordinary [obscene] movements. How the sea-captains used to colour up when she [Caroline] danced about, exposing herself like an opera girl; and then she gartered below the knee: she was so low, so vulgar!' Not content merely to observe, Lady Hester offered advice: 'I was the only person that ever told her the truth. . . . I plainly told her it was a hanging-matter, that she should mind what she was about.' What was more, she added, outdoing herself in venom, it was not only sea-captains with whom Caroline risked her neck: 'There was a handsome footman who might have been brought into the scrape.'[59]

Manby agreed to take two of the Princess's charity boys – one of them was the page Robert Hownam's son Joseph – with him in his frigate, the *Africaine*. In gratitude, she arranged for his cabin to be fitted out by her linen drapers. She also sent down numerous presents before he left in the spring of 1803, as Mr William Dillon, one of Manby's officers, attests in his memoirs.[60] He continues:

> One day a messenger of the Princess's called upon Capt. Manby's agent and left £300 to his account, declaring it publicly in the office before all the clerks. I mention these things that you may understand how much my Captain relied upon that lady's influence to obtain promotion.

In fact Manby's prospects were not advanced by his open association with the Princess and he remained a captain until 1825, after his retirement. The priggish Dillon further adds that the Princess's visits to the ship in the Dover Roads in the summer of 1803 'gave rise to many sayings'. When Caroline took a house on the sea at Ramsgate for three months that summer, she wrote again to the Lord St Vincent, this time asking him to order a frigate to attend her: 'She would be highly flattered, especially if his Lordship would order the *Africaine* for this purpose'.[61]

The Prince of Wales meanwhile had Moira and McMahon keep a close eye on his wife's doings. Lord Moira told McMahon, for instance, 'Were the Prince to offer the Princess to purchase the house at Ramsgate for her, she would probably (by what I hear) decline it. She has never wished it, they say, as a permanency. The attention would tell well.'[62] The Prince heard a report later this year that the Princess had behaved in an imprudent fashion with Captain Manby on a visit to Lord Eardley's house, the Belvedere, at Long Reach, downriver of Greenwich. Moira thereupon sent in June 1804 for Eardley's gardener, who was sadly uninformative on the subject.[63] The Prince, however, felt himself well justified, by his suspicions of the Princess with Captain Manby and other gentlemen, in doing nothing for her when his income was reviewed in Parliament – the nine years of deductions were nearly up at last – and increased to £100,000 a year. The King in December 1802 had had 'no doubt but his Royal Highness would make such comfortable addition to the Princess's allowance as would seem proper'.[64] The Prince, however, told Chancellor Eldon the following March that 'he was not the sort of person who let his hair grow under his wig to please his wife'. When the long-haired Eldon, who had literally done this, took offence, the Prince made an awkward apology: it was 'a proverbial way of saying a man was governed by his wife'.[65]

The Prince was much more interested in providing for Mrs Fitzherbert than for the Princess of Wales. He increased 'my Maria's' allowance from £3000 to £4000 a year. With his new moneys, he also proposed to Lord Hertford, Minnie's uncle, that Mrs Fitzherbert should keep the child. The Prince would then make Minnie a gift of £10,000 on her coming of age. Lord Hertford refused – Minnie was provided for in her father's will, and anyway Hertford himself was fabulously rich – and insisted on the return of the child.

The Prince was on no better terms with his father than with the Princess. The King continued to refuse the Prince promotion beyond the rank of colonel. The Prince ended by publishing his father's, the Duke of York's and his own letters on the subject in the autumn of 1803. Anguished by this betrayal, the King referred to his son as 'the publisher of my letters'[66] and refused to see him, but he was as affectionate to his daughter-in-law as he was unforgiving to his son. In February 1804 he sent to her at Carlton House a picture of her father. 'It will make certainly the finest ornament in my room,' she wrote in thanks.[67] The King's affection might have diminished had he known of a potentially explosive project Caroline had embarked upon. She was filling a 'large red-morocco book' with a frank account of her married life and character sketches of the royal family and leading politicians. It was not long before she was teasingly inviting her privy purse to 'transmit this stationery to Mr Canning' in exchange for a ransom paid out of Secret Service funds.[68]

A month later Lord Minto, back from Vienna, had 'a very pleasant, jolly dinner at Blackheath where we stayed till one in the morning. Lady Hester Stanhope was the principal personage. We played at pandemonium games, especially magical music. . . .'[69] Lady Hester, who was Pitt's niece, was less charmed, and she objected in particular to the antics of Willy Austin. 'He was a nasty boy,' she later recorded. 'Oh! how Mr Pitt used to frown, when he was brought in after dinner, and held by a footman over the table to take up anything out of the dessert that he liked.'[70] Then it was off to Southend for the Princess of Wales and her Household for a few weeks in April and May, and she made occasional excursions from there to Tilbury and Billericay.

Meanwhile the King, her protector, had become alarmingly deranged that February, though not so greatly that he did not 'dwell much upon the illegality of his confinement' when a 'mad-doctor', Dr Samuel Simmons, and other physicians were called to Kew to restrain him with a straitjacket.[71] Lord Eldon, who remained Lord Chancellor when Pitt returned as Prime Minister in May (the month in which Napoleon proclaimed himself emperor),* had no doubt, and the public followed him in believing, that the King's illness was brought on by his son publishing his letters. The King was not well enough to appear at the Birthday drawing-room in June. The Prince did not attend either, but 'drove through the streets upon the coach-box of his barouche'.[72] This callous behaviour did not endear him to the

---

* War between Britain and France had broken out again in May 1803, the Peace of Amiens having lasted little more than a year. Like the Revolutionary War, the Napoleonic War was characterized by shifting alliances.

country, and his friends advised him that he must heal the breach with his father.

In July, when the King was almost fully recovered, Lord Moira informed the Chancellor that 'From various quarters it had come round to his Royal Highness that his Majesty had expressed a wish to have the Princess Charlotte under his immediate care. . . . if such be his Majesty's inclination, nothing could be more gratifying to his Royal Highness than to see the Princess Charlotte taken under his Majesty's special direction.' Lord Moira made only one stipulation: 'he would solicit to commit the Princess Charlotte to the sole and exclusive care of the King'.[73] In other words, Caroline was to continue to have no powers of direction herself.

The King wrote immediately to Lord Eldon: the Prince's offer was 'the best earnest he can give' of his wish for a reconciliation, 'but it will require some reflection before the King can answer how soon he can bring himself to receive the publisher of his letters. . . . if he takes the superintendence of his granddaughter, he does not mean to destroy the rights of the mother. . . .'[74] The principal right which the King sought to uphold was that of a mother to live in the same house as her child. In the event, he delayed answering his son till 20 August, when Dr Simmons finally departed.

The King then agreed to receive the Prince before he set off for Weymouth, on Wednesday, 22 August, 'provided no explanation or excuses are attempted to be made by the Prince of Wales; . . . it is merely to be a visit of civility, as any retrospect could but oblige the King to utter truths, which, instead of healing, must widen the present breach . . .'.[75]

Meanwhile on Sunday the 19th, Lady Elgin had been startled (so she told the Prince) to receive a visit at Shooter's Hill from Caroline, in high spirits and with the information that she had 'great news to tell us'. Princess Charlotte immediately exclaimed, 'Going to Windsor!' 'Not just [exactly] that, but you are going to [the palace at] Kew,' the Princess answered her daughter, 'to see their Majesties, and the King has wrote to desire I would tell you to come in order to take leave of you and me' before he went to Weymouth. The King had written to his daughter-in-law, 'I trust I shall communicate that to you that may render your situation much more happy than you have as yet been in this country, but no more so than your exemplary conduct deserves.'[76]

Lady Elgin was made anxious by the informality of the invitation. When the Princess of Wales offered to take the Governess and her charge in her own carriage, she begged to be excused on the ground that Princess Charlotte would be too excited. She then wrote urgently to the Prince at Carlton House to inform him of the summons to Kew. Receiving no answer, she set off with her charge and was 'quite stupefied' when they arrived, in advance of the Princess of Wales, to find the King quite alone.[77] The old man embraced Princess Charlotte, said he came only to see her and her mother, took them into the eating-room and embraced Princess Charlotte again. 'He then added he was to take Princess Charlotte to himself as the Prince wished it, but he could say nothing yet.' Lady Elgin, who knew nothing of this, was astounded.

On the Princess of Wales's arrival, the King led her and Princess Charlotte to an inner room. Then out came Princess Charlotte 'with the King's private key of the garden', Lady Elgin recorded, 'saying his Majesty desired I would walk with her and Mrs Lisle'.[78] When the King and the Princess of Wales re-emerged, the party sat down to dinner, at which the King 'ate very well his pudding and dumplings, but I am afraid over-exerted himself'.[79] The King instructed Eldon that the Earl of Dartmouth (formerly Viscount Lewisham) should be consulted in the Princess's 'family arrangements' – so Caroline had at last won her point that the 'indolent' Colonel Thomas should be replaced. The King further reported to Lord Eldon that, at their interview, the Princess's 'whole conduct and language gave the greatest satisfaction. She will entirely be guided by the King. . . .'[80] This was not the first time that he had been impressed by her sobriety. In the presence of her fatherly sovereign Caroline always took care to comport herself correctly. Her misbehaviour at other times may thus have been less spontaneous, more wilful. As Malmesbury had said, 'with a steady man she would do vastly well'. From the day of their meeting, when the Prince had so uncouthly called for brandy, her husband's conduct had been like a red rag to a bull.

When the Prince heard that the King had seen the Princess of Wales, he became ill with rage. Lady Elgin for the first time in her life left Princess Charlotte alone in the care of her nurse Mrs Gagarin, at Shrewsbury House, and went to town to report to the Prince. She found him in 'violent agitation and distress of mind and body'. McMahon penned a memorandum of the griefs the Prince was labouring under:

> Regret to find that the Princess of Wales has been mostly consulted by the King. A house prepared for her; long interview at Kew. . . . That the Prince's objections to an interview may be summed up thus. The King does not grant it from affection . . . the object is merely to get possession of the child, which, as it would be bringing her more under the direction of her mother, the Prince cannot agree to after all that has passed.[81]

The upshot was that the King, with other members of the royal family, waited at Kew for the Prince of Wales at the proposed hour on 22 August – in vain. His father looked 'very pale and unusually thin and otherwise ill', wrote Prince Augustus, now Duke of Sussex, who had just returned to England. 'The Queen was much frightened as well as all my sisters.' The Prince did not appear. Instead, Moss, the old porter at Kew, brought a letter from him, which the Duke of Kent delivered to his Majesty.[82] 'The extreme agitation', wrote the Prince, 'into which the new approach of an interview with his Majesty under all the circumstances which have recently come to his knowledge has thrown the Prince, has produced a degree of indisposition which renders it impossible for him to present himself before him this day.'[83]

The King, 'after waiting a minute or two to read it', according to Sussex, 'said "the Prince is ill"', and proceeded to Weymouth without further comment. Sussex wrote from there to tell the Prince that he was mistaken in thinking his father meant to give the Princess of Wales a house of her own at Windsor. The idea their father entertained was to purchase a house there for Princess Charlotte. 'Whenever the Princess does by any chance come to Windsor she may have a room in it.'[84] The Prince, who was opposed to the Princess having any part in the 'direction' of Princess Charlotte, was not appeased. Rather than have that, he now withdrew his offer to entrust his daughter's care to his father.

Mr Charles James Fox, in this crisis, suggested helpfully to the Prince that 'the King may attempt to gain possession of the Princess Charlotte by violence or stratagem and take her to Windsor. . . . Send immediately without a moment's delay for your daughter to Carlton House, and . . . maintain the possession of her person by all legal means.'[85] Lord Eldon pointed out more calmly to the Prince that it had been settled in 1717 that the sovereign of the realm had superior rights to anyone else, parents included, in the care and education of all the royal family.[86]

The argument flourished through the summer and into the autumn. When the King and Prince met in November, the matter was still unresolved. The King wrote to the Princess on 13 November, 'Yesterday I and the rest of my family had an interview with the Prince of Wales at Kew, care was taken on all sides to avoid all subjects of altercation or explanation. . . . it leaves the Prince of Wales in a situation to show whether his desire to return to his family is only verbal or real. . . .' The King went on to say that he hoped soon to 'communicate some plan for the advantage of the dear child. . . . its effecting my having the happiness of living more with you is no small incentive to my forming some ideas on the subject.' He would decide nothing without her 'thorough and cordial concurrence, for your authority as mother it is my object to support'.[87]

The Princess of Wales duly received a paper the King had composed on Princess Charlotte's education, in which he proposed a bishop to superintend the whole, a clergyman to instruct her in religion and Latin 'and daily to read prayers', another tutor for 'history, geography, belles lettres and French, and masters for writing, music and dancing'.[88] He also saw the need for 'a governess whose age and activity may be more suited to the age of the Princess than the Countess of Elgin, and a sub-governess and assistant sub-governess'. Caroline accordingly wrote to Miss Hayman, 'My chief amusement and entertainment at present is hunting, not after hares or foxes, but after the most reverend fathers in God, ergo bishops to be a tutor for Princess Charlotte. . . .' The Princess dealt a side-blow to poor old Lady Elgin, the Prince's partisan, who was to be replaced: 'still she canters with one leg to the grave and the other after a pension. . . .'[89]

The Prince received the King's paper in November, and refused point-blank to relinquish the care of his daughter. Rumour abounded. The Paymaster-General Mr George Rose heard with distress that 'the Princess of Wales had a horror of her husband which neither Mr Pitt nor the Chancellor could erase, although they had tried'.[90] Mr Charles Abbott, now the Speaker of the House of Commons, wrote in October, 'The Princess of Wales gives great uneasiness by her unguarded conduct.'[91] The Prince of Wales told Lady Bessborough that he knew 'strong facts' against his wife which he had so far kept to himself. His confidante urged him 'either not to listen to any report at all . . . or at once to accuse her'.[92]

But there were other, more disturbing stories in circulation. The Princess's conduct had been more unguarded than anybody might have imagined, and it was not long before the repercussions threatened her very life.

## CHAPTER SEVEN

# THE ANONYMOUS LETTERS

## 1804–1806

*'The charge of high treason . . . the infamous crime of adultery'*

THE PRINCE OF WALES may or may not have known of a scandalous business into which his brother the Duke of Kent was drawn in the autumn of 1804. The Princess of Wales had asked the Duke to prevent her former Blackheath friends, Sir John and Lady Douglas, supported by Sir Sidney Smith, from pestering her with their attentions. After some nine months in Plymouth, Sir John had returned to town in August on the arrival in England of the Duke of Sussex, to whom he was groom of the bedchamber. Kent explained to the Princess that he did not know the Douglases, but he was acquainted with Sir Sidney and would see what he could do through that channel.

Sir Sidney, however, had a very different story to tell. The Douglases had received three anonymous missives, one with a seal identifiably that of the Princess, and all, they alleged, in her handwriting; two contained indecent drawings. One of these was entitled, in the same handwriting, 'Sir Sidney Smith, Lady Douglas in an Amorous Situation', the other, still more crudely, 'Sir Sidney Smith doing Lady Douglas your amiable wife'.[1] As Lady Douglas later recorded, in a statement also signed by Sir John:

> My husband with that cool good sense which has ever marked his character, and with a belief of my innocence, which nothing but the facts can stagger (for it is founded upon my having been faithful to him for nine years before we were married, and seven years since), as well as his long acquaintance with Sir Sidney Smith's character and disposition, and having seen the Princess of Wales's loose and vicious character, put the letters in his pocket, and went instantly to Sir Sidney Smith. . . . Sir John then told him, he put the question to him, and

expected an answer such as an officer and gentleman ought to give to his friend. . . .

It seems more likely that it was Sir Sidney's gallant 'character and disposition' which persuaded Sir John Douglas of the need for an immediate confrontation. At any rate, it was eccentric conduct for a husband convinced of the innocence of his wife and his friend. Lady Douglas continued:

> Sir Sidney Smith gave Sir John his hand, as his old friend and companion, and assured him, in the most solemn manner, as an officer and gentleman, that the whole was the most audacious and wicked calumny. . . . Sir Sidney added, 'I never said a word to your wife, but what you might have heard; and had I been so base as to attempt anything of the kind under your roof, I should deserve you to shoot me like a mad dog.'[2]

Smith then boldly suggested that the three of them should confront the Princess, but in response to their request for an audience Caroline declared herself indisposed. Lady Douglas thereupon sent her a letter of acknowledgement: 'Madam, I received your former anonymous letter safe; also your two last, with drawings.' A further anonymous letter was now sent, she stated, this time to Sir Sidney, 'saying, the writer of that wished for no civil dissensions, and that there seldom was a difference where, if the parties wished it, they could not arrange matters. . . . [Sir Sidney and the Douglases] were all satisfied it was from her Royal Highness, who, thinking Sir Sidney and Sir John might, by this time, be cutting each other's throats, sent very graciously to stop them. . . .'[3]

Judging by the matter-of-fact tone of the letter to Sir Sidney and by her apparent readiness to be identified as the sender of the letters, though she was later to deny that she had sent them, Caroline was out to make mischief. Sir John's unexpected attendance upon the Duke of Sussex at Carlton House, where he might have the ear of the Prince of Wales, must have been a source of anxiety to her. Her fear was that the Douglases would resurrect their enmity and expose her affairs with Sir Sidney Smith and Captain Manby. As we shall see, the motive attributed to her by the Douglases was a wish to conceal the existence of her supposed lovechild, Willy Austin.

The Duke of Kent, informed of his sister-in-law's scandalous correspondence by Sir Sidney, exclaimed, 'Abominable!' He nonetheless urged Sir Sidney to persuade Sir John to forget the insult and pleaded the King's delicate state of health, which would only suffer further if this affair were made public. Sir John consented, on the understanding that, should the Princess do any more mischief, he must speak out. The Princess's friend Captain Manby received coincidentally two anonymous letters this Christmas. The first promised a handsome reward if he revealed details of his relations with the Princess. 'The intimacy and proceedings ... at Lord Eardley's, Long Reach, Ramsgate, Southend' – Manby had visited the Princess here from his ship – 'can be easily proved.' The second expressed surprise that Manby had not replied. 'An offer of fortune to any amount is pledged to him.'[4] This second batch of anonymous correspondence almost certainly emanated from Carlton House, perhaps from McMahon.

The affairs of the royal family were in a sorry state. In December Mr Charles Abbott wrote:

> The King is harassed by family disputes. The Queen persists in living entirely separate. [Their relationship had deteriorated during his most recent illness.] The Prince of Wales was understood at first to have consented to the King having the education of the Princess Charlotte, but now he denies it. Mr Pitt assured the King that it was consented to on the authority of Lord Moira; but Lord Moira denies that he ever authorized Mr Pitt to say so. In the meantime the Princess Charlotte is removed to Carlton House, and the matter is to be litigated. The Prince, it is said, sometimes denies and sometimes admits that he had consented, but that it was before he had seen the King at Windsor.[5]

The implication was that the King was deranged.

Wild rumours went abroad. The Prince was furious at the prospect of losing the £5000 per annum which he received for the Princess's education. How strange it was that the Prince pressed the Hertfords to allow Mrs Fitzherbert to keep their niece, while he first gave away, then clung tenaciously to, his own daughter. Even Mrs Fitzherbert had her place in the rumours. It was said that she had offered to act as peacemaker between the Prince and Princess.

The King expressed his surprise to Lord Eldon that the Prince had not accepted the terms of his plan for Princess Charlotte in mid-December, and said that he had, 'with stoical indifference, waited the arrival of some information'.[6] An attempt was made to find a solution at a meeting at Pitt's house on 26 December. Moira represented the Prince: 'The point upon which the Prince rests is this: that it is requisite the arrangement should be entirely between the King and him, and that the Princess of Wales ought not to have, or appear to have, any interference in it.' Moira did not hand over another memorandum he made: 'The Prince's notion is that if the Princess of Wales shall appear to have interference in the original arrangement, or shall have the Princess Charlotte subsequently under her guidance, his Royal Highness will be liable to the misrepresentation that the King has sought to take his daughter out of his hands upon some charge of neglect.'[7]

The Chancellor represented the King, who continued to insist that 'in taking upon himself the care and management of the Princess Charlotte, he must be understood to do so in a sense consistent with all the attention due to each of the parents of the Princess'.[8] The King had his way, the 1717 precedent was upheld, and early in 1805 Princess Charlotte was settled at Windsor with a new governess, Lady de Clifford, and a new sub-governess, Mrs Alicia Campbell. Shrewsbury House on Blackheath was given up, and it was mooted that, in the summer season, Princess Charlotte should lodge at Kensington Palace, where both mother and father would have access to her. In the event, she spent her summers at Warwick House, where her mother was forbidden to set foot. Dr Fisher, Bishop of Exeter, was appointed to superintend her education, the Reverend Dr John Nott was her chief tutor, and a host of other masters visited from London. The King was well pleased with the arrangements – the Princess of Wales was to visit when she wished – and wrote from Windsor on 25 February 1805, 'It is quite charming to see the Princess and her child together, of which I have been since yesterday a witness. . . .'[9]

This was the first time since Princess Charlotte was three years old that mother and daughter had been permitted to sleep under the same roof. The King was less pleased with 'the language held by the Prince of Wales to Lady de Clifford', and with 'the very improper and unfair' paper that the Prince wrote for her and the Bishop of Exeter, containing instructions for their conduct with reference to the Princess of Wales. The Prince of Wales 'certainly means further chicane', his father wrote, but the King was grimly determined to have either exclusive care of his granddaughter or none: 'Windsor will be her residence for the greatest part of the year.... the advantage of excellent air and a retired garden ... will enable her, quietly and with effect, to pursue her studies, which certainly as yet have been but little attended to....'[10] Her grandmother the Duchess of Brunswick had the previous year made this very point, referring to Charlotte as 'a sheet of white paper'.

The Princess of Wales visited Charlotte at Windsor periodically this summer of 1805, and continued to grow in the King's esteem. The King was subdued, which Miss Hayman noticed on a visit he paid the Princess at Blackheath: 'it is seven years since I heard him speak and all the hurry of his manners is gone – he never said "hey!" once or "what!" twice together – and indeed was as quiet and collected as possible.'[11]

The friendship between his father and wife did not please the Prince. Lord Sheffield wrote, after his wife had dined at Blackheath in July, 'there is reason to believe that some of her servants have been spies upon her conduct'.[12] The visits of Mr Henry Hood, son of the naval hero Viscount Hood, who was now Governor of Greenwich Hospital, had attracted particular attention. In the autumn Lord Minto, with Windham, dined with the Princess and two of her ladies. 'It was very pleasant and good humoured as usual', Minto recorded,

> but she got me into one of her confidential whispers for the last two hours, which always distresses the patient, besides making my head ache desperately.... The King is as fond of her as ever, and has at last given her the rangership of Greenwich Park, which I am very glad of. They used to be very shabby and blackguard in refusing her half roods of green under her windows; now the whole is at her disposal.[13]

The Princess remained at Montague House, despite becoming Ranger, and the Queen's House or Ranger's House, in Greenwich Park, was leased to the newly founded Royal Naval School. (That way, the King could pay the Princess's debts from the Droits of

Admiralty as a notional purchase price for the House.)[14] The various houses and lodges in the park and around it, however, were now at the Princess Ranger's disposal, and for further sums she leased some of them to the School, or Asylum as it was known.

Many of the tenants in these park dwellings received notice to quit, some so that the Princess could install in their place various of her upper servants, others to make way for officials of the Asylum. Among those who received orders from Mr Charles Bicknell of the Asylum were the Princess's former friends Sir John and Lady Douglas, who occupied a house on Maze Hill. Three men arrived one morning, wrote Lady Douglas to the Duke of Sussex, 'with papers and pencils and informed me they were come to survey the place . . .'. It was to be converted, they said, into something useful for the asylum. 'I trust, rely and hope, we shall be protected . . .', wrote Lady Douglas, against these 'underhand merciless modes of warfare, which our enemies are making use of'. Sir John, she had told the surveyors in his absence, 'did not acknowledge the Ranger's power over his house'.[15]

The Princess of Wales unwittingly sealed her fate by leasing that particular lodge to the naval asylum officials. On 5 November Charlotte, Lady Douglas, gave a statement, in the presence of the Duke of Sussex, to whom she and her husband had first confided their story, and of the Prince of Wales, at McMahon's house in Charles Street, Mayfair, to the effect that Willy Austin, the Deptford boy whom the Princess had adopted in 1802, was the Princess's own child. Furthermore, Lady Douglas alleged, the Princess had told her that she would pass off the child as the Prince's own, as she had slept two nights at Carlton House at the relevant time.[16]

If the preposterous allegation that Willy Austin was the male child of the Prince and Princess of Wales were to be made and believed, the Deptford boy would usurp the position of their female child, Princess Charlotte. The matter went to the heart of the succession. According to Sir John Douglas, the Prince of Wales in his agitation scribbled down Lady Douglas's answers to his questions on sheets of notepaper.[17]

Mr Samuel Romilly, the Whig lawyer, had already acted for the Prince of Wales in the summer in an unsuccessful suit to have Mrs Fitzherbert officially appointed Minnie Seymour's guardian. Romilly was summoned to Carlton House, a few days after Lady Douglas had been questioned, to advise the Prince on a matter 'of the most confidential nature and of the greatest importance'. The Prince then recited, according to Romilly, the 'facts which had been communicated to him relative to the Princess of Wales, through the intervention of the Duke of Sussex, by Lady Douglas, the wife of one of the Duke's equerries'.[18]

A month later Lady Douglas gave a second statement about Willy Austin in the presence of the Duke of Kent and signed also by her husband. When he had read it, Romilly called in some perturbation on Lord Thurlow, whom the Prince had also consulted. Thurlow disbelieved the narrative, thought it a work of vengeance and highly circumstantial, while not according with his knowledge of the Princess. However, he suggested, 'it would be proper to employ a person to collect evidence respecting the conduct of the Princess'.[19]

As Thurlow was old, ill and plainly disinclined to pursue the matter, Romilly then visited another lawyer the Prince had consulted, Mr Thomas Erskine. Erskine was not much more impressed by the statement than Thurlow, and Romilly could not 'easily engage him to consider what I thought the matters principally deserving of consideration'. However, while the Princess of Wales spent Christmas with her friends Lord and Lady Sheffield at Sheffield Park, Romilly interviewed a solicitor, Mr Thomas Lowten – recommended by Thurlow – who, acting as a confidential agent, was to proceed to Cheltenham to question two of the Douglases' former servants regarding the allegation. At the request of the Prince, Romilly further questioned Lady Douglas at Lowten's chambers, in the presence of her husband and Lord Moira. Romilly recorded that Lady Douglas 'gave her answers with great coolness and self-possession, and in a manner to impress one very much with the truth of them'.[20]

Sarah and William Larpent, the Douglases' maid and manservant in Cheltenham, were duly interviewed by Lowten, accompanied by Sir John Douglas, in January 1806. William Cole, one of the Princess's pages of the backstairs at Blackheath at the time of her alleged pregnancy, was examined four times in January and February. There however the matter rested for a while, for in February, on Pitt's death, a new government headed by Lord Grenville and nicknamed the Ministry of All the Talents succeeded, and Romilly was appointed Solicitor-General in that administration.

Lowten continued his investigations in April and May, making 'many enquiries at Ramsgate, Southend and ... other places after the necessary evidence', at a cost of fifty-odd pounds. The curiosity about Manby's meetings with the Princess, first exhibited in the second batch of anonymous letters, had not diminished. Lowten also paid a Mr Wilkinson a similar sum 'for his attendance at sundry places, in town and country'.[21]

Towards the end of May, Romilly put this evidence – including the April depositions of another Montague House page, Robert Bidgood, of his wife Sarah and of the coffee-room woman, Frances Lloyd – before Lord Thurlow. Thurlow was apparently impressed by the quality of the supporting evidence. At any rate, he responded, 'the information had remained already too long in his Royal Highness's possession not proceeded on'.[22]

It was possibly Thurlow who advised that the Princess's physicians at Blackheath might usefully be questioned. Lord Moira asked Dr Edmeades to call on 20 May; at Moira's house the doctor found also Mr Conant, the Westminster magistrate. Edmeades indignantly counteredFrances Lloyd's testimony that one of the physicians had said he 'thought her Royal Highness in the family way', and that he had asked if the Prince 'had been down to Montague House'. He had 'never thought of such a thing as was suggested', let alone uttered it, Edmeades declared to Conant and Moira. According to the doctor's later account of this interview, 'Lord Moira, in a very significant manner, with his hands behind him, his head over one shoulder, his eyes directed towards me, with a sort of smile, observed, "that he could not help thinking that there must be something in the servant's deposition".' His partner Dr Mills had offered a similar denial six days earlier.[23]

The Prince ignored the doctors' denials. Romilly put the statements of all – except those of Edmeades and Mills – before Lord Grenville, the Prime Minister, on 23 May, and three days later sent him his opinion of the case against the Princess. Grenville went on the 28th to the King, to 'open the subject to his Majesty.... The King received the information with marks of considerable pain and concern,' but expressed 'his entire approbation' of the Prince's decision to lay the matter before him.

Erskine, now Lord Chancellor, the next day read to the King an abstract of the statements, and as a result the King gave his warrant that same day to appoint a Secret Commission of four Cabinet ministers – Lords Erskine, Ellenborough and Grenville and Earl Spencer (Secretary of State for the Home Department) – to launch an investigation. The King had 'expressed a strong wish that the whole should be kept as secret as possible until the result of our examinations shall be laid before him', Grenville told the Prince on the 28th.[24]

On the 31st, the Commission met with Romilly at Lord Grenville's house in Downing Street, and the following day they examined both Sir John and Lady Douglas. Grenville suggested to the Prince of Wales, who wished to call on him that day regarding Princess Charlotte's education, that another day would be more suitable. 'In a matter of such peculiar delicacy where appearances are to be watched and misrepresentations guarded against, some story might hereafter be grounded upon it, if it were known that immediately after these examinations and on the very same day I had received the high honour of your Royal Highness's visit here.'[25] The Prince took the hint and instead appointed McMahon to interview the Douglases immediately after their appointment at Downing Street.

What was to become known as the Delicate Investigation had begun, although the Princess of Wales, with the rest of the public, knew neither of the charges nor of the inquiry. She had only recently returned from a summer's visit to Devon with a party including Willy Austin and Lady Hester Stanhope, where she had been enjoying 'rambles amongst rocks, cliffs, and ruins', as she informed Miss Hayman. Caroline had visited Powderham Castle, she was going to Mount Edgcumbe to observe the beauties of the island and was disappointed only in an 'aquatic excursion', as no yacht was available. 'Nobody than me and little Willy have been well. . . . The climate is almost worse than Blackheath,' she added blithely; 'but it agrees wonderfully well with me.' Lady Hester was still disgusted by Caroline's indulgence of Willy. She recorded that the 'little, nasty,

vulgar brat' had been allowed into Lord Mount Edgcumbe's library
where he occupied himself 'turning over the leaves of a valuable book
of plates backward and forward' with inky fingers. She was no better
pleased at Blackheath: 'Once he cried for a spider on the ceiling . . .
then there was such a calling of footmen, and long sticks, and such a
to-do.'[26]

On the day that the Douglases were examined, the Princess's
suspicions were aroused. She wrote from Blackheath to Lady Townshend, her mistress of the robes, '. . . I am particularly uneasy at being
prevented going to Court' – for the Birthday – 'having lately heard
. . . that very unpleasant reports have been spread out from some very
malicious false and scandalizing tongues against poor me'.[27]

The following day Caroline received a letter from Princess
Elizabeth, to the effect 'That even I shall not have the honour of
seeing them at the Queen's House, nor in the evening, nor in the
morning . . .'. Caroline begged Lady Townshend to lend her her box
at the opera on 3 June, 'proving that sickness, nor any sort of illness
prevented my going to Court the next day'.[28] Four days later the
Princess's suspicions were amply confirmed when the Duke of Kent
visited her at Blackheath to prepare her for the fact that one Thomas
Lowten was on his way with a warrant to request the appearance of
several of her servants before a committee of peers, who were
investigating allegations against her.

'With surprise . . . but without alarm', the Princess later informed
the King, 'I received the intelligence that, for some reason, a formal
investigation of some parts of my conduct had been advised, and had
actually taken place.' When the Duke of Kent announced 'the near
approach of two attorneys to take away one half of my household, for
immediate examination upon a charge against myself, the Princess
prided herself that she 'betrayed no fear . . . manifested no symptoms
of conscious guilt . . . sought no excuses to prepare or to tutor my
servants for the examination which they were to undergo'. Of the
nature of the charge on which they were to be examined, 'I was then
uninformed. It now appears it was the charge of high treason,
committed in the infamous crime of adultery.'[29] The Princess asked
the Duke of Kent to remain with her till her servants were gone, 'that
he might bear witness that I had no conversation with them before

they went'. Later that morning Lowten and his colleague Wilkinson duly arrived with their warrants. (Lowten had earlier waited on the Duke of Kent to arrange 'the mode and time of serving the summons'.)[30]

They bore off to Lord Grenville's house six of the Princess's servants. In addition to Frances Lloyd, the coffee-room woman, whose evidence was already before the Commissioners, they took Mary Wilson, the housemaid who made the Princess's bed, and Charlotte Sander, Caroline's dresser who had come with her from Brunswick. John Sicard, the steward at Montague House, was forced to leave his duties, as was Thomas Stikeman, the page to whom Mrs Austin had originally applied with her son. Samuel Roberts, one of the footmen, was taken away as well.

The Princess was defiant in the face of the unknown charges. She had no doubt who were 'the instigators and accusers' in this matter, and she protested to the King on 8 June, the day after her servants' examination, that the Douglases were 'the most illiberal and vindictive people'.[31] She enclosed a paper, unhappily lost, describing their conduct which had led her to throw them over. Lord Eldon, she declared, was well acquainted with these circumstances. The King, anxious that the Princess should receive advice, yet reluctant to involve himself, asked Eldon to advise her.

The Princess kept all her engagements 'under this shock', dining in town at Lady Carnarvon's on the day her servants were taken away, and the following day hosting at Blackheath a large dinner for the French princes, the Comte d'Artois (later Charles X) and the Prince de Condé, who had led the emigration from France. This dinner was attended by Lord Minto, now President of the Board of Control, and by Mr William Windham, elevated to Secretary of State for War and the Colonies. Windham 'had heard, though the whole proceedings is very secret, that nothing material had come out. Some indiscretions, but nothing serious.' The Princess told Minto indignantly, 'there is no sort of question which was not asked of her servants, but as there is no truth there is nothing to tell'.[32]

Minto observed, 'there is reason to believe Sir John and Lady Douglas are at the bottom of this attack upon the Princess. Sir John Douglas had obtained a house in Greenwich Park, which the Princess took, or wanted to take, from them, to give, I think, to Miss Cholmondeley, when the Princess was made Ranger. Sir John was furious, and sent her, I hear, a threatening letter at the time.' Minto considered this circumstance fortunate, but was not sanguine. 'One can hardly conceive so strong and shocking a step to have been taken without a great deal of consideration and previous information. Yet all one knows of her unreserved and indiscreet manners may make one understand how an unfavourable judgment may have been formed without any real foundation.'[33]

Lady Douglas, whose statement was the foundation of the Delicate Investigation, had certainly formed a most unfavourable judgment of the Princess of Wales on the basis of her 'unreserved and indiscreet manners'. The Douglas narrative contained the material charge, 'viz. that her Royal Highness had been pregnant in the year 1802, in consequence of an illicit intercourse, and that she had in the same year been secretly delivered of a male child, which child had, ever since that period, been brought up by her Royal Highness, in her own house, and under her immediate inspection'. Whether or not this judgment was formed 'without any real foundation' was for the four Commissioners to decide. They were as one in believing that the Prince had no other course of action open to him but to give Lady Douglas's statement, and that of the supporting declarants, to the King.

Lady Douglas's statement, written down the previous December, utterly damned the Princess, 'partly on the ground of certain alleged declarations from the Princess's own mouth' and partly on her own 'personal observation'.[34] It stated: 'The Princess told me that if she were discovered in bringing her son into the world she would give the Prince of Wales the credit of it, for that she had slept two nights in the year she was pregnant in Carlton House.' Lady Douglas then recited in elaborate detail the history of her brief but intense friendship with the Princess.[35] She and Sir John had lived in a house on Blackheath from April 1801 with their baby daughter

very happily and quietly; but in the month of November, when the ground was covered with snow, as I was sitting in my parlour, which commanded a view of the Heath, I saw, to my surprise, the Princess of

Wales, elegantly dressed in a lilac satin pelisse, primrose-coloured half-boots, and a small lilac satin travelling cap, faced with sable, and a lady pacing up and down before the house, and sometimes stopping, as if desirous of opening the gate in the iron railing to come in.

Lady Douglas curtseyed at the window. 'To my astonishment she returned my courtesy by a familiar nod, and stopped. Old Lady Stuart, a West Indian lady who lived in my immediate neighbourhood ... was in the room, and said, "You should go out. Her Royal Highness wants to come in out of the snow." The Princess said, 'I believe you are Lady Douglas and you have a very beautiful child. I should like to see it.' Lady Douglas assumed that Sir Sidney Smith had spoken of them, as he often stayed with them on Blackheath and, indeed, had become 'part of the family'.

So the relationship between the Princess and Lady Douglas began. Lady Douglas then detailed the intimacy which the Princess thrust upon her. 'In a short time the Princess became so extravagantly fond of me, that ... it ... was very troublesome.' Exaggerating this claim to the point of suggesting lesbian advances, Lady Douglas instanced how the Princess ran into her bedroom, took her in her arms and said she had never loved any woman so much. At Montague House the Princess insisted that her new friend should take off her hat so that the Duke of Kent could see her beautiful eyes. The Princess 'walked about Blackheath and the neighbourhood' without livery servants, but 'only with her female attendants'. She soon saw, Lady Douglas recorded, that 'her Royal Highness was a very singular and a very indiscreet woman, and we resolved to be always very careful and guarded with her'.

In March 1802, Lady Douglas spent a fortnight at the Round Tower, at the Princess's request, and acted as her lady-in-waiting. (The Princess had lied, Lady Douglas believed, when she had said Miss Garth was ill.) Lady Douglas found the Princess 'a person without education or talents, and without any desire of improving herself'. She detailed in her statement a catalogue of sins the Princess had committed during this time. The Princess came to dine with her in a long red cloak, a silk handkerchief tied over her head and a pair of slippers 'down at the heels'. One evening after dinner at Mr

Windham's in town, when a lady was seated at the harpsichord, the Princess called out for 'oil' as she was very warm. Mrs Windham did not understand, so Lady Douglas had to advise her that ale was required, of which the Princess drank quantities.

The Princess also wrote to Prince William of Gloucester to inform him that there was a fair lady in the Round Tower who awaited his advances, and told Lady Douglas that she was foolish to be content with Sir John. The Duke of Gloucester called to protest 'how very free she permitted Sir Sidney Smith to be' – Smith was an almost daily visitor; 'as Sir Sidney was a lively, thoughtless man, and had not been accustomed to the society of ladies of her rank, he might forget himself, and she would then have herself to blame'. The Princess said she would have boxed Prince William's ears if he, rather than his father, had made these remarks. She declared, to Lady Douglas's horror, 'I will cheat him and throw the dust in his eyes, and make him believe Sir Sidney comes here to see you.'

On the day Lady Douglas left Montague House, the Princess sat her down on her bed and announced, 'I have the most complaisant husband in the world – I have no one to control me – I see whom I like, I go where I like, I spend what I please, and his Royal Highness pays for all.' She showed Lady Douglas a letter from the Prince authorizing this freedom and said that the Prince urged her, when she was at Carlton House, to 'select some particular gentleman for my friend'. He offered her £60,000 if she would go and live at Hanover. She then continued, 'I should have been the man, and he the woman. I am a real Brunswicker, and do not know what the sensation fear is; but, as to him, he lives in eternal warm water, and delights in it, if he can but have his slippers under any old dowager's table, and sit there scribbling notes; that's his whole delight.'

Lady Douglas moved on to the Princess's announcement of her pregnancy. The Princess called on her one evening and said she had a secret. She thought Lady Douglas had found her out, 'for you looked droll when I called for ale and fried onions and potatoes, and when I said I eat tongue and chickens at my breakfast'. When Lady Douglas 'affected not to understand', the Princess said, 'Well, I'll tell. I am with child, and the child came to life when I was breakfasting with Lady Willoughby. The milk flowed up into my breast so fast, that it came through my muslin gown, and I was obliged to pretend that I had spilt something, and go upstairs to wipe my gown with a napkin.' The Princess announced further, 'You will be surprised to see how well I manage it, and I am determined to suckle the child myself.' Lady Douglas was herself expecting a second child in July 1802, and she declared, 'After this we often met, and the Princess often alluded to her situation and to mine, and one day as we were sitting together upon the sofa, she put her hand on her stomach, and said, laughing, "Well, here we sit like Mary and Elizabeth in the Bible."'

Lady Douglas passed to her own lying-in. The Princess had often said she would attend it. 'I shall have a bottle of port wine on a table to keep up your spirits, a tambourine, and I'll make you sing.' A short while before her time came, Lady Douglas was at dinner at Montague House when the Princess disparaged a lady who had visited earlier as being 'ugly . . . a vulgar common milliner . . . and her daughter looks just like a girl that walks up the street'. When Lady Douglas would not agree, the Princess 'bawled out, "Then you're a liar, you're a liar, and the little child you're going to have will be a liar."' Lady Douglas alleged that, to her distress, when her time came the Princess pushed her way past locked doors and nurses to be present. First, she held Lady Douglas's hand, then, 'the moment she heard the child's voice she left me, flew round to Dr Mackie . . . and received the child from Dr Mackie, kissed it, and said no one should touch it until she had shown it to me'.

After this extraordinary affair, Lady Douglas received several visits from the Princess, who spoke of her own coming delivery. She said that, by constantly increasing large cushions behind her, no one would observe the difference at Court, or elsewhere. 'When you hear of my having taken children in baskets from poor people, take no notice; that is the way I mean to manage; I shall take any that offer, and the one I have will be presented in the same way. . . .'

The Princess, Lady Douglas observed, did not spare her abuse for the royal family. Her cousin Prince William of Gloucester she castigated as the grandson of a 'common washerwoman'. The Duke of Cumberland was a 'foolish boy'. All the rest were 'very ill made, and had plum pudding faces, which she could not bear'. The Duke of Cambridge, besides, looked like a sergeant, 'so vulgar with his ears full of powder'. She even declared that the King 'did not know what he was about', or was insane, when he gave his house to Mr Addington, the then Prime Minister – whom she abused as 'the son of a quack doctor'. Lady Douglas declared, 'Sir John and myself . . . regretted that . . . his Royal Highness the Prince of Wales should have lost any popularity when . . . her temper is so tyrannical, capricious, and furious that no man on earth will ever bear it. . . .'

The Princess, Lady Douglas declared, insisted that the christening of Caroline Sidney Douglas take place at Montague House. Dressed in a lace dress, 'pearl necklace, bracelets and armbands, a pearl bandeau round her head, and a long lace veil', the Princess chose to sit all evening upon the carpet while the company sat on the chairs, after the clergyman was gone. Sir Sidney was also present, and stood godfather. Then the Princess concluded by eating 'an amazing supper of chicken and potted lamprey'.

On 30 October 1802, Lady Douglas went to visit the Princess. There had been an estrangement since the August christening, because the Princess had quarrelled with Sir Sidney. The Princess was walking before her house 'dressed in a long Spanish velvet cloak and an enormous muff, but which together could not conceal the state she was in, for I saw directly she was very near her time'. Lady Douglas was then told not to visit, as there was measles in the house. Absent in Gloucestershire over Christmas, she did not see the Princess till January 1803, when she called and found the Princess with 'an infant sleeping on a sofa, with a piece of scarlet cloth thrown over it'. 'Here is the little boy,' the Princess said. 'I had him two days after I saw you last; is not it a nice little child?'

According to Lady Douglas, Mrs Fitzgerald then came in and 'sat down to tell me the whole fable of the child having been brought by a poor woman from Deptford, whose husband had left her'. Lady Douglas described how the Princess insisted on changing the child's 'napkins'. 'The drawing-rooms at Montague House were literally in the style of a common nursery. The tables were covered with spoons, plates, feeding-boats and clothes; round the fire, napkins were hung to air, and the marble hearths were strewed with napkins which were taken from the child.' The Princess also intimated that 'she had attempted to suckle' the baby, although he now was fed from the bottle.

Such was the burden of Lady Douglas's declaration, although there was a great deal more of it, all defamatory of the Princess, including a description of a dinner at which Princess Charlotte was made to play with the infant, and a description of the obscene and anonymous letters and drawings of 1804.[36]

The other depositions collected by the Prince of Wales and his agents, and now set before the Commissioners, confirmed the Princess's intimacy with Lady Douglas from 1801 till late 1802, the assiduity of Sir Sidney's visits to the Princess during that time, Lady Douglas's spell in the Round Tower in March 1802 and the arrival of Willy Austin in November of that year.[37]

William Cole had been twenty-one years in the Prince's employ and came as page with the Princess from Carlton House to Blackheath; subsequently he was sent back to duties at Carlton House. He declared that 'when the ladies have retired, about eleven o'clock, he has known Sir Sidney remain alone with the Princess an hour or two afterwards'. Further, 'One night about twelve o'clock, he saw a person wrapped up in a great coat go across the park, into the gate to the greenhouse' – which communicated with the Blue Room – 'and he verily believes it was Sir Sidney.'

Cole took some sandwiches the Princess had ordered into the drawing-room in March 1802, where he found Sir Sidney with her. When he returned to the room, 'he found the gentleman and lady sitting close together, in so familiar a posture as to alarm him very much, which he expressed by a start back, and a look at the gentleman'. A fortnight later he was dismissed. Cole saw the Princess, however, nine or ten times that year. 'She grew lusty, and appeared large behind. . . . at the latter end of the year . . . the Princess was grown thinner.' Robert Bidgood, the other page, added to this that Sir Sidney Smith was often at Montague House till three or four in the morning, although he did not know if the ladies were still up. Moreover, the Admiral was once in the Blue Room at ten in the morning, though no one had let him in.

Fanny Lloyd, the coffee-room woman, as we have seen, declared that one of Caroline's physicians had asked if the Prince visited the house, for, he asserted, 'the Princess certainly was with child'. In addition, Lloyd reported a story to which Cole and Bidgood both referred, that Mary Wilson, the housemaid, had 'found the Princess and Sir Sidney in the act'. Lloyd said she believed it was in the Blue Room that Wilson saw this. Cole and Mrs Bidgood, however, asserted that Fanny Lloyd told them it was in the Princess's bedroom that Wilson found the pair – 'in such an indecent situation, that she immediately left the room, and was so shocked that she fainted away at the door'.[38]

This ended the statements in the declarations set before the Commissioners adducing the 'material' charge of pregnancy against the Princess. However, the statements of Cole, Bidgood and Fanny Lloyd also provided what the Commissioners termed 'collateral evidence, applying to other points of the same nature (though going to a far less extent)'. In other words, besides the allegation of a pregnancy implying one adulterous relationship with Sir Sidney, the Princess was charged with a succession of adulteries, from 1801 to 1805.[39]

Lady Douglas had pointed the finger at Sir Sidney Smith. William Cole, the page, added the names of the politician George Canning (after rather than before his marriage) and of the painter Thomas Lawrence – both in 1801. From hearsay – Cole was dismissed in 1802 – he adduced Captain Thomas Manby, from 1802 till 1804, and Mr Henry Hood in 1805. Fanny Lloyd told him that the Princess went off for whole afternoons at Portsmouth with Mr Hood (he was now Lord Hood, after inheriting a barony from his mother), taking with her a luncheon of cold meat. 'They used to get out of the gig, and walk into the wood, leaving the boy' – their sole attendant – 'to attend the horse and gig.'[40]

Bidgood fingered Manby. The Princess paid for fitting out his cabin in 1803. When Manby was about to sail, Bidgood saw, in a mirror, 'Captain Manby kissing the Princess's lips; and soon afterwards he went away. He saw the Princess, with her handkerchief to her face, go into the drawing-room apparently in tears'. Fanny Lloyd said that, at Ramsgate later in 1803, she had been told to make breakfast at six in the morning for the Princess. Opening her shutters, she saw the Princess and a man walking in the garden. At Southend in 1804 Sicard kept watch for the arrival of the *Africaine*, Captain Manby's ship, and Bidgood believed Manby slept at the Princess's house. 'Towels, water, and glasses' were put in the passage outside her room in the morning.

Although Bidgood was not at Portsmouth with the Princess in the summer of 1805, he was a witness to Mr Hood's visits on her return from there. Hood came at midday for luncheon 'without his wife', and stayed to dinner 'sometimes in boots'. No one let him out.[41] Finally, Fanny Lloyd had heard of an incident at Lady Sheffield's this last Christmas, when the Princess late one night 'went out of her bedroom, and could not find her way back'.

The weight of the evidence amassed against the Princess presented her legal advisers with a formidable task. First they had to defend her against the material charges. Then, perhaps an even greater challenge, not least because Hood probably was her lover, they had to demolish the other allegations, whose cumulative effect would be to damage her in the eyes of the King and of the country. Without royal or popular favour, her position would be greatly weakened.

## CHAPTER EIGHT

# THE DELICATE INVESTIGATION

## 1806–1807

*'A Brunswicker never has been conquered yet'*

THE LORDS COMMISSIONERS had their instructions from the King on 29 May 1806, 'to enquire into the truth' of the 'written declarations, touching the conduct of her Royal Highness the Princess of Wales, an abstract of which has been laid before your Majesty, and to examine upon oath such persons as we should see fit, touching and concerning the same, and to report to your Majesty the result of such examinations'. The Commissioners first examined 'those persons in whose declarations the occasion for this Inquiry had originated; because, if they on being examined, upon oath, had retracted or varied their assertions, all necessity for further investigation might possibly have been precluded'.[1]

Lady Douglas was startled by being asked to take an oath at Lord Grenville's house in Downing Street on her first appearance there, as was Cole. Nevertheless, she 'positively swore' to all the important particulars contained in her former declaration. She was put out only, as she wrote to McMahon, that she had omitted to mention the incident regarding the Princess and Captain Manby at table, when the Princess had pressed her leg against his in full view of Sir Sidney:

> If such facts were not stated, it would be difficult for people who never saw her habits or manners familiarly to believe it possible. . . .
>
> I beg leave to say that when I was sent for last Sunday I thought I stood in too serious a condition to allow myself to converse freely, particularly as Lord Grenville judged proper to administer the oath.

Therefore she had only 'answered the questions asked. . . . I inspired poor Mr Cole with a good deal of courage at Lord Grenville's. I never saw a person so frightened. . . .'[2]

Once these preliminary examinations were concluded, the Commissioners, as we have seen, summoned the Princess's servants on 7 June. They hoped to learn 'particulars ... which would be necessarily conclusive on the truth or falsehood of these declarations. ... we entertained a full and confident expectation of arriving at complete proof, either in the affirmative or negative, on this part of the subject' – namely, the Princess's alleged pregnancy and motherhood of 'the Deptford boy'.

All the servants who had been summoned, bar Fanny Lloyd, denied the charges against their mistress of pregnancy or adultery. The Princess's dresser, the maid who made her bed, her steward, were all convincing witnesses. All agreed that Willy Austin was regularly visited by his mother, a woman who originally in 1802 'came to the door with a petition to get her husband replaced in the Dockyard'. She had a child with her, and Stikeman, believing that the Princess might take it, told her to return with it so that the Princess might see it. This she did, and, a few days later, 'the child ... was left, and has been with the Princess ever since'. Stikeman added that the child's father, 'whose name is Austin, lives with me at Pimlico. My wife is a laundress, and washed the linen of the Princess. Austin is employed to turn a mangle for me.'[3]

The Commissioners received their 'complete proof' later that day, when Mrs Austin, the child's mother, appeared before them. She corroborated Stikeman's story in every respect. She added that she was sent down to the coffee-room and given some arrowroot to wean the child, and the Princess agreed to take her son, little Willy. 'For I was suckling the child at the time, and when I had weaned the child I was to bring it and leave it with the Princess.' On 15 November 1802 she returned to Montague House with the child weaned, and left it there. 'I saw the child last Whit Monday, and I swear that it is my child.'[4]

Later in the month a copy of the Brownlow Street Lying-in Hospital registry was produced to certify that a child, William Austin, had indeed been born to Samuel and Sophia Austin on 11 July 1802, as Mrs Austin stated. The Commissioners hardly needed this confirmation. On the first day that witnesses were called, they proved to be witnesses for the defence, and Lady Douglas's story appeared one lengthy lie.

Sir John Douglas, when examined, revealed that he had received none of the confidences Lady Douglas alleged the Princess had made to her, and only heard of the pregnancy from his wife in 1804. His testimony was ambiguous: 'One day she leaned on the sofa, and put her hand on her stomach, and said "Sir John, I shall never be queen of England." I said, "Not if you don't deserve it." '[5]

The supporting evidence of William Cole, Robert Bidgood and Fanny Lloyd was thrown into doubt, especially when Mary Wilson, the maid who, it was thought, had caught the Princess and Sir Sidney *in flagrante*, denied it. Ten years later, when the Princess was dismissing some of her Household with either pensions for life or one year's salary, she was insistent that Mary Wilson be well paid. It seems possible that Wilson did indeed see the Princess in the act of adultery with Sir Sidney in 1802 and confided her information to all the upper servants. It seems equally likely that the Princess asked or paid Wilson, either in the summer of 1806 or earlier, to stay silent on the subject.[6]

Returning to the subject of Willy Austin and his parentage, later this month – June 1806 – both Dr Mills and Dr Edmeades denied having either of them told Fanny Lloyd that the Princess was with child. Either Lady Douglas's tale of the Princess's pregnancy had been a tissue of lies amounting to perjury, given the oath she took, or the Princess had deceived her erstwhile friend with a fantasy that she was pregnant when she was not – and perhaps had deceived herself as well.

It is possible that this fantasy amounted to a pseudocyesis, or phantom pregnancy – in other words, the Princess of Wales had all the symptoms of pregnancy, was nauseated, grew large and believed herself to be pregnant. Given Caroline's situation in 1802, this is perfectly possible. She adored babies and young children, and was denied the opportunity to have more after Charlotte – who was now six years old. Her new friend, Lady Douglas, with one young child, was pregnant with another. And so, perhaps Caroline became deluded that she too was pregnant. Or Caroline was pregnant by Sir Sidney Smith, and had a miscarriage. Pseudocyesis sometimes occurs in women who have miscarried.

What seems much more probable, given Caroline's peculiar sense of humour, is that she pretended to think herself pregnant as a joke. From Lady Douglas's own original statement it is plain that Caroline delighted in outraging her po-faced neighbour with references to her own and to Lady Douglas's supposed dalliances – and by such harum-scarum episodes as inventing her labour. Whatever the truth of Lady Douglas's claims that the Princess of Wales was pregnant, William Austin was certainly not her child – and, as certainly, was exactly who he was thought to be by everyone except Lady Douglas. (In later life he was like as a spit to his mother and to his brother Job.)[7]

On the seventh day of the Delicate Investigation, the succession to the throne was discovered no longer to be in doubt, and so there was every reason to curtail the Inquiry, given that the principal charge was proved groundless. Furthermore, the motives of the chief accusers were suspect, and their evidence was tainted respecting the principal charge. Lady Douglas had an axe to grind, as the Princess had tried to remove her from her house. There was also the very curious point that Lady Douglas, mother of a seven-month child in January 1803, believed Willy Austin, six months old at that date, to be, at most, ten weeks old.

Cole and Bidgood had been with the Prince of Wales twenty-one and twenty-three years respectively, and the Princess of Wales had dismissed the former from her employ. The failure of the Prince's agents, who had been so busy questioning others in early 1806, to question Sophia Austin was also remarkable. The identity of the mother, and her whereabouts, was no secret, as she visited Willy frequently. The Princess and her advisers, however, had no means of knowing that the principal charge had been countered, and Sicard, on his royal employer's behalf, was conducting a Spanish Inquisition among the other servants.

Caroline wrote to Lady Townshend on 18 June, 'their schemes are deeper than I had a right to expect. . . . Mrs Bidgood, wife of my page, whom I know even not by sight, has tried to corrupt the coffee-room maid named Lloyd, in the time when I was in Dawlish. . . . Lloyd swears that she will take the greatest oath' to that effect. Later, she announced, Fanny Lloyd had confessed to having been 'examined secretly, last winter, at the Temple, by Mr Lowten'.[8] Sicard effectively 'turned' frightened Fanny to become a witness for the defence.

Caroline had a ready explanation for anything 'old Dr Mills', who she heard was examined, might have said against her. Mills had been her physician when she first came to the Heath. Then the Duke of Cumberland had recommended, instead, Mills's partner, Dr Edmeades, whose wife's father was 'an intimate friend' of the Duke: 'Which of course affronted the old man Doctor Mills, and it is said that in one of his ill humours against me he said "Perhaps the Princess don't wish I shall be informed of her illness".'

The scandal-brewing Mrs Bidgood heard this, Caroline asserted, and assured Fanny Lloyd that the child to whom the Princess gave birth was taken in by Mrs Sicard. The steward's wife, to her great joy, had had a child at this time, after being married and childless a great many years, 'which I suppose has given rise to this scandal and calumniation'.[9]

One of Fanny Lloyd's remarks during her examination on 7 June – to the effect that a Mrs Towneley, who did the washing at Montague House, saw stains of a delivery or miscarriage on the Princess's bed-linen – decided the Commissioners not to end their inquiry then and there, for the succession was not yet out of danger. From now on, they occupied themselves more with the question of the Princess's possible adulteries – and therefore with other potential illegitimate children – than with 'the Deptford boy', or with his parentage, on either the maternal or the paternal side.

The examinations resumed on 23 June, when Willy Austin's Blackheath nurse Mrs Gosden confirmed the mother's story, that the child had already been weaned when he came to Montague House. Mrs Gosden also effectively destroyed Lady Douglas's tale that the drawing-rooms there were strewn with dirty nappies. Mrs Gosden had her nursery upstairs.

Mrs Fitzgerald, the Princess's woman, denied (possibly perjuring herself) that the Princess had been at Lady Douglas's labour, and Lady Willoughby declared stiffly that she had no memory of the Princess having to retire from her breakfast table four years earlier. Still the inquiry proceeded. The Princess of Wales wrote on 1 July, 'Now I am sorry to tell you that we go back to eight, nine and ten years which include poor little Edwardine. . . .'[10] The washerwoman Betty Towneley had appeared before the Lords Commissioners, to confirm that she had thought the Princess's linen marked with the signs of a miscarriage. She was further questioned about the arrival of Edwardine. Caroline was indignant: the child was a foundling, aged ten months with four teeth when discovered on the heath.

Bidgood was re-examined, and added that the Princess went out in her phaeton, with coachman and helper and accompanied by Mrs Fitzgerald, 'carrying luncheon and wine with her', when Captain Manby's ship was at Long Reach. 'The servants used to talk and laugh about Captain Manby,' he deposed.[11] Mrs Lisle, still the Princess's bedchamber woman, was examined on 3 July, and admitted that the Princess 'appeared to have greater pleasure in talking' to Captain Manby than to her ladies. She went on to damn the Princess's conduct further: 'She behaved to him only as any woman would who likes flirting. I should not have thought any married woman would have behaved properly who should have behaved as her Royal Highness behaved to Captain Manby.'[12]

Mrs Lisle confirmed that the Princess had driven out for hours at a time in Mr Hood's whisky at Catherington, with no other companion but his servant. She added two more names to the legion of the Princess's possible illicit admirers in Mr John Chester at Lady Sheffield's at Christmas 1805, and a Captain Moore, directly on the Princess's return to Blackheath. On the other hand, she remembered no instance on which Captain Manby or Sir Sidney Smith or any of the rest had remained with the Princess after her ladies had retired. Conduct unbecoming was her charge. One of the footmen at Montague House, Samuel Roberts – perhaps the 'handsome footman' implicated by Lady Hester Stanhope – had been more outspoken. 'The Princess is very fond of fucking,' he had said, an assertion treated by McMahon as a dispassionate observation, but it may well have been born of personal experience.

The Lords Commissioners concluded on 14 July 1806:

There is no foundation for believing that the child now with the Princess is the child of her Royal Highness, or that she was delivered of any child in the year 1802; nor has anything appeared to us which would warrant the belief that she was pregnant in that year, or at any other period within the compass of our inquiries.

Accordingly, 'the alleged pregnancy as stated in the original declaration . . . we cannot think . . . entitled to the smallest credit'.

'We do not however feel ourselves at liberty,' the Commissioners continued, 'much as we would wish it, to close our Report here. Besides the allegations of the pregnancy and delivery of the Princess, those declarations on the whole of which your Majesty has been pleased to command us to inquire and report, contain . . . other particulars respecting the conduct of her Royal Highness, such as must, especially considering her exalted rank and station, necessarily give occasion to very unfavourable interpretations.'[13] The Commissioners' Report did not mention Samuel Roberts's testimony but named Robert Bidgood, William Cole, Frances Lloyd and Mrs Lisle as:

> witnesses, who cannot, in our judgment, be suspected of any unfavourable bias, and whose veracity, in this respect, we have seen no grounds to question. On the precise bearing and effect of the facts thus appearing it is not for us to decide; these we submit to your Majesty's wisdom . . . as on the one hand, the facts of pregnancy and delivery are to our minds satisfactorily disproved, so on the other hand we think, that the circumstances to which we now refer, particularly those stated to have passed between her Royal Highness and Captain Manby, must be credited until they shall receive some decisive contradiction, and if true, are justly entitled to the most serious consideration.[14]

So the Report wound up an investigation which had confounded the spirit of British justice at every turn, despite the presence of the Lord Chancellor and the Lord Chief Justice among the four Commissioners. The Commission had masqueraded as a court of law, imposing oaths and summoning witnesses. The Princess was treated as a defendant in a court of law, yet she was not told what the accusations were against her, nor given the opportunity to defend herself against them.

The accusations were of capital crimes. Adultery, as Lord Malmesbury had informed Princess Caroline long before in Brunswick, was high treason for the Princess of Wales. By the relevant statute of Edward III, strictly speaking she was an accomplice in the crime of high treason against her person, but she was liable, like her partner, to the death penalty. Yet no formal charge was made in any court of law but this bastard court at Downing Street. Finally, the Commissioners were required, by their commission, only to give their view of the credibility of the original declarations, without giving chapter and verse in justification.

Yet it was a judgment that they made when they condemned the Princess, in her absence, as guilty until proven innocent for her conduct with Captain Manby, although they neither declared it the crime of high treason, nor named it something other than a crime, nor gave her the opportunity to prove herself innocent.

While the King meditated on the Report he had commissioned, the Princess of Wales remained in a state of severe anxiety. Excluded from Court indefinitely by her father-in-law, she was also prevented from seeing Princess Charlotte, and among those few who knew of the Secret Commission an assumption of her guilt was almost universal. On 25 June Lord Minto wrote to his wife:

> Miss Cholmondeley, who should not be quoted, told me today that yesterday and the day before she [the Princess of Wales] was extremely agitated and talked very seriously of going back to Brunswick. Windham dissuaded her strongly, saying it would be to plead guilty and abandon her reputation.
>
> For my own part, as nothing but humiliation and affronts attend her here ... I do not feel so clear that for her own comfort and tranquillity it would be so unwise a measure. I am really grieved for her. Her treatment from the beginning has been afflicting and insulting; and the prospect, instead of brightening, is more gloomy and threatening than ever.[15]

Other Tories – politicians and lawyers – out of office saw the Princess's cause as an opportunity to make mischief for the Ministry of All the Talents, which was predominantly a Whig government and under the sway of Moira, now in the Cabinet as Master-General of the Ordnance, and Carlton House. The Commissioners' conduct of the investigation against the Princess was undoubtedly influenced, if not directed, by the Prince's known wish for a damning outcome.

Lord Moira, on the Prince's behalf, attended at more than one of the examinations and suggested various lines of questioning. (From the most impartial stance, this fact would seem to damn the Delicate

Investigation as *ex parte*.) He wrote to the Prince, who had departed for Bibury Races on 21 June, 'It is now becoming generally understood that your Royal Highness takes no concern in the matter and the inference drawn from that circumstance has been of the highest degree important.' The Prince meanwhile supplied Romilly with samples of the Princess's letters, for comparison with the anonymous letters which the Douglases had produced.[16] (The issue was never resolved.) Moira wrote again, advising the Prince of Wales to stay out of London: 'All is going on well, and the delays have undoubtedly been useful.'

Chief among the Princess's advisers was Mr Spencer Perceval, lately the Attorney-General, but other distinguished lawyers (Sir Vicary Gibbs, Mr Thomas Plumer and Sir William Grant) were also on hand. In addition, the Duke of Cumberland, who had fallen out with his brother the Prince, took the Princess's part. Her spirits rose. Plumer dined with her on 22 June and was, in her view,

> rather inclined to pacific measures, and not wishing I should go to the bottom of this infernal accusation. . . .
>
> Tell Mr Perceval, Lord Eldon and Sir William Grant [she wrote to Lady Townshend] that a Brunswicker never has been conquered yet, and that my honour is more dear to me than all my jewels, that I am ready to pawn them all, to defend my own honour, and to discover all my accusers. . . . I am ready to meet them [Eldon and company] at the Duke of Cumberland's apartments. . . .[17]

Perceval and the others counselled the Princess to insist on occupying apartments again in Carlton House, which she was ready to do, 'so painful as it will be to find myself once more under the roof of my tyrant'. They held her back from attending the opera and encouraged her to write to her family in Brunswick, expressing her outrage at her treatment. The existence of the secret inquiry was leaked to *The Times*, and Perceval began preparing a defence against the probable charges. Captain Manby, on 8 July, completed an account of his lodging on Blackheath and of his innocent relationship with the Princess.

Next day the Princess sent a copy to Perceval of an angry letter she wished to send to the Commissioners, declaring that Mr Bidgood refused to speak of his second examination to her and furthermore 'was found by one of my servants coming out of Lady Douglas's lodge in the Park'. On receiving Perceval's 'kind reproof', she obediently 'put it [the letter to the Commissioners] to the flame'.[18]

Lady Townshend exhorted the Princess on 25 July, 'no time should be lost in preparing your letter to the King'. The Princess was now 'seven weeks without knowing the charges brought against you or [the] accusers except what your Royal Highness could collect from the ladies and servants of your family examined'.[19] The Princess wrote to Lord Eldon the same day, begging him 'verbally [to] explain and open his [the King's] eyes on the unjust and unloyal proceedings of his Ministers'. The Princess was 'quite resigned to her cruel fate, from the period that her honour was in the hands of a pack of ruffians, and who are only devoted, and slaves, to her most inveterate enemy'.[20]

The Report, however, stayed with the King for the good reason that he had not decided what to do, and the Princess of Wales waxed ever more indignant at her treatment. When she heard that Sir John Douglas meant to publish a pamphlet in reply to imputations in the – Tory – *Morning Post* against his wife's honour, Caroline wrote of 'my intention to prosecute him then as a libel and defamation writer'.[21]

The King had seen only the heads of the charges against the Princess. Now he was told of no precise or legal crime she had committed. He was in an awkward position – of his own making or of his son's, depending on how one viewed the matter. He asked the Cabinet to meet, discuss the Report and direct what steps he should take. They advised only that 'in the first instance' copies of the Report should be sent to both Prince and Princess of Wales.[22] It was not till the middle of August – two and a half months after the Princess first became aware of the inquiry – that she received a copy of the Commissioners' Report, which revealed the accusations against her. The King was still undecided how to proceed on 20 September when he wrote to his sister in Brunswick: 'Till the subject came officially before me I had not the smallest suspicion. I cannot possibly decide upon it, until I shall have acquired an entire knowledge of circumstances.'[23]

The Prince of Wales was furious with the Commissioners. On 5 August, even before he received his copy of the Report, he had told

McMahon that, from what Thurlow could gather, the Commissioners had shown 'too great a degree of lenity' to the Princess. If there was 'not quite sufficient to try her for . . . high treason, still,' he believed, 'that from the circumstances of her imprudence, they ought to follow it up by a recommendation to the King – (which he ought immediately to sanction) – of bringing in an Act of Parliament to dissolve the marriage'.[24]

The Princess's first complaint against the Report was that it was brought to her on 11 August by 'a common servant. . . . She is in great haste to read all this stuff and nonsense,' she wrote, begging her advisers to hurry over to inspect the Report after she had done with it. Next day – her husband's forty-second birthday – she wrote, 'Lord Eldon and the Duke of Cumberland are sitting this moment in my room to read over all the evidence.'[25] The result of that session at Montague House was an impious letter from the Princess of Wales to the King that very day. 'I can in the face of the Almighty assure your Majesty', she declared, 'that your daughter-in-law is innocent and her conduct unquestionable; free from all the indecorums and improprieties . . . imputed to her . . . by the Lords Commissioners, upon the evidence of persons who speak as falsely as Sir John and Lady Douglas themselves.' She denied solemnly 'the scandalous stories' of Cole and Bidgood.

'Recollect', she begged her father-in-law and uncle,

> that the whole of the evidence on which the Commissioners have given credit to the infamous stories charged against me was taken behind my back, without my having any opportunity . . . even to point out those persons who might have been called, to prove the little credit which was due to some of the witnesses, from their connection with Sir John and Lady Douglas, and the absolute falsehood of parts of the evidence, which could have been completely contradicted.

She looked only to 'that happy moment, when I may be allowed to appear before your Majesty's eyes again'.[26]

This letter, it hardly needs saying, was phrased by the Princess's legal advisers, although she declared five days later that she wanted 'no adviser, but my own heart, to express my gratitude for the kindness and protection which I have' – or rather had – 'uniformly received from your Majesty'. In this second letter, of 17 August, the Princess, however, supposed the King would 'not be surprised, nor displeased' that, as 'a woman, a stranger to the laws and usages of your Majesty's kingdom, under charges aimed, originally, at my life and honour', the Princess had taken advice.

Her advisers had observed that the copies of the Report and the accompanying examinations came unauthenticated. Furthermore, she had not received 'certain written declarations' which were the foundation of the proceedings, including those 'asserting facts of the most confirmed and abandoned criminality, for which, if true, my life might be forfeited'. (The Tower and scaffold were unlikely to be the Princess of Wales's fate in 1806, but there was no harm in making the point.) She still did not know, in short, 'the extent, and the particulars of the charges or informations against me, and by what accusers they have been made; whether I am answering the charges of one set of accusers or more'.[27]

The King, on receipt of this letter, rather uncomfortably directed Lord Erskine 'that he may lose no time in conforming to the Princess's wishes as far as justice may require'.[28] The original declarations of Lady Douglas and the rest, and the Report and examinations newly authenticated, were in the Princess's hands by early September – and were not sent, this time, by a 'common servant'. In the meantime, Perceval had shown to Mr Thomas Lawrence and to Captain Manby the examinations which incriminated them as possibly guilty of high treason. Sir Sidney Smith was at this time on active service in the Mediterranean and seems not to have been pursued for a statement of his own. Perceval also suggested that the Princess should write out her answers to the charges – he would supply her with an abstract of the evidence against her – from which he would draft a complete answer to be sent to the King. Lord Hawkesbury, a prominent Tory, and Canning should then look it over, because Perceval felt that their political friends should be apprised of the latest developments.[29]

When the original declarations arrived on 29 August, Perceval's view of the narrative of Lady Douglas and her husband was that 'A greater farrago of gossiping trash and malignant accusation can hardly be conceived.' He believed any 'impartial mind' would have distrusted

Lady Douglas's statement 'from the evident spirit [of rancour and resentment] with which it was written'. In his view also, however, and unfortunately, Lady Douglas could not be prosecuted for perjury, as the Delicate Investigation had not been enough of a judicial proceeding. Perceval had hopes, nevertheless, that she might be liable to judgment from the Privy Council, at least, for false oath. Lloyd and Cole, he noted, were 'in direct flat contradiction to each other'.[30]

Moira meanwhile told the Prince, 'the cry now is, "Since the Prince has had the evidence communicated to her [the Princess] let her publish it if she can face it."'[31] The Princess was keen as mustard to do so, although she complained of the labour this entailed for her. 'Mr Perceval has given me a very great task, in writing my own evidence,' she wrote on 9 September, 'and relating events which, in the time they passed, I looked upon as of no consequence and so perfectly uninteresting then [that] I can hardly trust them [now] to my memory to do them justice and to do them correctly. . . .'

She was taking precautions against further domestic treason. The bedchamber woman's maid, who 'dines, sups and sits a part of the evening with my own dressers', from now on – after the spite shown by Sandell, Mrs Lisle's maid – would dine in Hall.[32] Mrs Lisle herself was kept on as bedchamber woman, perhaps in recognition of the favourable tone of most of her statement.

Her defence moved towards completion. Meanwhile, Manby and Lawrence made depositions indignantly countering the charges against them.[33] Manby denied Bidgood's evidence that he had kissed the Princess at Montague House, or slept 'in any house occupied by . . . the Princess of Wales'. Lawrence rebutted Cole's testimony that he had stayed behind a locked door with the Princess. When he had stayed at Montague House to paint the Princess's picture, 'nothing passed between her Royal Highness and myself which I could have had the least objection for all the world to have seen and heard'.

Jonathan Partridge, gardener to Lord Eardley at Belvedere, stated that Lord Moira had questioned him as long ago as June 1804 about a visit the Princess had made some time before with some ladies and a gentleman, to look at the pictures and take their luncheon.[34] Edmeades, the surgeon, again implicated Moira, who, as we have seen, in May 1806 attempted to persuade the surgeon that 'there must be something in the servant's [Fanny Lloyd's] deposition'.

Two of the Princess's footmen, Philip Krackler and Robert Eagle-stone, deposed that they had seen Bidgood keep an assignation with Lady Douglas in Greenwich Park shortly after his second examin-ation.[35] All these depositions were designed to accompany the letter, of which, on 1 October, Perceval wrote to Lady Townshend, 'the task of drawing up the Princess of Wales's letter to the King falls on me. . . . it is, I assure you, a very laborious work'.[36] The following day this mighty counterblast (when later printed, 160 pages long) against 'the substance of the proceeding itself, and . . . the manner of conducting it' was dispatched to the King.

The Princess complained first that the original testimony, on which the charges against her depended, 'betrayed, in every sentence, the malice in which it originated'. She urged, as 'matters of serious lamentation at least', the following: that the King had 'been advised to pass by the ordinary legal modes of inquiry into such high crimes' in favour of a Commission; that the Commissioners, 'after having negatived the principal charge of substantive crime', had 'entertained considerations of matters that amounted to no legal offence, and which were adduced' only 'in support of the principal accusation'; that the Commissioners, 'through the pressure and weight of their official occupations, did not bestow that attention on the case which, if given to it, must have enabled them to detect the villainy and falsehood of my accusers, their foul conspiracy', and 'must have preserved my character from the weighty imputation which the authority of the Commissioners has, for a time, cast upon it'.

Above all else, the Princess complained that the Commissioners should 'upon this *ex parte* examination, without hearing one word that I could urge, have reported to your Majesty an opinion on these matters so prejudicial to my honour, and from which I can have no appeal to the laws of the country because the charges, constituting no legal offence, cannot be made the ground of a judicial inquiry'.[37]

The Princess then made her objections at length and in detail to the original declarations, the subsequent examinations, the witnesses' characters and the Commissioners' findings. In passing, she denied authorship of the anonymous letters. The letter closed with a reiteration of her strongest arguments. There was no precedent for, or 'legality of', a Commission, rather than a judicial court, being empowered to enquire into high treason or 'any other crime known to the laws of the country'. A concluding and positively Ciceronian peroration protested against the establishment or proliferation of 'such a court of honour, of decency and of manners'.

If Commissioners, Privy Council 'or any regular Magistrates, when they have satisfied themselves of the falsehood of the principal charges, and the absence of all legal and substantive offence, are to be considered as empowered to proceed in the examination of the particulars of private life, to report upon the proprieties of domestic conduct; and the decorums of private behaviour ...', thundered Perceval in the persona of the Princess, 'it would ... prove such an attack on the security and confidence of domestic life ... that no character could possibly be secure'. The letter wound up with a solemn warning:

> I trust new law is not to be found out, and applied to my case.... I fear no charge brought against me in open day, under the public eye, before the known tribunals of the country.... But secret tribunals, created for the first time for me ... till I am better reconciled to the justice of their proceedings, I cannot fail to fear.[33]

On the day that this was sent to the King, Lady Douglas received another visit from 'the surveyor's people' at her Greenwich Park lodge, and she appealed to the Duke of Sussex once more. They 'again appeared and measured all the outside of the wall of our garden and that angle of the park which is immediately adjoining to the cottage ...', she wrote. She was determined, however, although she lived in 'the very same park with the cruellest foe ever a woman had, and the other lodges filled with pages from Montague House ... never to quit the spot'. She walked about Blackheath, Lady Douglas told Sussex, to 'show people the confidence we have in them. This I have made a point of doing from the first moment that the Morning Post first held us up as marks for vengeance ... amidst all the human evils I had calculated upon contending with, I had never thought of anything so horrible as seeing my name branded in a public news-paper'.[39] The Secret Commission was secret no longer, and the Whig and Tory papers took up the causes of, respectively, the Prince and Princess of Wales. To add to Lady Douglas's woes, 'every person to whom we owed a farthing sent in their demands' after the *Morning Post* noticed her. In December 1806, Lady Douglas and her children were still under notice to quit.[40] But she had some compensation. The service she had rendered the Prince with her tales of his wife was graphically demonstrated by his paying her an annual pension for life of £200.[41]

The Prince was horrified to learn from Moira, at the beginning of November, that the Prime Minister Lord Grenville had not even looked at the Princess's letter, which the King had sent him. (There had been the trifling matter of a general election to occupy the ministers.) 'From what he [Lord Grenville] had heard of its tenor,' reported Moira, 'he said he thought nothing more could be done by Ministers.' Grenville suggested, in fact, to the Prince's rage, that he (the Prince) 'had only to signify to the Princess that her explanations were so unsatisfactory as to make it requisite for her not to revisit Carlton House'.

Moira had done his best to urge 'the unfairness of letting the interdict come from you when both had appealed to the King as the only competent judge'. And he had further insisted that 'nothing could satisfy the public but either a publication of the whole evidence, or such a decision on the part of the King as should give the world to understand what had been the bearing of that evidence'.[42]

Grenville's proposal, the Prince answered Moira, 'both astonishes and revolts me'. He 'could not have experienced a more entire want of support had the Government been composed of his greatest enemies'. The Prince declared that, unless the business was brought to 'an immediate conclusion', he would 'together with you and all the rest of my friends ... retire'. He would no longer be the Government's 'sheet anchor', the Prince fulminated, for 'a set of men who have evinced even a want of firmness and resolution to carry into effect their own opinion'.[43]

The Princess had new calamities to bear while she waited for a response from the King to her letter. In October on an expedition to Norbury, her carriage overturned, and Miss Cholmondeley, her companion, was killed. On her return to Montague House she heard the news (in a 'melancholy account' from Brunswick)[44] of the death of her eldest brother, Hereditary Prince Charles, following what *The Times* called a nervous colic. The Princess was ill for some weeks from the effects of the carriage accident, and 'nearly relieved her enemies from any further machination to get rid of her'.[45]

To add insult to injury, Robert Bidgood, still in her employ, appeared in 'The pew at church which is only appropriated for the Princess's servants ... close to her own at Greenwich [church]', not in mourning, as was prescribed for her Household after her brother's death. Distraught, Caroline begged Lord Eldon to have Bidgood and her other 'traducers' officially dismissed from her employ.[46]

Worse, far worse, was to come. The Princess's parents had both written in August, beseeching the King to publish the particulars of the investigation and to receive their daughter now that she was cleared of any crime. 'I close this letter with tears ...', the Duchess wrote. 'It is so delicate a thing to attack the honour of a woman.'[47] The Princess was heartened by her mother's demand that her innocence be 'publicly declared before the eyes of all Europe'. Her parents, however, had troubles of their own. In August 1806, King Frederick William III of Prussia finally decided to go to war against Napoleon and the French Emperor's Grande Armée. The Duke of Brunswick, despite his age and despite Valmy, was appointed commander of the Prussian forces. But France was in the ascendant at this time. In contrast to Trafalgar in October 1805, where Nelson (himself mortally wounded in the battle) defeated a combined French–Spanish fleet off southern Spain, the Emperor had inflicted defeats on the Austrians and Russians at Ulm (two days before Trafalgar) and Austerlitz (December that year).

Throughout November 1806 the Princess received, by degrees and from different informants, news of the catastrophic defeats which the Prussian armies had suffered at the battles of Jena and Auerstädt on 14 October. Her father had been badly wounded at Auerstädt and had been carried off to comparative safety on a litter. Her soldier brother Prince William had come through unharmed and was with Prince Hohenlohe's forces. Napoleon's Grande Armée was pressing northwards. The old Duke was near-blind in one eye from his wounds. Brunswick had fallen to the French.

The Duke of Brunswick asked Napoleon for clemency, begging that Brunswick might remain neutral. The Emperor of the French agreed, on condition that the aged soldier Duke quit the Prussian army. The Duke refused. 'As long as he could use his limbs and vital air was in him, he would defend his King and Country,' he replied, as his daughter Caroline informed the Reverend George Lock. But the Duke, for all his brave words, was desperately ill.[48] She was told he had been indifferent to all, hardly present, since the day of the battle, and he did not know that his state had been incorporated in the Confederation of the Rhine.

Then there was better news. 'My beloved father's eyes are quite saved,' she wrote, and her mother and the rest of the family – all except Prince William – had joined the Duke at Altona, Hamburg's port on the Elbe.[49] The Duchess, her imbecile and blind sons Princes George and Augustus, the widowed Hereditary Princess and Prince William's wife with her two sons carried with them as many portable treasures from the Great Library at Wolfenbüttel as they could.

The news got worse again. The Duke was too ill to be moved. His family had had to press on without him, the Duchess to Augustenburg, the Hereditary Princess to Holstein, Princess Marie with her two sons to her sister, the Queen of Sweden. On 27 November the Princess learnt that her father had died on the 10th of that month at Ottensen. It was said that a mistress had been with him in the field and had remained by his side till the end. If true, it would explain why the Duchess of Brunswick had departed from her dying husband.

The Princess of Wales was unmanned by this destruction of her homeland and by her family's exile. Her father's death was the worst blow. Lord Malmesbury was 'the only person I have yet been able to see', she wrote on 2 December, 'for our sentiments are very congenial upon the great loss I have just met with'.[50] Caroline was now without the shield of protection which she had always believed, if not with good reason, that her father constituted. She fell ill with 'nervous headaches'. Perceval saw her in December and thought her 'very much fallen away, though I think upon the whole she looks better than she did about a fortnight ago'. The Princess, he wrote, now believed 'it is intended that she shall never be permitted to see the King again, at least not to see him alone'.[51] And the King did not feel able, in the circumstances, to send his personal condolences to his niece on the death of her father his brother-in-law and the maternal grandfather of the future Queen of England.

Despite her grief, Caroline continued her attempts to vindicate her 'honour and innocence'. 'It is, Sire,' she addressed the King on 8 December, 'nine weeks today since my counsel presented to the Lord High Chancellor my letter to your Majesty.' The King would 'easily conceive what must have been my state of anxiety and suspense, whilst I have been fondly indulging in the hope that every day, as it passed, would bring me the happy tidings that your Majesty was satisfied of my innocence...'. She believed that the King had asked the Commissioners for 'their advice upon the subject' of her letter. She understood that 'their official occupations' excused the delay, but she urged 'the extreme prejudice' which it 'produces to my honour...':

> The world, in total ignorance of the real state of the facts, begins to infer my guilt from it. I feel myself already sinking in the estimation of your Majesty's subjects, as well as what remains to me of my own family into ... a state in which my honour appears at least equivocal and my virtue is suspected.[52]

Perceval was pleased with this letter. He reasoned: 'it plainly intimates that she cannot let the matter rest as it is, unknown to the public'. And: 'if she is obliged to publish the papers, she will do it more creditably to herself, if it should appear ... that she was absolutely driven to it, as the only resource which was left to her by which she could be redeemed from the disgrace in which her character is involved by the proceeding of which she complains....'[53] The Princess of Wales begged the King to receive her before the Queen's approaching Birthday, or 'the world will infallibly conclude ... that my answer must have proved unsatisfactory, and that the infamous charge have been thought but too true'.

Lord Grenville had, in fact, agreed to 'adopt handsomely any line which shall be recommended by the Cabinet', as Moira told the Prince on 11 November. Moira had no doubt 'what that line will be'. The individual members of the Cabinet to whom he had spoken wanted only to be convinced that the Princess's answer did not 'overturn the facts averred by Cole and Bidgood.... Then they will strongly urge the interdict from the King.'[54] This interdict, it will be remembered, related simply to her exclusion from Carlton House.

When the Cabinet was finally stimulated to bend its corporate mind to the Princess's letter of 2 October – in part because, as the new Foreign Secretary Lord Howick (soon to succeed as Earl Grey) told his Cabinet colleague Lord Fitzwilliam, 'the Princess's answer has been circulated'[55] – the proceedings were by no means as fluent or as unfavourable to the Princess of Wales as Moira had prophesied. The Cabinet minute of 23 December, which was the result of the ministers' deliberations, ran as follows: 'the facts of the case do not warrant their advising that any further steps should be taken in the business by your Majesty's Government, or any proceedings instituted upon it' – bar, perhaps, the prosecution of Lady Douglas for perjury. (Perhaps Perceval's opinion of the legality of such prosecution was more accurate; at any rate, Lady Douglas escaped indictment.)

The Cabinet – not surprisingly, as it included among its chief officers the four Commissioners – declared, on the other hand, that it could find no 'just cause of complaint' against the conduct of the investigation. As for the Princess's request that the King receive her and confirm to her 'by your own gracious words your Majesty's satisfactory conviction of her innocence', the Cabinet submitted, any 'personal declarations' the King made must be considered as depending solely on his 'own feelings and persuasion on the result of all that has passed'. Likewise, the Cabinet felt 'not properly competent to advise' the King on 'the degree of intercourse and access to your Majesty's person to which your Majesty may be graciously pleased to admit any member of your royal house'. In other words, the Cabinet passed the buck back to the King.[56]

It is clear from Windham's diary and from the Lord Privy Seal Lord Holland's notes of the discussions that there was no real unanimity of opinion in Cabinet. Windham insisted on offering a dissentient minute, in which he chivalrously stressed his belief in the Princess's complete innocence.[57] Lord Ellenborough, the Lord Chief Justice, and Lord Erskine, the Lord Chancellor, were keen to defend the justice of the investigation they had compèred. The Chief Justice, at one point, argued that the 'lascivious kissing' between the Princess and Captain Manby averred by Bidgood amounted on her part to incitement to high treason.

Lord Grenville, on the other hand, now 'seemed to have made up his mind to the Princess's innocence' of all 'levities'. Lord Moira, for his part, muddied the already murky waters by speaking of a box opened by a friend of Captain Manby's that contained a portrait of the Princess of Wales, 'with many souvenirs hanging to it'. Among them was a leather bag containing 'hair of a particular description and such as his friend said he had been married too long not to know that it came from no woman's head'. Ellenborough observed with heavy humour that, if this 'document' could be examined and compared in court with 'the record to which it was originally annexed', the law would admit it as evidence.[58]

For all its jocularity, the Cabinet had not got off the hook. The King, 'with characteristic sagacity', wrote Lord Holland, 'perceived our embarrassment, and ... pressed us for an explicit answer'.[59] ('Explicit or conclusive', the King had written to the Chancellor. A decision of innocence or guilt was required, he reminded his Cabinet of lawyers, for all who labour under accusation.)[60] 'He would never have been satisfied without one,' wrote Holland,

> and he did in fact by dexterity, although not in direct words or by command, extort one from us.
>
> The substance [of the Cabinet's eventual advice] was that he should admit the Princess of Wales to his presence, but should convey to her Royal Highness through the Lord Chancellor a strong admonition to be in future more circumspect and discreet in her behaviour.

The battles in Cabinet before this second minute was hammered out for the King towards the end of January 1807 raged the fiercer because of the Princess of Wales's declared intention, if she was not received, to publish all the material relating to the investigation.

Perceval was the prime mover behind publication. He was with the Princess on New Year's Day to ask 'whether I should be getting the papers printed to be ready for publication, as soon as we might think right to publish them'. The Princess told him on 27 January, 'she understands that the publication is the only thing which frightens the Commissioners'.[61]

The following day, the 28th, the King wrote to the Princess for the first time since the Delicate Investigation, to inform her of his

Cabinet's advice that no further steps were to be taken against her and that he would receive her. However, while none of the 'other matters' – besides the pregnancy – were 'legally or conclusively established', the King wrote, 'there have appeared circumstances of conduct on the part of the Princess which his Majesty never could regard but with serious concern'. (Unknown to her, the King had shown his customary mildness by substituting 'serious concern' for 'severe disapprobation' in the Cabinet's draft.)[62] His Majesty desired and expected that 'such a conduct may in future be observed as may fully justify those marks of paternal regard and affection which the King always wishes to show to every part of his royal family'.

The Princess gave her private opinion of this letter to Miss Hayman, while returning officially grateful thanks to her uncle: 'Honourably acquitted: but a reprimand. This is the sentence . . . which . . . I received in the name of his Majesty. . . .' And she claimed that the sword of Diogenes still hung over her head. The sentiment was accurate, if the Princess mistook Diogenes for Damocles. At any time, the investigation against her might be reopened.[63] She feared, besides, 'new mischief is going on at Windsor, which has been promoted through the visit of the Prince'.[54] Still, she looked forward meanwhile to her restoration to official grace and favour with the King, and to his reception of her into his presence.

Her fears were well founded. The Prince discovered – reluctantly – 'a degree of misconduct' in the Princess, he informed the Lord Chancellor, that made it his duty to lay the papers before his own law officers, 'so that I may not have to charge myself with any possible hazard affecting the interests of my daughter and of the succession . . .'.[65] At the same time the Prince represented to his father that he thought of retiring into his former neutrality from the active – and Whiggish – line in politics he had lately pursued. The King, with this inducement, wrote to the Princess on 10 February regretting that he could not receive her while the Prince's own investigation went forward.[66]

The Princess's reaction was swift. A preliminary letter was fired off expressing her 'inexpressible pain' at this news.[67] Perceval then constructed a lengthy letter for his royal client which the King received on 16 February, stating 'the various grounds' on which the Princess felt 'the hardship of my case'. The Princess protested, 'the justice due to me is to be suspended, while the judgment of your Majesty's sworn servants is to be submitted to the revision of my accuser's counsel'. Here, for the first time, she was pulling aside the veil that obscured the Prince of Wales's role in promoting the invest-igations into her conduct. As she went on to point out, the ministers' judgment had hardly been arrived at hastily. 'This revocation of your Majesty's gracious purpose has flung an additional cloud about the whole proceeding,' she continued, 'and the inferences drawn in the public mind from this circumstance ... will leave so deep an impression to my prejudice as scarce anything, short of a public exposure of all that has passed, can possibly efface.'[68]

And so the threat of publication was formally made. However, the Princess dissimulated, 'a female mind must shrink from the act of bringing before the public such charges, however conscious of their scandal and falsity ...'. She must have been alive to the danger in which her threat placed her. The King had, after all, broken with the Prince of Wales, 'the publisher of my letters', after he had published their Army correspondence in 1803.

The Princess of Wales next asked to be restored to her 'former respect and station' within the royal family and requested, to that end, either her old apartments at Carlton House or apartments in some other royal residence. She enclosed the Prince's letter of 30 April 1796 to show that, thereafter and for no fault of her own, she had been banished 'into a sort of humble retirement'. Was she to be blamed, the February protest demanded, if, 'without the check of a husband's authority, without the benefit of his advice ... a stranger to the habits and fashions of this country', she had, 'under the influence of foreign habits and foreign education', observed a conduct 'in any degree deviating from the reserve and severity of British manners'?[69] In correspondence with the King, Caroline yet again turned to her advantage a letter which she had previously chosen to regard as licensing her to take lovers. Here she played the victim, rather than the beneficiary, of that document.

Mr Richard Ryder, the MP, commented, 'I hear the Prince insists on separation or divorce.'[70] The Prince's principal lawyer, Mr William Adam MP, Chancellor of the Duchy of Cornwall, was certainly of the opinion that the evidence against the Princess constituted grounds for a separation *a mensa et thoro* (from bed and board).[71] But the Princess and her advisers, notably Mr Spencer Perceval, were in earnest when they threatened publication. It seemed the only avenue that might lead to vindication for the Princess and, of course, to the extreme political embarrassment of the Ministry of All the Talents.

Others had their doubts, and Eldon wrote to the King at the beginning of March of his anxiety regarding 'the mischief which, I perceive, is arising'. If the Princess published, it would be 'an event more deeply to be deplored and deprecated' than any which he could imagine. Eldon had heard, furthermore, that she was to include 'reports or facts of reciprocal crimination.'[72] In plain English, the Princess meant to bring counter-charges of adultery against the Prince. (The Prince had not confined his attentions to Mrs Fitzherbert. In the year in which he listened to Lady Douglas's tales against the Princess, the Prince paid the bills of a Mme de Meyer, whom he visited after dark, and in the same year apparently impregnated a boarding-house woman at Weymouth.)[73]

Although adultery in the Prince of Wales did not constitute high treason, a discussion of his relationship with Mrs Fitzherbert would be highly embarrassing to the dignity and honour of the royal family. It would, of course, also raise, as the Wily Austin allegation had done, the dangerous question of Princess Charlotte's claim to the throne – not to mention that of her father. Eldon begged the King to receive the Princess of Wales and so prevent such a harmful outcome.

The Princess wrote again to the King on 5 March 1807 with this threat: 'the publication of the proceedings referred to will not be withheld beyond Monday next'. (Perceval had written to Lady Townshend on 26 February, 'The question of publication stands just as it did. The printer is in progress. . . . The booksellers of course will have the pamphlet for sale at the same time [as the printer], and I shall find it necessary to communicate with them, before I make use of their names as publishers.')[74] As for any unpleasant consequences which should arise from this publication, the King's 'most unhappy and most injured daughter-in-law, subject and servant' assured him, 'they must be incalculably less than those which I should be exposed to from my silence'.[75]

The Book, as it came to be known, was actually printed, by Mr Edwards of Crane Court, Fleet Street, and Lady Townshend sent to the bookseller, Mr Lindsell, next day on 6 March for a copy, mistakenly believing that it had been published as well.[76] However, in the event, it contained no references to the Prince's adultery or to Mrs Fitzherbert. And then, as suddenly as the Delicate Investigation had come to the boil, the matter was at an end. 'It is not yet finally determined whether the publication will come out or not,' Perceval wrote on 29 March. 'I have a closet full ready to issue out at a moment's warning.'[77] Lord Grenville's ministry fell, and was replaced by the Princess's friends, the Tories, under the Duke of Portland. Lord Eldon once more became Lord Chancellor, and Perceval came into office as Chancellor of the Exchequer. Publication of the Book could only be an embarrassment to the incoming ministers, and it was abandoned.

As one of their first acts on entering into office, the Tory ministers on 21 April submitted a minute to the King stating that there was no reason for him not to receive the Princess. Not only the pregnancy and delivery, but 'all the other particulars ... to which the character of criminality can be ascribed, are either satisfactorily contradicted, or rest upon evidence of such a nature ... as render it ... undeserving of credit ...'. (One of the outgoing ministers' last acts had been to write their own minute, standing by the Commissioners' July 1806 Report.)[78]

The King duly informed the Princess that he would receive her 'with as little delay as possible', as the Cabinet had advised. Further, he would appoint apartments for her use in Kensington Palace, in place of those she had occupied at Carlton House.[79] And so, like many other questions in English political life at this time, that of the Princess's conduct proved not one of morality but purely one of party.

The Princess wrote to Miss Hayman in April, 'At last the comedy has ended and the curtain drops: "Much ado about nothing." I only think my grandchildren will look upon it as being indeed a parody to Shakespeare.'[80] Mrs Emilia Boucherett, one of the Lock–Angerstein connection, spent the evening with the Princess of Wales after she had received the order to meet the King next day at Buckingham House. 'She was in a state of tempered joy, as if she feared to be too happy,' wrote Mrs Boucherett:

> We spent a quiet, pleasant evening, surrounded by her little Court – such a one as Queen Catherine [of Aragon] might have had – her

physician Bayley [Baillie], Walter Scot[t] the poet, and Lord Rivers; Boucherett, Mrs Lisle and myself in the characters of attendants. Great happiness is no friend to noisy mirth, and we were all very grave though very happy: the Princess uncommonly so.[81]

The day after the reception Caroline wrote, 'I am worried to death with writing abroad to announce these happy tidings. . . .'[82]

The Prince, meanwhile, railed against the new ministers and their minute, as he had railed against the old. He had been 'arranging some detailed observations' on the new minute when he heard that his father had proceeded to adopt his ministers' advice and receive the Princess. 'That purpose . . . I now forgo,' he wrote. With little grace, he added, 'After this declaration [about the reception] it ceases to become me . . . to engage in controversial discussion either with the legal advisers of the Princess or with the confidential advisers of your Majesty; characters now so blended as to render the possibility of an equitable decision from them upon this subject rather questionable.' To this there was an obvious response, with reference to the relations of the Prince, Romilly and the previous ministry.

He informed his father that 'a large edition' of the Book was 'now in the possession and in the habitation of one of your Majesty's present confidential servants'.[83] This was absolutely true, or had been. Following the decision not to publish the Book, Perceval had made a great bonfire of the 500 copies of that publication locked up in a cupboard in his house at Lincoln's Inn Fields. He had also advertised anonymously in *The Times* in May for stray copies.[84]

Not satisfied with the promise of apartments for his wife in Kensington Palace, the Prince still hoped for a formal separation from her and, in a draft letter, he declared, 'those considerations of piety which call equally upon your Majesty and upon me to secure the mind of my daughter from taint cannot but decide your opinion that the intercourse between Princess Charlotte and her mother should be allowed only under due limitation'.[85] He was furious to discover that on 18 May the Princess of Wales had dressed for Court – it was incidentally the day after her thirty-ninth birthday – at Warwick House, where she visited Charlotte. He wrote to his father of 'the line which I am bound to adopt . . . the rules to be observed.

... the Princess must never be under the same roof with me'. He regarded Warwick House, where Princess Charlotte now resided, as 'the same as my own house, there being a communication between that house and mine'. Charlotte, he decreed in addition, might visit her mother at Blackheath. However: 'The boy the child of a pauper must not be introduced into the company of Charlotte.'[86] The Prince, for all his hostility to the boy, had evidently been persuaded that Willy Austin was not after all the child of his wife.

The Prince had the satisfaction of receiving 'a very friendly note' from his father. Yet, far from sanctioning these arrangements, the King wrote as follows to the Princess of Wales:

> The King cannot but lament the differences which still unfortunately subsist between the Prince and Princess of Wales. It is painful to his Majesty to signify to the Princess of Wales that the Prince has expressed to the King his determination that the following rule must be observed – that the Princess must abstain from going to Carlton House, or to Warwick House considered as a part of the same.
>
> The King desires not to be understood to give his sanction to such a rule, or to admit the reasons which appear to have influenced the Prince.

On one point, however, the King was firmly in agreement with his son: the child 'under the protection of the Princess' should never appear when Princess Charlotte visited. The Prince further informed Lady de Clifford that, when she took Charlotte to Blackheath, the young Princess was never to be 'out of your sight'.[87]

In the matter of popularity the Prince was always the loser to the Princess. She appeared at the opera to tumultuous applause and was cheered on her way to Court when she appeared for the first time at the King's Birthday. The Prince attended the Birthday as well. Husband and wife 'did not speak, but coming out close together, both looked contrary ways', wrote Lady Bessborough, 'like the print of the spread eagle'.[88] This was nothing new, but the devastating effects of the Delicate Investigation had yet to become apparent.

## CHAPTER NINE

# SHIFTING ALLEGIANCES

## 1807–1810

*'Everybody must love something in this world'*

T HE DOWAGER DUCHESS OF BRUNSWICK, a widow and a refugee, was in search of asylum. Disingenuously she wrote in May 1807 to her brother, the King of England, from Schleswig-Holstein to declare that her daughter had taken a house for her at Blackheath. 'Her whole happiness seems to depend on my being with her,' she claimed. 'I have wrote over and over again that without your permission I could not think of coming there.'[1] With the Princess received at Court, the King showed no further hesitation to extending an invitation to his sister to reside in England. At the beginning of July, the elderly Duchess landed with a group of attendants at Harwich and proceeded to Montague House, Blackheath, to lodge with her daughter. There they received visits from the King and Queen and other members of the royal family.

The international political scene was shifting. That same July Alexander, Emperor of Russia, signed at Tilsit a treaty of alliance with Napoleon under which, after Britain's forecast defeat, he was to rule an empire of the East, leaving an empire of the West to the French. One consequence of this treaty was that the late French King's brother Louis XVIII and members of his family would soon leave their Russian refuge for England.

The Princess of Wales wrote in a letter to Miss Hayman on 14 July, a week after her mother arrived, of living in 'a perfect bustle. . . . all the visits of the royalties went off remarkably well, and it is settled that my mother don't go to the royal family without me. By that means it will come all again upon the footing as it was two years ago. . . .'[2]

In this she was deluded, or was putting a brave face on an

unpalatable truth. It never came 'all again upon the footing as it was two years ago' with the King, although Malmesbury and Plumer (now Solicitor-General) had prevailed on the Duchess, as the Princess noted, to 'make it a rule' not to go to the royal family without her daughter. According to a statement made by Queen Charlotte six years later, the King, on returning from giving his audience to the Princess, declared that all intimacy was at an end, and only the outward signs of civility were to obtain.[3]

The King had been outraged by the near publication of the Book. The remarks Lady Douglas alleged the Princess to have made on the subject of the King's derangement were certainly not calculated to appease him. He objected vehemently to any public airing of a royal quarrel, any appeal by any member of the royal family to fickle public sympathy, in place of his royal authority. The Princess's close, near-filial relationship with the King, which the Delicate Investigation had so efficiently interrupted, was over. Not only was the Princess's own father dead and her homeland in enemy hands; her uncle the King, who had been her protector, a friendly court of appeal in her battles with her nominal protector, her husband, was henceforward deaf to her further appeals.

The King no longer consulted Caroline about the care and education of Princess Charlotte. The house at Windsor, originally proposed for her visits when her daughter was in residence there, was given over to Princess Augusta and renamed Augusta Lodge. The King now came to Blackheath not for cosy chats with his daughter-in-law, but to see her mother.

The Duke of Clarence, who knew his aunt's prudish nature of old, had prophesied before her arrival, 'The report of the Commissioners will have a very severe effect on the Duchess whenever she is in possession of it, and, believe me, the frail fair one at Blackheath will shudder at the sight of her mother if she comes over.'[4] In fact, whether or not the Duchess, who abhorred scandal, read the Report, she was as little eager as the King to discuss it. According to Caroline, the Duchess was 'very deaf, and looking much older than she ought. ... her memory fails her very much, and her whole system is very much shook'.[5] She had lost her home of forty years, her English dowry there and her husband. She was dependent on her brother's bounty for a pension. Who can blame the trembly old lady if she preferred never to mention, as Queen Charlotte later averred, the Delicate Investigation?

The Princess and her mother found common cause during the early days of renewing their acquaintance in lamenting the Duke's death and the collapse in fortune of the Brunswick ruling house. The Princess of Wales was to give Mr Walter Scott a silver cup for his honourable mention of her father in his celebrated poem *Marmion*, which he published in 1808:

> Lamented Chief! . . .
> Valour and skill 'twas thine to try,
> And, tried in vain, 'twas thine to die.[6]

Caroline looked to her brother William, the new head of the family, as 'the hope of Brunswick'. In fact, he was a landless exile. She had an idea, which came to nothing, of adopting his younger son Prince William, aged one and a half, and bringing him up for 'the English service'.[7]

A temporary pattern of life established itself for mother and daughter. 'I have my mornings to myself,' the Princess of Wales wrote in July 1807, 'and the rest of the day we have constantly company.' Maternal grandmother and granddaughter were to meet for the first time the day she wrote – Princess Charlotte was coming to dine, before she departed with Lady de Clifford for Worthing. Caroline was expecting, besides, 'three Graces of ancient dates', old friends of the Duchess.[8]

The honeymoon period did not last long for Augusta and Caroline. After only a month a certain strain was showing itself, and the Princess referred briskly to 'not much gêne and etiquette between us. . . . each likes to live her own way'. The Duchess rose from her bed and retired to it early. She drove out with one of her German ladies in the morning, while the Princess took her own airing after lunch. ('A sort of shower bath which I take every morning prevents, I believe, my getting any cold, and is the case of my having been free from spasms,' she added.) 'Seldom before two o'clock I am visible,' she wrote to her privy purse.[9]

The ancient friction between mother and daughter reasserted itself. Caroline wrote in irritation, '. . . I am not reasonable, and have not been under any sort of control since ten years, no check has been laid upon me or my entire independent spirit. . . .' The Duchess found it difficult to reconcile the outwardly obedient young woman who had been hemmed about by the restrictions she had imposed before she left Brunswick with the strong-willed and certain woman her daughter had become. It was something of a relief to both ladies when the Duchess moved into the house adjacent to Montague House in September – originally Chesterfield House, now renamed Brunswick House. There she invited her brother to the first of many dinners 'of all the German dishes that you like – send me your bill of fare that it be to your taste'.[10]

A new pattern of life evolved. On Mondays and Wednesdays the Duchess walked round to her daughter's to dine, when 'particularly old fogrums and old cats are invited'. On Thursdays and Saturdays the Princess dined early at her mother's, then escaped to greet company for cards, and gave a dinner herself besides every Sunday at Montague House, which her mother did not attend.[11]

Among the Princess's regular visitors was Mr Walter Scott, who had earlier this year won her approval by his verse in her defence in his 'Health to Lord Melville'.

> Be damn'd he that dare not
>     For my part, I'll spare not
> To beauty afflicted a tribute to give:
>     Fill it up steadily,
>     Drink it off readily –
> Here's to the Princess, and long may she live![12]

'As soon as she saw me,' Scott noted, 'she cried out "Come, my dear Walter Scott, and see all my improvements," and accordingly she whisked me through her grotto and pavilion and conservatory and so forth asking me slily at the same time if I was not afraid to be alone with her.'[13] She showed the poet two statues of herself and of Princess Charlotte in the saloon, respectively titled *Resignation* and *Hope*. In other words, the Princess's spirit – and sense of humour – had not been entirely cowed by her ordeal. Nor indeed had her sense of decorum been reformed. Scott continued an occasional visitor when down from Edinburgh.

In October he was persuaded to recite some verses from his friend

Mr Robert Southey's poem, 'Queen Auragua, or howsoever you spell her name' – Queen Orraca – at the Princess's request, till she had them by heart. He suggested to Southey, 'if you wish to oblige her', that he should send a copy of the poem to this friendly royal patron. Scott himself took care to send a copy of *Marmion* 'with some ornaments' – or illustrations by Mr James Skene – to the Princess, well in advance of its publication.[14]

The Princess, despite her irritation, was duly conscious of the benefits her mother's presence brought her at Blackheath. When Princess Charlotte returned from Worthing, she was allowed to come to her grandmother's every Saturday. 'It is such a protection to me, more than I am ever able to express,' she wrote in the autumn. 'The royal family, all the different branches, often come to see us.'[15] The Prince of Wales alone kept away, after writing to his aunt that he would be very pleased to see her when she was in her own house.[16]

What the Duchess made of Willy Austin, Caroline's 'Moses in the bulrushes', now five years old, is not known. Lady Townshend, who had supported the Princess during her trials over the last year, found her royal mistress in stubborn mood when she broached the delicate subject in September 1807:

> My anxious wish for you prompts me again to entreat, implore the removal of Willy from Montague House. I do really think that his Majesty's returning affection has been entirely stopped by your keeping that boy, even to the risk of Princess Charlotte's never being permitted to go to Blackheath, and if your Royal Highness persists in it, the world at large will condemn.[17]

The Princess was firm in reply. She had 'strictly adhered' to the King's orders, and Willy never appeared when Princess Charlotte came to the house: 'which, in truth, I only relinquished in compliance to my daughter's wishes – which she [I?] would have done in case a favourite dog or bird had been in my house'. (Princess Charlotte confirmed later that she only sometimes saw the boy on the staircase; he was sickly looking and blue-eyed.) 'After all that scandal's tongue has said,' Caroline wrote, 'I think that the more equal and the more uniform my conduct is to that child – by following the same plan of education with all the other boys who are under my care – going from home and to school and is to be trained for the Navy when age and circumstances are adequate to it – would be the most natural in my opinion.'

The Princess refused to pension the child off with a sum of money to the Austin parents, as Lady Townshend suggested. It 'would be related by my enemies as if I wished to stop their tongues. . . . Besides, as I have never had the comfort to have had my own daughter under my care or roof, I always had poor orphans or poor parents' children with me of all ages and sizes. . . .' She informed Lady Townshend that, when Willy went to school, she meant to take another child. 'It is my only amusement and the only little creature to which I can really attach myself, as I hate dogs and birds, and everybody must love something in this world. I think my taste is the most innocent and the most natural. . . .' She concluded by taking the moral high ground: 'I wish every lady in England had put their affection in no other beloved objects as in those innocent little beings – they would have escaped from committing many follies if not even to criminality.'[18]

Lady Townshend, nevertheless, resigned her position as mistress of the robes in January 1808. The Princess lost another ally, and an influential one, that spring in a similar dispute. One Saturday in March she was to stand godmother to Perceval's youngest son in company with the Duke of Cumberland. In the interval between invitation and christening, however, the Princess fell out with the Duke, and they did not speak at the ceremony. The Duke had, like Lady Townshend, remonstrated with the Princess about Willy Austin, and she had returned him a 'very impertinent' letter.[19]

With her sister Lady Sheffield already in waiting, Lady Glenbervie agreed to take on the duties of Lady Townshend, and soon found that the Princess still enjoyed teasing her attendants about the boy. During a tête-à-tête dinner with Lady Glenbervie at Blackheath, Caroline appeared to fall into a 'sort of reverie'. As Lord Glenbervie, who acted as Surveyor-General of Woods and Forests and kept an amusing diary, recorded, 'Little Willy' was in the room playing with an orange which Lady Glenbervie had given him. 'After looking at him steadfastly', the Princess said, referring to her supposed maternity, 'in her imperfect English, "It is a long time since I brought you to bed, Willy."' When the boy did not understand, she repeated her remark. Thinking she meant to reprove him for not being already in bed, he left the room, while Lady Glenbervie, 'prepared as she is for many strange things, was astounded and confounded beyond measure'.[20]

The Prince of Wales had agreed to the appointment of Lady Glenbervie: 'no person can be more truly respectable in every point of view than her Ladyship'. The Princess of Wales commented, 'this may be the first symptom that in the year of our lord 1808 our sentiments will be always in unison for the future'.[21] There were, in fact, rumours that 'an attempt is making', early in this year, 'to bring about a reconciliation quelqu'onque between the Prince and Princess'. Lord Glenbervie believed that Lord Malmesbury, 'the prime oracle of the Princess', and the Prince's new confidante, Isabella, Lady Hertford, had promoted it.[22] With his wife, Glenbervie speculated whether the Prince had consulted Lady Hertford before approving Lady Glenbervie's appointment: 'He visits every forenoon when they are both in town and often dines en famille with her and Lord Hertford, and it is said that when absent, and often when both are in London, he employs a great part of the morning every day in writing to her. What can be the topic of conversation? She is near fifty and has been a grandmother more than twelve or fourteen years.'[23]

Lady Hertford might be a grandmother (her son, the Earl of Yarmouth, was in his thirties), castigated by different contemporaries as 'stately, formal and insipid' and 'forbidding, haughty'. But her ample figure was beautifully dressed, and her dignified manner appealed to the Prince as much as it repelled others. Both Lord Hertford and his son Yarmouth were congenial to the Prince in their passion for French furniture and paintings. Moreover, Hertford, on an income of £70,000 a year, and Yarmouth, who married a double heiress, could afford to indulge their passion. The Hertfords lived in easy splendour and pomp at Hertford House in Manchester Square and at Ragley in Warwickshire. The contrast with the Prince's uneasy existence at Carlton House and with Mrs Fitzherbert's domestic charms could not have been greater.

Lady Hertford had championed the Prince and Mrs Fitzherbert in their successful bid to win custody of Minnie Seymour, Lord

Hertford's niece, the previous year. Ironically, the confidential friendship with Lady Hertford, and her husband's appointment as guardian
to Minnie, led the susceptible Prince to fall victim to that lady's
charms, the more so as, while encouraging his attentions, she refused
him 'the last favours', in the then fashionable phrase. And, as ever
when his feelings were overwrought by romantic sentiments, the
Prince fell violently ill. 'I understand that Ragley will be called the
royal dispensary,' the Princess of Wales had noted in September
1807.[24] Lady Bessborough suffered an attack by the Prince when he
was in this disordered state of mind. She wrote in half-disgust, half-
pity of 'that immense grotesque figure flouncing about half on the
couch, half on the ground'.[25]

Cruelly, Mrs Fitzherbert was still summoned to the Pavilion at
Brighton, and to gatherings at Carlton House, so as to preserve Lady
Hertford's reputation. The Prince no longer went to Mrs Fitzherbert
at her own houses, as he had been used to do. In the early summer of
1808, he informed a friend that 'he intended to go about a good deal
in future, having found out that living with one person was like living
alone, and of that you know one very soon grows tired'.[26]

Hertford had the power to remove Minnie from Mrs Fitzherbert's
care if she complained about her treatment. Finally, that summer, she
declined an invitation to the Pavilion and left Brighton. The Prince
protested that 'the sad affair [with Lady Hertford] was quite at an
end'.[27] Less than a week later, however, it had begun again. Even so,
the Prince wrote to Mrs Fitzherbert, 'Every thought and every idea
of my existence and of my life never leave and never quit thee, for the
smallest particle of an instant.'[28] The following year, however, Mrs
Fitzherbert's patience was at last exhausted. She wrote to the Prince
of the 'very great incivilities' she had received at Brighton. 'It is well
known your Royal Highness four-and-twenty years ago placed me in
a situation so nearly connected with your own that I have a claim
upon you for protection. I feel I owe it to myself not to be insulted
under your roof with impunity.'[29]

So Mrs Fitzherbert won Minnie and lost the Prince to Minnie's
aunt. She kept on her houses at Brighton and in London, but the
Prince ceased to visit her and Minnie, the child who had taken her
place on his lap and called him 'Prinny' with proprietorial affection.

Meanwhile, the Princess of Wales moved into Kensington Palace shortly before her fortieth birthday. It had taken the Office of Works a good year to prepare her apartments there. This was not sheer dilatoriness. Mr John Yenn, the clerk of the works, wrote that the building was 'originally of bad construction and of a composition of the worst and most inferior materials'. Unused by royal occupants in the second half of the eighteenth century, it was 'decayed by mildews, damps and rottenness'. Mr James Wyatt, the Surveyor-General, confirmed in 1811 that the dry rot was making considerable inroads. Even the Duke of Kent, who was as exacting a tenant as he was a general and had kept apartments in the palace from 1804 onwards, was unable to rectify matters, and complained that he could store no meat in his larder, as the ceiling dripped. [30]

The Princess of Wales was allotted rooms in the north-eastern section, which had last been used by an earlier Queen Caroline – Caroline of Anspach, Queen Consort to King George II. They were situated behind the Queen's state drawing-room, dining-room and Gallery overlooking Kensington Gardens and Bayswater Gate.[31] 'Kensington gains ground over my heart,' Caroline – of Brunswick – wrote, early in her occupation.[32]

She revelled in her new life at Kensington, where she established herself in the spring of 1808. In the daughters of Lord North – Lady Charlotte, recently married to Colonel John Lindsay, joined Lady Sheffield and Lady Glenbervie – the Princess had three congenial ladies-in-waiting who were sociable, broad-minded and interested in literature and the arts. With their aid, she entertained intensively, and a regular Court developed at Kensington, which numbered among its members lawyers and politicians, artists and writers, travellers and 'professed wits'.

Caroline generally received her guests in a circle in one of the three principal rooms – the dining-room and two drawing-rooms. Among her Kensington courtiers were Sir William Scott, Mr William Windham, Lord Henry Fitzgerald, Mr Brownlow North, Mr Matthew 'Monk' Lewis, Sir Harry Englefield, Sir William Gell and Mr Richard Keppel Craven.

Above lay the state apartments, dark and disused with a serendipitous array of royal paintings and curiosities. One room was entirely filled with fine cork models of the principal Roman ruins. The Princess delighted in leading guests on impromptu tours above while awaiting dinner, although they could make out little by the meagre light of a couple of candles, 'held in different hands'.[33]

Dinner – plain, but accompanied by good wines – was served on an array of Crown plate, gold and silver, which the King had lent the Princess. After dinner the company, if intimate, sometimes retired to a small morning-room usually 'looking full of litter'[34] and very comfortable, or there might be music and dancing. All agreed that the Princess gave 'agreeable dinners'. Politics, poetry and personalities formed the diet of conversation. Her only fault, as at Blackheath, was to prolong the pleasure till it turned to pain, and her guests wished themselves safe in bed.

With the Glenbervies and a new vice-chamberlain, Mr Anthony St Leger, the Princess still went about much with her Tory friends and supporters. In March 1808 she remained in the gallery of the House of Commons listening to a debate from eight in the evening till six in the morning. The following Saturday, Mr William Wellesley-Pole, Secretary to the Admiralty, gave a great dinner and supper in her honour. The ensuing week she supped at Lord Dartmouth's and dined at Sir William Scott's. 'It is astounding how her Royal Highness has taken to ask for those dinners and suppers of late . . . chiefly since Lady Glenbervie's waiting began,' that lady's husband noted. 'Lady Glenbervie has her conjecture about the reason. Lord Rivers has been of all the parties.'[35]

Lord Rivers of Stratfield Saye and Sudeley Castle was a fifty-seven-year-old bachelor and, according to Lady Charlotte Campbell's 1838 *Diary*, 'a pleasant and an elegant man – one of the last of that race of persons who were the dandies of a former century'.[36] He had been a Tory MP, and was to remain one of the King's lords of the bedchamber till 1810. As we have seen, he had been present at Blackheath in the summer of 1807 to celebrate the Princess's restoration to the King's favour.

Whether or not Caroline granted him 'the last favours' can no more be substantiated than whether Lady Hertford accorded that same prize to the Prince of Wales, as no correspondence between either couple exists. Rivers was as often called the Princess's 'lover' as

Lady Hertford was dubbed the Prince's 'mistress'. However, the Princess took a certain malicious pleasure in denying a sexual relationship between the Prince and Lady Hertford; 'it is only a liaison of vanity of her part', she declared.[37] The Prince himself, characteristically, had Lowten, his 1806 private detective, investigate the Princess's relations with Rivers some years later. A maid reported that one afternoon she had seen 'the pillows of the sofa on the floor, the floor covered with hair powder'.[38] Suffice it to say that Rivers was a constant escort to the Princess in her new and sociable London life.

The Tory ministers were still dogged by the business of the Book. Shortly before the christening of his son, it became clear that Perceval had not succeeded, at his bonfire in Lincoln's Inn Fields, in burning all the copies. He himself had lent copies to all the Cabinet; Richard Edwards, who printed the book, had also lent out copies.

A black comedy developed when, in February 1808, Mr Francis Blagdon, editor of the *Phoenix*, advertised the forthcoming publication in that newspaper of some highly interesting proceedings. Mr James Perry, editor of the *Morning Chronicle*, confirmed two weeks later that Blagdon had a copy of the Book. McMahon wrote to William Adam, the Prince's lawyer, stressing the Prince's anxiety that news of the threatened publication 'should this very night be communicated to Mr Perceval' so that something might be done to prevent it.[39] On 11 March the Lord Chancellor, Lord Eldon, granted, on the application of Gibbs, Sir Arthur Piggott and Romilly, a Chancery injunction against publication of the Book, on penalty of a fine of £5000. The Treasury solicitor, Mr Henry Litchfield, recovered later, at further cost, the offending copies from Blagdon, who was given in compensation Treasury patronage for a new newspaper.

In a vain attempt to stem further trouble from the awkward appearance of stray copies of the Book, Litchfield had inserted at the end of March in several newspapers the following carefully worded advertisement: 'Any person having in their possession a certain book, printed by Mr Edwards in 1807, but never published ... and will bring it to W. Lindsell, Bookseller, Wimpole Street, will receive a handsome gratuity.' Apparently, the Tory Government spent over £10,000 of Secret Service money in purchasing half a dozen copies of the Book of their own devising from enterprising bibliophiles.[40]

Princess Charlotte was no longer the 'sheet of white paper' her grandmother the Duchess of Brunswick had dubbed her in 1804. She was growing up fast and taking stock of her parents, her relations and the world outside Warwick House, just as much as they took stock of her. The brouhaha surrounding the Delicate Investigation had been officially kept from her, but she was ten when the proceedings began, eleven and a half before her grandfather again received her mother. Her mother was renowned for her indiscretion, and cramped Warwick House, where Charlotte lived cheek by jowl with a houseful of ladies and servants, was a Tower of Babel. Carlton House next door was a zoo of gossip. She did not know the details, but Charlotte was aware that her parents were feuding.

When she was with either parent, Charlotte was reserved and unsure of herself, and the stammer from which she had come to suffer became more pronounced in their presence. Most of the time, however, she spent at her solitary lessons with her tutors, or with the ladies of her establishment. On her pet birds and dogs and ponies the lonely child lavished much attention, but she loved best her nurse Mrs Gagarin. Of her two sub-governesses, she was fond of Mrs Campbell, but Mrs Udney attracted her unqualified loathing. Her venerable preceptor, Dr Fisher, now Bishop of Salisbury, was no better liked. The young Princess took vengeance on him, mimicking the ponderous stress he gave to each syllable. She referred to him as 'the Great U.P.', after his habit of pronouncing the word 'bishop' as 'bish-up'.[41] She enjoyed going to art exhibitions with him, however.

She could recognize moral authority – her lessons 'chiefly in religion and principles'[42] had inculcated some of each. She wanted to be an attentive pupil, and a good one, when Dr Nott taught her, but she was more often contrite than conscientious. At the age of fourteen in 1810 she was still unable or unwilling to spell correctly, her handwriting was a mire and her Latin appalling.

With Lady de Clifford, her governess, Princess Charlotte rubbed along very well, without feeling the least respect for her, as the old lady never attempted to thwart or discipline her. Governess and pupil sometimes went out shopping together – Charlotte was allowed £10 a month pocket money – and the pupil delighted in passing under the sobriquet of Lady Sophia Keppel, one of Lady de Clifford's granddaughters.

Lady de Clifford's grandson George Keppel, later the Earl of Albemarle, first encountered Princess Charlotte in the spring of 1808, when he was a new pupil at Westminster School. George was very fond of his grandmother, who was as lenient to him as she was to her royal charge. Princess Charlotte, too, made something of a pet of the younger boy, and brought to him at school sandwiches of her own making. One day she watched some boys fighting at Westminster with great interest, and learned to square up to George, with her fists raised.[43]

Over the next few years George spent many Saturdays at Warwick House. On Sundays, Princess Charlotte generally came with his grandmother to George's parents, the Albemarles, at their house in Earl's Court, or he joined them in Lady de Clifford's villa at Paddington. On one occasion in the villa Charlotte and George turned their hand to cookery, unbeknown to Lady de Clifford, who rang the dining-room bell sharply to enquire why her mutton chop was so very peppery. At Earl's Court, Princess Charlotte delighted in tumbling George's younger sisters from a mound in the orchard down to a bed of nettles. If they did not cry, she rewarded them with a doll.[44] These japes with George and his sisters constituted almost all the childish fun Princess Charlotte knew.

As her Aunt Württemberg pronounced later, 'she has been a little too much accustomed to act for herself'.[45] Those who saw Charlotte at Warwick House, at her mother's or at Windsor were unanimous in expressing their surprise that the future Queen of England was so deficient in manners, learning, even deportment. She slouched in her chair, and her walk was awkward.

It was not entirely Charlotte's fault that she was so ill educated. When she was thirteen, in the spring of 1809, her tutor Nott was dismissed – because she liked him too much. Charlotte had childishly made a will in which she left 'all my best books, and all my books', to Dr Nott, as well as 'all my papers'. She added, 'I hope the King will make him a bishop.' To Mrs Campbell she left her three watches and half her jewels. She remembered her other sub-governess, only to write, 'Nothing to Mrs Udney, for reasons.' Mrs Udney spitefully contrived to have Dr Nott removed, charged with obtaining an undue influence over his pupil. He was also accused of keeping back, among other documents which the Prince of Wales had demanded for his own cynical purposes, a paper in which Charlotte described her mother as a 'monster' in the grip of both 'pride and the Devil'. She had written this after her mother had ignored her when they were both taking airings in the park. Caroline probably did not see Charlotte, but this was anyway at the time of the Delicate Investigation when she was forbidden to contact her daughter. The distraught child, already convinced that her parents did not love her, rushed home to compose that indictment of a 'monstrous' mother. When she came to the word 'Devil', she struck the paper again and again with her pen, crying, 'There, I do this to show how many devils there were that took hold of her!'[46]

A substitute master was not produced for a full year, and in October her German master bravely 'represented' to Queen Charlotte that the Princess was 'losing a great deal of time, without receiving the useful instruction requisite for her age and situation'. According to Charlotte, 'the Queen remarked, "it was of little consequence whether she learned a little more or less".' Charlotte was furious. 'I know what she means by this,' she told her mother, the Princess of Wales. 'She means to keep me in ignorance that she may govern me. But I am determined never to be governed by anyone of my own sex. I shall always be happy to hear your opinion, my dear mamma, but even you shan't govern me.' The Princess of Wales considered that this outburst showed a great deal of character.[47]

At Blackheath, a donkey, with a chariot to draw the Duchess round Greenwich Park, joined the Brunswick House establishment. 'He supplies the place of nightingales, cuckoos, larks etc. and his thrilling voice wakes me every morning,' Princess Caroline wrote, but, in love with her new salon of friends at Kensington, she was rarely there to be woken.[48] Even Willy Austin was off her hands, dispatched to Dr Burney's school in Greenwich. At least he was 'so fond of school that he goes away when the time comes with great cheerfulness'.[49] Caroline nonetheless took him about with her everywhere in his holidays.

The Princess's behaviour was no more and no less indiscreet than it had been before the Delicate Investigation. More than spies and informers, though, she feared her creditors. £34,000 had earlier been provided from the Droits of Admiralty, ostensibly as a purchase price for the Ranger's House in Greenwich Park, but in fact to clear the Princess's debts. It was generally accepted that the income the Prince had afforded her since 1797, £12,000 a year, together with her £5000 a year pin-money from the Treasury, fixed on her marriage, was inadequate to the needs of her separate establishments. The Princess had high hopes of Perceval when he came into office in 1807. In August of that year she wrote to Miss Hayman, her beleaguered privy purse, 'I can tell you in a whisper that my debts will be all paid.'[50] A month later she confided, 'In February you will find me no longer a beggar and trying to hide my face from my creditors.'[51] In the meantime, of course, her expenditure did not diminish.

In June 1808 the solicitors Blagrave and Walters wrote to the Princess of Wales begging for payment on behalf of many creditors, including the jewellers Rundell, Bridge & Co., their own 'repeated applications having failed of effect'.[52] Two months later Messrs Blagrave and Walters called on the Duke of Portland, the Prime Minister, as he informed the Prince of Wales. The Princess's debts to their clients totalled more than £40,000, and the government, Portland said bluntly, could do nothing.

Mr Adam, the Prince's lawyer, replied next day that his master had no idea why Portland had called on him: 'The creditors of the Princess of Wales can have no demand or claim on his Royal Highness.'[53] The King, however, declared that the Prince was indeed responsible, like any other husband in the country, for his wife's debts. Moreover, ministers and King prevailed upon the Prince to see that, given the state of the economy, the Droits of Admiralty could not again be applied in relief of the Princess's debts. Such relief required the House of Commons' assent, and on the Prince, rather than the Princess, would very likely fall the blame for failing adequately to fund his wife.

There was much to be said on either side, and the rights and wrongs of it were argued by the Tory ministers and by the Prince's lawyers for many months. The Prince had not increased his wife's income when, under Addington's administration, he had gained access to his full income, and for some years his quarterly payments to his wife had been in arrears. On the other hand, the £34,000 more than compensated for those omissions. The Prince was already tarnished this year by the pusillanimous part he had played in the scandal of the sale of army places by his brother the Duke of York and his mistress Mrs Mary Anne Clarke. He at last agreed in May 1809 to increase his wife's income by £5000 – bringing her total income to £22,000 a year.[54]

Perceval and Adam discussed the Princess's debts on 25 May. Her creditors, the clients of Blagrave and Walters, included a French bookseller, a painter on velvet, the oil man at Kensington, a nursery-man and a tea merchant. The total now was £41,000.[55] Adam composed a paper for Lord Eldon in which he insisted on a 'legal indemnity' for the Prince of Wales against any debts the Princess of Wales might incur beyond the sum of £17,000 a year. It was a case of the pot calling the kettle black. 'The prodigious excess of her Royal Highness's expenditure beyond her income', argued Adam, 'makes this security indispensably necessary to enable the Prince to do justice to his own creditors.'[56]

It was agreed that, if at any point the Princess exceeded her income, a Parliamentary Bill would immediately be enacted to indemnify the Prince. The following day it was learnt that the Princess owed above £8000 to additional creditors, who had not given in their accounts to Blagrave and Walters. The Prince, fearful of further public obloquy, buckled and 'spontaneously' agreed to pay up the full figure of £49,000.[57] When in mid-June the total sum was disclosed to be £51,056, rather than £49,000, everyone lost patience. It was agreed that the extra should be paid from the Princess's privy purse by instalments over four years.[58]

Adam sounded out the Princess's creditors on the Prince's behalf to see if they were open to payment by arrangement or instalment. They were ready to come to whatever arrangement he proposed, Adam reported, and had apparently been sent into transports of admiration on hearing of the Prince's generosity and sense of justice.

The Prince had a talent, which he had displayed during the Delicate Investigation, for maintaining a double standard. At that time, the Princess's 'levities' had offended the Prince, a libertine. Now the Prince declared elaborately, 'should the consideration of these subjects be forced upon the public .. he never will submit to shun enquiry or to purchase, by increased burdens either on the public or on himself, only a short respite until fresh excesses shall create fresh debts and fresh debts shall produce fresh demands'.[59]

He ignored his own excesses. For instance, the stable and riding house which Mr William Porden had constructed in the Indian style for him at Brighton had cost £55,000 and had taken three years to build, from 1805 to 1808, so dilatory was he in paying the Brighton tradesmen. 'The naked timbers of the roof of the riding house stand exposed to all weathers, a monument of disgrace to his Royal Highness and all concerned,' Yenn wrote reproachfully.[60]

While the matter of her debts remained unresolved, the Princess of Wales did not let up the exhausting social programme to which she submitted her ladies. She dined at Mr John Julius Angerstein's on 2 June, and stayed after a rout till half-past three in the morning. Mr Samuel Lysons, the topographer and antiquary, 'remarked that the Princess is grown very coarse, and that she dresses very ill, showing too much of her naked person . . .', the painter Mr Joseph Farington reported. A large lady was followed into the rout room by 'a little man of the name of Parrot. The Princess said, "She should have brought him on her finger."'[61]

The following day saw the Princess at a woodland breakfast given by Lady Glenbervie at the Pheasantry, her shooting box in Bushey Park. Miss Mary Berry, another guest, had already encountered the Princess in May of this year at Mr Henry 'Anastasius' Hope's house, when the Princess had stood godmother to Hope's second son. 'I don't think she was taken with me,' Miss Berry recorded,

as she saw, when I did not suppose she did, the move which I made to Lady Sheffield when she first proposed it to me – the presentation [of Miss Berry to the Princess of Wales] – which I changed for a proper Court face the moment I saw her looking, and the thing inevitable. The last dance before supper she danced herself with [William] Lyttelton.

Such an exhibition! but that she did not feel at all for herself one should have felt for her! Such an over-dressed. bare-bosomed, painted eye-browed figure one never saw. G. Robinson said she was the only true friend the Prince of Wales had, as she went about justifying his conduct.[62]

The Princess unfortunately took a fancy to Miss Berry, editor of Mme du Deffand's letters, and to her sister Miss Agnes Berry. Throughout the summer the unwilling Miss Berry was bidden to attend the Princess at different functions. She altered her opinion of the Princess, however, when Caroline came to inspect Strawberry Hill, Walpole's Gothic mansion now in the care of Mrs Damer, the sculptress. It was 'a surprise' visit – of which Mrs Damer was notified two or three days before.

> She was on her very best manner, and her conversation is uncommonly lively, odd, and clever. What a pity she has not a grain of common sense, nor an ounce of ballast to prevent high spirits, and a coarse mind without any degree of moral taste, from running away with her, and allowing her to act indecorously and ridiculously whenever an occasion offers!
>
> Were she always to conduct herself as she did here today, she would merit the character of having not only a remarkably easy and gracious manner, but natural cleverness above any of her peers [members of the royal family] that I have seen, and a good many have at different times fallen under my observation.[63]

By November 1809 Miss Berry and the Princess of Wales were fast friends, and it was quite possibly at the prompting of 'Berrina' that soon thereafter the Princess of Wales offered the post of lady-in-waiting to the Duchess of Argyll's daughter, Lady Charlotte Campbell, mother of a large family and newly widowed. Miss Berry promised Lady Charlotte 'agreeable dinners' at Kensington.[64] In the event, Lady Charlotte wrote, or provided the material for, such vicious accounts of those dinners in the 1838 *Diary of a Lady in Waiting* that she effectively destroyed any reputation Caroline had left.

In the summer the Princess of Wales had turned against Mr Spencer Perceval. Although he had done his best to help with her tangled finances, his insistence that she herself pay her last debt of

£2000 rankled – as, apparently, did his refusal to allow her to take over additional apartments at Kensington.[65]

The Princess's political allegiance to the Tories was anyway changing – Perceval replaced Portland as Prime Minister in October. Lord Glenbervie believed the 'agent of her conversion' to be Lord Henry Fitzgerald, son of the Duke of Leinster and a fervent Whig, who had replaced Lord Rivers in her affections. In the winter of 1809 the Princess was very active for the Whig leader Lord Grenville in the contest for the Chancellorship of Oxford University against Lord Eldon, her chief legal adviser in her 1806 troubles. This university election became a desperate political contest between Tories and Whigs. The Princess sought to make her Blackheath neighbour the Reverend George Lock vote against Eldon, and she boasted that she had secured Grenville seventeen votes. Through Eldon, she meant to strike against Perceval, although 'she must know', remarked Sir William Scott, 'that they saved her from total ruin and disgrace'.[66]

The Princess of Wales was soon, noted Glenbervie, 'an avowed partisan of Lord Grenville, Lord Grey, etc. She laughs at Perceval as a presumptuous, foolish lawyer, at Lord Eldon as a vulgar bore and the whole Ministry as drivellers.' At the end of 1809 Glenbervie added: 'Her affair with him [Lord Henry Fitzgerald] is become the universal talk, and is never talked of but with disgust.'[67] Lord Henry was in his opinion 'a good-natured and very well-bred man but weak, and under agreeable manners covers, in society, as violent and absurd politics as those of . . . his late brother, the Duke'.[68] Lord Henry, a passionate Whig, had certainly acted in a 'violent and absurd' fashion during the harrowing days of his other brother Lord Edward's imprisonment and death in Dublin after the Irish rebellion in 1798. His antagonism to Tory administration had only deepened since, and he was among those who favoured thoroughgoing electoral reform and, in due course, supported Radical Parliamentary candidates.

Through consorting with Lord Henry Fitzgerald, the Princess of Wales found a new pool of political excitement and a new clutch of admirers in the Whig Opposition. However, Sir Robert Wilson, who was much with Mr Henry Brougham, Mr Francis Horner, Romilly – her old adversary – and other leading Whigs, told Glenbervie that, though the Princess of Wales courted that party, 'the Opposition don't want her'. Sir William Scott, brother of Lord Eldon, wrote sadly of the Princess 'giving up her old and tried friends for her old and tried enemies'.[69] Nevertheless she persisted, and in the course of 1810 the Whig Opposition came to see her enthusiasm for their cause as potentially advantageous.

Under Lady Hertford's Tory influence, the Prince of Wales was no longer so committed to Whig measures such as Catholic emancipation, which his friendship with Fox, as much as his intimacy with Mrs Fitzherbert, had led him earlier to espouse. Ever since Fox's death in 1806, the Prince had veered away from the Whigs. He thought Grenville had betrayed him by not condemning the Princess of Wales in the 1806 Report more strongly and getting him a divorce. Grey was anathema to him. The Whigs were in danger of being left without any royal patron.

Mr Walter Scott was acute in his judgment two years later, when he remarked that 'the Opposition picking up the Princess of Wales so soon as they had lost' the Prince was like a game of commerce, a popular card game, in which exchange or barter was the chief feature.[70] But Caroline, relying on her popularity with the public, thought she held all the cards – a belief which was to be rendered nugatory by a dramatic turn of events, the advent of the Regency.

## CHAPTER TEN

# A REGENCY COURT

## 1810–1813

*'Don't you think I am very naughty?'*

AN UNEXPECTED PLEASURE for the Princess of Wales in the autumn of 1809 had been the arrival of her brother, the Duke of Brunswick, in London. He was greeted in the capital as 'a second Xenophon' after a heroic march across Germany with the corps of Black Brunswickers that he had himself raised – their uniforms were black (in mourning for the Duke's father, fallen at Auerstadt in 1806) with light-blue facings, and a death's-head and crossbones were emblazoned in silver on the shakos. 'His beard will be cut and his black coat be changed into a red coat,' the Princess lamented, when the Duke joined the English army in the spring of 1810.[1]

The Duke sent for his sons from Glückstadt on the Elbe, where they had been living with their maternal grandmother, following their mother's death in 1808. Their presence in England, first at Brunswick House at Blackheath, and then at Belmont House in Vauxhall, led their other grandmother, the Duchess of Brunswick, to alter her will. (Previously she had left Brunswick House to her daughter Caroline.) The Princess had her reward for her neglect of her mother, her canvassing for Lord Grenville and her flirtation with Lord Henry. The Duchess abruptly decided that her Brunswick grandsons should inherit her house at Blackheath. The Princess of Wales, 'now not inhabiting Blackheath' (she was mostly at Kensington), could have no need of her house, declared the Duchess.[2]

Caroline meanwhile complained of her mother, who was lonely at Blackheath. However, she wrote of the Duchess, 'she is so afraid that I intend to rule over her, that were I to suggest ... for variety' taking a house (in town) for a few months, 'it would be enough to prevent it entirely.'[3] The Duchess of Brunswick did in time rent a town house, and the 1838 diarist records a visit to the Duchess there:

> We were ushered into the dirtiest room I ever beheld, empty, and devoid of comfort. A few filthy lamps stood on a sideboard; common chairs were placed around very dingy walls; and, in the middle of this empty space, sat the old Duchess, a melancholy specimen of decayed splendour.[4]

Once in 1809 the Duchess of Brunswick had declined to dine at the Queen's House unless her daughter, who had not been included, were invited also; Princess Elizabeth wrote a note of apology, 'ascribing the omission to a mistake'. This year the Duchess again received an invitation to dine at the Queen's House in March, and this year she went alone. It was some revenge, Glenbervie suggested, for 'The manner in which her daughter treats her, the disrespect and contempt for her she is at no pains to conceal, the reluctance with which she goes to dine with her twice a week, her impatience to depart early after dinner.'[5] The Princess affected to rejoice, he wrote, 'in having escaped the corvée of the dinner'. A few days later the Duchess sent a note asking her daughter to come to dine the next day, as the Queen was coming. The Princess, on reading the note, said, 'I won't go.' She turned to Lady Glenbervie and said in a show of defiance, 'I am going to be very naughty. But I am determined not to go. Don't you think I am very naughty?'

It might have been better for the Princess if she had not gone, but go, of course, she did, with Lady Glenbervie in attendance. The Queen was 'very distant to her during the repast', then took advantage of a discussion of the Duchess of Argyll's attempts to have her daughter Lady Derby received in company after 'the éclat with the Duke of Dorset' to make the following pronouncement: 'She thought it quite right in a mother not to abandon her daughter though she lost herself in that manner, but she could not think it a duty, or right, to live with such people.' The Princess looked grave.

The Duchess of Brunswick's lady, Mme de Haeckel, told Lady Glenbervie after the Queen had departed that she had been ready to sink to the ground from mortification. The Duchess of Brunswick, although not abandoning her daughter, had unsympathetically asked

Caroline if anything had been said about the failure to invite her to the Queen's House. The Princess replied, 'Yes, by Princess Sophia.' Her sister-in-law had said, 'It was a pity.' It was not said this time, Caroline added, that it was supposed the omission was by mistake. To this the Duchess answered querulously, 'They said nothing to me, and I could say nothing. It was very different when you and I lived under the same roof. I see nothing of you now, I know nothing about you and what you do, and I don't desire to know.' Lady Glenbervie was so shocked by this that she could not help crying. The Princess herself spoke of nothing else all the way back to Kensington, but she did not remedy her conduct, political or personal. In fact, she wrote boldly to the King in May 1810 to ask if she might come with her mama to pay him her respects at Windsor. The King was evasive. Next time the Duchess came, the Princess should likewise.[6]

The Princess had to seek consolation in the King's decision to consult her about the appointment of Dr Short of Westminster School to take the place at last of Dr Nott as tutor to Charlotte.[7] The 'Bish-up' had, in the interregnum, been the young Princess's chief instructor, to no apparent profit. Charlotte was horse-mad and an animal lover – unlike her parents. Among her pets were a Maltese dog and a greyhound, and at Bognor, where she summered for some years, she had a team of grey ponies that she galloped over the fields and lanes, ignoring Lady de Clifford's remonstrances.

In January 1810 Miss Berry had noted, among the men present at a dull party at Kensington Palace, Lord Grey and Mr Henry Brougham, both leading lights of the Whig Party. Later in the month came Mr Douglas Kinnaird and Sir Robert Wilson, as well as Lord Henry Fitzgerald. This last continued the favourite. In July Lord Glenbervie entered the principal drawing-room at Kensington to find the Princess 'tête-à-tête with Lord Henry Fitzgerald, but ... on two opposite sofas with a table between. How proper, or rather prudish. I had been announced indeed some time, and had remained in the hall franking a letter to Miss Hayman. But what then!'[8]

One Sunday the Princess desired the Reverend Sydney Smith – the witty cleric and cousin of Sir Sidney, who claimed that St Paul's Cathedral had 'pupped' to produce Brighton Pavilion – to preach his sermon on toleration in Kensington Palace chapel. 'The tendency of it', noted Glenbervie, was 'political and in co-operation with the anti-ministerial and revolutionary party of the day'. Afterwards the church-goers, including the Misses Berry, walked in Kensington Gardens, and the Princess was 'loud in her encomiums on the subject and sermon'.[9]

By now the Princess was committed to the Opposition. A few months later Mr John Hookham Frere affected surprise when she was disparaging of the ministers: 'What, then, your Royal Highness is in Opposition?' 'To be sure I am,' she replied, 'most decidedly.'[10] In fact, the Princess's circle at Court was not exclusively 'in Opposition'. Some of the Whigs wanted nothing to do with her, and she endeavoured in vain to get Lord Holland and Horner. Canning, for the Tories, still visited, although he spoke his mind, Glenbervie reported, as the Princess discovered when, 'engouée with the wit and agreeableness and wit [sic] of Sydney Smith', she asked Canning what he thought of one of Smith's sermons. 'Execrable,' returned Canning. On another occasion, the Princess, pursuing her 'system of seeing all remarkable persons', asked Lady Glenbervie to enquire of Canning where Mr Henry Salt, the intrepid traveller, was to be found. Canning replied, 'Mr Salt lodges at the Raas's (I do not know the name nor the number) somewhere in Abyssinia. Ever, dear Madam etc.'[11]

A representative selection of the Princess's friends dined in March 1810 at Kensington. The Glenbervies and Miss Hayman were of a party which included Canning, Mr John Ward, Mr Richard Payne Knight and Lord Archibald Hamilton. Ward represented the 'professed wits', whose company the Princess enjoyed, others being Lyttelton and the Reverend Mr Smith. Their 'wit' took curious forms. Ward said to Lyttelton that he thought the Princess had cast a favourable eye upon him. Lyttelton replied, 'No. I only fan the flame which you have kindled.' Ward rejoined with one of his arch and malicious looks, 'I had much rather be the bellows than the poker.'[12] Lyttelton, on the other hand, replied to the Princess, who had said 'she hated ceremony and never thought of taking things ill or being affronted by inattentions', 'No, your Royal Highness never minds how rude people are to you.'[13]

Lord Archibald Hamilton, a reforming Whig MP, represented with Canning two sides of the political coin. Those of Lord Archibald's political persuasion, however – and especially those on the wing of the Whig Party who favoured radical electoral reform – predominated at the Princess's table, as did beaux over belles.

Of the females who formed part of the Princess's Court, Jane Harley, Lady Oxford, whose love of Radical men was as great as her love of radical causes – Sir Francis Burdett had been her lover, and Lord Archibald was now in favour – was a regular visitor. Her children were by so many different fathers that they were known as the 'Harleian Miscellany', after a celebrated collection of seventeenth-century manuscripts.

Mr Richard Payne Knight was also reputed once to have enjoyed the favours of Lady Oxford, his country neighbour. His role at the Princess's table, however, with Sir William Gell, Mr Richard Keppel Craven, Sir William Drummond, Sir Harry Englefield, Lord Aberdeen and many others was that of 'traveller' and antiquarian. All of these men belonged to the 'Dillys', or Society of Dilettanti, and most to the Society of Antiquaries. The more elderly among them had travelled in Italy before the Napoleonic War. The younger Dillys had, perforce, conducted their excavations and explorations, or served as diplomats, in Greece, Turkey, Syria, Palestine and Russia.

Just as the Princess had relished Sir Sidney Smith's tales of his own heroism at Acre, or Manby's accounts of Newfoundland, she lionized these adventurers, and encouraged them to tell of their travels and give their erudite – and often contrary – opinions at her table. Payne Knight declared, for instance, that Lord Elgin had 'lost his labour' in bringing home the eponymous marbles.[14]

'I am in great favour with Sir Harry Englefield,' the Princess wrote contentedly to Miss Hayman. Sir Harry was President of the Society of Antiquaries. 'I supped with him at his own house, and he is now my Cicisbeo to carry me to all the sites of the arts and sciences. I go today to the British Museum, another day to the Liverpool Museum, and afterwards to Lord Elgin's fine collection of statues. On your return to Kensington you will find that I am a virtuoso.'[15]

A no less colourful element among the Princess's favourites were the writers like Mr Thomas Moore, Mr Matthew 'Monk' Lewis and Mr Samuel Rogers. Caroline read omnivorously, Lewis remarked, and she enjoyed the excitement of publication. When Lady Oxford

forsook Lord Archibald for Lord Byron and brought the stormy one
to Kensington, the Princess was in ecstasy, though Byron had savaged
many of the other writers at her table in his *English Bards and Scotch
Reviewers*.

So assiduously did the Princess court her own courtiers, so
interested was she in all her guests and their doings, it was hardly
surprising that her assemblies at Kensington were well attended. Lord
Glenbervie considered the company at one fête she gave for the
Persian Ambassador 'very numerous and . . . in general, the best in
London'. On this occasion, the Princess first received her guests 'very
graciously and gracefully' in 'a sort of circle' in the first room. Then
she and her cousin Princess Sophia Matilda of Gloucester seated
themselves on a sofa in the dining-room, with the Persian Ambassador
on another, while the singer Signor Giuseppe Naldi accompanied on
the harpsichord Mme Angelica Catalani, who sang for the company.
Later two professional dancers performed a Court minuet and a
gavotte.[16]

Her train of thought, indeed her *train de vie*, became steadily more
erratic under the influence of her new friends, the whole thrust of
whose writings and actions and politics was to challenge convention.
The Whig reformers decried the rotten state of Parliament. Sir
William Drummond believed the Old Testament was all allegory.
Payne Knight and his fellow antiquaries, in their love of all things
Greek, ridiculed Christian religion and its sacraments.

The Princess revelled in this topsy-turvy world, and, infatuated by
the licence afforded her, opened a letter addressed to Lady Glenbervie. She 'does not seem to believe in attachment of any husband and
wife to one another, nor in the chastity of any married woman. She
has anecdotes of intrigues without end of all the women of her society
or acquaintance,' Lord Glenbervie complained.[17] Most of these stories
concerned these ladies granting 'the last favours' to gentlemen not
their husbands, and the Princess, not to be outdone by others,
declared of herself that the King had all but ravished her. 'Being alone
with her' at Montague House, 'in the room communicating with the
conservatory, he threw her down on one of the sofas, and would
certainly have ravished her, if, [it] happening to be without a back,
she had not contrived to get over it on the other side.'[18]

As the Princess of Wales became increasingly careless – of her dress, which was sometimes scanty, sometimes soiled and often juvenile, of her behaviour and of her conversation – she also took few pains to guard her tongue and others' in front of her daughter. The Duchess of Gordon tangled one evening at supper with Sir William Drummond, who was expressing his usual heretical views, while Princess Charlotte was present. The Duchess ended by saying, 'If you cannot help your infidelity you deserve to be pitied. If you try to shake the faith of others you deserve to be hanged.' Princess Charlotte, who had likewise come under attack from Sir William, then also summoned up courage to reprove him.[19]

In November 1810, Lord Henry Fitzgerald was called away to his wife, known as Lady de Ros, and his children, who were ill in the country. Towards the end of that month a package came to Kensington for the Princess, 'a large packet, sealed with black, by the post' – one of the Fitzgerald boys had since died, and Sir Henry was in mourning. Later that day she spoke in some agitation to the Glenbervies of 'a rupture, a total breaking off between two remarkable persons, I do not choose to mention names, between whom a connection, what man [untranslated German 'one'] calls an intimate very intimate friendship, has subsisted.'[20]

The Glenbervies pretended to believe she meant Lord Archibald Hamilton and Lady Oxford. Privately they had no doubt that Lord Henry had sent back the Princess's letters and ended their liaison. So it proved. When at home with his wife, 'to whom he was a most kind and attentive husband', and with his children, Lord Henry had finally had the courage to end his affair with the Princess, which had given rise to such comment, and 'the reign of good King Henry' was over. It was a wise move, if painful to the Princess. She told Lady Glenbervie that the Prince had sent her notice: 'if she were not more circumspect in her conduct, he would send her to Holyrood House [in Edinburgh]. She quite expects to be sent there if he is made regent.'[21]

The youngest of the Sisterhood at Windsor, Princess Amelia, whose health had always given cause for concern, became gravely ill in the autumn of 1810. Her father the King was deeply affected by her suffering and, his resilience perhaps weakened, his own mind succumbed to its old malady, even before Amelia died in December. The Princess of Wales, according to the 1838 *Diary*, could find little pity in her for the Queen and the princesses in their distress at this double blow. She only regretted having to abandon an expedition to the Lyceum Theatre, where, Lord Glenbervie feared, a certain actor, by name Raimondi, had taken her fancy.[22]

The consequences for the Princess of Wales when the King's health did not improve were far greater than a little curtailment to her entertainment. For on 5 February 1811 the Prince of Wales was at last appointed Regent, albeit for only a year and with limited powers. All at once, the King's despotic powers over the royal family and his formidable social authority were vested, not in her good-hearted father-in-law, but in her husband, who more than anyone in the world wished her ill. He lost no time in expressing that ill-will. He seemed equally decisive in writing to Mr Spencer Perceval that he intended to retain, out of filial respect, his father's ministers during that year. Hardly had the commotion over this craven *volte face* from 'Fox's fat friend' subsided than the new Prince Regent decreed in April that Princess Charlotte should, henceforward, see no company at her mother's. He had come to hear of Sir William Drummond's heretical performances.

Miss Berry had a glimpse of Charlotte at Kensington shortly before this edict fell. The fifteen-year-old Princess was playing 'at a round table at a foolish game, of calling the cards by the name of Ninycum-twit, or something like that', with a group of her mother's intimates, including Sir William Drummond. Miss Berry lamented, 'She knows no creature, but the royal family and their attendants: she has never yet seen a play or an opera; and whenever she is her own mistress, what must be her first idea but to satiate herself with pleasures. . . .'[23] That evening Charlotte's chief pleasure was swapping ghost stories with Lady Charlotte Campbell, while her mother said gnomically that she had 'the second-sight, and sees a great deal that is coming, nothing that anybody expects, and a great deal that nobody thinks of'.

The Princess of Wales talked a good deal to Miss Berry about her memoirs – that red morocco book for which she had once wished Canning to pay Secret Service money. She suggested 'in joke' – though she may have been perfectly serious – that Miss Berry publish them.[24] One fine moonlit night this June, walking in the Blackheath garden with Miss Berry, the Princess talked of 'her own story'. She began:

> from her early youth, and continued in detai. to the epoch of her marriage, and in still greater detail since. Every circumstance of the Prince's behaviour to her at and after her marriage; every circumstance of the contrivances for getting her out of Carlton House; his character, which she knows perfectly; the Queen's, which she abhors, and whom she believes to be her greatest enemy. . . .[25]

When the Prince Regent gave a great fête, ostensibly for the French royal family, at Carlton House that month, Charlotte was exiled to Windsor on grounds of youth. The Princess of Wales was not invited to this celebration, which in effect inaugurated the Regency. Miss Berry had 'a long and almost affecting conversation with her, because for the first time she seemed to feel her situation, while she continues very good-natured to others'.[26]

Caroline had not expected to be invited to the fête, or to any of the entertainments surrounding this showpiece. She had written to Miss Hayman a month earlier, 'my private society is sadly shivered to pieces'.[27] Her husband had let it be known that no friend of the Princess's would be welcome at the Regency Court, and Miss Berry was one of many to whom he avoided speaking or even 'letting his eye fall upon. . . . I am satisfied that Kensington sticks in his throat, and qu'il se venge des grands sur les petits,' she wrote.[28] 'My mind is much quieter than it has been for some time,' mused the Princess of Wales, however, 'though I cannot help thinking that many irons are now lying in the fire to blow up the edifice of tranquillity which I have erected for myself.'[29]

On the evening of the Carlton House fête, surprisingly, the Prince Regent invited all the Princess of Wales's ladies – though not his wife. Caroline responded by sending them in her own carriage, and Miss Berry gamely elected to keep the Princess company, taking on 'the office of dragon [or chaperone] . . . for fear any stories were to be made on the only evening when the Princess was without any of her ladies. . . . The Princess played the piano [that night] in a manner to convince one that she had once played very well.'[30]

Caroline's spirits were never oppressed for long, and she exaggerated to Miss Hayman some of the features of the Carlton House fête from which she was barred (there had been a stampede and many women had been stripped almost naked in the ensuing panic; one of the Regent's brothers had tried to restore order):

> the broken limbs – the lives lost – the fine speeches made at the head of the pillory to which the Duke of Clarence ascended by a ladder to harangue the populace. . . . – Such a scene as Carlton House was for the last three days . . . the running stream [water-filled channels built into the dining tables] in which the goldfishes acted the most conspicuous part at the great fête. . . .
>
> All the benefit I have had from these fine doings has been that the chickens, turkeys, guineafowls etc have been cheaper than ever before this season – as the fête was put off so often, that all the poultry died and were sold off at half price.

The Princess was determined to entertain the French royal family at her own fête, 'which in my humbler way will only end in a breakfast – and I dare say they will think it is the remains of the crumbs that are dropt from the table of the rich man'.[31] In the event Louis XVIII pleaded a fit of gout – brought on by the Regent's fête; his niece Mme d'Angoulême, a 'fluxion de tête'. The Prince de Condé felt bound to remain with Louis, his guest at Wimbledon. On the morning of the Princess's 'déjeuner à fourchettes', accordingly, the Duke of Cumberland ill-naturedly informed Caroline's brother the Duke of Brunswick at a military review that he need not hurry to his sister's, as none of the French princes was going. Happily, he was misinformed. The Princess's apartments at Kensington were graced by four princes in all and forty of their gentlemen.[32]

The Princess of Wales was ill equipped to win this war of attrition. On becoming Regent, the prince had announced that he meant to 'eclipse Napoleon' in splendour. He certainly eclipsed his wife, and her 'agreeable dinners' became a thing of the past. Guests, when invited, failed to appear. Her particular dilettanti friends, Gell and Keppel Craven, were gone to Aphrodisias in Turkey for the Society of Antiquaries. The Whig politicians – Brougham, Grey – courted the Regent once more, in the hope that, when he attained full powers the following year (the King's mania had not diminished) he would turn out the Tories for the allies of his youth.

In October 1811, the Princess admitted defeat and removed 'all her plate, Household, batterie de cuisine, and servants to Montague House to remain an indefinite time', Lord Glenbervie reported. 'She seems tired of Kensington, and disgusted with it, and complains that nobody comes to her there.'[33] Caroline herself wrote to Miss Hayman, mocking her 'completely sedentary, quiet and dull country life'. For 'the metropolis', she said, 'I have such a thorough contempt that I certainly shall not grace it again till after Easter'. Miss Berry, Miss Mary Gell (Sir William's sister), Lady Charlotte Lindsay and Miss Garth had been the only inhabitants of 'this sequestered bower . . . my daughter and Princess Sophia now and then to dinner. . . . This has been the usual train of my rural life.'[34]

Miss Berry confirmed that the Princess, for a wonder, had no men at dinner when she went to stay at Montague House in November. Caroline and her ladies talked and read in 'the drawing room which opens into the greenhouse, a very warm and comfortable room'. They walked to Lee Church and inspected the Princess's kitchen garden across the heath, where she had once so contentedly lectured the Abbé Campe under an arbour of honeysuckle on the appropriate education for the poor.[35]

Of Princess Charlotte, Lady Glenbervie observed, 'she is grown tall and very graceful – but . . . she is forward, dogmatical on all subjects, buckish about horses, and full of exclamations very like swearing'. A Dutch diplomat likened the adolescent Princess Charlotte to a mutinous boy in skirts.[36] Understandably, Charlotte champed at the bit. On one occasion she had a comical set-to with Lady de Clifford. She had a habit of sitting with her legs stretched out and showing her drawers. (She was not above wiping her nose on her sleeve, either.) Her governess remonstrated, Charlotte responded that the Duchess of Bedford showed hers – pantaloons beneath shorter skirts were then fashionable – and poor Lady de Clifford subsided in a fluster.[37]

The year 1812 began badly for Princess Charlotte. She passed her sixteenth birthday on 7 January 'upon thorns', as she told her friend Miss Mercer Elphinstone.[38] She had first to dine with her father at

Carlton House, then eat another dinner with her mother at Black-heath. There was spiritual as well as physical indigestion to follow. She was the heir presumptive, who might, given the nervous vagaries of her father's health and her grandfather's illness, succeed to the throne in two years' time. And yet the repressive, ineffective, edu-cational regime and the narrow bounds of her existence, which had been prescribed when she was eight in 1804, were still largely in place.

The general suspicion that the Prince had no serious thought of bringing in a Whig administration on attaining his full powers as regent was confirmed when he kept Perceval and the Tory ministers. Charlotte, a budding Whig, rode in mute reproach back and forward past the garden-front windows of Carlton House, while her father within signed the papers. When the Prince inveighed against the Whigs at a dinner he gave at Carlton House in February, she burst into tears.[39] Whereupon Lord Byron gleefully penned the lines:

> Weep, daughter of a royal line,
> A sire's disgrace, a realm's decay;
> Ah! happy if each tear of thine
> Could wash a father's fault away.[40]

Retribution followed swiftly. Charlotte was forbidden by her father to have any further intercourse with Miss Mercer Elphinstone, the Whiggish young lady whose friendship she so prized and whom the Regent suspected – quite rightly – of influencing his daughter. Her father, moreover, dispatched her to spend the summer at Lower Lodge at Windsor, under the watchful eye of her grandmother Queen Charlotte. Lady de Clifford was not far off when she described this manoeuvre as kidnapping, although she was misguided enough so to describe it to Princess Charlotte.[41]

The long-standing rapport between the Prince Regent and his mother had been much in evidence at her Birthday in January, and the newly political Charlotte, aware that the Queen was a diehard Tory, wrote to Mercer, 'All good Whigs tremble.'[42] In May Queen Charlotte repeated to the Prince Regent the advice she had given her granddaughter: 'she ought to look upon you as the only source of her happiness, she ought at no time to consider herself as aggrieved when you disapproved of anything in her conduct ... she ought to be careful about fancying particular friendships at her time of life. . . . political friendship never could be depended upon . . .'[43] These words were hardly likely to appease Charlotte, who now, like her mother, viewed the Queen, blind worshipper of her son, as inimical to her interests. She undertook, reluctantly but determinedly, a clandestine correspondence with Mercer, and Lady Charlotte Lindsay served as postmistress on Princess Charlotte's weekly visits to her mother.[44]

At the end of March some of the Whig Opposition had taken up the Princess of Wales's cause in the House of Commons, and condemned Perceval for deserting her. Mr George Tierney, leader of the Whigs in the Lower House, suggested that the Princess be known as the Princess Regent and be accorded an income to match her husband's.[45] The Duke of Northumberland, a Tory intimate of the Regent, remarked, not without reason, that these Whigs' 'understandings appear to be driven from them by their disappointed ambition'.[46] The majority of the Whigs, however, did not so firmly espouse the Princess's cause. Grey and Grenville discussed in a desultory fashion publishing the Book, to embarrass the Tory administration. (It surely would have also embarrassed Grenville.) They were merely casting round for any stone to throw at the Regent, anything with which to discredit the Tory ministers.

Mr Henry Brougham was one Whig MP who saw a possibility of glorious advantage accruing to him from the rift between 'young P' and 'Mrs P' and 'old P', as he referred to Princess Charlotte and her parents.[47] His intimate friendship with Lady Charlotte Lindsay smoothed his way, and both royal ladies hearkened to his advice. In June an opportunity to make mayhem arose.

Perceval, Caroline's former champion, had been assassinated in the lobby of the House of Commons in May by a commercial agent ruined by the war.* As prime minister, he had been sustained in his

---

* Since 1806 Napoleon had directed economic warfare against Britain by means of the Continental System, designed to exclude British trade from continental Europe. It was soon to be defeated by the all-powerful Royal Navy. Meanwhile, the land war had spread to the Iberian Peninsula, from where Viscount Wellington was attempting to expel French troops under Marshal Soult. Russia's withdrawal from the Continental System provoked Napoleon's disastrous Moscow campaign, launched in June 1812, which in turn caused troops to be removed from the Peninsular War, fatally weakening Soult's forces.

difficult relations with the Regent and the Princess of Wales by an exceptionally strong religious belief in the sanctity of marriage, and by feelings of chivalry towards the oppressed Princess. Lord Liverpool (formerly Lord Hawkesbury), who replaced Perceval as premier, was a pragmatist; he served his political master rather than God, and he kept public opinion, rather than morality, ever in view.

The Regent took immediate advantage of this moral laxity in his new Minister and enjoined Lord Eldon to write to the Princess of Wales on 17 June with the message that her daughter, while in residence at Windsor for the summer, would visit her only once every two weeks.[48] The Princess of Wales consulted Brougham about this new restriction on her intercourse with her daughter, and it was on his advice that she proceeded down to Windsor on 10 July to see Charlotte at Lower Lodge, in defiance of Eldon's injunction. 'Our gracious Queen Charlotte expressed herself in the most delicate way upon that subject', the Princess of Wales wrote, 'by saying that Lady de Clifford ought to have the power ... if the Princess had again the impertinence to come to Windsor to turn her out of the house: this elegant speech shall make its first appearance in the Examiner [Mr Leigh Hunt's newspaper].'[49]

Caroline's spirits were up again, her taste for battle returned and she relished a message – from Lord Liverpool this time. She was not to visit her daughter at Lower Lodge. The Prince Regent kept apartments there and regarded it as one of his own houses – where he chose not to receive her. Liverpool was summoned to Kensington next day, 16 July, and, in the presence of her vice-chamberlain, Mr Anthony St Leger, the Princess of Wales threatened to return to Windsor if her daughter did not come to her once each week.[50] The Princess won this skirmish and her point, and Princess Charlotte duly appeared at Kensington the following week.

Caroline monitored her daughter's visits carefully and kept a 'dossier'. Charlotte called on her grandmother, the Duchess of Brunswick, at Blackheath on the old lady's birthday, 11 August – 'for which reason I don't expect her this week, but the week after, and the week following', Caroline informed Miss Hayman. 'If she does not come, I shall certainly go to Windsor and shall have the honour to be turned out by her gracious Majesty.'[51]

In the interval, Caroline went to enjoy herself at Tunbridge Wells. Lady Charlotte Campbell warned Miss Mary Berry, who was staying there with her sister and father, 'Samson, the Philistines be upon thee.' Miss Berry must use her black eyes to search out some stray males in this fashionable watering-hole, as 'there being a dearth of men throughout the land at present, we have none alas to bring'. Otherwise, Lady Charlotte continued, 'we shall be heavy in hand on you and ourselves without a little male aid'. Old Mr Berry, who 'liked the fun of gallanting her about', was the Princess of Wales's chief escort about town. On the Pantiles promenade and at a ball given in honour of Wellington's victory at Salamanca on 22 July, the Misses Berry were forsaken by their usual beaux.[52] The Princess of Wales had become a laughing-stock, an object of ridicule, with her outlandish ways and bizarre dress sense. And the ridicule, the whispers and the contempt were sanctioned by the highest authority, the Regent himself.

Caroline returned to London and threatened yet again to come down to Windsor, as Lady de Clifford was ill and could not escort Charlotte. The Queen declined, on her son's behalf, and on the ground that it would interrupt Charlotte's studies. She then lent one of her own ladies, Miss Cornelia Knight, to chaperone Charlotte to Kensington, and the crunch was once more averted.[53] Charlotte journeyed up to visit her mother on 22 September and told her all, which was duly 'added to the dossier'. The Regent and Princess of Wales were riding roughshod over their nervous daughter and her feelings.

The young Princess was due to visit her mother again on 1 October, barely a week later. However, in the meantime and advised by Brougham, the Princess of Wales set out for Windsor – on a Sunday morning this time, and without giving prior notice to the Queen beyond a note sent after she departed Blackheath. The Princess was coming specially on a Sunday and after church, her new lady of the bedchamber Lady Anne Hamilton wrote, so as not to disturb her daughter's studies or devotions. Lady Anne conveyed this same message to Lord Liverpool.[54]

By the time Caroline arrived at Windsor, set up camp in Augusta Lodge and sent an unctuous note to Lady de Clifford begging her to bring Charlotte to her there, pandemonium had broken loose. Before Lady de Clifford, panic-stricken, could inform the Queen of this request, the Queen, having received Lady Anne's letter, had reported to the Regent – who would undoubtedly have told Liverpool, had that confidential servant not informed his master of his own note from Lady Anne.[55] Thereupon the Regent instructed the Queen, who informed Lady de Clifford, as well as the Princess of Wales, that the invasion should be prevented. The barbarian at the gate of the castle should not enter – although, strictly speaking, both Lower Lodge and Augusta Lodge lay outside the walls of Windsor Castle. The Princess of Wales begged an interview with the Queen. This was granted, the Queen informing her that, while she was 'sorry they met on so unpleasant a subject', it was out of her power to release Lady de Clifford from her son's orders. As for Augusta Lodge, 'the Princess must be well aware that His Majesty had never asked her to it since the unfortunate business'.[56]

Caroline started back to London, on the whole pleased with the day's events, and leaving her enemies to recriminate with each other over the handling of her visit.

The question of the Princess of Wales's access to her daughter, to which the Regent was opposed, was intertwined with that of Princess Charlotte's growing desire for freedom, to which her grandmother was opposed. The Duke of York stressed to the Queen later in October 'the necessity of her enjoying more liberty and passing a part of her time in London', and suggested that his sisters, the princesses, should chaperone her in the world: 'Charlotte was to all intents and purposes without a mother or, if possible, in a worse situation, and therefore she required the support and protection of the female part of her family.'[57] To this sensible proposal, however, the Queen was reluctant to agree. Charlotte was left to the none too strict governance of old Lady de Clifford.

Charlotte was taking liberties of her own accord at Windsor, liberties that her relations never dreamt of – though she was her mother's daughter. She had developed into an attractive young woman with shining chestnut hair and infectious high spirits. In the course of a few short weeks in the autumn of 1812, she had encountered by appointment, out on her airings with Lady de Clifford, first one young officer, Captain George Fitzclarence, stationed at Windsor with his regiment, then, on his departure and in his place, Captain Charles Hesse. Both were, so to speak, family affairs. Fitzclarence was the son of Charlotte's uncle the Duke of Clarence and Mrs Jordan the actress. Hesse was reputedly an illegitimate son of another of her uncles, the Duke of York. Perhaps on that account, Lady de Clifford made no objection to Fitzclarence or Hesse riding alongside the Princess's carriage for several weeks. Then she regretted her forbearance, and ordered Charlotte to have no further communication with Hesse.[58] Charlotte, however, exchanged love letters and presents with Hesse. She later told her father that Caroline had encouraged her in this liaison and once locked her in a bedroom with Hesse, saying 'I leave you to amuse yourselves.' Nonetheless Charlotte was never sure whether the handsome officer was her own lover or her mother's.

Charlotte's return to London and to Warwick House was the occasion for a new passage to arms between Queen and Princess of Wales. Caroline wrote on 21 November that she had assumed she would see her daughter, when Charlotte was in town, once a week, and that she knew of no reason why her intercourse with her daughter should be so restricted.[59] This lofty letter was the work of Brougham, now chief among her advisers, although he was out of Parliament. Mr Samuel Whitbread and Mr Thomas Creevey were at this time her chief supporters in the Commons (Brougham, changing constituencies, had failed to win a seat at Liverpool in the October election).

Caroline's letter and the Queen's reply were duly published in December as the letters of 'Illustrious Personages', despite government attempts to suppress them.[60] Byron wrote that month of Caroline's claims: Lady Oxford, his inamorata, 'thinks I agree with her in all her politics. . . . She insists always upon the Princess's innocence, but then as she sometimes reads me somewhat a tedious homily upon her own, I look upon it in much the same point of view as I should upon Mary Magdalen's vindication of Mrs Joseph or any other immaculate riddle. . . .'[61] Byron did not like Caroline any the less for that, and she told a correspondent in January 1813, 'he was all couleur de rose last evening and very pleasant; he sat beside me at supper, and we were very merry; he is quite another person when he is with people he likes, and who like him. . . .'[62]

Meanwhile, Brougham had had a thundering *succès d'estime* – his clients went to jail – when he defended Mr Leigh Hunt and his brother in November 1812 against the accusation that they had libelled the Prince of Wales as 'fat, foolish and fifty' in the *Examiner*. Temporarily barred from Parliamentary politics, Brougham was led to believe that he might accomplish as much out of the Commons as in it, and now turned his hand to pamphleteering. He wrote a letter in January 1813 for the Princess of Wales to send to the Prince Regent, and she declared it 'quite perfect'. However, the Regent declined to receive it, and it was returned unopened the following day.

Brougham was well pleased. 'The most curious is young P's letter to old P which gave rise to all the row at Windsor,' he told his friend Creevey.[63] While the Princess of Wales's letter was receiving its finishing touches, Lady de Clifford had honourably, if foolishly, told the Prince Regent of Princess Charlotte's assignations in the park at Windsor with Captain Hesse. The Regent and the Queen were outraged. The Queen at first wanted all the servants at Lower Lodge removed, and Lady de Clifford was ordered to resign her position as governess on the strange ground that she felt she had lost Charlotte's confidence.[64] The Duchess of Leeds was selected as governess in her place.

When Charlotte was told that Lady de Clifford was to be replaced, she wrote to her father on 10 January the 'curious' letter Brougham mentioned. Her chief complaint was that 'other young people of my age ceased to have governesses at seventeen'.[65] She had no objection, she said, to the Duchess of Leeds forming part of her establishment, but as one of her ladies, not as a governess. The 'row' which followed was painful. The Prince Regent took Lord Eldon with him next morning to inform his daughter that she was legally bound to obey him. What would you do with your daughter if she behaved in this manner? the Regent enquired solemnly of his Lord Chancellor. And Eldon, no less solemnly, replied, 'I would lock her up.'[66] Sir Henry

Halford, Charlotte's doctor, made more progress when he reminded her that male heirs to the throne were also subject to governors until they were eighteen.[67]

The Duchess of Leeds was duly appointed governess, and a furious Charlotte had for companions the Duchess's schoolgirl daughters, when her ardent wish was to escape the schoolroom. The Regent made only one concession: Miss Cornelia Knight, wrested from the Queen, became Charlotte's lady companion and not her sub-governess.

All through January the Princess of Wales agitated that the Regent should read her letter, and he as stoutly refused to do so. Finally the document was presented to Liverpool and Eldon, with the plea that 'she should not be the only subject in the empire whose petition was not permitted to reach the throne'.[68] The ministers signalled that its contents had been made known to the Regent. Had it actually been read to him, she persisted, and what was his pleasure upon it? No answer came to this letter of 19 January, and eight days later she wrote again to demand an answer.[69]

Liverpool at last informed Lady Charlotte Campbell that the Prince Regent, 'having permitted the Lord Chancellor and Lord Liverpool to communicate to his Royal Highness the contents of the letter which they had received from the Princess in such manner as they might think proper, the letter of the Princess had been read to his Royal Highness'. Liverpool added, 'His Royal Highness was not pleased to signify any commands upon it.'[70]

This was not the case when a copy of 'The Regent's Valentine', as the spurned letter became known, was published in the *Morning Chronicle* on 10 February. (Brougham and the Princess of Wales both swore that they had not been responsible.) The impact on the public was enormous, the sympathy for the Princess of Wales widespread, and for a time Regent's Valentine prints, plates and jugs were on sale, with some of Brougham's more choice expressions inscribed thereon.[71]

'Sir, there are considerations of a higher nature than any regard to my own happiness,' the letter read, 'which render this address a duty both to myself and my daughter.' She had begun by saying that she would have preferred to 'continue in silence and in retirement', consoled by the reflection that that retirement was no fault of her own.

> There is a point beyond which guiltless woman cannot with safety carry her forbearance. If her honour is invaded, the defence of her reputation is no longer a matter of choice; and it signifies not whether the attack be made openly, manfully, and directly – or by secret insinuation, and by holding such conduct towards her as countenances all the suspicions that malice can suggest. If these ought to be the feelings of every woman in England, who is conscious that she deserves no reproach ... how much more justly they belong to the mother of ... her who is destined ... to reign over the British Empire.

She referred to 'The separation which every succeeding month is making wider' between mother and daughter. She said 'nothing [or rather a great deal] of the deep wounds which so cruel an arrangement inflicts upon my feelings ... cut off from one of the very few domestic enjoyments left to me ... the society of my child ...'.

She begged the Prince not to incarcerate Charlotte at Windsor. Excluded from all intercourse with the world, 'She ... enjoys none of those advantages of society which are deemed necessary for imparting a knowledge of mankind. ...' She feared lest Charlotte might be 'called upon to exercise the powers of the Crown, with an experience of the world more confined than that of the most private individual'.[72]

The day after the *Morning Chronicle* published this appeal, the Princess of Wales was stepping into her carriage at Blackheath on her way to meet Charlotte at Kensington as promised, when she was told that her daughter would not be coming. 'In consequence of the publication in the Morning Chronicle of the 10th instant of a letter addressed by your Royal Highness to the Prince Regent,' Liverpool wrote in reply to her enquiry, 'his Royal Highness thought fit by the advice of his confidential servants to signify his commands that the intended visit ... should not take place.'[73]

Caroline's reply to this was to attack the ministers. The 'insidious insinuation' – that *she* had published that letter – was 'as false as all the former accusations of the traducers of her Royal Highness's honour in the year 1806'. They 'ought to feel ashamed of their conduct . . . in avowing' to her their advice that 'upon unauthorized and unfounded suppositions – a mother and daughter should be prevented from meeting – a prohibition . . . positively against the laws of nature'.[74]

Four days later, on 19 February, Addington, now Lord Sidmouth and Home Secretary, told the Privy Council that the Prince Regent wished them to consider the Princess's letter and all the Delicate Investigation papers, and report their opinion 'whether under all the circumstances of the case it be fit and proper that the intercourse between the Princess of Wales and her daughter the Princess Charlotte should continue to be subject to regulations and restrictions'.[75] To nobody's surprise, when the Privy Council reconvened on 23 February, they concluded after two days' discussion that the restrictions should remain in place. The Privy Councillors, among whom were the Princess's chief defenders in 1806, even concluded that 'the inquiry in 1806 . . . appears to have been pressed upon your Royal Highness in consequence of the advice of Lord Thurlow, and upon grounds of public duty . . .'.[76] This episode – the revival of the Delicate Investigation and its consequences – represents perhaps the nadir of British party politics.

The uproar was considerable, and the Princess's new 'trial' was regarded as monstrous. Charlotte was resigned to the outcome. Brougham wrote:

> Notwithstanding the opening of all letters, which we at first thought under the Duchess of Leeds would have been terribly inconvenient, things have got back nearly into their own channel, for young P contrived to send her mother a letter of twenty-eight pages, and to receive from her the Morning Chronicle with all the articles about herself – as well as the examinations. Now these, I take it, are exactly what old P had rather she did not see.
>
> She takes the most prodigious interest in the controversy [he added happily], and I am going to draw up a legal opinion respecting her case. . . .[77]

Small wonder, when Princess Charlotte was kept so assiduously supplied with information, that, on being presented with the Privy

Council Report, she told her trembling governess that it did not add anything.[78]

To embarrass the Tory administration as much as to clear the Princess's name, the Whig press now serialized, and later booksellers published copies of, the Book, which Perceval had suppressed in 1807 on gaining office. Pandora's box was fully opened at last, though its lid had been loosened in 1811 by the publication of Mr Thomas Ashe's *Spirit of the Book*, purportedly a confessional work composed by the Princess herself. (Ashe later claimed that Carlton House had paid him to write it.) There was now a call for Lady Douglas to be prosecuted for perjury. On 26 March the old Duchess of Brunswick died. Caroline's relationship with her mother had always been marked more by mutual irritation than by affection, and they had sought to score points off each other right to the end. When the new Regent had invited the Duchess to Carlton House one day, without including her daughter, the old woman had carefully voiced the hope that it would be possible to carry her litter up the stairs there. The Princess had riposted, 'The state rooms were on the ground floor in my day.' But she reacted to her mother's death with some tenderness, writing the next day, 'We must with gratitude acknowledge His clemency that she did not suffer long.' The burial of the Duchess at Windsor and the publication of the Book brought Caroline more public sympathy than ever before. As a result, the Prince of Wales sent Charlotte to pay a visit to her mother, in the hope of abating his own public odium.

In April Caroline, standing at the windows of Kensington Palace, bowed to the Mayor and aldermen of the City of London, who had come to present her with an address expressing their sympathy for her sufferings.[79] (Brougham wrote her gracious answer to the City delegates; he baulked at composing the address as well.)

The Prince Regent, sent into a rage by his wife's popularity, demanded to have his – hitherto unpublished – Law Officers' Report of 1807 printed. It utterly condemned the Princess of Wales, in his view, and countered her defence as set out in the Book. His ministers pointed out that it was apparent from that document, his Law Officers' Report, that the Prince had pursued the Princess for a divorce, which was not generally known.[80]

Even Brougham, that political opportunist *par excellence*, was faintly sickened by the political humbug of this period. By April he was less cock-a-hoop about the Princess of Wales's affairs, and had grown wary of Whitbread's schemes for her further defence. 'Do not listen to Sam,' he warned Creevey. 'He has NO HEAD. Depend upon it, he has not. He is good for execution, but nothing for counsel except indeed as far as his courage and honesty go, which are invaluable, but not of themselves sufficient.'[81] Brougham now had 'a degree of dislike of the whole concern' – which he himself had whipped up. In May he discovered from Lady Charlotte Lindsay that 'there is an idea of another letter from the Princess to Prinny, and that Whitbread has written one. Pray try to impress upon him', he begged Creevey, 'the fatal effects of any more letters. She will be called the compleat letterwriter and become generally despised.'[82]

The Regent and the Princess of Wales skirted round each other. The Regent had every intention of gracing a grand fête at Vauxhall, which he had sponsored, until he heard that his wife intended to go. 'Mother P certainly goes to the tea garden tomorrow night, to meet her husband,' Brougham confirmed. 'It was her own idea, but I highly approve of it. . . . The consternation of Prinny is wonderful. I'll bet a little money he don't go himself. . . .' Brougham was proved right: the Prince Regent indeed failed to attend.[83]

But this victory was not only a petty one, it was pyrrhic too. The Prince Regent's campaign to exclude Caroline from Society was to drive her, with disastrous effect, into choosing her lovers from outside it.

## CHAPTER ELEVEN

# CAROLINE AND CHARLOTTE

## 1813–1814

*'She has a spice of her mother's spirit'*

THE PRINCESS LIVED an increasingly isolated existence, and her intercourse with Charlotte was still subject to restriction. 'The state of things at that prosecuted Court is deplorable,' wrote Lord Glenbervie after a visit in June 1813 to the Princess at Kensington. (The writer Mme de Staël was one among many who wooed the Prince Regent and declined invitations to his wife's salons.) A few days later, Glenbervie wrote, after another evening there, of 'our scanty party. . . . The affairs of the Princess go worse and worse, which means a sad life for Lady Glenbervie, and, if her virtue, spirit and prudence were not those of Egidia, a life quite impossible.' Caroline, ignored by Society, had begun to take pleasure in flouting the most elementary conventions of her caste. She was described as 'keeping a sort of open house, receiving visitors in a dressing-gown, and sitting [incognito], and talking about herself with strangers on the benches' in Kensington Gardens.[1] For some months she had been renting two cottages on Craven Hill in Paddington. In one lived her lady-in-waiting Lady Charlotte Campbell and her children. To the other cottage Caroline was herself an almost daily visitor, ostensibly taking singing lessons from a handsome Italian musician, Pietro Sapio. But Sapio had in fact become her lover, a circumstance made only too evident by the constant presence at Kensington Palace of his parents, a ramshackle and impoverished count and countess. Dubbed the Squallini by the 1838 diarist, the family were all earning their living as singers. Conte Antonio Sapio – 'Old Orang-utan' to Lady Charlotte – claimed a distinguished past. The Prince Regent's agents investigated, and to their chagrin found that he did indeed appear to have tutored Queen Marie Antoinette.

Princess Charlotte suspected the existence of this new liaison, but her own affairs of the heart were coming to assume a greater importance. 'Young P and her father have had frequent rows of late, but one pretty serious one,' Brougham informed Creevey later in the summer. 'He was angry at her for flirting with the Duke of Devonshire, and suspected she was talking politics. This began it. . . . In the long run', Brougham forecast, 'quarrel they must. He has not equality of temper, or any other kind of sense, to keep well with her, and she has a spice of her mother's spirit; so interfere they must at every turn. . . .'[2]

In August Charlotte was ill, alternately overwrought and moping at Windsor. 'Studdy', she had uncharacteristically told Mercer, was her chief amusement there.[3] In a desperate attempt to restore order and certainty to her wearisome existence, she announced that she wished to marry – and to marry the Duke of Gloucester, or Slice as he was known, who had succeeded his father in 1805. Nobody took this declaration very seriously, least of all her designated bridegroom. The Duke had been for years, in an ineffectual way, attached to her aunt Princess Mary (whom indeed he ended by marrying).

The catalyst for this sudden partiality was the hints thrown out about William, the Hereditary Prince of Orange, whom Lord Malmesbury had canvassed as a possible bridegroom for Charlotte earlier in the year. Charlotte had managed to avoid him when he came as the messenger with dispatches containing news of Wellington's victory over Soult in the eight-day Battle of the Pyrenees which had ended on 1 August. However, 'the plagues about him' did not let up once he had returned to his commander.[4] Charlotte was the first to comment upon the absurdity that her father believed her still to require a governess, while he also believed her ready to marry.

Charlotte knew Billy. He had grown up in exile in England, attended Oxford University and joined the British Army. Only now was his father's United Orange Kingdom restored to him. Silly Billy, as he was known, was not a prepossessing youth – short and skinny and indecisive in character – but by November 1813 Charlotte had come round to the idea. She would gain her own establishment, and financial independence – this was an important consideration, as following in her parents' footsteps she had built up debts of £22,000.

She would, moreover, be independent of her father – as she thought. But an enquiry on this account in December to Lord Grey, leader of her favoured party, the Whigs, elicited the disappointing news that she would remain dependent on her father till she reached the age of twenty-one.[5]

The Regent formally presented the Hereditary Prince of Orange to his daughter on his return to London in December, and they marched solemnly up and down a side room, making a very odd trio. Young William was quite overshadowed by the tall and buxom Charlotte, and by her elegant, if enormous, father. Charlotte agreed that very evening to an engagement and, Miss Knight recorded, was quite calm about it. Two days later, however, she was in tears. She had discovered that she would be required to spend half the year in Holland.[6]

Meanwhile, Wellington's successful conclusion of the Peninsular War had been matched by a decisive allied victory over the French at Leipzig in October. A combined British, Austrian, Prussian, Russian and Swedish army had defeated Napoleon, already gravely weakened by his failed invasion of Russia. Forced to abandon France's conquests in Germany, the Emperor himself was soon back in Paris.

At the start of 1814 the Princess of Wales was a little less despondent about her own future than her daughter. No doubt keen to enjoy greater freedom with her operatic lover, she rented a house near Craven Hill (she gave up the cottages there). She was 'now just arranging all my pictures' in the new house, 'halfway to town. It is in "Connaught Place" at the top of Oxford Street, Cumberland Gate – at no. 7. . . . the rooms are large and lofty – but like all town houses', Caroline informed Miss Hayman, 'there are few rooms for attendants'. Sicard and others, as a result, kept their apartments at Kensington Palace. 'All your old acquaintances at Blackheath – even the greenhouse', Caroline continued, 'will be moved to Connaught Place.'[7] The two Blackheath houses (in the event, she had inherited her mother's) were to be let. 'It was advisable to take the house entirely unfurnished, with the greatest economy it will come to £1500 (independent of having all the furniture carried there from Blackheath).' She foresaw no change in her income or situation, 'which I confess makes me sometimes very low-spirited. . . . I reckon that I shall remain in this purgatory at least ten years longer.'[8] Here she apparently looked forward to a day when her daughter would be Queen.

To cheer Caroline up, Gell and Keppel Craven had returned this winter from Turkey, and in December 1813, Miss Berry had noted, the Princess was 'screeching with Craven'.[9] This fondness for singing had been fostered by her supposed lessons with Sapio.[10] Princess Charlotte saw the Italian on horseback outside her mother's house in Connaught Place, and he was also the subject of an investigation by Lowten, the Regent's confidential agent. Lowten was able to prove nothing, and Sapio continued to delight his royal mistress until his departure for Paris later in the year. Caroline remained fond of the whole family and invited them to stay with her on Lake Como in the winter of 1816/17.

The Opposition lawyers had been considering, at Charlotte's request, the precedent for an heir apparent's leaving the country, and supported her wish for an article in her marriage contract to restrict her absence. 'She has been induced to insist upon conditions being inserted in the contract of marriage of which she never thought until recently,' wrote Lord Liverpool, the Prime Minister.[11]

And then, at the end of March 1814, came news of the allied occupation of Paris and Napoleon's abdication, and of peace after twenty-one years of European war. After several battles, allied armies had converged on the French capital, and the Emperor was banished to Elba. Under the Treaty of Paris, France's frontiers were to be those prevailing in 1792, before the French Revolutionary War. London was illuminated for three days in April, and amid the public rejoicing Grey advised Charlotte to go cautiously, not to be too publicly the Whig. He advised her merely to ask to see a copy of her marriage contract, and enquire why no provision had been made for a house in London or in the country.[12] The Prince Regent replied that William and Charlotte should live with him at Carlton House.

Great celebrations were to be held for the peace in June. The Tsar of Russia and the King of Prussia were both coming to grace the city with their presence. A flurry of announcements of public events followed, and cards were sent out for balls, public and private. Among the entertainments, it was announced, there were to be two drawing-rooms. 'As it is necessary that some positive cause should be established by the journalists of the day for every action performed by any branches of the royal family,' wrote a contemporary slily, 'it was immediately ascertained that the reason of holding two drawing-rooms could be no other than to allow an illustrious female to appear at Court without meeting her husband, and vice versa. . . .' It bore comparison, he wrote, with 'the Dutch toy, in which when the lady is within, the gentleman turns out, and when the latter chooses to enter, the lady briskly retreats'.[13]

The Princess of Wales, however, received a letter from her mother-in-law on 24 May, informing her that her presence was not required at either of the two drawing-rooms which were in view. Miss Berry was summoned, a few days later, to Connaught House to hear Lady Charlotte Campbell read aloud this letter and the correspondence which followed. Of the Princess's letters to the Queen, Miss Berry wrote, 'They were good, but too long, and sometimes marked by Whitbread's want of taste, who dictated them.'[14]

The Queen had written on 23 May:

> her son, the Prince Regent . . . considers that his own presence at her Court cannot be dispensed with; and . . . he desires it may be distinctly understood, for reasons of which he alone can be the judge, to be his fixed and unalterable determination not to meet the Princess of Wales upon any occasion, either in public or private. The Queen is thus placed under the painful necessity of intimating to the Princess of Wales the impossibility of her Majesty's receiving her Royal Highness at the drawing-rooms.[15]

The Princess begged the Queen to acquaint those 'illustrious strangers', to whom she was closely related by birth as well as marriage, with her motive – consideration for the Queen – for abstaining from 'the exercise of my right to appear before your Majesty . . .'. She added, '. . . I do now, as I have done at all times, defy the malice of my enemies to fix upon me the shadow of any one imputation, which could render me unworthy of their society. . . .' She ended by declaring that she intended to 'relieve myself from a suspicion of disrespect towards your Majesty by making public the cause of my absence from Court, at a time when the duties of my station would otherwise peculiarly demand my attendance'.[16]

To this, the Queen replied that she would have felt no hesitation in informing the Tsar and King of Prussia of this intelligence, 'if her Royal Highness had not rendered her compliance with her wish to this effect unnecessary, by intimating her intention of making public the cause of her absence'.[17]

Events now moved swiftly towards a climax. The Princess fired off – she was indeed the complete letter-writer – another missile to the Regent, rebuking him for choosing 'This season' for 'treating me with fresh and unprovoked indignity'. She was to express neither her joy at the peace nor indulge 'those feelings of pride and affection permitted to every mother but me'. Princess Charlotte was finally to be presented at Court, and the Prince of Orange 'has announced himself to me as my son-in-law.... Since his Majesty's lamented illness I have demanded, in the face of Parliament and the country, to be proved guilty, or to be treated as innocent. I have been declared innocent; I will not submit to be treated as guilty.' She then enquired angrily, 'Can your Royal Highness have contemplated the full extent of your declarations – never to meet me upon any occasion, either public or private? Has your Royal Highness forgotten the approaching marriage of our daughter, and the possibility of our coronation?'[18]

Charlotte was duly presented at Court. The Princess of Wales herself was loudly cheered at the opera on 3 June, but this could hardly assuage her wounded feelings. When the Tsar and the King of Prussia – both her near relations – arrived in London but made no effort to see her, her last hopes were disappointed. Whitbread wrote to Creevey on the 11th: 'The Emperor [of Russia] has as yet returned no answer nor returned any civility to the Princess's message and letter by St Leger....'[19] In fact, Tsar Alexander wrote a reply dated 10 June, but cravenly sent it only on his departure from London:

> if I was not able to present my compliments to your Royal Highness I hope you will attribute it only to the state in which I found matters on my arrival in this country. Delicacy imposed on me obligations which it was impossible for me to throw off. This is the only reason which prevented me from carrying out my duty to your Royal Highness. I beg you to accept assurances of my highest consideration, etc.[20]

'She is sadly low,' Whitbread reported, 'poor body, and no wonder. What a fellow Prinny is!'[21]

The Princess of Wales had, in fact, lost heart, and had written two days earlier on 9 June to her brother William in Brunswick, newly restored to his duchy under the Peace of Paris, asking if she could visit him there. This very evening at the opera the Prince Regent, who was basking in the reflected popularity of his royal guests – but was execrated when 'caught alone', according to Creevey – stole her thunder when she entered her box to the now habitual applause. For the first time in many years, he bowed to her across the house and won his own cheers. While the Princess of Wales awaited a reply to her letter to her brother, and began making arrangements privately for her departure, Brougham made what Creevey called 'one of the most brilliant moves in his campaign'.[22]

Brougham was aware that Caroline planned to leave England, although he did not know of her letter to her brother. He wished, at all costs, to prevent Charlotte following her out of the country. Combining blackmail and an appeal to self-interest, he sought an interview with 'the young one', at which he stressed that Charlotte was the only object keeping her mother in England. If she, Charlotte, left the country, as leave she must by the terms of her marriage contract with the Orange Prince, her mother would also go abroad. He impressed upon her 'this fact, that if her mother goes away from England, as she is always threatening to do from her ill usage in this country . . . then a divorce will inevitably take place, a second marriage follow, and thus the young Princess's title to the throne be gone. This has had an effect upon the young one almost magical!'[23]

Charlotte broke her engagement to the Prince of Orange on 16 June, and before doing so she informed Lady Charlotte Lindsay, whom she asked to witness the event, that 'she was determined to support her mother, and felt that both she and her mother should remain in England, and support and protect each other'. When the Prince of Orange arrived at Warwick House, she told him that she was resolved not to leave England, but would 'avail herself of the discretionary power promised her in the contract'. In those circumstances, young Orange, though 'very unhappy', seemed to admit that 'the marriage must be off'. This bore out Charlotte's conviction that 'they meant to play a trick and get her out of England as soon as she should be married'.[24]

Her former suitor refused to tell her father of the rupture in their relations, and attended all the festivities, from dinners in the City to balls to a military review in Hyde Park his pleasure in them apparently undiminished by his broken engagement. Princess Charlotte, however, behaved with great dignity now that her mind was made up. Her letter that evening to the Prince of Orange included the declaration: 'From recent circumstances that have occurred I am fully convinced that my interest is materially connected with that of my mother, and that my residence out of this kingdom would be equally prejudicial to her welfare as to my own.'[25]

When it became known that Princess Charlotte had ended her engagement, and when her motives were revealed, there was much sympathy for both Princesses, and their names were continually 'coupled in the popular applause' which greeted their individual appearances. A projected ball at White's Club was broken off, after some of the members of the Committee vetoed the sending of tickets for the event to the Princess of Wales and others swore they would send all theirs to her; the Prince Regent then declined to attend. Caroline, meanwhile, was 'quite transfixed with astonishment that my daughter at last has resumed her former character of intrepidity and fortitude: ... her father frightens her in every manner possible,' threatening that her character would be lost in the world by her fickleness in breaking off the marriage.[26]

The continued absence of the Regent's wife – and now of his daughter in disgrace – from all the festivities in honour of the allied sovereigns and the peace was repeatedly remarked upon. Brougham and Whitbread had great hopes of sowing further seeds of discontent, and reaping further political harvest. Even as the sovereigns departed, preparations were in train for a series of balls to honour Wellington, who arrived in July from Paris.

Earlier in the month, there had been a fierce debate in the House of Commons about the Princess's predicament, with one Whig asking if Caroline was 'to be content in the cold shade of obscurity and neglect'. Parliament then decided that her income should be increased. Lord Castlereagh, the Foreign Secretary and Leader of the

House of Commons, 'laid upon the table on Wednesday papers relating to the Princess of Wales's pecuniary situation, which were ordered to be referred to a Committee of the Whole House' on the following Monday. That same Wednesday evening, 30 June, the Princess sent to Whitbread, at the Commons, a note which she had received from Castlereagh. He proposed to increase her allowance – on the ground that she intended to travel abroad – from £22,000 to £50,000.[27] It would now be administered by trustees on her behalf rather than by the Regent. This was a splendid opportunity to embarrass the government, and Whitbread debated with Brougham how best, how most magnificently to refuse 'this insidious offer made in so unhandsome a manner'. He sent word the next morning to Connaught Place that later in the day he would bring to the Princess of Wales 'the result of our counsel, in the shape of a letter to the Speaker'.[28]

Judge of the disarray of Whitbread's and Brougham's plans to discredit the government when the Princess of Wales, as she informed Whitbread in answer to his letter of 1 July, decided that 'there are moments in life when every individual is called upon to act for themselves'. To Whitbread's 'infinite surprise', just as he was setting out for Connaught Place, he received the Princess's declaration that she intended to act for herself, and, with it, a copy of a letter she had already sent to Castlereagh, accepting the £50,000 annual provision.[29]

Brougham's 'convulsions ... were very strong' when Whitbread told him at Westminster Hall of the Princess's independent action. He told Creevey he was outraged at 'Mother P bitching the thing so completely – snapping at the cash, and concluding with a civil observation about unwillingness to "impair the Regent's tranquillity"!! et cetera.'[30] Lady Charlotte Lindsay 'burst into tears'; St Leger was 'thunderstruck and mortified to the greatest degree'.[31]

Finally, Whitbread went to the Princess herself, and was received very civilly. He lamented that 'the crisis had just arrived which would have put her in possession of all she wanted ...'. Now the words in 'the last paragraph of her letter [her reference to the Regent's tranquillity] appeared ... to have surrendered everything, and ... would be retorted upon her whenever she wished to assert the rights of her station'.[32]

Caroline, however, replied that she had relinquished nothing, and meant to assert her rights by going to the national thanksgiving service at St Paul's the following week, on 7 July. Brougham approved the Princess's plan for St Paul's, although he typically made it appear his own. 'Though she deserves death, yet we must not abandon her, in case P gets a victory after all. Therefore I have made her send St Leger to the Bishop of Lincoln [who was Dean of St Paul's] to ... demand proper seats for her and her suite.'[33]

When she was informed – by Lord Hertford of all people, who was Lord Chamberlain – that there was 'no place for her' at the national thanksgiving, Brougham wrote joyfully, 'So the game is alive once more. ...' He and Whitbread were to see the Princess that day, 'and get, if possible, a letter or message from her ... setting forth this new indignity, and I trust spurning the money upon such terms. So we shall recover from the scrape she placed us all in. ...'[34]

Brougham designed a most affecting letter to be sent by the Princess to the Speaker,

> in which Mrs P takes the highest ground, saying she had accepted it [the £50,000] in the belief of its being an earnest of a new system of treatment, et cetera, and in order to show her conduct to the P was only because she must vindicate herself, and not arising from any vexatious views. ...
>
> Now she finds she and the offer and all have been wholly misconstrued, and that her conduct has been supposed to proceed from an unworthy compromise; and, in short, throwing up, on the ground of the treatment continuing et cetera. ... This is decisive, I think, and gives us the game again. ...

To ensure that the Princess did his bidding, Brougham wrote her 'a long and very severe epistle' in which he accused her, as he told Creevey, of everything. She was the better for his threats, he found, 'and [his] promises'.[35]

In fact, the Princess paid no attention to Brougham. She took Whitbread's more palatable advice, which was to accept a reduced amount of £35,000 a year, rather than send Brougham's radical letter and lose all her gain. She was anyway reluctant to burden the taxpayer overmuch. Brougham blamed alternately Whitbread and Canning, the latter having advised her to go abroad.[36] The Duke of Brunswick, in response to Caroline's letter of a month before seeking sanctuary at his Court, had cravenly refused to commit himself till he had obtained the Prince Regent's approval. This was given all too readily, and Caroline was able to forge her plans for departure. She sent her new man of business, Mr Moses Hoper, to secure the rental of Sompting Abbey, at Worthing, near where she would embark, and had him also make a list of the pensions he was to pay on her account while she was away.[37] Brougham had failed to make 'Mother P' dance to his tune.

A new scandal had broken out within the damp walls of Warwick House. Miss Cornelia Knight was possessed of no less a 'romantic' idea than that Princess Charlotte should govern her own conduct, and had 'contrived' several visits to her charge from Prince Augustus of Prussia, a well-known womanizer of thirty-five and 'the only black sheep in his family'. Miss Mercer Elphinstone on one occasion found Charlotte and Augustus alone together at Warwick House, and Miss Knight most reluctant to let her interrupt them.[38]

Charlotte had heeded neither Dr Fisher's well-meaning advice at the end of June that she should agree to marry the Prince of Orange at a later date nor Grey's counsel that 'patience and submission ... are, I am persuaded, your best, perhaps your only arms. This is a hard lesson for a person of your Royal Highness's age, and born to such prospects ... ,' he added kindly. 'But resistance would be even less effectual.'[39]

When the Regent heard of these meetings – and there were rumours, too, that Charlotte had gone out in her carriage without a chaperone – he acted swiftly. First, he had his mother privately appoint new ladies for his daughter. Then he had her seek out a 'place of confinement' for Charlotte. She fixed on Cranbourne Lodge, a house in a remote part of Windsor Great Park.[40] When she informed him that it was ready, he summoned his daughter and Miss Knight to Carlton House on 11 July. In her memoirs published in 1861 Miss Knight sought to exculpate herself. The Prince Regent had never come near Warwick House. She had acted night and day in Charlotte's best interests. She had rarely had an evening out. The Duchess of Leeds was negligent of her duties. And so forth.[41] Miss Knight was quite right in her chief complaint, that there had been no one to guide her – but what folly she had committed while neglected! She can hardly have been surprised when on the 12th she was summarily dismissed.

That day the Prince Regent went to his daughter at Warwick House after she had pleaded that a bad knee prevented her from attending on him next door at Carlton House. With no information to the contrary, she assumed that the measures the Prince now announced to her were being taken as a result of her refusal to marry Orange. The Duchess of Leeds, like Lady de Clifford before her, was to be turned off. Lady Ilchester and Lady Rosslyn had been dragooned into service and were to carry off the disgraced young Princess to Cranbourne Lodge. There she was to have no visitors except her grandmother once a week. In the meantime, she was to sleep at Carlton House.

Miss Knight, waiting anxiously below while the conference between father and daughter took place, was scarcely relieved when Princess Charlotte emerged in the late afternoon wild-eyed and crying, 'God Almighty grant me patience!' to some well-meaning remark of Cornelia's. Forgetful of her gammy knee, the girl snatched up a bonnet and rushed from the room; a surprised servant at Connaught Place opened the door some minutes later to discover Charlotte asking for her mother. She had jumped into a hackney carriage in Cockspur Street, promising the driver a sovereign if he hurried.[42]

This dramatic flight lost a little impetus, however, because Caroline was dining at Blackheath. Messengers were dispatched to summon her and Brougham. Charlotte's absence had meanwhile been dis-covered at Warwick House. Cool-headed Mercer had been dressing for dinner there when Charlotte fled, and she and Dr Fisher were sent by the Regent to Connaught Place to try and bring Charlotte to reason.

Brougham arrived – he was reluctant to come at first, thinking it was the Princess of Wales who had summoned him – to find Charlotte. The girl ran to him, seized his hands and exclaimed, 'I have just run off!' Mercer was with her. Dr Fisher had been dispatched with Charlotte's ultimatum to her father, that she would return only when Miss Knight had been reinstated, and Mercer allowed full access to her. Meanwhile Charlotte had ordered dinner. As the Regent hastily summoned his own advisers to discuss the legal position – Dr Fisher was sent back with a statement to Princess Charlotte that her unconditional surrender and return were required – Caroline arrived at Connaught Place with Lady Charlotte Lindsay and joined the dinner party. Princess Charlotte was 'in high spirits', Brougham noted, 'seeming to enjoy herself like a bird set loose from its cage'.[43]

Dr Fisher arrived, closely followed by a team of the Regent's advisers – the Lord Chancellor, Ellenborough (the Chief Justice), Mr William Adam (the Chancellor of the Duchy of Cornwall) and Mr John Leach (the Vice-Chancellor of the Duchy). The committee of diners upstairs decided who should enter the house and who should not. That some of these supplicants had, like Charlotte, come by hackney carriage raised their spirits to a pitch of hilarity, and they affected to believe that all had so journeyed. Only Dr Fisher was allowed into the house, and he had to wait in a room below while they finished dining. The Regent's legal advisers sat impotently in their conveyances outside, for all that they had the might of the law on their side. (Indeed, Ellenborough had with him a writ of habeas corpus, though those inside did not know it.) The Duke of Sussex, however, whom Brougham had summoned, was admitted, and was there to witness Brougham explaining to Charlotte that she must return to her father that night.[44] The Prince Regent, he said, had absolute authority over her until she was twenty-one years old, and she must obey him. Her mother agreed that this was the case.

Wicked Brougham. He wrote that Charlotte 'was affected beyond description. I have told many a client he was going to be convicted, but I never saw anything like her stupefaction.'[45] Brougham and Grey, for their own ends, had encouraged the Princess to think that she was all but independent of her father. And now – condemned to a prison existence – she had acted on that belief, only to find that her adviser now told her the opposite. Small wonder that Princess Charlotte accused Brougham of deserting her, when the people, she claimed, had supported her.

She was also bitterly upset that her mother had not supported her more – but the Princess of Wales was, in her words to Whitbread, 'weary of all the trouble she has endured herself, and been the occasion of to her friends'.[46] Caroline was, in spirit, once more on the Continent, not in the drawing-room of Connaught Place. It was only Brougham who had deluded Princess Charlotte into believing that Caroline would stay in England if her daughter, her chief protector, stayed – and thought of leaving only because her daughter did. As her friend Mr John Ward put it, 'this poor woman . . . it is evident, can never pass one hour of peace and happiness in this island'.[47]

The Duke of York was waiting below – it was three in the morning – to carry Charlotte back to her father. Brougham took her to a window overlooking Cumberland Gate and Hyde Park. Day was breaking. 'I have but to show you to the multitude which in a few hours will fill the streets and that park,' he said. Voting for a by-election was to take place later that morning in Hyde Park:

> And possibly Carlton House will be pulled down, but, in an hour after the soldiers will be called out, blood will flow, and if your Royal Highness lives a hundred years, it will never be forgotten that your running away from your home and your father was the cause of the mischief; and, you may depend upon it, the English people so hate blood that you will never get over it. . . .[48]

These words – curiously prophetic, as we shall see, of another scene at that same gate, though one not involving Princess Charlotte – decided the Princess. She went with her uncle York, after making Brougham draw up a minute stating that she could never willingly marry the Prince of Orange, and that if such a marriage was announced it would be without her consent.[49] On her return to Carlton House, the arrangements for her removal to Cranbourne Lodge were put in hand, and the bird, so recently uncaged, was more confined than ever.

The Whigs, discomfited by the Princess of Wales's intended departure, made a meal of it in the Commons, remonstrating with Lord Castlereagh at the end of July 1814. They had not helped to secure an increased income for the Princess, Tierney said, only for her to quit the country. Castlereagh easily countered this. All he knew was that her Royal Highness had 'signified to one of his Majesty's ministers . . . her Royal Highness's intention to go to the Continent'. (The Princess of Wales had written her formal request to Liverpool on 25 July.) Castlereagh was persuaded, he said, that the House, in voting for the addition to the income of her Royal Highness, had no design of imprisoning her in the country, nor of preventing her from residing wherever her pleasure or convenience might indicate.[50]

Tierney replied, lamely, that the step which her Royal Highness was about to take was against the direct advice of Whitbread and of everyone who had her interests at heart. Brougham, Grey and Tierney still (correctly) suspected Canning of having instigated Caroline's plan for foreign travel,[51] and ignored the explanation, which she gave both publicly and privately, that she had been humiliated and abused by the Regent and his ministers long enough. To quote Ward once more, 'Dear, disinterested patriots! And do they really think that none but a faithless hired adviser could think of persuading this poor woman, to retire to some spot where she may be free of vexation and disappointment?'[52]

Charlotte, who knew nothing of her mother's correspondence with Brunswick, was mortified when she heard that Caroline was to quit England. Furthermore, when Charlotte was allowed to pay a farewell visit to her mother, Caroline took her leave so casually that her daughter was deeply offended. Charlotte wrote that it was impossible to impose maternal feelings where there were none.[53] Yet Caroline was in holiday mood, intent on escaping for a time not her daughter, but all the restrictions, the humiliations, the lonely existence which had so oppressed her spirits. And the Prince Regent asserted, as Liverpool informed her, that he did not wish to 'interfere in any plan which may be formed by your Royal Highness for your present or future residence ...'.[54] Privately, the Regent was said to have toasted her imminent departure, 'To the Princess of Wales's damnation and may she never return to England.'

Accounts in the newspapers of the Princess of Wales's short stay at Sompting Abbey tell of her walking with one of her ladies and attendants to Worthing, where she sat for nearly two hours on the beach: 'The moonbeams danced on the waves, and the pleasure-boats glided at her feet.' At a distance lay at anchor the *Jason* frigate, which, in a few days, was to convey her to her natal shores.[55]

Caroline, Princess of Wales, now forty-six years old, embarked on the *Jason* at Lancing on 8 August 1814, wearing a 'dark cloth pelisse, with large gold clasps, and a cap of velvet and green satin, of the Prussian hussar costume, with a green feather'. The cap was not dissimilar to that which she had worn on her arrival in England twenty years before. Then, Lady Jersey had had her remove it at Greenwich; now, there was no one in the world with authority over her, and it is clear from her correspondence, even before she left England, that Brunswick was to be a springboard for adventure. Conspicuous among her effects was a large tin box marked 'Her Royal Highness The Princess of Wales: To be kept always with her'. Inside was her red-morocco book of memoirs – evidence perhaps that she envisaged some colourful new chapters.[56]

'She is about to take the most important step in her life,' she informed Whitbread. 'No person, possessed of pride and feeling, could endure to be degraded below her rank in this kingdom ... bear to be so hated by the Sovereign, as to be debarred from his presence both in public and in private. The Princess of Wales knows not how to support so much debasement and mortification.' Her fervent wish for her daughter Charlotte was that 'great and powerful as she may be, she will not tyrannize over anyone, because they have not the good fortune to please her'.[57]

But Charlotte was not destined to be 'great and powerful', and Caroline was to bring upon herself fresh 'debasement and mortification', to exceed any that had gone before.

## CHAPTER TWELVE

# THE LONG VOYAGE

## 1814–1817

*'I am like Aladdin . . . with his enchanted lamp about me'*

O N BOARD the *Jason*, the Princess of Wales was at first 'considerably annoyed by the sea', then recovered enough 'to have
danced and been merry'. Captain James King, the ship's commander,
was very attentive, perhaps stimulated by a letter supposedly
written to him by the Duke of Clarence encouraging him to pay
gallantries to the Princess, whose husband, the Duke assured him,
would readily excuse his presumption. Knowing nothing of this, the
Princess desired Mr Moses Hoper to send the Captain a piece of plate
– 'anything pretty' for £80.[1] Lady Charlotte Lindsay was with her till
Brunswick; Lady Elizabeth Forbes was a new lady-in-waiting, an
unknown quantity. On board also were Willy Austin and Edwardine
Kent, that girl of mysterious parentage who had been educated at
Bath.

The gentlemen of the Princess's suite were delighted by the
prospect of travel, and of travel in areas which had been out of bounds
since the wars with France began over twenty years before. Sir
William Gell – his friend Mr Richard Keppel Craven was to join
them at Brunswick – urged the Princess to consider wintering in
Naples. Dr Henry Holland, who had travelled with Gell and Craven
in Greece, had been persuaded by his 'Athens friends' to accompany
the Princess as her medical man. He noted that the route from
Hamburg – which was 'occupied by a swarm of Cossacks' – to
Brunswick was 'a toilsome travel of two days over heavy sands,
through marshy thickets, on roads rudely fashioned'.[2] For Caroline,
it was the route home, and fortunately she had brought her experienced English coachman Charles Hartop in her train, as well as
Sicard, his assistant John Hieronymus and her footman Philip Krackler.

Not only the English were delighted at their newfound ability to roam the Continent. The people of rural Germany were thrilled by their release from French domination, and welcomed the German-born English Princess as the first swallow of a golden new summer. The royal party was received everywhere 'as emperors and grand duchesses are in England', wrote Gell, with reference to Caroline's late exclusion from the peace celebrations in London. 'Nothing would be more splendid than our entry into this place,' he wrote on 18 August 1814 from Brunswick, 'with torches, hussars, artillery and a most numerous mob.'[3]

The Duke of Brunswick greeted his sister with enthusiasm, since the English Government had assured him of its complete acquiescence in the Princess's visit. However, Dr Holland wrote, 'Each manifestly felt the disparity' of character between them. The Princess was 'still under the joyousness of early travel, and not altogether mindful of the wonted proprieties of the place'. As a result, the Brunswick Court was 'a good deal disturbed in its grave decorum'.[4]

The Princess was at first elated by her escape from England – 'We live upon excursions, plays and balls,' wrote Gell[5] – but she found soon enough that the Brunswick Court of 1814 was no more diverting than it had been when she left it twenty years before She described it to a friend as deadly dull, and full of dreary old spinsters. Only six days after her arrival she gave orders for the uniforms she meant her gentlemen to wear to be sent direct to Naples, where she had decided to spend the winter, and she arranged for all the baggage – following on another frigate – to go there also. Meanwhile, she managed to marry off the teenaged Edwardine Kent to one of her brother's aides-de-camp, Captain de Normann. Edwardine later wrote bitterly that the marriage had taken place after an acquaintance of two hours. Gell declared that it was 'a very good sale of a very bad piece of goods' – £200 down and £60 a year was the price paid from the Princess's exchequer.[6]

Further financial business was apparently transacted, according to a document which the Princess was to produce in 1817. This details a loan which she made to her brother of 15,000 louis d'or on 24 August, repayable with interest after three years. No record of it exists in her accounts, or indeed in the Brunswick state papers. It was a transaction of which apparently none besides the Princess and her brother had any cognizance.[7] It seems reasonable to doubt that any loan was made: at this time, Caroline told Sicard that her £5000 advance from the English Treasury was untouched.

While his sister travelled to Italy, the Duke was off to Vienna, for the great Congress of allied powers, set to open on 1 October, where he hoped to win further prizes. Meanwhile, in England Hoper had the unenviable task of turning off most of the Princess's servants at Kensington Palace and Connaught Place. 'The scene I underwent with some of the persons ... was distressing, several of them shed tears,' he wrote to Gell. 'It is but justice to them to remark that they really appeared to me to flow as much from a sense of deep and sincere attachment ... as from a feeling of complaint.'[8]

The royal party set out south, swollen by Keppel Craven and Captain Charles Hesse (Hesse having taken leave of absence from his military duties), two Brunswick country girls and two German menservants. Lady Charlotte Lindsay went off to join her sister and Lord Glenbervie on their way to Coblenz. Keppel Craven sardonically listed the 'triumphs' the Princess enjoyed, as her party wended its way south. Dr Holland noted the Princess's pleasure in the company of Marshal Kellermann at Strasbourg. Kellermann himself was uncomfortably aware, as he hosted a review of 8000 troops for Caroline, that he had defeated her father at Valmy.

'Her knowledge of the events amidst which she had lived as well as of their antecedents was curiously vague and inconsecutive,' Holland noted, 'and the quick succession of places and persons in travelling did not amend this deficiency.'[9] Still, as Lord Glenbervie observed, Caroline's later reference to the sixteenth-century Archbishop of Milan, San Carlo Borromeo, whose statue stood on the shores of Lake Maggiore, as 'Sir Charles Burroughs' was astonishing even by her slipshod standards.

'A word to the wise', Gell would write to Hoper on 15 October from Milan. He enclosed a summary of the different monarchs, empresses and literati who had entertained her Royal Highness in the German states and in Switzerland. 'Make the best use of this you can. I have not time to reduce it to a proper form, so do it in England as it may be very useful'[10] – for publication. He had earlier written from

Geneva, 'We saw and feasted with the Empress Marie Louise at Berne, the Emperor of Austria's daughter [and Napoleon's wife], and also the Grand Duke Constantine [of Russia]'s lady.' Much was made by the English in Switzerland of the curious stroke of fate whereby the victorious Regent's wife lodged side by side at the Hôtel d'Angleterre and sang duets with the defeated Emperor's wife. Nothing was said between them, apparently, of the captive on Elba.

'We have Saussure, Sismondi and other literati to meet Lady Westmorland at dinner today,' Gell wrote after they had reached Geneva.[11] The Princess of Wales was resuming her system of seeing all notables, in whatever field, and she met with few refusals. Everyone was curious to see this vagrant Princess of Wales – except Mme de Staël. As in 1813 in London, she was a lion who avoided capture, declaring she had no wish to consort with the woman who brought shame on the name of England.

'Naples must be a very inconvenient residence for the Princess of Wales . . .', Lord Liverpool protested on 18 September, 'as this country and Naples are not at peace (an armistice only existing at present between them). I should think therefore her Royal Highness would upon reflection take up her residence under present circumstances in the territories of any other sovereign in Italy.'[12]

The Princess of Wales paid no attention. Over the Alps the party progressed, with a new lady's maid, Louise Demont, obtained at Geneva. 'The old London and Dover coach' which housed the servants and baggage, Holland recorded, was 'a whimsical sight . . . with all the old English designations still upon its panels'.[13]

At Milan the Princess was received with all honour by Comte Henri de Bellegarde, the Austrian Governor (Austria had regained its Italian territories), and by his chamberlain, Conte Filippo Ghislieri. Rapturous receptions awaited her in the streets, as well as at La Scala, where she graced the Viceregal box. The people of Milan, under an Austrian yoke again, hoped that the imminent Congress of Vienna would bring a settlement under which the English might be their masters rather than the hated Austrians. High in Caroline's favour too were General Pino, a former officer of the Napoleonic Grand Army, and his wife, the Contessa Calderara Pino, whom she visited on Lake Como. The Contessa's first husband, Conte Calderara, another Napoleonic soldier, had discovered her when she had been a dancer at La Scala. He had settled with her at an enchanting house on the edge of the lake, the Villa Garovo. She had had toy fortifications built on the hill above the villa in imitation of those at Tarragona to surprise her husband when he returned from his siege of the original in Spain. She now lived here with her second husband, and Caroline departed back to Milan with the declared intention of returning to Lake Como the following year.

Before she left Milan, the Princess turned to Ghislieri and his friend Pino for advice. She felt in need of a courier who knew the country and the language and who could arrange lodgings and transport on her journey south. The candidate whom they ordered to present himself at the Palazzo Borromeo where she lodged by the Porta Ticinese was one Bartolomeo Pergami, aged thirty, who had served Pino in the Russian campaign. More recently, he had acted as the Contessa Calderara Pino's courier.

Pergami (or Bergami, as he was sometimes known) was a startlingly handsome man, well over six feet tall, with black curling hair, dark eyes and a splendid physique. According to Pergami's own account, he entered the Princess's lodgings to find nobody in attendance. Wandering through a suite of rooms in search of help, he found a lady struggling vainly to disentangle the skirt of her dress from a piece of furniture. Pergami courteously assisted her and discovered, if he had not guessed it, that this was his prospective employer.[14] The Princess rewarded his gallantry by hiring him forthwith, and Pergami duly rode ahead of the royal entourage to secure a change of horse and lodgings for the party.

The Whigs Lord and Lady Holland and their family had hoped to avoid the Princess of Wales on their travels in Italy, as they had successfully avoided her in London. But in an inn ('a wretched place') outside Loiano on the road to Florence, they found themselves face to face with Caroline after both parties had been forced to take shelter from a storm – 'Wind, rain in torrents and no moon'. A 'dragoon' – possibly Pergami – had entered the inn and announced that the Princess of Wales was approaching. 'With some . . . difficulty,' Lady Holland reported to her sister-in-law, 'I got your brother to go out and propose that she should come and warm herself by the only fire. . . .' Fortunately for these reluctant Samaritans, the Princess behaved 'with great civility and good taste and unaffected good humour'. And on the way down to Florence next day Caroline's doctor was of help with the Hollands' young daughter Mary Fox, who suffered badly from travel sickness. Once in the city Lady Holland retreated: 'I wrote my name at her door here but have avoided as far as I could and hitherto with success being invited to her parties. . . .'[15]

Lord Sligo, a former travelling companion of Byron known to Caroline – he was Sir William Scott's stepson – saw her at Florence. Gell and Keppel Craven, he noted, looked like 'two jack puddings', dressed as they were 'in the most extraordinary costume that can be imagined'. (The strange tabards the Princess had designed for her suite owed, in one critic's view, something to Henri IV and something to the Tower Beefeaters. Caroline's own appearance was now somewhat outré. At Geneva she had bought a heavy black wig, which she wore constantly. In an effort to assimilate her colouring, she drew in a pair of startling black eyebrows. She also rouged up her pale skin.) Sligo, relying on 'malicious people here', had his own ideas about 'the intimacy' between Captain Hesse, who was permitted to wear his hussar uniform, and the Princess. He objected moreover to Willy Austin's presence at the opera with the Princess – 'Now really it was too bad to have that little bastard sitting in front while everyone else was standing up'[16] – and to the presence of Prince Borghese, Princess Pauline Bonaparte's husband.

On 31 October the Princess reached Rome, while the Hollands remained at Florence. The Roman nobility had awaited her arrival with curiosity and sympathy. 'The trial she had to undergo, and still more a work in the form of confessions supposedly written by the Princess herself – a mediocre and fantastic work – which they read with avidity, turned the heads of the Italian ladies,' Baron Ramdohr, the Hanoverian Minister in Rome, reported, referring to Ashe's *Spirit of the Book*.[17] However, even before her arrival, reports of her conduct on the road had done something to abate this enthusiasm.

Her suite were not happy either. They were incensed when they discovered in October that the royal party's luggage had not yet been embarked on the *Clorinde*, the frigate appointed to bring it out to Italy. 'We shall be in great distress for clothes and everything else if this ship does not soon arrive in Italy,' wrote Gell, 'the whole party absolutely counted upon it.'[18] A functionary from the Lord Chamberlain's Office had intervened to remove, from the packages awaiting dispatch at Kensington, eleven cases of Crown plate – 'it having been ascertained', wrote Lord Hertford the Lord Chamberlain, 'by official vouchers, that the plate in question was Crown property'.[19] The King had loaned it in 1808 to his daughter-in-law for her use at Kensington Palace.

Poor Hoper was then forced by his indignant royal client to dispute the matter, with the result that the rest of the baggage was detained. From Milan, Gell warned him to desist: 'We [he meant the Princess] are unfortunately sincere to nobody and we do nothing but make false or half confidences which hamper us in a thousand ways and expose us to a thousand misfortunes ...', he wrote bitterly. 'All the plate belongs to the Crown entirely and even I am afraid we have sold a quantity which was not quite our own. . . . The affair must be given up. . . .'[20] In the event, the *Clorinde* and its baggage, which included everything from clothes and books to harps, did not reach Naples till February 1815, by which time the Princess and a good part of her suite were at daggers drawn.

At Rome, Ramdohr said he had difficulty in recognizing the Princess of Wales, whom he had known before her marriage. She had put on a lot of weight, her complexion had coarsened, while her black wig and eyes and 'her assured expression make her face appear hard, which it was not formerly'. He noted her two favourite casts of expression: 'alternately of studied dignity and of an insouciant nonchalance'. He concluded, 'her toilette is rich but bizarre, and recalls the dress of Guercini's sibyls' (whose tunics often slipped from their shoulders).[21]

Caroline's first visit was to Prince Lucien Bonaparte, of all people, who had retired to Italy after playing a vital role in his brother's 1799 coup. The next evening the banker Signor Pietro Torlonia, whom Napoleon had created Duca di Bracciano, entertained her. 'In short,' observed Sligo, who had followed the Princess to Rome, 'to be Bonaparte's friend or relation appears to be a claim upon her friendship.'[22] The Princess of Wales's hatred of England after this summer of humiliation is well attested. She was hardly better disposed towards the other allied sovereigns than towards the Regent, because they had ignored her in London. What more natural – given her strange, fanciful mind – than that she should conceive herself with Napoleon a victim of the allied powers and show this mysterious fellow-feeling to his family and friends? The enthusiasm of Mr Samuel Whitbread for all things Napoleonic seems to have infected her. In her eyes, she had been a state prisoner in London, as Napoleon now was on Elba. Presumably, just as she had forgotten that Kellermann had defeated her father, she bore no grudge against Napoleon and his family for the death of her father and the rape of her native land.

Anecdotes about the Princess during her stay in Rome multiplied. To the Queen of Spain's consoling remark, 'Never mind, the Regent may die and you can marry again', the Princess was reported to have responded, 'Oh, no, I want to be Queen of England.' On the other hand, when Prince Poniatowski asked her if she intended to return soon to England, she was said to have replied, 'Not before my daughter is queen.'[23] One evening she was dancing with the former King of Holland, Louis Bonaparte. Her diamond crown fell off, she recovered it before it fell to the ground and, quitting the line a moment, with a vivid pantomime gave it to the King who had lost his own. Ramdohr criticized the enormous pleasure she took in dancing, which was as much as anything a reaction to her enforced retirement in London. 'She did not quit her place all evening. Waltzes, contredanses, English, French . . . all executed with pretensions and graces, and with a frivolity hardly fitting her age and figure.'[24]

Caroline saw the Pope on her arrival in the Holy City – and apparently said of this encounter to the inventor Sir Humphry Davy, 'you will see evident symptoms of it in nine months' time'. Ramdohr summed up the Princess's nature ably, given his short exposure to her charms: 'a need for vague activity, a desire for distractions, quite a strong dose of vanity. . . . One understands as easily how the most serious accusations could be lodged against her as how she was able to get so many to leap to her defence.'[25] From now on, Caroline paid less and less attention to her position as Princess of Wales.

Sligo conceded that the Princess had received 'the greatest possible attention from everyone, indeed I doubt whether Marie Louise [Napoleon's empress] in the full plenitude of her husband's power would have met with more civility'.[26] However, the applause they gave, in his opinion, was to 'the credit in which the nation' stood. Dr Holland described the week at Rome as 'one of toil'.[27] Everyone asked, according to Sligo, whether Willy Austin was her son, 'and really from the immense protuberance of her ventre (if such things were possible) I should guess that she were pregnant at this moment'.[28]

For all their delightful qualities, the Princess's suite did not include a single individual who felt able or inclined to warn her about her behaviour. Lady Elizabeth Forbes was unsure of her ground. Lady Charlotte Lindsay had left at Brunswick. Dr Holland did not consider it part of his medical duties to diagnose or remedy his patient's eccentricities of behaviour. Gell and Keppel Craven contented themselves with writing accounts home of her unseemly activities. Captain Hesse, far from warning Caroline about her misconduct, abetted it.

Gone were the restraints of ladies like Lady Townshend or the outspoken Miss Hayman, who had felt moved to speak out. Gell and Keppel Craven were no more moralists than the Princess herself. They wished only to enjoy themselves with their antiquarian friends at Rome, and they looked forward to Naples, the next stop, which they saw as an enchanted city. They regarded their attendance at the endless stuffy receptions and assemblies which their duties as the Princess's chamberlains imposed upon them, and their ridiculous costumes, as quite enough to complain about, and were both far too European in character to worry about the resonances of the Princess's behaviour in England.

Mr Henry Brougham in England was still furious about what he regarded as the Princess's betrayal of his interests and was concentrating his wiles on her zealously Whig daughter Princess Charlotte. He regarded the Princess of Wales as a lost cause from the Whigs' standpoint. Moreover, he was still out of Parliament, having failed to secure the Lonsdale nomination, and was occupied with attempts to find a seat through another patron.

The Prince Regent in England was privately reluctant to restrain his errant wife's behaviour. Though it might not redound to the nation's credit, he wished it to continue, and to a point where he would be entitled, even obliged, to call for a divorce. Ramdohr sent his report to Count Ernst von Münster, the Hanoverian Minister in London and the son of Caroline's old governess in Brunswick. Like Münster, Prince Metternich in Vienna, Cardinal Consalvi in Rome and the other chief ministers of Europe received daily reports from police spies in their own territories, and from diplomats and ministers in the different cities of Italy, Switzerland and Germany not under their sway. Along with information about suspicious characters, and about crimes of passion and politics, these now included surveillance reports of that distinguished personage, the Princess of Wales. Eager to please the Prince Regent and to bring him into closer alliance with their masters' absolutist regimes, Consalvi forwarded the reports concerning the Princess to the Foreign Secretary in London, and Metternich gave his to Castlereagh's brother Lord Stewart, British Ambassador to Vienna. They soon discovered that their access to information on the Princess's misconduct enabled them to entice the Regent into greater co-operation. To Metternich and Consalvi, the Regent wrote those magniloquent letters which were his speciality, praising them for the care they were taking to protect the good name of England, and pressing them on to further endeavours.

Brooding on the matter, and not after all content with the European powers' efforts on his behalf, the Regent decided to take action himself – and how better than in his guise as Regent of Hanover, with Count Münster as his deputy? Fortunately, under the terms of the Peace of Paris, the Regent's brother Dolly (Adolphus, Duke of Cambridge) acted as governor, supported by a council of three ministers. In effect, at Hanover not only did the United Kingdom have a very useful source of income, the Regent also had what amounted to a private bureaucracy of whose doings the English Parliament remained largely unaware. It was a connection which he now decided to exploit.

The matter of the Princess's movements, meanwhile, was still agitating Lord Liverpool and other members of the English Government. War might break out at any time, and the Congress of Vienna, now assembling, had yet to decide the fate of Naples. Wellington, the new English Ambassador in Paris, fulminated against Caroline's folly in going to Naples,[29] but the Princess of Wales had the Government over a barrel. Short of summoning her back to England – and they had only just got rid of her – they were powerless to restrict her movements. Or rather, if they cut off her money supply, they could be sure she would come haring back to harass them, and promulgate her woes. Caroline, not a whit alarmed, proceeded on her way south. It is remarkable that the Government had failed to anticipate the headstrong Princess's wish to travel further afield than Brunswick. In the delicate state of affairs which still obtained – with the coming Congress crucial for England as well as for the other states of Europe, with new alliances being forged and boundaries drawn – the English ministers' want of foresight might well prove calamitous. The royal husband, a latter-day Pontius Pilate, had eschewed all jurisdiction over his wife, and the royal wife herself, Caroline, Princess of Wales, the most carefully closeted female under the laws of England, assault on whose body was high treason, had escaped from under the net and had attained perhaps the greatest liberty which any English woman enjoyed.

Without the knowledge of his Cabinet, although Castlereagh was privy to the deed, the Regent ordered his Hanoverian Minister, Count Münster, to appoint an individual to proceed to Italy, there to fulfil a double mission. The appointee was to survey the state of Italy, with special reference to sedition and dissenting factions, and, secondly, he was to survey the conduct of the Princess of Wales, reporting fully on both points to Münster. Münster's choice fell on a former Hanoverian chamberlain, Baron Friedrich Ompteda, whom Münster apprised on 25 October – while Caroline was still on the road to Rome – of his opportunity to 'give proof to the Prince Regent of Great Britain and Hanover of his zeal and devotion'.[30]

Ompteda's second objective, to 'obtain exact information on the conduct of the Princess of Wales' in Italy, required

> the greatest prudence and discretion. The Prince Regent is far from wishing to place any obstacle in the way of the Princess of Wales and her contentment. Separated from her by an Act sanctioned by his father the King, his Royal Highness allows the Princess full liberty to live wherever she pleases. But his Royal Highness owes it to himself and his people that a Princess who bears his name should do nothing which derogates from his dignity ... and that the rumours about her

conduct, and surmises which may be bred of mere malevolence, should be clarified.

Münster's instructions continued, 'The Baron is to approach as near as he can to the Princess, and write an exact account of her conduct. If that conduct is not as it ought to be, it is extremely important to obtain sufficient proofs to legitimate the fact.... In pursuit of this end naturally Baron Ompteda is authorized to employ all honest means thereto – given that this is with moderation and discretion.'

The Princess of Wales and her suite were met at the frontier of the Kingdom of Naples by a guard of honour, and at Terracina King Joachim Murat himself appeared, resplendent in military uniform, with a corps of Neapolitan officers at his back to escort Caroline into the city. The elaborate reception afforded by Murat to the Princess was no more disinterested than had been the court paid to her at Milan. Murat hoped, somewhat naively, that his attentions to Caroline would be reflected in a favourable view of his claim to the Kingdom of Naples being taken by Castlereagh among other ministers at Vienna. He was dashing beyond description, so perhaps it was for propriety's sake that the Princess insisted on twelve-year-old Willy's presence in the gala carriage with herself and the King.[31] A fearless cavalry officer, Murat looked impressive even seated. Like some figure from Versailles, he sported a long curling wig, black as Caroline's own. (She fancied that she resembled him.)

Without many brains inside his bewigged head, Murat was affable in conversation, courtly to ladies and possessed of a strong sense of self-preservation, if not of animal cunning. He was in appearance a character from *opera buffa*, a sort of pasteboard king – just like the Bourbon Ferdinando IV before him. In consequence, always ready to indulge the Neapolitans' passion for display and festivities, he was immensely popular.

The Princess had rented apartments in advance in the Villa Maresche, one of a row of commodious houses on the Riviera di Chiaia, which looked on the Bay of Naples across a strip of public gardens planted with palm trees. The house had a salon facing the seafront and promenade, a terrace and large secluded garden at the back behind the dining-room. Caroline was well content at first, and wrote of Naples 'that it was a Paradise', and 'The King and Queen are quite delightful people and quite adored by this nation. I shall soon be very rich. . . . Naples is a place without expenses at all.'[32]

Caroline's gay sentiments obscured a development whose consequences were to be as tumultuous for her country as they were to be fatal for the Princess herself. Her newfound contentment owed much to the closer attentions of Bartolomeo Pergami. There can be no doubt that this former quartermaster, now her servant, became her lover, ousting Captain Hesse. Sixteen years her junior, he was following in Sapio's footsteps. It was later suggested that the night of their arrival in Naples was the first they spent together. She returned early that evening from the opera displaying clear signs of anticipation, and rose late the next day. For the first time, Willy Austin did not sleep in her room, and the Princess gave orders that Pergami should occupy a chamber near hers, ostensibly to protect her from robbers – a need which seems not to have struck her before.[33]

'Although he is a very good sort of person in some respects he is as mad as a March hare in others,' Gell wrote of 'Hat Vaughan',* the alias he employed for his Royal mistress.[34] He and Keppel Craven moved out of the cramped apartments to which they had been appointed following the game of musical bedrooms at the Villa Maresche and rented rooms near by – where they kept a kettle permanently on the hob for other English who wished to drop in. Lady Elizabeth Forbes was one of their most frequent visitors.

The invitations which the King and Queen showered on the Princess of Wales delighted their recipient, but not her chamberlains or Lady Elizabeth. Dr Holland was pressed into service as an additional escort when Gell and Keppel Craven kept out of the way. One evening the Princess went off to a masquerade at the San Carlo Opera House with her Swiss maid, Louise Demont, and the courier Pergami.

The Princess of Wales was too busy with her hero-worship of King Joachim Murat to care whether her suite were fulfilling their duties or not. 'He was raped by the Princess, it is impossible to find another word to describe the excess of her extravagance,' wrote Baron

---

* The original 'Hat' Vaughan was Mr J. T. Vaughan, a convivial member of Brooks's.

Ompteda in one of his reports.[35] Dr Holland put it differently: 'The four months we passed in Naples – the closing period of his reign – were coloured in every way by the personal character of the man. It was a time of continuous fête and revelry.'[36]

Queen Caroline Murat, Napoleon's sister, was a more complex character, and bore the Princess of Wales's passion for her husband with a calm bordering on indifference. The Princess nonetheless extended her enthusiasm to the Queen, writing to England for fifty bottles of Colley's Chemical Cream – at a guinea each – to be dispatched 'for the Queen of Naples'.[37]

Although the Queen of Naples was prepared to entertain the peculiar English Princess, she was reluctant for her daughters to be over-exposed to her, according to Princess Louise Murat, the eldest. However, at a shooting party in the Neapolitan woods, the Queen was taken ill with a headache and accepted the Princess of Wales's offer to take the girls into her carriage. Princess Louise believed that Caroline was more pathetically pleased with this mark of favour than with any of the lavish receptions afforded to her at Court.[38] Louise was a year or two younger than Princess Charlotte, and it is not difficult to guess why the Princess of Wales enjoyed her company and that of her sisters.

Miss Catherine Davies, their English governess, took more kindly than their mother to the Princess of Wales. Caroline, with her usual curiosity and lack of form, singled out the English governess at Court as her 'compatriot'. Miss Davies must come to her apartments, said the Princess, where an English clergyman, the Abbé Taylor, held a Protestant service each Sunday.[39] (It does seem typical of the Princess's judgment that this venerable cleric should subsequently have been imprisoned in England for sodomy.)[40]

But it was not long before her growing tendency to lounge around at home with Pergami led to resentment among the Murats after her failure on occasion to attend Court functions in her honour. Members of her suite were no less antagonized as Pergami began to usurp the functions not only of the steward Sicard but also of the chamberlains. Now that they were settled in Naples, Pergami's duties as courier were extinguished. Exploiting his subsidiary role as interpreter, he displayed considerable skill in finding work for his idle hands and so rendering himself indispensable. Even when she dined alone with Willy Austin, Pergami waited at table. 'We enjoy one of the finest cities, climates ... and societies the world produces,' wrote Gell philosophically, 'and it is not my fault if all the world is not happy. ... he [Hat Vaughan] is very much liked here by the people of the city and might do very well. ...'[41]

Lord Sligo, seizing the opportunity to further a diplomatic career, had followed the Princess of Wales to Naples, from where he wrote to Lord Lowther, a Lord of the Treasury, suggesting that he should send reports on her conduct to England for the Prince Regent and Lord Castlereagh. (He had hopes of becoming English minister in Naples when, as seemed probable, Naples was taken from the Murats and restored to the Bourbons.) After receiving a cautious reply in the affirmative, Sligo bombarded Lowther with information: Queen Caroline Murat had by her bed a copy of the Princess's supposed confessions, Ashe's *Spirit of the Book*. Caroline of England had told Caroline of Naples that her husband the Prince Regent was fit company only for gamblers and grooms. But Sligo was more enthusiastic than able as an informant. He described Murat as a 'most capital sort of fellow' and committed his choicest gossip to paper in 'lemon juice'. While Baron Ompteda was hotfooting it to Naples, Sligo wrote, 'Her conduct has been so strange that there is already a great coolness between her and the Court and it will very soon be a downright quarrel.'[42]

Sligo boasted that he had a 'prime channel' in the Queen. His first suspicions, that Hesse was Caroline's favourite, faded: 'I don't know who is rogering the Princess now.' Then his own courier told him that Bartolomeo Pergami has a 'good place'. He was remarkably handsome, six foot three and had suddenly become rather rich. 'In short I think it very likely that he does the job for her.' On 16 December Sligo had further news: 'The courier's room is next to hers ... he never now goes to the bawdy house. ...' By now Pergami had been promoted to equerry and, Sligo noted, 'he always rides by the side of her carriage when she drives out in a most superb hussar's dress'.[43] Gell and Keppel Craven noted disloyally that Pergami's and the Princess's rooms both had windows giving on to the terrace which ran the width of the house.[44]

To Sligo's astonishment, the Princess of Wales sent for him in December. She was in tears, having heard that the Regent was beginning divorce proceedings against her. She had had no letters from Charlotte since she had left Brunswick She would appeal to the people of England. Sligo believed that he was on the point of constructing an arrangement, where all others had failed, between Princess and Regent, and he wrote accordingly – and excitedly – to his stepfather Sir William Scott.[45]

The Princess had no sooner spoken of an 'arrangement', whatever it may have been, than she forgot it. Her spirit was up again, and her relations with the Murats improved. On New Year's Eve she gave a ball to the King and Queen and 300 others, in the royal casino on the seashore at Chiatamonte. The gardens were illuminated, then further lit up by a fireworks display. One room was set aside as a Temple of Glory, with a bust of Murat presiding. The Princess of Wales, dressed as Fame, crowned the bust with laurel, while a Muse of History and other lesser divinities traced the letters 'Joachim Napoleon'.[46]

On 22 January 1815, the Princess wrote further to Liverpool, threatening an early return to England and demanding to know who was the source of the rumour about a divorce and 'what new grounds could be made out'. Hoper told her after taking Brougham's counsel: 'he attaches but little importance to the attempt of . . . a divorce'.[47] However, these rumours had their effect. 'The repugnance to returning to England is quite gone off,' Gell noted.[48] The Princess was well aware that, in her agent Hoper's words, 'all the world is mutable and even John Bull . . . might half forget this august and injured Princess if she forgot to return for a long period to old England'.[49] In fact, the Princess of Wales demanded a frigate in February to take her back to London, or possibly to the north of Italy, where she also – and contradictorily – thought of summering on Lake Como. Liverpool, in England, and Murat – supposedly on a 'hint' from Sligo – refused her.[50]

Ompteda pursued his investigations, while his quarry continued to make a spectacle of herself. During the Carnival in February, a Neapolitan diarist observed, the Princess played the merry devil and threw confetti with abandon from her coach in the Toledo, the wide main street of Naples. Her dress, Ompteda complained, was often improper – the diarist reported that she went as an 'immodest Sultana' to a masked ball. Ompteda was, however, initially dismayed to hear that 'the man in question [Pergami], following his campaigns in Russia, underwent different operations ... and is wholly deprived of the means of satisfying a woman'. He would try to get 'an ocular inspection'.[51] Eventually Ompteda had no real doubts about their affair, but he had no proof. On 1 March he rebutted in the most formal manner his earlier assertion that the Princess's conduct was 'exempt from any reproach, if remarkable for extravagance'. He now declared, 'She is the talk of the Court and town. . . . Her unguarded conduct, especially towards men, exposes her to scandalous suspicions ... in a town where chastity has never had much of a ministry.'[52]

As if in confirmation, Gell had written to Hoper on 4 February, 'Your friend Vaughan is very unruly,' and forecast her 'running headlong into ruin'. Not only had the Princess paid for three extra months the rent of the house she now planned to quit – she had decided to summer on Lake Como – and paid for liveries of servants who were shortly to be turned off, she was also 'throwing away the money in other and of course less respectable channels now in agitation and God knows what will be the end'. As long as 'hope is left', he and Keppel Craven would not abandon attempts to keep things in order.[53]

Four days later Gell resigned his post as chamberlain. The Princess had written in December 1814, 'the cheapness of Naples is certainly true but ... the Princess has very extravagant gentlemen at her Court who make most exorbitant demands ...'.[54] This was not the quirky creature who had entertained them at Kensington Palace and made them laugh with her malapropisms and enthusiastic misunderstanding of their scholarly projects. The Princess now complained of their extravagance, sending poor Sicard to question the cost of a new suit of clothes for Keppel Craven, berating them for the high rent of their rooms. That same month, Sicard wrote to Hoper, telling him no longer to address all correspondence for the Princess to Gell but care of the banker at Naples, M. Falconnet. Things 'have strangely altered', he hinted darkly.[55]

In the next ten days it was settled that Gell should remain at Naples for his health – and he was indeed a martyr to gout – and Keppel

Craven too, who intended later to join his mother the Margravine of Anspach. The Princess and Lady Elizabeth Forbes had long since agreed not to prolong their acquaintance, and Lady Charlotte Lindsay was on her way from Germany to Naples – but only to act as an escort for the Princess's journey northwards.

The Princess's lust for independence was astonishing. In Gell's considered opinion, 'his [Hat Vaughan's] wish was to jockey all his friends and show the world he could walk alone without falling into the fire'.[56] Only her assistant steward Hieronymus remained with her of a household which had been twenty years together. John Sicard left Naples to attend to business in London. She expected him to join her with his wife and family later in the year, but Pergami, as the Italian speaker, had already supplanted him. Various of the Princess's English servants had returned to London. Philip Krackler and his pregnant wife had left at Geneva. As the time of the Princess's departure neared, it became apparent that her Brunswick maid Annette Presinger would have to be left at Naples, as that country innocent was also pregnant. (The Princess's Swiss maid Demont arranged for her sister in Lausanne to join them in the north.) Two menservants acquired at Brunswick were now returning there, and, in their place, Pergami recommended two fellows with whom he had struck up acquaintance at Naples. Moritz or Maurice Crede was taken on as *ecuyer*, or head of stables. Teodoro Majocchi, big and burly and formerly employed in Murat's stables, joined the indoor establishment under Pergami's direction. For the courier, in the course of his usurpation, was on his way to becoming the Princess's equerry and was dressed in a new costume to stress his position. Ompteda sent to Münster charming watercolours of the upstart courier resplendent in his different dresses in saloons and on the seafront.[57]

Despite the bold show, the Princess was well aware that she would lose considerable esteem in the world's eyes if she did not have a suite of English ladies and gentlemen to support her dignity. She therefore wrote to Lady Charlotte Campbell, asking her to join her at Milan. She made the same request of her old protégé, her London page's son, now a lieutenant in the navy, Mr Joseph Hownam.

In the midst of these preparations, on 5 March, the Princess of Wales attended a ball given by the Finance Minister, Count Mosbourg.

'That vague whisper which often precedes an event close at hand' began to circulate the ballroom. For, among the guests, to their astonishment, was Napoleon's mistress, the Countess Walewska, recently arrived from Elba. At eleven o'clock, while the King and Queen were engaged in the figures of an English country dance, Count Mosbourg was summoned from the room. He returned to whisper in Murat's ear, whereupon they left the ballroom together. Seven days before, Napoleon had escaped from Elba.[58]

Napoleon had sailed to Nice, where he promptly declared himself Emperor once more and called all Frenchmen to rally to his standard. He was soon gaining support daily, and an allied army was hastily formed to defend the restored Bourbon monarchy against him. The Congress of Vienna, though depleted by the hasty departure of the army commanders, was nonetheless carried forward by its own bureaucratic momentum, as the diplomats continued with their drafting of the Final Act. Naples was in an uproar, and Hesse abandoned his idle life to return to his regiment. The Princess of Wales gleefully hinted to all who would listen that the Murats had made her privy to the secret of the Emperor's approaching escape. Ompteda was among the few who took this claim seriously, and he devoted hours of his time and pages of his lengthy reports to the unlikely hypothesis that Princess Caroline had in some way instigated Napoleon's escape.

Lord Sligo had paid a visit to Elba in the previous autumn. 'From what I made out I have no doubt that Napoleon will make another attempt whenever he has an opportunity.' Sligo was privileged during his visit to catch a glimpse of 'the Emperor as he was returning from his drive. He was in a little yellow phaeton drawn by four grey ponies with two postillions. He was dressed in a green uniform with epaulettes and faced literally with snuff. He is very like the engraving ... only fatter a good deal. ... he appears to be very popular here. He saluted everyone of those who took off their hats to him.'[59]

The Murats had certainly known privately of the project for escape and had heard of its accomplishment a matter of days before the news became public knowledge. Napoleon counted on their support in his venture. The Princess of Wales was the last person to whom they would have confided the news, on grounds both of her English ties and of her personal indiscretion. The Murats were anyway far too busy fighting between themselves about what to do, as the Hundred Days wore on – Caroline Murat was all for sending Neapolitan troops immediately to her brother's aid, Joachim Murat counselled caution. The march might end in Napoleon's defeat, for which they would have sacrificed a kingdom. They wavered to and fro – if privately – increasingly inimical to each other, while the English in Naples expected them any day to declare for Napoleon.

The English Government understandably felt aggrieved that its doubts about the advisability of Naples as her Royal Highness's residence had proved justified. However, it could not risk the capture and imprisonment of the Princess of Wales's person, and a frigate, the *Clorinde*, was sent to Civitavecchia, with Captain Samuel Pechell in command, with orders to embark the Princess immediately.

Lady Charlotte Lindsay arrived to take a temporary grip on the Princess's affairs. Till now Caroline had recommended Lady Elizabeth Forbes to dine with Gell and Keppel Craven, and she told the newcomer, 'She thought her attendants preferred being by themselves.' Manfully Lady Charlotte dined with the Princess and Willy, and the courier waited on them.[60]

Even under the threat of becoming French prisoners, Gell, Keppel Craven and Lady Elizabeth declined to accompany the Princess, preferring to take their chance with the fortunes of Naples. The Princess of Wales and Lady Charlotte were driven to Rome and then to Civitavecchia, where in mid-March they boarded the *Clorinde*.

Typically, Caroline regretted not at all what she left behind her, and looked forward to the delights of Genoa and the north that awaited her. She was glad to leave Naples. Her one irritation on board was that Captain Pechell gave her 'only half of the cabin, with only a green baize partition between him and her [Royal Highness]'. This 'want of accommodation led to a shyness between them'. Pechell's brother also annoyed the Princess by practising the flute all day long in the Captain's half. When a shipboard dance was prepared and the officers and ladies stood up, the numbers proved to be insufficient. The Princess thereupon ordered Louise Demont and Pergami to join in. But Captain Pechell, offended by the servants' participation, stopped the music.[61] Possibly he was anyway out of temper, for it was he who had been detained by the lengthy plate dispute in England. Lady Charlotte Lindsay observed later that it was 'not unusual in England for the upper servants to join to make up a dance', and Pergami was 'much in the confidence' of her Royal Highness.[62]

Caroline was 'very happy to be out of Naples', she informed Miss Hayman from the *Clorinde*, 'which I hate dreadfully, the locale is certainly beautiful and that I enjoy much but ... the sham Court it was such ludicrous appearance for a real Princess of Wales that I thought the whole time I was in fairy land. Thank to heaven my illusion is gone and I am no longer under the influence of ... a Syrien [siren] or perhaps the devil ...'. On the matter of her troubles with her suite she preserved 'a profound silence'. Sicard would tell all. 'I am now just opposite the lion's den the island of Elba, and Corsica,' she wrote zestfully.[63]

The Princess was surprised to find the Glenbervies at Genoa – and in a most agitated case. They had escaped a few days earlier from Nice, where Napoleonic enthusiasm was at fever pitch. Lady Glenbervie's health was in tatters, but she and her gregarious lord rallied themselves to greet the Princess. Appreciating at once her plight in having no English attendants of rank, if secretly sympathizing with her deserters, they agreed to act informally as her lady-in-waiting and chamberlain during her stay at Genoa. The Princess rented from the Durazzo family the Palazzo Scogliette, an imposing edifice outside the walls on the western side of the merchant city. She soon declared Genoa to be a paradise, which she had formerly believed Naples to be. 'I am like Aladdin', she wrote to Gell, 'sitting in his beautiful palace with his enchanted lamp about me, namely Lord and Lady Glenbervie.... The situation is the most enviable in the world as it is close to the sea with a most charming wood at the back.'[64] Perhaps the Princess would settle there, despite Gell's prophecy that 'we shall be condemned to traverse all Italy ... in search of a better place ...' and then return to Naples by default.[65] She rode a donkey every day and had sent the *Clorinde* to fetch Lady Charlotte Campbell, who was stranded, unable to afford the fare, at Nice with her many children and governess. The party, the Princess felt, was now complete. After all, the principal constituents of her suite appeared to be those of her establishment at Kensington Palace. And she hoped that Lady Charlotte and the Glenbervies would accompany her to Milan in May.

The Glenbervies declined at once on grounds of age and health. Lady Charlotte accepted, then changed her mind after she had been jolted up and down along remote roads to ramshackle farmhouses as companion to the Princess, who spoke of her wish to live a secluded life at Genoa. There could be no more delightful residence than the Palazzo Scogliette. Lady Charlotte confided to a correspondent that she fancied the wish for seclusion was not unconnected with her predilection for 'The Man'. He had made himself even more popular by affecting one night in the garden to save the Princess from ruffians who were no more real than the rogues in buckram suits who fell upon Falstaff at Gadshill.[66]

A description of the phaeton in which the Princess was carried through the streets of Genoa marks the high point of her – not unsuccessful – attempt to make England a laughing-stock abroad. (Apparently Murat gave her this vehicle in return for the Dover mail coach.) A child dressed up as an operetta cupid in flesh-coloured tights led two tiny pied horses, which drew an illuminated phaeton made in the form of a conch shell, decorated with mother of pearl. Within sat a vast woman of fiftyish, short, round and high in colour, wrapped in a gauzy *décolleté* gown with a pink bodice. The pink feathers of her headdress floated in the wind, and a short white skirt came to scarcely past her knees, leaving on view fat pink legs. At her side perched Willy Austin, whom everyone in Genoa believed to be her son. She increased their suspicions on purpose by referring to him as the little Prince. This procession was preceded by a great handsome brute on horseback – Pergami – dressed exactly like King Murat, whom he attempted to imitate in gesture and manner.[67]

At Milan in mid-May the Princess found her old friends the Governor Bellegarde and his chamberlain Ghislieri. Lady Charlotte Campbell did her best to find a lady-in-waiting to succeed her when she left in June. She herself was promised to Mrs Damer at Nice, if the outcome of the war now threatening in France was satisfactory. 'If Italy goes to the dogs', the Princess of Wales thought of visiting Canning, newly appointed minister to Portugal.[68] There were few enough Englishwomen in Milan, let alone Italy, free to wander in the Princess's wake. By a happy chance, Lady Charlotte, according to her diary, discovered a Miss M—, probably Lord Montgomerie's daughter, impecunious and reluctant to return to England. The lady addressed a letter to the Princess, who forbore to reply to it, raising the objection that she had never cared for Miss M—. The diary has the entry: 'When this was her chance for salvation, so foolishly to dismiss it.' This much is true. Lady Oxford did recommend a French lady in September, hearing that the Princess was without attendants – and got a sharp reply: the Princess was very well attended.[69]

In fact, the Princess had her own ideas on what would suit. She wrote to Hoper to announce that she had been 'obliged to take a Milanese countess as her lady of the bedchamber'.[70] To another correspondent she announced Contessa Oldi to be a Venetian noble-woman. This lady's name before marriage proved to have been Angelica Pergami, sister of Bartolomeo. Her husband belonged to an ancient Cremascan family and, fallen upon hard times, he made a living as an innkeeper. The reference to Venice might reflect the Venetian origins of the Pergamis' mother, a Foresti by birth.

The Contessa Oldi was not blessed with her brother's good looks. Her portraits show a sheeplike countenance and a foolish smile, crowned by incongruously girlish ringlets. Accounts of her personality show that in this case the outer was a mirror of her soul. The Princess herself was said to refer to the Contessa as the 'dumb woman'.[71] As a companion, she was far from perfect, for she spoke no English or French. Her speech, when speak she did, revealed her provincial origins, for it was heavily tinged with the Lombard accent so unacceptable in polite Milanese society. Nevertheless the Princess lauded her to all her correspondents.

Louise Demont, her Swiss maid, a pretty, black-haired girl, was more a lady-in-waiting to the Princess than was the Contessa Oldi. 'She is quite a treasure to me,' the Princess wrote of Demont, 'always good spirited and ready to do everything for me as she makes even my gown.'[72] Demont and her sister Mariette Brun also acted in Contessa Oldi's place as secretaries. (The Swiss maid later declared that she never saw the Contessa with a pen in her hand, and had suspicions that she was illiterate.)[73] Fortunately Caroline's protégé

Mr Joseph Hownam came out as bidden from England and could conduct the English correspondence with her bankers and advisers.

Ompteda hinted darkly that her wish, ever since the advent of Pergami, had been to dispense with the vigilance of an English suite. It was more that she had found new interests in her own life and had become less inclined to indulge the whims of Gell and Keppel Craven. Her behaviour was now guided less than ever by the demands of English Society. She was no longer occupied with the politicking which had directed her appearance in England. If her conduct was not markedly German either, the Princess thought she had acquired a new personality in Italy. Certainly she was under a spell in that country, but it was a spell of energetic self-indulgence.

There was no stopping the Princess's appetite for travel. 'I arrived with thunder and lightning at eleven o'clock the night at Venice in a fine ornamental barge,' she wrote after a month at Milan. Then she undertook a tour of funerary sculpture. At Ferrara she saw the tomb of Ariosto, 'the tomb of all my dear ancestors of the noble [Guelph] family of Este and even the famous Princess Beatrice [Blessed Beatrix II of Este], who now still does much wonders at the superb church of St Antonia'. At Bologna she met Abbé Mezzofanti, the celebrated librarian who spoke forty-six languages. At Ravenna she inspected Dante's sepulchre.[74] Four months later she wrote of another tour recently completed: 'I have been to see all the lakes in Switzerland. . . . I was absent about three weeks and since that time I have travelled all over Lombardy – un voyage pittoresque!'[75]

All this time, however, the Princess of Wales had been pursuing a plan to purchase the Countess Calderara Piro's house on Lake Como, the Villa Garovo. Pergami's domestic virtues – he was a practical man who could equally order a dinner at an inn and administer a household – proved invaluable in this project. While this transaction was in train, Brougham, at last returned to the House of Commons as MP for Winchelsea, was addressing her sternly on her financial affairs. Mr Samuel Whitbread's recent suicide had left him in the position of her principal trustee (for the administering of her Parliamentary annuity), and it was his painful duty to inform her that she was in serious danger of going bankrupt. In March Hope had written, 'most unfortunately I know the Princess herself has drawn rapidly and heavily' on her Coutts account.[76] Brougham beseeched her to sign a power of attorney, which he enclosed, enabling him in London to untangle her troubled affairs. Coutts were refusing to advance any further sums, and he exhorted her to spend no more than £6000 a quarter.[77] The Princess of Wales did not sign the power of attorney, and, far from limiting her expenditure to the sum Brougham named, she signed the treaty of sale for the Villa Garovo on 16 July 1815.[78]

While the documentation was being prepared by notaries, the Princess had moved with her caravanserai into the Rotonda, or Villa Villani, on the outskirts of Como. The notables of that town, including Count Alessandro Volta, the discoverer of electricity, flocked to her salon as the notables of Blackheath and its environs had to Montague House.

Baron Ompteda visited the Villa Villani from Milan with such regularity that he was given a room of his own, and naturally furnished full particulars of the Princess's visitors and their characters to Münster. He observed that the Princess relied greatly on the courier, who now directed the household. There were, however, to Ompteda's chagrin, no outward signs to show that intimacy existed between them. He repeated his mournful dirge: the only way to get evidence of an improper relationship between them was to force the royal bedroom door. Leaving aside the scandal that would ensue if this was done, Ompteda reported that Pergami had such a reputation for strength, credited as he was with nigh superhuman powers by all who knew him, that it would be difficult to find anyone to act against him.[79]

The Princess was still at the Villa Villani when news came of the final days of Napoleon's bid to regain power, as the allied armies clashed with the French in the farming districts outside Brussels. Fanny Burney, Mme d'Arblay, was in that city on her way back from the post office when she heard a clatter of a thousand hoofs and the clash of armour, the heavy rumbling of guns being dragged over cobbles. Turning, she saw a sight which struck fear into her heart – a death-black corps of riders, with silver death's-head and crossbones flashing on their shakos. When the ghostly band had passed by, Mme d'Arblay ascertained that she had seen the Black Brunswickers, with the Duke at their head, riding through the city.[80] The Duke fell later that day, 16 June, at the Battle of Quatre-Bras. His courage and his family military record were to be recalled by Lord Byron in his roll-call of the dead on the Belgian plain. 'There was a sound', the poet recounts, 'of revelry by night', suddenly disturbed by distant cannon-fire:

> Within a window'd niche of that high hall
>> Sate Brunswick's fated chieftain; he did hear
>> That sound the first amidst the festival,
>> And caught its tone with Death's prophetic ear;
>> And when they smiled because he deem'd it near,
>> His heart more truly knew that peal too well
>> Which stretch'd his father on a bloody bier,
>> And roused the vengeance blood alone could quell;
> He rush'd into the field, and, foremost fighting, fell.[81]

The Duke of Brunswick's name appears often in the sorrowful letters written home by British survivors. He was to be the last of his line to die in battle. Arrangements were made for his young sons in London to proceed to Brunswick, where the Duke's body was brought home to join those of his father, his uncle Ferdinand and that earlier warrior Henry the Lion in the cathedral crypt.

On 18 June, the great struggle for European hegemony was concluded on the fields of Waterloo outside Brussels. There Wellington, in command of British, Dutch, Belgian and German troops, crucially supported by Blücher's Prussians, routed the French army. A few days later Napoleon surrendered to the British, and soon afterwards he began his final exile on the island of St Helena in the South Atlantic. Britain's pre-eminence in Europe was now unchallenged, and the Final Act of the Congress of Vienna, although completed on 9 June, nine days before Waterloo, was signed on the 19th, duly rewarding the triumphant allies with new dispositions of territory.

The Princess of Wales received the news of her brother's death, according to Ompteda, with a shocking degree of calm. In fact, as one of her ladies was later to lament on an occasion of far greater loss, the

Princess considered it a matter of honour or pride never to exhibit weakness. Gell was astonished to hear that she had got it into her head that she would be called to Brunswick to act as regent to her eldest nephew during his minority. Any plan more unlikely to have entered the heads of the English Regent and Lord Castlereagh is hard to imagine. The Princess considered it a real worry, and fretted in anticipation.[82]

The fancy had left her head a few weeks later. She reported that, after all, she had escaped the burden. Her ties with Brunswick were now effectively at an end, and with the purchase of the Villa Garovo her new fancy was to extol the blood of her Guelph ancestors who had reigned at Este. Caroline had become interested in the Guelph branch of the Brunswick family since her arrival in Milan. The Guelph secret societies there in 1815 were dedicated to throwing off Austrian rule. The cards sent out for her first reception at Lake Como on 24 August bore the name of Caroline d'Este.[83] Moreover she renamed Garovo the Villa d'Este to press home her point. Fortunately, it escaped most people's attention that the 24th was the Feast of San Bartolomeo, Pergami's name-day. The Prince Regent also prized his Guelph ancestry, and indeed instituted the Hanoverian Guelphic Order. One of its first recipients was Count Münster. Meanwhile, Ompteda excitedly tried to discover links between the Princess and the Guelphs in Lombardy – Mr Douglas Kinnaird, among other Englishmen in Milan, was suspected of playing a part in the secret societies – but had to conclude that the Princess was not involved in any subversive political activity.

Always on the look-out for plots and conspiracies, where a simple explanation would have sufficed, Ompteda rejoiced in the information that the Princess had burnt a stack of papers in the fireplace at Villa Villani before her departure. He immediately linked this to the recent death of Murat, who had been shot at Pizzo in the aftermath of Napoleon's failed campaign, and suggested that it was correspondence with Murat and Queen Caroline which had nearly caused the chimney to take fire. He could, however, find no evidence of correspondence passing between the suspects and had to leave the matter there.[84]

'I have now settled myself in a most beautiful grot[to] upon the Lac of Como,' Caroline wrote to Gell with her usual enthusiasm. 'The place is romantic, superb. . . . I have seven barges with boats . . .

grand cascades, fountains in abundance, all possible fruit trees. . . .'[85] Upon her arrival, there were also in the grounds a Temple of Minerva, some 'Elysian fields' and, on the hill above the house, the system of battlements and castellations modelled on those at Tarragona. The party at the Villa d'Este was a tremendous success, she informed Gell. For the occasion a local poet, Bellini, wrote an ode in her honour, detailing the many joys which her residence brought to the community of Como.[86]

The Princess informed Gell that she had initiated a grand project: following in the footsteps of Napoleon and Caesar, she was turning her attention to improving the communications of her empire. Access to the villa could be gained only by boat or by a rough lakeside path along the hillside, where carriages could not pass. The Princess ordered that the carriage road, which finished a few miles out of Como at Cadenabbia, should be extended to Cernóbbio and the Villa d'Este. Disbanded soldiers and unemployed labourers formerly engaged in the construction of Napoleon's tunnel through the Alpine foothills at Simplon had begun work. It was forecast that the project would be completed in a year at a cost of £2000. 'I have made myself important in Lombardy,' she wrote with naive pleasure.[87]

She took little note of her financial position in this project. Her income was already depleted by the purchase of the villa, with a down-payment of £1000 and the balance of £4000 to follow over the next eighteen months. There were, besides, the pensions to be paid to her former attendants, her debts in England – and her mounting debts in Italy. Coutts had refused to pay her quarterly allowance in July 1815. Brougham wrote to her, again demanding the power of attorney as her trustee, and enclosing a plan of economy. She ought to spend only £22,000 a year of her £35,000, and the remainder would be put aside to pay her debts. In a year she would be clear of them.[88] The Princess paid no attention: she could get money from Signor Luigi Marrietti, her Milan banker.

'It being necessary to repair and beautify it different artists were employed,' she later wrote of the Villa d'Este.[89] Among them was one Monticelli – pre-eminent in Lombardy, she declared – who painted the Apotheosis of Venus and Psyche on the ceiling of one of her grottos.[90] She did not stint on the decoration of her new home, and architects, painters, workmen and gardeners from Milan and Como as well as from the local village of Cernóbbio scurried all over the estate, remodelling interior and exterior, refurbishing the rooms and reappointing the grounds. If she imitated Napoleon in her empire-building, she imitated the Prince Regent in her extravagant decorative schemes at Como. On her payroll of household and outdoor servants, she had a caretaker, three footmen, cooks. The local boatmen, carriers, blacksmiths, laundresses, woodmen, tailors, hairdressers, butchers, bakers and candlestick-makers in Cernóbbio and other nearby villages were kept fully supplied with work. She would have been 'important' enough even without engaging in the munificent project to build a new road.

The household at the Villa d'Este had been enlarged by the addition of Pergami's brother Luigi and cousin Bernardo. Moreover a child appeared, three or four years old, Pergami's daughter Vittorine. (His wife, a shadowy figure, continued at Milan with a younger daughter.) Luigi acted as steward, Bernardo as accountant. Willy Austin and Hownam were now the lone John Bulls among a herd of Italians. The Princess told Gell, 'We now all speak much Italian – which is quite delightful.'[91] Caroline's passion for Willy diminished as she found other targets for her love – if not Pergami himself, then certainly his little daughter. Hownam wrote to Lady Cumming, one of Lady Charlotte Campbell's daughters, who had visited the Villa d'Este in his absence, 'Amusements I have none.' Lady Cumming and her husband Sir William, according to Ompteda, found that they were expected to dine 'with persons who seemed to them not made to be seated at table'. They departed abruptly.[92]

'Independence, curiosity and also economy are the real motive of my travelling at the present moment,' the Princess wrote in November. Despite her purchase of the villa, she was off again. Where economy came into the picture is unclear. The Princess was arranging for an entire new wing to be added to the Villa d'Este, in her absence, and a theatre. Meanwhile she was off to Sicily, 'to Malta, to Sardinia and then to Tunis to deliver the poor slaves which are now retained there. Jerusalem is my great ambition,' she wrote, 'to see Jan [St Jean] d'Acre, and Cairo.'[93] Also on her itinerary were Greece and Turkey, and she was duly to reach all these destinations, with the exceptions of Sardinia and Cairo. Lady Hester Stanhope, who had acted as lady-in-waiting to the Princess on that 1805 ramble in Devon, now lived in Syria, and though she might be eccentric she was not lost to propriety. When she heard a rumour that Caroline meant to call on her, she fled her convent at Sayda for Antioch.[94] In the event, the Princess never set foot in Syria, but she had contemplated visiting Greece even before she left England. The accounts by her travelling friends – Gell, Keppel Craven, Byron, Englefield – had stimulated her already potent wanderlust, as had Sir Sidney Smith's earlier tales about his heroism in the Holy Land, and Napoleon's Egyptian campaigns. Tales of the 1172 pilgrimage to Jerusalem by her ancestor Henry the Lion reinforced Caroline's determination.

The Princess of Wales was setting off on her Levantine pilgrimage with no one of the calibre of Gell or Holland, who would, in different company, have leapt at the chance. Her behaviour had ruled out their attendance. At last she signed the power of attorney for Brougham. She spoke of equipping her home with furnishings and materials from the cheap markets of Constantinople. Hoper in London was ordered to ask the Government for a ship to transport her and her entourage on her travels. The Admiralty protested, as they had when asked for a vessel to take her to Genoa, but once more they complied.[95] The Princess's trump card, which gained her this astonishing freedom, was that she could always threaten to return to England. So the Government continued to pay her annuity, and she tested, indeed exceeded, the limits of acceptable behaviour for a European woman, let alone the Princess of Wales.

Ompteda was dismayed to hear of the Princess's voyage, and followed her to Genoa, where she was to embark. Desperate to continue his surveillance of his subject – it had now become more an obsession than an office – he followed a crew member to his mother's home in the town and attempted to bribe him to act as his spy on the voyage. When this met with no success, Ompteda reconciled himself to waving the ship goodbye, and reflected that the reminiscences of the party might be bought on their return. Meanwhile he bribed the German stableman, Moritz Crede, to filch for him a set of keys to the Villa d'Este – and to the Princess's bedroom – against her return.[96] He also used the absence of the Princess to compile a report on her activities, and sent it with the hope that it would be useful to Münster.

When Ompteda's early reports had reached London in the summer, they were deemed utterly useless by the vice-chancellor Mr John Leach, for none of the hearsay evidence would stand up in an English court of law. In their enthusiasm, Münster and Ompteda had not thought to consider that the rules of evidence in German law were very different from those of English common law. Castlereagh's brother Lord Stewart, on his passage through Milan, *en route* to Vienna, was detailed to advise a chagrined Ompteda of the short-comings of his laborious researches.[97] Witnesses and their written depositions were needed to substantiate his detailed personal reports. An English lawyer had already been sent out to advise and aid Ompteda in this task, and Ompteda thought of travelling to Naples to obtain the depositions of some of her former servants there.[98]

Unaware of the machinations in Milan and England against her, the Princess on 14 November embarked happily for Sicily on Captain Thomas Briggs's ship, the *Leviathan*. This had been summoned to Genoa after the Princess of Wales had refused to sail with Pechell again. At dinner the Princess summoned Pergami to sit beside her at the Captain's table, an elevation which had already offended Sir William and Lady Cumming. Hownam, unable to hide his feelings, remonstrated with his royal patron, then left the cabin. Captain Briggs was astonished, but found himself unable to put a stop to this new arrangement.[99] This was only the beginning of a passage of arms between the Princess of Wales and the Royal Navy which would prove her undoing. She further outraged Briggs by insisting on going ashore at Elba, visiting Napoleon's former palace and taking away a billiard cue as a souvenir.[100]

Having learnt her lesson at 'that brilliant sham Court' at Naples, Caroline wrote from the Palazzo Butera at Palermo, 'I have actually made a solemn promise never any more in my whole course of my life to go to a Court.'[101] She had arrived in Sicily on 26 November to find to her distress that the Court of King Ferdinand was no longer in mourning for his wife Queen Maria Carolina, a turn of events which threatened her with royal assemblies. She therefore left for Messina, where Briggs had to depart, and Pechell in the *Clorinde* was summoned. After hearing from Briggs of Pergami's promotion on board the *Leviathan*, Pechell absolutely refused to keep table, or to bear the expense of the board, for his royal guest and suite. He was, however, happy to do so, as he wrote to his commander-in-chief Admiral Lord Exmouth, 'provided her Royal Highness would be pleased to make a sacrifice which my duty and feeling as an officer compelled me to exact, by not insisting on the admission to my table of a person of the name of Pergami, who, though he is now admitted to her Royal Highness's society, was, when last her Royal Highness embarked on board the *Clorinde*, in the capacity of footman.'[102] The Princess of Wales at first refused to discuss the subject. Then an unhappy Hownam informed Pechell that her Royal Highness would bring her own cook on board and keep her own table. A disgruntled Pechell reported that he had taken the Princess to Syracuse on 10 January 1816, after she had passed a month in Messina. He was now at Malta making essential repairs to his ship, including to the main mast, in preparation for the journey to Palestine.[103]

In the event, Caroline, having travelled northwards up the coast from Syracuse to Catania, arranged with a Captain Vincenzo Gargiulo, owner of a *polacca* – a three-masted trading ship – to carry her east. The *polacca* was a very different vessel, stained from its travels to Africa and Asia with cargoes of olives and currants and wine, from the smart British warships which had been her former transport, but there would be no officious Royal Navy captain on board. Further honours came the way of Pergami during their months at Catania. The Grand Master of the Order of Malta at that place wished to honour the English Princess by conferring the prestigious decoration in his gift on the two Englishmen, Flynn and Hownam, in her suite. (Lieutenant John Flynn, who had been commanding a gunboat in the Royal Neapolitan Flotilla, had been appointed captain of the *polacca*.) The Princess replied that their Protestant religion forbade them to accept, but that Pergami would be pleased to be their substitute.[104]

On 25 February, she left Captain Gargiulo to fit out the ship to her specifications, and departed south with her entourage overland to the small town of Augusta. She or Pergami had apparently heard that there was an estate with an accompanying barony there for sale.

The Princess had it in mind to elevate Pergami to the rank of chamberlain, and according to the rules of English Court etiquette – which she was still observing, which indeed she had followed in appointing the Countess Oldi as her lady of the bedchamber – only a nobleman could fill this honourable position (Sir William Gell and the Hon. Richard Keppel Craven had been vice-chamberlains). The purchase and transfer of title and land was accomplished in two days.[105]

So it was on the arm of her new chamberlain, Barone Pergami della Franchina, Order of Malta – it was now 1 April – that the Princess of Wales leant as she stepped on to the *polacca*, the former *Industria*. Its new name, *Royal Charlotte*, cribbed from the royal yacht of George III, was shining on its bows. The Princess's sleeping arrangements on board were eccentric, even bohemian, and were eventually to become the focus of a *cause célèbre*. 'I remained night and day upon deck,' she wrote, ' – a sort of tent was contrived for me; I lay there without ever taking off my clothes, and the rest of the persons who remained on deck with me did the same.'[106] Within that tent slept Pergami too. Contrary to Caroline's assertion, no one else slept on deck.

The Princess's grandiose intention in visiting Tunis, the first port of call after Sicily, was to free the Christian foreigners who had been sold into slavery by Barbary pirates. Such corsairs, who at this time were in league with Tunisia's ruling Bey, had infested the waters off North Africa for 500 years. At Tunis the Princess of Wales first stayed with the French Consul, then, on being offered the loan of a sparkling new palace by the Bey, somewhat modified her opinion of her host. In fact, she abandoned her plans to crusade for his captives' freedom, in favour of picnics at the ruins of Utica and Carthage, and enjoyed a tour of the Bey's harem.

She wrote to Gell on 21 April, just before leaving Tunis, 'I am as happy as the Day is long [the Dey of Tunis was a local governor], and I have received most superb presents in horses.' (These horses proved a nuisance on the cramped *polacca*.) 'After I had visited all Sicily for the sake of the antiquities, I came here and had the pleasure to release [a] great many slaves, before the English fleet arrived which came only a week later. . . . I am quite in astonishment that all the wonderful curiosities of Carthage, Utica, Savonny [Zaghouan] ... never have been taken much notice of. ... as England has ever behaved so ill to me not to give me another ship to continue my voyage I shall certainly send them no antiquities, not even my own self.' She concluded, 'the soi-disant Barbarians are much more real, kind and obliging to me than all the civil people of Europe. ... I have been three times in the seraglio and received most kindly. I have seen the dancing of the country. ... I am living a perfect enchantment. The dear Arabians and Turks are quite darlings.'[107]

Just as Mr Samuel Whitbread's influence could be seen in the Princess's sudden declaration for all things Bonaparte, so Brougham's influence – he was the leading campaigner for the abolition of slavery – may be seen in this venture. Like a child the Princess got it mixed up – Brougham campaigned to free Africans from European or American slavery, not Europeans or Americans from Arab slavery. And, like a child, she lost interest when offered a piece of sugar candy.

Accompanied by a guard of honour, she visited the ruins of the city of Utica on 8 April, sleeping at the country houses of the Bey's younger son. Four days later she was off to Zaghouan to see the Roman aqueduct, when Lord Exmouth arrived off Tunis. A year previously the United States had sent a strong force into the Mediterranean and had settled accounts with the Barbary pirates. At the same time the release by the rulers of the North African seaboard of all American captives, or slaves, was secured. Exmouth was now on his way to effect the same for the British slaves, with nineteen British and six Dutch ships of the line. His intention was to bombard Tunis, by way of forcing the Bey to agree to abolish Christian slavery throughout his territories. The Bey abruptly terminated the entertainments laid on for the Princess when the armada arrived. Fresh from success at Algiers, it was to bombard Tunis in its turn for a full twenty-four hours, before proceeding to Tripoli to dole out the same treatment. The Princess expressed extreme displeasure that politics had interfered with her social calendar – Exmouth nonetheless ordered her to depart Tunis.[108] Very likely she relished the possibility of being sold into slavery – or ransomed, as in the affecting story by Mrs Crisp of Minorca, *The Female Captive*, in which Mrs Crisp told how she 'underwent a mortifying examination' in the harem and was then begged to become the Sultan of Marrakesh's 'concubine'[109] – quite as much as she gloried in her earlier role as a crusader against the Saracen or later a pilgrim bound for Jerusalem to capture the golden city.

Wishing a fond farewell to the Bey, the royal thorn in Lord Exmouth's side departed on 23 April for Athens. Via Malta and the island of Milos, the *Royal Charlotte* ploughed across the eastern Mediterranean to reach Athens on 8 May. The Princess owed her craving to see Greece to the Gells and Byrons of her Kensington circle, but without them she found it had little to offer. A couple of weeks sufficed for her to recover from the journey and to take stock of the antiquities and the sights in Athens and its environs. Then it was off again, via Corinth, to Constantinople, where the Princess found an old acquaintance, Mr William Windham's great friend Mr Bartholomew Frere, now English Minister to the Ottoman Porte. At Constantinople the Princess enjoyed a frenzied bout of shopping – four dresses of 'embroidered gold brocade, and other gold clothes' were among the goods she bought, and arranged to have shipped back to Italy to await her return[110] – before Frere urged her to leave. The plague had broken out in Constantinople, so the Princess sojourned near the Ottoman Court on the Bosphorus for a month, before taking ship for a leisurely sail down the eastern Mediterranean seaboard.[111]

On 2 July she arrived at St Jean d'Acre, as her earlier hero Sir Sidney Smith had before her. And then she disappeared into the land of the Old and New Testaments: '. . . I travelled on horseback through Palestine to Jerusalem, Nazareth, Bethlehem, Canaan – by the Dead Sea, and the rivers of Jordan and Jericho – and I returned by Jaffa. . . .'[112] Her most remarkable venture – her entry into Jerusalem on an ass – she was to commemorate, on her return to Milan, in a grand portrait by Carloni as *The Entry of St Caroline into Jerusalem*.[113] And at Jerusalem the pilgrim Caroline founded an order in her name.[114]

She had certainly endured all the privations of earlier pilgrims to Jerusalem. Travelling always by night to avoid the sun, she had slept 'under boughs' at Ephesus, in a cowshed and under canvas.[115] She had left unseen no place of interest – though she did not find them very interesting. The birthplace of Homer, the great statue of Diana at

Ephesus, the Mount of Olives – she had inspected them all. And again and again she noted that she was the first European, or first European woman, or first lady of her rank (if her former attendant Lady Hester had been there before her) to do so. Failing anything else, she was undoubtedly the first Princess of Wales to make this long voyage to Jerusalem.

On 17 July the pilgrim party left Jerusalem for Jaffa, where they embarked. On the voyage back to Italy – another outbreak of the plague prevented an assault on Cairo – the Princess of Wales lay all day, all night, in a happy daze out of the heat of the summer in her shipboard tent, lost to the world. She went below, apparently, only to bathe, and in and out of this canvas boudoir went her Court – Pergami, Hownam, Flynn, Contessa Oldi and Demont – while the *Royal Charlotte* battled its way homeward against the wind, frequently delayed by storms and periods of quarantine imposed on travellers returning from the Levant. At last, on 10 September, they docked at Capo d'Anzio, south-east of Rome.[116]

On 16 September the Princess of Wales returned to the Villa d'Este after an absence of ten months with a suite now including 'Turks, Arabs, Negroes', as well as English, Italian 'and above all natives of Crema' – the Baron's home town. There was 'nothing more singular than this assembly of sinister figures', ran a Milan police report in December.[117] At the Villa d'Este, where building work was now complete, the Princess had hoped to settle down to a peaceful existence. 'I have a charming theatre at my house and very often we play French charades and Italian opera.'[118] Willy Austin was sent to the Collegio Gallio, a school founded at Como in the seventeenth century by a philanthropic cardinal, the man who built the Villa d'Este.

The Contessa Oldi's two small children arrived to keep Vittorine company, and a tutor from the Collegio was employed to give them lessons. With the children came Signora Pergami, mother of 'il Barone' and Contessa Oldi. Despite her noble Venetian ancestry, Mme Mère, as she was called after Napoleon's mother, happily employed herself as laundress to the household and sat silently at table by her equally silent daughter. While Pergami dined at table, his brother Luigi and Bernardo ate with the upper servants. Despite

the open misalliance with her chamberlain, the Princess still expected
to receive the honours due to her rank. But the visits she made in
pursuit of this gratification were not always successful. At the Parma
Court of the Empress Marie Louise, an inelegant yawn caused her
and her chair to topple backwards together. She promptly dissolved
into laughter, with only her feet visible to an unamused Empress.

And then a scandal erupted. 'Mr Ompteda had bribed my piqueur
[groom] named Moritz Crede,' she wrote indignantly to Gell, 'a
German who had been formerly in Joachim [Murat]'s family.'[119]
Hownam returned from a trip to find 'the house in confusion, and
Moritz Crede dismissed'. It was a complicated story. Annette Presinger,
the Princess's maid from Brunswick, was pregnant again, and Crede,
the father, was therefore turned off. Hoping for a reference, he plea-
bargained, revealing that he had been bribed by Ompteda's agent in
the Villa d'Este, a kitchen hand called Ambrogio Cesati, to show him
the Princess's bedroom and provide him with keys for a later attempt
to surprise their mistress *in flagrante*. Cesati was also dismissed, as
was Presinger, who, it was suspected, had given information to Crede
about Caroline's sleeping arrangements.[120]

Pergami, who had imagined himself protecting the Princess from
ruffians in Genoa, now had a more serious threat to oppose. 'Mr
Pergami', Caroline wrote, 'rarely took his clothes off, but constantly
walked two or three times during the night round the house to see
that all was safe.'[121] The Princess fired off a letter of furious complaint
to Count Francis von Saurau, the new Austrian Governor of Milan.
Ompteda had received nothing but hospitality from her in their year's
acquaintance from 1814 to 1815. This was a gross breach of friendship, as well as of the law. A farce developed. Hownam wrote to
Ompteda, challenging him to a duel if the miscreant would not
apologize publicly and leave the state of Lombardy. Ompteda eventually replied that duelling was forbidden in Austrian territories. Saurau,
after consultation with Metternich in Vienna, had meanwhile told
Ompteda he would do best to leave Lombardy. However, Ompteda
accepted the challenge and with his second awaited Hownam at
Mannheim in Germany. When Hownam did not appear, Ompteda
wrote in December that he considered the matter closed and Hownam's honour as an Englishman sullied.[122] He wrote a sorrowful letter

to Münster, in which he detailed the embarrassing tale, and resigned from his espionage activities. The Regent and his ministers would have to find another channel of information about the Princess's activities.

Ompteda's betrayal came as a severe shock to the Princess, and she was losing the respect she had gained in Como. She successfully petitioned the Como authorities for a posse of soldiers to stand guard outside her gates, but fights broke out between these soldiers and the Princess's servants.[123] She attended a dance with Signor Tamassia, the former Prefect of Como under Napoleon, at which he wore, it was alleged, a monk's costume. The authorities were shocked by this sacrilege. The Princess rebutted this charge, and, perhaps to make amends, subscribed, with her household, a large sum to make good fire damage in Como.[124] The parish priest was apparently not appeased. He conducted a sermon in Cernóbbio in which he advised mothers not to let their daughters go near the foreign Princess's villa.[125]

In October Mr John Cam Hobhouse noted, 'She had ruined herself with the Italians.' He nonetheless wrote a letter of recommendation for Byron's former companion Mr John William Polidori, a conceited youth who had hopes of becoming the Princess's physician. He heard that, at an entertainment she had given, she had had a donkey brought to the table, which she had caressed and crowned with roses before the assembled company. When Hobhouse told the Duke of Devonshire in Venice that the Princess had 'a Mameluke outside her carriage', the Duke replied that 'it was not so bad as having a courier inside'.[126]

An interested English observer of the Princess's activities at the Villa d'Este was the Tory poet Mr Walter Savage Landor. He had taken up residence with his wife and brother on Lake Como during the Princess's absence in the east. The poet Southey – another ardent Tory – came to stay with Landor at Como and he suggested that it might do some good if Landor published these lakeside rumours. With encouragement from McMahon, Southey's friend and the Regent's private secretary, Landor cobbled together a book, mainly a translation of a seventeenth-century Italian historical account of Lake Como. He prefaced it, however, with his own notes on the current

state of the area, including some observations on the Princess of
Wales's disgraceful entourage.[127] The Princess wrote blithely of the
Englishman whose name she did not know, 'This Mr Lindon has
never wished to be presented to me and even if he meets my carriage
he never takes even his hat off.' She thought him sinister. He kept his
young and pretty wife in seclusion 'with a pair of pistols', but she
believed he had written favourably of her and of her house in an
account of the lake, which she had not seen.[128] She never did discover
the nature of his observations. Indeed, it seems the book was never
published.

Always eager for a new project, and increasingly under the sway of
Pergami, the Princess that December purchased for him a derelict
house and grounds near Milan, once part of his father's lands. New
Year 1817 saw a house-warming party, when the entire Villa d'Este
household debouched in pouring rain and in a welter of mud outside
the new residence, renamed, to hammer home Pergami's recently
acquired title, La Barona. To the festivities were bidden, given that
more distinguished company refused to attend, the local farmers and
their wives and daughters.

The party continued for some days, the Princess at her most high-
spirited and amiable, her entourage sodden with wine. The story
circulated in Milan and further afield that the whole had ended in an
orgy, and that several farmers' daughters hurriedly had to be found
husbands in the succeeding months.[129] Caroline, not a whit disturbed,
had a new plan to visit her great-aunt in Germany, the Margravine of
Bayreuth.

She had received the news of her daughter's approaching marriage
to Prince Leopold of Saxe-Coburg before she left Tunis in April
1816, without resentment that she was not expected to grace the
celebrations.[130] She would never return to England, even when her
daughter was on the throne, she now wrote, and she eagerly studied
reports in the foreign newspapers of the Regent's frequent bouts of
illness.[131] (His father remained lost in his shadowy world in the
northern apartments at Windsor.) Friends sent Caroline prints of the
daughter whom she had not seen for two and a half years, and of
handsome Prince Leopold. She was informed that a Parliamentary
grant had been made to the young couple, to allow them to purchase

Lord Clive's old house, Claremont, near Esher in Surrey. The nation rejoiced that the 'Daughter of England' had found happiness. Princess Charlotte was devoted to her Leopold and regretted only that her mother could not be present on 2 May 1816 when she wed him. The Princess of Wales, noting with perfunctory interest that she had not been informed of the coming event by the British Government, returned to her own affairs.

The Princess's creditors in Milan and even in Como were growing restive, not to speak of her creditors in England. Marrietti, her banker in Milan, was increasingly difficult about allowing her credit. Her impulse was to flee, an impulse which she disguised as a wish to tour the towns of Germany and visit her aunt. She engaged a German-speaking courier, the Chevalier Carlo Vassalli – his father was an important gold-lace manufacturer in Milan – to accompany her party, and set out in February via the Tyrol. Munich held her interest for some days, for here apparently she sold 'my fine antiquities' to the Prince Royal of Bavaria.[132] Then she continued her journey to her aunt at Nuremberg.

A secret purpose to her journey became clear only when she arrived in Karlsruhe, a fief of her cousin the Grand Duke of Baden, where he was then resident. She asked him to purchase from her the supposed deed whereby her deceased brother, the Duke of Brunswick, had sworn to redeem in three years from 1814 the sum of £5000 which she claimed to have lent him. It would be easier for the Grand Duke, she argued, to obtain the money from the Brunswick Government than for her, a lone woman. The request astonished the Grand Duke – he was also apparently perplexed by the Princess's insistence on wearing half a pumpkin on her head to keep it cool – but he agreed to send the bond to the Brunswick Government.[133]

Satisfied with the apparent success of her plan, the Princess proceeded to Vienna, by way of Linz and Nuremberg. Purposeless as the Princess's wanderings had become, this one was humiliating. The Emperor Francis was unable to receive her because he was in mourning, she was informed by Lord Stewart. And a fine caricature, showing Caroline and her heterogeneous entourage being turned away, was published in England.[134] The Princess withdrew to Trieste, then to Monfalcone, and finally returned to the Villa d'Este. She

wrote from there in May to her old supporter Sir William Gell in
Naples. She was *en route* to Rome, and she begged him to meet her
there, to take up his lapsed duties as her vice-chamberlain. The
Austrian Government ministers, incidentally, were 'quite horrible
brutes and despots'.[135] They were more ruthless than she knew. Her
husband was planning to investigate her conduct yet again, and the
Austrian authorities in Vienna and Milan were to offer the Regent
their eager assistance.

## CHAPTER THIRTEEN

# THE MILAN COMMISSION

## 1817–1819

*'No more scandals can be created about poor me'*

THE PRINCESS OF WALES reached Rome in June 1817 to find Gell there to welcome her, and established herself in the Villa Rufinella, a massive white building belonging to Prince Lucien Bonaparte on a hill above Frascati, an hour from the city. Frascati, long a fashionable summer retreat for the Roman nobility, was dominated by the vast and elegant Villa Aldobrandini, rising above the main square. The Villa Lancelloti flanked it, on the road leading up to the Villa Rufinella, and Caroline's Roman banker, Torlonia, occupied a smaller villa across the square in beautiful gardens. These villas looked over the flat Roman plains; and this view ended, on a clear day, with the dome of St Peter's shining on the horizon – constant reminder of the power of the Papacy, and of Cardinal Ercole Consalvi, the Pope's right hand in the Papal States, which stretched northwards to Bologna, east to the Marches and south to the border with the Kingdom of Naples. Gell preferred the situation and view westward of the hills from Rufinella, though the house was not so elegant as the others.[1]

The principal purpose of the Princess's visit to Rome was to sell the Villa d'Este to Torlonia, who had earlier expressed an interest. Ompteda's betrayal had made her conscious that her lakeside home was open to the inspection of any passing boatman or vigilant emissary of her husband. Moreover, she owed enough money in the neighbourhood, and to her Milan banker Marrietti, to make her reluctant to return to Como. Perhaps too she had at last recognized a difficulty which Gell had expressed two years earlier:

Hat Vaughan I am afraid has sunk into total neglect and oblivion in his present state and nobody takes the least notice of him.... Why a person should select low company and then go and live just in the spot where that company was born I cannot think because it affronts all the gentry of the place who might otherwise be very well disposed, but will not and cannot for their own sakes sit down with the lower classes who live at their own door and under their windows. It is not for want of being told that Mr Vaughan makes these mistakes....[2]

Caroline moved always with lightning speed, and rarely gave the truthful reason for her decisions. At Frascati and later at the Villa Brandi, a former convent in Rome, she enjoyed the same lavish attentions from the Papal officials as she had received from the Milan authorities in 1814. Her Roman project was successful, for in July 1817 she signed a treaty with Torlonia, transferring the Villa d'Este to his name, for a sum of 150,000 louis d'or.[3]

Caroline made her farewells to Gell in August and led her party across the plains of Rome and over the Apennines to the small Adriatic town of Senigallia, in the Marches, to attend the annual fair for which the town was famous. A few days later the Princess moved some twenty miles up the coast to Pesaro, where she took the lease from a young widow, the Marchesa Mosca, of an elegant villa on the San Bártolo hill above the town. The Mosca villa, Villa Caprile, was one of a number of *casini di delizie*, or pleasure houses, on Colle San Bártolo, built in the seventeenth century by Pesarese families of note, at a time when a flourishing Court had existed there.[4]

The Villa Caprile enchanted the Princess, with its three tiers of terraces, adorned with box hedges and fruit trees, looking inland. She kept a boat in the Gulf of Pesaro, and bathed there till October. An avenue along the hillside led to a little open-air theatre – constructed, stage, pit and seats alike, from flattened box-cypress hedging – and the Princess lost no time in staging recitals from French plays here.[5] The hill of San Bártolo, moreover, was crisscrossed with paths leading to other villas – Cardinal Giuseppe Andrea Albani was a near neighbour – and to stretches of woodland where Pergami and his brothers amused themselves with rough shooting.

The Villa Caprile itself was dominated by a large cupola above two floors of apartments. Marble pillars adorned the hall, the *salon d'honneur* boasted frescoed ceilings, and there was a fine stucco gallery where the household could promenade in bad weather. The Princess wrote to Gell, chattering gaily as ever of her latest residence; the expenses at Pesaro were moderate, and she wished only to live a life retired, though there was an amusing circle of poets and intellectuals in the neighbourhood.[6]

It was no fancy of hers that poets existed in this remote part of the Papal States. At another colony of villas beyond Pesaro to the south lived a most poetic couple, Signor Giulio Perticari and his wife Costanza Monti Perticari. Costanza was the beloved daughter of the philosopher Signor Vincenzo Monti, and her friendship for the Princess soon expressed itself in an ode to her Royal Highness. Costanza's and Giulio's enthusiasm for the eccentric Princess diminished somewhat when they were bidden sometimes four times a week to dine at the Villa Caprile. The Princess's performances in the theatre, with Costanza's cousin Signor Francesco Cassi as her partner, were enough to make you laugh, wrote Costanza. Monti in Milan, meanwhile, wrote anxiously when he had not heard from his daughter in some weeks. There were rumours at Milan, he wrote, that the Princess's life was in danger from poison, and the want of letters from his daughter made him fear for her safety also.[7]

The summer of 1817 passed contentedly for the Princess, and only domestic disturbances ruffled the household. Teodoro Majocchi, the crony of Pergami employed in her service since Naples, was turned off 'having quarrelled with my other servants'.[8] At Pesaro she was safe from spies: no strangers could appear in the small town without the news reaching the Villa Caprile at once. Moreover Cardinal Consalvi in Rome had instructed the police chief Capitano Luigi Bischi and authorities in Pesaro to afford the Princess every courtesy. (This was more in the hope that they might learn something of the Princess's household than from any great warmth that he felt towards the troublesome royal resident of Pesaro.) The Princess wrote contentedly in October that she was awaiting the news that she was a grandmother.

Princess Charlotte and her consort had settled down together at Claremont to a life of tranquillity and regularity. Claremont was a commodious house, with an elegant entrance hall designed by Sir

John Soane, and airy rooms with high ceilings and views of the leafy grounds outside. The grounds had been rolled into harmony by Capability Brown fifty years earlier, and specimen trees overhung a small lake below the house. The estate was surrounded by a quin-tessentially English landscape, with wooded Surrey hills stretching south to Dorking. According to Sir Thomas Lawrence, the Princess delighted to drive in a phaeton by the lake, with Leopold walking at her side, in the months approaching her confinement.[9]

Charlotte was intensely happy with her new domestic role, and fussed over her china and linen with all the avidity of a new bride in humbler circumstances. She extended open invitations to her friends to visit. 'It is Liberty Hall here,' she wrote confidently, as her circumscribed childhood and restricted adolescence faded from her mind. In fact, those who visited found that they were condemned to spend the evenings in an uncomfortable circle of chairs, in German fashion. Their hostess, who spoke so fondly of her husband's wish being her rule, was inclined to ignore him when he suggested that she might go to bed to rest.[10]

Princess Charlotte looked forward to her confinement with con-tentment and her own brand of courage. Relations between the Regent and his daughter had never been better. The young couple had spent Christmas 1816 in the tropical heat of the Pavilion, and the Princess suffered none of her former nerves in her father's presence now that she had a protector in Leopold. Old Queen Charlotte emerged from her seclusion at Windsor to give her granddaughter sound advice about the layette and nurses for the coming infant. There had been no – legitimate – royal birth in the House of Hanover since Charlotte's own entrance into the world twenty-one years earlier. Public moralizers, such as Mr William Cobbett, lyrically expressed their hope that the virtues of Princess Charlotte and a new generation would expiate the sins of the Regent and his brothers.

The Princess of Wales diverted herself in Pesaro by inviting herself to dinner with a poor curate, and then arriving at the flustered man's house with two wagons loaded with dishes in her train – and bags of gold.[11] England's great officers of state meanwhile prepared to be summoned to Claremont for the royal birth. In November the message came from Charlotte's *accoucheur*, Sir Richard Croft. Lord

Chancellor, Lord Great Chamberlain and Prime Minister hastened to the Princess's side at Claremont, and found themselves condemned to a long and cramped wait in the antechamber between the hall and the Princess's bedchamber.[12]

The Princess had just come in from a walk with Prince Leopold on 3 November when she felt the pains begin. Casting bonnet and cloak aside, she took to her bed, and fifty hours of painful labour began. Throughout the night Leopold rushed distractedly to and fro between his own bedroom, where he attempted to read, and his wife's bedchamber, on the other side of the bathroom. At seven in the morning on 5 November the officers were called in to witness the protracted birth. The royal infant, born at nine o'clock that night, was a boy – stillborn.

Princess Charlotte bore the loss with remarkable courage. Her instinct, despite her exhaustion, was to comfort her husband, and they talked hopefully, in their grief, of more children to come. The officers of state departed for London, bearing the unwelcome news to the Regent. The Princess urged Leopold to rest, and Croft settled her that night with a sleeping draught. After discussions with the nurses, he himself returned home. The household settled to rest, after the day of sorrow.

At four in the morning of 6 November dreadful cries rent the house of mourning. Charlotte had awoken from her drugged sleep with agonizing stomach pains. Croft was summoned in haste. He was too late. The Princess, in the grip of post-partum haemorrhage, bearing the terrible pain to the last, expired at five in the morning. Leopold's grief was terrible to see. Hardly had the shock of the stillborn child died away than his beloved wife was horribly deprived of life. Leopold would allow nothing of Charlotte's to be touched. Bonnet and cloak were to remain where she had cast them. He wrote to his father-in-law to break the news, then retreated to his bedchamber to mourn in private.[13]

In late October the Princess of Wales had written serenely to Gell of her lot at Pesaro. The weather was beautiful and she bathed most mornings. The house was comfortable, the Papal authorities respectful. With Pergami a vigorous chamberlain and lover, she had serious thoughts of remaining in this paradise for the rest of her life. 'I shall now soon be a grandmother,' she continued, 'and I trust to heaven that then all libels about me will be at an end. I am then a well-established old lady' – she was nearing her fiftieth birthday – 'and no more scandals can be created about poor me. . . .'[14] This complacent, not to say eccentric, reverie was ruptured by the calamitous news from England. The manner of the Princess of Wales's learning it was undeniably cruel. The Prince Regent felt unable to break his rule, made shortly after their daughter's birth, that he would not enter into communication with his wife – even in this tragedy of their daughter's premature death. 'Some inconvenience might arise to the Regent after all that has passed, in renewing any communication of this nature,' Lord Liverpool instructed Prince Leopold's equerry. It was therefore for Leopold to write to his mother-in-law, as Liverpool conceded that umbrage might be taken if no notice were given.[15]

Leopold, stricken by grief, did not write immediately, and, by chance, an English Cabinet courier passed through Pesaro on his southward journey to Rome, where he was to inform his Holiness the Pope of England's loss. As Brougham was later to observe with masterly irony, it was far less important to inform Princess Charlotte's mother than to inform the Pope – that historic friend and ally of the English sovereign since the days of Henry VIII.[16] The Princess and her household in Pesaro were on the *qui vive* for news of the accouchement in England. The courier was seized and brought out to the Villa Caprile. According to reports in Rome, on hearing the unexpected and fatal news the Princess fainted dead away.[17]

The Prince Regent preferred to believe that his wife first learnt of poor Charlotte's demise from the Radical MP and former Lord Mayor, Alderman Matthew Wood, and that she at first took no notice. When informed with the rest of the public, 'she then made a fuss about it and had leeches put on to her temples and head,' he commented in the margin of a letter from Sir William Knighton.[18] Ompteda in Rome was similarly dismissive of the Princess's grief. Her sorrow was already calmed, he wrote in mid-December. He had the evidence of Pesaro police reports to show that she had invited Cardinal Albani to dinner.[19] It did not strike the Hanoverian Minister that she might derive some spiritual benefit from the prelate's visit.

A prurient crowd jostles for a view of a 'loyalist' printseller's display of 'anti-Queenite' caricatures.

James Gillray's response to the Prince's intended second marriage. Mrs Fitzherbert, with tattered feathers, flees at the left, while an idealized Princess Caroline appears at the right.

With this broadsheet, Catnach the publisher milked the remains of public feeling for the dead and buried Queen.

In his view, this was frivolous behaviour, on a par with her card-playing at Como after her brother Brunswick's death.

It seems more likely, from sources close to her, from her own writing on the subject and especially from her subdued subsequent existence, that the death of Princess Charlotte dealt a severe emotional blow to the Princess of Wales. She had lost not just her only child, but her anticipated prosperity and position as mother of the Queen. The numerous brothers and sisters of the Regent, however, ensured that no succession crisis would arise for the time being. In November Hownam wrote to Gell, 'Her Royal Highness's state I leave to your imagination. My pen is unequal to the task.' She had fixed her determination. She was 'not under any consideration returning to England'. Hownam, the last remaining 'respectable' – or English – member of the Princess's suite, thanked Gell on her behalf, but declined his offer to visit, for she wanted no company. She preferred 'remaining without counsel which she is convinced can only tend to make her more unhappy'.[20] There was much sympathy for her in England.[21] Wrote one supporter, 'We hear her sighs wafted on the gales, and we feel the crash of the thunderbolt which tore asunder the last tie that bound her affection to the British Isles.'

The Princess of Wales wrote to Brougham, her old adviser – and Charlotte's – in January 1818. 'She has been all her life a child of misfortune and wretched and miserable for so many years, that this last blow for her future prospects of life has been almost the death warren [warrant] to her feelings. The rest of the few years which may perhaps have been allotted to her by the Almighty' she trusted 'to passe tranquille without any farther [further] persecution and insultes. Her political interest for England and also for Europe is now for ever at ende. . . . She must for ever,' she concluded, triumphant and bitter, 'look as a very severe punishment upon the English nation the dreadful melancolique death of the hope and glory of the British nation.'[22] The shock had struck 'too deeply', wrote Hownam. The Princess suffered from very severe headaches and endured 'moments of melancholy which distresses much'.[23]

The Princess of Wales's usual response to affliction was a great show of 'jocularity and indifference', as Lady Charlotte Campbell had lamented. This stance made people think her 'an unfeeling and light-minded person'.[24] This was not the case now. The Princess retreated into a lethargy, a depression of the spirits, somewhat akin to her stuporous state after her father's death eleven years before. Then her ladies at Blackheath had been strong in support. In her weakened state at Pesaro the Princess's dependence on Pergami and his close-knit Italian family grew.

All that Pergami and his brothers and sisters knew of Charlotte were the portrait and prints which she had sent to her mother. They entered into the Princess of Wales's plan to erect a monument in the garden in memory of her daughter, and they respected her grief – Pergami had lost his younger daughter at Milan earlier that year.[25] They managed the house, and they encouraged the Princess's fondness for Pergami's six-year-old, Vittorine, who was at an age which perhaps recalled sweet moments of bright, curly-headed Charlotte in the Blue Room at Montague House.

A domestic fracas, about the time of Princess Charlotte's death, had deprived the Princess of Wales of her elegant maid Louise Demont, who had so recently likened her mistress to Christ. Giuseppe Sacchini, a courier, had been dismissed for thieving gold napoleons from the Princess's box; Demont had then been discovered to be his accomplice – and in addition a scandalmonger, who had suggested that the Princess was infatuated by Sacchini.[26] With Demont's tearful departure home to Lausanne, the Princess lost her secretary, as well as the only woman of intelligence in her suite.

Since her marriage, and before, the Princess had relied for her letter-writing on a succession of ladies-in-waiting to correct her more outlandish turns of speech, offer suggestions and write the whole in a legible, educated hand. Now, with Demont gone and with Charlotte dead, the English correspondence, which had been her delight, noticeably falls off, as does her interest in playing a part in English affairs. Such correspondence – financial, political, social – as remained fell on *il Barone*, so that he came to know every detail of his royal mistress's intentions.

A later report by an agent sent to enquire into the 'general opinion entertained in Pesaro' of the Princess is of some interest. The subject generally showed 'affable and courteous manners' to all, the writer observed. However, 'sometimes she was troubled with an ill humour that rendered her silent and reserved, beyond the limits of her rank and polite deportment ...'. She evinced 'a public weakness' for Pergami, who is described as 'the most perfect master of her house and even of her will. . . . all deliberations and agreements were made before Mr Pergami, and her Royal Highness was for this reason inaccessible and passive'.[27]

This new passivity is seen in the circumstance that the Princess, that energetic and curious traveller, remained at Pesaro for nearly two years together. Dashing Italian colonels – Olivieri, Vassalli and Schiavini – came and went in the role of equerries, Hownam departed for England in the spring of 1818. She was principally alone with the Pergami family, or those 'in his absolute confidence', who now constituted her whole household.

The daily scene rarely varies. While old Mme Mère supervises the laundry and a second daughter, Faustina Martini, a newcomer, counts off sheets, Bernardo Pergami wrestles with the week's accounts, and Luigi, the majordomo, receives the morning's deliveries from Pesaro in the kitchen. Meanwhile the Princess is seated in the salon, with Vittorine playing at her feet, and Contessa Oldi a silent companion. In the late afternoon a horn is heard, in bounds *il Barone* from his rough shooting, and dinner soon comes steaming to the Princess's table.

If the preponderance of Pergamis in the household was open to the worst possible interpretation, besides making for a monotonous and rustic existence of the mind, there were great advantages for the Princess of Wales. 'There is only one family at Pesaro,' Ompteda wrote gloomily,[28] and he could see no way of penetrating Caroline's defences to obtain conclusive proof of the scandalous intimacy which the situation suggested.

The most conclusive proof that the Princess was now in low spirits and, at the same time, deeply under Pergami's influence lies in her failure to show interest in politicking after Charlotte's death, despite Gell's urging: 'She says she never was ambitious and that now she is less so than ever – neither does she sigh for that throne you point out the possibility of her possessing one day or other, in her own right.' Her political life was now finished, 'except that of embroiling herself in party, whereby she herself is not at all interested'.[29] Was it low spirits, or did *il Barone* actively dissuade her? It was obviously to the financial advantage of the Pergami family that the Princess should remain among them at Pesaro.

Equally it could be argued that it was in her financial interest to return to England, and profit from the political unrest and confusion obtaining there. The Radical wing of the Opposition, with Alderman Wood at their head, would have welcomed her as a useful tool with which to make mischief. The Princess of Wales, however, preferred to remain in her 'nutshell' at Pesaro. She was under the spell of *il Barone*, and she repeatedly stated that she wished only to live quietly at Pesaro.

The spectre of his enemy's appearance in England, for all her declarations to the contrary, continued to haunt the Regent. On New Year's Day 1818, writing from Brighton, he informed Lord Eldon, the Lord Chancellor, 'Much difficulty in point of delicacy being now set aside in my mind by the late melancholy event which has taken place in my family . . .', the Chancellor could not be surprised if he therefore turned

> my whole thoughts to the endeavouring to extricate myself from the cruellest as well as the most unjust predicament that ever even the lowest individual, much more a Prince, ever was placed in, by un-shackling myself from a woman who has for the last three and twenty years not alone been the bane and curse of my existence, but who now stands prominent in the eyes of the whole world characterized by a flagrancy of abandonment unparalleled in the history of women, and stamped with disgrace and dishonour.

Was it to be tolerated that 'such a monster' was to be suffered to continue to bear the Prince's name, that 'this country and I' should be expected to submit to the degradation?[30] The Prince told Eldon that he had it in mind, 'to enable me under the show of a Council being held at the Pavilion, to throw a mask to the public over the real object, to assemble such of my confidential servants about me as I wished to whom I meant to state my intention, of shortly laying before them a paper, accompanied by other papers and vouchers, respecting the . . . conduct of the Princess of Wales'.

Charlotte's death had given her father fresh heart in the battle for divorce. It would matter less now if he was to bring about the disgrace of the dead girl's mother, and he believed that the Government would encourage him to secure the succession by taking a new wife. The Regent was also spurred by the enthusiasm of his trusted Carlton House advisers – Sir William Knighton, Sir Benjamin Bloomfield, Sir John Leach and Mr Frederick Watson. (McMahon had died the previous September.) Appointed personal physician, private secretary, vice-chancellor of the Duchy of Cornwall and member of the Duchy's Council respectively, they made themselves beloved by raising hopes in their royal master's splenetic breast of an end to his 'most unjust predicament'. In the autumn of 1817, according to the vice-chancellor's own statement, a large – and by now dog-eared – collection of papers, some from Carlton House, some from the Foreign Office (including Ompteda's reports), had been laid before Leach. He declared himself optimistic that a judicial procedure might come of it. Knighton was zealous: 'I am silently, but with great industry, arranging every weapon of defence, to weaken, resist and overthrow whatever opposition may arise whenever the question comes fairly before the public.' By 16 December 1817, Leach had added to the papers an opinion written on the evidence to date; the Regent had corrected it and suggested the addition of a narrative of the Princess's general conduct.[31]

These were the papers which the Regent placed before his ministers on New Year's Day 1818. Confidently he waited for their approval. A resounding negative to proceedings of any nature against the Princess was the Cabinet's answer. Its argument remained the same as that which it had put forward in 1813 and in 1816.[32] In addition, the state of the nation, beset by sedition and discontent with the Government and monarch, precluded any unpopular measures that were not strictly necessary. The country, far from appreciating the Regent's point that Princess Charlotte's death removed an obstacle to his plans for divorcing his wife, would see any proceedings thereto as a hounding of a woman now unprotected by her daughter's glorious future prospects. Cabinet ministers ended with the usual animadversions on the evidence submitted – the bulk of it already well known to them. Most of it was inadmissible in

English law, and none of it furnished conclusive evidence of the Princess's adultery with Pergami – the only conceivable grounds for divorce.

The Regent, baulked, turned back to Sir John Leach. By mid-March, the vice-chancellor, ever the toady, had formed the view that what was needed was a commission of trained lawyers to proceed to Milan and elsewhere, there to assess the witnesses examined by Ompteda and question others. They should then transmit the evidence to England, with their opinion on the form the proceedings should take.[33] The Prince Regent welcomed this scheme. The ministers, however, declined to send any such commissioners. Again they urged the malignity of the times, and invoked public opinion as a deciding factor against the scheme.

In fact, the period from the summer of 1817 till the summer of 1819 was one of comparative calm, and the Government may have used the fear of disturbances as an excuse. There was even a small trade boom. However, Lord Sidmouth, the Home Secretary, could easily point to the mass of reports from his much decried system of agents all over the country to show just how malignant the spirit was. Although there were no outbreaks of violence, he argued that the state of the nation was far from tranquil. The Radicals were, according to his reports, meeting secretly and training for future assaults, while openly promulgating their revolutionary doctrines in the newspapers.

The Regent, baulked again, suggested that he send his own commissioners out to Milan. Lord Liverpool and Lord Eldon sanctioned this new proposal and agreed to supply it from the Secret Service Fund, on the understanding that it was 'not a Cabinet measure' and that proceedings against the Princess would not automatically follow the Commission's report. As Leach later put it with some delicacy, 'the privity and approbation of the Lord Chancellor and Lord Liverpool to this Commission is a private and in some sense an irregular act'.[34] These negotiations show the uneasy nature of the alliance between Regent and Cabinet at this time.

The Commissioners whom Leach appointed in August 1818 were three: a solicitor, Mr John Allan Powell; a King's Counsel, Mr William Cooke; and a military attaché seconded from the British Embassy in Vienna, Major James Browne. Powell's journal is preserved, and gives a scrupulous account of the manner of his appointment. Aware of the delicacy of the material, he identified each of the principals by a number: the Princess of Wales no. 1, the Prince Regent no. 2, the country no. 6, the House of Commons no. 8, appearing alongside Prince Metternich no. 13 and no. 10 'the pseudo Baron Pergami'. Cooke, who had written the standard work on the bankruptcy laws, had now all but retired from the Bar, and accepted the post without hesitation. Powell was a younger man. He had commenced his legal career in his native Dublin, superintending the affairs of the young Duke of Leinster, and was still making his way in the world. Nonetheless, on his first visit to Leach at his house in South Street on 5 August, he had grave doubts about the mission to Italy, but he was tempted by the prospects of future government employment which Leach promised, not least in the event of charges being brought against the Princess. 'It would lead to results highly advantageous to me, by bringing me immediate contact and making me known to persons the most capable of serving me,' Powell wrote.[35]

On reading Leach's March 1818 report, Powell found the evidence 'very loose' and not proving the 'intimate connection between no. 1 and [no.] 10'. He was influenced by Cooke, however, to accept the commission. The only condition that Cooke, the older man, made was that they should be in possession of a clear and 'sufficient authority' for their mission, be it from the Regent, Leach or the Government. 'The whole affair would certainly be much canvassed by no. 8 [the House of Commons] and no. 6 [the country].' The difficulty they had extracting this authority for their commission might have warned them of hazards to come.

The spheres in which they now moved were so exalted that it was hard not to be overawed. At one meeting in South Street 'to confer on the plan of operation' was Lord Castlereagh's brother and Ambassador in Vienna, Lord Stewart, no. 12, who promised that every assistance would be given them by the Austrian authorities in Milan. Stewart said that he himself would write to Prince Metternich, no. 13, to inform him of their mission and 'obtain from him an order to no. 14 [Count Julius Strassoldo, new Governor of Milan] to give us all the assistance in his power, to put us immediately in communication with no. 15 [the Austrian police]'.[36] So the resources of the

British Government and of the effective ruler of the Austrian Empire were at their disposal.

Powell satisfied himself that what he was being asked to do was a job worth doing, to bring British legal expertise to a mess of Italian evidence inadmissible in England. In fact, his role was not far off that of a spy or private detective for the Regent. The odium heaped on Oliver the Spy, one of Sidmouth's agents uncovered the previous year, might have encouraged him again to remain safely in Lincoln's Inn. The Government ministers' reluctance to allow their names to appear on documents in the case was a further pointer, although Leach said that, if it came to divorce, 'the delicacy of these noble Lords must end'.[37]

The Regent was graciously pleased to approve the employment of Cooke, Powell and Browne. The whole of his Carlton House bureaucracy, with Bloomfield at its head, was assiduous in furthering this mighty enterprise. Münster and the Hanoverian Government were ready with all help, and Ompteda, now Hanoverian Minister to the Vatican, was to meet them at Milan, to be employed as they chose within the Papal States. The Papal Government itself was eager to assist. Reports were to be sent in the diplomatic bag. But all three appointees were deceived, or deceived themselves, in thinking that the Milan Commission, as it was dubbed, had any legal authority whatsoever, and that the authority they obtained possessed any force to prevent them incurring the obloquy reserved for those who walked, in Wilberforce's famous phrase, the 'crooked paths' of espionage.

Armed with their authority from Leach – 'you are hereby authorized to proceed forthwith to Milan'[38] – the Commissioners went to Coutts Bank on 8 August to present specimen signatures so that they could draw at Marrietti's. Having agreed to arrive in Milan in the guise of 'chance travellers who had become acquainted with each other on the road', the Commissioners dispersed, and Powell left England on 16 August. They were so well satisfied with the probity of the arrangements that they even left it to Leach to settle the amount of 'generous recompense' on their return.[39]

All this took place while the Princess of Wales remained at Pesaro. In June, with the lease of the Villa Caprile coming up for renewal, she had acted on her boast that she would settle in Pesaro for good, and bought a property. Her choice fell on the Villa Gherardesca, a house barely a quarter of a mile across the San Bartolo hill from the Villa Caprile. The new villa – which she renamed the Villa Vittoria, presumably after Pergami's daughter rather than Wellington's victory of that name – was much smaller. Mr James Brougham, Henry's brother, called it a cottage, but it was more a large farmhouse, and greatly inferior in elegance to its neighbour, or indeed to the Villa d'Este at Como. It offered considerably more privacy, however, than either of the Princess's former homes, as its modest façade and gardens were hidden from the road below by a series of orchards and a wilderness garden. An avenue of cypresses led up to the house. This consisted of a stone principal building, with a large cupola. A colonnaded gallery stretched to the north along a paved terrace. Immediately to the south of the house a smaller avenue of cypresses led towards other properties on the hillside.

The Princess's architect friend, the Marchese Andrea Antaldi, conceived the idea of filling in the northern colonnade to make a suite of rooms and replacing the first part of the avenue with a covered colonnade. A small Italian garden lay behind the open colonnade, and the Princess imagined herself creating an English garden of the wilderness below the house. The interior of the house had none of the grandeur, either, of the Villa Caprile. The kitchen lay directly behind the entrance hall, a small stairway led up to the bedchambers. There were plans to create, in the new suite of rooms, a hall of statues and a music room. Incongruously, a room immediately off the hall was appointed the Princess's bathroom, and in time boasted a sunken bath of grey marble, complete with a mirror let into a frescoed ceiling. Upstairs were to be apartments for all the household.[40] For the moment, most of the attendants and servants lodged elsewhere, while the Princess and the principal Pergamis camped as best they could in the house.

It would have been an inconceivable dwelling for a noblewoman, let alone the Princess of Wales, twenty years before, but times had altered. The Princess had found a kind of peace in her provincial paradise. The society she kept consisted of the local nobility and Papal authorities of the little town. 'We have as many princesses and duchesses here as man can wish for,' she had informed Gell, who was

still in Naples, soon after her arrival in Pesaro, 'and all more beautiful
and charming than at home.'[41] She was accustomed to provincial
society, from Brunswick to Blackheath to Como, and she found at
Pesaro that her ways were tolerated. She had all the comforts of a
devoted household, the resources of a large stable and a crew to man
a little yacht. The climate was fine, existence was cheap and Pesaro
was far removed from the route of English Grand Tourists, who had
snubbed her at Como and Milan.

Other English natives, all of them chary in some sense of Society's
gaze, had found the same advantages. The Shelleys' ménage at Lerici,
although a purely English household, was far off the beaten track.
Lord Byron experienced a provincial paradise with Contessa Teresa
Guiccioli at Ravenna remarkably similar in some aspects to that of
the Princess of Wales at Pesaro. All three households were located far
from the galleries and statues which had drawn eighteenth-century
English dilettanti to Italy, and which now attracted numberless
tourists. Byron wrote disparagingly of English travellers who 'Flor-
enced and Romed – and Galleried – and Conversationed it' for a few
months, then home again. 'Now I have lived among the Italians,' he
wrote, '. . . been of their families – and friendship – and feuds, and
loves in a part of Italy least known to foreigners – and have been
amongst them of all classes, from the Conte to the Contadino; and
you may be sure of what I say to you.'[42] Caroline at Pesaro could have
made the same claim.

While the Regent encouraged other heads of state not to receive
her and while he refused to receive her at his own Court, the
Princess's retreat was in many ways an excellent compromise. The
Regent would have done better to leave her alone, despite her liaison
with Pergami.

Her friends the Perticari were busy restoring an old theatre beside
their town house in Pesaro. The Princess took a great interest, and
was present in September when the town's most famous son, the
composer Signor Gioacchino Rossini, came specially from Naples to
inaugurate the new theatre. Rossini stayed with the Perticari, and in
due course received a note from the Princess inviting him to dine at
the Villa Vittoria. Rossini, aged twenty-three, unchivalrously and
improbably pleaded rheumatism: unable to make the courtly bow

which her rank demanded, he had to decline From then on the Princess refused to attend the theatre when Rossini's music was performed.[43]

In October, confirming that the Princess had no wish to return to England, she offered, via Anthony St Leger, her rooms at Kensington Palace to the Duke of Kent and his new bride.[44] (The offer was accepted, and thus the future Queen Victoria, the Kents' daughter, in due course was born and grew up in the former apartments of Caroline, Princess of Wales.) The Regent did not, however, contemplate calling off his hounds. The Milan Commissioners had met, according to plan, in mid-September at the Albergo Reale.

Ompteda came up from Rome to meet them, burning with enthusiasm for the new concerted effort against the Princess, to inform them of details of her conduct, of names and addresses of the witnesses he had examined, of further potential witnesses.[45] He had particular hopes of Teodoro Majocchi, Giuseppe Sacchini and the maid Louise Demont. That these were all servants and had been turned off by the Princess was, in his view, compensated for by the bedchamber secrets that they knew. As for the present goings-on at Pesaro, he expressed himself confident that the Papal authorities and Cardinal Consalvi himself would render all the assistance they could want, and all would soon be revealed.

The Commissioners, cheered by Ompteda's assurances of Papal co-operation, dispatched him back to Rome to urge on his friend Consalvi. He was then to proceed to Ancona, to investigate information sent by Sir John Coxe Hippisley that, in all the inns up and down the Adriatic coast, the Princess's adultery was a scandal. Meanwhile, they themselves would examine the body of witnesses who could testify usefully to the Princess's transgressions at the Villa d'Este. Ompteda took to his demotion from chief spy to messenger boy without much fuss.

Baron Sardanha, seconded from his post in the Austrian Government, appeared equally helpful. As secretary to Count Saurau, formerly Governor of Milan, Sardanha had had dealings with the Princess. Moreover, he was as well acquainted as anyone with the tardy and byzantine Austrian government machinery, which inhibited all activity in Milan. Every petition, request and report had to be sent to Vienna for Metternich himself to consider, refuse, grant or comment on, before the authorities in Milan could return an answer.[46]

From the Milan Government the Commission wanted, apart from general assistance, several official documents. One was the *fede criminale*, or Government certificate, for each witness they examined, to show whether they had a criminal record.[47] They also envisaged, in the event of proceedings, requiring passports for the relevant witnesses to travel to England and permits to release Government employees from their posts for the appropriate period. Major Browne, who in his post at Vienna had seen how slowly the Austrian mills ground, was delighted to have Sardanha's promises of assistance in removing bureaucratic obstructions from their path.

Cooke and Powell paid more attention to the Milanese lawyer or notary Signor Francesco Vimercati, whom Sardanha recommended to them as honest and respected. With Vimercati the three Commissioners worked out several 'formulas', to discourage bribery, perjury and bad evidence, before they began their examinations. Under Cooke's and Powell's direction, Vimercati and his clerks spent a good part of October making careful notes, gleaned from Ompteda's and Leach's papers, from Milan police records and from local gossip, on each of the twenty-four witnesses the Commissioners proposed to examine. It was settled that the examinations should be held at Browne's lodgings, No. 660 Porta Orientale. (Cooke meanwhile undertook the feeding of the Commission at his quarters.)

When the witnesses arrived, they would be asked to swear on a crucifix. Bribery and reward were inadmissible in this high-principled court of inquiry. It was agreed that a small sum to meet the expenses of travel from their home, board and lodging in Milan if necessary, and a sum for loss of earning during their absence at Milan, would encourage the witnesses to appear. Curiosity would do the rest.

The hope was, as the Commissioners' first dispatch to Leach on 18 October declared, that all of the examinations would be conducted within two weeks and the Commissioners on their way home by mid-November. Granted, it was a laborious process – the examinations had to be conducted in Italian, then translated into French before being copied into English – and one which could easily lead to improper accusations from antagonists once the matter of their examinations became generally known. However, the Commissioners felt that 'by these formulas' they had taken all necessary precautions against any impropriety.[48]

The first witnesses arrived at Browne's lodgings on 26 October: a groom, an innkeeper and a hotel waiter.[49] Almost at once the cheerful prognostications of the Milan Commission were routed by the disposition of the witnesses to see the Commissioners as eager to enrich anyone who would say anything against the Princess of Wales. The orderly examinations degenerated into farce. The lake of Como, where twenty of the twenty-four original witnesses resided, was soon ablaze with rumours.

Perhaps unwisely the Commissioners encouraged their original twenty-four witnesses to discover and produce new witnesses to further disgraces of the Princess. These agents were nothing if not enthusiastic. 'You will never have to ply those oars again,' was the inducement held out to one marvelling boatman. Filippo Riganti, a tobacconist, for example, came forward to give fascinating information about Pergami's depredations, in an earlier career as tax collector, on the wine sellers of Monza. Then the tobacconist brought in a tailor of Como, Gaetano Sacchi, who had gone up to the Villa d'Este once or twice to measure the Princess's servants for coats. Sacchi became an especially active agent himself, bringing his assistant Gaetano Negri and many others. Giorgio Corticella, a cook who deposed to seeing the Princess and Pergami come into the kitchen at the Villa d'Este and take a mouthful of the dinner being prepared, sent back a bricklayer, and so it went on. The grand total of inhabitants of Como and Milan who gave testimony at No. 660 Porta Orientale numbered eighty-two – and more were instantly sent back home as being of bad character.[50]

For some time the Commissioners, busy with the paperwork of reports, translations, dispatches, and with the examinations themselves, had no idea of the damaging rumours spreading in Milan and round the lakeside of Como. The Milanese authorities tried to stem the gushing mouths. Pietro Biretta, for instance, a boatman, was hauled off to jail after he had spoken of his visit to the Commissioners at an inn on the way back to Como and had claimed that Vimercati was after divorce evidence.[51]

It was a hopeless task, trying to restrain the wagging tongues. The witnesses, after giving their evidence, would repair with their recompense to the inn below Browne's Milan apartments and regale the other drinkers with tales of 'the stern Englishmen in black suits upstairs', as one witness had it. 'One of them stood by Vimercati and his clerk, who wrote it all down at the table, two stayed in the shadows of the big dark room.'[52] And, when the witnesses left their coach at the halts, let alone when they reached Como and the local inn, the tales lost nothing in the telling.

In Pesaro, the Princess of Wales was well informed about the activities from 'my lawyer, [Avvocato Pietro] Codazzi' in Milan and gave this sanguine account to Gell: 'Lord Stewart from Vienna took the pain to come up to Milan to call for all the servants which during a year or longer had been dismissed. M. Ompteda paid also a visit to the Apostolic Delegate Luigi Gandolfi, for further much interesting questions. By great expense Lord Stewart at last succeeded to have a few vagabond of servants who speak ill of me and he took them to Vienna. . . .'[53]

The story of the Italian witnesses lodged in Vienna would be farcical if there were not more serious implications to their sojourn there. The Commissioners in Milan heard with delight that Teodoro Majocchi in Vienna had been persuaded to testify by their confederate at the British Embassy there – Browne's former colleague Lieutenant-Colonel George During. After he had made an excellent deposition, they dispatched him back to Colonel During in early November, with another five witnesses for safe keeping. It was a move which sheds unflattering light on the opinions they held of their witnesses' characters. It was a reckless move, moreover, because the subsistence pay awarded to their families was open to misinterpretation. Two of Majocchi's relations went with him, his wife Maria and old Battista, his father. He had allegedly, as coachman to the Princess, followed the Princess and Pergami when they went off to make wild love in a woodland glade.[54]

The group of six – the tailor Sacchi and his assistant Negri, the three Majocchis and a chambermaid Maria Soleri – set out for the Embassy in Vienna. They were under the care of an Austrian Army brigadier, Domenico Contini, and were wrapped in greatcoats and

winter clothes newly purchased by the Commission. (The Princess
was delighted to obtain the tailor's bill some months later.)[55] With
these valuable witnesses on the road, the Commissioners turned back
to the other examinations, and also to searching out potential
witnesses further afield.

They were thwarted in their project to question Moritz Crede, the
groom who had been dismissed for thieving and whom Ompteda had
suborned. His successor Giuseppe Restelli who had himself been
turned off in 1817, was dispatched to seek him out at Cassel, where
he was now head of the Grand Duke of Baden's stables. The Elector
of Hesse-Cassel, however, refused to give Crede permission to leave.

They had greater success with Giuseppe Sacchini, the equerry who
had been dismissed with Demont. First he testified, then he agreed to
go and search out Demont herself in Switzerland. (Although from
Erba like the tailor Sacchi, Giuseppe Sacchini was of higher social
standing and, in particular, had expectations from two rich uncles in
Milan. He had to keep his testimony and his journey a secret from
them, which suggests that the Commission and the quality of its
witnesses was not highly regarded in Milan society.)[56] When Sacchini
reached Lausanne, the depth of the misunderstanding between agent
and employer was seen. After a series of boozy Christmastide evenings
treating all the lads of Lausanne and after a series of rides in a hired
charabanc around the lake, Sacchini discovered that his former
colleague Demont was living with her father and stepmother in
poverty in the small village of Colombier near Morges, high above
Lake Léman.

Poor though she was – the younger of her two half-sisters and her
father worked in the fields – Louise Demont was not to be won easily.
In a series of conversations with Sacchini just outside the village, or
bowling along in his carriage between Colombier and Morges, she
demurred at the idea of deposing against the Princess. Her other
sister Mariette, who was still working for Caroline, would be sacked
and would have to work in the fields at Colombier, and she herself
would be abused – suspected of pregnancy was the delicate implication
– if she disappeared to Milan. Also, she declared, she was in mid-
negotiations with a suitor in Lausanne. Some financial guarantee,
Sacchini wrote, was needed before she would come. To this, Browne

replied firmly, 'No bribery.' Yet the Commissioner was increasingly anxious for Demont to testify, and the charabanc plied assiduously between Morges and Colombier, according to later testimony of the *voiturin* Jean Linder. Finally in January 1819 came the welcome news that Louise had consented to appear before the Commission in Milan. 'Like a second Cicero', Sacchini had held forward to Demont – in place of gold – 'the noble opportunity of revenge'.[57] Apart from her privileged position as lady's maid, Demont was also the witness, with Sacchini, last in contact with the Princess.

The Commission had increasingly less dependence, despite Ompteda's bluster, on evidence or witnesses emerging from Pesaro. None of the Pesarese nobility, it became clear, would consider deposing against the Princess to such a Commission, and the only other people she saw were 'the one family'. The fact was, as Ompteda lamented, the Princess provided riches for the people round about with her extravagant style of living, and she was popular, wherever she went, for the lively interest she took in the other inhabitants, great and small, as much as for her familiar tone and dispensations to charity. While the Pesaro authorities – Bischi, the police chief, and Gandolfi, the Papal Delegate – dutifully filed reports to Rome on her movements, they also appeared with her proudly in public, and sent a detachment of guards each day to the Villa Vittoria. Their interest in discovering evidence against the Princess, Browne raged, was lukewarm at best.[58] Hence the Commissioners' relief that Demont, who at least knew the Villa Caprile, if not the Villa Vittoria, would testify.

At the end of December 1818, with the Commission's approval or without, a further concerted attack had been made on the lakeside inhabitants at Como. Antonio Augustoni at Chiasso near Como wrote to Pergami, 'For some days past, there have been people here, lurking about, and running from one person to another with questions. . . . they have even found those who have dared to tell untruths. . . . the most respectable of them are but porters and watermen.'[59]

Dragoni, the Princess's factor at Como, was pursued by Restelli. His brother-in-law in Milan was simultaneously offered a bribe to obtain this useful witness. The gardener and washerwoman at the Villa d'Este were 'attacked' at their home in Cernóbbio by a small man with a round face, probably yet another agent called Dottore

Ciceri. Their methods were apparently crude, and certainly unknown to the Commissioners.[60]

In fact, on 22 December Vice-Chancellor Leach remonstrated with the Commission on the quality of the evidence: 'It is reasonable to expect that testimony with respect to domestic transactions should be found amongst the servants and dependants of the family, but it would be very fortunate if their statements could be confirmed by many witnesses of a different description.' The evidence of a cellar-maid at Karlsruhe, Barbara Kress, had raised a 'great expectation that it may be established that the conduct of the Princess was equally imprudent at other places'. Less than two months later, Leach was making the same point. There was enough evidence now from boatmen and couriers about carriages and embraces.[61] The Commissioners succeeded in halting their agents, and Lake Como resumed its former placidity.

Her lawyer Avvocato Codazzi reassured the Princess on 31 December, 'It was not a Milanese Government process against her, but an illegitimate and irregular process' by Vimercati and Lord Stewart, under the orders of the Prince Regent. Codazzi, well informed up to this point, thought the Milan Government might not know of it.[62] The Princess bided her time.

As the Commission dutifully bent to finding new witnesses in German inns and berated Ompteda for his inability to find the Captain of the *polacca* who had ferried the Princess to the east, Louise Demont arrived in Milan in February 1819. She captivated her examiners from the moment she appeared. Powell seems to have been especially smitten. This was no ordinary girl from a Swiss hamlet. One can see, in Demont's hard-headed aspirations, in the pains she took to achieve a demure and genteel exterior, how eager she was to forget her origins. In character she was a Continental Becky Sharp, who worked her way up through a combination of allure, sly wit and, above all, an ability to please while pleasing herself.

Louise Demont had been treated as friend, rather than maid, by the Princess of Wales, had been taken by her to the opera, the theatre. When she had been dismissed at Pesaro, she had written and published a journal of the Long Voyage, in which she had heaped praise on her former employer. It had caused a stir in Lausanne, and

she had been taken up and lionized by the local ladies. Now the
Commissioners were her prey. They wrote excitedly that she was an
excellent witness, and they were delighted to have got her. In fact,
she was a dismissed lady's maid, but Mlle Demont made herself a
great lady, who had condescended, in the pursuit of truth and justice,
to come down from the cold mountain heights and testify sorrowfully
against the employer who had got rid of her. Her examination
occupied all of twenty-two days, 'to allow her time for recollection
and not to fatigue her by too long attendance at one sitting', Powell
wrote tenderly.[63]

Her story led the Commissioners from the point of Pergami's
employment as courier in Milan in 1814, through his rise to honours
beyond his station, to her dismissal in November 1817, when he
presided over the Caprile household. Her position as lady's maid
meant that she had had the opportunity of inspecting the Princess's
bed linen, of observing marks, stains and impressions suggesting the
presence or absence of one or two in the Princess's bed during the
night. Thus the two points which the Commissioners sought to
establish – that Pergami's rise to honours could only have an amorous
explanation, and that he had had the opportunity of conducting such
exploits – were both met by the Swiss maid's evidence. It dovetailed
with Majocchi's, yet they had had no way of communicating. (The
fact that it did not adhere to the adulatory tone of her Lausanne
journal was not at this point thought relevant.) On 27 January the
Commissioners sent their fifth dispatch to Leach, suggesting that
some agent should be appointed to superintend the witnesses at
Milan: 'to counteract any attempts that may be made to influence
them to vary the facts which they have already stated'. They cited the
witnesses' 'proneness to be acted upon by menaces and bribes'.[64]
Leach replied that Browne should remain at Milan while Cooke and
Powell dealt with the German witnesses on their way home to
London.

Meanwhile, in Vienna, there were ructions from the witnesses
lodged there. Hardly had the group reached that city at the beginning
of December 1818 before the complaints began about Sacchi the
tailor. According to his assistant Negri, Sacchi was keeping a whore
at the Three Crowns Inn within ten days of his arrival. Maria Soleri,

another of the witnesses, was pregnant by her brigadier escort and proved untruthful as a witness. Sacchi, a bombastic fellow with a high opinion of himself, wrote that Riganti, the tobacconist agent in Milan, had promised him six florins maintenance in Vienna, and During had reimbursed him only at a rate of three a day.

Then there was the vexed question of whether old Battista Majocchi's wife was getting more money subsistence at Milan than Signora Sacchi. In fact Sacchi was generally contented. After three months in Vienna, he wrote to his wife that he had put on so much weight that his Milan waistcoats were all too small, and he had a double chin.[65]

As the Commission's work neared an end in March 1819, the agents were sent out again – with an architect apiece – on an important task. They were to make ground-plans of the relevant houses and inns where the witnesses' evidence turned on an arrangement of rooms. These plans still exist, ranging from the crude to the flower of the Italian architect's skill. The Princess in due course was to commission plans of her own. A beautiful representation of the Villa d'Este includes a coloured plan of all the gardens, grottoes, temples, as well as a fine front elevation of the house on the lake.[66] The circumstances in which these plans were made were not always easy.

To check that a plan of the Barona was correct, Louise Demont and Vimercati's wife and son – the lawyer himself was ill – arrived after Restelli had approached Filippo Pomi, the doorkeeper there. He agreed to let them in after money had changed hands. They would have to be quick, he warned them, to avoid detection by his wife. Louise Demont then 'ran through the bedrooms', as she put it, with the architect making hasty sketches as she went.[67]

The occasional employ of a *bel regalo*, or bribe, by their agents was perhaps suspected by the Commissioners. But it took them by surprise when they discovered that Codazzi's clerk was copying all his master's papers regarding the Princess for the purpose of offering them to Vimercati.[68]

The Princess of Wales did not begin her campaign against the Commissioners until the early part of 1819. From this point on, it would seem, she was cured of the lethargy which had gripped her since her daughter's death in 1817. She began by demanding attestations to her good conduct from her friends in Como and by discharging her Pesaro gardener, in the hope that the Commissioners would accept false testimony from him which she could later disprove. Apparently she was now expecting the Commissioners to approach her direct with an offer of terms for separation or even divorce. She had read this news in the *Gazzetta di Milano*, Ompteda thought, and had abandoned an aquatic expedition she had spoken of to Istria, south of Trieste.[69]

That March, while the two Commissioners Cooke and Powell packed their bags and Browne prepared to remain in Milan to superintend the witnesses, the Princess had a visitor in Pesaro. Mr James Brougham, Henry's brother, had been deputed by a committee of her trustees in London to travel to Pesaro and discover the full extent of her liabilities and assets. He had also to devise a scheme for putting her financial affairs on a sounder footing.

In the course of two weeks at Pesaro, James Brougham gained a very detailed picture of the Princess's finances, her relationship with Pergami and her surprising thoughts for the future. His first impression was that the Villa Vittoria, the Princess's pride and joy, was unfitted to her situation – more of a cottage than a palace. The two large wings Antaldi was building were not finished. 'The confusion of buildings makes it look worse,' he wrote. The style of the whole thing was more 'hospitable and plentiful than dignified, elegant or even comfortable'. There was company to dinner every night, the guests were very respectable people from Pesaro and the neighbourhood – not much of a selection. Cardinal Albani on summer visits and the Pope and Consalvi in Rome were very civil to her. The permanent household, besides *il Barone*, consisted of his sisters and brothers, Willy Austin and the two Italian colonels, Alessandro Olivieri and Carlo Vassalli. Old Mother Pergami occasionally took her seat at dinner, and they ate off common white stoneware. 'Everything is "le Baron",' wrote James Brougham. His picture was in every room. The establishment was huge, some eighty people, including grooms and stablefolk to service forty-eight horses. And then there was the yacht with a captain and crew of eight maintained.[70]

The Princess received James Brougham with the greatest attention and kindness, spoke confidentially on all subjects and had *il Barone* lay all the books before him. Brougham found them quite regular; Pergami evidently understood figures well and superintended everything, with written orders for every last shilling's disposal. Brougham thought him 'a plain straightforward remarkably good sort of man . . . very active'.

The Princess of Wales spoke frankly about the reasons for the strange seclusion of her household. She had come to Pesaro originally for economy and to pay her debts. Now she liked it and wished to stay; she had promoted Pergami because she found him useful. Her gentlemen and servants had been incompetent in Naples and had spent a fortune. If her English ladies and gentlemen would not stay with her, what could she do? She had to have an Italian household, with Italian ladies and gentlemen and Italian servants.

Brougham's assessment was that she owed in total about £17,200 abroad – she also had debts in England. There was the most cordial hatred of Marrietti, principally because when she was living at Como he had paid, without orders from the Princess, whoever had applied to him. The Milan Commission rumours made her agree that she would pay him in two lump sums, while Brougham fended off creditors with £4000 immediately. 'She is solvent if she were to die tomorrow, the Villa d'Este, horses, jewels, et cetera would much more than pay her debts. . . .' If she lived, 'the debt compared to her income is a flea bite'.[71]

On the vexed question of her relationship with Pergami, Brougham at first considered that 'There is enough to justify reports, but still all may be right, and though the whole thing might be ridiculed, yet there is much to be said in her favour, and everything has been much exaggerated.'

He changed his opinion about this after a grand dinner for all the principal people of Pesaro, about thirty of them. They ate off plate – 'ye shabbiest sort, light plain things that scarce looked like silver' – and all with the Baron's arms. 'Nothing can appear more revolting to propriety than the Princess of Wales with her large fortune using another person's plate. . . . His house and grounds, his plate, his ordering everything, he even buys her bonnets, this I saw, and all his family quartered upon her!'[72]

The Milan Commission had very much annoyed the Princess of

Wales, he wrote. She had wanted to write to the Austrian Emperor in Vienna to demand that he put a stop to it, but he had dissuaded her. He had also prevented her having all the people of Pesaro examined. In opposition to these very Carolingian plans, he had suggested that she seek advice. She was well informed, he said, about the whole Commission, and dreaded chiefly Louise Demont, 'a great w—', she said, 'and undoubtedly bribed'. She also feared that Ompteda had plotted to poison her. As a result, there were pistols in Brougham's bedroom, and guard dogs prowled outside.

The Milan Commission had annoyed – or frightened – the Princess so much that she made a very surprising proposal before Brougham left. She wished to obtain a divorce from the Prince Regent – on terms.[73] She wanted an immediate final payment. James Brougham suggested an initial payment and an income to follow. She was really happy in Pesaro, she said, and received no insult from Rome, as there was no English minister there. Her support for the Whigs made her odious to the Prince, and she genuinely wanted not to return to England. Divorce seemed best now, Brougham added drily, before the Milan Commission reported. By now he was able to state that Pergami's bedroom was in the Princess's part of the house. They lived as man and wife.[74] It is not unlikely that Caroline wished to formalize that comfortable state of affairs by marriage, though Pergami's wife in Milan would have been something of an impediment to such a scheme.

The Princess's debts, and her fears of the Milan Commission, now opened the way for a calm and comparatively dignified ending to the most undignified royal marriage in English history. However, while the English ministers would undoubtedly welcome any concord between the royal pair, there was no longer any theoretical need for a divorce to ensure the Hanoverian succession beyond the Regent's own generation. For this very month, 26 March, occurred the first royal birth since Princess Charlotte's twenty-three years before – a son, Prince George, for the Duke of Cambridge and his new wife. Within two months followed, in indecent haste, the Kents' daughter Princess Victoria and the Cumberlands' son, another Prince George.

The Princess of Wales was hoping to achieve her aim of 'peace and money enough to live' by agreement; the Prince Regent, on the other hand, still strongly favoured divorce by trial. There were various options, as we shall see, but the most straightforward and amicable route seemed to be dissolution of the marriage by Parliamentary Bill. However, after Henry Brougham had consulted the Regent's friend Lord Lauderdale both men concluded that it would be 'totally impracticable to pass an Act unless on proof of guilt or confession of the party'. When James Brougham reported this to Caroline,

> she said, I feared it would be so. I then said she might get a separation by mutual consent, though not a divorce – she said that was doing nothing. She seemed so anxious, and spoke so confidentially that I asked her whether she would consent to allow as a reason for passing the Bill that she had been guilty of infidelity – to which she answered 'that is impossible'.[75]

Though the Princess did not deny her adultery to James Brougham, her refusal to admit it while at the same time brazenly living with Pergami as man and wife represented an audacious challenge to the Regent. She was shortly to modify her objective and pursue a separation by agreement. The challenge, however, still stood, and in making it she was hoping to find a champion in Henry Brougham. But it was Henry Brougham's subsequent performance which was to lead to the supreme crisis of her life.

## CHAPTER FOURTEEN

# PLANS FOR DIVORCE

## 1819–1820

*'Laws . . . strong enough for the times'*

Mr James Brougham's proposal of a divorce or separation was a practical acknowledgment of the intractable difficulties prevailing between the royal Titans. The Regent's venomous animosity towards his wife, countered by her vengeful feelings towards him, prevented any easy solution. Unfortunately, the new peace plan was destined to founder and its architect take his place in the long chain of disappointed and disinterested advisers. James Brougham clashed – as had Malmesbury and Cholmondeley, and Eldon, Perceval and Whitbread, and all the Princess's ladies wringing their hands – with those who sought to extract political advantage from the royal disaffection.

In 1819, besides the royal couple's mutual antagonism, and the Government's reluctance to take any firm action in the matter, there were several political opportunists ready to bring the negotiations to naught. And the brightest and best of these was James's own brother Henry, who affected to represent the Princess's interests. We shall see that the only interests we can be certain he represented were his own. The negotiations of 1819 and 1820 shed a fascinating light on Henry Brougham's crooked ambitions – or rather throw a fascinating shade. Into the lucubrations of his mind we can see only dimly, for Henry Brougham was frank with no man, at least on paper, although he conducted a vast correspondence.

Whenever Brougham enters the picture, he clouds it, partly because he rarely revealed what his object was, partly because he generally had several he was prepared secretly to pursue as well as several others he was openly pursuing – in sum, because he was a man of too many parts. He wore the two principal hats of lawyer and

Whig politician, but there were other and more laudable ones, such as Parliamentary reformer, educationalist, slave abolitioner, man of letters. Some of these interests were incongruous, even incompatible for anyone but Henry Brougham – a man with no fixed principles.

In the course of the negotiations he began by acting in the Princess's interests, and treated with the Tory Government, ignoring Lord Grey's decree that the Whigs should steer clear of the Regent's marital difficulties[1] (the Whigs, as a party, had little hope of office). He then secretly abandoned the Princess's interests, while ostensibly continuing to act as her agent in the negotiations. He hoped thereby to obtain the silk gown of a King's Counsel – a prerequisite for the office of Lord Chancellor, to which he aspired. But he did not only aspire to be Lord Chancellor, he had hopes of the premiership. It was common knowledge that the Regent detested Lord Liverpool. Brougham would be led to a point in his Parliamentary ambitions where he wondered if he could not give the Regent what he wanted, get rid of his wife and then form a government himself.

The Princess of Wales confirmed, soon after James Brougham's departure from Pesaro in March 1819, that she was enthusiastic about the scheme for a divorce despite the apparent obstacles. She saw the Milan Commission as 'the Regent . . . maliciously at work so that he can remarry'. In fact, the Regent was eager only to extricate himself from his present ties, without much thought of what might come after. However, Caroline was soon concluding that separation by agreement had its advantages after all, not least as a pre-emptive strike. 'I will take a petition to Parliament,' she declared, 'so as to be quit at last for always of this tyrant and blackguard of a husband.' She urged Lady Charlotte Lindsay, the recipient of her letter, to chivvy Henry Brougham in the matter.[2]

Henry Brougham hardly needed encouragement. At the beginning of June, James having returned to London in June, Henry put in hand the negotiations for a separation. His object seems to have been to impress the Regent with his power over the Princess of Wales rather than do well by his client.

Brougham followed his brother's suggestions closely in the terms he offered. The Princess would remain abroad, renounce the right to be crowned in the event of the King's death, and meanwhile use a title other than that of the Princess of Wales – this would have the effect of freeing the country of further embarrassment arising out of her loose conduct. In return, she would receive the full annuity of £50,000, instead of the £35,000 she had deemed it politic to accept in 1814. He chose to follow his own line, however, in two important areas. First, he dispensed with the established charade whereby the Princess's advisers addressed the Government in her royal persona. Secondly, he did not approach the Government directly with the suggestion for a separation. He wrote instead first to Lord Lauderdale to invite him to put the offer to the Prince Regent. Lauderdale refused. Brougham then wrote to Lord Hutchinson, another personal friend of the Regent although nominally a Whig, but now he dissembled a little. He intimated that the suggestion for a separation emanated from him, and that he alone could get the Princess to agree to it. Thus was introduced the idea of his paramount importance in any negotiation that might follow, the idea that the Government would reward him in due course for his services.[3]

Hutchinson communicated the offer to the Government and to the Prince Regent. But the Regent was incensed by this talk of a separation 'by arrangement'. Divorce alone would satisfy him. The Milan Commission's Report was almost ready, and he was eagerly anticipating the public charges against the Princess which must surely follow in its wake. However, on 16 June he conceded that there were certain virtues in the proposal, not least because it suggested to him a marvellous compromise – a divorce 'by arrangement', instead of by adverse proceedings.[4] But this idea was anathema to the Government, and it lost no time in putting an end to the Regent's hopes. On the 17th it dispatched to him a forthright minute: a divorce 'never could be accomplished by arrangement, nor obtained except upon proof of adultery, to be substantiated by evidence before some tribunal in this country', which must pose, in these turbulent times, a 'serious hazard to the interests and peace of the kingdom'. Ministers suggested that a separation might be rendered complete 'by some arrangement upon the principles suggested ...' in Brougham's original proposal, and without the need for public proceedings, which they dreaded.[5] Whereupon the Regent, ignoring the Cabinet's last remarks, on the 22nd reverted to his original contention, that divorce proceedings were absolutely necessary to the nation's honour. The Milan Commissioners' Report, he prophesied, would convert the ministers to this view. Meanwhile, the ministers encouraged Brougham, although they stipulated that the offer must appear to come from the Princess herself.

Astonishingly, Henry Brougham never informed the Princess of these dealings. Thus she never knew that the Prime Minister and Cabinet approved the plan for a separation.[5] Instead he frightened her, first in June and at intervals in the succeeding months, with misleading reports that proceedings would take place against her in November, after Christmas, early in the New Year. Nothing, as we have seen, could have been further from the Government's mind, and nobody knew that better than Henry Brougham. It seems that he genuinely wished in June to please ministers by accomplishing the separation, and he created these alarms in her mind to make her more pliable to his will. By the end of the negotiations, however, as his correspondence with Hutchinson makes plain, he had abandoned the interests of the Government, as well as those of the Princess – both were for a royal separation – to serve the Regent secretly.

On 24 July, the Cabinet considered the Report. The Commissioners' proud boast was that 'this great body of evidence' that they had collected 'establishes the fact of a continuous adulterous intercourse'.[7] The Government did not hesitate to disagree, determining that the evidence was not strong enough to make the outcome of proceedings inevitable.[8] (Even had there been witnesses to half a dozen separate acts committed *in flagrante delicto*, one feels they would still have reached that conclusion.) The Government and Regent were never willing to compromise with each other on this issue. Nevertheless, as a sop to the Regent, it was settled that Cooke and Powell, released from the colossal labour of preparing the Report, should interview a few more witnesses – the naval captains Briggs and Pechell – and that the state law officers should consider the Milan Commission papers, with the Regent's own law officers, and recommend proceedings. The Government hoped that the matter could thus die away.

Brougham, on the other hand, was now playing a deep game. Without the knowledge of the Tory ministers, he encouraged the Regent, when he baulked at a separation, in hopes that he, Brougham, could secure a divorce. His political peers guessed at, rather than knew of, his underground communications with Carlton House. It was always of the utmost importance to him to hide his hand, but in this he outdid himself. Hutchinson reported to him from Stroud on 29 July that he had had a very long audience – three hours – with the Regent before he left London. Hutchinson believed that 'the Lady acquires courage from delay, and that she will not be inclined to yield' till Parliament reassembled. Hutchinson pressed Brougham to take to the Princess 'any proposal which might facilitate this ... he [the Regent] is by no means desirous of wounding the feelings of the Princess in any unnecessary degree, and still cherishes the hope that something may be accomplished through your interference.... Of this I am sure,' Hutchinson concluded, 'that they [the ministers] will always bring forward the measure with reluctance.'[9]

The Government's relief that the matter was in abeyance and Brougham's new relationship with Carlton House were both jeopardized in August by the startling news that the Princess of Wales was on her way to London to 'confront her attackers'. According to Hutchinson, the ministers were 'thrown into the greatest state of anxiety and alarm' by this development. They especially dreaded the appearance of the Princess in London, bursting with her wrongs and ready to be taken up as a cause by her friends, who ranked among the Radical reformers and urged her to return.[10]

The ministers were increasingly worried by the general spirit of disaffection in the country, as trade fell back into depression and discontent with Liverpool's ministry increased. The populations of several cities, including Glasgow and Birmingham, were alleged in Parliament to be starving. There were outbreaks of violence and affray in the poorer manufacturing areas of the country. The increasing 'outdoor' agitation for Parliamentary reform dismayed the ministers still more. The proposed reforms included widening the electorate, abolishing rotten boroughs (those with no electorate to speak of) and creating Parliamentary seats in large towns and cities which lacked representation. The assemblies and meetings called by the Radicals frightened the ministers most of all.

In fact, because the leaders of this Radical movement hoped to show that they were fit to enter Parliament themselves, and their supporters fit to cast votes, respectability and orderliness were the keynotes of most of the assemblies, and of most of the literature. Mr Samuel Bamford was one of the heterogeneous group of individuals who followed trades varying from weaver to tailor, from bookseller to shipwright, and who united in their outdoor Radical work. Bamford reveals in his autobiography that there was even a code of dress for the meetings, at which speakers such as Mr Henry 'Orator' Hunt and Sir Francis Burdett addressed mostly peaceful crowds. When they drilled, it was to march in an orderly fashion to assigned meeting places.[11]

Radical extremists, and extremist tracts, speeches and slogans, naturally existed. Still, the audiences which assembled in the country-side to hear the speakers in support of reform – and in large towns as well as London – included the odd peer of the realm, a gaggle of MPs and a variety of persons of the middling class, although the indus-trious or working classes were in the preponderance. There was an impatience for change in Parliament.

Most Radical meetings assembled and dispersed quietly, as requested by the speakers and in accordance with the Radical tenets. The nationwide network of Hampden Clubs, where issues were thrashed out in smaller groups, caused no incident. The literature with which the Radical groups sought to advance their cause among right-thinking men and women was effective, but hardly immoderate. Women, incidentally, were allowed a vote at Radical meetings, though there was no thought of their voting at Parliamentary elections. Home Office agents, nevertheless, sent reports that confirmed the ministers' worst fears: of turbulent mobs mouthing violent sentiments against King, country and especially Government; of wild and sedi-tious ideas promulgated in bloodthirsty tracts and fulminating broad-sheets. Lord Sidmouth at the Home Office was apt to shake his head and tap one of these documents whenever a colleague suggested that the mood of the country was on the mend.[12]

Interestingly, the Government saw the reform movement in Parlia-ment itself as far less threatening – although Lord John Russell and a few other Whig MPs had regarded reform as the great issue since before the Regency. Many others, including Brougham, had promised support in 1811 at a famous Crown and Anchor tavern dinner.

Moreover, at recent elections several MPs had been elected on a Radical ticket, including Aldermen Wood and Robert Waithman and Sir Francis Burdett. These Radical Members, with Russell, pressed motions to transfer the representation of rotten boroughs to more populous areas. But these motions had yet to succeed, and the Government felt safe in Westminster. The sins and abuses in Parliament of which the reformers complained had established an apparently invincible Tory majority, so Parliament could never reform itself until that majority so agreed. And that the Tories were disinclined to do, nor was most of the Mountain (an element of the Whig Opposition) as yet persuaded.

With this stalemate in Parliament, the Radical and reformist MPs joined in the outdoor agitation and so redoubled the ministers' worries about the state of the country. One can now see just why the ministers so feared the Princess of Wales's return. The persons with whom they suspected she was in contact in London were none other than the Radicals – Brougham, Burdett, Wood, Waithman. The thought of her reappearance in England, which had for so long haunted her husband, now became a frightful spectre for the ministers too in the climate of disaffection in which they imagined themselves to live, beset by revolutionaries and rioters; they saw that the Radicals might fashion out of the Princess and her claims about the Milan Commission a very useful stick with which to beat them. They envisaged the Radicals promoting her cause, airing her wrongs at public meetings. Couriers were dispatched to urge the governments of France, Austria and elsewhere to prevent her passage to England, and the British ministers waited uneasily.

Brougham's reaction was equally agitated. The return of the Princess, he wrote to Hutchinson on 5 August, would be 'pregnant with every sort of mischief', and he added, with scant respect for his client, '(not to mention the infernal personal annoyance of having such a d—l to plague me for six months)'. He had not believed her occasional intimations that she would come over, and in June he had told her not to. Now it seemed she really was on her way. He went on to say that he hoped the Regent would protect him from the clamour of the mob, a further indication of the double part he meant to play. He had written to Caroline at Pesaro, he told Hutchinson in a further letter on the 12th, instructing her to stop at Lyons and await his arrival.[13]

On receiving this letter, Hutchinson wrote from Ireland to Bloomfield, the private secretary at Carlton House:

> I should hardly think that the Lady would venture over and I agree in opinion with the writer [Brougham] that it is probably only a demonstration on her part, but however she is so strange a woman that he [Brougham] cannot venture to calculate upon anything or to suppose that she will not perform any act because the impudence and imprudence of it be self-evident. . . .[14]

An erratic series of requests and announcements trickled into London in August, all indicating that the Princess was indeed in earnest and that she would appear in the capital in September. Rumours flew about among members of her erstwhile suite and household. Lady Charlotte Lindsay received a letter from Pesaro in which the hope was expressed that she would be at Dover on an unspecified date in September to meet her mistress – from whose employ she had resigned in 1816. Lady Charlotte sent the letter to Brougham in Cumberland, and voiced her doubts that 'the Lady' would keep the appointment.[15] Others were more trusting. Sicard, walking in Kensington Gardens, was asked by Miss Hayman if it were indeed true, and declared that he was sure she would come. Mr Moses Hoper interrogated Brougham's housekeeper in Hill Street.[16]

Confirmation came from Italy. The Princess had left the Villa Vittoria on 17 August for an unknown destination. Moreover, the Milan authorities had been tricked into sending her, under the alias of Contessa Oldi, a passport for France. Metternich wrote personally to the Prince Regent to apologize for his Milanese officials' folly, and to inform him that the Princess had now been traced to a remote and decaying residence, the Villa San Bono, in the Duchess of Parma's territories near Piacenza. If she would not give back her passport for France, if the frontier officials let her through, couriers he had already sent would ask the French Government to stop her from crossing the Channel. Lord Stewart had warned Sir Charles Stewart, the British Ambassador in Paris, to scrutinize all passport applications.[17] As the frontier guards of Europe armed against her coming, we must return to Pesaro to see why, against Brougham's advice, the Princess had taken this dramatic step.

Just as Brougham's intentions this long summer were cloaked in ambiguity, the Princess behaved in a manner to puzzle her contemporaries, as well as those who have come after. When James Brougham left her in March, she was still contentedly embellishing her 'cottage' at Pesaro. She had fitted out the rooms upstairs with a library and a music-room for her pianoforte, harp, hand-organ and other musical instruments. The saloon was apparently in Turkish style, to judge from the number of 'pillows' recorded in an 1821 inventory of the house and from a contemporary's observations on the dress of the tapestried figures on the walls. Lustres and lamps, pier-glasses and sofa-tables testify to a degree of comfort, without, as James Brougham remarked, much elegance. The most lavish room in the house was probably the Princess's bathroom, with its mirrored and painted ceiling and sunken marble bath. Not that the house was completely finished. The Princess always had a fresh scheme afoot, and when she left she was apparently thinking of turning an upper room into a billiard-room – perhaps to display Napoleon's billiard cue.[18]

In May, the Princess was busily involved in a local project, without a thought of foreign travel. Perticari's new theatre in Pesaro had proved a great success, and companies from Bologna and Florence had appeared during the two previous seasons. The Princess became a public benefactor this season, and paid for a troupe from Bologna to appear – with the proviso that they sing no music by Rossini. By chance, Rossini himself came back to Pesaro this season, and prevailed on his hosts the Perticari to take him to the opera. The Princess and her household were forewarned of this, and when Rossini entered the pit of the theatre a loud hissing was heard. No one could tell at first at whom it was directed, and there was an undignified scramble on the part of several likely victims to leave the theatre. The Princess sat implacably in her box – no. 25. (It is still to be seen, at the side of the stage.) Then a voice was heard at the back of the gallery: 'It is for you, Rossini.' There was a general mêlée, as Rossini and the local police and the claque in the gallery, as well as other opera-goers, tussled together. By the following day, it had been established that the malevolents in the gallery were drinking-companions of *il Barone*.

According to Browne in Milan, it was settled by the citizens that Pergami had set them on to their task and that the incident dishonoured all Pesaro, as well as its famous son. A group of townspeople then marched on the Villa Vittoria and expressed their disapproval of the household's behaviour by applying sticks and stones to the window-glass.[19]

Browne asserted that this exhibition of disfavour so alarmed the Princess that she then and there left Pesaro. In fact, Rossini's momentous visit to the theatre occurred on 23 May, and the Princess did not leave Pesaro till mid-August. Nevertheless, it seems plausible that the incident at the theatre, and her consequent loss of popularity in the town, made the Princess of Wales uncomfortable there. At any rate, she wrote her letter, announcing her return to England, to Lord Liverpool only a week after the incident, and before Brougham had suggested the plan of separation to the Government.[20]

In June and July, for the first time since her daughter Charlotte's death, the Princess went travelling, to Como and to Lodi, near Milan. Browne described her as unusually active and restless. Her residence in the Casino d'Olza – a 'miserable town house' in Lodi, he said – while Pergami conducted his business transactions, reawakened in the Milanese nobility all the feelings of disgust they had felt during her residence at Como.[21]

Certainly, the Princess's instinctive remedy for unease or dissatisfaction was to escape and travel. However, the journey to England which she meditated was hardly on a par with the tours which she undertook on a whim or on feeling a whiff of malaise in Italy, in Switzerland or in the German states. All through June and July she was laying careful plans for her journey. She arranged to hire two houses, stopping-places in Italy on the way to the port of Genoa. She engaged at Lodi a caretaker for the Villa Vittoria during her absence.[22] And, as we have seen, she corresponded mightily with England about her coming visit. Did she have advisers besides Brougham in London, as Liverpool suspected, and were they the Radicals?

The Princess knew full well that a formal separation with an additional £15,000 a year would bring her a measure of relief, and deliver her from fears of the Milan Commission and proceedings. So why in June did she announce her return, when the Brougham brothers had promised to try and get her the separation which in March she had wanted? At a guess, she felt, rather like the Prince Regent, that such an anodyne measure gave no vent to her anger against her spouse, while a dramatic return to England appealed to all her love of histrionic gestures. Possibly some of the Radical MPs encouraged her in this move. Just as the Whigs, and the Tories before them, had adopted the Princess's cause, so now one may guess that she served as a useful symbol of oppressed virtue to the Radicals. Firm evidence that they advised her at this date to return to London is lacking.

The idea of a return had always been at the back of her mind. On James Brougham's departure in March, she had informed Gell that, if the Government's answer was not favourable, she would go in her little vessel to London.[23] In the event, she set out by carriage. On 12 August she was ensconced at Pesaro, and writing to Gell. She was expecting a visit from Keppel Craven, with whom she had resumed contact.[24] But on 17 August she was away, and most of her household with her – packed into three post-chaises and bound for none knew where.

The authorities and Browne in Milan were horrified when the Papal authorities communicated this news. For all they knew, she might have taken ship already for England. In fact, her flight, though dramatic – and for several days the Princess of Wales succeeded in vanishing entirely from official view – was short. At the beginning of September Metternich received a stiff letter from Count Albert Neipperg, Prime Minister of the Duchy of Parma, which included Piacenza. He had been villeggiaturing at Sala Bagnaria with his royal mistress (in both senses of the word), Marie-Louise, Duchessa di Parma and former Empress of Napoleon. The holiday atmosphere was seriously disturbed, and the Duchessa sorely vexed, when police reports from Parma and Piacenza intimated that the Princess of Wales had entered her territories and apparently had every intention of remaining there.[25]

The Princess's identity had been exposed when the size and boisterousness of her party brought the city guards running to demand passports at a posting-house just outside the walls of Parma. Then word reached the outraged Duchessa that the Princess had hired a house in the Piacentine Hills – the Villa San Bono – from a Parmesan banker, Signor Ghizzoni, and had taken up residence there. The Duchessa di Parma, wrote Neipperg from her country retreat, considered that her territories, ceded to her at the Congress of Vienna, had been violated by the entry of the Princess of Wales.[26] (The two ladies had not met since the Princess of Wales had fallen off her chair at Parma in 1816.)

For once the Princess showed none of her usual enthusiasm when travelling for making new acquaintances among the local nobility. She remained quietly at San Bono, while the authorities buzzed with agitation, and police chiefs, civil authorities and dragoon guards attempted to discover the purpose – and proposed length – of her visit. Rumours flew about. Lights burnt up on the hill late at night. It was thought that she expected visitors from England. Had they arrived? From the house led a multitude of tracks and paths through the hills – into Tuscany and to the port of Leghorn, or into Piedmont, where Genoa lay just across the Apennines. How to stop her? Metternich suggested that Count Julius Strassoldo, the Austrian Governor of Milan, should go to San Bono and ask for her passport back, because it was made out in Contessa Oldi's name.[27]

Whom was the Princess expecting in her mountain eyrie? Not Brougham, for sure, and we have some pointers that it may have been members of the Radical party. Moreover, the arrival of her lawyer Codazzi from Milan and her household's frequent comings and goings between Piacenza and Como suggest that she was hoping to marshal a defence, or even draw up charges against the Milan Commission. At Piacenza post office, clerks scrutinized her correspondence and found that she had written letters to the following in England: Sir Francis Burdett and Aldermen Wood and Waithman. Moreover, the names of two English travellers, 'Guglielmo Wood' and 'Joseph Broadley', were inscribed in the police records at Parma.[28] These men arrived the very day the Princess reached the villa. The son of Alderman Matthew Wood was called William. Why the son, and not the father, if Guglielmo Wood proceeded to San Bono? And why did nothing come of the meeting?

On 12 September, a courier with a letter for the Princess arrived from England in Piacenza, and that same night the post-coaches rolled down the hill, bearing the Princess away to another mysterious destination.[29] What was in that letter, who had written it and was the Princess now making her dash for England?

To provide some answers to these questions, we must return to England and to the infamous proceedings at the Manchester Meeting of 16 August – today generally known as Peterloo – which effectively distracted the ministers from their fears of the Princess's arrival. Orders were given by the Manchester magistrates for the dispersal of an assembly of Radical reformers in St Peter's Fields. The Radical leaders at the meeting included Mr Henry 'Orator' Hunt. The various contingents of the meeting had drilled for weeks before, and some of the crowd held banners proclaiming 'Votes for All' and 'Reform or Death'. The magistrates felt that this 'Jacobin' meeting was intended as 'a display of the organized power of the unrepresented' – which it was. But Lord Eldon's Actonian aphorism – 'Numbers constituted force, and force terror, and terror illegality'[30] – applied more to the mayhem which followed than to this peaceful assembly. The magistrates decided that 'the whole bore the appearance of insurrection',[31] and made out a warrant for Hunt's arrest. Forty yeoman cavalry broke into the tightly packed crowd, estimated later at some 60,000 strong, and including women and children. They literally cut a path with their sabres through the frightened mass of bodies – or the horses' hoofs pounded such a path – to reach the platform, where Hunt had been about to speak. Hussars were called in to help the yeomen, and the scene became a confusion of fleeing citizens, plunging horses and flashing swords. Within fifteen minutes, eleven people were dead and four hundred injured.

Feelings ran high against the magistracy, and against the Government. On Hunt's platform there had been, unusually, newspaper reporters from the London and provincial press, and the proceedings were reported in detail. The Whigs seized the tragic occasion to lecture more of the middling class of the urgent need for some degree of Parliamentary reform. Meanwhile, Hunt languished in jail for the best part of a year, awaiting trial.

The Government, however, fought back. Earl Fitzwilliam was dismissed from his lord-lieutenancy for urging an inquiry into the magistrates' conduct, and the Regent publicly congratulated them.

This attracted not a little odium. As Sir Francis Burdett said, 'For what . . . ? . . . their promptness in shedding the blood of their countrymen?' Home Secretary Lord Sidmouth was confirmed in his belief that 'The laws were not strong enough for the times.'[32]

For the Radicals, including Burdett and the Princess's two other September correspondents, Wood and Waithman, Peterloo was not only a 'massacre' but superb political capital, and the Radicals made of it one of the most emotive symbols of governmental oppression of the nineteenth century. The Radical press condemned the Government for 'high treason against the people'. Burdett presided over meetings condemning the 'massacre'. Wood and Waithman orchestrated the City response. And the matter did not end there. As the calls for an inquiry in the country increased, the Parliamentarians prepared for their own battle. The Government announced, and set the state law officers to devising, 'laws . . . strong enough for the times'. These bills were to become the notorious Six Acts, to be debated in emergency session in November.

If Burdett and Wood and Waithman had planned to meet with the Princess of Wales in San Bono in September, they had no time for it now. If they earlier had had plans to incite the people to clamour and dissent by promoting the Princess as a symbol of oppressed virtue, they had no need of her now. Possibly Mr William Wood was a messenger to tell Caroline of the subsequent engagements which detained his father. And the letter which sent her off? Although it is difficult to interpret accurately the chain of communication between the Princess in Italy and her correspondents in London, it may be that this was Brougham's letter of which he wrote to Hutchinson on 12 August, wherein he warned her not to approach England but to go to Lyons, where he would come to her.

Caroline certainly followed Brougham's instructions and proceeded in due course to Lyons. Before she journeyed in France, however, she spent a month at the ramshackle castle of Montuè de' Gabbi belonging to the Conte Giuseppe Candiani-Rota in the province of Alessandria, in the King of Sardinia's lands. Browne in Milan commented that the arrival of the Princess of Wales caused consternation in her host governments similar to that occasioned by brigands. The local Sardinian officials were privately instructed to do all they could to make her stay uncomfortable. They stopped clearing the road leading up to the castle and removed the guard they had initially afforded her, as inducements to her departure.[33]

The Princess remained here till early October, notwithstanding this frigid welcome, receiving no visitors nor apparently any communications from England. Pergami and William Austin, Vassalli and the rest went back and forwards to Como and Milan, as the police records and reports attest, in search of witnesses to depose against the Milan Commissioners and in favour of the Princess. Apparently, from this mountainside in Savoy she was organizing further details of her defence. She asked for a passport for Avvocato Giuseppe Marocco, her Como lawyer. She wished him to conduct her defence in England, she told the Governor of Milan. She also wrote to Sir Charles Stewart in Paris, intimating that she looked forward to a reception at the French Court on her arrival and requesting a passport for England.[34]

As suddenly as she had arrived at the Castel di Montuè, one day she was gone. Now, for the first time since she had settled at Pesaro, the Princess of Wales left Italy. Was she on her way to England at last, after these false starts? Metternich, and Lord Stewart on the English Government's behalf, were in a frenzy again. They instructed the Milan authorities, and implored the Sardinian and French governments, to block her journey at every point from Alessandria itself to the Simplon Pass, to Paris and to the English Channel. Despite the willing co-operation of all the authorities and governments, on 12 October the fugitive Princess of Wales slipped through the various nets and arrived at Lyons. There she pursued her usual practice of inserting a paragraph in the newspaper announcing her presence. To everyone's great relief she seemed to have no immediate intention of progressing further north. To dissuade her from thoughts of Paris, Sir Charles Stewart wrote her a letter in which he regretted that her not being received at the Regent's Court meant that the French King felt unable to receive her at his.[35] The Princess was duly indignant, but remained at Lyons to await Brougham.

When Henry Brougham had suggested meeting her at Lyons, the political watershed of Peterloo was still a few days off. With the debate on the emergency legislation coming up in November, Brougham could hardly get away – and so he wrote to the Princess in

Lyons on 5 November. He was marshalling, with the rest of the Opposition – Whig and Radical – every fact, figure and argument that could be found against the proposed measures. Moreover, he was helping to mastermind, or at least encourage, opposition in the country.

In his letter to the Princess, Brougham did not fail to add, 'there is nothing more certain than some [divorce] proceedings – though they may be delayed till after Christmas'.[36] He promised to come to her before that time. This information was, just as before, wholly false, and, as before, he knew it to be so. With calls for a Peterloo inquiry, the ministers wanted less than ever to pursue the Princess. They were still afraid that she would continue her journey over to England. In October and again in November Lord Hutchinson, on their behalf, begged Brougham to go to the Princess in Lyons to reinforce his counsel that she stay away.[37] Brougham impatiently refused. The political opportunities presented in the wake of Peterloo had weakened his interest in the Princess's affairs and in colluding with the Regent. He judged that fear of proceedings would keep the Princess out of England, while he devoted his attention to attacking the government bills. After the session was over, he might give the matter some thought.

Caroline's hopes were raised when she received a visit from two Whig peers, Lords Whitworth and Essex. Imagining that they brought a political offer of some kind, she welcomed them. Lord Essex later commented that she appeared very dirty and wore liquid rouge. On discovering that they were merely passing through on their way from Italy to the November Parliament, she rose abruptly and dismissed them.[38] Presumably she understood then that Brougham was not coming out to her.

At any rate, she had left Lyons for Marseilles, 'as it was too cold to wait there in the bad season', before Brougham's letter reached her.[39] In London, the Regent spoke in Parliament of 'the seditious practices so long prevalent' which necessitated these six bills. 'A malignant spirit is now fully manifested,' he declared, '. . . aiming at the subversion of the rights of property and all order in society.'[40] Brougham, Burdett, Wood were among many who spoke forcefully against the bills. In December – inevitably with the Tory majority in both Houses – the Six Acts were passed, restricting meetings, gagging the sixpenny press, empowering the seizure of arms in disturbed districts, preventing drilling and hastening misdemeanour trials. And still Brougham did not go out to the Princess.

In December, she was still expecting him, and she still had half a mind to go to England, as she informed Gell. She missed her cottage in Pesaro. If she had a chance of winning, she would go to England, otherwise she would wander the globe, she wrote wildly. Less wildly she enclosed a statement of the varying amounts, terms and conditions of her annuity from England, from the £5000 pin-money on her marriage to the current £35,000.[41] She had heard rumours from England that her uncle King George III was not expected to last the winter. With his death, all the royal annuities would lapse, and her annuity as Queen of England would have to be considered afresh by Parliament.

The King of England, in his rooms overlooking the North Terrace at Windsor, had caught a cold, and it had gone to his lungs. As the doctors' prognostications became increasingly gloomy, his son, the Prince Regent, was haunted by the spectre of his estranged wife coming to claim her crown as Queen. He urged on the state law officers, who still had in their hands the Milan Commissioners' Report, to reconsider it – and, with it, some useful additions. After a lengthy search, Browne in Milan had finally discovered in Amalfi the Captain of the *polacca* which had taken the Princess to the East, and he had pressed into service the British Minister in Naples, Sir William à Court. Grumbling, à Court negotiated with the Captain, and his secretary, terms on which they were prepared to leave their ship and go to testify before Browne in Milan. The sum Captain Gargiulo asked was so enormous, à Court wrote testily, he only hoped the Captain's testimony would be worth it.[42]

In Vienna, Lord Stewart had interviewed Hesse, the Princess of Wales's erstwhile equerry and possibly lover of both herself and her daughter. On this occasion, to Stewart's annoyance, Hesse proved a model of loyal discretion, and had seen nothing at any time to compromise his royal mistress. He had left her service only when called away by his regiment for the Waterloo campaign.[43] Even without Hesse, the witnesses protected by the British Embassy at

Vienna were a matter of anxiety to Stewart and to Browne in Milan. Majocchi was dispatched to England in December, as travelling valet to a Mr William Hyett, in whose service he continued on their arrival in Gloucester. He had been growing restless, and a change of scenery was thought advisable.[44] Stewart and Browne had also been made anxious by the Princess's autumnal activities round Lake Como.

In July 1819, the Milan Commissioners had seen fit to dispatch Louise Demont, Majocchi's former fellow-servant, and Sacchini to London for safe keeping. To disguise themselves, they adopted the elevated titles of Comtesse Colombier and Conte Milani. Demont plagued the life out of poor Powell, whose unenviable task it was to supervise her accommodation. Barely a week went by without a plaintive note from her arriving at his chambers. 'Je n'ai plus d'argent' was the constant refrain – she had an appetite for food and drink, not to mention clothes, of a quality to match her new title. She changed her lodgings frequently, generally after her landlady or the housemaid had in some way insulted her. She took English lessons, kept a maid, dined out regularly and lay abed late. She had, in addition, brought with her as chaperones her youngest half-sister and a Mlle Raimondi from home.[45] And all this the public purse bore unawares.

Sacchini retreated to the country in September with a doctor's certificate that the London air was bad for him. He remained at Aston in Kent till November, as the paying guest of a Reverend Philip Godfrey. Godfrey so relished the amiable Count's company that he took him with him when he went out to dinner in the neighbourhood. Still Sacchini complained, and begged Powell for leave to return to Milan – he was terrified that his rich uncles there would disinherit him now that they had learned of his presence in England on the Princess's business. Reluctantly, as proceedings seemed, in November, far off – contrary to Brougham's letter to the Princess – Vice-Chancellor Leach gave permission for him to depart for Italy.[46]

Apart from the deposition of the *polacca* Captain and his mate, and some further depositions of Captains Briggs and Pechell, there was little for the Advocate-General (Sir Christopher Robinson), the Attorney-General (Sir Robert Gifford) and the Solicitor-General (Sir John Copley) to consider which the Cabinet had not seen and rejected in July 1819. The Regent hoped, however, with the Six Acts in place and the agitation in the country subsiding, that a clear case against his wife would be discerned. On 17 January 1820 the law officers of the Crown, and on the 21st those of the Duchy of Cornwall, agreed that a Parliamentary bill of divorce was the appropriate measure, given the options.[47]

The Princess of Wales's adultery, if proven, did not constitute high treason, they argued. 'If a man do violate the ... wife [of] the King's eldest son and heir,' Edward III's statute ran, he committed high treason. Chief Justice Coke had added the gloss: '*Violare* is here taken for *carnaliter cognoscere* [to obtain carnal knowledge]. . . . And if the wife of the King do yield and consent to him that committeth this treason, it is treason in her.'[48] Pergami could commit no treason against a king or crown not his own. Therefore, 'if the Princess do yield and consent to him', she committed no treason either.

Next, the law officers of Crown and Duchy advised delicately, an ecclesiastical measure – granting a separation *a mensa et thoro* – was not advisable, for the petitioner had to show 'clean hands' (as the maxim required), unblemished by adultery – which, as everyone knew, was out of the question for both parties. It was not, they considered, a matter for an attainder. So they plumped for a bill of divorce as the least problematic measure. But they could not recommend it, in view of the scandal it would bring on the Prince Regent. Impervious to cautious counsel, the Regent handed on the law officers' opinions to the Cabinet for consideration.[49]

Meanwhile, the Misses Mary and Agnes Berry saw the Princess of Wales at Marseilles and reported that she was in reflective and quiet mood.[50] Staying at a small hotel, and keeping relatively incognito, she had at last all but given up Brougham. She was merely waiting for better weather to sail back to Italy and her 'cottage' at Pesaro. At the end of January 1820, resigned to the futility of her wait, she departed by ship from Toulon. Bad weather and near-shipwreck caused her to put in at Monaco, where she recovered for several days at the palace of Prince Honoré V. She then proceeded to Leghorn, instead of Genoa, her earlier proposed destination. On account of this, her old steward Sicard had some difficulty in locating her to give her momentous news. King George III had died on 29 January, and she was Queen of England. When she had written as 'Princesse de Galles' on 1 February 1820 to thank Honoré for his Governor's attentions in Monaco, she was, in fact, Queen Caroline, Queen Consort to King George IV of Great Britain.[51] But would she be crowned? Sicard brought with him to Leghorn a letter from Brougham which pressed her in peremptory terms to make for London as quickly as she could.

## CHAPTER FIFTEEN

# QUEEN

February–June 1820

*'Uncrowned and unprayed for'*

'ON MY ARRIVAL at Leghorn I found Mr Sicard with a long letter from Brougham,' the new Queen of England informed her vice-chamberlain Gell, 'communicating the demise of our good old King and the new title I had obtained.'[1]

Queen Caroline dispatched Sicard obediently to England with the warrants which Brougham had requested for his and Mr Thomas Denman's appointment as her Attorney- and Solicitor-General. (There were seventy places, 'some of them very fat ones', as Brougham put it,[2] in the gift of the Queen Consort.) However, the Queen herself did not depart for northern France, where Brougham had urged her to proceed with all haste and where he had promised to meet her. The previous four months had hardly inclined her to believe his promises. Furthermore, she had no wish to be neglected by the French officials as Queen, as she had been as Princess of Wales. At Rome her quarterly pension waited; at Rome the Papal authorities had always treated her with respect.

On 20 February 1820, Cardinal Consalvi accordingly received a missive from the new Queen's chamberlain, Barone Pergami di Franchina, to the effect that her Majesty the Queen of England would shortly arrive in Rome.[3] The Cardinal confided to a sympathetic Duchess of Devonshire in her apartments near the Quirinal the difficulties this royal visit posed. She wrote in her diary, 'I don't see how he can avoid calling upon her.'[4] The Duchess and her English coterie of friends, including Mrs George Canning, would have to follow suit, repugnant as the idea might be. Queen Caroline, equally not doubting her welcome, rattled up two days later to the Villa Brandi on the Aventine Hill, where she had stayed before. Now she hired superb apartments complete with Great Hall and suitable for a travelling Court.

Caroline had a position at the head of English female society as Queen Consort, whether in Rome or in England, quite other than that which she had occupied as Princess of Wales. Her powers in England would revolve, like those of Queen Charlotte before her, around the drawing-rooms which she held. The Duchess of Devonshire and her friends speculated that, if the Queen returned to London, the King would shut up Court, so that his Queen could hold no drawing-rooms. Worse still, the Court of St James, presided over by such a Queen, might find itself short of company. Either way the English throne was disgraced, the tone of English Society greatly lowered and the example to the lower orders far from uplifting. Still, the Queen was the Queen, and the Duchess and Mrs Canning prepared to do their duty and pay their respects.

The Duchess of Devonshire was gratified to learn from the Cardinal, in one of their cosy tête-à-têtes, that the Queen would not remain queen for long. Consalvi had consulted with Baron Reden, Ompteda's successor as the Hanoverian minister, and with the Comte de Blacas, the French Ambassador. Reden advised that no deference need be shown to 'the Queen, or Princess of Wales – one knows not what to call her'. Reden assured Consalvi that proceedings were about to be brought against 'Caroline of Brunswick' and the title of queen stripped from her.[5] Consalvi, in the mistaken belief that he was following Foreign Secretary Lord Castlereagh's directives – rather than the King of Hanover's wishes – then acted towards Queen Caroline with an insolence which was regrettable in a cardinal. From a diplomatic point of view, it was a disastrous display of spleen.

Consalvi began by refusing Pergami's demands on the Queen's behalf for a guard of honour and a Papal audience. He wrote, 'As there has been no communication from the English Government, the Papal Government does not know that the Queen of England is in Rome.' The Queen sent Pergami back next day with an angry letter: 'I demand the guard of honour which your Government gave me on my other visits.' This royal person, said Consalvi suavely, must see that as Contessa Oldi, on whose passport she travelled, she had no right to Papal audience or guard of honour. If she asked for the guard as Princess of Wales, it would be sent to her straight away.[6]

The Queen was outraged and initially bewildered by Consalvi's antagonistic stance. She held that she, in contrast to Consalvi, had been informed officially of her new titles. In this she prevaricated a little, as Brougham and not the English Government had dispatched Sicard to her with the news. Consalvi was technically in the right, as he reminded Mr Charles Dodwell, an English expatriate and her next emissary. It was not etiquette for Courts to accord titles to visitors until informed officially. 'Wretched woman, what a situation she had brought herself into,' commented the Duchess of Devonshire. The Duchess then herself received a visit from Dodwell, who, with Gell, had joined the Queen in Rome. Dodwell begged the Duchess to intercede with the Cardinal. He said that the Queen had cried very much, that she said she had come to Rome to pay her debts and that Consalvi seemed to think her an adventuress by referring to her as that royal person.[7]

Thus the pleasant life which the Queen had envisaged unfolding at Rome under the canopy of her new titles did not materialize. She wrote to Gell in great discontent at the beginning of March, 'I cannot go out neither receive company till it has been mentioned in the papers that the King's funeral is over.' She compromised by placing a visitors' book 'open in the Great Hall' of her palace on the Aventine Hill 'for any strangers to leave their names'.[8]

A great quantity of English travellers were in Rome at this time for Holy Week as the visitors' book, an elegant marbled volume preserved at Windsor Castle, attests. John Gandy and the rectors of the Scotch and English Colleges, Lady Westmorland, Sir Humphry and Lady Davy all left their names, as did the Prince de la Paix and Torlonia.[9] The Queen sat in lonely state in the apartments above, waiting for visitors who did not call and for the Papal Government to relent. Consalvi considered that he had triumphed when he effectively barred the Queen of England from any form of public life.

In fact, in his wish to ingratiate himself with Castlereagh, the Cardinal made a serious error in listening to Reden. It was the wish of the King and his Hanoverian tools, not of the British Government, to start proceedings against the Queen and to strip her of her royal dignities. Consalvi apparently mistook the wistful wishes of the Hanoverian Minister for the British Government's firm statement of intent. As we have seen, the ministers were desperate to prevent proceedings against the Queen, and keen for her to remain abroad. The question arises – was Consalvi in fact eager to mistake Reden's word for Government gospel, and ingratiate himself with the King by insulting the Queen? The Queen believed this. Consalvi, she wrote, was 'in great hope that by behaving impertinent to the Queen a part of the Coronation oath would be left out against the Pope . . .'.

'He also, this worldly Cardinal,' the Queen went on, 'assures everyone that Lord Castlereagh has been the sole person who restored the Pope to his holy state, for which reason he could not act against his particular wishes.'[10] Yet, in insulting the Queen so grossly that she could not stay in Rome or the Papal States, Consalvi ensured, more than anyone, that she returned home to England – which was Castlereagh's and the ministers' nightmare. As we have seen, it was impossible to please both King and ministers in the matter of the Queen. It would appear that Consalvi chose to oblige the King.

At the beginning of March the diplomatic bag brought to the Duchess of Devonshire a letter from her sister Lady Liverpool and to Mrs Canning one from her husband George. The King had prevailed on the Government and the Archbishop of Canterbury to omit, by Order in Council, his wife's name and titles from that part of the liturgy where prayers were offered up for the royal family individually and collectively. No proceedings were to take place against her, however, unless she ventured over to England. Furthermore, the King had sought out precedents for excluding the Queen Consort from the Coronation. 'The Queen is to remain queen, but uncrowned and unprayed for,' was the Duchess's conclusion after she and Mrs Canning had pooled their information. They discussed anxiously whether they ought to visit. Mrs Canning said, 'Degradation should be avoided as much as possible . . . the better her existence was on the Continent the less inclined she would be to return and raise a cry for herself in England.'[11] The Duchess agreed, and pronounced herself ready to visit, if some lady or an English gentleman were present, and her name duly appears in the Lista di Visite. It is one of the last entries on 8 April.

Queen Caroline's fury at her reception in Rome was exacerbated by the news of her exclusion from the liturgy. 'I believe it may bring her good luck,' she wrote grimly to Gell.[12] Her reaction to this second attack on her royal titles was to end her plans to reach England some time at the end of the year. She instead prepared for an immediate return.

First, she framed a letter to Lord Liverpool. Lord Castlereagh had spoken in the House of Commons of his support for her queenly privileges, she wrote, yet her new name and titles were omitted from the liturgy.[13] She wrote on the same day, 16 March, to the Foreign Secretary himself to protest that Reden had called her 'Caroline of Brunswick' in the presence of a large gathering.[14] She then sent separate letters to Brougham and to Alderman Wood to announce that she was on her way to England, and despatched Luigi Pergami to Pesaro with the news that she would shortly arrive there.

On 12 April, Cardinal Consalvi informed the Duchess of Devonshire that the Queen had gone – 'in such anger', recorded the Duchess, 'that she has vowed vengeance in every paper French and English and that it would not stop there'.[15] According to the Queen, the French Ambassador, the Comte de Blacas, had refused to sign her passport. 'Mr Park [the English Consul at Rome] with trembling hand much afraid of losing his place at last was obliged to give me a pass-port for London,' she wrote to Wood. 'The 30th of April I shall be at Calais for certain,' she added. 'I have seen no persons of any kind who could give me any advice different to my feelings and my sentiments of duty relatif of my present situation and rank of life.'[16]

The King's insistence on the omission of his wife's name from the liturgy together with Consalvi's insults were responsible for her abrupt departure for England. But Reden's extraordinary and repeated references in public to Caroline of Brunswick had acted as a goad. 'To be obliged to submit to the great insolence from [the] Hanoverian Minister which can know nothing of the constitution or of the real rights of the Queen of England', wrote Queen Caroline grandly, was out of the question.[17] Did Reden have secret instructions from Münster and ultimately from King George IV to urge the Queen to return to England? Why did Castlereagh not write to countermand Consalvi's reliance on Reden's information, and inform him officially of the Queen's presence in Rome? The answer is that neither Consalvi nor Reden gave him any account of their actions. With only an English consul in Rome, Castlereagh knew nothing of the Queen's complaints till her letter to him arrived at the end of March. His hurried response, informing Consalvi of the old King's death, the Queen's new title and her presence in Rome, arrived the day after she left Rome. It was a colossal shambles on the English Government's part. Ministers – and Brougham besides – had taken a foolishly complacent view of the Queen's likely reaction to her exclusion from the liturgy.

On 30 January, the day after his father's death, King George IV had attended church. He returned home in sombre mood, according to Castlereagh: 'The horror of having the Queen made an object of the prayers of his people haunted his imagination and distracted his rest.'[18] At the proclamation of the new reign next day outside Carlton House, according to Brougham, the King was disgruntled again. Brougham wrote to Creevey, 'The change of name which Mrs P [the Queen] has undergone has had a wondrous effect on public feeling. She is extremely popular. ... the cry at the proclamation was God save the Queen! but Perry [editor of the *Morning Chronicle*] durst not put it in his paper. ... he told me all this in private.'[19] The political significance of Caroline's popularity was reinforced by the imminence of a general election, necessitated by the change of monarch.

The King was 'very agitated' in council with his Cabinet on 2 February, as he pressed for the omission of his wife's name from the liturgy. The matter then lapsed when he fell victim to pneumonia or pleurisy. For some days it was believed the illness would prove fatal. 'I never prayed so heartily for a Prince before,' wrote Brougham, dreading the succession of the ultra-Tory Duke of York, and the rupture of his plans.[20]

The King recovered slowly, after his doctor Sir Matthew Tierney had relieved him 'at different times [of] about 80 ounces of blood'.[21] While still on his sick-bed, he resumed the campaign for divorce proceedings against his wife which his father's death had interrupted. In an attempt to influence the Cabinet's discussion of the law officers' opinions, he sent to his ministers the evidence collected since the Milan Commission's Report of July 1819.

On Saturday night, 5 February, the King recollected that the prayers to be said on the next day in church were not yet altered. 'He immediately ordered up all the prayer books in the house of old and new dates, and spent the evening in very serious agitation on this subject, which has taken a wonderful hold of his mind,' wrote the Secretary to the Admiralty Mr John Wilson Croker. Meanwhile, that Sunday the clergy prayed for 'our most gracious Queen' or for 'all the royal family', as they wished.[22]

The King had an excellent library, but, unfortunately, for all his thumbing of prayer books, he found no useful precedent. Furthermore, Cabinet ministers and prelates did not see the matter as clearly as he. The Archbishop of Canterbury Dr Charles Manners-Sutton protested, and his son, the Speaker, was in favour of praying for her, simply because she was Queen. The ministers were in two minds. They dreaded a public outcry, on the one hand, if the Queen's name were omitted; but they were aware that their report on the latest Milan evidence would enrage the King, and they were eager to oblige him in the matter of the liturgy, if they could.

On 10 February, at breakfast with Lord Lowther, Croker had the happy thought, 'If she is fit to be introduced to the Almighty, she is fit to be received by men, and if we are to pray for her in Church we may surely bow to her at Court.' Inclusion of her name would be 'a final settlement of all questions in her favour'. Removal of her name was therefore a matter of urgency. As Croker reported in his journal, Lowther said that 'in all the discussions he had never heard the matter argued from this religious point of view', and they went together to Carlton House, where Bloomfield was also much struck by this argument.[23]

The Cabinet agreed on the 10th to the omission from the liturgy, despite Canning's protests that, if there were to be proceedings, omitting the Queen's name from the liturgy was condemning her in advance. He was overruled with the argument that she was adequately prayed for in the expression 'all the royal family'. The Tory Government was aware that it was fighting to stay in office. In the same minute, it had returned objections similar to those in the minute of 17 June 1819 and in addition emphasized the inadvisability of proceeding in these times of distress and factiousness.[24]

The King was barely placated by the Cabinet's decision on the liturgy after its treacherous minute of 10 February, in which, according to Croker, 'They offer to assist to keep the Queen out of the country by the best mode, namely, giving her no money if she will not stay abroad. . . . The King will have a divorce or nothing.'[25] When the King ordered Castlereagh on 13 February to call Stewart and Münster to England, it was not hard to guess why. Both were chief players in the Milan Commission. Castlereagh wrote to Stewart on the 13th, 'I consider the Government as virtually dissolved. . . .'[26] The King had told Lord Liverpool to 'get out' of one Council meeting. He had sworn he would change his ministers and obtain a divorce, or go to Hanover and get one there.

Castlereagh considered the chief difficulty to be that, whereas previously they could stall, it really had to be decided now, about 'the Princess' as he called her, on three counts – the liturgy, financial assistance and the Coronation. He had hoped that, by excluding her from the liturgy and from the Coronation, the Opposition could be got to propose a Parliamentary inquiry into her conduct, and spare the ministers that disagreeable duty. Time was running out.

Croker in his journal wrote, 'It looks like a very serious breach.' The King said that his ministers had left him in the lurch. His health suffered. He ate only dry toast and drank a little claret and water.[27] 'It is said that the King applied . . . to some of the leaders of the Opposition,' Mrs Arbuthnot confided to her diary. 'But this is only street talk.'[28] Whether the Whigs were approached or not, the King yielded to his Tory ministers' view expressed on the 14th and grudgingly abandoned the notion of divorce, especially after Castlereagh had represented Prince Metternich's disapproval of the proposed measure. (Metternich had told the British Foreign Secretary at Aix-la-Chapelle two years earlier that he regarded any divorce in one of the ruling houses of Europe as most unwise.) Lord Stewart told Metternich that Castlereagh had informed the King of these views, and they had carried great weight. The King exacted only one concession: were the Queen to come to England, the Government would move against her and begin proceedings.[29] It is clear, from a letter Wellington wrote at this time, that the ministers thought this very unlikely.

Liverpool summoned Brougham as the Queen's adviser on 18 February, and stated the Government's decision not to proceed against her – unless she came to England – and to omit her name from the liturgy. The Prime Minister mentioned the provisions of the June 1819 proposal for a separation as still suitable for the Queen's comfort. Brougham, without disclosing that he had failed to communicate the proposal to Caroline, remarked that it would be more difficult to make her give up what she now had but which was then only in prospect. Liverpool retorted that she was destitute till Parliamentary provision was agreed. Brougham, aptly echoing Iago, dismissed the liturgy question as 'trifles light as air'.[30]

At the end of February 1820 there was one last scuffle over the Queen in the House of Commons, before the country went to the polls. The Radical Mr Joseph Hume asked what financial assistance was to be given to the Queen. Tierney, leader of the Whigs in the Lower House, got up to protest at a woman being paid out of public funds when she was not fit to be prayed for, of such a character that a commission in Milan had investigated her conduct. Let there be a frank assessment of her conduct, he thundered, by means of a Parliamentary inquiry. Either the King was betrayed, he said, or the Queen insulted. The Opposition, in short, behaved just as Castlereagh had hoped they would.[31]

Brougham rose to confuse the issue and confound Castlereagh's hopes, for he wished to have the Queen near at hand or just over the Channel before he raised her standard. He had never heard of the Milan Commission, he declared, and his client was anyway of unblemished virtue. Lord Holland was almost admiring: 'he did not simply deny it [that he had been negotiating with the Queen for a divorce or separation] but by vehement declamation and argumentative contradiction of collateral parts endeavoured to involve all that had passed between him, his client and the Government in obscurity'.[32]

Castlereagh answered that he felt only the warmest feelings of chivalry towards the Queen and that he guarded, on her behalf, her queenly privileges. There, Canning hoped, 'the Queen's business' had ended. Financial assistance would be arranged in the Civil List in the new Parliament – and, if they could add a condition that she receive it while abroad, so much the better. 'What is wanted is to unqueen her, but how is it to be done?' murmured Countess Lieven, echoing many a minister's sentiment.[33] On 7 March, Metternich wrote to congratulate Castlereagh on avoiding 'the damage that the scandalous process of divorce would have done to every throne'.[34] Castlereagh and Metternich had no idea of the Papal Government's over-zealous behaviour in Rome.

The discovery of the Cato Street conspiracy, by which Arthur Thistlewood and other desperadoes had hoped to assassinate the Cabinet while at dinner, created a national commotion that drove all other subjects off the public stage. In the election, held on 25 March, although the Radicals gained ground, especially in the north and in Scotland, the House of Commons remained largely unaltered in political complexion. The ministers were now sanguine. Even the question of the Civil List did not unduly plague them. They had determined not to raise the King's allowance. 'Time will be requisite to reconcile the King's mind to the arrangement,' wrote Liverpool philosophically on 29 March,[35] when the King first learnt of his disappointment, and, although his Majesty was 'pretty well disposed to part with us all', as Eldon wrote, he could find no one willing to replace them.[36]

Then Caroline's steward Hieronymus arrived at the end of March with the letters which she had directed in Rome on 16 March to Liverpool, Castlereagh and Brougham. It seemed the Queen was on her way to England, although the official intelligence that she had left Rome did not arrive till the end of April. They panicked, all of them, Brougham, King, Government, and there was a frenzied interchange of letters and interviews.

'Our Queen threatens approach to England,' wrote Eldon; 'but, if she can venture, she is the most courageous lady I ever heard of. The mischief, if she does come, will be infinite.' Brougham told Hutchinson he could not keep the Queen away for long. Hutchinson urged Brougham to go to her, but Brougham only sent off Hieronymus with a message that he would be at Aix-en-Othe or Lille at the end of April.[37] Next, Bloomfield and Leach informed Liverpool in early April that the King wanted Hutchinson to go with Brougham to the Queen. Would Liverpool see both men? A few days later, on the

15th, accordingly, the interview took place at Fife House, the Prime Minister's private residence. Brougham asked for a proposal to show the Queen, and Liverpool duly wrote a memorandum – a replica of the June 1819 proposal, but with the additional clause that proceedings would begin the moment the Queen landed in England. Brougham declared that he could not deliver this ultimatum to the Queen. On the 22nd Liverpool wrote out a supplementary letter for Hutchinson to carry.[38]

Brougham saw the Queen's promised arrival as a useful opportunity to acquire for himself the silk gown of leading counsel. He pressed upon Hutchinson the sinister argument that a silk gown from the King would solve all the difficulties in the case. If he presented his warrant as the Queen's Attorney-General and was duly sworn in the law courts, 'such a formal recognition of their [Brougham's and Denman's] and her rights' would make it very difficult to argue that she was no queen but a private citizen.[39] If, however, he were offered the silk gown of King's Counsel before 19 April, when the legal term began, then he would not put forward his warrant.

The only difficulty with this traitorous argument was that Eldon, in whose gift were the silk gowns, detested Brougham. Liverpool and Canning pleaded with him. At a time when the trials of Hunt and Thistlewood were arousing large-scale sympathy for the 'miscreants', the last thing needed was the arrival of the Queen. The feeling 'outdoors' had not yet concentrated on the Queen, but it would happily do so. Cardinal Consalvi's letter to her was published in the English newspapers, to cries of outrage. Surely a government never hung by a silk gown before, expostulated Canning. He suspected that Brougham had heard rumours that the silk gown was not forthcoming. 'The delay, and still more the rumours which he must have heard ... of an indisposition [by Eldon] to comply at all – have naturally and necessarily given time to the Opposition to work upon him, and have led him to doubt whether he has not a better game before him in fighting the Queen's battle than in conspiring with us to keep the peace. The silk gown ... would have fixed him,' Canning ended sadly.[40]

In the event, Brougham presented his warrant as the Queen's Attorney-General, with Denman as her Solicitor-General, on 20

April. 'I feel above all things anxious that HM the King should be informed', wrote Brougham secretly to Hutchinson, '. . . that I do this involuntarily and after having done all I could to avoid it, and that whatever consequences follow are imputable to others and not to myself.' He finished by lamenting how often his Majesty's interests had been 'neglected or postponed. . . . We have frequently seen it together and lamented it.'[41]

Brougham continued to hedge his bets, or 'keep both King and Queen open', as he put it. He promised the King and Government that he alone could keep the Queen away, yet he wrote to the Queen without mentioning any memorandum or Government proposal – which might have kept her away. He boasted in April that he would be Prime Minister, and spoke in the House of a possible coalition government in May.[42]

On 28 April, Liverpool told the King that the Queen was definitely on her way, and the ministers began to prepare in high indignation for her possible arrival. They had still apparently not understood that her coming was her own indignant reaction to the denigration she had suffered at Rome and to the omission of her name from the liturgy. But then the ministers thought that she had rejected the 15 April memorandum and the June 1819 proposal, which Brougham had never shown her. As Castlereagh wrote grimly on 6 May, 'If she is wise enough to accept the pont d'or [the £50,000 offered] which we have tendered her, the calamities and scandal of a public investigation will be avoided. If she is mad enough or so ill-advised as to put her foot upon English ground, I shall, from that moment, regard Pandora's box as opened.'[43]

A week later Leach directed Powell to prepare English copies of all the Milan Commission evidence. Brougham felt uneasy when his rival as Caroline's champion, Alderman Wood, in apparently casual conversation, said he might go abroad to visit his son. The next moment he was gone – 'Wood is certainly gone to get her,' Lord Grey heard.[44] Brougham himself, although implored by Hutchinson and others, preferred to keep her at arm's length.

When the Queen left Rome on 8 April, she found a general welcome at Pesaro, in defiance of the Papal Delegate Gandolfi, who had refused the magistrates' request to illuminate the town and salute her arrival with cannon-fire. 'All the high authorities and all the different classes of people came to meet me on the road,' she told Gell: 'More than eighty carriages,' including 'the good old Vesco [Bishop] ... and all the magistrates'. Next day, the Delegate himself came toiling up to the Villa Vittoria to pay his respects, and the Queen had the satisfaction of telling him herself from her window that she was not at home. She then succumbed for some days to a rheumatic fever, recovered, and occupied herself, while waiting for Hieronymus to return, in doling out cash to the poor of the place and hosting what she called a quiet dinner for all the magistrates and nobility of the area.

On 13 April, Hieronymus returned from London with Brougham's promise to meet her at Aix-en-Othe or Lille, and with copies of the English newspapers carrying the Cardinal's 'clever letter', which she had sent for publication. 'It is at least a small revenge for all evil dealing, and the Hanoverian Minister is also well mentioned,' she wrote triumphantly, and set out that day for Milan.[45] With her went baggage coaches and all her carriages. This was no ordinary journey, and the caretaker at the Villa Vittoria later testified that she took with her from Pesaro all her clothes, her jewels, her plate, her china and most of her personal possessions. She was on her way to present herself as their queen to the people of England, and a respectable appearance and style of life were necessary.

Leaving her more gauzy items at Pesaro, Queen Caroline commissioned several new dresses from Alderman Wood in London on the day she set out, sending him the patterns for some silks. 'Them which are in gold [perhaps she sent her Constantinople dresses] should be made in all sort of collers [colours],' she wrote. She recommended that Mrs Webbe, her former mantua-maker opposite Pall Mall, send her a white silk gown and hat, 'made exactly of the english fashion as ... the present franche [French] mode do not please me much'.[46] The hatred for English ways which the Princess of Wales had expressed when she left for the Continent in 1814 was no more. Her role as lady traveller or as Italian exile was put aside for the moment, although she expected to be back in Pesaro by the late summer. In fact, she was never to see Italy again.

Caroline was seeking to present herself on her return to England as a queen hardly less English than Good Queen Bess herself, and sending out directions hither and thither. Lady Charlotte Lindsay, she hoped, would meet her, and Keppel Craven too. 'I think really Mr Craven should not lose any time to meet me at Calais,' she instructed Gell on 13 April, 'as by the first or second of May I must be at Calais.'[47] In the event, the Queen was detained by her rheumatic complaint both at Milan (where she stayed at La Barona and was rejoined by Colonels Olivieri and Vassalli) and at Turin. No one visited. The Queen felt 'quite miserable at not being able to keep my word by being by this time in London, but Heaven ordained it otherwise'.[48]

While crossing the Alps into Switzerland, on the freezing heights of Mont Cenis she suffered from 'a most dreadful spasm in my stomach' – spasms which she was soon to experience in a more ghastly form – and had to rest on the mountain.[49] By the time she arrived in Geneva on 7 May 1820, she was thoroughly exhausted and had no strength left to continue her journey.

There was to cheer the Queen's convalescence Mr William Wood, Alderman Wood's son, her probable visitor the previous year. A Radical after his father's heart, he had been expelled from Winchester for a schoolboy revolt and was completing his education at Geneva. Brougham had urged Lady Charlotte Lindsay to write and advise the Queen not to listen to Alderman Wood, but during her month at Geneva it was Wood's son with whom she was closeted. When she at last departed north, young William seized the chance to interrupt his Swiss education and go with her.[50]

Like any general on the move, the Queen formed her plans and issued her directives as she went. Still at Geneva, on 12 May, she sent letters with Vassalli to Wood and Brougham regarding a London residence. She declared the Duke of Kent's house at Ealing inconveniently far from the metropolis and thought of the Angersteins' house at Blackheath instead. She considered taking a country house later, but had no wish for apartments at Windsor, where her daughter and mother were buried. It would bring back 'dreadful recollections of my former misfortunes and trials'.[51] The King was no doubt relieved by this renunciation.

On 25 May, with Vassalli returned, the Queen heard that

Brougham and, separately, Alderman Wood and Lady Anne Hamilton (her former lady-in-waiting, a keen Radical) would meet her on her way to Calais. Now she travelled swiftly down the Rhône valley to Lyons. From there she wrote to Brougham, and again from Dijon. On 27 May at Montbard her first champions from England, Wood and Lady Anne, joined her party. When she reached Villeneuve, close to Aix-en-Othe, however, there was no sign of Brougham. She now wrote to Liverpool requesting a royal yacht and residence.[52]

The agitation at the end of May when the Queen's various letters arrived, intimating her approaching descent on England, was general. 'The town here is employed in nothing but speculation whether her Majesty will or will not come,' wrote Lord Eldon to his daughter from London. 'Great bets are laid about it. Some people have taken fifty guineas, undertaking in lieu of them to pay a guinea a day till she comes, so sure are these that she will come within fifty days: others again are taking less than fifty guineas, undertaking to pay a guinea a day till she comes, so sure are they that she will not come.' Lord Eldon held to his old opinion: 'she will not come, unless she is insane'.[53] The Radicals, planning to exploit the wrongs done to the Queen, were in a state of high excitement.

The King was still more exultant, and reminded his Cabinet of its promise to start proceedings against her the moment she set foot on English soil. Believing that the question admitted of no argument, he summoned Eldon on 28 May to discuss details of his Coronation, which he judged a more urgent and interesting question. After some thought – and against the advice of the Privy Council – he had decided that peeresses – though not his wife – should attend the ceremony.[54] Eldon was little exercised by any detail to do with the Coronation, as he firmly believed it would shortly have to be postponed.

Meanwhile, the Cabinet hoped the Queen's business, with Brougham's promised help, might still be resolved without proceedings. Brougham came back from the House of Commons at four in the morning on 31 May to find Caroline's Dijon letter. He immediately wrote to Hutchinson to say that he had ordered a carriage to be ready 'at a moment's warning', as the Queen expected him at St Omer this day. However, he could not travel immediately as he was appearing 'in a cause' in the House of Lords.[55]

Hutchinson went down to confer with Brougham in a private room at the House of Lords later that day. According to the note he had received, said Brougham, the Queen was in no mood to accept compromise. He felt that he could use his personal influence and win the day. However, Hutchinson must secretly travel with him, to present the more unpalatable of the Government proposals (that she use a different title), which the Queen would not accept from him, Brougham. Hutchinson and, later, Liverpool agreed to this, just as they agreed that he might have to vary the terms of Liverpool's 15 April memorandum. 'Lord Liverpool has never doubted that it was Mr Brougham's sincere wish to prevent the unpleasant consequences which must arise from the arrival of the Queen.'[56]

The discussions took place, as Hutchinson later lamented, in a confounded hurry. The King's household at Carlton House was privy to them, with his private secretary Sir Benjamin Bloomfield making known the King's wishes, and Liverpool presenting the Cabinet's directives. On 31 May, Liverpool wrote urgently to Brougham with the information that the Queen had now demanded a yacht. How so, if she was awaiting his arrival? Brougham protested that he had never undertaken that the Queen would not come, although his private wishes were that she would not. Now for the first time he spoke of his duty to his client, and admitted the possibility that she might yet come. He could safely undertake one thing, however. He never upon any account, he wrote solemnly, would sanction any one step being taken either in Parliament or out of doors, and no part of the Queen's proceedings ever should be made subservient either to popular or party purposes – by him. He added pointedly that the Queen's courier Vassalli had confirmed that Alderman Wood was with the Queen.[57] Liverpool anyway urged Brougham to depart: 'The landing of the Queen in this country . . . will render all arrangement impracticable,' he threatened.[58] Finally on 3 June Brougham and Hutchinson departed for Dover, Calais and St Omer. Brougham had his 15 April memorandum, and Hutchinson the other proposals contained in Liverpool's letter of 22 April as bargaining counters. The mystery is that Liverpool and Carlton House should have trusted Brougham in the matter.

The Queen had arrived at St Omer on 1 June, having previously commanded beds at the Hôtel de l'Ancienne Poste. The innkeeper had laid a carpet in readiness on the steps of the hotel near the foot of the hill which led up to the Corn Market. He was in attendance when the Queen, with Lady Anne Hamilton behind her, descended from a yellow-bodied post-chariot with the royal arms. The Queen was dressed, noted the onlookers, in a pelisse lined with ermine, and wore a white willow hat.[59] She, Lady Anne and Vittorine ascended to their bedchambers. More carriages and calashes rolled up, and out stepped a 'tall, robust military-looking man', who was later judged to be 'respectfully attentive to her Majesty's person'. This was Pergami. William Austin, who as a child had attracted such attention, was deemed 'a modest lad, remarkably plain in his dress, of quiet and diffident manners'.[60]

The Queen passed her time, until Brougham should appear, in 'repeated interviews' with Alderman Wood. Wood apparently dissuaded her from any plan of a compromise and said that the House of Commons would never vote her £50,000 in these times of hardship. She would do better to return and fight for her good name. She was said to be calm and composed, and refused a guard of honour from the captain on duty at the gates of St Omer, citing the 'studied neglect' she had received everywhere from the French authorities. Hutchinson, however, said she had such a guard at her hotel.

At three o'clock in the afternoon of 3 June, Brougham and Hutchinson arrived at St Omer and put up in different hotels. Brougham saw the Queen first for two hours, and disingenuously said that he believed a Government emissary was arriving, then presented Hutchinson, who drank tea with the Queen. 'Both the Queen's manners and the behaviour of the foreigners in her suite', declared Brougham, 'drew from him [Hutchinson] a very positive declaration that matters have been grossly misrepresented.'[61] He told Liverpool that he himself had never seen such a display of propriety. 'She appeared calm and collected,' noted Hutchinson, 'and I entertained a distant hope that she might be induced to listen to reason.'[62] Brougham's view of this matter was less optimistic. In his letter to Liverpool, dispatched after the meeting with the Queen and unbeknown to Hutchinson, he wrote, 'I never saw a resolution more fixed than that which she has taken to go to England without loss of time.'[63]

Brougham had told Queen Caroline that 'the moment she landed the Government had come to a clear and unequivocal determination of sending a message to Parliament, which must at once put an end to all negotiations'. She had appeared undeterred. 'The principal cause of her positive determination to go to England is the treatment she has received abroad,' wrote Brougham, as if surprised by what the Queen had repeatedly written to Liverpool, Castlereagh and himself.[64] Nine parts in ten of her complaints turned, he said, upon the insults in Rome from Consalvi, Park and, especially, Reden and de Blacas. 'They give her the name of Caroline of Brunswick, and, still more absurdly, Caroline of England, with other indignities too long to detail. . . . It is easy to see that this has driven her home.' (Brougham was hardly likely to cite his own careful neglect of the Queen.) As a result, he had not dared mention the proposed condition that she renounce her title as queen. 'The bare mention of the thing would have been followed within five minutes by an order of post-horses to go to Calais.' However, he believed that Hutchinson meant soon to propose it.

'The only chance of preventing her Majesty's immediate return,' wrote Brougham, was for Liverpool to dispatch a courier at once with an assurance that the Government would send 'the most ample instructions to our ministers abroad to treat her as queen'. It was a matter of urgency. The Queen's attendants had all got passports – to accompany her to England or to return to Italy – and Brougham had with difficulty persuaded her to delay setting out for England till after she had heard the complete Government proposals.[65]

On the following day, 4 June, 'The negotiation, if negotiation it can be called,' wrote Hutchinson, 'commenced a little after twelve . . . and ended about half-past four.'[66] It began in an 'abrupt and unexpected' manner. Brougham sent a note by Vassalli, asking Hutchinson on behalf of the Queen to put in writing the King's proposals which she believed he had brought with him. Hutchinson correctly believed that Brougham, who was awaiting Liverpool's answer, meant to gain time. He replied accordingly that he expected a courier, and that he had meanwhile to look over his documents.[67] Half an hour later, at two o'clock, while Hutchinson was eating his lunch, Brougham wrote

back. He had to express the Queen's surprise that his proposals were
not ready. The Queen would wait only till five o'clock.[68]

Hutchinson was put in a quandary, and it was all of Brougham's
making. Not only was he anxious 'to screen Brougham from the
imputation that he was acting in concert with us'; he had never
thought that he rather than Brougham would have to make the
proposals. Now he had been cast in the role, not of adviser, but of
Government negotiator. Moreover, he thought Liverpool's 15 April
memorandum was in Brougham's pocket, and he doubted his own
recollection of its specific terms and conditions, as he had not seen it
since April. 'I felt the absolute necessity of making her some proposition,' he wrote.[69] Accordingly, he drew on his memory of the terms
of the memorandum, which proved reasonably accurate. Unfortunately, in one of his few errors of recall, he went further than the
memorandum and proposed that the Queen renounce all titles of the
British royal family. (The memorandum had allowed for her to use a
royal title other than Queen.) Still, by four o'clock he had cobbled
together a document and sent it over to Brougham and the Queen.
What he wrote was 'very indistinct, informal, and not the best sort of
English', he later admitted, but her post-horses were at the door, and
she was furious. In the event, he was 'not in possession of any
proposition . . . in a specific form of words', Hutchinson wrote to the
Queen, but he could give the substance of many conversations. On
condition that she remained abroad and used no English royal titles,
he wrote, the Government proposed to grant her an annuity of
£50,000. If she did proceed to England, and here he echoed
Brougham, the decision was taken to proceed against her as soon as
she landed.[70]

An hour later, at five o'clock, back came the Queen's decision.
Brougham was empowered to assure Lord Hutchinson that 'It is quite
impossible for her Majesty to listen to such a proposition.' Hutchinson swiftly sent over a note to Brougham, asking for 'a more detailed
explanation' of the Queen's refusal. He was willing to send a courier
to England to ask for further instructions if the Queen would
communicate 'whether any part of the propositions which I have
made would be acceptable to her; and if there is anything which she
may wish to offer to the English Government on her part . . .'.[71]

It was too late. The negotiations were over, although Brougham dispatched the note after the Queen. Her Majesty had left for England the moment she had replied to Hutchinson's proposed terms, and apparently without taking leave of Brougham. He watched impotently from a window of the hotel as her carriages drove off through the rain, bound for Calais. So determined was she now to cross the Channel that she did not stop when a Government courier, heading for St Omer, passed her on the Calais road.

Pergami and others of her Italian suite set off as smartly for Italy. It was no part of Caroline's plan to arrive in London attended by Italians, least of all by the man whose appearance in England at her side might bring down on her head a charge of high treason. Although it was true that a charge of high treason did not lie against an alien, an alien venturing on to English soil was deemed to have accepted the protection of the Crown and so made himself subject to the Treason Act. Those advising the Queen were no doubt only too aware of this ramification, no matter how difficult it might be for the authorities to prove fresh adultery on English soil. At any rate, Pergami parted from Caroline at St Omer, never to see her again.

A disconsolate Brougham and Hutchinson were left to chastise each other for their part in the shambles of a negotiation. Brougham blamed the meddling Alderman. Hutchinson wrote to Liverpool castigating Brougham and, implicitly, the ministers' dependence on his influence with the Queen. He believed she took counsel from her own presumption and obstinacy.

> Before our arrival she had organized everything for stage-effect: her chief performer was that enlightened mountebank Alderman Wood. . . . on this occasion we have been entirely out-generaled – the violence and the determination of this woman have had the effect for the moment of wisdom and arrangement and she has completely succeeded in all her plans.[72]

Hutchinson had earlier written, 'It is impossible for me to paint the insolence, the violence and the precipitation of this woman's conduct. I never saw anything so outrageous, so undignified as a queen, or so unamiable as a woman. . . . She has really assumed a tone and hauteur which is quite insufferable. . . . She has set the King's authority at defiance, and it is now time for her to feel his vengeance. . . .'[73]

After this outburst, Hutchinson fell ill and remained at St Omer. Brougham set off after the Queen and chased her to London. Meanwhile, Mr Thomas Barnes, 'principal editor of the Times', who had crossed the Channel in an open boat, raced an *Observer* reporter back to the printing presses of London and published the first account of the negotiations, complete with copies of the St Omer correspondence, probably provided by Alderman Wood.

Brougham's plans had been confounded. His boast that he could keep Caroline away from England had proved empty. In desperation he sent a letter after the Queen, begging her to reflect calmly and impartially on the step she was about to take. He advised her not to accept the present offer, but to await another offer, namely, of an annuity with no renunciation of rank, title or rights, and with a Government pledge of her honourable reception abroad. These terms were here more explicitly stated than they had been in his letter to Liverpool of 3 June. In any event the Prime Minister's reply, conveyed by the courier whom Caroline had encountered, arrived too late. 'There are some persons whose advice is of a different cast and who will be found very feeble allies in the hour of difficulty,' Brougham hinted to the Queen. If she insisted on returning to England,

> I earnestly implore your Majesty to proceed in the most private and even secret manner possible. It may be very well for a candidate at an election to be drawn into towns by the populace – and they will mean nothing but good in showing this attention to your Majesty – but a Queen of England may well dispense with such marks of popular favour. . . . I shall consider every such exhibition as both hurtful to your Majesty's real dignity, and full of danger in its probable consequences.[74]

Brougham enclosed a copy of this letter to Liverpool, then wrote on the Monday morning again, begging him not to send a message to Parliament till he, Brougham, was back in his place there. 'How much I regret the failure of this negotiation . . .', Brougham continued, adding that he was 'at all times . . . ready to lend my aid in case it is renewed' in England.[75]

Barnes of *The Times* had preceded Caroline to Calais, to observe that, despite the heavy rain, the people were in a high bustle and filling up every avenue to the hotel where the Queen was expected to sleep. Instead she drove straight to the pier and embarked directly on board the *Prince Leopold* packet or ferry, in the absence of the royal yacht she had requested. Her baggage and carriages went on board the *Lady Jane*, and she settled down to wait.

'Neither at the landing of William the Conqueror,' ran Barnes's 'Queenite' text next day, 'nor at that of William III' had any arrival in England caused such a sensation.[76] *The Times* increased its circulation dramatically after Barnes scooped all the other newspapermen with the St Omer correspondence, and outdid the rest with his chivalrous speeches in favour of the Queen.

The *Prince Leopold*, with the Queen and Lady Anne Hamilton, Wood and Austin aboard, and the *Lady Jane* worked out of Calais harbour at six in the morning of 5 June. Despite the inclement weather, the Queen remained for the most part on deck, 'conversing chiefly on the present political condition of the country' with the officers. It was not till eleven in the morning that a breeze blew up from the south and allowed the packets to make headway across to Dover. Here, since early in the morning, a multitude had been assembling, many of them 'dressed as if for a fête'. There was 'a conspicuous number of females' among them, on the beach, on the heights, and in the avenues leading to the principal hotel, and all looking anxiously for the Queen's arrival.[77]

Shortly before one in the afternoon, the *Prince Leopold* appeared in the Dover roads. Colonel Monroe, commandant of the garrison, flustered by the arrival of the Queen of England, gave orders for the royal salute to be fired. So Caroline's return to England, after six years' absence, with proceedings promised against her, was greeted, to the satisfaction of the assembled crowd on shore, by a roar of cannon from Dover Castle. On hearing that the packet could not dock at the pier till 5 p.m., the Queen decided, with Brunswicker courage, to risk an open boat. She landed at one o'clock to cries of 'God bless Queen Caroline!'

A sentimental glass picture exists of the Queen being helped from the craft at Dover beach. It is the first of a stream of Queenite confections for which the public appetite was insatiable in the next six months. The angular figure of Lady Anne Hamilton is seated behind the Queen, calmly surveying the people milling about the boat.[78] Lady Anne, for all that she was a duke's daughter, was also the sister of the Radical MP Lord Archibald Hamilton, and ardently took up the Queen's cause, the only one of her former ladies to do so. *The Times* described the Queen as she walked towards the Ship Hotel. 'Her blue eyes [were] shining with peculiar lustre, but her cheeks had the appearance of a long intimacy with care and anxiety.' The newspaper noted that she was not so *embonpoint* as formerly and was dressed with elegance.[79]

The Queen was so set about with rejoicing crowds that, to the horror of the Ship Hotel's proprietor Mr Wright, she was forced to seek refuge within the York Hotel. With commendable presence of mind, Mr Wright sent an open carriage to carry her off from the rival establishment to the bosom of his own. Even on this short journey, the horses were taken from their traces, and the populace drew the carriage themselves. A band preceded it, with some of the leading tradesmen carrying large banners inscribed 'God save Queen Caroline'. It was all as bad as Brougham had feared; on reaching the Ship Hotel, the Queen bowed from the principal window, just like any candidate seeking election.

A guard of honour had been provided outside the Ship. When this show of arms met with signs of disfavour from the populace, Wood appeared with a soothing message: the Queen's 'firm reliance was on the just principles and cordial attachment of her people'. As Denman later acknowledged, Wood had an instinctive knowledge of the English character and mind. The Queen rested at the Ship Hotel, then rose in the late afternoon and prepared to depart for Canterbury, where she meant to sleep. The jealous people of Dover would not let her go, however, before a deputation had given her their congratulations on her arrival. She replied graciously, and they responded by drawing her carriage right out of the town.

In Canterbury, although it was nearly dark, the gates of the ancient cathedral town were illuminated by a hundred flambeaux, and a shadowy mass of some ten thousand people awaited their Queen. At the Fountain Hotel she found the Lord Mayor and a Corporation of seven aldermen, the Sheriff, the Town Clerk and sixteen common councillors waiting to pay their respects. Once again she bowed from the principal window, and then retired, although the street was still filled and every window thronged, despite the heavy rain.[80]

The respectable and cheering crowds, a significant number of women among them, at Dover and Canterbury, the support of the Lord Mayor and Corporation, the addresses and replies were all typical of the enthusiastic behaviour her cause would elicit, not just on her way to London but throughout England over the next few months. Cannon-fire and cheering crowds were, in a sense, what the Queen had craved when she was deprived of recognition in Rome. The whole did indeed resemble an election. The question was: would the candidate be successful or not?

The next morning, the Queen departed Canterbury. She appeared greatly affected by the acclamations about her and 'repeatedly put her head out of the window', waving her handkerchief and crying 'Long live George IV!' in cordial fashion. Officers of a cavalry regiment stationed at Canterbury accompanied her to Sittingbourne, a development which alarmed the authorities. The army and its officers were supposedly the chief suppressors of local disturbances, not their supporters.

If the Queen was surprised by the warmth of her reception, the Government and the local authorities were not. The MP Mr Robert Peel had written to Croker in March of this year, 'Do you not think that the tone of England – of that great compound of folly, weakness, prejudice, wrong feeling, right feeling, obstinacy, and newspaper paragraphs, which is called public opinion – is more liberal – to use an odious but intelligible phrase – than the policy of the Government?' Peel spoke of 'a feeling, becoming daily more general and more confirmed ... in favour of some undefined change in the mode of governing the country ... public opinion never had such influence on public measures, and yet never was so dissatisfied with the share which it possessed. It is growing too large for the channels that it has been accustomed to run through.' He ventured a guess that the Tories would sooner or later combine with the Whigs for some moderate Whiggish reforms, so as 'to oppose the united phalanx to the Hobhouses, and Burdetts, and Radicalism'.[81] Though it was now but three months later, had the moderate Tories and Whigs left reform too late?

The Radicals, who included the Queen's former Kensington courtier Sir Francis Burdett and Byron's friend Mr John Cam Hobhouse, with Brougham himself, were to prove the Queen's chief Parliamentary supporters in the coming struggle 'indoors'. But, as she saw at Dover and Canterbury, the Queen had another useful source of support in the 'outdoor agitation', which was the weapon of the common people. Excluded from Parliament by the net of patronage and interest, many saw her cause as mirroring their own. In their eyes, she was an injured queen, wife and mother, and a weak woman who needed their help to fight against a tyrant king, as they fought against a tyrant government. The Queen was to be a symbol of their own oppression, and a tool with which to dig at the Government. She had, in her early days of marriage, shown herself an adept manipulator of public opinion, though her part was confined to appearances at the opera house. It would seem that she appreciated immediately the greater power that public opinion, and the 'industrious classes', now represented.

In London the failure of the negotiations was made known to the Government on the evening of 5 June, while the Queen slept at Canterbury. In the House of Commons, the Cabinet was absent from the debate of an important motion, to disfranchise Grampound, a rotten borough. The Chancellor of the Exchequer, Mr Nicholas Vansittart, asked Lord John Russell and Mr John Lambton, instigators of the motion, for an adjournment, on the ground that the ministers were in Cabinet 'upon a subject of high importance'.[82] The atmosphere in the House of Commons was charged. Everyone knew to what he referred, for the news was that the Queen had landed. Russell, Lambton and the reformers in the Commons agreed reluctantly to the adjournment. One speaker agreed that the borough in question was corrupt. Nonetheless, he likened 'the present constitution of the House, with all its imperfections', to Aladdin's lamp, 'which, though covered in rust, still retained its charm.'[83] On this abject note, Parliamentary reform was for the moment abandoned.

At that Cabinet meeting, the ministers were deciding their tactics. They had no option but to make a show of beginning proceedings

against the Queen, on their declared word to the King. In a last-ditch
attempt to delay, they included in the message which they had to
send down to Parliament provision for a Secret Committee to inspect
the Milan Commission papers. This would leave some time for
compromise and negotiation, before the 'Pandora's box' of which
Castlereagh had spoken had at last to be opened.

Leach sent urgently to Powell: the Queen had landed that day.
The following morning – the 6th – he instructed Powell to gather
together all the original reports and copies, depositions and translations, for dispatch to the Houses of Parliament that evening. Accordingly, he began a laborious trawl round the different Government
departments, collecting papers from Liverpool in Downing Street,
from the Foreign Office next door and from Mr Henry Hobhouse at
the Home Office.[84]

At Sittingbourne, though forbidden to mention her by name in the
liturgy, a deputation of clergymen in full gowns turned out to greet
the Queen, and the bells of the churches rang. At the bottom of
Chatham Hill, the Queen had to ask the populace to refrain from
pulling her carriage out of the town, as she was anxious to reach
London that day. At Rochester and Strood, and in every town through
which she passed, her arrival had the same electrifying effect on the
people gathered to acclaim her.

In London, the King came down to the House of Lords to give his
assent to the Civil List, among other bills. It was in everyone's mind
that he hoped to give shortly his assent to a bill of divorce. He
returned to Carlton House as his royal wife was just approaching
Shooters Hill, near her old home at Blackheath. At Gravesend the
people had insisted on delaying her by drawing her carriage through
the town. From Dartford on, the cavalcade surrounding her had
increased steadily in number, until at Shooters Hill the descent was,
except for a narrow pathway, crammed with hundreds of stationary
vehicles, with well-dressed females among their occupants. These
vehicles later formed part of the procession which accompanied her
to London.

Sir Francis Burdett and Sir Robert Wilson, the Radical soldier
MP, had come on horseback to greet her. Cobbett was also at
Shooters Hill, holding aloft a laurel bough in her honour. Blackheath

resembled some great Continental fair, wrote *The Times*. Some of the
riders had come all the way from Dover with her.[85]

The rain had stopped when she resumed her journey, and her
carriage was thrown open. Mr Charles Greville, who rode out as far
as Greenwich to meet her, judged that the fifty-two-year-old Queen
looked exactly as she had done before she left England six years
before and seemed 'neither dispirited nor dismayed. She travelled in
an open landau, with Alderman Wood at her side and Lady Anne
Hamilton and another woman opposite.' The acclamations redoubled
and continued without interruption until she reached the metropolis,
when they swelled into a yet louder strain as the carriages proceeded
over Westminster Bridge. 'Carriages, carts, and horsemen followed,
preceded, and surrounded her coach the whole way. . . .' Women
waved pocket handkerchiefs, and men shouted wherever she passed.
At Carlton House, Wood cried out, 'Long live the King!' and the
soldiers were made to salute. Greville reported that the King said,
'That beast Wood,' disgusted like everybody else by the Alderman's
vulgarity 'in sitting in the place of honour while the Duke of
Hamilton's sister was sitting backwards in the carriage'.[86]

The Queen later declared herself gratified by her husband's
concern on this point. As she passed by White's she bowed and smiled
to the men standing at the window. She was seen to be wearing a
black twilled gown, 'a fur tippet and ruff, with a hat of black satin and
feathers'. 'Nobody either blames or approves of her sudden return,'
Greville wrote, 'but all ask, "What will be done next? How is it to
end?"' When the Queen had last entered London ceremonially, Lady
Jersey had sat opposite her. Then she had been a bride on her way to
St James's Palace. Now, her mock-Elizabethan royal progress concluded, she was on her way to take up residence in a City alderman's
house in South Audley Street. Alderman Wood and his family had
gladly agreed to vacate it for Fladong's Hotel.

While the Queen's procession wound slowly towards South Audley
Street through the crowded thoroughfares, Powell had completed his
labours, copying – with Hobhouse at the Home Office – 'all the
depositions and the papers'. At five o'clock Powell stowed the Milan
Commission papers with the 1806 and 1813 papers in two green
barristers' brief-bags, one for each House of Parliament. Accordingly,

Lord Liverpool, in the House of Lords, had the first of these bags on the table before him when he stood up that evening to deliver the King's message which had been sent down to the House. 'The King thinks it necessary,' Liverpool said, 'in consequence of the arrival of the Queen, to communicate to the House of Lords certain papers' – he here motioned towards the object on the table, identified by Hansard as 'a green bag, sealed, and apparently filled with papers' – 'respecting the conduct of her Majesty since her departure from this Kingdom, which he recommends to the immediate and serious attention of this House. The King has felt the most anxious desire to avert the necessity of disclosures and discussions which must be as painful to his people as they can be to himself; but the step now taken by the Queen leaves him no alternative.' Liverpool said that he meant to move an address next day to thank the King for his message. He further intended, the day after, to table a motion referring the papers on the table to a Secret Committee. This decision of government, he intoned, was 'guided by precedent, as far as precedent (and that of a very old date) can avail', where no precedent for the present case existed. The Secret Committee would point out what proceedings, if any, were fit to be adopted.[87]

Papers set on the tables of the Houses of Parliament were often stowed in innocuous green lawyers' brief-bags – the papers on the suspension of habeas corpus had gone down to Parliament in such a one in 1818. However, the green bags in which Powell had placed the Milan Commission papers now caught the imagination of the public and of the influential cartoonists of the day as a synonym for Government dirty business. The events of the summer of 1820 were a gift to satirists, who played with every possible permutation of green baggery. There were cats let out of bags, money bags, scatological references to night-soil – with the inevitable title 'A dirty business' – which was carried away in bags. Perhaps first prize should go to the cartoonist Mr William Hone, who devised a monstrous cartoon of two green bags swelling in dignity, with the portly bodies of the King and Queen encased within, and their crowned – and outraged – heads protruding from the top.[88]

In the House of Commons, the King's identical message on the evening of 6 June caused considerably greater uproar. Castlereagh, as

Leader of the Commons, read it in so low a voice as to be nearly inaudible – an indication of how much he wished not to be heard – and moved to consider the message next day. He was then met by strong criticism from a succession of MPs seething at the St Omer negotiations, a knowledge of which they had culled from *The Times* that morning. Mr Grey Bennett asked if the reports of the St Omer talks were true. He was astonished that a British Government, without the authority and consent of Parliament, had

> dared to call upon the Queen of Great Britain to divest herself of that title which she holds by the same right as the King himself does his title, for a bribe of £50,000 a year – a bribe, too, not to be paid by the King himself, but to be taken out of the pockets of the people of England, labouring under the severest distresses, to be given to a person who, if the statements circulated against her were true was ... unworthy to be Queen of England. . . .

Creevey, the Whig wit, said he saw that the King now had the same objection to being with the Queen in the same country as he had previously had to a meeting in the same drawing-room. From the time of Henry VIII on, he warned more seriously, it had been the rule for Parliament not to interfere in the affairs of the queens of England. Sir Robert Wilson objected that the Queen had been obliged to 'sail in a common passage boat' and that, once in London, she had had to take shelter in the house of an honest citizen. Lord Archibald Hamilton observed that, following the omission of her name from the liturgy, the Queen appeared to be the only person in the island denied the right of innocence until proven guilty. Denman asked why this matter was to be referred 'not to the ordinary tribunals of the country' but to a Secret Committee, and he asked 'what was the nature of the proceedings which it was intended to institute against her Majesty'.[89]

Now at this point Denman imagined that he was the Queen's sole appointed law officer. He had received a highly disgruntled letter from Brougham, who had crossed to Dover that morning and taken the Maidstone route so as to avoid his client and her triumphal progress. Brougham announced his intention to give up the Queen. 'I suppose she will have Wood for her Attorney-General,' he wrote

venomously. Denman had already offered to a protégé, Mr John
Williams, the post of Queen's solicitor-general. He was consequently
somewhat astonished to see Brougham, who he had not known was
in the House, rise and champion the Queen. Brougham had entered
the chamber while Castlereagh was still speaking and had said to
some persons near him that 'the ministerial threat prevented him
from retiring [as Queen's attorney-general]'.[90] In fact, quite possibly
the showman in Brougham could not resist the limelight. Creevey
believed that his and Denman's defence of the Queen had shamed
Brougham into continuing as her attorney-general. If they had not
spoken, Creevey thought, Brougham would have denounced her. He
may have been swayed also by the publication that day of his St Omer
correspondence with Hutchinson. Either he defended the Queen or
he appeared the creature of Carlton House. Brougham's fortunes
seemed at a low ebb; he seemed to have gambled with every party and
interest, and lost. For the Tories, Wellington declared that he had
betrayed everybody – King, Queen, ministers and Lord Hutchinson.
It was probably now in his own best interests to exert himself to the
utmost on behalf of his client.

The Opposition leaders were anxious to know what Brougham
would do next; Lords Grey and Holland dreaded having the Whigs
dragged into supporting the Queen. 'For the life of me I can feel no
interest and little curiosity about these royal squabbles, degrading no
doubt to all concerned, and disgusting and tiresome I think to the
bystanders,' wrote Holland.[91] Grey, resigned to opposition, thought a
change of ministers the dream of a Bedlamite[92] – though the Tories,
Liverpool and Canning for instance, were convinced the affair would
bring them down. There were less fastidious, less lymphatic Whigs,
however, who seized on the Queen's business from its beginnings.
'Radical Jack' Lambton and Lord John Russell, denied their Parliamentary reform measure, took up the Queen's cause with vigour.

Croker noted in his diary that the general opinion at Brooks's Club
the night before was that Brougham had acted basely by the Queen –
and the Whig rank and file and the Radicals were convinced of it.[93]
When Brougham rose in the House of Commons, there was thus a
good deal of sympathy for the Queen, and a distaste both for the
proposed Government measure against her and for his dealings. In

the event he said rather lamely that the reports from St Omer were garbled – a claim indignantly denied next day by *The Times* – and that his lips would be unsealed when he had spoken with his client.[94]

Brougham took a calculated risk in his short speech. There was some reason to doubt that he still had a client in the Queen. By her abrupt departure from St Omer, she had shown that she herself suspected him of acting basely by her. How basely was not yet apparent. The Queen, on her way into London, still did not know of Brougham's failure to tell her that the Government had agreed to the separation plan in 1819. She did now suspect, at least, that he had acted at St Omer for the Government and the King rather than in her interests. Brougham gambled on her still wanting his skills as an orator and advocate. Did he feel a moment's unease in the House when Denman, shortly after, was summoned by the Queen to meet her on her arrival at Alderman Wood's house? The courier was 'a low person (an election agent of Wood's)', noted Denman, and drunk to boot. After delivering his message, he was forcibly ejected from the lobby of the House of Commons by the officers in attendance.

Denman proceeded directly to South Audley Street and, having squeezed through the crowds into the Alderman's house, had an excellent view from the drawing-room window of the Queen's procession. Among the carriages and vehicles, carts and horsemen absolutely stationary in South Audley Street below, there was 'Hardly a well-dressed person . . . to be seen in the crowd', recorded Denman. Of those on horseback with a respectable appearance he saw a bankrupt cousin of his and a sheriff's broker. When the Queen's procession appeared, her progress was 'slow through the countless populace', he wrote, 'her travelling equipage mean and miserable'. Her open barouche, 'of shabby appearance', still with Wood at her side and the ladies opposite, was followed by six or seven carriages – on the box of one a man with a turban, in another Hieronymus, her steward, and Carlo Fortis, her courier, with immense mustachios. In another sat Mariette Brun, sister of the disgraced Louise Demont and dresser to the Queen. 'What a melancholy contrast to regal state!' wrote Denman. 'Nothing ever gave me a deeper impression of sadness than the aspect of this forlorn-looking court . . .'.[95]

It was some time before the Queen could descend, and climb the steps of the house. 'The enthusiastic shouts of the people and the courage that shone in the fixed eye of the Queen' somewhat raised Denman's spirits. From the balcony of the house, she acknowledged the cheers of Londoners. 'Her Majesty, with a deportment peculiarly graceful, walked from one end of the balcony to the other, and, having bowed to all around, withdrew from the ardent gaze which had fed upon her presence.' Sketches and cartoons in plenty exist of this scene. The Queen is a small, tense figure seemingly overwhelmed by the rapturous crowds in the narrow street beneath.[96] Where Alderman Wood is shown beside her, his lanky awkward figure does not so much diminish her as dignify her still further.

The Queen received Denman with favour, and spoke repeatedly and animatedly of the Government's conduct, which, she declared, had forced her home: 'If they wished me to stay abroad, why not leave me there in peace? No woman of character could submit to the insults they have offered.' After reciting different circumstances which had left her, as she saw it, no alternative, 'she often repeated, like the burden of a song, "And so here I am."' She was very much exasperated by Brougham. When Denman said he awaited her commands, 'she said very coldly that she should be glad to see him, but her opinion of him was much altered – she even spoke of his betraying her'. She agreed that he should bring Brougham to her after dinner. So Brougham had his client, and the Queen had a powerful agent, but their good opinion of each other's usefulness was tempered by a greater than ever mutual distrust. When Denman went to Brougham at nearby Hill Street to report the Queen's invitation, Brougham was downcast: 'in the most solemn and alarming manner, he [Brougham] laid open to me all his apprehensions on the subject of the Queen's case'. He spoke of sinister reports, which he said it would have done no good to communicate earlier. Denman would 'never forget the tone and manner with which he said to me . . . "So now we are for it, Mr Denman."' The Solicitor-General did not waste much time on recriminations. 'All our thoughts were directed to the future. . . .'[97]

They went together to the Queen. Nothing remarkable occurred – the Queen and Brougham were throughout frigidly polite. She detained Denman a moment after she had dismissed Brougham, though, and said, 'He is afraid.' 'She was certainly right,' wrote Denman, 'but his fears were on her account, not on his own.' These forebodings were to be all too amply justified.

## CHAPTER SIXTEEN

# THE SECRET COMMITTEE

## June–August 1820

*'A mass of evidence to fill a green bag'*

AS DARKNESS FELL on the night of 6 June, the mob rampaged outside Wood's house – according to Croker, obliging some neighbouring householders to 'illuminate', or put candles in their windows, in honour of the Queen. The clubs of St James's illuminated voluntarily. Lord Sidmouth's house was attacked, his son-in-law Mr George Pellew reporting that one 'intrusive missile' after another hit the window shutters. Dr Matthew Baillie, who had assisted at Princess Charlotte's *accouchement* in 1817, was inside on a professional visit to one of the family, and in the circumstances struggled to give his instructions.[1] Meanwhile, the mob broke the windows of Wellington's carriage. Croker, Secretary to the Admiralty and an experienced Parliamentarian, concluded his account of the evening's disturbances, 'I think the ministers wrong, that is, injudicious in proposing a Secret Committee.'[2]

'How deeply interested all are,' wrote the philanthropist MP Mr William Wilberforce in his diary. 'Indeed I feel it myself, about her! One can't help admiring her spirit, though I fear she has been very profligate.'[3] Fanny Burney, Mme d'Arblay, wrote to Mrs Lock next day from lodgings near South Audley Street, 'All London now is wild about the newly arrived royal traveller. . . . Our part of the town is surprised and startled every hour by the arrival of some new group of the curious. . . .'[4] Two days later, on the 9th, Lady Jerningham echoed the fears of many: 'This country is I fear nearer disaster than it has been since the days of Charles 1st . . . a constant mob cheering her and for two nights past breaking every window which did not illuminate. . . .'[5]

The drama of the Queen's royal progress to London concluded, the morning of 7 June saw ministers and Treasury officials gathered at Lord Liverpool's office in Downing Street. It was a mark of the ministers' lack of feeling for 'the times', as Peel had put it in March, that they never considered for a moment granting the Queen's request for a royal residence. Yet this refusal aggravated the public grievance about the liturgy, that the Government had treated the Queen as guilty until she was proved innocent. It was fortunate that the public did not know that the decision was taken on the 7 or 8 of June to send for the witnesses. 'Couriers were accordingly dispatched for them,' wrote Powell.[6]

That it was incongruous for the Queen of England to be lodged in the house of a City alderman, past Mayor of London and Radical MP struck many. It did not strike the ministers. This choice of refuge conveniently confirmed the Queen's declaration that 'her reliance was on the people', but that did not weigh with them, nor did the ease with which public demonstrations in support of the Queen were effected in the public thoroughfare of South Audley Street – and public emotions fomented by her balcony appearances. In the comparative privacy of a royal residence, be it Kensington Palace or distant Hampton Court, where empty apartments abounded, the Queen could have had no such ready audience. As it was, Eldon reported, 'Alderman Wood . . . has in South Audley Street . . . a pretty numerous levée of the family of John [Bull] and my Lady. . . .'[7] Louise Demont, the soi-disant countess, was greatly excited by the arrival in London of her former mistress, against whom she hoped to testify. She sent her younger sister, who had come with her to England, 'to take a walk in the environs', and she plainly saw Mariette their sister at a window in the house with a young man.[8]

The ministers and officials who gathered at Downing Street were all connected to the Treasury Office, which itself occupied a building in Parliament Street close by. Their aim was to settle financial provision for the Queen before the debates in Parliament resumed that night. Accordingly, they summoned to their assembly Mr Andrew Dickie, confidential clerk to the Princess's banker Mr Thomas Coutts (Coutts lay ill in the country at Salt Hill). From Dickie's conscientious account of the 'interview, which fell to my lot today', it is apparent that the ministers were anxious not to incur charges of misusing the

Queen, but naively believed that generous financial terms would put them in the clear.[9]

Present at Downing Street were Liverpool, First Lord of the Treasury, Vansittart, Chancellor of the Exchequer, Mr George Harrison, Deputy Chief Secretary to the Treasury, and Mr William Huskisson, a minister without portfolio. They ordered Dickie to inform the Queen that the allowance which she had received as Princess of Wales would be continued for the present and that 'any reasonable temporary advance' would be forthcoming upon her demand.

Dickie proceeded directly from Westminster to South Audley Street. Glaziers and carpenters were hard at work *en route*, repairing the damage done, in the 'excesses' of the mob's fervour for a general illumination the night before, to the residences of ministers and known friends of Crown and Government. At South Audley Street the banker's clerk found 'about 2000 people about his [Wood's] dwelling'.

Fighting his way through the crowds of merrymakers, Dickie gained the front door and sent up his name. He was immediately ordered upstairs and into the Queen's presence. She received him 'very kindly and with much good nature' and graciously acceded to the Government's proposals, asking for £1000, in notes, to be brought to her that day.

Her Majesty then enquired if Mr Coutts, while he was out of town, would allow her and her 'few servants' to occupy some rooms in his house in Stratton Street – '(not in front) in the most retired part'. She had her own cook, she informed Dickie, and 'would purchase all the necessaries she should want'. She felt that she could not long trespass on the kindness of her present host, who had 'very politely gone with his family to a hotel'.

Dickie was swift to disabuse her Majesty of her notion that she could now trespass on Mr Coutts's kindness instead. The house in Stratton Street, he declared, was 'repairing, painting, etc. and could not afford suitable accommodation'. He departed with celerity to obtain the draft she required, and at the end of a long day wrote to Coutts to inform him that 'the subject' was at rest: 'I could not help thinking that both you and Mrs Coutts would wish to be excused

from such an honour.' Although keen to defend his employer's right
to a quiet life, Dickie was troubled by the question of the Queen's
residence. He confided in Harrison, the Treasury Secretary, that he
wished 'the house part as well as the money part had been agreed' by
the ministers. Harrison concurred.[10]

The failure to provide a royal residence, coming hard upon the
failure to supply a royal vessel for her transport from Calais, exacerbated the general feeling originally aroused by the omission of the
Queen's name from the liturgy, that she was being deprived of her
royal rights, or prerogative, through the misuse by the King, aided by
the Government, of his own royal prerogative.

In the question of royal prerogative were muddled up the concept
of divine right and various other nebulous notions, of which few who
spoke on the subject had a clear understanding, but of which many
had much to say. To royal prerogative was added, moreover, the
fundamental principle of English law that the prosecution bears the
burden of proof – that is, that a person is held to be innocent until
proved guilty. The Government's treatment of the Queen appeared
to be in clear contradiction of this venerable cornerstone of English
justice.

These questions, of the Queen's prerogative as queen consort and
her rights as a subject of the Crown, were not surprisingly confused
in the debates on the King's message in the Houses of Parliament this
evening of 7 June. In the Lords, the proceedings were relatively
urbane, in keeping with the impregnable Tory ascendancy there.
Liverpool, after thanking the King for his message, moved for the
appointment of a Secret Committee to consider the contents of the
green bag. Holland likened the prospect of a Secret Committee in
the Lords to that of a grand jury which would first decide on the
charges, then vote on them as petty jurors.[11]

Eldon replied from the Woolsack that no judicial proceeding could
follow from the findings of the Secret Committee, except in the
House of Commons, where the Queen could be impeached – but
then the Lords would not be jurors. Impeachment would be for high
treason as accessory to an adulterer (accessories in cases of high
treason were treated as principals). However, by the statute of Edward
III, 'the act of a person owing no allegiance to the British Crown

could not be high treason'. Therefore the acts of Pergami and the Queen, whatever they might be, did not constitute high treason, and impeachment was inappropriate. The Secret Committee, Eldon declared, was to meet to consider what, if any, legislative proceedings might seem appropriate in the light of the evidence set before it. The more orthodox route to divorce, judicial separation followed by Parliamentary bill, was of course blocked by the 'clean hands' doctrine – or, as Eldon loftily put it, 'The difficulties ... would strike those who were acquainted with legal subjects.'

Lord Lansdowne questioned the appointment of a committee on the ground that 'the other House' might move for an impeachment, and on grounds of the *ex parte* or one-sided nature of the green-bag contents. Eldon replied that the Queen would have full opportunity to defend herself against all charges. The peers yielded to Eldon's authoritative exposition of the law, the Secret Committee was duly appointed and ballot-glasses were ordered for the next day to determine which fifteen peers should comprise its membership.

Back in the Commons (which in theory would conduct its own investigation parallel to that of the Upper House), Brougham, after his lame showing the night before, had commandeered – virtually hijacked – the debate. He began by reading a poignant address, of his own composition, from the Queen to the House.[12] She had returned to defend her character and rights against measures pursued against her honour and her peace for some time past by secret agents abroad, and lately sanctioned by the conduct of the Government at home. She declared herself surprised by the proceedings in Parliament.

> It is this day fourteen years since the first charges [in the Delicate Investigation] were brought forward against her Majesty. Then, and upon every occasion ... she has shown the utmost readiness to meet her accusers, and to court the fullest inquiry into her conduct. She now also desires an open investigation, in which she may see both the charges and the witnesses against her, a privilege not denied to the meanest subject of the realm.... she solemnly protests against the formation of a secret tribunal to examine documents privately prepared by her adversaries.... she relies ... upon the integrity of the House of Commons....

Furthermore, she protested against the way in which she had been treated 'even before any proceedings were resolved upon'. The omission of her name from the liturgy, the absence of royal convey- ance and residence, the slights of English ministers abroad and the ministers of foreign allies of England were 'measures designed to prejudice the world against her, and could only have been justified by trial and conviction'.[13]

Castlereagh objected to insinuations that the ministers came down to address the House 'with a tone of persecution or prosecution'. He regretted much that 'criminal advice' which had led her Majesty, unbeknown to her chief legal advisers, to 'appeal to the lowest orders of the populace' by publishing the St Omer correspondence.[14]

Brougham then rose to stress the point contained in the Queen's message, and to confound the 'oily rhetoric' of the Government with some passionate, not to say inflammatory, arguments that the Com- mons try further negotiation before proceeding to open the green bag.[15] He referred to her treatment as Princess of Wales in England and, later, her enforced removal from the country, and stated admiringly that her 'sagacity . . . and the propriety of her mind' had not been impaired by her 'absence from her family' nor by 'the withdrawing of that salutary control which . . . was the best preserver of female propriety and delicacy'. Why blame her, after six years away, 'for listening to certain recommendations [to return to England] . . . not those of Absolute Wisdom'? This was a very popular sally at the expense of Alderman Wood, widely known as 'A.W.'. He turned his attack on the Milan Commission and on Cooke: 'On what sort of evidence did [the Secret Commission] proceed? . . . Was it on papers, on letters, on anonymous scraps of information, transmitted from beyond the Alps by a secret commission, sent out God knows when, and for what purpose till now a secret. . . ?' He was

at a loss to understand how . . . one of the King's counsel – a man universally respected for his learning and acquirements . . . how such a man could be induced so to let himself down to the level of agents of a very different description, as to accept a commission to go to a foreign country, there to collect the tittle-tattle of coffee-houses and alehouses; the gossip of bargemen on canals and ferrymen on rivers, and porters of châteaux, and cast-off servants . . . to employ himself, month after month, in taking down the calumnies of a class of human beings so degraded that their appearance in any court of law was always stamped with infamy, and in collecting from such polluted sources a mass of evidence to fill a green bag for the noble Lord opposite!

Brougham's denunciation of the Milan Commission and of the green bag ended, 'Let no man dip a finger in such filth who was not born to degrade the human species,' and he begged that the country should be spared the calamity to which an inquiry would lead.[16] Powell wrote four days later to Leach, having waited 'to see if the ministers would say anything in our justification'. They had not, and he begged Leach to ask the Government to 'protect us and repel the calumny'.[17]

Canning was next on his feet, to pay an extraordinary tribute to the Queen which lost him any favour he had won from the King. He declared the Queen to be 'Of fascinating manners, of easy access, of an open, generous and unsuspecting disposition'. Although he went on to say that, on account of these very virtues, 'faction had marked her as its own', that he had seen this and begged her to go abroad in 1814 as he begged her now, this did not mitigate his offence in the King's eyes.[18]

Wilberforce made his first contribution to the discussions when he now moved to adjourn the debate on a Secret Committee till the Friday 'in order to give the parties time to effect an amicable accommodation'. The House approved the motion without a division. Wilberforce's aim was to prevent the inquiry altogether, 'an object which could only be attained by such an amicable adjustment as should give neither party cause for triumph'.[19]

When the Commons rose at midnight, Denman hurried to South Audley Street to tell the Queen of Brougham's triumph in the House, and of the adjournment. But the building was in darkness: she had retired for the night. Her royal husband was also in his bed at Carlton House, but he nonetheless agreed to receive Liverpool and Wellington. Their dutiful account of the proceedings in Parliament, especially of Wilberforce's motion, astonished him. 'He was extremely angry with them, behaved very rudely to the former [Liverpool], and when the Duke [of Wellington] interposed an observation, commanded him to hold his tongue.'[20] The brunt of the King's rage fell on the absent Canning. He told his Prime Minister that he expected Canning to resign from the Board of Trade. Liverpool responded that his own resignation would follow.

The same evening, while the King's case against the Queen, and hers against him, were being debated in the Palace of Westminster, there were worrying displays for the second consecutive night of mob violence against the residences of ministers and intimates of the King. Placards posted by Mr William Benbow, the Radical printer, at strategic street corners had appeared early in the day, with the simple injunction to 'illuminate for the Queen this night'.

The mob had had splendid fun all day. They commanded all approaches to South Audley Street, pelting passers-by with mud if they would not raise their hats and huzza for the Queen and yelling 'Queen! Queen!' and 'Balcony! Balcony!' at intervals, with gratifying results. When the Queen retired for the night and the house lay in darkness, the same spirited and youthful groups of her supporters, now at a loose end, decided to police the metropolis and urge those whose houses were unlit to 'illuminate'.

At about midnight or so a mob of a hundred revellers set out from South Audley Street. The cries of 'Lights! Lights!' were continually heard in the streets, accompanied by threats. Where a house remained in darkness, stones and other missiles followed. Soon the 'fine large squares of the parlour and first-floor windows were entirely broken' in many of the houses in Curzon Street, Dover Street and Clarges Street. The mob's path led them along Piccadilly and down to St James's Square, where they 'hooted and pelted' Lord Castlereagh's house. Then 'a new direction was given to their fury by a solitary exclamation of "Carlton House! Carlton House!" – to the propriety of an attack upon which all seemed to agree.'[21]

At Carlton House, however, were gathered within the forecourt a large company of soldiers and constables, under the direction of Sir Robert Baker, chief magistrate of Bow Street. After a rush *en masse* at one of the gates, which they failed to force open, the party broke up in disorder.

Crown, Cabinet and their partisans were all equally under attack. Lord Sidmouth's house in Clifford Street was again assaulted. At Lady Hertford's house in Manchester Square, all the windows fell victim to mob rage. The rioters even managed to gain entrance to the hall before they were repelled. As Society had not seen fit to inform the 'lower orders' of the King's change of affections, the windows of his new favourite Lady Conyngham escaped unscathed. The Misses Fitzclarence, daughters of the Duke of Clarence, had their front door thumped, their railings broken and every square of glass at the front of their house destroyed.[22]

Violence in any form was antipathetic to the Radical cause. Respectability, industry and moral virtue, on the Commonwealth model, were the grounds on which they requested political representation. Correspondingly, corruption and moral turpitude on high formed the basis on which they condemned the present ministers, borough-monger peers and placemen MPs – which was why the Queen's case was so appealing. The pen and the printer's press were the Radicals' weapons, not stones and mud. Strictly speaking, though, they were disingenuous in claiming that they had no part at all in the nocturnal turbulence, for it was Benbow's placards calling for an illumination of the metropolis which had led to the violence.

Violence, however, was the prerogative of that peculiar disorganized and sporadic phenomenon, the London mob, which had most memorably come to life in the Gordon Riots of 1780. On this occasion it seems to have included a great many 'juveniles' or apprentices to different trades, shopkeepers' assistants and even schoolboys. It was an impetuous and aggressive force at the best of times.

This same night Sidmouth and Eldon were returning with Wellington in his carriage from Parliament. As they neared the Home Secretary's house in Clifford Street, an extraordinary sight met their eyes. Sidmouth's son-in-law Mr George Pellew and George's father Lord Exmouth – with whom Caroline had tangled in Tunis – had made up a family dinner party in the house. Now the powerfully built Exmouth stood framed in the light of the open front door, brandishing a sword at a large crowd gathered in the street below.[23]

Pellew had left earlier for his lodgings close by, after withstanding with the rest of the company a 'feeble attack' on the house by the mob. Hearing the mob coming back, he returned too, and with the Watch was an eyewitness to what followed. A carriage dashed rapidly down the street and drew up at the door. Pellew heard Sidmouth say from within, 'Let me out; I must get out,' but his father-in-law was forestalled by the Duke, who had taken to locking his carriage doors ever since he had been shot at in Paris. Wellington's commanding voice answered, 'You shall not alight; drive on.' The order to move was speedily obeyed by the coachman as a stone broke the carriage window.[24] As Master of the Ordnance, Wellington was aware that, if his instructions had been followed, a posse of Guards should be patrolling nearby Piccadilly. So indeed it proved, and the mob dispersed as the carriage returned triumphant with an attendant company of Guards. One 'juvenile printer' was taken prisoner and spent the night in jail.

Next morning, Denman came with Brougham to consult with the Queen. When he exulted over Brougham's speech of the previous evening, the Queen replied coldly, 'I saw he would make a good speech.' In her distrust of her Attorney-General, she was not to be placated. Denman regretted this, but believed that her remark proceeded from her 'general sense of the inutility of speeches'.[25]

Meanwhile, Wellington profited by his night's adventure and issued detailed instructions to all barracks for companies of six or nine soldiers to patrol nightly the affected areas of the metropolis.[26] This had its effect and, after the following night had passed without incident, Eldon was at last able to assure his daughter in the country that the town was quiet and likely to remain so. 'The Queen has gone from South Audley Street to Portman Street, quite out of our neighbourhood.'[27] (Caroline had moved to Lady Anne Hamilton's house.)

The mob's ardour for the Queen also diminished after Castlereagh had announced in the House of Commons on the evening of Friday the 9th that Liverpool had received 'at a late hour that day' a communication from the Queen which rendered it impolitic to debate this evening the appointment of a Secret Committee of MPs. To expostulations from Opposition MPs, Brougham rose to confirm the Foreign Secretary's announcement. The Queen had 'directed the most serious attention to the declared sense of Parliament as to the propriety of some amicable adjustment of existing differences being attempted'. He added, 'The strong and earnest remonstrances of her legal advisers had overcome the reluctance which the illustrious individual in question felt to being the first to negotiate.'[28]

The Queen's letter to Liverpool placed the Cabinet in a very difficult position. Eldon had written to his daughter that while Parliament hoped for 'a pacific settlement', 'The King is determined and will hear of nothing but thorough investigation, and of ... thorough exposure of the Queen, and divorce. To this extent Parliament will not go.' Eldon prophesied then that the King would try to find 'an administration which can bring Parliament more into his views than the present ministers; I don't see how matters can go on a week longer, with the present Administration remaining'. Indeed, Eldon believed, 'no administration, who have any regard for him, will go the length he wishes, as an administration'. If any tried to do so, they would not take Parliament with them. 'That body is afraid of disclosures – not on one side only – which may affect the monarchy itself.'[29]

However, Liverpool, after receiving a letter from the Queen which betrayed her ignorance, was able to convey to her his 'extreme surprise' that he was the first to inform her, in June, that 'a memorandum delivered by Lord Liverpool to Mr Brougham on the 15th April last contains the proposition which Lord Liverpool was commanded by the King to communicate through Mr Brougham to her Majesty'.[30] To that he, Liverpool, had received no answer.

If the Queen had doubted Brougham at St Omer, now all her suspicions were confirmed by this dramatic revelation. The thought of what might have been – while now she faced a Secret Committee and Parliamentary proceedings – hardly endeared him to her. But, presented with a *fait accompli*, she was phlegmatic. She wrote an uncomfortable reply to Liverpool: her advisers had not had the opportunity till she came to England of presenting this memorandum, 'now submitted to her Majesty for the first time'. These terms did not, however, accord with her 'dignity and honour'.[31] Liverpool responded peaceably: the suggestion was that she abstain from exercising her royal rights, not renounce them. 'Any proposition ... must have for its basis her Majesty's residence abroad,' he added firmly.[32] The Queen seemed ready to negotiate. The King meanwhile was happy to have his ministers discuss the Queen's departure abroad, as long as 'they will persevere in their endeavours to obtain that inquiry which he considers absolutely essential to his Honour'.[33]

Ever since the debate on the 7th, the King's anger had focused on Canning's compliments to the Queen. He refused to consider any arbitration till he had had a full apology and explanation from Liverpool on the subject. Throughout the first weekend after the Queen's arrival in London, his pique continued. A letter from Wilberforce on the 9th begging him to restore the Queen's name to the liturgy, 'suggesting the ferment which would be occasioned; that [if he did not] the country would be in a fury, and perhaps the soldiers might take the Queen's part', hardly appeased him. Wilberforce wrote sadly in his diary on Sunday:

> I fear lest it should please God to scourge this nation through the medium of this rupture between the King and Queen. If the soldiery should take up her cause, who knows what may happen – and is it very improbable? O Lord, deliver us! Thou only canst, who hast the hearts of all at thy disposal. Yet how gracious God is to me, giving me the acceptable service of putting off the discussion![34]

On the Sunday, Liverpool, Castlereagh and the Secretary of Patronage Mr Charles Arbuthnot spent the whole day at Carlton House, 'vainly endeavouring to procure an interview with the King'. On the Monday, after Castlereagh had again adjourned a noisy Commons, the three men saw him, but 'found him so much irritated' that Liverpool told Canning he must seek an interview. At the levée on Tuesday the 13th, Canning finally had his audience. It 'lasted fifty-two minutes by Lord Yarmouth's watch', and the President of the Board of Control's apology was accepted.[35] The King, however, remained convinced that Canning's speech had betrayed his former liaison with Caroline. At last, and in the nick of time – in the Lords that day Liverpool had to postpone the meeting of the Secret Committee, while 'more communications' took place – the King grudgingly agreed to the negotiation the Queen offered, and Liverpool stiffly advised Brougham.[36]

The ministers were aware that the King had, as Eldon feared, in these last days made overtures to the Whig leaders, Grey in the Lords and Tierney in the Commons. Grey, in Hawick, was perturbed to receive a letter from Tierney, written on the 12th. Lord Donough-more, brother of Lord Hutchinson, had approached him, as well as Lansdowne and Holland. 'The ministers would be immediately dismissed,' wrote Tierney, 'if I would say that I advised him [Don-oughmore] to press the King to do so. He offered to return to Carlton House and to finish the business in an hour.' The King was graciously pleased to forget all his grievances against the Whigs, added Tierney, and was disposed to grant the Catholic emancipation the Whigs sought. 'I am sure Grey may be Minister if he chooses' were Donoughmore's words.[37]

Grey departed south at once. 'I shall be very probably laughed at, for having gone on a fool's errand,' he recorded, but it was a political opportunity he could hardly refuse to investigate. In the event, he found in London that the King had agreed to negotiate. Moreover, the divisions within the Whig party, as ever was the case, made forming a government next to impossible.

Wood, her former host, was inconveniently opposed to the Queen's new plan. In the two back drawing-rooms at Lady Anne Hamilton's house, she consulted with Brougham and Denman, and here on the morning of the 10th she received an expostulatory letter from Mr William Cobbett. He urged her not to yield to Parliament's wish for a negotiated peace with the King. Her reliance should be on the people, not on Parliament, and she should fight for her rights.[38]

In this advice, he was joined by Alderman Wood, who continued to make the point that he had raised originally in St Omer. She would find Parliament loath to vote her £50,000 a year with her name uncleared. The difficulty was that Wood had, as Brougham had sharply reminded the Queen, little knowledge of the evidence con-tained in the green bag or of her history. Brougham advised her in the strongest terms – playing on her fears of the Milan Commission's findings – to accept the Government proposals.

But Cobbett's advice was not to be lightly dismissed. Before he had fled to America in 1817, fearing the consequence of the suspension of the Habeas Corpus Act, his *Weekly Political Register* had been the bible of every aspirant 'statesman at the loom and politician at the spinning jenny' of the educated lower class. The *Register* had a large circulation and a far greater readership. All coffee houses, public houses and inns

– where informed public debate was the desideratum – subscribed to one or more copies. The local Hampden Clubs and different trade societies subscribed – and, besides, a good many regular readers clubbed together to obtain a single copy. Cobbett was the great disseminator of political information. His views were robust, patriotic and critical of Government and Crown only because the individuals in question failed to meet the high standards he required. He was the roast beef of Old England, John Bull incarnate.

On his return from America in the wake of the Six Acts, Cobbett found that the duty of sixpence under the new Stamp Act – designed to eradicate the 'Great unstamped' wash of Radical broadsheets and newspapers – put his *Political Register* effectively out of the reach of his earlier readership. Furthermore, under the new Act, the mail coaches now would not carry his *Register* to the distant parts of the country his firebrand variety of dogged conservatism had once influenced so greatly.

The Queen's cause was thus a perfect platform from which Cobbett might air his views, with the nation interested and the metropolis obsessed. Cobbett had lately appointed Benbow publisher of the *Register*. The two worked closely together over the next few months propagandizing for the Queen. Cobbett filled the pages of his paper with denunciations of King and Ministers, and probably helped Benbow with the composition of pamphlets and placards in the same cause. Londoners were their main targets, but their products reached further afield. Benbow advertised that collections of literature about the Queen could be had in places fifty miles from London, by application to particular taverns.[39] While pamphleteering was Cobbett's genius, Benbow's particular contributions to the Queenite agitation were exuberant and mordant caricatures, satirizing Crown and Cabinet and their machinations against the Queen, which he commissioned and sold.

Cobbett, with Benbow, occupied a place on the soft edge of Radical politics. Both men openly attacked the King's morals and inveighed against his treatment of the Queen. Yet neither looked, in their exertions over the Queen's rights, to the overthrow of the monarchy, as did the 'ultra' Radical politicians. Francis Place, the influential Westminster tailor, Richard and Jane Carlile, publishers of the

*Republican*, and Thomas Dolby the bookseller all hoped for convulsion.[40] Cobbett and Benbow confined their attentions, as did the octogenarian reformer Major John Cartwright, to emphasizing the parallels between the oppression of the Queen by the King and the struggle of the unrepresented of England for Parliamentary reform. Cobbett's letter to the Queen shows him confident that he spoke for a majority outside Parliament when he advised her to resist all compromise. It also demonstrates his belief that public opinion was a real force for the Government to reckon with – and, implicitly, for the Queen to reckon with, if she did not heed Cobbett, its mouthpiece.

On the 14th Brougham and Denman, for the Queen, went to the Foreign Office to begin the negotiations with Castlereagh and Wellington, for the King. 'We were received by Lord Castlereagh', wrote Denman, 'in his parlour, after he had entertained a party of foreign ambassadors.' The Foreign Secretary was consequently 'covered with diamonds, stars and ribands; the Duke of Wellington was equally splendid.' Two 'meagre lawyers' faced these imposing figures. Castlereagh, despite his magnificence, assumed an air of 'agreeable frankness', and declared that they were eager to meet 'as men of business, rather than persons of high station and formality'.[41] Although the matters for discussion centred on and assumed the Queen's residence abroad, Brougham continually introduced the subject of the liturgy, and suggested that the restoration of her name to it might reconcile her to living on the Continent. Castlereagh promptly replied, 'You might as well try to move Carlton House.'

Four further meetings at the Foreign Office and at Castlereagh's St James's Square residence had no greater effect. On the 19th the negotiations had failed, and Leach told Powell urgently to prepare for proceedings.

The agitation in Parliament when the protocols of the five meetings were laid before the House of Commons paled besides the outdoor agitation, which had been steadily fomented this last week. There was a dramatic development which Wilberforce, for one, had foretold. 'The extinguisher has caught fire,' wrote Mr Henry Luttrell to Greville.'[42] Public order in London was maintained at this time by the military, with the insubstantial addition of a small civil force of constables and watchmen. Sir Francis Burdett four years earlier had spoken eloquently of the power of the people matched by 'an essential power at Hyde Park, at Knightsbridge, at the Tower, at Woolwich, at Hounslow, at Deptford and at Chatham. We are in fact in this metropolis, in the midst of a circumvallation of forces'.[43] Then he had been protesting against the encircling barracks. If these troops became 'infected' by the Queenite agitation, if the power of the people combined with this essential power, this 'circumvallation of forces', what then?

A number of regiments drafted into London in the wake of the Queen's arrival found themselves placed in new barracks in the old King's Mews at Charing Cross. The conditions there were exceedingly cramped, the extra duty was wearing. Furthermore, orders came not only from Wellington but also from a variety of commanders ranging from the Duke of York, Commander-in-Chief of the army, to Bloomfield for the King at Carlton House, and conflicted more often than not. The regiments' officers rarely came near their men. The soldiers had a specific complaint and no one to address it to: they felt entitled to extra pay for the extra duty. In the confined conditions their grievances rumbled.

On the evening of 15 June rumblings of discontent in the Mews came to a head, and the men of the 3rd Foot Guards laid down their arms. York and a number of ministers, including Wellington, were attending a drawing-room at the Queen's house. To their mortification, they were summoned downstairs to be told of the agitation at the Mews some hours after it had begun. They took swift action, and ordered the mutinous units to be removed from London. Early next morning one battalion was marched off in disgrace to profit from the soothing sea breezes of Portsmouth.

Later that day, crowds gathered outside the Mews, with women predominant, clamouring for the remaining battalion within to come out and join them. It was known to the Home Office that, at certain taverns near the barracks, ale and meat were being provided gratis to the soldiers if they would drink the Queen's health. This alliance between people and troops was a dangerous development. Sidmouth called out the 2nd Life Guards under Captain Cranstoun Ridout, instructing him to read the Riot Act and disperse the crowds. This was successfully done, and the second battalion marched out of

London next morning without incident. But the affair of the soldiers added an element of real danger to the 'convulsions' about the Queen.[44]

References abound, in diary entries of this week, to Catherine the Great and to other usurpers who employed the military to overthrow the existing administration. Few believed a General Order, issued by the Duke of York to army and public, which claimed that the symptoms of discontent had been confined to one battalion, and even to some few individuals in that. The truth of that statement Wellington disproved in an important memorandum to Liverpool on the condition of the Guards. 'I feel the greatest anxiety respecting the state of the military in London,' he wrote; '. . . the men in their march [out of London] joined in, and made use of, the cry of disaffection of the day.' Rumours were rife respecting the loyalty of all the Guards, both cavalry and infantry – 'whether true or false, no man can tell. . . . We know not . . . whether seeds of discontent are laid or not in other corps. . . .' The Duke of York, for all his General Order, was uneasy about the Coldstream Guards, the Cabinet was informed.

Wellington recommended certain procedures to combat the discontent in the Guards. First, the confusion of the troops by numerous and conflicting orders from different persons should cease. 'Nobody knows who is on or who off duty, all the troops are harassed. . . .' Furthermore, as the sergeants and corporals of the Guards were 'taken from the ranks, and of the class of the people, and liable to be influenced by the views and sentiments of the people', he advised that the officers of the Guards should go constantly among their men to discover their opinions and combat their inclination to disaffection. Wellington proposed the establishment of 'a police in London, or military corps'. Feelings of emulation would then prevent 'the breaking out of these mutinies' in the Guards battalions.[45]

On the fifth anniversary of the Battle of Waterloo, Sunday the 18th, the Duke of York was stoutly cheered at the Knightsbridge barracks, and Wellington's measures appeared to have alleviated the discontent. However, at Hampton Court the troops were still reported to be drinking the Queen's health, and this same night in Brighton a somewhat farcical display of support for the Queen took place at a dinner of celebration given by some sergeants of one regiment, the 51st, for those of another. One of the guests, a sergeant of the Guards, drunk, proposed the health of the Queen, 'with three times three'. Ejected from the dinner by the loyalists of the 51st, he returned with a mob and proceeded to lay about his hosts and turn them out of their own dinner.[46]

The King was vexing the ministers again. Some ragged cheers greeting his appearance at the Chapel Royal at St James's on the Sunday led him to believe that the hearts of the people were with him. Sidmouth was dispatched to disburden his Majesty of this hope, which he did with such vigorous effect that the King spoke of going to Hanover and leaving his brother York as regent. He was persuaded instead to retire to Royal Lodge at Windsor, after vainly urging Sidmouth, whom he favoured, to form an administration and secure the divorce in the place of Liverpool.[47] The King now detested Liverpool almost as much as his wife, and suspected that his enthusiasm for proceedings against the Queen was not strong.

It was in this uneasy atmosphere that the Parliamentary debates on the failure of the negotiations began on the 19th. Grey was one of those in the Lords who censured the Government for its endless postponements of the Secret Committee – 'Tomorrow and tomorrow and tomorrow' – for which it had so blithely moved two weeks earlier. (The King wrote to Grey to express his approval of this speech a few days later.) Burdett in the Commons applied to the green bag, which still lingered on the table, Lord Buckingham's theatrical order to an incompetent actor, 'Get off on your knees, but get off.'[48]

By Tuesday the 20th, Wilberforce had concluded that it was his duty to move an address to the Queen begging her to give up the mention of her name in the liturgy as the 'only material difference which remained' between King and Queen.[49] 'I hope I am averting a great evil,' he wrote, although he knew that he exposed himself to 'extreme odium and misconstruction'. He hoped that if his proposition of an address was carried in the Commons by a great majority, the Queen would yield to 'the will of Parliament'. Accordingly, he gave notice that he intended to bring on a motion next day.

That night, on going up to bed, Wilberforce heard a knocking at the door. A letter from the Queen was handed to him, 'a warm, expostulatory letter – her own ebullition!' Her opposition to his plan had been prompted by a mischievous account of it given to her by Alderman Wood.[50]

The following day, Wilberforce responded, and resolved to put off his motion to the Thursday, when the Queen would have had time to consider his answer. The House was impatient with him but that evening Brougham brought him a 'more moderate' letter from the Queen. Accordingly on the 22nd, in a noisy House, he moved for an address to the Queen, begging her to yield on the question of the liturgy, assuring her that giving way would not be construed as 'any wish to shrink from enquiry, but would only be deemed to afford a renewed proof of the desire, which her Majesty had been graciously pleased to express, to submit her own wishes to the authority of Parliament'.[51]

In his hopes for the success of his address Wilberforce was shored up by Brougham, who wrote to him on this day, 'She will accede to your address, I pledge myself.' Wilberforce had another source of support. 'God in whom I trusted,' he wrote of his speech introducing the motion, 'graciously blessed me, and enabled me to go through my business not discreditably.'[52] His motion engendered some memorable speeches. In response to a remark that the Queen was sufficiently prayed for in the liturgy 'as included in the prayer "all the royal family"', Denman rose to protest that, if the Queen were mentioned in the liturgy, it was in the prayer 'for all who are desolate and oppressed'. And Castlereagh, seeking to frighten the country gentlemen into acceding to the motion for fear of arousing the King's ire, said that, 'the King himself in his closet' (rather than in council) had made the decision to omit his wife's name from the liturgy. Thus for the first time the King's animus against the Queen was on public display. Burdett was 'bitter and violent' in reply. He was not aware that in this country the King had a closet, or that he made any decisions before consultation with ministers.[53]

'That ill-timed insult' in Castlereagh's speech was immediately reported to the Queen – by Wood – and Denman received a furious letter from her later in the debate, stating that she refused to consider entering into 'any further stipulation after such an avowal'. Denman believed that Castlereagh's speech did indeed have the effect of closing up her mind to all negotiation.[54]

At five o'clock on Friday morning the House rose, after Wilber-force had secured a sizeable majority for his motion. It was settled that he and three other MPs – Acland, who had helped draft the resolution, Wortley, who had seconded the motion, and Bankes – should go to the Queen on the 24th, Saturday morning, with the address. Wilberforce wrote to his wife on the Friday, buoyed up with hope: 'What a blessing it is to have been led by a Gracious God into paths which—' He broke off, as Brougham and Denman, the Queen's law officers, arrived at his house.[55]

His interview with this couple somewhat dimmed his hopes, fostered by Brougham only the day before – he was now 'not very sanguine that the Queen would assent to his petition'. Nevertheless, on the Saturday morning Wilberforce attired himself 'in full Court costume' at Acland's and went with his fellow-deputies to Portman Street. A lively crowd was assembled in the narrow street, and the four men were hooted and hissed as they entered Lady Anne's house.

There was great anger against the House of Commons and against Wilberforce, who for his efforts won the name of Dr Cantwell. To the unrepresented people of England, the Parliamentary address was further evidence that not only the Cabinet and the King but, as they had suspected, the House of Commons also were persecutors of the woman the press loved to call 'the injured Queen'. Wood had declared he would not vote a shilling of public money for the Queen if she went abroad (which hardly endeared him to that royal personage).

In Lady Anne's drawing-room upstairs, Wilberforce found Queen Caroline flanked by Brougham and Denman, in their great wigs and long gowns.[56] The appearance of unity was misleading. An interesting scene had taken place shortly beforehand at Denman's house. Denman had remarked that the Queen's 'own feeling appeared to be unfavourable to any terms of compromise'. Brougham, reverting to his earlier view, swore she would accept the House of Commons' suggestion for her graceful retirement from the country. Denman composed a letter in the Queen's name, rejecting the proposal; Brougham drafted an acceptance. On their arrival at Portman Street, they found that Caroline had determined to 'decline the mediation', and she presented them with an ill-written letter – apparently the composition of a Miss Grimani, who was 'much with the Queen'.

Denman and Brougham considered its language eccentric and were busy trying to cobble together an amalgam of Miss Grimani's and Denman's epistles when the Parliamentary deputies entered.[57]

Wilberforce thought the Queen cold, Denman considered her magnificent. After the deputies had read their resolution to her, Brougham immediately read Denman's reply. 'Alas, the answer most decidedly rejected our mediation,' Wilberforce confided to his diary.[58] The deputies knelt, kissed the Queen's hand and retired.

The deputies' emergence on to the street with Brougham and Denman was the signal for anxious enquiries from the crowd and for general rejoicing when the Queen's refusal was made known. Those nearest the deputies relieved their feelings by jostling and spitting on them, while others further afield jeered and hooted in derision. Wilberforce and the others, their coats and hair damp with spittle, were forced to seek crowded sanctuary in the coach of the Queen's law officers.

Wilberforce bore with patience the accusations in the press that he had trifled with the House of Commons and had attempted to deceive the people with his earlier avowals that the Queen would agree to his resolution. He later implicitly admitted that his proposal was wrong-headed. He should have moved for an address to the King, begging him to revoke the Order in Council omitting the Queen's name from the liturgy. He had perhaps forgotten that, in his letter of the 9th to the King, he had already made that suggestion, to no effect. In the Commons, however, when the Queen's answer to the deputies was read later that day, the anger of the House was directed principally against Caroline. Denman was revolted, and his vivid account of the House's temper makes uncomfortable reading.

The country gentlemen, who had so fearfully supported Wilberforce's original motion for an adjournment in the hope of negotiation, were now as eager for proceedings to begin from motives of wounded pride. As Denman put it, the general sentiment was 'I am for proceeding now, are not you for going on with the business [the inquiry]?' He added, 'Their address had in effect proposed to recognize her innocence. . . . Now that she asserted that innocence, they instantly took the green bag for gospel and were delighted at the prospect of crushing her with its contents.' He concluded, 'the shame of that disgusting inquiry . . . now, like a pestilential vapour, impended over the country'.[59]

The failure of the Parliamentary address, and the dangerously increased popularity of the Queen consequent upon it, alerted the Government to the need to move fast. On Sunday the 25th, after a Cabinet meeting, Arbuthnot hosted a dinner at Whitehall Place, and Canning, determined to distance himself from the imminent proceedings, went direct from there to the King to offer his resignation.

In a coded memorandum to a friend abroad, Canning described this audience. He had expressed the view that Mars (the King) had put himself completely in the right since the arrival of Juno (the Queen), and ought to make no further concession. However, 'it was impossible for Marcus [Canning] to take any part in criminatory proceedings against a person to whom he had stood in so confidential a situation. . . . he could not become one of Juno's accusers'. Mars had a right to 'his entire services' now that negotiations were at an end and hostile proceedings unavoidable. Therefore, either Marcus continued in Mars's service 'altogether silent and inactive on this particular question', or else he resigned. He thought it would be more useful to Mars if he resigned. Mars received this with 'perfect cordiality', although he intimated that Marcus had not told all his reasons for declining to take an active part against Juno. Mars and Marcus parted on amicable terms, and the next day Canning heard through Liverpool that the King insisted he remain in office.[60]

On 27 June, the Secret Committee met for the first time, and Caroline's scandalous adventures over so many years, from Blackheath to Naples, from the Levant to Pesaro, came under the hostile scrutiny of fifteen peers determined to recommend proceedings. The green bag was at last carried from the table in the House of Lords and its contents spilled out in a secluded committee room. Liverpool feared that 'the Queen's popularity was at the zenith, the faith of the people and her faith in them restored by her answer to Parliament, execrations now reserved for Cabinet, King and Parliament. Now a new spirit was at work in London and in provincial centres.'[61] This spirit was then called 'disaffection'. The Queen had protested to the House of Lords the day before, articulating all the grievances voiced by defendants arraigned before the criminal courts. It was agreed that her counsel should be heard, and they begged the House first to postpone all proceedings for two months to allow her to prepare a defence. She objected to the secret tribunal which had assembled the evidence against her in the green bag and to the composition of the present Secret Committee, of which all but two members were attached to the Government.[62]

On the 20th, Powell had returned from the country to find two urgent notes from the vice-chancellor: 'English translations of all the depositions will be immediately needed,' now that the negotiations with the Queen had ruptured. For nineteen hours a day for seven days Powell – and Mr Thomas Brooksbank, Lord Liverpool's secretary and a good linguist, 'nearly as much' – laboured to complete this task before the Secret Committee met. An angry conference with Leach and Cooke interrupted this work on the last evening, the 26th. They were engrossed by the continuing reluctance of the ministers to defend the 'Mission' to Milan, and by Denman's attack in the Commons on Leach himself, adapting Emilia's words from *Othello*: 'some busy and insinuating rogue, some cogging, cozening slave to get some office must have devised this slander'.[63] Cooke declared that, as he had retired from the Bar, he would act in whatever proceedings followed as chamber counsel only, leaving the Government Attorney- and Solicitor-General to find other counsel to support them. Powell stated that he would not act as 'agent' in the affair unless he received a 'specific authority' from the Government, and 'that their past conduct to us was a bad guarantee for the future.... to save themselves they would sacrifice both him [Leach] and us'.[64]

In the course of this meeting, 'quite unexpectedly', Mr Adamberger, a courier from Lord Stewart in Vienna, was announced. 'He had brought with him the three Majocchis, Negri and Sacchi,' and they were lodged at Ibbotson's Hotel in Vere Street. 'From the state of the public mind and the fury of the populace it [was] evident to us all that it would be highly dangerous for them to remain here,' Powell wrote. Mobs were going through every coffee house, accusing foreigners of being witnesses. He was furious that the Italians had been brought to him. He had before told Leach, 'I neither could nor would take upon myself the personal charge of the witnesses.' He was moreover dismayed that Sacchi and Negri, whose characters he doubted, had been called to England.[65]

Powell and Adamberger went together to Liverpool at Downing Street. Here it was agreed that Mr Joseph Planta at the Foreign Office should arrange for Lord Clancarty, Ambassador to The Hague, to receive the witnesses in Holland, and Adamberger was sent off to Planta, with a letter to this effect from Liverpool's secretary, Brooksbank. When he heard from Harwich that the *Princess Charlotte* packet had departed with the bewildered Italians for Holland, Powell hoped that he had thus seen off all further attempts to make him responsible for the witnesses in England. It was now 'a national and a Government measure', Leach agreed, and it was for the Government to look after its witnesses. Powell represented forcibly to Liverpool that the witnesses now on the road from Milan should be intercepted at Calais and Boulogne by 'a confidential person' and dispatched direct to The Hague. This also was agreed to, and Powell resumed his task of translating and copying the evidence for the Secret Committee. By working closely with Hobhouse, Powell at last completed the work the following day and sent the papers to Liverpool. The Prime Minister thereafter sent instructions for Powell to have Demont's and Sacchini's depositions sworn before a magistrate.[66] So much for the Cabinet's repeated contention that foreign servants who had been dismissed would not be adequate witnesses. Powell duly took these sworn statements on 1 July down to the House of Lords, and Liverpool himself came out from the Committee Room into the Robing Room to receive them.

Powell, for all his misgivings, was an indispensable 'agent' to all the parties interested in ridding England of the Queen. At the Home Office Bloomfield engaged in a fruitless discussion about the lack of good English witnesses 'to give greater credit to the foreign'. The following day they were to mull over the question of calling Hownam for the prosecution – but the Duke of Clarence gave Hownam 'the highest character as an officer', and it would be, Powell believed, 'a dangerous experiment'. Now he went off again from Home Office to the Admiralty, to Carlton House and thence to South Street, Leach's house.[67]

While the Secret Committee met, and the King threatened to

change his ministry if they should not decide in favour of a prosecution, his legal officers were exercised to decide just what form the
proceedings should take if a case for the Queen's adultery could be
made out from the papers. Over all such discussions loomed the
terrifying possibility that the Queen's counsel might bring charges of
recrimination. Since Gillray had first published in 1786 his 'The
Morning After Marriage', showing the Prince of Wales and Mrs
Fitzherbert yawning and attending to their morning toilette, rumours
of a secret marriage had continued to grow, despite Fox's denials in
the House of Commons, despite the later marriage to Caroline, the
tatters of which were now before the public, and despite the Regent's
estrangement from Mrs Fitzherbert. If Brougham stopped short of
making such an assertion it was in his interest that his royal client
should be the lawful Queen. There was besides the King's record of
mistresses and less salubrious liaisons for Brougham to exploit. The
abdominous King's relationship with his present favourite, the cor-
pulent Lady Conyngham, was generally thought to stop short of
impropriety. Most imaginations were daunted by the notion of the
twin mountains of flesh conjugating.

The procedure which Lord Eldon decided ultimately to invoke was
a Bill of Pains and Penalties to remove the Queen from the Kingdom,
and deprive her of her titles. This would, satisfactorily, afford no
opportunity for recrimination. Such bills made use of Parliamentary
procedure to impose penalties where recourse to the criminal courts
was deemed unsuitable. After passage through both Houses the
measure would be enacted and the punishment enforced.[68] Eldon
satisfied himself that, contrary to what some might think, it was not
an unconstitutional expedient. Bills of Pains and Penalties were of
ancient usage, and had been implemented at irregular intervals in the
course of the previous century, most notably during the Jacobite trials
following the Stewart Rebellion of 1745. Even so, it was a sinister-
sounding instrument. As Lady Cowper wrote of its application to
Caroline, 'A Bill of Pains and Penalties is an awkward name; it sounds
to the ignorant as if she was going to be fried or tortured in some
way.'[69]

The Government was thus well prepared when the Secret Committee returned its solemn findings to Parliament. To no one's

surprise, its members found that there was material evidence to warrant proceedings against the Queen.[70] So it was that on 4 July Lord Liverpool gave notice that he would propose that a first reading of the Bill of Pains and Penalties should begin next day. The Bill was to begin in the House of Lords, and go down to the Lower House for its consideration when the second and third readings had been completed 'above'. Castlereagh wrote a relieved letter to his brother in Vienna. On the whole, he did not think that 'matters ... could have worked more favourably', so the British Government had the advantage.[71] The advantage, in fact, was *all* the Government's.

The Bill's title stated its purpose all too clearly: 'An Act ... to deprive her Majesty Caroline Amelia Elizabeth of the Title, Prerogatives, Rights, Privileges and Exemptions of Queen Consort of this Realm, and to dissolve the Marriage between his Majesty and the said Caroline Amelia Elizabeth.' Its preamble related her engagement in 1814 of Pergami, 'a foreigner of low station' whom she had promoted, and alleged that she had conducted herself towards him 'with indecent and offensive familiarity and freedom, and carried on a licentious, disgraceful and adulterous intercourse' with him.[72] For the Bill to be passed, the allegations in the preamble had to be proved to the satisfaction of the two Houses of Parliament. For this reason, the second reading (which would begin on 17 August) would take a form similar to that of a trial, with examination and cross-examination of witnesses and speeches by counsel and indeed by peers. The word 'trial' soon came to be popularly applied to the proceedings, and the participants themselves used forensic vocabulary. Lord Chancellor Eldon, as Speaker in the Lords, would have the difficult task of adjudicating between counsel who sought to rely on court procedure and peers anxious to guard the traditions of their House.

Brougham and Denman, the Queen's Attorney- and Solicitor-General, now advised her solicitor, Mr William Vizard, who had often acted for her before, on the instruction of additional counsel. In consultation with Caroline herself, they settled on four distinguished practitioners: Mr Thomas Wilde, Mr John Williams, Mr Nicholas Tindal and Dr Stephen Lushington. For the other side, the Government Attorney-, Solicitor- and Advocate-General (Gifford, Copley, Robinson) would likewise soon be augmented by Dr James Parke and

Mr William Adam; the Treasury Solictor, Mr George Maule, would be assisted by Powell.

On 8 July, it was announced that the Coronation had been postponed indefinitely: the King was of course anxious to get his wife out of the way before that solemn event took place. In the debates that started two days later on the first reading of the Bill it was pointed out angrily, with reference to the Milan Commissioners' activities in Italy, that the Queen's lawyers had to marshal in less than six weeks a defence to what Government agents had been preparing over a space of two years. Furthermore, the decision not to supply her counsel with more than the heads of the charges against her, with no list of specific times and dates on which impropriety might have taken place, and no list of witnesses against her, ran contrary to fundamental tenets of British justice. Her Majesty had the impossible task of providing evidence, in this short space of time, to counter unknown specific charges which might refer to any place, any time and any event in the 'long period of time' after 1814 identified in the preamble. Quite apart from the difficulty attached to recollection of episodes which had long ceased to hold any significance for her, there was the burden posed by the extended travelling which Caroline had undertaken in these years.

Lord Liverpool blandly replied that the Queen would be afforded every assistance in her task by the governments of all of the countries through which she had journeyed. In previous bills of this nature, he added, it had not been the practice to furnish the defendants with anything more than the heads of the charges.[73] Later in the month, the Government agreed with Vizard a sum of money to fund the search for defence evidence abroad, and Mr Jabez Henry, a former colonial judge in the Ionian Islands, was appointed to conduct that search. On 4 August, Castlereagh wrote to ask the Austrian authorities to facilitate Henry's efforts in Milan.[74]

At home the Government had an additional advantage over the Queen and her team of lawyers in the shape of the Alien Officers, posted in all the ports to notify the Home Office of all foreigners who entered the country. The Alien Act, a wartime measure, had been renewed early in June of this year, in the face of general disapprobation. It was to prove a useful tool to the Government in the Queen's affair, and Sidmouth assiduously scanned the Alien Officers' daily reports.

Meanwhile, it emerged that the Government's plans for the interception of the Milan witnesses at Calais had gone awry. On the night of the 5th, Powell had been summoned by his clerk to his chambers in Lincoln's Inn. He found skulking there a courier from Milan with five more witnesses. No one had been at Calais to meet them, and the courier had merely followed Colonel Browne's instructions at Milan in crossing to Dover and proceeding to Powell's chambers. Powell dispatched the party back to the inn in the City where they had alighted from the Dover coach and wrote a furious letter to Lord Liverpool. The courier had informed him that twelve more were to cross the Channel the next day. 'It is impossible to tell what the consequences may be,' he wrote. Apparently no orders had been given to the British Consul at Calais, and Powell insisted that some 'confidential person' in London be approached to take care of these arrivals. He, Powell, had no objection, he told Liverpool next day, to communicating with the 'confidential person' or giving directions, but 'I neither can nor will take charge of the witnesses. . . . The negligence and want of enquiry with respect in this most important subject . . . is painful and provoking beyond measure.'[75]

From Milan Browne wrote a few days later, having only just received Leach's letter informing him of the British Government's intention to intercept the Italian witnesses in France and send them overland to The Hague. 'Heaven and earth are at work here to intimidate our witnesses and the [anti-Austrian] radicals of Milan are literally mad,' Browne wrote. 'Every batch of witnesses which departs increases their rage. . . . Heaven grant that nothing may happen to them, or we are ruined here,' he warned.[76]

His prayer came too late. Without a word of English among them, and no interpreter, Restelli and his band of Italian workmen, cooks and confectioners had landed at Dover on the night of 6 July. The witnesses' dark skins and foreign appearance made them immediately suspect to the crowd, which regularly gathered now at the quay with the precise intention of discovering 'bugs and frogs' who came against the Queen. The visitors were set upon by their English hosts and hostesses and were mauled all the way up the beach with sticks. The assembly of ill-wishers steadily increased along the route to Mr Wright's Ship Hotel, where the witnesses finally took refuge. As a result of what became jovially known as the 'Dover massacre', the workman Brusa had been partially deafened by a blow. Restelli was badly beaten and all were left with a horror of the English and England. 'Chief among their attackers were women, who scratched and pummelled in good fishwife fashion.'[77]

The bill for the damage to Mr Wright's carriage, which he rented out for the Italians for their journey to London, is a testimony to the irate temper of John Bull and his lady, which the miserable witnesses had aroused by their arrival. While Powell and Planta at the Foreign Office attempted to soothe the terrified 'aliens' in London and immediately dispatched them after their fellows to Harwich and The Hague, xenophobia reigned in the streets. The rout of the pathetic Italians was seen as a national glory to equal any military triumphs of the late war.

The repercussions abroad were enormous. A batch of witnesses from Lugano were at Paris *en route* for Calais, and they turned back for home, as did another batch which had set out from Milan on the 4th. When the news of the 'massacre', grossly exaggerated, reached Milan later in the month, there were widespread rumours that the Queen was on the throne, Restelli dead and the witnesses all in prison condemned to death. In this climate of opinion, Browne found it impossible to convince the witnesses who had been about to set out that the truth was otherwise. He wrote begging for Restelli to return to prove he lived still, and to bring with him letters from every one of the witnesses at The Hague to convince their relatives that they were safe. Finding witnesses required, said Browne, 'the patience, good humour, firmness and rage (though suppressed) of an angel and devil combined'. He wrote further, 'The infamous work carried on by the partisans of the Queen in England, can be equalled only by that of a similar description by wretches here. ... there is a desperate struggle, between what is high and respectable and what is despicable. It would seem as though the whole of Italy were tied to the Queen's apron string, although everyone, at the same moment, admits her misconduct.'[78]

In England, too, many of the Queen's partisans believed her to be guilty of misconduct. But as Henry Brougham declared:

The strength of the Queen's case lay in the general demurrer which all
men, both in and out of Parliament, made, viz., admit everything to be
true which is alleged against the Queen, yet, after the treatment she
had received ever since she first came to England, her husband had no
right to the relief prayed by him, or the punishment sought against her.[79]

This 'general demurrer' or 'public opinion' made the Government loath
to implement the repressive press legislation of the Six Acts, designed
specifically for such a state of affairs as had now arisen – though a
torrent of newspaper invective against the ministers, verse-satires, penny
broadsheets and scurrilous prints swelled against and overflowed the
banks of propriety. The King was to write to Eldon of the caricatures
which vilified and mocked him: 'If the law as it now stands has not
the power to protect the Sovereign against the licentious abomin-
ations of this description, it is *high time* that the law should be amended.'[80]

This disaffection accounted for the fantastic popularity of Hone's
verse-satire, *The Queen's Matrimonial Ladder*. Sold with a toy wooden
ladder for a shilling and published in August, it told the Queen's
wrongs from marriage onward in picture and verse and reached its
twelfth edition three days after the 'trial' of the Queen began, its
fifty-first edition in 1821.[81] 'Satire', wrote Dolby, the Radical politician and publisher, 'is torpid unless hatched into animation by some
ruling vice or folly.'[82] The 'ruling vice' was the King's and his
ministers' Bill against the Queen; her supporters hatched satire into
'stinging activity'.

The 'general demurrer' against the handling of the Queen was the
reason why the walls of London were daubed, 'The Queen for ever,
the King in the river', why Radical politicians like Dolby and Benbow
turned publisher and why their boys, and Hone's, were out with their
horns on the street corners, advertising the latest graphic effluxion
against the Crown and ministers. 'No man could go through the
streets of London', adverted Sir Matthew Cholmeley, 'without having
his eyes insulted by the most offensive placards and comparisons of
an odious kind between the highest personage and the greatest of
tyrants.'[83] Cholmeley presumably referred in particular to parodies of
the King as Kubla Khan, as Henry VIII and as Nero. Shelley's
*Swellfoot the Tyrant*, one of the most offensive or most satirical

publications, was in fact suppressed in August after only seven copies had been sold. The poem – the King is Swellfoot, Lady Conyngham Adiposa – pays homage to the caricatures and verse-satires which found their way even to Shelley's Italian retreat.[84] The printing press was newly adopted in August as the symbol of freedom of speech, while the green bag continued to represent repression, conspiracy and, in particular, the perjured evidence of the Italian witnesses.

Although the leading cartoonists such as Williams, Rowlandson, Cruikshank and Lane – Gillray had died in 1811 – were not politically attached to any party, their satirical imaginations were naturally attracted towards scenes derogatory to his Majesty and his Majesty's Government. One cartoon depicts Liverpool, Castlereagh and Sidmouth, as the Three Witches from *Macbeth*, stirring a green bag into cauldron and chanting, 'All that's evil, all that's sin', with the King himself a bloated Macbeth, standing by.[85]

The public disorder in London was steadily fomented by skilled agitators such as Mr Francis Place, the Radical tailor and pamphleteer. Broadsheets flew off the presses, often consisting of little more than some rude verses accompanied by crude woodcuts. Public meetings to decry the treatment of the Queen were proclaimed with printed advertisements, tacked to the walls at street corners and the doors of coffee houses. Countrywide, the Radical MPs and some Whig MPs responded to Henry Brougham's urging to make the affair a national issue. It was a bold concept. England, despite the 1801 Act of Union, was still politically divided from Scotland. Brougham, making use of his Scottish connections, wrote splendid letters to his *Edinburgh Review* and to his Edinburgh University friends, urging the justice of the cause. It is noticeable that, among the addresses which are preserved, the Scottish towns and communities feature largely.[86] Much was written about the Government's supposed iniquity in withholding from the Queen the Crown plate snatched from the *Clorinde* in 1814, the return of which had been requested by her lawyer Lushington in the Commons this July. Although the refusal was hardly unjust, many of Caroline's supporters throughout the country, organized by the Queen's Silver Plate Committee, proposed to purchase a service to be given to her as a mark of loyalty.[87]

It was of no avail for the editor of *Flyndell's Western Luminary* to write, 'Shall a woman who is as notoriously devoted to Bacchus as to Venus – shall such a woman as would, if found in our parent, be committed to Bridewell and whipped – be held up in the light of suffering innocence?' The answer was, yes, she was, and this out-spoken *Luminary* was prosecuted for a libel on the Queen in 1821.[88] Certainly, cries of 'Prince Austin' and crude jokes against the Queen and Pergami were heard among the crowds; those who marched in such seemly fashion across London with their addresses to the Queen were known to drink themselves stupid at the taverns in Hammer-smith afterwards. Brougham himself, when asked at London dinner parties about Caroline's relationship with Pergami, would reply, 'She is pure in-no-sense.'[89] It made no difference. The Windsor journalist Mr Charles Knight was no friend to the Queen, but he had no doubts about the question. She was 'a depraved woman, but an injured wife'.[90]

Peel was to consider the question in late August: 'I do think the Queen's affair very formidable. It is a famous ingredient in the cauldron which has been bubbling for a long time, and upon which the Government could never discern the least simmering. They applied a blow-pipe [bellows], however, when they omitted the Queen's name in the liturgy: where they established a precedent of dethrone-ment for imputed personal misconduct.'[91] His meaning was clear. If a queen were to lose her privileges, guilty of such crimes, what to do with a king guilty of similar crimes? The Cabinet had not thought the matter through. The theatre manager at Brighton informed his Majesty that he could not, without fear of violence, ask the audience to sing 'God Save the King'. His Majesty remained at Windsor through July and August with Lady Conyngham and daughters in his new Royal Lodge, fished from the Chinese pavilion, boated on Virginia Water and busied himself with details of his deferred Coronation ceremony. (Some wondered if it would ever take place.) One expedition on the water in a long-oared barge with Lady Conyngham and one of her daughters gave rise to a remark by a courtier, 'So we too have our Lake of Como.' The King apparently laughed heartily.[92]

At the end of July, Mr John Gast, a Radical shipwright, held a meeting of artisans of the mechanical trades at the Cart and Horses in Goswell Street, a meeting which the Lord Mayor had refused to allow within the bounds of the City. Gast spoke for an hour to a packed house, condemning 'spinnage' or espionage in all its forms, recalling Oliver the Spy who had penetrated the Manchester reform associations, and castigating the Milan Commission as more of the same. A resolution was carried to present an address to the Queen on 15 August, and copies of it were laid at taverns and public houses for her Majesty's well-wishers to sign: 29,786 signatures were added in the space of two weeks.[93] Although the greatest agitation in the Queen's affair occurred in the metropolis where she lodged, to that metropolis came the delegates of her supporters with addresses confirming the indignation against her treatment felt in Newcastle, the provincial centres of Birmingham, Manchester, Glasgow, Bristol, Edinburgh, as well as in smaller parishes nationwide.

Although the Government and its friends spoke of the Queen 'putting herself at the head of the Radical party', although some of the answers the Queen returned to the addresses presented to her were judged 'seditious', many of the Radicals felt ambivalent about her case. Their objective was Parliamentary reform, which would not be achieved under Liverpool's Government. The Queen's case was a useful tool for embarrassing the Government, possibly for felling it. Yet her behaviour was quite the reverse of the respectability and propriety the Radicals urged on their followers, and there were obvious difficulties, besides, for committed republicans among the Radicals in supporting a royal cause.

At the beginning of August the Queen decamped from Portman Street to Brandenburg House, a splendid seventeenth-century mansion on the Thames at Hammersmith belonging to Keppel Craven's mother, the Margravine of Anspach, who now lived abroad. The news that Queen Caroline was about to favour the parish of Hammersmith with her residence put the local inhabitants into a fever of excitement. If the Queen hoped for quiet and rest, she did not find it. As at the Villa d'Este, watermen and lightermen plied their trade in clear view of the house. With no bridge between Kew and Fulham and only a ferry at Chiswick, the market gardeners of these western environs of London and the ferrymen who landed at Hammersmith Hole in the Wall grew used to seeing the Queen walking on the lawns.[94] However, there was no Pergami here to take the Queen's arm. It was lawyers and political advisers and – increasingly, as the second reading approached – Italian supporters from Pesaro who paced with her in the shrubberies.

Caroline was unsettled and unsure of herself. She even wrote to her counsel to suggest that she reserve her defence for the Commons. Five of her barristers signed an indignant letter that this would be quite at variance with the 'tone' of all her pronouncements to date.[95]

Meanwhile, in his chambers in Lincoln's Inn Fields her solicitor Mr William Vizard and his clerks were buried beneath a flood of half-literate letters, offering delusive aid, sightings of witnesses and information to the Queen's cause.[96] Brougham saw himself as master-minding the operations, which he believed would in due course bring down the Tory Government and render the Queen his pawn. But ever since she had discovered his failure to tell her of the June 1819 Government proposal, Caroline had been understandably wary of him. His quip, 'The Queen is pure in-no-sense', had become well known. Yet the Queen needed Brougham, the finest forensic advocate of the time, and a Parliamentary speaker whose skills were not in doubt. And he needed her. Nevertheless, it was an uneasy alliance, and the Queen infuriated him by appearing to lean as heavily for her advice on Alderman Wood – castigated by Hutchinson as 'that mountebank' – as on himself.[97]

In fact, Brougham and Wood offered very different strengths to the Queen's cause. Wood had the might of the City of London behind him, with its wealth to bestow. This was perhaps no small consideration for the Queen. Brougham, on the other hand, was invaluable in his orchestration of the MPs, both Radical and Whig, whom he urged to obtain signatures to petitions in the Queen's favour, to organize public meetings and to flood the local and national newspapers with news of nationwide support for the Queen. There had never been a metropolitan issue which so inflamed the minds of the British living far north and west of the capital. To Brougham goes the credit for this national propaganda.

If the Queen headed any party, it was a royalist party. As Lord Holland wrote, the 'Queenite frenzy' was 'strong proof of the childish love of royalty still prevalent in this country . . .'.[98] The essayist Mr William Hazlitt commented, 'Here were all the patriots and Jacobins of London and Westminster . . . ready to worship the very rags of royalty. . . . it was the mock equality with sovereign rank, the acting in a farce of state, that was the secret charm.'[99] Miss Anne Cobbett gently derided the care her father took with his dress for appointments at the Queen's house. Hazlitt referred to cartoonists' wives visiting the Queen – which cartoonists they were we do not know. Denman, however, despite his eloquent support for Caroline, did not feel that she was a fit person to receive his wife. While he conferred with his client at Brandenburg House, he obliged his wife to remain outside in her carriage, where she made lace by the yard. He later regretted that his loyalty had not been more whole-hearted, for a visit from Mrs Denman might have encouraged other ladies to call.[100] Theodore Hook this December was to compose a song hostile to the Queen entitled 'Mrs Muggins Going to Court at Brandyburg House'. Satirizing the women who took up her cause, and enjoyed gin and gingerbread on the lawn at Brandenburg House after bringing up addresses, it anticipates all the simpering faces, cheap lace and frumpish feathers familiar to us in the works of Thackeray and Dickens.[101] Social ambition was certainly an element in the enthusiasm that some showed for the Queen. Her position was greatly strengthened at this time, odd though it may seem, by the decisions of her former lover Henry Hood, who in 1816 had added his father's viscountcy to his mother's barony, to join her retinue as chamberlain, and of his wife to become her mistress of the robes. These posts had been vacant since the departure of Pergami and Contessa Oldi.

For those royalist supporters who were moved by something more than the charm of association with 'the very rags of royalty', the Queen's affair was a dangerous abuse by the monarch of the Crown's privileges. The King was allowed by means of the Bill of Pains and Penalties to achieve what no adulterous subject of his could achieve – divorce without 'clean hands'. Where no law of the land or statute, as all knew, applied to the Queen's case, this odious Bill of last resort was brought against her. On the morning of 17 August, when the second reading in the House began, Gillray's 1786 cartoon, 'The Morning After Marriage', was republished.[102] It was almost the only reference to Mrs Fitzherbert. The press preferred to concentrate on the King's simpler relations with Lady Conyngham, Mrs Quentin (a colonel's wife), Lady Hertford, where recrimination was limited to adultery. In fact, nobody wanted to raise the larger issue of the King's relations with Mrs Fitzherbert. It suited nobody to enquire into prior marriages, bigamy and the legitimacy of Princess Charlotte.

The leaders of the principal Whig factions, Lord Grey and Lord Holland, considered Brougham's advocacy of the Queen's cause unprincipled and self-serving. Parliamentary reform, they considered, showing rare unanimity, would not be advanced one jot by inflaming public opinion against the monarch and his ministers. If the Tory Government was brought down by this disgraceful business, it would leave the people with a deep mistrust of Parliament of any kind. They castigated the Queen for returning to England, the Government for responding with this unparliamentary Bill, and Brougham and the Radical adherents for orchestrating the Queen's defence. Parliamentary reform would come only by reasoned debate within the Lords and Commons, they argued, and they stood by, Parliamentary ostriches, while passion raged about them on the streets and in the public prints.[103]

The hearts of Caroline's supporters were further inflamed by publication in *The Times* and other Queenite newspapers of a letter from her to her husband dated 7 August. This masterly document, composed by Cobbett, berated the King:

> From the very threshold of your Majesty's mansion the mother of your child was pursued by spies, conspirators and traitors. . . . You have pursued me with hatred and scorn, and with all the means of destruction. You wrested me from my child. . . . You sent me sorrowing through the world, and even in my sorrows pursued me with unrelenting persecution. . . .[104]

As August and September were traditionally the season when the peers repaired to their estates to administer their affairs there and to indulge in sporting pursuits, this summons back to London represented a very disagreeable interruption to their pleasant summer plans. However, the extraordinary nature of the proceedings and their own important judicial role alleviated their discontent.

In any case their attendance was compulsory. The House of Lords had itself resolved to fine absent members £100 a day for the first three days and £50 a day thereafter, defaulters 'being taken into custody'. No excuse would be allowed, except age (seventy years upwards), sickness, bereavement and absence from the country either continuously since 10 July that year or on Government service. Of the 367 on the roll, 109 peers were thus excluded, including many of those most familiar with Caroline's story. Malmesbury pleaded both age and sickness, Byron was in Italy writing *Don Juan* but keeping an eye open for potential witnesses in the Queen's cause, and Moira (now Marquess of Hastings) was Governor-General in India. Sligo, embarrassed by his role as a spy in Naples, absented himself without leave but escaped with a reprimand.

From the unseasonable occupation of the town mansions and houses of the nobility, usually deserted till October, the vast London service industry of washerwomen and purveyors of fuel, comestibles and liquor derived great advantage. Many persons of London Society besides, without a foothold in the Lords, made a point of vacationing in London, and the chamberlain's office was besieged by demands for tickets to the Strangers' Gallery. The Office of Works had a more immediate problem. The chamber of the House of Lords was unable to accommodate the full complement of peers in comfort. Only on the State Opening of Parliament did a sizeable number throng the chamber, and then only for a few hours. For the second reading, the House was due to sit from ten till four in the summer heat, for an unknown number of weeks. Moreover, the Queen herself had to be suitably enthroned at the Bar of the House, and counsel, interpreters for the foreign witnesses, shorthand writers, newspaper reporters, had all to be thought of. The architect Sir John Soane, directed to alter the chamber to detailed specifications, to accommodate all, built two temporary and somewhat fragile galleries, supported on iron struts, on either side.[105]

Meanwhile, Powell, Hobhouse of the Home Office, Leach and the Government law officers were busy. Powell's duties included visiting a temporary building in Cotton Gardens adjacent to the House of Lords, where were assembled by 15 August sixty-odd witnesses come over from the Holland depots. They persecuted Powell with complaints about their asylum. The first group, which had landed after nightfall at Parliament Stairs on the 13th had been supplemented by a further five furtive boat-parties. At The Hague, Lord Clancarty awaited orders to send other batches dispersed about the Low Countries to the crowded dormitories of Cotton Gardens.[106]

Evidence of the obsessive public interest in these unfortunates appears in the detailed newspaper accounts of that 'sinister depot' in Cotton Gardens, which, the *Morning Chronicle* informed its readers, had originally been intended as extra kitchens for the postponed Coronation banquet.[107] The Coronation cooks had been put to work as servitors for the Italian guests.

In a cartoon, 'Preparing the Witnesses', which appeared the day before the second reading, Castlereagh and Sidmouth battle to bathe dirty fops of villainous appearance.[108] This follows logically from the cartoons which had likened the green bags containing the witnesses' evidence to sacks of night-soil. The implication was clear. Whatever the Italians' evidence, the Queenites intended to discount it.

The King came off no better in this latest batch of cartoons. He was the Pig of Pall Mall, with Castlereagh and Sidmouth, again seen as the chief ministers of the theatrical 'piece', attempting to wash a huge boar with the facial features of the King. It was, Castlereagh gasps, a harder task than cleaning the Augean Stables.[109]

On the streets and in the coffee houses, the discussion centred on the burning question of the day. Was the Queen guilty or pure, and would her innocence, if proved, bring down the Tory Government? Mr Charles Greville wrote that you could not meet a man on the street without his asking, 'Have you heard anything new of the Queen?'[110] From hour to hour the rumours flew, the newspaper compositors busied themselves and the cartoonists exercised their mordant wit.

In preparation for her ordeal, Queen Caroline had taken a house belonging to Lady Francis in St James's Square. A neighbour there, Lord Castlereagh, was persuaded for fear of the mob to camp for the duration at the Foreign Office.[111] The determining moment of Caroline's life was at hand. The blame for this predicament she laid not at her own door, nor even at that of the King, but at that of her chief adviser. 'If my head is on Temple Bar,' she had said, 'it will be Brougham's doing.'

## CHAPTER SEVENTEEN

# TRIAL

## August–November 1820

### 'Upon the brink of a precipice'

T HE WEATHER WAS appropriately threatening on the morning of
Thursday, 17 August 1820, when the proceedings against the
Queen began in the House of Lords.

The security precautions for Palace Yard and Westminster were
modelled on those taken for the trial in Westminster Hall of Mr
Warren Hastings, the former Governor-General of Bengal,
impeached in 1788. In addition, Lord Sidmouth had ordered all
magistrates, Bow Street runners, beadles, watchmen, constables and
other law-enforcers with responsibility for the different parishes of
London – and especially for the Queen's route between St James's
Square and the House of Lords – to be at their posts early in the
morning.

Around Palace Yard, before the House of Lords, a double row of
timber fences was erected, stretching from St Margaret's Church
north to the King's Bench Office in Parliament Street and south to
Abingdon Street. By seven in the morning a very large body of
constables was established inside the timber palisades while footguards
piled their arms in the piazza under the arcaded front of the House of
Lords. A troop of Life Guards rode in to form a further line of
defence, while another patrolled towards Abingdon Street and the
river, and a Surrey mounted patrol rode over Westminster Bridge to
parade down Parliament Street and into Charing Cross. A police hulk
and gun boats on the river by Westminster Hall completed the
immediate protection for the peers due to take their places in the
Lords at ten o'clock.[1]

This show of force was reviled at the first opportunity in the House
of Commons by Mr John Cam Hobhouse. The Lords, he said, had

literally hedged and paled themselves in by a standing army. In the same way, he supposed, the Commons would be required to act in due course, 'until at last the sentence was verified – "obsessam curiam et clausum armis senatum." What a figure must England cut in the eyes of Europe,' he exclaimed, 'when her representatives should be obliged to fence themselves round with bristling bayonets, because there was no sympathy between them and the people!'[2]

'The people' were not deterred from assembling outside the barricades, some ten or twenty thousand of them bearing banners and placards, with white favours in the men's hats denoting their allegiance to the Queen. The number of women – their badges were white handkerchiefs, which they waved vigorously – was remarked on by all, as was the peaceable spirit of the crowds and the good-humoured conduct of the soldiers. By half-past nine Westminster Bridge was thronged and the avenues between St James's Square and Palace Yard choked with pedestrians, equestrians, carriages, carts and wagons – some owners of vehicles were letting out seats on top at a shilling a head. Moreover, 'the windows and tops of the houses' along the route the Queen was expected to favour, past Carlton House, 'were filled by fashionable and respectable people, chiefly ladies', according to the newspaper reports next day.[3]

At a quarter to ten the peers began to arrive, on horseback or in carriages. The crowds amused themselves, while they waited for the Queen, by cheering or booing those they recognized. The peers alone were allowed to approach the House of Lords from the riverside, down Abingdon Street, and permission was also afforded them alone to pass through the royal parks and enter Parliament Street through the Life Guards entrance. Lord Eldon, the Lord Chancellor, who had the dubious honour of presiding over the chamber of peers, took his usual route through the park at eight o'clock, on horseback, with his son and grandson, who wished to see the show. He had refused an offer of an escort of Bow Street runners, and, somewhat to his surprise, arrived unmolested.[4] As the peers now passed through the narrow gap, a carriage width, in the timber fences and presented their credentials issued by the Clerk of the Office of Works – 'Admit the bearer of this at the North Door of Westminster Hall' – many of them sent messages home to announce their safe arrival and allay their families' fears. The Dukes of York and Clarence were loudly cheered, and 'God save King Frederick' called out more than once. Wellington was hissed, for his part in the June negotiations. Lord Anglesey, a notorious adulterer, fared no less badly.[5]

In all, 258 peers passed up the double stairs within Westminster Hall and along the corridor into the House of Lords, where the calling over of names began promptly at ten. Within the double doors the chamber had been substantially altered since the peers had recessed in July. A sketch which the painter George Hayter made of the scene is preserved, and shows that the alterations carried out by Soane had been all too necessary to accommodate the packed crowd of peers, bishops, members of the legal profession and spectator MPs.[6] Soane's temporary galleries, which partly hide the Armada tapestries above the peers' benches, dominate the wings, and here some eighty of the more nimble peers have ascended, among them the Duke of York on the Tory side. The throne appears to float in the recesses of the chamber, the bullion and lace on its canopy and curtains evoking the glory of the Crown, the vast royal arms and monogrammed 'GR' potent reminders of the absentee monarch and husband. A scarlet chair is placed beside it in readiness for the Queen – enabling her, during the call-over, to assert her right to sit here, before joining the counsel. Around the steps of the throne cluster a number of the eldest sons of peers, there by right, and a throng of Members of Parliament, who have entered by the Long Gallery which connects the two Houses.

In the middle ground before the throne is visible the lappeted wig – and the nose – of the Lord Chancellor. He has forsaken his seat on the Woolsack for a stool at the table of the House in front of the throne and is almost hidden by the judges who flank him. Directly in front of the table come the archbishops – Canterbury, York and Ireland's Tuam – and the bishops. To the left of the Lord Chancellor are the Government peers – Liverpool, Sidmouth, Wellington – and the Tory benches. Castlereagh, Leader of 'the other place', watches the proceedings through a ventilation aperture in the underpinnings of Soane's galleries.

On the other side of the table, the Whigs are assembled, with Holland and Grey, Erskine and Lansdowne all destined to play a major part in the proceedings, for all Grey's earlier determination not to make a party issue of the Bill. And finally, in the foreground, is the Bar of the House, which divides peers from commoners: from our left to our right, the Government law officers, the shorthand writer to the House of Lords, the interpreters, the witnesses and the Queen's defence counsel. For the Queen, after she has registered her right to sit beside the throne, another chair adorned with scarlet cloth is set beside her counsel's place at the Bar. Sir Thomas Tyrwhitt (Black Rod) and clerk, and Mr William Dorset Fellowes (Lord Great Chamberlain's acting deputy) and clerk, have places assigned beside her.[7]

Other interested spectators – such as the newspaper editors, including Mr Thomas Barnes of *The Times* and Mr Peter Stoddard of the *New Times* – stand below the Bar, within railed enclosures on either side of the folding chamber doors. On the first day, each duke, marquess and earl was allowed to vouch for one stranger's admittance to the proceedings; on the second day this privilege was granted to members of the lower orders of the peerage. Thereafter this pattern was repeated.

After he saw this initial sketch, the Whig MP Mr George Agar Ellis commissioned Hayter to paint a full-scale portrait of the 'trial' of the Queen in the House of Lords. As the proceedings progressed, Hayter visited the House assiduously and sketched continually – peers, bishops, counsel and the Queen. These dated sketches, preserved in the National Portrait Gallery archive – counsel in rhetorical flight, the peers lazing, yawning, leaning forward or backwards to hear a friend's quip, judges conferring – are more telling of the long days' hearings than the large finished oil. His scribbled *aides-mémoire* show how scarce was any colour in the chamber, other than some spashes of red and gold, to relieve the sobriety of the peers' morning coats and the lawyers' robes. 'Cravats much whiter than wigs,' ran one note – 'some black cravats.'[8] Apart from the gilt pillars supporting Soane's galleries, and the brass chandeliers above the peers' heads, there were few points of brilliance in the chamber, and the area around the throne was at all times in shadow. It was not, in short, a painterly scene, but, as the Bishop of Llandaff read prayers shortly after ten o'clock, there was no doubt in anyone's mind that it was a momentous occasion.

And what of the Queen, whom Hayter sketched repeatedly in her seat at the Bar, and who is central to his great painting? While the peers were still being called over, there occurred a forcible reminder that a very different spirit obtained outside, as shouts were heard in Palace Yard. The Queen had arrived, and the muted cries of 'God save Queen Caroline!' and 'The Queen, God bless her!' yielded to a general huzza – and then to roars and shrieks, which seemed to promise some general disturbance.

The Queen's journey had begun at Brandenburg House earlier that morning, with only a few local inhabitants standing at the railings of the house to wish her well. With Lady Anne and Alderman Wood, she drove through increasingly crowded streets into London and to St James's Square. At Lady Francis's house were waiting her vice-chamberlains Gell and Keppel Craven. They had arrived that morning from Naples, and were in full Court dress, wigs and knee-breeches. Outside, besides the cheering spectators on cart- and wagon-tops, waited the Queen's state carriage, with chocolate facings and the royal arms, provided at last by the Government.

The Queen's carriage procession from St James's down to Westminster was a popular triumph. First came the Radical Mr Samuel Waddington as avant-courier, holding aloft a mock green bag on a pole. Alderman Wood's carriage headed the vehicles, then came the Queen with Lady Anne Hamilton inside her 'superb and beautiful coach with six horses – the coachman driving in a cap, like the old King's coachman', as the newspapers reported.[9] The crowds strained to see her, but the weather was inclement, and they saw only the trademark bobbing plumes atop her hat within the misty glass. The Queen's vice-chamberlains followed in another fine carriage, and William Austin, the Hoods and Vassalli brought up the rear.

As the Queen's carriage turned into Pall Mall and passed Carlton House, the sentries hesitantly presented arms. The ladies at the windows along the route waved their handkerchiefs frantically. Into Charing Cross and down Parliament Street the carriages turned, encumbered at every point by the jostling onlookers. The sentinels at the Treasury, the Foreign Office and the Home Office – where so many of the Departments' officials had laboured, and continued to labour, against the Queen – presented arms as the procession lurched past Whitehall. On the arrival of the Queen's carriage in Palace Yard at the gap in the timber defences, her supporters' enthusiasm was so great that the barriers were broken down, and a mass of people surged behind her to the doors of Westminster Hall.[10]

It was the hullabaloo consequent on the Queen's arrival, and this surge, which had disturbed the proceedings in the chamber of peers. But the constables and Life Guards stood firm, the encroachers were pushed back and the barriers hastily re-erected, while the Queen and her party presented themselves at the door cut only days before for her entrance.

Sir Thomas Tyrwhitt was in attendance at the door, in his official black and silver dress as Black Rod. Creevey had reported the day before Tyrwhitt's defiant stance: 'the Government is stark, staring mad ... they want to prevent his receiving the Queen tomorrow at the door as Queen, but ... he will'.[11] He had been dismissed for less when in the year of Caroline's marriage he had taken her part against Lady Jersey, and now, as then, stood firm – with the Lord Great Chamberlain's deputy lurking behind him, eager that Black Rod should usurp none of the rights of his mistresses Lady Cholmondeley and Lady Willoughby, who shared the hereditary office of Lord Great Chamberlain. As the royal party crossed Westminster Hall and proceeded up the peers' double stairway, Fellowes heard the Queen say to Tyrwhitt, 'I am sorry indeed that the people make so much noise,' and she repeated her apology.[12] The party proceeded along the passage behind the peers' chamber, then paused while the Queen entered Lord Shaftesbury's room. Here the Secret Committee had first met; now it was fitted up for the Queen's use as a robing-room. The Queen removed her bonnet, and wound about her head and around the bosom of her 'richly twilled black sarsenet dress' several thicknesses of white veiling. Thus bundled up, and accompanied by her attendants, she entered the chamber by the door behind the throne.[13]

Creevey had obtained a place among his fellow-MPs within two yards of the chair set for the Queen by the throne. 'Two folding doors within a few feet of me were suddenly thrown open, and in entered her Majesty. To describe to you her appearance and manners is far beyond my powers,' he wrote to his stepdaughter. 'I had been taught to believe she was as much improved in looks as in dignity of manners. . . . the nearest resemblance I can recollect to this much injured Princess is a toy which you used to call Fanny Royds.' (This is the tilting Dutch doll, apple-cheeked, black-banged, round-bottomed and weighted with lead, that always jumps erect from whatever position it is laid in.) The manner in which the Queen 'popped all at once into the House, made a duck at the throne, another to the peers, and a concluding jump into the chair which was placed for her', Creevey likened to the performance of another toy, a rabbit or cat, 'whose tail you squeeze under its body, and then out it jumps . . . off the ground into the air'. She squatted in her chair, continued Creevey, 'with such a grace that her gown is at the moment' – the MPs were provided with pen, ink and paper outside the Long Gallery – 'hanging over every part of it, both back and elbows'.[14]

Hayter's study in oils of the Queen in her chair bears out Creevey's impression of her defensive, awkward posture. Her dress is bunched up about her waist, and from her shoulders, hunched about her ears, full, 'perfectly episcopal' sleeves depend like monstrous panniers. The 'handsome white veil', which Creevey described as 'so thick as to make it very difficult . . . to see her face', is thrown back in Hayter's study, but the 'few straggling ringlets on her neck', which Creevey doubted were her Majesty's own, are faithfully represented.[15]

Behind the Queen stood Lady Anne. 'For effect and delicacy's sake she leans on her brother Archy's [Lord Archibald Hamilton's] arm,' wrote Creevey, 'though she is full six feet high, and bears a striking resemblance to one of Lord Derby's great red deer.'[16] Keppel Craven and Gell stood beside the Hamilton stalwarts. Among the 258 peers gazing curiously upon their Queen were men who had accused her (Erskine and Ellenborough, launchers of the Delicate Investigation), men who had loved her (Hood, now her chamberlain, and Rivers) and men whose wives or mothers had loved her husband (Conyngham and Jersey). When the calling over of the peers' names was resumed, the Lord Chancellor read a letter from the Duke of Sussex, begging to be excused from attendance on grounds of consanguinity to both the principals named in the Bill. His brother York, who had been forced by the King to attend, rose and, in a very marked and angry tone, said, 'I have much stronger ground for asking leave of absence than the Duke of Sussex' – the Duchess of York had died in early August – 'and yet I should be ashamed not to be present to do my duty!' Clarence, the King's firm supporter, remained also.[17]

After the calling over had been concluded, it occurred to several peers just how difficult it would be to prove every allegation in the preamble, and how repugnant was the divorce clause. The Duke of Leinster moved that the order just given 'that the House do proceed with the Bill' should be rescinded. This attracted only forty votes in favour. A further motion from Lord Carnarvon that the House decide if high treason was not applicable held up proceedings, while the judges retired before emerging to announce, what everyone knew, that no law or statute of the land was applicable to the Queen's case. Finally, the Bill was read, counsel were called in and the Queen prepared to suffer the consequences of the King's obdurate hostility and of her own recklessness.

From the door nearest the stations at the Bar prepared for them appeared the Queen's counsel and solicitors, Brougham, Denman, Lushington, Tindal, Wilde and Williams, with Vizard bringing up the rear. A moment after, the Government law officers, Gifford, Copley and Robinson, came through the double doors, followed by their brother counsel Parke and Adam and the solicitors Maule and Powell.[18]

As the Queen's defence counsel received permission from Eldon to criticize the principle or 'nature' of the Bill, what Lord Holland called the 'decorous and solemn etiquette of the august chamber', in contrast to the partisan rancour of the Commons, added to the gravity of the occasion. Brougham rose to speak, his full-bottomed wig and long silk robe muffling with authority his wiry figure, which, in the less orderly Lower House, the Radical Bamford had compared to a stag at bay.[19]

The success of Brougham's speech was not in doubt. 'I will not now advert to any topic of recrimination . . . I dismiss for the present all . . . questions respecting the conduct or connections of any parties previous to marriage,' he began menacingly, but he warned that he did not waive his right forever. 'Be the consequences what they may . . . an advocate is bound to do his duty' to his client, he reminded the House. This brought him to the magnificent rhetorical question: 'Are we arrived in this age at that highest pitch of polish in society when we shall be afraid to call things by their proper names yet shall not scruple to punish by express laws an offence in the weaker sex which has been passed over in the stronger?'[20] Brougham then instanced the Duke of York's admission in 1809 of adultery with Mrs Mary Anne Clarke when the Duke had escaped impeachment.

If the Queen had been tried when the offences took place, Brougham said, her husband would have needed 'clean hands'. Nobody in the House required reminding of the ascendancy of Lady Hertford over the then Regent while the Princess of Wales had toured Europe. And why this Bill of Pains and Penalties now, thundered Brougham, when the succession to the throne was not threatened? The Bill was an *ex parte*, odious, unjust Bill. It was true that the Secret Committee had judged there was evidence to support it, but the Government had brought it in only because it had announced that the Queen's arrival entailed proceedings. 'He is the greatest of all fools who consults his apparent consistency at the expense of his absolute ruin,' Brougham concluded. The House was duly shaken by this attack.

After Denman had spoken further next day against the principle of the Bill and reiterated the right of a royal consort to recrimination, the Government Solicitor-General defended the Bill and implicitly attacked the Queen's attempt to seek escape in her husband's own moral turpitude. The purity of women was prized in society, said Copley, precisely because men could not aspire to that honour and grace which embellished women, especially English women. Hence, to safeguard that purity, adultery in women was a crime, and a ground for divorce, while it was condoned in the stronger sex.[21]

The Queen had risen and left the chamber after Brougham had spoken, and was escorted by Tyrwhitt to her carriage. Her exit from Palace Yard and her return to St James's Square were loudly cheered. No attempt was made to disperse the crowds, which faded away gradually from Palace Yard after the last of the peers had departed in the late afternoon.

On the 19th, the Attorney-General began to detail the heads of the charges against the Queen. 'Silence can no longer be preserved,' Gifford began, against deafening claps of thunder – which the

Opposition papers the following day took to be a sign of divine disapproval of his speech. Referring to 'scenes which must disgust every well-regulated mind', the Attorney-General followed the wandering Princess chronologically from Naples to Genoa, to Milan, to Como, on the Long Voyage to the Holy Land, and back to Italy and Pesaro. It was now for the first time revealed that the Princess was accused of committing her first adulterous act with Pergami after returning, excited and nervous, from the theatre at Naples on her second evening there in November 1814. There were imprints of the two bodies on the bed the next morning to confirm it, and the Queen lay abed and refused to receive morning callers. At a masquerade later that month in the San Carlo Theatre attended by the King and Queen of Naples, the Princess appeared on her courier Pergami's arm immodestly attired, and at a New Year's Eve ball she wore a still more indecent costume, and it was Pergami who had dressed her. On her voyages in the Mediterranean, during which all manner of improper behaviour was observed, British sea captains refused to have Pergami at their table; at Aum in Syria she slept apart from the suite with Pergami. On the voyage back to Italy, she slept alone with Pergami under a tent on board, and he alone was present when she bathed below decks.[22]

The heads of the charges made astonishing reading. Ladies stopped their maids from seeing the newspapers; soon peers would stop their ladies' own supply of newspapers. The question was whether the heads of the charges could be proved by the witnesses. At first it appeared only too likely.

On Monday, the 21st, the first witness was called, Teodoro Majocchi, and the first major excitement of the trial was produced. As the familiar burly figure of her former servant appeared, the Queen uttered some indistinct exclamation. She then rose, stumbled towards the door and left the chamber of the peers. Her cry was interpreted by the interested spectators variously as 'Teodoro!' and 'Traditore!', or 'Traitor' in Italian. ('Teodoro' would have come more naturally to the Queen, whose Italian was limited.) Moreover, it was surely the shock of recognition, rather than what she saw as Majocchi's perfidy – she had known of it since early 1819 – which occasioned her cry.[23]

The Queen's reaction to Majocchi was felt by all to be occasioned by a bad conscience, to tell against her and damage her case. He appeared a straightforward and honest witness, who, through the interpreter Marchese Spineto, told a simple tale under questioning by Gifford. (Spineto, the assistant to a Cambridge professor, became something of an entertainment to the peers and spectators. His hands gesticulated wildly – Hayter sketched his flashing fingers – and he acted every point, so that with Majocchi he performed something of a burlesque show.)[24] Majocchi had been with the Queen at Naples, at Como, on the Long Voyage to Jerusalem. During this time the courier Pergami had been promoted to equerry, to chamberlain. Pergami had first waited at the Queen's table with Majocchi himself, then he began to dine with her. The Queen had apparently bought Pergami a barony and an estate to go with the title. His mother, child, sisters and brothers joined the suite. The details were no less baldly told. Pergami's room was always close to the Queen's, the rest of the suite was always 'lontano', or distant, at Como, at Naples, at Genoa, at Milan and on the road. On the way back to Italy on the Long Voyage, the Queen slept under a tent on deck with Pergami. He, Majocchi, had received the lantern from under the canvas at night. He had finally left the Princess's employ because she was 'surrounded by bad people'. The evidence Majocchi gave so disconcerted Denman and Wilde that they went round to Brougham's house in Hill Street, Mayfair, at midnight to offer suggestions for the cross-examination.[25]

The Queen herself was in a state of shock. 'She was copiously bled that night,' reported Denman, 'and when she took her seat the following day in the House of Lords I never saw a human being so interesting. Her face was pale, her eyelids a little sunken, her eyes fixed on the ground. . . .'[26] This spectacle prompted her counsel later that day to advise her to stay away except when her presence was specifically requested. Thereafter she appeared only occasionally, and then reluctantly: a note survives, addressed to Henry Brougham, enquiring whether her attendance was required at 'the House of Correction'.[27] Overcome by the heat in the chamber one day, she fell asleep in her chair, prompting Lord Holland's epigram:

> Her conduct at present no censure affords
> She sins not with couriers but sleeps with the Lords.[28]

Usually it was not long before she withdrew to her robing-room –
there, it was rumoured, to play at whist or backgammon with
Alderman Wood. She retained in public the severe expression which,
one observer noted caustically, she seemed to feel appropriate to her
queenly status.[29]

She, Denman and Wilde need have had no fears about Brougham's
cross-examination. On Tuesday, 22 August, he had Majocchi speak
the phrase 'Non mi ricordo,' 'I do not remember,' over eighty times
in answer to his questioning. Perhaps most damaging of all these
admissions of forgetfulness, in contrast to his excellent memory for
the facts required of him by the King's Attorney-General the previous
day, was his repeated answer, 'Non mi ricordo,' to Brougham's
questions about the location of the suite's bedchambers at Naples.[30]

Hardly less astonishing was his 'Non mi ricordo' to the question,
'Was a new wing added to the Villa d'Este during your absence on
the Long Voyage?' Yet he remembered in detail an alteration to the
disposition of the Queen's and Pergami's sleeping chambers on their
return from Palestine. Brougham was merciless with the prosecution's
star witness. Had Majocchi not asked to be taken back into the
Princess's service after he left? 'Non mi ricordo.' How many crew
were there on board the *polacca*, where the tent had been erected?
'Non mi ricordo.' Two? 'Non mi ricordo.' Twenty-two? The same
answer. And Brougham established that Majocchi had spoken to no
one of what he had observed of the Queen and Pergami till he told
all to the Milan Commission. (This avowal of discretion was, for
Brougham's purposes, tantamount to an admission of inventing the
whole.) Finally Majocchi, beaten and bewildered, broke down
entirely, when asked whether, on his journeys between Vienna and
Milan, he had received money from both Lord Stewart and the Milan
Commissioners. The interpreter complained, 'He does not understand the most common words, he is frightened out of his wits.'[31]
Majocchi withdrew – his testimony, so steadfast and assured the day
before, now in tatters.

The next two witnesses were Paturzo and Gargiulo, mate and
Captain of the *polacca*. They testified, like Majocchi, to the erection
of a tent on deck on the way back from the Holy Land. Paturzo had,
like Majocchi, received the lantern from under the canvas handed out

by Pergami at night. Moreover, he had seen the Queen and Pergami sit on a gun on deck and embrace. Gargiulo spoke of the bath which the Queen had taken on board in the room off the dining-room, with Pergami her only attendant. Gargiulo had sent Paturzo away one day when the Queen was bending over Pergami, stretched on one of the two beds within the tent.[32]

The cartoonists had a field day with Majocchi as the Cock of Cotton Walk – Hone's response *Non mi ricordo*, was soon as popular as his *The Queen's Matrimonial Ladder*.[33] In the Lords, Brougham attacked the sums paid by the British Minister at Naples to the Captain and his mate in compensation for their absence from their vessels. He also raised the dubious objection that a Catholic Italian's oath in a foreign and Anglican law court was no more binding than the act of an English seaman on trial in a Chinese court in breaking a plate after the custom obtaining in that distant land. The trickier questions of law such as this, and there were to be many of them, were referred to the panel of judges who sat in the chamber as advisers to the peers. Now for the first time they retired to deliberate and determined that the present form of oath was satisfactory.[34]

While the press filled their pages with the details of the evidence, Majocchi was brought forward once more at the request of Brougham to answer charges that he had lived at Gloucester earlier this year and had told an acquaintance there, Mr Hughes, a banker's clerk, that the Queen was a good woman and a chaste one. After a good deal of prevarication, Majocchi was forced to admit that he might have said this.[35] The examination of various witnesses, including Captains Pechell and Briggs, a cellarmaid from Karlsruhe and a waiter from Trieste, then proceeded.

Briggs's and Pechell's evidence was damaging to the Queen's cause, especially where Pechell stated that he had refused to keep a table for the Queen on the second journey if Pergami sat at it, on the ground that the Italian had waited at table on the first journey. Cross-examination failed to shake the witness, although Denman did his best to prove the Captain hostile to the Queen.[36]

Equally, the cellarmaid Barbara Kress remained unchallenged in her evidence that she had seen the Queen sitting on Pergami's bed with her arm around his neck, and that she had later found the

Queen's cloak in the bed. Kress admitted that the Württemberg Minister Baron von Grimm had gone running through the Queen's apartments directly her entourage left the inn, and had peered into beds in an undignified manner.[37] This evidence of Governmental zeal did not, however, undo her damning testimony.

There was only so much that Brougham and his team of counsel could do, in cross-examination of witnesses, about some of whom (or about some of whose evidence against the Queen) they knew nothing till the witnesses appeared at the Bar. They had to wait till the defence to bring forward their own witnesses to contradict the present assertions. In cross-examination, they concentrated on undermining the value of the testimony offered by referring again and again to the witnesses' transactions with the Milan Commission, to their being herded together across Europe and to their confinement together in Cotton Gardens, as contrary to justice.

The appearance of Louise Demont at the Bar offered a splendid opportunity for Brougham and Denman. The testimony elicited from her ran over the same ground as that of Majocchi, and Brougham, with Williams, was successful in obtaining from her the French equivalent of 'Non mi ricordo': 'Je ne me rappelle pas.' When they produced Demont's letters written, after her dismissal in 1817, to the Queen pleading to be reinstated, and to her sister speaking highly of the Queen, Caroline's former maid argued that these were 'double entendre'. Brougham remarked drily that there was a short Saxon word which better described Demont's evidence.[38] (He meant 'lies'.)

There were besides a host of Italian workmen, masons, painters and boatmen to speak of disgraceful scenes at the Villa Villani and the Villa d'Este at Como, and of specific examples of the Queen's licentious behaviour. Among these were instances of her kissing Pergami, watching Mahomet the Turk perform an obscene dance, and an occasion when she lifted the figleaf attached to a statue of Adam in a grotto and laughed with Pergami. They spoke also of seeing the Queen walk arm-in-arm with Pergami and go upon the water alone with him at Como, and of numerous presents she made to him, besides her attendance at scandalous parties at la Barona.[39] Then it was the turn of the last witness, Giuseppe Sacchini, the equerry dismissed with Demont. He testified that he had opened the curtains of the Queen's carriage on a journey from Senigallia to Pesaro, to find the Queen and Pergami asleep within, the former's hand resting on the latter's private parts. Brougham found him out in a lie about changing his name to Conte Milani. He had claimed it was prompted by fear of discovery after the Dover riot, only for the Queen's Attorney-General to point out that that riot took place one year after the adoption of the Milani title.[40]

Emboldened by information just received from the household of Majocchi's late Gloucestershire employer, Brougham then recalled that Italian for the second time to enquire whether he had been to Carlton House, and elicited the admission that he had taken letters (these were from Lord Stewart in Vienna) to a large house in London with Greek pillars on the day the King was buried.[41] This caused a sensation, for the mood in the House was still angry after the Attorney-General requested that the House allow him the favour of an adjournment. Some material witnesses, who had been frightened away by the Dover riots, were on the road and would arrive shortly. Brougham did not neglect the opportunity for a speech in denunciation of the Attorney-General's request, but before it could be granted or refused, Gifford withdrew. He had heard from Milan that the witnesses were too far off to make an adjournment expedient.[42]

Powell, in a letter to Browne instructing that no further witnesses be sent as the case for the prosecution was concluded, fulminated against Brougham and against 'his usual style of bravado and humbug – you cannot imagine how insulting and bullying his conduct has been to the House'. He mentioned that Lord Sidmouth had said to him, of the Milan Commission, 'that ghost is laid and everyone sees the more it is enquired into, that the Milan Commission has done its duty honourably and well'.[43] He ignored the fact that the witnesses had again and again been skilfully led by Brougham to admissions which awakened the Lords to the possibility that the Italians had perjured themselves to the Commissioners in Milan, but feared to do so in the House of Lords. The Commissioners, in short, were suspected of too credulous, not of dishonourable, conduct.

Pergami's elevation from courier to chamberlain as alleged in the preamble had been proved. The propinquity of his bedchamber to that of the Queen's in half a dozen residences and his sleeping under the tent on board the *polacca* were matters which, unless disproved by the defence, could lead to only one conclusion. Arbuthnot said gleefully, 'She is blasted.'[44]

On 9 September, the Solicitor-General summarized the charges against the Queen, declaring them wholly substantiated by the testimony of his witnesses. It was now Brougham's turn to apply for an adjournment, to allow the defence time to conclude the collection of evidence. A number of peers objected to this interruption of the proceedings, but an adjournment until 3 October was eventually granted. The peers were asked to keep an open mind till the defence was under way, but for most of them at this point the Queen's guilt was not in question.

Outside the Lords, however, as the crowds assembled with un-remitting enthusiasm to watch the comings and goings, the question of the Queen's guilt or innocence apparently mattered 'not a straw', as Cobbett remarked.[45] When Wellington or Anglesey – the sources differ – was urged by the crowd to pull off his hat for the Queen, he complied with the words, 'God save the Queen! – and may all your wives be like her!' This sally provoked a burst of laughter from the predominantly Queenite crowd.[46] Caroline's supporters concentrated on Brougham's skilful cross-examination and the damaging pointers towards subornation of and perjury by the witnesses. Croker agreed that the disgusting acts of which she was accused appeared not to have shaken the people's adherence to the Queen one iota.[47]

Meanwhile, in Milan the affairs of both Browne and the Queen's agents grew increasingly tangled. James Brougham came out to Italy in September to prime Mr Jabez Henry on the case to date in the Lords, and to take over in Milan, while Henry proceeded to Pesaro. Their increasingly urgent attempts to obtain the necessary per-missions for their chosen witnesses to depart for England might be likened to a game of spillikins, where the spills or sticks they hoped to remove from the pile were the witnesses, and the obstructing spills the rules and regulations of the Austro-Milanese bureaucracy, coupled with the witnesses' own fear of that bureaucracy and of the suspicion of Jacobinism which might fall on them if they agreed to go.

There was no doubting the sincerity of Castlereagh's official letter of 4 August asking the Austrian authorities to give every assistance to

Henry. (Castlereagh had no wish to be seen to impede the Queen's defence after the furore over the Milan Commission's work.) Nor was there any doubting that the two months from Henry's arrival in Milan at the start of August to 3 October were a wholly inadequate period in which to circumvent the byzantine by-roads of the Austrian bureaucracy and arrange matters between Milan, Vienna and London, each city ten days' distance from the others. It did not help that Henry had left in London the document declaring his power of authority from the Queen.[48] Browne meanwhile wrote angrily of every coffee house in Milan being awash with radicals, who scared his people with threats against their lives.[49] The Milanese authorities – who regarded the Italian Jacobins' fervour for the Queen as a threat to the state, the recent Neapolitan and Spanish revolutions in their minds – put every difficulty in Henry's way, Castlereagh's letter notwithstanding.

Before the proceedings had opened, the Queen had written personally to all the officials in Milan and Como whom she had befriended asking them to come forward on her behalf. Brougham and the defence, conscious of the prejudice in London against foreign menials, suggested as witnesses other Italians in high office, all attached to the army, the universities or Government departments. But, to all Henry's and James Brougham's tentative applications for their attendance in London, the Milanese Governor Strassoldo replied that they were needed at their posts. He added that, following the Dover riots, it was impossible that the Generals Pino, Balabio and Galimberti should attend in military rig for fear that the Emperor of Austria's uniform be insulted.[50] There was also the officials' own unwillingness to go: the congé which they eventually received from Strassoldo – after pressure was brought to bear on Metternich by Castlereagh and Stewart – they felt to be ambiguous, given that 'congé' denoted both leave of absence and dismissal. Although Metternich wrote to confirm that none of the Emperor's employees could be dismissed except for a crime, all the witnesses the Queen requested were slow to make their applications to the Government for leave to proceed to England, and two of them pleaded ill-health. This lack of enthusiasm Henry discovered not from the reluctant witnesses themselves, but from the Milanese police after he had been told nothing for a month, merely invited again and again to return, as there were no orders from

Vienna.[51] The Italians anyway felt a horror of travel over the Alps in the winter season, in no way diminished by the bloodcurdling reports of their compatriots' handling at Dover.

In the event Henry was thrown back on the very boatmen, couriers and servants whose employ as witnesses by the prosecution the defence counsel had so derided. And these menials were no less alive to the fears of reprisals from the Milanese Government and from the English crowds on their arrival. Moreover, each year at the Michaelmas Fair on 3 October, when the annual leases expired, much of the Lombard populace moved house, so the lower class of witness was reluctant to be away at this time of bargaining and transmigration.

Slowly the tangle of public and personal objections to the witnesses' journeys unravelled, and by the end of September Henry had thirty witnesses on the road. But he had been reduced to the very system of blandishments and promises, and payments for loss of time and subsistence of families, which the Milan Commissioners had been forced to operate. Moreover, Pergami and Vassalli had at Como and Pesaro behaved exactly as – or worse than – Restelli and Riganti and the Commissioners' agents had done.[52]

Browne observed Henry's and James Brougham's efforts with an indignation which sometimes gave way to sardonic satisfaction, when he felt he had firm evidence that their methods were improper. 'There is some strong secret fund at work,' he wrote when he heard that the banker Torlonia had offered Cardinal Albani 16,000 louis to go over to London to speak up for the Queen.[53] The Cardinal rejected the offer. The Pope had decreed that none of his subjects should leave the Papal States, claiming to feel uneasy about the volatile state of Italy following the revolution in Naples.

Browne and Brougham, who had begun as enemies, came to feel some common cause. Powell, despite his earlier letter to Browne, wrote again advising him to prepare witnesses for hearings in the House of Commons. Now both sides had to fight against the dark rumours surfacing in the Italian press of a revolution in London, with the Queen on the throne and the King in the Tower, witnesses assassinated and the letters of reassurance brought by Restelli in September faked by the English authorities.

Restelli had been sent by Powell to Browne in Milan immediately the Solicitor-General concluded the Government evidence, with orders that he return to England by 3 October. As the time for his departure neared, Browne became increasingly worried. Restelli had taken to his bed, and, pleading a severe attack of jaundice, was refusing to comply with Powell's directive: 'I much fear Restelli is shuffling – he is in bed and says he has a fever from crossing the water and he is heartily sick of the manner in which the witnesses are conveyed to England.' Browne added, 'The trouble is, he has like all Italians a horror of crossing water, and moreover fears the English winter.'[54]

In England, and knowing little of the difficulties in Milan, Henry Brougham was largely confident of his case, except for the troublesome evidence of Kress, the Karlsruhe cellarmaid. Now that the places and dates and witnesses were all known, his plan was to continue the tenor of his cross-examination and to use the defence witnesses to discredit further the characters of the most damaging prosecution witnesses.

Denman had been suffering from ill-health since early August, and went, immediately the Government case closed, to Cheltenham to recuperate before the defence began. He was not safe even there from the strain of the 'Queen's affair'. Caroline's supporters first drew his carriage into the town, then surrounded his house crying 'Queen! Queen!' He was next asked to use his authority to prevent their breaking the windows of a parson who had refused to allow the church bells to be rung in Denman's honour. As Denman later recalled, 'Going among the mob, I prevailed upon them to disperse and spare the few of his windows that remained unbroken.'[55]

During the recess, the Queen took daily airings with Lady Anne and William Austin in the royal parks. She had also been writing to Pergami in Pesaro, a matter of some concern to her lawyers. Quite apart from the chance of the letters being seized and published, the expense of sending couriers back and forth across the Alps was considerable, and they warned that the Treasury might well question these items in the final account.[56]

The addresses which the Queen received – Wednesday became the appointed day – also perturbed Vizard, for the tenor of her replies was, under the influence of Dr Samuel Parr and the Reverend Robert Fellowes, increasingly inflammatory. Her reply to the Addresses of

the Inhabitants of Wakefield and of Ilchester – the latter was supposed
to have been written by Mr Henry 'Orator' Hunt in his prison cell –
caused particular anxiety. The Queen's own interest in these affairs
was characteristically sporadic. On one occasion she stood behind
Alderman Wood as he read out her answers and made 'ridiculous
faces' at the painter Lonsdale and others.[57] The addresses and replies
were all printed in full and were distributed nationwide. In Milan,
where they were reprinted in the Government *Gazzetta di Milano*, the
'revolutionary' tone of the texts made the Queen's supporters still
more reluctant to travel in her cause.

The procession to present the Address of the Married Ladies of
Southwark and Westminster was a remarkable event. A meeting had
been held by Hobhouse and Mr Samuel Whitbread (son of Caroline's
late champion) at the Crown and Anchor Inn, where a motion was
supported to congratulate the Queen on the end of the prosecution
case. On 19 September a mill of ladies, dressed in white and wearing
the white favours which Gast had made popular as emblems of the
Queen's purity,[58] walked from Westminster to Hammersmith. Caroline's chief appeal to these ladies, judging from the text of the address,
lay in the injurious treatment she had received during her early
marriage and in Cobbett's claims that she was driven, babe in arms,
from her home.

On 2 October, Hobhouse went to Brandenburg House to tell the
Queen of his industry on her behalf. He confirmed that the mood of
the public was still 'universally' for her. When she asked him what the
state of the army might be, Hobhouse replied that it was loyal to
the Crown, and they left that delicate subject alone.[59] There had
been, in fact, no hint of open disloyalty to the Government since the
July near-mutiny, and Wellington could afford to ignore reports
that stray soldiers toasted the Queen in their messes. In fact the
violent feeling against the Government, King and Milan Commissioners had somewhat abated. The 'people' had found more
congenial objects of vilification in the inhabitants of Cotton Gardens.
The predominant mood of the caricatures and verse-satires from
September onward was xenophobic. The Government and Commissioners were seen as dupes of the greedy Italians, Cotton Gardens
was caricatured as a chicken coop, and Majocchi and Demont,

recognizable with mustachios and bonnet, were among the feathered friends who pecked at gold coins poured into the feeding-troughs by the ministers.[60]

In fact, the evidence of the prosecution witnesses had led some of the Queen's original supporters to doubt their allegiance to her cause. The Common Council of the City of London had delayed hanging the portrait by Lonsdale, which the Queen had presented to them, till the result of the trial was known.[61] Equally, a number of those who had earlier pledged to subscribe to a service of plate for the Queen had determined to wait till her acquittal before stumping up, and activity within the Queen's Silver Plate Committee was at a standstill. Moreover, for the first time caricatures and verse-satires against the Queen now appeared. Most striking was *The Radical Ladder*, a parody of *The Queen's Matrimonial Ladder*. Published by the Loyalist Association, it was illustrated by Cruikshank himself.[62]

The morning of 3 October, the day appointed for the opening of Queen Caroline's defence, was bright and sunny. Her carriage was thrown open as she processed along the now familiar route, and she was welcomed at the House of Lords as before by Tyrwhitt and Fellowes. Brougham's opening speech lasted two days. At its finale, the aged Lord Erskine, former Lord Chancellor, rushed from the chamber in tears. Denman thought it 'one of the most powerful orations that ever proceeded from human lips'.[63] It was a masterly performance.

Brougham began with a veiled threat, referring to 'those millions of your Lordships' countrymen, whose jealous eyes are now watching us'. He passed swiftly to the question of recrimination, which again he said the case did not at present require. But he intimated that he only postponed 'the statement of that case of which I am possessed . . . if hereafter I should . . . feel it necessary to exercise that right. . . . an advocate . . . knows . . . but one person in the world', his client. He repeated his threat of August: 'separating even the duties of a patriot from those of an advocate, he must go on reckless of the consequences, if his fate it should unhappily be, to involve his country in confusion for his client'.[64] But that, said Brougham, changing tack, would be to give up 'the higher ground of innocence'. It was 'foul and false and scandalous in those who have said . . . that there are improprieties admitted to be proved against the Queen'. The only charge proved against the Queen, Brougham asserted, was that she moved in inferior and foreign circles, and the responsibility for that he proceeded to lay at their Lordships' own feet.

> You ... have ... been the instigators of that only admissible crime. While she was here, she courteously opened the doors of her palace to the families of your Lordships.... She condescended to court your society – and, as long as it suited purposes not of hers ... she did not court that society in vain. But when changes took place – when other views arose [at the start of the Regency] ... then her doors were opened in vain ... it is not in the presence of your Lordships I must expect to hear anyone lift his voice to complain that the Princess of Wales went to reside in Italy, and associated with those whose society she ... ought not to have chosen ... had she been in other or happier circumstances.

After this attack, Brougham moved on to the emotive subject of Princess Charlotte, and was at his most acerbic when referring to the failure to inform Caroline of her daughter's projected marriage – 'An event ... which ... most excites the feelings of a parent'. That Charlotte had become pregnant she heard by chance from a courier *en route* to the Pope. The girl's death the Queen learnt of by a similar accident, but – and here he was at his most sardonic – 'she would, ere long, have felt it; for the decease of the Princess Charlotte was communicated to her mother by the issuing of the Milan Commission'.*

Brougham pointed out that each of the attacks on the Queen, since her marriage, followed on the deaths of valued protectors. Instancing Pitt, Perceval, Whitbread and Princess Charlotte, he ended with the death of King George III. On the day 'which saw the venerable remains of our revered sovereign consigned to the tomb ... her constant and steady defender ... that same sun ushered the ringleader of the band of perjured witnesses [Majocchi] into the palace of his illustrious successor!'[65]

Brougham now turned to the 'getting up of a story', which was how he characterized the evidence in support of the charges against

---

* Nor indeed had she been informed of Queen Charlotte's death in 1818.

the Queen. He derided the Solicitor-General's assertion that the evidence had proved the substance of the Attorney's opening statement. The witnesses had lied to the Commission, Brougham said, but had feared to lie in the House of Lords. The Attorney-General had stated that the evidence would come down almost to the present day. Yet it fell short of that by three years. He had spoken of the Queen's 'extremely indecent and disgusting' dress at the masquerade in Naples, had claimed that she was booed from the theatre. Yet Demont had said only that the dress was 'very ugly'.

Again at Naples, the Attorney-General had seized on 9 November as the night the 'adulterous intercourse' began, and had spoken of 'clear, decisive marks' of two people having slept in the bed, of the Queen's unusually late rising: Demont had corroborated none of this. The Queen and Pergami had been heard kissing a long time: Majocchi, when questioned, had heard whispering for ten minutes. Again and again Brougham undermined the Attorney-General's assertions, and ended devastatingly that he did not doubt that his learned friend had all these stories in his brief. But, when the witnesses were called, 'they now recollected only the part that was true, and forgot what was untrue'.

As for the tale that her suite had left her at Naples, Lady Charlotte Lindsay joined her there; Lady Glenbervie, Gell, Craven, acted in her suite thereafter. Was she neglected by the royal houses of Europe? Scarcely. She was received by the Duke of Baden, the Bourbons of Palermo, the King of Sardinia. Only at Vienna, where Lord Stewart was the British representative, was she neglected.[66]

'It was remarkable that, considering that the prosecution had both valet and waiting maid, such a case should have been left so lame and short ... when contrasted with their opening,' Brougham observed. It was not 'from any over-caution of the parties [Caroline and Pergami]. ... If you believe the evidence, they had flung off all regard to decorum, all trammels of restraint. ... Just in proportion as the different acts alleged are ... of an atrocious nature, in exactly the same proportion do the parties take especial care ... that there shall be good witnesses.' They waited for a witness to re-enter before they kissed, they sat on a gun together before eleven crew of the *polacca*. Brougham demanded to know 'whether folly was ever known so extravagant'. And then the parties dismissed the spectators of their guilt, causelessly, and furthermore refused to take them back. Let this 'folly' operate on their Lordships' minds as a check, he counselled. Finally, the Queen returned to England to confront her accusers and refused the Government proposals – 'the opportunity of an unrestrained indulgence of all her criminal propensities. . . . If this is the conduct of guilt, then I have misread human nature,' Brougham declared.[67]

He passed to a consideration of the methods employed by the Milan Commissioners – the 'drilling' at Milan, the 'herding' of witnesses in Holland and in Cotton Gardens – and of the value of the evidence given by those who cared nothing for their reputations in England. He compared the efforts in Milan by King, Commissioners and witnesses to make out a case against the Queen to the efforts of King Henry VIII to secure by bribery approval from the 'doctors [lawyers] of Bologna' for his divorce from Queen Catherine of Aragon. He ended with a reference to a distinguished Neapolitan diplomat, who wrote in 1792 of 'the free and public sale of false evidence' in that Kingdom. 'If you would support a [law] suit,' wrote the Italian, 'alter a will . . . the shop of perjury is always open.' Brougham called on the Lords to dismiss this case, supported by witnesses from 'the country of Augustus and Borgia . . . [where] in all ages perfidy could be had for money'. The House then adjourned.

When Brougham resumed the following day, he detailed the contradictions and omissions in the prosecution evidence. He exposed numerous inconsistencies, some small, some large, and succeeded in injuring the credit of all the witnesses. The evidence of the 'great witnesses', Majocchi and Demont, he quite undid. Demont he laughed at for her 'candour' about her untruths and 'double entendres', Majocchi he presented as 'of happy memory'. Paturzo's flippancy when asked if a gun he had mentioned had been on deck – 'On the deck, we could not carry it in our pocket.' – he recognized from his experience in the lower courts as characteristic of a witness who was lying. As for the Italians' insistence that they had never discussed the Queen's behaviour prior to deposing before the Commissioners in Milan, that was proof that they had thought up their stories only as they travelled to Milan. And as for their denials of collusion and colloquy in 'the magazine of evidence', Cotton Gardens, Brougham was glad to know that there was 'one spot on the face of the island, one little land of Goshen, sacred from the squabbles which surround it'.[68]

After a reference to the prosecution's reluctance to call forward the members of the Queen's English suite, Brougham passed briefly to a consideration of Pergami's elevation. He could not avoid it, and so he attempted to show that his rise from courier to equerry to chamberlain was 'the sluggish process with which merit finds its way in the world'.

It was the hand of Providence, Brougham declared, which had found out the witnesses in the lies – such as Sacchini changing his name, Demont about her letters, Majocchi about Mr Hughes – and embellishments which invalidated their evidence. These falsehoods went not 'to the main body of the cases' but 'to the main body of the credit of witnesses'. He referred to 'that great passage . . . in the Sacred Writings' – 'History of Susanna' in the Apocrypha – where the Elders, though telling a clear and uncontradicted story, were discovered in a plot against their victim 'by the trifling circumstance of a contradiction about a mastich tree'. The witnesses' falsehoods were not accidents, but 'dispensations of that Providence which wills not that the guilty should triumph and which favourably protects the innocent'.[69]

Brougham went on to summarize his objections to the Bill of Pains and Penalties: 'inadequate to prove a debt – impotent to deprive of a civil right – ridiculous to convict of the lowest offence – . . . monstrous to ruin the honour of an English queen! What shall I say, then, if this is their case – if this is the species of proof by which an act of judicial legislation, an *ex post facto* law, is sought to be passed against this defenceless woman?'

He ended with this extraordinary imprecation:

My lords, I pray your lordships to pause. You are standing upon the brink of a precipice. It will go forth on your judgment, if it goes against the Queen. But it will be the only judgment you ever will pronounce which will fail in its object, and return upon those who give it. Save the country, my lords, from the horror of this catastrophe – save yourselves from this situation – rescue that country, of which you are the ornament, but in which you could flourish no longer, when severed from the people, than the blossom when cut off from the root and the stem of the tree. Save that country, that you may continue to adorn it – save the Crown, which is in jeopardy – the aristocracy which is shaken – the altar itself.... You have said, my Lords, you have willed – the Church and the King have willed – that the Queen should be deprived of its solemn service [by exclusion from the liturgy]. She has indeed, instead of that solemnity, the heartfelt prayers of the people. She wants no prayers of mine. But I do here pour forth my supplications at the throne of mercy, that that mercy may be poured down upon the people, in a larger measure than the merits of its rulers may deserve, and that your hearts may be turned to justice.[70]

The peers had already been outraged by one of Benbow's productions, *A Peep at the Peers*, satirizing the many diagrams of their august chamber which the newspapers had printed. Keyed in to Benbow's plan were identificatory notes containing gross calumnies against a number of peers and their wives, alleging corruption and cuckoldry. It represented a month's work for Cobbett and his daughter Anne.[71] This menace from within, by the Queen's counsel, alarmed them all the more for its apparent foundation in republican feeling outdoors. The Lord Chancellor later rebuked Brougham most weightily for his threats to the House.

Brougham rested from his labours at last, and Williams succeeded him, to anticipate some of the evidence for the defence which would follow. Williams left oratorical fancy to his leader, save for a reference to the King, 'a name which ... flames in front of this Bill', and to the Queen, 'shorn of her beams'. He concentrated on reminding the peers of the Queen's initial difficulties in answering the Bill, with no lists of witnesses provided or specific dates or places where her offences might have taken place, with none of the wealth, authority and power which supported the Bill. 'There is reason to apprehend in this case, from the unequal conflict between the parties, that there may not be impartial and equal justice between them,' he reminded the peers, taking his text from Cicero.[72] With the uneasy suspicion that that might well be true, the peers settled to hear the defence witnesses and to decide on the Queen's guilt or innocence, which Brougham had so brilliantly brought into question again.

The first witnesses called for the defence, on 5 October, were former and present English members of the Queen's suite and circle. The testimony, 'given ... with their manner of dexterous explanation ... made a very great impression on the House', wrote Powell to Browne.[73] Like the monkeys who see no evil, hear no evil, speak no evil – first Lord Guilford (the former Mr Frederick North, who had succeeded his brother in 1817), then his sister Lady Charlotte Lindsay, Lord Glenbervie, Gell and Keppel Craven had attested to their high opinion of the Queen's virtue, to her conduct beyond reproach and to their impeccable excuses for leaving her side.

Lord Guilford admittedly said that Pergami was suited to his station as a courier, that the Contessa Oldi had 'not particularly vulgar manners'. Lady Charlotte admitted that she had stayed on in the Queen's employ for the sake of her husband's finances, and had quit her post eventually after hearing rumours of the Queen's behaviour. But rumours were not evidence, and everyone in the chamber had heard these rumours. Gell and Keppel Craven did especially well, testily recalling the long hours spent at the Murats' concerts with the Queen, and comparing the Queen's dress as Fame or the Genius of History in Naples (accounts differed) to the respectably draped antique statues in Mr Thomas Hope's collection or in the British Museum.

From these vice-chamberlains' evidence emerged a very different picture of life at Naples from that drawn by the servants Demont and Majocchi – and one which the peers recognized. The arrangements of bedchambers, the antics of Italian lackeys and couriers, were of no interest to members of the English suite. Lady Charlotte could not remember if the Queen had walked arm-in-arm with Pergami, or if she had offered him food from the carriage. She supposed, loftily, she might have done.[74]

The next group of witnesses produced a more ambiguous effect. Sicard said that the Queen was 'uncommon kind, almost to a fault' to her servants. He recalled that she had offered him her arm in Greenwich Park. He was forced in cross-examination, however, to confess that, in twenty-one years in her service, he had never known her elevate a servant to dine at her table.[75]

William Carrington, Gell's valet, had heard Majocchi in the

courtyard at Rufinella say that he would kill Ompteda like a dog for his ingratitude to the Princess. John Whitcomb, Keppel Craven's man, intimated that he had slept often with Demont at Naples. Carlo Fortis, the courier, caused a sensation when he averred that he, and not Sacchini, was the equerry on the route to Pesaro from Senigallia, and that the carriage the Queen had used had been an English land-aulet with sprung blinds, not curtains. Moreover, in the carriage with her had been, besides Pergami, the Contessa Oldi and little Vittorine.

The matter of the tent on the *polacca*, and of the Karlsruhe cellar-maid's testimony, had still to be investigated. Lieutenant Flynn came first, and seemed determined to rebut the idea that he knew that Pergami had slept under the tent with the Queen. Yet he had no idea where Pergami had spent the night. However, under skilful cross-examination from Copley, he tied himself in tangles over a matter of a logbook and ended by fainting there and then in the chamber.[76]

Lieutenant Hownam, also determined to play ignorant about the sleeping arrangements on the *polacca*, was forced finally to admit – in a very low voice – that, yes, he believed Pergami had slept there inside the tent. To guard the Queen.[77] These witnesses' reluctance to implicate Caroline made their admissions all the more damaging. The case against the Queen had recovered its strength. The ministers, who regarded each day, each witness, as a battle in a campaign or siege, according to Countess Lieven, were cock-a-hoop. But then came the 'godsend' – as Powell termed it – for the Queen and her defence.[78]

On 13 October, Brougham applied to have Restelli brought forward, to be re-examined on his attempt to suborn a witness. It was then revealed that he had been sent abroad and had not yet returned. By whose orders, Brougham asked? The answer came, 'Mr Powell sent him.' When Powell himself was brought to the bar, Brougham asked, 'Who is your client or employer in this case?' This pertinent enquiry was shouted down, whereupon Brougham made an indignant and most effective speech. He was never permitted throughout this case to ask the name of the plaintiff, but was told he could not ask this or that: 'up to this moment I have never been able to trace "the local habitation – the name" of the unknown being who is the plaintiff in this proceeding. I know not it may vanish into thin air. I know not under what shape it exists.' Citing Milton's *Paradise Lost*, Brougham expressed his wish to meet this 'shape',

> If shape it might be called that shape had none
> Distinguishable in member, joint or limb,
> Or substance might be called that shadow seemed;
> For each seemed either . . .
> What seem'd his head
> The likeness of a kingly crown had on.[79]

This apposite quotation shocked a House already convinced that Brougham was dangerously close to sedition. When the King heard a report of this speech, he commented with bitter wit, 'He might at least have left my shape alone.'[80] Naturally, the satires of the Cotton Garden inhabitants as pecking chickens flourished anew, with Restelli 'flown from the coop'.

Restelli's absence compounded the growing suspicions of conspiracy, and increased the distaste for the proceedings among the peers. Brougham now invited the peers to conclude that the defence's case was injured beyond redemption. Lord Grey got up to agree, but the Lord Chancellor ruled that, though Powell's action in sending Restelli away was 'ill-judged', it did not mean justice could not be done. Lord Grey objected that it was not so much ill-judged as 'most iniquitous'. Lord Carnarvon moved that the Bill be taken a second time six months hence – which was to say that it should be dropped. 'There is proof', he argued, 'that an extensive system of subornation of perjury existed, which [the Lords] were prevented from probing to the bottom. . . . The case, if indeed it could be rendered more odious, or rather disgraced, was by this last excrescence reduced to the lowest pitch of infamy.'[81]

The case rumbled on, but the peers were growing restive. Mr Charles Greville was one among the spectators who found his interest in the case waning after Codazzi's clerk Signor Bomfiglio Onati testified on the 16th that he had sold to Vimercati a batch of his master's documents relating to the Queen.[32]

The case for the Crown lay open to charges of false evidence, subornation of perjury and – in the case of the Commissioners – a criminal lack of control over their agents. Louise Demont was recalled to face the testimony of a bonnet-maker from her native Swiss canton,

Mme Martigny, who quoted her as hotly defending her former mistress in 1818. 'She is nothing but a gossip,' Louise wrote agitatedly to Powell,[83] but the 'gossip' had done further damage to Demont's credibility, if it were needed. Filippo Pomi, the Barona caretaker, had earlier testified that Demont had encouraged him to give evidence to the Milan Commissioners, declaring that in doing so herself she had 'made a good day's work', meaning that she had been well paid.[84]

When evidence was given that a defence witness, the chamberlain to the Grand Duke of Baden, had been prevented from coming by the authorities, though they had forced Kress to attend, Brougham protested on 23 October that he could and would proceed no further.[85] To the relief of all, Denman and Lushington then summarized the defence – Denman likened the King's treatment of the Queen to that of Nero of Octavia[86] – and the now unpalatable case was nearly at an end. No one was more relieved than Brougham, as the certain fact of the Queen and Pergami sleeping within the tent on the *polacca* and the testimony of Kress about the Queen's cloak in Pergami's bed were now lost in the general revulsion against the methods used to obtain this testimony. Mrs Arbuthnot wrote that there was no question about the Queen's guilt but nobody knew whether or not the Bill would pass.[87] Vizard, on the other hand, immediately dispatched all the remaining witnesses back to Italy, as he was sure it would not go down to the Commons.[88] The matter had ceased to be one of morality and become an occasion for Whig and Tory peers to score political points off each other.

And what, in all this, of the Queen, who had sat stony-faced while the House erupted about her? Some of whose existence she was unaware had appeared and testified against her, some falsely, some truly. Some whom she did know and had trusted had proved her enemies. 'Her down-sitting and her up-rising', as Denman had it,[89] had been searched out over four years, the relationship with Pergami which she had so valued derided. 'Much rather would I hand her to the scaffold', said Denman in his closing speech, 'than consent to see her leave this country, or live in it a degraded and miserable outcast, the object of general pity or more general scorn, and one whom, though we could not but look upon as brought to it by the misconduct of others, we could but consider as one of the strongest evidences of the degradation of rank and female character.' He urged mercy, and closed with words which he regretted ever after: 'Go and sin no more.'\* Yet, for all Denman's impassioned plea for clemency, before it came to the vote on the second reading numerous peers rose to express their conviction of the Queen's guilt, while warning that they would not be able to vote for the Bill if it still contained the divorce clause. When the count was taken, the result on 6 November was a majority for the Bill of only twenty-eight. The shadows of the charges must, as Denman said, loom over her for all the remainder of her life.[90]

After a spirited piece of politicking, the Whig peers voting to keep the divorce clause in the Bill – so that the bishops and peers with religious scruples would have to vote against the Bill proper – the third reading resulted in a majority for the Bill of only nine. On 10 November, Lord Liverpool rose to his feet in the Lords and, as Carnarvon had suggested, moved 'that the further consideration of the Bill be adjourned six months'. Lord Grey declared that the Bill, no longer before the House, was 'still before the country, and would long live in its memory'. He charged ministers with 'the grossest neglect of duty, in listening only to *ex parte* evidence, giving a willing credence to the most exaggerated and unfounded calumnies'. He reprobated the conduct of the Milan Commission and demanded an inquiry into its origin.[91] The proceedings, which had so mesmerized the nation and beset the peers, were finally at an end. The Queen, though widely believed to be guilty, was 'acquitted'. Denman danced round her robing-room with Lady Charlotte Lindsay, and Brougham was chaired to Brooks's Club, the hero of the hour.

The Queen was greeted by uproarious crowds as she left the 'House of Correction', uncorrected, for the last time. Illuminations and transparencies that night decked out the houses of London. The Queen had triumphed, and the King was undone. The printmakers, the booksellers, the purveyors of china and pottery wares outdid

\* This Christian imprecation spawned the popular ditty: 'O Gracious Queen we thee implore / To go away and sin no more. / Or, if the effort be too great, / To go away at any rate.'

themselves in the production of goods commemorating the vindication of the Queen, friend of the oppressed. Accounts of the proceedings were rushed out, the closing speeches of all the counsel printed on broadsheets.

And the King, that shape that had no form? He spoke wildly of resigning the ungrateful kingdom to his brother York and retiring to live in Hanover. When the Queen had signed her name to a formal protest against the Bill, after the second reading, she had written 'Caroline Regina' – adding aloud, 'Regina in spite of him.'[92]

## CHAPTER EIGHTEEN

# SUDDEN DEATH

November 1820–August 1821

*'The total eclipse'*

FOR GUILT OR INNOCENCE, as Cobbett had remarked, the people did not in the hour of triumph care a straw. 'Caroline was an injured wife, although I could not doubt that she was a depraved woman.' This was the private opinion of Charles Knight, publisher of the *Windsor and Eton Express*, and much the same sentiment was writ large on a cotton handkerchief printed with a woodcut of the House of Lords 'trial' and sold in numbers. Into this depiction of the Parliamentary scene was inserted a handsome bust of Pergami wearing a cluster of decorations. 'What effect can reasoning have with people', wrote one editor, 'who, having printed handkerchiefs in commemoration of the Queen's innocence . . . place a colossal portrait of Pergami over the throne of England?'[1] Though the peers might believe that the evidence of adultery with Pergami under the shipboard tent was overwhelming, though they had many of them risen solemnly to express that conviction, the popular consensus was that the Queen was 'acquitted', and that that acquittal had been brought about by the efforts of the press and by the addresses of the public. Some of her supporters were violent in their enthusiasm. Creevey heard that 'the river below the bridge today is the most beautiful sight in the world; every vessel is covered with colours, and at the head of the tallest mast in the river is the effigy of a bishop, 20 or 30 feet in length, with his heels uppermost, hanging from the masthead'.[2]

For five nights the chief cities of Britain were illuminated. In London, wrote one observer, occurred 'all the unmitigated extravagances of a popular triumph; popular meetings, addresses, illuminations, squibs, bonfires, and breaking of windows . . . together with much other ebullitions of gaiety, as his Majesty the mob, when tickled, delighteth to indulge in.'³ Mr William Cooke gave orders 'to remove my tin boxes' from his chambers, and left town, after receiving information that a mob was collecting for an attack.⁴ Among the ebullitions was Dolby's and Isaac Cruikshank's 'The Total Eclipse: A Grand Politico-Astronomical Phenomenon, which occurred in the year 1820'.⁵ There was in addition a rumour that Caroline was to publish her red-morocco memoirs; had they been as frank as she often claimed them to be, their revelation must have undermined the public's belief that she had been justly acquitted even more than their recriminatory passages must have damaged the King. But no such publication took place.

Only a few days after the Bill had been abandoned, a Sicilian, Iacinto Greco, who had acted as cook to the Queen in 1816 at Syracuse, came forward with startling new evidence, of the very kind which Ompteda and the Milan Commission had so zealously sought. Had his testimony been produced in the Commons, the Queen's supporters might have found it difficult to argue her innocence. Greco told a lieutenant detailed by the Foreign Office to seek out further evidence in South Italy that after dinner one evening he had opened the door of the saloon beyond which lay the principal staircase. He saw

> the Princess on the sofa at the further end of the saloon – Pergami was standing between her legs which were in his arms – his breeches were down, and his back towards the door – at which I was. I saw the Princess's thighs quite naked – Pergami was moving backwards and forwards and in the very act with the Princess.

Pergami turned his head and saw the cook. The next day Greco was discharged.⁶

Asked why he had not come forward before, Greco explained that his wife had been told that if he went to England her husband's head would be cut off. But it was too late. The case was closed.

Fresh from her triumph, Caroline made a series of demands. Still intent on being crowned, she further required an increased annuity now that she was Queen, a royal residence and restoration of her name to the liturgy. She declared that, unless the latter omission were made good, she would not accept a single penny from the state. The

King, who had written of his wife more than twenty years before that he would 'rather see loads of vipers crawling over my victuals than sit at the same table with her',[7] now faced the prospect not only of Caroline's continued presence in England but of her being crowned with him. And these horrors he was determined to prevent. He urged his ministers to settle the question of the Queen's annuity before the Parliament session ended. 'If the matter be settled speedily, I have every reason to believe the departure of the Queen will be equally so.'[8] But the ministers insisted that he prorogue Parliament until January, without previously considering the Queen's three demands, following Lord Lauderdale's advice that 'the lapse of time will rather abate the elation and triumph at what is called the Queen's success than the weight which is due to the judicial decision of guilt in the House of Lords'.[9] The ministers told the Queen, however, that the King would not assign the royal palace which she had requested (in her view, 'an arrangement so necessary to the support of her station and the honour of the Crown').[10] The King bowed to the ministers' advice, but told Liverpool spitefully that he considered himself 'under the necessity of taking measures for the foundation of a new administration'.[11] In this project the King was baulked by the reluctance of the Grenville Whigs, who had been informally supporting the Tory Government, to co-operate with the main body of the Whigs under Grey. In any case Grey had put himself beyond the pale when he had announced during the third reading his firm belief in the Queen's innocence. And he would insist on the inclusion of her name in the liturgy.

In a final bid to get rid of Liverpool, on 26 November the King called Grenville himself to Windsor hoping to lure him out of political retirement and into office. But Grenville could not stomach the King's extraordinary proposal that he publish the memorandum drawn up in 1814 by Princess Charlotte, detailing Caroline's connivance in her daughter's affair with Captain Hesse and Charlotte's suspicion that he was her mother's lover as well. The King hoped to rely on this document as ground not only for the continued omission of the Queen's name from the liturgy but also for fresh proceedings for divorce.[12] But, no less than any other Whig, Grenville was reluctant to inherit the poisoned chalice of the 'Queen's affair' from the Tory ministers. Particular matters still outstanding were whether to prosecute Government witnesses for perjury and whether to investigate the Milan Commission, as well as decisions on the liturgy and Coronation among other 'dirty pickings'.

For Brougham, despite the acclaim which followed his forensic defence of the Queen, these developments meant that he had failed in his larger design: the Government had not been overthrown. Moreover, the supposed vindication of his client had done nothing to advance the greater cause of Parliamentary reform, nothing to undo the Alien Act and the other repressive measures of Liverpool's Government.

With Grenville obdurate, the King was forced back into the arms of Liverpool and his colleagues. The monarch's gloomy expectation was that during the prorogation the Radicals would 'work double tides to keep treason and tumult afloat through the medium of the press, and all the collateral engines which we know are resorted to for the most wicked purposes.... Hence, no tranquillity.'[13]

Caroline was no less dismayed that her rights and favours as Queen Consort were not to be discussed before January. Without a settled income she could not return to Italy and to Pergami, waiting for her at Pesaro. Domestic contentment must be postponed. As in the summer of 1814, when she had skipped abroad immediately on receiving her increased Parliamentary allowance, paying no attention to the fury of MPs who felt they had not given her money to be spent out of the country, she would care not a whit more now for the political censure that would attend her departure for Italy. This would be so even though this time she would be returning to a lover, an act which would unmask her affirmation of virtue and innocence, and even though she now had a mass of supporters who would raise a storm of protest if she abandoned them. When it suited her, Caroline was wonderfully indifferent to the opinions of others.

At this time she confided in no one but Pergami, with whom she corresponded mightily. Her confidential couriers Luigi Camera and Carlo Fortis went back and forth between Pesaro and Hammersmith at vast expense.[14] These letters, and the sentiments and plans contained in them, have vanished.

While she awaited the January debates in Parliament, Caroline acquiesced in her supporters' plans for a thanksgiving service in St Paul's. The idea was 'to return thanks for her escape from a conspiracy', but when the Dean of St Paul's denied that there had been any conspiracy, she had little alternative but to attend ordinary morning service on that day and treat it as her thanksgiving.[15]

The Queen's Cavalcade Committee, which had been formed by Radical MPs after her 'trial' to arrange presentation to her of the innumerable congratulatory addresses, also organized her procession to the Cathedral. A banner bearing the slogan 'The Queen's Guard: The People' aptly described the throng – 500 horsemen rode before her carriage and an equal number behind, escorting her through a crowd estimated at 50,000. All Hammersmith was shut up and, as the state carriage passed the church of St Peter's, charity children in 'holiday gear' strewed flowers in the road. The Queen wore white, symbolizing innocence – a silk pelisse extravagantly trimmed with white fur and 'a close turban covered with a white veil'. Hordes of spectators occupied the walls and trees of Hyde Park to watch her go by. At Temple Bar the Lord Mayor and Sheriffs and Common Council received her and conducted her to the Cathedral, where she sat among a committee of sixty ladies, also veiled and in white. Denied official sanction for her visit, the Queen listened with satisfaction to the morning service. The psalm appointed was number CXL, which begins 'Deliver me, O Lord, from the evil man'.[16] But no peers except her chamberlain, Lord Hood, were present; even her defence lawyers stayed away. The Government papers could thus call the Queen's companions a 'mere rabble', but Countess Lieven, no friend to the Queen, thought the procession to St Paul's 'beautiful, absurd, frightening, all at once'.[17]

The following month Brougham sent a circular letter to the principal signatories of every address received by the Queen begging them to ask all the persons in their town who had put their names to that document to sign a petition to the House of Commons, praying for the restoration of the Queen's name to the liturgy and the affirmation of 'all her other rights and dignities'.[18] This 'private suggestion' was an enormous success. As Creevey had observed, 'The people have learnt a great lesson from this wicked proceeding: they have learnt how to marshal and organize themselves, and they have learnt at the same time the success of their strength.'[19] But whereas Brougham had expected the petitions to be restricted to demands respecting the Queen's rights, Alderman Wood and other Radicals organized their own letters with additional pleas for Parliamentary reform and for prosecution of the Milan Commission – and these letters were often couched in highly inflammatory language. Whigs and Radicals, so recently and powerfully allied in their support of the Queen, were beginning to diverge, much to the Government's glee.

The single greatest advantage the Government had was that it had not till now gone on the attack. Harrison at the Treasury was now suggesting publishing a *Collectanea*, a collection of tracts against the Queen,[20] and in December there arose a champion of the 'rational part' (the Government's term for its own supporters), a hero of the counter-revolution – Theodore Hook, the anonymous editor and publisher of *John Bull*, a new weekly paper, who combined a taste for satire with a facility for composing topical lyrics to be set to well-known tunes. Hook also delighted in giving salacious information about the ladies who visited the Queen, and inveighing against their morals. The criticisms are now harmless as dried snakes, but so effective were they at the time that many of those ladies stayed away, afraid for their reputations. An astonishing 9000 copies of *John Bull* were sold weekly, half the circulation of *The Times*, and back numbers were rapidly reprinted.[21]

Another weapon used in support of the Government was the loyalist caricature. Theodore Lane produced for the printseller Humphrey a series of fantastical cartoons – possibly inspired by Hook's fertile imagination – later collected in a volume entitled *The Attorney-General's Charges against the Queen*.[22] To remind the public of the main allegations against Caroline he depicted her bathing with Pergami's assistance, gambolling with him on the lawns by Lake Como and sitting in the carriage with her hand on his private parts. Two other cartoons were hardly less damaging. One shows an imaginary scene at 'Brandyburg House' where a stuporous Queen and Court slumber at the dinner table; empty bottles lie all around, and Lady Anne Hamilton's Scotch bonnet has slipped from its moorings.[23] In another, above a crazed Queen surrounded by her advisers savagely depicted (Wood is a naked, hairy devil in alderman's robes, Brougham is a broomstick wigged and gowned) flaps an owl wearing a fool's cap with bells and carrying in its beak the cross of the Order of St Caroline; a portrait of Pergami is on the wall.[24]

If the Queen was dismayed by these satirical attacks, which equalled in venom those inflicted earlier in the year on her husband, she made no public display of her feelings. But, although the number of visitors of rank fell off, she received with good humour those who did call. Prince Leopold was one of them, venturing to Hammersmith to make the acquaintance of his dead wife's mother. Scathing comment in the Whig papers was his only reward. But with the approach of Christmas, when peers and ladies left London, the Queen was left more than ever to her own devices. A Government spy posted at the gates of Brandenburg House reported in February 1821 that Lady Anne Hamilton was quarrelling with Contessa Oldi, and the Italian members of her Court were more concerned with recovering their travelling expenses from Vizard so that they could set off home than they were with the Queen's further struggles in England.[25] Gell had already escaped to Italy, and Keppel Craven was anxious to join him there.

While she waited for the new session to bring down retribution on the Milan Commission, the Queen may have been tempted to take her own prior vengeance. On 8 January 1821, far away in Milan, Colonel Browne was set upon outside his lodgings by would-be assassins armed with stilettos. He was slow to recover from his wounds, but had no doubt who was the instigator of the violence. He reported that Vimercati, the Commission's lawyer in Milan, fearing for his own life, was nearly dead 'of fright'; he had ordered his wife to cook all meals behind locked doors and to taste them before he did.[26] If Pergami in Pesaro had hired the ruffians to attack Browne, it was the nearest thing to revenge that the Queen was to wreak on the Commission.

With the Parliamentary debates imminent, a succession of Whig politicians from both Houses visited Brandenburg House. If they were to support the Queen in Parliament, they could scarcely stand aloof from her in private life. In the event the King's Speech on 23 January took them by surprise, for it recommended that an annuity be provided for the Queen to replace that which she had been given as Princess of Wales. This took the wind out of the Whigs' sails, and Lord Archibald Hamilton's motion on the 26th that the omission of the Queen's name from the liturgy was 'ill advised and inexpedient' was defeated.[27] The petitions to Parliament which Brougham had drummed up were duly read out – but this was a device that misfired. Too many of them were violent in their demands for the reform of the Commons and therefore incensed many of its Members. The Whigs were still reluctant to link the Queen's cause with that of reform.

The Queen had by now entered into negotiations with Prince Leopold for the purchase of his town residence, Marlborough House. These were soon to fall through, and she leased instead Cambridge House in South Audley Street for a term of twenty years. But, never comfortable there, she retained Brandenburg House. Lady Francis was meanwhile trying to restore the house in St James's Square which the Queen had rented since August. The carpets had been ruined, 'with wax, ink, oil and other things thrown over them'. In the reception rooms the tassels had been ripped from several 'rich scarlet coverings', which were themselves 'dirtied and spotted'; glazed calico covers were likewise rent. Moreover the blinds had never been drawn in the day, so the blue silk furnishings in the drawing-rooms were all faded. Ornaments, furniture and lustres had been broken, keys lost, and the silver 'much bruised and damaged from the servants always throwing them down on the stone floors or steps when done with'. The bedding and blankets all had to be 'sent to the scourers from total neglect'.[28]

The House of Commons voted on the liturgy question in January and February produced solid victories for the Government, thereby confirming the Queen's exclusion. But her annuity was duly increased to £50,000, and when she received news of this on 2 March she agreed to it at once, abandoning her earlier vow to accept nothing without liturgical recognition.[29]

This was the end of her political power. Her grabbing at the money exposed her selfish motives and the emptiness of all her phrases about alliance with the people. The Whigs and Radicals both abandoned her cause for what it was, a selfish cause – as theirs had been. From now on it was a lone battle, horns locked, between King and Consort. There were no further appeals to the people. The addresses, the petitions, the country and borough and public metropolitan meetings slowly diminished in number, before dying out altogether.

Now that her annuity was forthcoming, Caroline wrote of her wish to 'recruit her health by an excursion on the continent', having for many months suffered 'an extreme state of anxiety'.[30] A Hammersmith carpenter was called to Brandenburg House to make fifty packing cases, each to bear a tin plate 'chased as follows – Her Majesty the Queen of England'.[31]

She continued to press for reinstatement of her name to the liturgy, which the Government was determined not to yield. She asked Liverpool to inform the King of 'the Queen's intention to present herself next Thursday in person at the King's drawing-room'.[32] She meant to present a petition to her husband asking him to restore her name. An extraordinary Cabinet minute of 19 March shows the perturbation which the Queen had always been able to cause the King and his ministers. They judged it unlikely that she would come to Court. If she did, however, she should not be blocked on her way to Queen's House for fear of 'creating general confusion in the Metropolis, and . . . shedding quantities of blood'. She should be shown into a ground-floor room, and the Lord Chamberlain should be sent to receive the petition. If she insisted on coming upstairs, the King should descend to her with his ministers.

In the event the Queen did not attend the drawing-room but presented her petition the day before. With great relief the King sent it back: he saw no reason to depart from his decision of February 1820. The matter of the omission of her name was at last settled.[33]

However, Caroline was now objecting to certain initial deductions that had been made from her annuity. She had sent Lushington to the Prime Minister to complain, but without effect. With the lease of Cambridge House, she was once more short of money. On 29 April she wrote again to Liverpool, stating that, as she was under the financial necessity of remaining in the country, she planned to attend the Coronation. The threat was clear, as was the offer to be bribed to return to Pesaro. At the same time she launched a last attack on the King, writing direct to him to ask him to appoint ladies of the highest rank to attend her and to name her train-bearers.[34] On 1 May the King told Liverpool that he never opened letters from the Queen, 'a resolution adopted more than twenty years ago'. The Prime Minister would have to tell the Queen that she was not to attend the Coronation, 'else she might have some sort of colour to assume that it had never been formally notified to her' and that her request had been 'contemptuously disregarded' by the King and his ministers. The King then commanded Liverpool to say 'that it is his Majesty's prerogative to regulate the ceremonial of his Coronation in such a manner as he may think fit; that the Queen can form no part of that ceremonial except in consequence of a distinct authority from the King; and that it is not his Majesty's intention under the present circumstances to give any such authority'. The King, he added, had dispensed with the attendance of all ladies at his Coronation.[35]

The Queen replied that she was much astonished at Liverpool's letter: to be crowned was one of her rights and privileges. Liverpool sent this to the King, suggesting that 'the threat is an empty threat, which the Queen has evidently not the power of carrying into execution, and must appear to have been made solely with a view of extorting money'.[36]

That same day, the Government spy at the gates of Brandenburg House reported the Queen's response to the intransigence of the King and his ministers: 'It's terrible, shocking, too much to bear. I see they wish to get me gone.' She still spoke of taking the waters on the Continent, and her friend Prince Ercolani and Willy Austin went so far as to purchase two travelling desks for her carriages. The spy added that when 'two country-looking men' stopped opposite her gates, one remarked, 'How does Mrs Innocence get on? How long does she mean to carry on this farce?' His companion answered sagely, 'I suppose she is at this time of day tippling with some of the humbug Italians.'[37] The Queen, well aware that she was widely believed to drink, was said to have imbibed two decanters of cold tea one evening, passing it off as wine so as to lend credence to the claims that the King's wife was a drunkard.[38]

On 5 May, Napoleon Bonaparte, whose cause Caroline had once so vigorously espoused, at last died on St Helena. King George IV received the news: 'Sir, your bitterest enemy is dead.' 'Is she, by God!'

was his tender reply.[39] But the Queen was not only very much alive, she now seemed to be planning an extended stay in England. Still dissatisfied with Cambridge House, she contemplated buying Brandenburg House, where the 'various articles of furniture and pictures' packed up by the carpenter gathered dust in the mangle-room.[40]

On 9 June, it was proclaimed that the Coronation, delayed for a year, would be held on 19 July. Four days later, at Cambridge House, Caroline gave a lavish dinner party for the leading Whigs, among whom were her counsel Brougham, Denman, Williams and Wilde, together with their wives. The Queen was mustering her forces for an attack on the King's claim that it was his prerogative to decide whether she should be crowned. On the 25th the Home Secretary Lord Sidmouth received her formal application. Claiming that coronation was her right, she appealed to the precedents of previous queens consort. Sidmouth fobbed her off with the reply that the Government law officers would be consulted.[41]

The matter was now raised in the Commons, where Castlereagh, now Marquess of Londonderry, stated that ministers had advised the King that he should be crowned alone. But the Queen's obstinacy now forced the matter on the attention of the Privy Council, where Brougham and Denman, fortified by Vizard's researches, were heard – for the last time, as it transpired – for the Queen, with Gifford and Copley against. On 12 July the case was resolved against her – it was the King's prerogative to decide.[42]

Still not prepared to admit defeat, Caroline on the 15th addressed a letter to the Archbishop of Canterbury petitioning to be crowned the day after her husband. This ploy was no more successful than its predecessors.[43] Nevertheless, Hieronymus declared himself certain that his mistress would attend the Coronation: 'he had been with her seven years and never knew of one instance of her Majesty altering her resolution when once she had made up her mind if even it would have cost her her life.'[44] The King meanwhile was busying himself with his costume for the great day, ordering new jewels and a fine crown. The Queen too had her dressmaker attend on several occasions, to fit her and her ladies, Lady Hood and Lady Anne Hamilton, in their splendid dresses.[45] But whether she would actually go, merely to witness her husband's Coronation, no one knew.

The morning of the Coronation, 19 July 1821, was fair and there was a breath of wind early on, when the Queen and her party arrived at the Abbey to make her ill-fated attempt to attend the ceremony. Turned away from entrance after entrance, she uttered her poignant cry to the sentry at Westminster Hall, 'Let me pass; I am your Queen.' It was then that the pages slammed the door in her face – a resounding affront which, more than all the magnificent show devised by King George IV, gave his Coronation its place in history.[46] Caroline retreated at once to Cambridge House.

The excitement aroused by the Queen's attempt to storm the Abbey and Hall was forgotten by her fickle supporters in the enthusiasm for the Coronation procession, which emerged from the Hall at eleven o'clock. First came the heralds, trumpeting their King. There followed herb-women, including Caroline's former woman of the bedchamber, Miss Garth, strewing flowers and handfuls of lavender and rosemary before the monarch. The Lord Great Chamberlain preceded the portly princes of the blood. Next came the great officers of state, with the diminutive Sir Thomas Tyrwhitt in his elegant black suit side by side with the Lord Chancellor holding the mace. The Kings' gentlemen came next, and then finally the figure of the sovereign, nodding and bowing gracefully to his subjects.

The King's robe-makers, and his no less talented corset-makers, had excelled themselves. His great girth was held in by a complicated apparatus of strings and stays, which only added to the stateliness of his progress. On his bosom flashed the Garter star, the Golden Fleece dangled from his neck and knocked against insignia of other Orders – the Bath, the Thistle and the Guelphic (designed by himself). From his vast shoulders a mantle of ermine and velvet dipped in graceful folds, its hem borne aloft by four pages. As he stepped slowly onward, his feet were seen to be encased in velvet shoes tasselled and embroidered in gold and silver thread. The whole magnificent outfit was assembled at a cost of £24,704 8s 10d.

The procession disappeared into the Abbey, where the waiting peers and peeresses rose to their feet with a great rustling of cloth. The King marched, with his royal brothers his supporters, to the altar, where the Archbishop of Canterbury and other clergy waited. The ancient minster echoed to the music of organ and choir as the

Archbishop placed King Charles II's crown on the anointed head of the new monarch.[47]

Outside the Abbey the crowds, when they heard that all was done, roared their appreciation. It was all that the showman King could have hoped. He turned, the ceremony for which he had waited so long triumphantly ended, and processed back down the long aisle. As he passed, the ladies curtseyed with difficulty in the confined pews and their husbands bowed low, before filing out after their sovereign. As the King emerged, his magnificent bulk framed in the door of the Abbey, he received the first spontaneous marks of respect from the public he had feared and reviled since he had ascended the throne, and with whom his relations had been difficult ever since he had married the troublesome Princess of Brunswick.

While the King and his guests moved on to Westminster Hall for the banquet, Caroline made her way to Brandenburg House, where she retired to her bedroom, remaining alone for four hours. That night at supper, Lady Anne Hamilton recorded, 'her Majesty put on the semblance of unusual gaiety, but the friends who were around her observed that though she laboured hard to deceive them, she only deceived herself, for while she laughed, the tears rolled down her face – tears of anguish so acute that she seemed to dread the usual approach of rest'.

The party broke up only at three in the morning, when the Queen called for 'a tumbler of water and some magnesia, putting in such a quantity of the latter that it was literally a tumbler of paste, to which she superadded a few drops of laudanum'. (Magnesia is an antacid and purgative.) The Reverend John Wood, another of the Alderman's sons, now Queen's Chaplain, and Lady Anne tried to dissuade her from taking 'so strange a mess, but in vain; with the aid of a spoon she contrived to get it all down, and not till then did she retire to bed'.[48]

Sir Walter Scott, writing the next day, declared that the Queen's cause was 'a fire of straw which has now burnt to the very embers, and those who try to blow it into light again, will only blacken their hands and noses, like mischievous children dabbling among the ashes of a bonfire'.[49] But Caroline had hopes of igniting support in Scott's native Edinburgh and in Glasgow, and she informed Lord Liverpool of her intention to visit there. She had been impressed by the determination of the Kirk to pray for her and by the vigorous demonstrations mounted by Scottish Queenites after her 'acquittal'.

But her health was not good. Denman went to Brandenburg House a few evenings after the Coronation and found her with a large party, 'dancing, laughing and romping, with spirits frightfully over-strained'.[50] But by now she had quarrelled with Lord and Lady Hood, and with Lady Anne. In her febrile state, she saw slights and affronts where none existed, and she went so far as to dispense with the services of the Hoods. In their place as chamberlain and mistress of the robes she appointed, most irregularly, the commoners Mr John Wood and his wife. Brougham ascribed this odd nomination to the Queen's passion for their child, which, following her similar attachment to Willy Austin and Vittorine Pergami, prompted him to dub her a 'child-fancier'.[51]

The Hoods had still not left Brandenburg House when, on 30 July, Caroline insisted on attending a representation of the Coronation performed at the Drury Lane Theatre, despite feeling unwell. It was to be her last public appearance. On her return she was 'very sick, and had much pain in her bowels', an obstruction having set up an inflammation. Dr Holland, calling by chance the next afternoon, was shocked by her condition. 'Do you think I am poisoned?' she asked him, seeming 'much surprised herself at her illness'. Dr Holland found that the acute inflammation of her bowels had persisted for two days 'without even attempt at relief'. As he later reflected, 'There was a sort of irrational bravery in the character of Queen Caroline, leading her to disregard all common precautions, not solely in reference to public opinion, but even where personal suffering and risk were concerned.'[52]

The next day he brought to Brandenburg House Dr Richard Ainslie, one of the King's physicians, and on the following day another, Dr Warren, attended with them. They concluded that the Queen was dying, but decided nonetheless to bleed her. If she had any papers of consequence, they advised her, she had best dispose of them. 'At this she astonished them all by the greatness of her mind; for her Majesty did not betray the slightest agitation, but immediately and coolly answered, "Oh yes, I understand you; it shall be done."'[53]

She stayed up nearly the whole of that night with Mariette Brun, 'burning letters, papers and MS books'. She then called Hieronymus and made him swear to burn more documents in the kitchen fire. In particular she gave him to consign to the flames 'a large folio book, full, or nearly so, of her own writing'. These were her memoirs. After sorting 'all her little trinkets, [she] wrapped them in separate papers' for different friends, and at last rested.[54]

The propriety of making her will was now accepted by the Queen. On Thursday, 2 August, all four of her counsel attended to hear her wishes. Denman reported, 'We ... were received with the most unselfish kindness. The Queen was lying on a sofa-bed without curtains; she sat up in it, her head bound with a silk handkerchief, the face flushed, the eyes remarkably bright. She spoke cheerfully, though sensible of her danger. ...' Lushington then conferred alone with the sick woman. Wrote Denman, 'I shall never forget the feeling with which I heard from him that she desired to be buried in Brunswick and her tomb to bear no other inscription than that simple one, "Caroline of Brunswick, the injured Queen of England".'[55] (These two wishes were later embodied in codicils.) Willy Austin was to be her residuary legatee; to Vittorine Pergami she left the Villa Vittoria in Pesaro. Only now was her illness made public. The King, however, on 31 July had left London for Ireland, the first monarch to visit that country since William III in 1690, and news of her condition did not reach him until he arrived at Holyhead on 9 August for the crossing to Dublin.

Meanwhile on 3 August the lawyers returned with her will ready for signature. While waiting for her to recover sufficient strength, they 'wandered listlessly over the apartments and gardens, in restless uncertainty'.[56] Lady Anne and the Hoods, despite their dismissal, were in constant attendance. In the course of the day, the doctors came to believe that they saw signs of improvement. That night, when the lawyers were ushered into her bedroom, Brougham recorded, he asked her if it was her pleasure now to execute the document. '"Yes, Mr Brougham; where is Mr Denman?" she replied in the tone of voice of one in perfect health.' Denman then opened the curtains of her bed and, in the presence of Lushington and Wilde, appointed her executors, and two proctors from Doctors' Commons, her will was read to her. 'She put her hand out of bed and signed her name ... in the steadiest manner possible. In doing so she said with great firmness – "I am going to die, Mr Brougham, but it does not signify."' Brougham said, 'Your Majesty's physicians are quite of a different opinion.' 'Ah,' she replied, 'I know better than them. I tell you I shall die, but I don't mind it.'[57]

On the Saturday, Brougham and Denman both visited. Brougham noted that 'The obstruction still continued in spite of thirty-five grains of calomel in her, besides twenty more supposed to have been rejected, and castor-oil and jalap etc enough to physic a hundred people.'[58] Her pulse was steadier, and her doctors felt they could now bleed her again. (She had lost sixty-four ounces of blood altogether.) Reassured by her progress, her two lawyers left London to go on circuit. By the following afternoon, 'she was supposed to be safe', as Lord Liverpool explained later to the King.[59]

But Caroline wept and asked continually for Willy Austin, saying 'How odd it is that he never comes near me.' In fact he was himself weeping bitterly outside her room, repeatedly told by her doctors that she was asleep or too ill to see him. Her cries of suffering, Lady Anne Hamilton wrote, 'could be heard in all the adjacent rooms'. She expressed a wish to take communion, but the clergyman never came. She charged Mariette Brun to tell her sister Louise Demont that she forgave her, and she had one moment of happiness when, Hieronymus and Brun having announced their engagement, she joined their hands over the couch on which she lay.[60]

When her old doctor, Matthew Baillie, arrived on the Monday morning, he 'saw no cause for excessive alarm'. The obstruction seemed to have gone. But when Lushington and Wilde visited for a long interview later that day her condition had deteriorated. She talked incessantly on every subject for three hours. As they told Brougham, perhaps without much accuracy, 'She was then in no pain, mortification having commenced, and she had altogether lost her head.' The only names she mentioned were those of Vittorine and the Wood child.[61]

On Tuesday the 7th, she became much worse and moaned terribly with pain from four in the morning till ten at night. For the last two hours she was delirious, and Wilde, who was with her, later told

Denman that 'the name of Pergami never passed her lips'.[62] At twenty-five minutes past ten Dr Holland, standing with 'the awful watch in his hand, feeling her pulse, at last closed her Majesty's eyelids and declared, "All is over." '[63]

The turbulent life of Caroline, Princess of Brunswick and Queen of England, thus with great suddenness came to an end. Her battles, fought with unremitting courage and gusto for most of her fifty-three years against far mightier forces, were now concluded. Lord Hood, his loyalty undiminished, wrote shortly afterwards, 'I never beheld a firmer mind, or anyone with less feelings at the thought of dying. . . .'[64]

Dr Ainslie believed that the cause of death was a 'considerable lodgement of indurated and indissoluble magnesia in the stomach, forming an impediment to the transmission of food or medicine by choking up the intestines, and thereby producing inflammation'.[65] Dr Baillie, so sanguine only two days before, on the Wednesday suggested that the body be opened, only for Hood to point out that the Queen had expressly forbidden it.[66] Two hours after death, her body was black and swollen, which gave rise to rumours that she had been poisoned, but modern medical opinion concludes that Caroline died of natural causes, perhaps a gastrointestinal disorder such as a tumour, which would have produced the complication of obstruction. Another complication might have been infection of the blood, which could account for some blackening of the body.[67] Suggestions, however, that Caroline shared with her uncle King George III the metabolic disorder of porphyria, not least because of her history of cramps and erratic behaviour, are unconvincing – as proponents of this theory themselves concede.[68] Whatever the cause of death, Caroline no longer had a strong urge to live, and this may have had a morbid effect.[69]

The King received the news of his wife's death on 11 August on board the steam packet in St George's Channel. Croker, the Admiralty Secretary, heard that 'the King was uncommonly well during his passage and gayer than it might be proper to tell; but he did not appear upon deck after he heard of the Queen's death, and, though it would be absurd to think he was afflicted, he certainly was affected at the first accounts of this event. He walked about the cabin the greater part of the night on which the news reached him.'[70]

## CHAPTER NINETEEN

# LAID TO REST

August–September 1821

*'A system of persecution . . . continued to the grave'*

THE KING ARRIVED IN DUBLIN on 12 August 1821, his fifty-ninth birthday. Wrote Byron in *The Irish Avatar*:

> Ere the daughter of Brunswick is cold in her grave,
> And her ashes still float to their home o'er the tide,
> Lo! George the triumphant speeds o'er the wave,
> To the long-cherish'd isle which he loved like his bride![1]

But the Irish were willing to forgive their neglect and welcomed 'George the triumphant' with festivities. The principal dinner was to be held on the 14th, the day allotted to the Queen's funeral procession in London, after which her body was to be conveyed to Brunswick. The King told Liverpool he saw no need for any general mourning, not even the shortest period, but he compromised and agreed to a Court mourning.[2]

However affected he had been by the news of Caroline's death, his lasting sentiment was relief. Many were to speculate that he would seek another bride, but when he died in 1830, to be succeeded by his brother Clarence as King William IV, he was a widower, still enjoying the ample charms of Lady Conyngham. Around his neck when he was buried was placed a miniature of Mrs Fitzherbert, who survived him by seven years. As an extraordinary token of respect for her, on his brother's death King William ordered her to wear widow's weeds as if for her husband.[3]

Caroline's funeral procession on 14 August 1821 was a much less dignified affair, marked by riots, affray and manslaughter. The day after her death her executors Lushington and Wilde had handed to Lord Liverpool copies of her will and codicils. The Government readily agreed to arrange the conveyance of her body to Brunswick – to be embarked at Harwich – and to defray the expenses.[4] The route taken by the procession through London would steer north of the City, where Queenite demonstrations had been most ardent. The Government was reluctant to embark the body at Hammersmith, for fear of a demonstration on the river by the seamen and watermen, who had been among the Queen's most loyal supporters. Wellington said later, 'I would have embarked her in her own garden [at Brandenburg House]. I would have filled it with troops, and would have sent her in one tide from Hammersmith to Long Reach.'[5]

To one of Caroline's testamentary wishes the Prime Minister did not accede: that a plate engraved 'Here lies Caroline of Brunswick, the injured Queen of England' should be affixed to her coffin. Nevertheless, a silver plate was made and engraved, and on the eve of the funeral Caroline's executors removed the one with a sober Latin inscription which had been attached by the Lord Chamberlain's officials to her coffin. They were not permitted to affix any other 'while the body is under the jurisdiction of this country', they were informed by the Government.[6]

In drizzling rain on the morning of the 14th, the procession set out, headed by a troop of the Blues. The hearse, drawn by eight black horses, was preceded by three mourning coaches, including the Queen's state carriage, in which rode Sir George Nayler, Clarenceux King of Arms. He carried her crown on a black and gold-embroidered cushion – a queenly privilege denied her in life.[7] Behind the hearse followed seven further mourning coaches bearing members of her household, her executors, Willy Austin and her chaplain, Alderman Wood's son. At the rear, the Queen's Cavalcade Committee, still in being, joined a large number of other carriages, which were steadily augmented all the way to town. Brougham and Wood himself formed part of this tail.

At Kensington Church, where the Government had intended the procession to turn north for Islington, the horse soldiers came to an abrupt halt. Two carts blocked the road north, placed there by Queenites determined to force the procession to the City. No sooner were these vehicles removed than others were manoeuvred into position. Their scheme seemed likely to succeed when after an hour or more Sir Robert Baker arrived 'on a trooper's horse' and with a squadron of Life Guards led the procession towards Knightsbridge.

However, at Hyde Park Corner the Life Guards (characterized as 'butchers' for their part in quelling earlier protests) contrived, despite further barricades, to turn the procession north into the Park. Queenites raced for Cumberland Gate in a bid to block exit from the Park. As the cavalry galloped ahead, with hearse and carriages swaying wildly behind, crowds streaming in pursuit from every direction, violent skirmishes developed. The defenders at the Gate hurled bricks and stones at the hated Life Guards, who responded by discharging pistols into the crowd. Several men were wounded and two killed.[8] (The troop of soldiers was later paraded before witnesses but those responsible for the manslaughter were not properly identified.)

With the passage of the procession through the Gate and the dismissal of the Life Guards by Sir Robert Baker, who now read the Riot Act, peace of a kind was restored. Baker led the cortège north and east towards Islington, but at Tottenham Court Road a mass of carriages and carts chained together obliged him to turn south and into the City.[9] Thus was achieved, over the remains of the Queen, a final victory for her headstrong supporters.

At St Peter's Church in Colchester, where the coffin was laid overnight, new indignities befell it. That evening, a Government spy reported, Alderman Wood attended to pay his respects, 'with the executors' plate under his coat'. By some accident this slipped out, which so amused the Ladies Hood and Anne Hamilton as to astonish the watching throng, who could see no cause for merriment. A cabinet-maker then proceeded to affix the plate. Clarenceux King of Arms, on discovering this, called for it to be removed. Lushington swore that it had been done with Lord Liverpool's concurrence, but was politely disbelieved. At last, around midnight the wrangle – 'shocking considering the occasion' – was resolved. The offending plate was removed and confiscated by Clarenceux; 'the one with the Latin inscription' put in its place. Meanwhile a mob outside, angered by the closing of the church door, tried to gain entry by way of the vicarage. A gentleman emerged to reason with them, whereupon they tore his coat and stole his hat. 'He unhappily became very angry and said their Queen was an infernal —— [whore].'[10]

The embarkation of the body at Harwich next day provided, according to Brougham, 'the most touching spectacle that can be imagined – the day magnificently beautiful – the sea as smooth as glass – our officers by land and sea all full-dressed'. The piers were crowded, the harbour choked with boats of every size, as the frigate *Glasgow* prepared to receive its sombre cargo. 'The contrast of a bright sun with the gloom on every face was striking, guns firing at intervals made a solemn impression.' What struck Brougham most was the sight of a naval captain, who had been long in the Queen's service, sitting on a pier and refusing to leave it. 'He was deeply affected and wept exceedingly. . . .' (Brougham was being discreet; this was Captain Manby.) Brougham later explained to Creevey that 'if he had gone with the Queen's body to Brunswick' it would have been over-acting his part, 'it being very well known that through the whole of this business he had never been very much for the Queen! Now upon my soul,' added Creevey, 'this is quite true, and, being so, did you ever know anything to equal it?'[12] Despite this display of ambivalence, Brougham never gained preferment under King George IV, though he became Lord Chancellor at the start of the next reign – and all the Queen's other counsel achieved similar eminence.

On board the *Glasgow* the conversation turned much upon the character and exploits of the late Queen. The parentage of the unfortunate Willy Austin was once more brought into question when a Hanoverian baron on board judged him the image of the late Prince Louis Ferdinand of Prussia.[13] Willy himself never doubted his Austin blood and after he had subsisted for several years on what the insolvent Caroline had left to him, it was his brother Samuel Austin who rescued him in 1846 from a Milan lunatic asylum to which he had been committed.[14] Edwardine Kent, who married Lieutenant Flynn after divorcing her Brunswick husband, later made a gallant attempt to blackmail King William IV and Queen Victoria by claiming to be the rightful Queen of England.[15] Caroline's other protégée and legatee, Vittorine Pergami, grew up to marry an Italian noble, Conte Belluzzi, of the Fano district near Pesaro, and it was on a visit to her there in 1842 that her gregarious father, *il Barone* Pergami, fell from his horse. The man who had both provided for Caroline her greatest comfort and brought about her downfall was buried in his daughter's orchard. In the town of Pesaro, where he had made his home following the Queen's death, the site of his house is still known as *el spiazz del baron*.[16]

On 20 August 1821 the remains of his royal mistress were landed at Stade and taken by stages to Brunswick. A last scene of mayhem preceded the consignment of Caroline's body to the Cathedral vault. A mob broke through the ranks of footsoldiers, and some of the mourners were badly crushed. On the command of the reigning Duke, Caroline's nephew, a hundred maidens holding flowers and lighted tapers lined the aisles. In the vault the coffin was placed on a bier recently occupied by the coffin of her imbecile brother George. Here the Reverend Mr Wolff delivered a prayer in German and the maidens gathered in a circle around the bier and extinguished their candles.[17]

Still to be seen in the vault today, long after the incorporation of Brunswick into a greater Germany, Caroline's small coffin is covered in faded and rubbed crimson velvet, and next to it there stand the great coffins of her father Duke Charles, her great-uncle Duke Ferdinand and her brother Duke William, beneath a flag of the Black Brunswickers. 'A Brunswicker has the heart of a lion.' It was a heritage which had made it impossible for her to submit to a capricious husband or to the rules which then governed female conduct in England. The eccentric nature of her rebellions afforded an excellent burlesque for all Europe, and later prompted Max Beerbohm, connoisseur of comedy, to remark: 'Fate wrote her a most tremendous tragedy, and she played it in tights.' However, her sister Augusta's incarceration in a Baltic fortress should have been sufficient signal to Caroline of the wisdom of abjuring – except for propaganda purposes – the part of injured wife. Her high-spirited, even reckless, response to her predicament brought her unprecedented liberty, as she confounded the machinations of her husband and of governments in England and on the Continent to bring her to book. But in the end Caroline's breathtaking audacity had fatal consequences, contributing to the loss of her daughter, her crown and her life.

# REFERENCES

For full bibliographical details, see Sources, pp. 510–19.

### ABBREVIATIONS

| | |
|---|---|
| AS | Archivio di Stato |
| ASC | Archivio Storico di Commune |
| Asp/C | Aspinall, ed., *Letters of the Princess Charlotte* |
| Asp/G | Aspinall, ed., *Later Correspondence of George III* |
| Asp/K | Aspinall, ed., *Letters of King George IV* |
| Asp/P | Aspinall, ed., *Correspondence of George, Prince of Wales* |
| BL | British Library |
| LEF Journals | Journals of Lady Elizabeth Foster, Duchess of Devonshire |
| T. C. Hans. | Hansard, *Parliamentary History . . . to 1803* |
| Hansard | *Hansard's Parliamentary Debates* |
| HLRO | House of Lords Record Office |
| LGC | Lord Great Chamberlain's Papers |
| RA | Royal Archives |

Prologue
### Coronation Day, 19 July 1821

1. George: *Catalogue*, x, pl. 14255
2. Westminster Abbey Muniments, 63503, 12 July 1820
3. Fox: *London*, 251
4. *Annual Register*, 1821, 346; RA 22670–84, July 1821
5. Fox: *London*, 46

6. Ibid., 250
7. Trench: *Remains*, 449–50
8. HLRO, LGC II
9. Westminster Abbey Muniments, 51309A–11A
10. Ibid., 51272–3
11. Print Room, Royal Library
12. Maxwell: *Creevey Papers*, ii, 16–18
13. Fox: *London*, 44–6
14. RA Geo. Box 8/19, 13 March 1827
15. Maxwell: *Creevey Papers*, ii, 17–18
16. Nightingale: *Memoirs of Caroline*, iii, 129
17. Maxwell: *Creevey Papers*, ii, 18
18. Brougham: *Life and Times*, ii, 422
19. Richardson: *Disastrous Marriage*, 207–8
20. RA Geo. Box 8/19, 13 March 1827
21. Richardson: *Disastrous Marriage*, 208

Chapter One
PRINCESS CAROLINE, 1768–1794

1. Droysen: 'Aus den Briefen', 193
2. Niedersachsisches Staatsarchiv iv, 1 Alt. 24/313, May, June 1768
3. Frederick the Great: *Mémoires*, i, 489
4. RA 51961, 16 September 1760
5. Ibid., 51978, 19 February 1764
6. Mirabeau: *Secret History*, i, 251
7. Droysen: 'Aus den Briefen', 176
8. RA 51988–9, 8 February 1765
9. Ibid., 51984–5, 14 January 1765
10. Ibid., 51991, 1766?
11. Ibid., 52008, 22 April 1769
12. Royal Library, inv. K485
13. RA 52013, 25 July 1769
14. Ibid., 52030–31, 24 December 1771
15. Ibid., 52034, 13 March 1772
16. Ibid., 52050, 3 July 1772
17. Ibid., 52010–11, *c.* 5 June 1769

18. G.E.C.: *Peerage*, iii, 24
19. RA 15975, 8 May 1772
20. Massenbach: *Memoiren*, i, 233
21. RA 52082–4, 21 July 1777
22. Malmesbury: *Diaries*, iii, 189
23. RA 52082–4, 21 July 1777
24. Bury: *Diary*, i, 15
25. RA 52088–9, 12 December 1777
26. Ibid., 52080–1, 26 November 1777
27. Bury: *Diary*, i, 132
28. RA 52136, May 1787
29. Ibid., 52096, 14 June 1781; ibid., 52097, 8 June 1781
30. Bury: *Diary*, i, 19, 132; Asp/K, ii, 359
31. RA 52099, 7 December 1781
32. Adeane: *Early Married Life*, 25ff.
33. RA 52107–8, 7 November 1782
34. Ibid., 52109, 10 December 1782
35. Ibid., 52111, 1783 [?]
36. Ibid., 52107–8, 7 November 1782
37. Malmesbury: *Diaries*, iii, 164
38. Weigall: *Princess Charlotte*, 4–5
39. Melville: *Injured Queen*, i, 12
40. Niedersachsisches Staatsarchiv iv, 1 Alt. 24/315
41. Ibid
42. Ibid.
43. Bury, *Diary*, i, 10
44. Niedersachsisches Staatsarchiv iv, 1 Alt. 24/315
45. RA 52120–21, 19 December 1783
46. Ibid., 52122, 10 February 1784
47. Walker: *Miniatures in the Collection of Her Majesty*, pl. 243; Walker: *Regency Portraits*, i, 99
48. Niedersachsisches Staatsarchiv iv, 1 Alt. 24/315
49. Mirabeau: *Secret History*, i, 252
50. Huish: *Memoirs of Caroline*, i, 8
51. RA 52135, 1 May, 1787
52. Ibid., 52131–2, 25 February 1787
53. Westminster Abbey Muniments, 60009
54. Baron: *A la Cour de Brunswick*, 240
55. Argyll: *Society Letters*, i, 260

56. Baron: *A la Cour de Brunswick*, 240–1
57. Nightingale: *Memoirs of Caroline*, i, 35–8
58. Mundy: *Journal of Mary Frampton*, 85–6
59. Bury: *Diary*, i, 107
60. Huish: *Memoirs of Caroline*, i, 30
61. Asp/P, ii, 407
62. Huish: *Memoirs of Caroline*, i, 15
63. Asp/P, iii, 9
64. Huish: *Memoirs of Caroline*, i, 13
65. Buchez and Roux: *Histoire parlementaire*, xvi, 276
66. Duntzer: *Life of Goethe*, ii, 107
67. Biro: *German Policy*, ii, 117
68. Malmesbury: *Diaries*, iii, 158
69. Asp/P, ii, 407 n. 1

Chapter Two

THE BRUNSWICK BRIDE, 1794–1795

1. Langdale: *Mrs Fitzherbert*, 134
2. Russell: *Fox Correspondence*, ii, 278–85
3. *Edes* v. *Bishop of Oxford* (1667), Vaugh. 18 at p. 21
4. *Heseltine* v. *Lady Augusta Murray* (1794), 2 Add. 390; *Sussex Peerage Case* (1844), 11 Cl. and Fin. 85
5. Asp/P, ii, 133
6. George: *Catalogue*, vi, pl. 7298; ibid., pl. 6932; Argyll: *Society Letters*, 255–6
7. Castle: *Jerningham Letters*, i, 33
8. RA 41854, Estimate to Lady Day, 1786
9. Tooke: *Letter to a Friend*
10. T. C. Hans., xxvi, 1048–9
11. Ibid., 1066–8
12. Langdale: *Mrs Fitzherbert*, 123, 172
13. Buckingham: *Court of George III*, ii, 2, 6–7; Macalpine and Hunter: *George III*, 173
14. Historical Manuscripts Commission, 2nd Report (1871), 14
15. Ibid., 90; Musgrave: *Pavilion*, 95
16. Macalpine and Hunter: *George III*, 186

17. Asp/P, ii, 453
18. Hibbert: *Prince of Wales*, 125, 127
19. Asp.P, ii, 453
20. Ibid.
21. *Heseltine* v. *Lady Augusta Murray* (1794), 2 Add. 390
22. Asp/P, iii, 16; Mundy: *Journal of Mary Frampton*, 84; Wheatley: *Wraxall*, v, 36
23. Langdale: *Mrs Fitzherbert*, 125
24. Asp/P, ii, 444
25. Bladon: *Diaries of R. F. Greville*, 304–5
26. Ibid., 325
27. Asp/P, ii, 454
28. Stanhope: *Pitt*, ii, appendix
29. Oman: *Gascoyne Heiress*, 207
30. Asp/P, iii, 169
31. Ibid., ii, 453
32. Ibid., 465; RA Queen Charlotte's diary, 22 November 1794
33. Asp/P, ii, 460
34. RA 52160, October 1794
35. RA 32466, November 1794, accounts signed 2 December 1795
36. Asp/P, ii, 492
37. Malmesbury: *Diaries*, iii, 153
38. Asp/P, ii, 511
39. Ibid., 510
40. Malmesbury: *Diaries*, iii, 163
41. Asp/P, ii, 513
42. RA 52159, 8 October 1794
43. Malmesbury: *Diaries*, iii, 164
44. Ibid., 165–6
45. Ibid., 182
46. Ibid., 166
47. Ibid., 167–8
48. Ibid., 189
49. Ibid., 193
50. Ibid.
51. Ibid., 195–7
52. RA 52163, 26 January 1795
53. Malmesbury: *Diaries*, iii, 203
54. RA 52164, 24 March 1795

55. Malmesbury: *Diaries*, iii, 235–6
56. Asp/P, iii, 23
57. Malmesbury: *Diaries*, iii, 207–8
58. Ibid., 211
59. Ibid., 214
60. Ibid., 216
61. Ibid.
62. Albemarle: *Fifty Years*, i, 271; Melville: *Injured Queen*, i, 50
63. Malmesbury: *Diaries*, iii, 217
64. Ibid., 218

Chapter Three
MATRIMONY, 1795

1. Malmesbury: *Diaries*, iii, 219
2. Asp/P, iii, 169
3. Lewis: *Walpole Correspondence*, xii, 139
4. Morrison: *Hamilton Papers*, i, 209; ibid., 264
5. Bury: *Diary*, i, 4
6. Asp/P, iii, 198; Stanhope: *Memoirs*, i, 311–12
7. George: *Catalogue*, vii, pl. 8610
8. Asp/P, iii, 38; ibid., 47
9. Ibid., 38–9; ibid., 41
10. Ibid., 45
11. Whitley: *Artists*, ii, 205–6; Millar: *Later Georgian Pictures*, i, 33
12. Asp/P, iii, 50–51 n. 5
13. Hibbert: *Prince of Wales*, 146
14. Ibid., 147; Malmesbury: *Diaries*, iii, 220
15. Castle: *Jerningham Letters*, i, 75
16. Wheatley: *Wraxall*, v, 391
17. Browning: *Leeds Memoranda*, 220
18. Castle: *Jerningham Letters*, i, 75–7
19. Bessborough: *Georgiana*, 212
20. Bury: *Diary*, i, 21
21. Asp/P, iii, 123
22. RA Geo. Box 12/39, Evidence in support of the charge of recrimination [1820]

23. Minto: *Life*, iii, 14
24. de Bellaigue: *Carlton House*, 12, 219–20
25. Ibid., 22
26. RA Geo. Box 12/39, Evidence in support of the charge of recrimination [1820]
27. Bessborough: *Georgiana*, 213–14
28. Bury: *Diary*, i, 14
29. Malmesbury: *Diaries*, iii, 219–20
30. RA Geo. Box 8/1, press cutting [12 April 1795]
31. RA Add. 11/27, 23 May 1795
32. Fitzgerald: *Life of George IV*, i, 291
33. Minto: *Life*, iii, 14
34. RA 52165, 21 August 1795
35. RA Geo. Box 8/1, 20 May 1795
36. RA 52167–8, 31 May 1795
37. T. C. Hans., xxxii, 90–91
38. Ibid., 4, 96–7, 100
39. Asp/P, iii, 71
40. T. C. Hans., xxxii, 125
41. Asp/P, iii, 69
42. Ibid., 70
43. Ibid., 71
44. RA 52169–70, 3 July 1795
45. Adeane: *Girlhood of Maria Josepha Holroyd*, 327
46. Greenwood: *Hanoverian Queens*, ii, 260
47. Lewis: *Walpole Correspondence*, xii, 149–50
48. Asp/P, iii, 104
49. Bessborough: *Georgiana*, 215
50. RA 52171–2, 7 October 1795
51. Melville: *Injured Queen*, i, 61–5
52. Lewis: *Walpole Correspondence*, xii, 150

Chapter Four

THE CARLTON HOUSE SYSTEM, 1795–1796

1. Asp/P, iii, 172
2. Ibid., 191

3. Colchester: *Diary*, i, 137
4. Asp/P, iii, 125
5. Ibid., 126–7
6. Ibid., 127 n. 1
7. Ibid., 132–9
8. Colchester: *Diary*, i, 37
9. RA Add. 21/8/16, February 1796
10. Asp/P, iii, 144
11. RA Add. 21/8/17, March 1796
12. Ibid., 21/8/20, 1796; ibid., 21/8/21, 1796
13. Colchester: *Diary*, i, 52
14. Ibid., 44
15. Asp/P, iii, 172
16. Ibid., 159
17. Browning: *Leeds Memoranda*, 222
18. Asp/P, iii, 168
19. Ibid., 170–71
20. Ibid., 172
21. Ibid., 173
22. Ibid., 176
23. RA Geo. Box 8/1, 27 April 1796
24. Asp/P, iii, 176
25. Ibid., 178
26. Ibid., 179
27. RA Geo. Box 8/1, 7 May 1796
28. Browning: *Leeds Memoranda*, 223
29. RA 42115–16, 9 May 1796
30. RA 39184–5, 13 May 1796
31. RA 16708–9, 16 May 1796
32. Ibid.
33. Asp/P, iii, 185–6
34. RA 39132–3, 18 May 1796
35. Browning: *Leeds Memoranda*, 221
36. Ibid.
37. Lewis: *Walpole Correspondence*, xii, 186
38. Ibid., 187–8
39. Browning: *Leeds Memoranda*, 222
40. Asp/P, iii, 196–7
41. Browning: *Leeds Memoranda*, 223

42. Asp/P, iii, 197–8
43. Ibid., 200
44. Ibid., 204
45. Ibid., 200
46. Ibid., 212
47. Ibid., 211
48. Ibid., 216
49. Ibid., 220
50. Ibid., 223
51. Ibid., 224
52. Colchester: *Diary*, i, 61
53. Browning: *Leeds Memoranda*, 228–9
54. Ibid., 229
55. Asp/P, iii, 240; Melville: *Injured Queen*, i, 75
56. Asp/P, iii, 241
57. Ibid., 244
58. Granville: *Leveson Gower Correspondence*, i, 122–3
59. Melville: *Injured Queen* , i, 76–7
60. Browning: *Leeds Memoranda*, 231
61. Lewis: *Walpole Correspondence*, xii, 200

Chapter Five
UNOFFICIAL SEPARATION, 1796–1798

1. Asp/P, iii, 283
2. Ibid., 281
3. Ibid., 272
4. Ibid., 275
5. Browning: *Leeds Memoranda*, 233
6. Asp/P, iii, 279
7. Ibid., 300
8. Ibid., 280
9. Ibid., 281–2
10. Ibid., 283
11. Ibid., 285
12. Ibid.
13. Ibid., 298

14. Ibid., 297
15. Asp/G, ii, 535
16. Asp/P, iii, 309
17. Ibid., 312
18. RA Add. 21/8/26, [1797]
19. Ibid., 21/8/30, end of April 1797
20. RA Add. 37/5, 2 June 1797
21. Ibid.
22. Ibid.
23. RA Add. 37/6, 3 June 1797
24. Ibid., 37/6, 3 June, and 37/7, 5 June 1797
25. RA Add. 37/9, 11 June 1797
26. Ibid., 37/8, 7 June 1797
27. Ibid., 37/9, 11 June 1797
28. Ibid., 37/13, 6 July 1797
29. Ibid.
30. Ibid., 37/14, 22 July 1797
31. Ibid., 37/10, 21 June 1797
32. Ibid., 37/11, 25 June 1797
33. RA 42350–2, 27 June 1797
34. RA Add. 37/12, 28 June 1797
35. Ibid., 37/14, 22 July 1797
36. Weigall: *Princess Charlotte*, 20
37. Asp/P, iii, 357; ibid., iv, 223 n. 1
38. RA Add. 37/15, 13 August 1797
39. Ibid., 37/12, 28 June 1797
40. Ibid., 37/15, 13 August 1797
41. Asp/P, iii, 374
42. Ibid., 371; RA Add. 37/17, 17 October 1797
43. Asp/P, iii, 375 n. 1
44. RA Add. 37/18, 21 October 1797
45. Ibid., 37/37, 1 November 1797
46. Asp/P, iii, 374–5
47. RA Add. 37/23, 10 November 1797
48. Asp/P, iii, 375
49. Ibid., 377
50. Ibid.
51. Ibid., 378
52. Ibid.

53. Ibid., 379
54. RA Geo. Box 8/3, enclosure of 10 December 1797 in letter of 18 February 1807
55. Asp/P, iii, 389
56. Ibid.
57. Ibid., 381
58. RA Geo. Box 8/15, 15 December 1797
59. Asp/P, iii, 382
60. RA Geo. Box 8/15, 20 December 1797
61. RA Add. 21/8/48, 6 January 1798
62. Asp/P, iii, 390–1
63. Asp/G, iii, 6
64. Asp/P, iii, 495
65. Ibid., 497
66. Minto: *Life*, iii, 10
67. Ibid., 13
68. Ibid., 18ff
69. Ibid., 36

Chapter Six
MONTAGUE HOUSE, 1798–1804

1. Asp/P, iii, 452–3
2. Ibid., 478
3. Ibid., 501
4. Minto: *Life*, iii, 21
5. Bury: *Diary*, i, 16
6. Trevelyan: *Grey*, 191 n. 2
7. Asp/P, iv, 13
8. Ibid., 16
9. Ibid., 57
10. Ibid., 55
11. Ibid., 56
12. Ibid., 61
13. Minto: *Life*, iii, 61
14. Ibid., 63
15. Granville: *Leveson Gower Correspondence*, i, 251, 255

16. Quennell: *Lieven Letters*, 98
17. Minto: *Life*, iii, 64
18. RA Add. 37/99, 12 February [no year]
19. Asp/P, iv, 85
20. RA Add. 37/27, 7 January 1820
21. Walker: *Regency Portraits*, i, 100
22. Millar: *Later Georgian Pictures*, i, 61
23. Walker: *Regency Portraits*, i, 98
24. Fairburn: *Inquiry*, 104–5
25. RA Add. 37/29 [watermark 1801]
26. Melville: *Injured Queen*, i, 99–101
27. RA Add. 21/90/15, 1 July 1806
28. Melville: *Injured Queen*, i, 98
29. RA Add. 37/29 [watermark 1801]
30. Bury: *Diary*, i, 72
31. RA Add. 21/8/58–65, *c.* 25 March–7 April 1801; ibid, 21/8/67, 2 June 1801
32. Malmesbury: *Diaries*, iv, 20
33. Bickley: *Glenbervie Diaries*, i, 224–5; ii, 87
34. RA Add. 21/179/5, 6 June 1801
35. Asp/P, iv, 217
36. Ibid.
37. RA 52208–9, 16 July 1801
38. Ibid., 52210–11, 3 August 1801
39. Asp/P, iv, 221
40. RA 37073; RA 32482
41. Asp/P, iv, 223
42. RA 21/8/72, summer 1801
43. Asp/P, iv, 239
44. Ibid., 240
45. RA 37073
46. Asp/P, iv, 283
47. Ibid., 285
48. Ibid.
49. RA Add. 37/29 [watermark 1801]
50. Fairburn: *Inquiry*, 76
51. RA 49256, 11 December 1801
52. Fairburn: *Inquiry*, 76
53. Bunbury: *Narratives*, 232; Minto Mss, 11054, 29 March 1802
54. Fairburn: *Inquiry*, appendix B, 72

55. RA 49258, 4 August 1802
56. Fairburn: *Inquiry*, 17
57. Romilly: *Memoirs*, ii, 130
58. RA Geo. Box 8/2, Memorandum by Lady Douglas, after 1 June 1806
59. Stanhope: *Memoirs*, i, 308
60. Lewis: *Memoirs of Dillon*, ii, 18–20
61. RA 51365, 1 June 1804
62. Asp/P, iv, 414
63. Fairburn: *Inquiry*, appendix A, 193
64. Asp/P, iv, 344
65. Twiss: *Eldon*, iii
66. Ibid., i, 462
67. Asp/P, iv, 488
68. RA Add. 37/30 [1804]
69. Minto: *Life*, iii, 308
70. Stanhope: *Memoirs*, i, 309
71. RA Add. 21/179/55, 25 May 1804
72. Colchester: *Diary*, i, 517
73. Asp/P, v, 55
74. Twiss: *Eldon*, i, 462; RA Add. 21/179/57, 18 July 1804
75. Twiss: *Eldon*, i, 462–3
76. Asp/P, v, 69 n. 1
77. Ibid., 76
78. Ibid., 77
79. Ibid.
80. Twiss: *Eldon*, i, 463
81. Asp/P, v, 82
82. Ibid., 86
83. Ibid., 79
84. Ibid., 86
85. Ibid., 93
86. Ibid., 94
87. RA Geo. Box 11/32c, 13 November 1804
88. Twiss: *Eldon*, i, 474
89. RA Add. 37/30 [1804]
90. Harcourt: *Rose Diaries*, ii, 169–70
91. Colchester: *Diary*, i, 529
92. G.E.C.: *Peerage*, i, 460

Chapter Seven
THE ANONYMOUS LETTERS, 1804–1806

1. Fairburn: *Inquiry*, appendix B, 86–9
2. Ibid., 86–7
3. Ibid., 88
4. RA Add. 21/90/90 (n.d.); ibid, 21/90/91, December 1804
5. Colchester: *Diary*, i, 531
6. Twiss: *Eldon*, i, 474
7. Ibid., 476
8. Ibid., 479
9. Ibid., 481
10. RA Add. 21/179/70, 2 December 1804; Twiss; *Eldon*, i, 482
11. RA Add. 37/32, 30 January [1805]
12. Adeane: *Early Married Life*, 281
13. Minto: *Life*, iii, 371
14. Asp/P, vi, 391 n. 2
15. RA Geo. Box 8/2, Tuesday morning [September 1806?]; Gray: *Perceval*, 79–80
16. Fairburn: *Inquiry*, appendix B, 49
17. Asp/P, v, 288 n. 1
18. Romilly: *Memoirs*, ii, 129
19. Ibid., 131
20. Ibid., 131–2
21. RA Geo. Box 8/3, Lowten's accounts, 29 April 1808
22. Romilly: *Memoirs*, ii, 147
23. Fairburn: *Inquiry*, 186–7, 190–91
24. Asp/P, v, 384
25. Ibid., 390
26. RA Add. 37/38, 22 April 1806; ibid., 37/39, 28 April 1806
27. RA Add. 21/90/6, 31 May 1806
28. Ibid., 21/90/6, 1 June 1806
29. Fairburn: *Inquiry*, 26–7
30. RA Geo. Box 8/3, Lowten's accounts, 29 April 1808
31. RA Add. 21/90/1, 8 June 1806
32. Minto: *Life*, iii, 388
33. Ibid., 388–9

34. Fairburn: *Inquiry*, 2
35. Ibid., appendix B, 49
36. Ibid., 49–91
37. Ibid., 98–108
38. Ibid., 106
39. Ibid., *Inquiry*, 3
40. Ibid., appendix B, 100–101
41. Ibid., 104–5

Chapter Eight
THE DELICATE INVESTIGATION, 1806–1807

1. Fairburn: *Inquiry*, 1–4
2. RA Geo. Box 8/2, Memorandum by Lady Douglas, after 1 June 1806
3. Fairburn: *Inquiry*, appendix A, 17
4. Ibid., 24–5
5. Ibid., 8
6. RA Add. 21/122/83, recd 3 November 1814
7. Austin family papers, 13 May 1846
8. RA Add. 21/90/11, 18 June 1806
9. Ibid.
10. Ibid., 21/90/15, 1 July 1806
11. Fairburn: *Inquiry*, appendix A, 29–30, 40
12. Ibid., 42–6
13. RA Geo. Box 3/2, Wm Cole's Evidence of January 1806; ibid., McMahon's memorandum, 3 January 1806
14. Fairburn: *Inquiry*, Appendix A, 8
15. Minto: *Life*, iii, 391
16. Asp/P, v, 396
17. RA Add. 21/90/12, 23 June 1806
18. Ibid., 21/90/18, 7 July 1806
19. Ibid., 21/90/84, 25 July 1806
20. Twiss: *Eldon*, ii, 25
21. RA Add. 21/90/24, 2 August 1806
22. Asp/P, v, 407
23. RA Geo. Box 8/20, 20 September 1806
24. Asp/P, v, 408

25. RA Add. 21/179/97, 11 August 1806; ibid., 21/179/26, 12 August 1806
26. Fairburn: *Inquiry*, 9
27. Ibid., 11–13
28. RA Geo. Box 8/20, 20 August 1806
29. RA Add. 21/179/527, n.d.
30. Ibid., 21/90/55, 31 August 1806
31. Asp/P, v, 423
32. RA Add. 21/90/29, 9 September 1806
33. Fairburn: *Inquiry*, 182–5
34. Ibid., 193
35. Ibid., 194
36. RA Add. 21/90/57, 1 October 1806
37. Fairburn: *Inquiry*, 122–4
38. Ibid., 174–7
39. RA Geo. Box 8/2, 2 October 1806
40. Ibid., 24 December 1806
41. RA 29819–55, Correspondence about Lady Douglas's pension, 29 April 1816–29 November 1830
42. Asp/P, vi, 39
43. Ibid., 42–3
44. RA Add. 37/40, 6 October 1806
45. Ibid., 21/179/533, n.d.
46. Twiss: *Eldon*, ii, 27
47. RA Geo. Box 8/15, 25 August 1806
48. Ibid., Box 13/83, 15 November 1806
49. RA Add. 21/90/32, 21 November 1806
50. Ibid., 21/90/33, 2 December 1806
51. Ibid., 21/90/59, 10 December 1806
52. Fairburn: *Inquiry*, 195–8
53. RA Add. 21/90/59, 10 December 1806
54. Asp/P, vi, 46
55. Ibid., 103 n. 1
56. Ibid., 105
57. Ibid., 110
58. Ibid., 110 n. 1
59. Holland: *Whig Party*, ii, 152–3
60. RA Geo. Box 8/20, 29 December 1806
61. Asp/P, vi, 128 n. 3
62. Ibid., 127, 129

63. RA Add. 37/43, 21 February 1807
64. Asp/P, vi, 136–7 n. 1
65. RA Geo. Box 8/3, 1 February 1807
66. Sermoneta: *Locks of Norbury*, 232
67. Fairburn: *Inquiry*, 213–16
68. Ibid., 216–19
69. Ibid., 220–31
70. Asp/P, vi, 137 n. 1
71. RA Add. 21/179/187, 24 February 1807
72. RA Geo. Box 8/20, 7 March 1807
73. Ibid., Box 12/39, Evidence in support of the charge of recrimination [1820]
74. RA Add. 21/90/63, 26 February 1807
75. Fairburn: *Inquiry*, 244–6
76. RA Geo. Box 8/3, enclosure, 6 March 1807
77. RA Add. 21/90/64, 29 March 1807
78. Asp/P, vi, 162; RA Geo. Box 8/20, 20 March 1807
79. RA Geo. Box 8/3, 21 April 1807
80. RA Add. 37/45, April 1807
81. Sermoneta: *Locks of Norbury*, 232–3
82. RA Add. 37/46, 5 May 1807
83. Asp/P, vi, 181; RA Geo. Box 8/4, 1 May 1807
84. Asp/P, vi, 151
85. Ibid., 181–2
86. RA Geo. Box 8/3, 18 May 1807
87. Asp/P, vi, 185n.; RA Geo. Box 8/3, n.d. [May 1807]
88. Granville: *Leveson Gower Correspondence*, ii, 251

Chapter Nine
SHIFTING ALLEGIANCES, 1807–1810

1. RA 52247, 17 May 1807
2. RA Add. 37/48, 14 July 1807
3. RA Geo. Box 8/5, Queen Charlotte's answers to Lord Liverpool, 16 February 1813
4. Asp/P, vi, 511
5. RA Add. 37/55, 29 November 1807
6. Douglas: *Familiar Letters*, i, 103; Scott: *Poetical Works*, 63

7. RA Add. 37/49, 31 July 1807
8. Ibid., 37/48, 14 July 1807
9. Ibid., 37/50, 3 August 1807; ibid., 37/51, 17 August 1807
10. RA 52252, 3 September 1807
11. RA Add. 37/54, after 7 September 1807
12. Scott: *Poetical Works*, 379
13. Lockhart: *Life of Scott*, ii, 272
14. Ibid., iii, 23
15. RA Add. 37/54, after 7 September 1807
16. Castle: *Jerningham Letters*, ii, 5
17. RA Add. 21/90/39, 4 September 1807
18. Ibid., 21/90/40, 7 September 1807
19. Bickley: *Glenbervie Diaries*, ii, 106
20. Ibid., 18
21. Ibid., 3–4
22. Ibid., 8
23. Ibid., 5
24. RA Add. 37/54, after September 1807
25. Granville: *Leveson Gower Correspondence*, ii, 349
26. Asp/P, vi, 275 n. 1
27. Wilkins: *Mrs Fitzherbert*, ii, 109
28. Hibbert: *Prince of Wales*, 256, quoting Brighton Pavilion Mss
29. Leslie: *Mrs Fitzherbert*, ii, 133–4
30. Crook and Port: *King's Works*, 341–2
31. Ibid., 344
32. RA Add. 37/58, 26 September 1808
33. Lewis: *Berry Extracts*, ii, 405
34. Ibid., 404
35. Bickley: *Glenbervie Diaries*, ii, 18
36. Bury: *Diary*, i, 25
37. Ibid., i, 22
38. RA Geo. Box 8/5, 9 November 1812
39. Gray: *Perceval*, 86–7
40. Asp/P, vi, 151
41. Albemarle: *Fifty Years*, i, 295
42. Asp/P, vi, 39
43. Albemarle: *Fifty Years*, i, 292–3, 299, 290
44. Ibid., 299–300, 306
45. Asp/K, i, 467

46. Asp/C, x–xi
47. Bickley: *Glenbervie Diaries*, ii, 20
48. RA Add. 37/58, 26 September 1808
49. Ibid.
50. RA Add. 37/52, 28 August 1807
51. Ibid., 37/54, after 7 September 1807
52. RA Geo. Box 8/25, 13 June 1808
53. Ibid., 14 August 1808
54. Asp/P, vi, 387 n. 1
55. Ibid., 390 n. 2; RA 37059
56. Asp/P, vi, 391 n. 2
57. Ibid., 395
58. Ibid., 403
59. Ibid., 400; RA Add. 21/179/122, 29 May 1809
60. RA 33593–4, 22 January 1807
61. Greig: *Farington Diary*, v, 177
62. Lewis: *Berry Extracts*, ii, 379–80
63. Ibid., 388–9
64. Ibid., 294
65. Bickley: *Glenbervie Diaries*, ii, 36
66. Ibid., 35
67. Ibid., 35, 44
68. Ibid., 36
69. Ibid., 37
70. Douglas: *Familiar Letters*, i, 252

Chapter Ten

A REGENCY COURT, 1810–1813

1. RA Add. 37/63, 29 September 1807
2. Ibid., 21/179/130, 22 March 1810
3. Ibid., 37/58, 26 September 1808
4. Bury: *Diary*, i, 2
5. Bickley: *Glenbervie Diaries*, ii, 57
6. Ibid., 57–61
7. RA Add. 21/179/131, 8 May 1810
8. Bickley: *Glenbervie Diaries*, ii, 69

9. Ibid., 65–6
10. Ibid., 67
11. Ibid., 56
12. Ibid., 75
13. Ibid., 74
14. Clarke and Penny: *Arrogant Connoisseur*, 13
15. RA Add. 37/34, 21 July [1809?]
16. Bickley: *Glenbervie Diaries*, ii, 64
17. Ibid., 81
18. Ibid., 86
19. Ibid., 81
20. Ibid., 89ff.
21. Ibid., 110
22. Ibid., 114–15
23. Lewis: *Berry Extracts*, ii, 452
24. Ibid., 454
25. Ibid., 479
26. Ibid., 478
27. RA Add. 37/72, 27 May 1811
28. Lewis: *Berry Extracts*, ii, 481
29. RA Add. 37/72, 27 May 1811
30. Lewis: *Berry Extracts*, ii, 479–80
31. RA Add. 37/73, 11 June 1811
32. Sichel: *Glenbervie Journals*, 130ff.
33. Ibid., 152
34. RA Add. 37/79, 28 December 1811
35. Lewis: *Berry Extracts*, ii, 487ff
36. Sichel: *Glenbervie Journals*, 153; Müller: *Stockmar Memoirs*, i,
    42 n. 1
37. Sichel: *Glenbervie Journals*, 153
38. Asp/C, 22
39. Buckingham: *Memoirs of the Regency*, i, 250
40. Byron: *Poetical Works*, 65
41. Asp/K, i, 192
42. Asp/C, 21
43. Asp/K, i, 78
44. Asp/C, 36
45. Asp/K, i, 68
46. Ibid.

47. Maxwell: *Creevey Papers*, i, 182
48. Asp/K, i, 116
49. RA Add. 37/83 [August 1812]
50. Asp/K, i, 131–2
51. RA Add. 37/83 [August 1812]
52. Lewis: *Berry Extracts*, ii, 306–7; Russell, *Moore Memoirs*, i, 119
53. RA Geo. Box 8/15, Pss of W to Queen, 2 September 1812; ibid., Pss Elizabeth to Pss of W, 3 September 1812
54. Ibid., Lady Anne Hamilton to Lord Liverpool, 27 September 1812
55. Ibid., Pss of W to Lady de Clifford, 27 September 1812
56. Ibid., Box 8/5, Memorandum of Conversation between Q and Pss of W [27 September 1812]
57. Asp/K, i, 175
58. Ibid., 518
59. RA Geo. Box 8/5, 21 November 1812
60. Asp/K, i, 190
61. Marchand: *Byron*, i, 381 n. 2
62. Bury: *Diary*, ii, 239
63. Maxwell: *Creevey Papers*, i, 179
64. Asp/K, i, 203
65. Ibid., 204
66. Albemarle: *Fifty Years*, i, 342
67. Asp/K, i, 208
68. RA Geo. Box 8/5, 19 January 1813
69. Ibid., 27 January 1813
70. Ibid., 28 January 1813; Maxwell: *Creevey Papers*, i, 177
71. May: *Commemorative Pottery*, 23–4; George: *Catalogue*, ix, pl. 12011
72. Brougham: *Life and Times*, ii, 157ff.
73. RA Geo. Box 8/5, 14 February 1813
74. Ibid., 15 February 1815
75. RA Geo. Box 8/3, quoted in Privy Council Report, February 1813
76. Ibid., Box 8/5, 31 March 1813
77. Maxwell: *Creevey Papers*, i, 179
78. Asp/C, 58–9
79. Lewis: *Berry Extracts*, ii, 534
80. RA Geo. Box 8/5, 31 March 1813
81. Maxwell: *Creevey Papers*, i, 181
82. Ibid., 182
83. Ibid.

Chapter Eleven
CAROLINE AND CHARLOTTE, 1813–1814

1. Sichel: *Glenbervie Journals,* 171–2; Leigh Hunt: *Austin Dobson*
2. Maxwell: *Creevey Papers,* i, 182
3. Asp/C, 64
4. Ibid.
5. Ibid., 80
6. Knight: *Autobiography,* i, 266–9
7. RA Add. 37/86, 24 August 1813
8. Ibid., 37/88, 12 October [1813]
9. Lewis: *Berry Extracts,* ii, 546–7
10. RA Geo. Box 8/5, 25 September 1813
11. Webster: *Castlereagh Foreign Policy,* i, 54
12. Asp/C, 114–16
13. Place Papers, set 18
14. Lewis: *Berry Extracts,* iii, 24
15. Knight: *Autobiography,* ii, 345
16. Ibid., 347
17. Ibid., 348
18. Ibid., 344–5
19. Maxwell: *Creevey Papers,* i, 195
20. Sichel: *Glenbervie Journals,* 224
21. Maxwell: *Creevey Papers,* i, 195
22. Ibid., 198
23. Ibid.
24. Brougham: *Life and Times,* ii, 208–9
25. Asp/C, 117
26. Melville: *Injured Queen,* ii, 308
27. Maxwell: *Creevey Papers,* i, 199
28. Ibid.
29. Ibid., 199, 201; Melville: *Injured Queen,* i, 298–9
30. Maxwell: *Creevey Papers,* i, 201
31. Ibid., 199
32. Ibid., 200
33. Ibid., 201–2
34. Ibid., 203

35. Ibid., 203–4

36. Asp/K, i, 461; Maxwell: *Creevey Papers*, i, 204

37. RA Geo. Box 13/77, Mr Hoper's Account, 5 July 1814–June 1816

38. Strachey and Fulford: *Greville Memoirs*, ii, 319

39. Knight: *Autobiography*, i, 286; Asp/C, 122

40. Asp/K, i, 460–61

41. Knight: *Autobiography*, ii, 15

42. Ibid., i, 304

43. Brougham: *Life and Times*, ii, 226–7, 233

44. Ibid., 228–9

45. Ibid., 235

46. Maxwell: *Creevey Papers*, i, 201

47. Romilly: *Letters to 'Ivy'*, 249–50

48. Brougham: *Edinburgh Review*, i, 470

49. Asp/K, i, 468

50. Hansard, 1st series, xxviii, 874–8

51. Melville: *Injured Queen*, ii, 323–4

52. Romilly: *Letters to 'Ivy'*, 249–50

53. Asp/C, 137

54. RA Add. 21/122/12, 28 July 1814

55. *Morning Chronicle*, 3 August 1814

56. *The Times*, 10 August 1814

57. Melville: *Injured Queen*, ii, 318

Chapter Twelve
THE LONG VOYAGE, 1814–1817

1. RA Add, 21/122/63, 14 August 1814

2. Holland: *Recollections*, 116–17

3. RA Add. 21/122/64, 24 August 1814

4. Holland: *Recollections*, 117

5. RA Add. 21/122/64, 24 August 1814

6. Ibid., 21/122/68, 12 September 1814

7. RA Geo. Box 13/49; ibid., Box 9/3b, Chancery Proceedings, 24 December 1817

8. RA Add. 21/122/66, 2 September 1814

9. Holland: *Recollections*, 118–19

10. RA Add. 21/122/82, 15 October 1814

11. Ibid., 21/122/72, 28 September 1814

12. Ibid., 21/122/70, 18 September 1814

13. Holland: *Recollections*, 122n.

14. Clerici: *Queen*, 53–4

15. Keppel: *Sovereign Lady*, 206–7

16. White: 'Lost Correspondence', 232–3

17. RA Geo. Box 8/6, 5 November 1814

18. RA Add. 21/122/81, 9 October 1814

19. RA Geo. Box 8/12, n.d., Lord Hertford

20. RA Add. 21/122/83, 3 November 1814

21. RA Geo. Box 8/6, 5 November 1814

22. White: 'Lost Correspondence', 233

23. RA Geo. Box 8/6, Extract, 12 November 1814

24. Ibid., 5 November 1814

25. Ibid.

26. White: 'Lost Correspondence', 237

27. Holland: *Recollections*, 127

28. White: 'Lost Correspondence', 233–4

29. Wellington: *Supplementary Despatches*, xii, 137

30. RA Geo. Box 8/6, Vienna, 25 October 1814

31. RA Geo. Box 8/6, 29 January 1815

32. RA Add. 21/122/22, 30 November 1814

33. Hansard, 2nd series, ii, 1112–14

34. RA Add. 21/122/98, 15 July 1815

35. RA Geo. Box 8/6, 1 March 1815

36. Holland: *Recollections*, 131

37. RA Add. 21/122/27, 26 December 1814

38. Spalletti: *Comtesse Rasponi*, 193

39. Davies: *Eleven Years*, 27

40. RA Geo. Box 13/47, 7 August 1820

41. RA Add. 21/122/26, 13 December 1814; ibid., 21/122/92, 21 December 1814

42. White: 'Lost Correspondence', 236–8

43. Ibid., 238–9

44. Adolphus: Trial, 251

45. White: 'Lost Correspondence', 239–40

46. RA Geo. Box 8/6, 4 February 1815

47. RA Add. 21/122/34, 22 January 1815

48. Ibid., 21/122/96, 4 February 1815
49. Ibid., 21/122/75, 6 October 1814
50. RA Geo. Box 8/6, 10 February 1815
51. Weil: *Murat*, ii, 339; RA Geo. Box 8/6, 2 March 1815 (back page of 1 March 1815)
52. Ibid., 1 March 1815
53. RA Add. 21/122/96, 4 February 1815
54. Ibid., 21/122/37, 30 December 1814
55. Ibid., 21/122/131, 30 December 1814
56. Ibid., 21/122/98, 15 July 1815
57. RA Geo. Box 8/6, Vienna, 8 April 1815
58. Holland: *Recollections*, 133
59. White: 'Lost Correspondence', 233
60. RA Geo. Box 10/28, Brief for the Queen (1820), f. 32
61. Ibid., ff. 30–31
62. Ibid., f. 33
63. RA Add. 37/92 [1815]
64. Ibid., 21/102/3 [1815]
65. Ibid., 21/122/96, 4 February 1815
66. Bury: *Diary*, i, 300; Clerici: *Queen*, 77
67. Nicoullaud: *de Boigne*, ii, 39–40
68. Lewis: *Berry Extracts*, iii, 47
69. RA Add. 21/102/7, 21 September 1815
70. Ibid., 21/122/51, 31 May 1815
71. Bury: *Diary*, ii, 136
72. RA Add. 37/92 [1815]
73. RA Geo. Box 23/34, n.d. [1820], begins 'Je vous envoye le plan'
74. RA Add. 21/102/9, 22 June 1815
75. Ibid., 21/102/9, 20 October 1815
76. Ibid., 21/122/99, 18 March 1815
77. Ibid., 21/122/148, 29 July 1815
78. ASC, Como, Notarile carteggio 4988 [18 July 1815]
79. RA Geo. Box 8/7, 26 January 1816
80. Hughes: *Burney Letters*, viii, 422
81. Byron: *Poetical Works*, 206
82. RA Add. 21/102/6, 30 July 1815
83. Bury: *Diary*, ii, 137
84. RA Geo. Box 8/6, 15 December 1815; ibid., 8 December 1815
85. RA Add. 21/102/9, 20 October 1815

86. Clerici: *Queen*, 83

87. RA Add. 21/102/9, 20 October 1815

88. Ibid., 21/122/55, 1 December 1815

89. Asp/K, ii, 349

90. RA Add. 21/102/10, 28 November 1815

91. Ibid., 21/102/6, 30 July 1815

92. RA Geo. Box 8/6, 3 November 1815

93. RA Add. 21/102/10, 28 November 1815

94. Cleveland: *Lady Hester Stanhope*, 195–6

95. RA Geo. Box 8/6, Exmouth–Pechell correspondence, December 1815

96. Ibid., n.d. [November 1815]

97. Ibid., Box 8/7, 3 January 1816

98. Ibid., Box 8/6, 25 June 1815; ibid., Box 8/7, 26 January 1816

99. Clerici: *Queen*, 72

100. RA Geo. Box 8/8, 9 December 1818

101. RA Add. 21/102/10, 28 November 1815

102. RA Geo. Box 8/7, 18 December 1815

103. Ibid.

104. RA Geo. Box 12/39, 28 August 1820

105. Ibid.

106. Asp/K, ii, 350

107. RA Add. 21/102/11, 21 April 1815

108. Ibid.; Demont: *Journal*, 74

109. Crisp: *Female Captive*, i, 43; ii, 36

110. RA Geo. Box 8/9, 9 April 1819

111. Ibid., Box 23/36, chronology; Demont: *Journal*, 35–8

112. Asp/K, ii, 350

113. RA Geo. Box 8/9, 9 April 1819

114. Ibid., Box 12/39, 28 August 1820

115. Ibid.

116. Ibid., Box 23/36, chronology; Demont: *Journal*, 62

117. RA Geo. Box 8/7, 12 December 1816

118. RA Add. 21/102/13, 20 November 1816

119. Asp/K, ii, 350

120. RA Geo. Box 10/28, Brief for the Queen (1820), ff. 13–14

121. Ibid., Box 11/32c, 9 December 1816

122. Asp/K, ii, 351

123. ASC, Como, 17 September 1816

124. Ibid., 5 November 1816

125. RA Geo. Box 23/8, 22 September 1819; ibid., 13 October 1820
126. Broughton: *Recollections*, ii, 46, 81
127. RA Geo. Box 8/19, 18 August 1817
128. RA Add. 21/102/14, 8 January 1817
129. RA Geo. Box 8/7, 25 January 1817
130. RA Add. 21/102/11, 21 April 1816
131. Ibid., 21/102/23, 29 October 1817; ibid., 21/102/18, [1817]
132. RA Add. 21/102/16, 25 May 1817
133. RA Geo. Box 9/3, 18 April 1818, f. 3
134. George: *Catalogue*, ix, pl. 12889
135. RA Add. 21/102/16, 25 May 1817

Chapter Thirteen
THE MILAN COMMISSION, 1817–1819

1. *Guida d'Italia: Roma e Dintorni*, 704
2. RA Add. 21/122/98, 15 July 1815
3. ASC, Como, Notarile carteggio 4988 [1819]
4. Martufi: *Diletto e Maraviglia*, 59–78
5. Borgese: *Perticari*, 114
6. RA Add. 21/102/23, 4 December 1817
7. Borgese: *Perticari*, 113
8. Asp/K, ii, 351
9. Holme: *Prinny's Daughter*, 237
10. Bury: *Diary*, ii, 272, 154
11. Borgese: *Perticari*, 114–15
12. Hibbert: *George IV, Regent and King*, 98
13. Ibid., 100
14. RA Add. 21/102/23, 29 October 1815
15. Richardson: *Disastrous Marriage*, 109–10
16. Asp/K, ii, 282
17. RA Add. 21/102/24d, 25 November 1817
18. Asp/K, ii, 222 n. 2
19. RA Geo. Box 8/7, 13 December 1817
20. RA Add. 21/102/24c, 20 November 1817
21. Brougham: *Life and Times*, ii, 332
22. Coutts & Co. Archives, 4544/5 Box 41, 20 January 1818

23. RA Add. 21/102/24e, 4 December 1817
24. Bury: *Diary*, ii, 145
25. Borgese: *Perticari*, 135
26. RA Geo. Box 10/30, 19 November 1817
27. Ibid., Box 23/11, n.d., Pesaro agent, 'The person whose name is hereunto subscribed . . .'
28. Ibid., Box 8/8, 6 December 1818
29. RA Add. 21/102/24f, 11 December 1817
30. Ibid., 21/179/159, 1 January 1818
31. RA Geo. Box 23/52, 31 January 1821; Asp/K, ii, 222
32. RA Geo. Box 8/5, 31 March 1813; ibid., Box 8/7, August 1816
33. Ibid., Box 9/3, 23 March 1818
34. Asp/K, ii, 252, n.1; RA Geo. Box 23/54, 15 November 1818
35. Ibid., Box 23/40, loose page; ibid., 5 August 1818 entry
36. Ibid., 6 August 1818 entry; ibid., 5 August 1818 entry; ibid., 6 August 1818 entry
37. Ibid., Box 23/54, 15 November 1818
38. Ibid., Box 8/8, 8 August 1818
39. Ibid., Box 23/40, 7 August 1818 entry; ibid., 8 August 1818 entry
40. Clerici: *Queen*, 113n. and 114–15
41. RA Add. 21/102/23, 29 October 1817
42. Marchand: *Byron Letters*, vii, 180
43. RA Geo. Box 23/11, n.d., Pesaro agent, 'The person whose name is hereunto subscribed . . .'; Clerici: *Queen*, 130
44. RA Geo. Box 8/8, 19 October 1818
45. Ibid., 30 September 1818
46. Ibid., 28 October 1818
47. Ibid., Box 23/14, *Fede Criminale* for Pietro Cuchi, 25 September 1820
48. Ibid., Box 23/55, 18 October 1818
49. Ibid., Box 23/5, 26 October 1818
50. Ibid., Box 23/5, 26 October 1818–February 1819
51. Ibid., Box 13/57, 25 September 1819
52. Ibid., Box 13/57, *passim*
53. RA 21/102/26, 24 December 1818
54. RA Geo. Box 23/8, 22 January 1819
55. Ibid., Box 8/9, 11 November 1819
56. Ibid., Box 23/69, 18 December 1820
57. Ibid., 16 December 1818
58. Ibid., Box 23/65, 4 December 1818

59. Ibid., Box 13/57, 13 December 1818
60. Ibid., Box 13/53, Printed depositions, pp. 146–8, 132–4
61. Ibid., Box 23/54, 22 December 1818; ibid., 14 February 1819
62. Ibid., Box 13/57, 31 December 1818
63. Ibid., Box 23/54, 1 March 1819
64. Ibid., 27 January 1819
65. Ibid., Box 23/8, 24 January 1818; ibid., Box 10/8, 22 February 1819
66. Ibid., Box 23/44; ibid., Box 13/60, portfolio
67. Ibid., Box 23/36, 'Malheureusement je n'ai jamais connu . . .'
68. Ibid., Box 8/9, 26 March 1819
69. Ibid., Box 8/8, 29 March 1819
70. Asp/K, ii, 272–3
71. Ibid., 275
72. Ibid., 277
73. Ibid., 278–81
74. Ibid., 281
75. Ibid., 357–8

Chapter Fourteen
## PLANS FOR DIVORCE, 1819–1820

1. Smith: *Grey*, 228
2. New: *Brougham*, 229
3. Yonge: *Liverpool*, iii, 15–16
4. BL Add. Mss 38190, f. 31, 16 June 1819
5. Yonge: *Liverpool*, iii, 17–19; RA Geo. Box 8/8, 17 and 22 June 1819
6. Brougham: *Life and Times*, ii, 354
7. RA Geo. Box 9/1, 13 July 1819
8. BL Add. Mss 38368, ff. 306–11, 24 July 1819
9. Brougham Mss 43188, 29 July 1819
10. BL Add. Mss 38277, ff. 202–3; Brougham Mss 14260, 14 August 1819
11. Bamford: *Life of a Radical*, ii, 150–51, 141–2
12. Phipps: *Plumer Ward*, ii, 16–17
13. Stapleton: *Canning*, 265–6
14. RA Geo. Box 8/8, 12 August [1819]
15. RA Add. 21/122/153, 13 August 1819
16. Ibid. 21/122/142, n.d. [1819]

17. RA Geo. Box 8/8, 13 October 1819
18. ASC, Pesaro, Inventorio di Villa Vittoria, 1821
19. RA Geo. Box 8/9, 17 September 1819; Clerici: *Queen*, 130–31
20. Clerici: *Queen*, 132
21. RA Geo. Box 23/57, 18 September 1819; ibid., Box 8/9, 17 July 1819
22. ASC, Pesaro, Inventorio di Villa Vittoria, 1821
23. RA Add. 21/102/32, 28 March 1819
24. Ibid., 21/102/30, 12 August 1819
25. RA Geo. Box 8/9, 31 August 1819
26. Ibid., 4 September 1819; AS, Milan, Presidio di Governo, 1819
27. RA Geo. Box 8/8, 13 October 1819; Clerici: *Queen*, 132–9
28. Clerici: *Queen*, 138–9
29. Ibid., 139–40
30. Hansard, 1st series, xli, 38
31. Ibid., 260
32. Ibid., 177; Pellew: *Sidmouth*, iii, 249; Asp/K, ii, 782
33. RA Geo. Box 8/8, 10 October 1819; ibid., Box 8/9, 30 September 1819
34. Clerici: *Queen*, 144
35. Ibid., 145
36. Asp/K, ii, 297
37. RA Geo. Box 8/8, 21 October 1819; ibid., 10 November 1819
38. Jennings: *Croker Papers*, i, 150; RA Geo. Box 8/8, 20 October 1819; ibid., 12 November 1819
39. RA Add. 21/102/34, 18 December 1819
40. Hansard, 1st series, xli, 1
41. RA Add. 21/102/34, 18 December 1819
42. RA Geo. Box 8/9, 1 December 1819
43. Ibid., Box 8/8, 23 December 1819
44. Ibid., Box 8/9, 6 January 1820; Hyett of Painswick Papers, Gloucestershire Record Office
45. RA Geo. Box 8/8, 16 August 1819; ibid., Box 23/34, August 1819–August 1821
46. Ibid., Box 23/55, 13 September 1820
47. Ibid., Box 8/6, 17 January 1820; ibid., 22 January 1820
48. 25 Edw. III, c./2; Coke, 3 *Inst.* 9
49. RA Geo. Box 8/10, 10 February 1820; ibid., 14 February 1820
50. RA Add. 21/122/157, 19 December 1819
51. Ibid., 21/148, 1 February 1820, copy of letter in the Palais de Monaco Archives

Chapter Fifteen
QUEEN, February–June 1820

1. RA Add. 21/102/36, 3 March 1820
2. Maxwell: *Creevey Papers*, i, 298
3. RA Geo. Box 8/10, 20 February 1820
4. LEF Journals, 23 February 1820
5. Ibid., 24 February 1820; RA Geo. Box 8/10, 23 February 1820; ibid., 26 February 1820
6. Ibid., Box 8/9, 25 March 1820; ibid., Box 8/10, 24 February 1820
7. Ibid., 6 March 1820; LEF Journals, 24 February 1820; ibid., 29 February 1820
8. RA Add. 21/102/36, 3 March 1820
9. RA Geo. Box 13/64, Visitors' Book, 1820
10. RA Add. 21/102/35, 29 March 1820
11. LEF Journals, 5 March 1820
12. RA Add. 21/102/36, 3 March 1820
13. Melville: *Injured Queen*, ii, 411–12
14. Ibid., 410–11
15. LEF Journals, 12 April 1820
16. Yonge: *Liverpool*, iii, 52
17. RA Add. 21/102/35, 29 March 1820
18. Londonderry: *Castlereagh Correspondence*, xii, 211
19. Maxwell: *Creevey Papers*, i, 296–9
20. Ibid., 297
21. Aspinall: *Henry Hobhouse*, 3
22. Jennings: *Croker Papers*, i, 159
23. Ibid.
24. Stapleton: *Canning*, 266–74
25. Jennings: *Croker Papers*, i, 160
26. Londonderry: *Castlereagh Correspondence*, xii, 213
27. Jennings: *Croker Papers*, i, 160
28. Bamford and Wellington: *Mrs Arbuthnot*, i, 2–3
29. Londonderry: *Castlereagh Correspondence*, xii, 220, 259; Yonge: *Liverpool*, iii, 54; RA Geo. 8/10, 10 February 1820; ibid., 14 February 1820
30. *Othello*, III, iii, 323
31. Hansard, 1st series, xli, 1623ff.

32. Stavordale: *Further Memoirs*, 277
33. Quennell: *Lieven Letters*, 47
34. Londonderry: *Castlereagh Correspondence*, xii, 220
35. Aspinall: *Arbuthnot*, 19
36. Twiss: *Eldon*, ii, 363
37. Ibid., BL Add. Mss 38565, f. 86; Asp/K, ii, 318–19
38. Yonge: *Liverpool*, iii, 56–8
39. Asp/K, ii, 320–21
40. BL Add. Mss 38193, f. 114
41. Asp/K, ii, 321
42. Maxwell: *Creevey Papers*, ii, 23
43. Londonderry: *Castlereagh Correspondence*, xii, 259
44. BL Add. Mss. 30123, ff. 163–6, 24 May 1820
45. RA Add. 21/102/37, 13 April 1820
46. Yonge: *Liverpool*, iii, 52
47. RA 21/102/37, 13 April 1820
48. Melville: *Injured Queen*, ii, 415
49. Ibid., 415–16
50. Atlay: *Victorian Chancellors*, ii, 336–7
51. Melville: *Injured Queen*, ii, 416–17
52. RA Geo. Box 8/8, 29 May 1820; Asp/K, ii, 339
53. Twiss: *Eldon*, ii, 366
54. Asp/K, ii, 329; Twiss: *Eldon*, ii, 365–6
55. Asp/K, ii, 338
56. Yonge: *Liverpool*, iii, 64
57. Ibid., 65–7
58. Asp/K, ii, 339
59. Barron: *Memoirs of Caroline*, 17
60. Ibid.
61. Yonge: *Liverpool*, iii, 65
62. BL Add. Mss 38285, f. 172
63. Yonge, *Liverpool*, iii, 65
64. Ibid., 66
65. Ibid., 67
66. Ibid., 72
67. Asp/K, ii, 340
68. Brougham: *Life and Times*, ii, 357–9
69. Asp/K, ii, 341, 343
70. Asp/K, ii, 343; Brougham: *Life and Times*, ii, 359–61

71. Ibid., 361
72. Asp/K, ii, 340–41
73. BL Add. Mss 38285, f. 172
74. Brougham: *Life and Times*, ii, 362–3
75. Ibid., 365–6
76. *The Times*, 7 June 1820
77. Barron: *Memoirs of Caroline*, 36–7
78. Walker: *Regency Portraits*, i, 101
79. Barron: *Memoirs of Caroline*, 37
80. Ibid., 46
81. Jennings: *Croker Papers*, i, 170
82. Hansard, 2nd series, i, 867
83. Ibid., 866
84. RA Geo. Box 23/40, 5 June 1820 entry; ibid , 6 June 1820 entry
85. Barron: *Memoirs of Caroline*, 48–51
86. Strachey and Fulford: *Greville Memoirs*, i, 94–5; Barron: *Memoirs of Caroline*, 51
87. RA Box 23/40, 6 June 1820 entry; Hansard, 2nd series, i, 870ff.
88. George: *Catalogue*, x, pl. 13735
89. Hansard, 2nd series, i, 872–80
90. Arnould: *Denman*, i, 144; Maxwell: *Creevey Papers*, ii, 29
91. Aspinall: *Brougham and the Whig Party*, 111
92. Ibid., 111 n. 3, quoting Lambton Mss
93. Aspinall: *Croker Papers*, i, 172–3
94. Hansard, 2nd series, i, 880–1
95. Arnould: *Denman*, i, 144–6
96. Walker: *Regency Portraits*, i, 101
97. Arnould: *Denman*, i, 146–7

Chapter Sixteen

THE SECRET COMMITTEE, June–August 1820

1. Pellew: *Sidmouth*, iii, 327–8
2. Jennings: *Croker Papers*, i, 174
3. Wilberforce: *Life*, v, 55
4. Hemlow: *Burney Letters*, xi, 161
5. Castle: *Jerningham Letters*, i, 168–9

6. RA Geo. Box 23/40, notes for June 1820
7. Twiss: *Eldon*, ii, 373
8. RA Geo. Box 23/34, 9 June 1820
9. Coutts & Co. Archives, 3143 Box 43, 7 June 1820
10. Ibid.
11. Hansard, 2nd series, i, 886–902
12. Ibid., 905
13. Ibid., 908
14. Ibid., 932–40
15. Ibid., 928
16. Ibid., 932–40
17. RA Geo. Box 23/53, 11 June 1820
18. Hansard, 2nd series, i, 962
19. Wilberforce: *Life*, v, 55
20. Aspinall: *Henry Hobhouse*, 27
21. *The Times*, 10 June 1820, BL Place Collection, Set 18; Nightingale: *Memoirs of Caroline*, i, 628
22. Strachey and Fulford: *Greville Memoirs*, i, 96; *The Times*, 10 June 1820, BL Place Collection, Set 18; Nightingale: *Memoirs of Caroline*, i, 630
23. Pellew: *Sidmouth*, iii, 327–8
24. Ibid.
25. Arnould: *Denman*, i, 148
26. Pellew: *Sidmouth*, iii, 330–31
27. Twiss: *Eldon*, ii, 373–4
28. Hansard, 2nd series, i, 1008–9
29. Twiss: *Eldon*, ii, 372
30. Brougham: *Life and Times*, ii, 371
31. Ibid., 370
32. Ibid., 371–2
33. Asp/K, ii, 345
34. Wilberforce: *Life*, v, 56–7
35. Bamford and Wellington: *Mrs Arbuthnot*, i, 22–3; Strachey and Fulford: *Greville Memoirs*, i, 97
36. Hansard, 2nd series, i, 1034, 1039
37. Smith: *Grey*, 229
38. Melville: *Injured Queen*, ii, 43–9
39. Aspinall: *Politics and the Press*, 29–31
40. BL Place Collection, Set 18; Hone: *For the Cause*, 308–9
41. Arnould: *Denman*, i, 153–4

42. Strachey and Fulford: *Greville Memoirs*, i, 100
43. Hansard, 2nd series, iii, 57
44. Wellington: *Despatches*, i, 127; Aspinall: *Henry Hobhouse*, 26; Pellew: *Sidmouth*, iii, 331
45. Wellington: *Despatches*, i, 127–9
46. Phipps: *Plumer Ward*, ii, 57
47. Aspinall: *Henry Hobhouse*, 27–8
48. Hansard, 2nd series, i, 1098, 1104
49. Ibid., 1185
50. Wilberforce: *Life*, v, 57–60
51. Hansard, 2nd series, i, 1202–13, 1228
52. Wilberforce: *Life*, v, 60, 65
53. Hansard, 2nd series, i, 1270–71
54. Arnould: *Denman*, i, 155
55. Wilberforce: *Life*, v, 61
56. Strachey and Fulford: *Greville Memoirs*, i, 99; Wilberforce: *Life*, v, 61
57. Arnould: *Denman*, i, 156
58. Wilberforce: *Life*, v, 61
59. Arnould: *Denman*, i, 157
60. Stapleton: *Canning*, 290–2
61. Bamford and Wellington: *Mrs Arbuthnot*, i, 26
62. Melville: *Injured Queen*, ii, 454–6
63. RA Geo. Box 23/40, notes for June 1820; *Othello*, IV, ii, 130
64. RA Geo. Box 23/40, notes for June 1820
65. Ibid.
66. Ibid.
67. RA Geo. Box 23/40, 1 July 1820 entry; ibid., 2 July 1820 entry
68. Cookson: *Liverpool's Administration*, 245–8
69. Smith: *Queen on Trial*, 78–9
70. Hansard, 2nd series, ii, 167–8
71. Alison: *Castlereagh*, iii, 122–3
72. Hansard, 2nd series, ii, 212–13
73. Ibid., 307
74. RA Geo. Box 13/59, bundle 35, 4 August 1820
75. Ibid., Box 23/56, 6 July 1820; ibid., Box 23/55, 7 July 1820
76. Ibid., Box 23/57, 10 July 1820
77. *Republican*, 7 July 1820, BL Place Collection, Set 18
78. RA Geo. Box 23/57, 18 July 1820
79. Brougham: *Life and Times*, ii, 385–6

80. RA Add. 21/179/161, 6 November 1820
81. George: *Catalogue*, x, pl. 13790–808
82. Dolby: *Memoirs*, 149–50
83. Hansard, 2nd series, v, 118
84. White: *Shelley*, ii, 224–6
85. George: *Catalogue*, x, pl. 13787
86. RA Geo. Box 10/2, List of addresses
87. Addams: *Lushington*, 146
88. Aspinall: *Politics and the Press*, 132n.
89. Quennell: *Lieven Letters*, 68
90. Knight: *Working Life*, i, 258–9
91. Jennings: *Croker Papers*, i, 176–7
92. Ilchester: *Journal of Henry Fox*, 38
93. Prothero: *Artisans and Politics*, 139
94. Draper: *Hammersmith*, 42–3
95. Asp/K, ii, 354–5
96. RA Geo. Box 12/41; ibid., Box 12/42
97. Arnould: *Denman*, i, 162–3
98. Stavordale: *Further Memoirs*, 179
99. Swinnerton: *Northcote*, 89
100. Arnould: *Denman*, i, 149
101. Berkeley: *Recollections*, iv, 162
102. Collection of Andrew Edmunds
103. Trevelyan: *Grey*, 193
104. Queen's Letter to the King, 4, 16
105. Crook and Port: *King's Works*, 520; Soane Museum Drawings, 51/3/60, 25 July 1820
106. RA Geo. Box 9/5, 14 August 1820; ibid., 31 July 1820
107. *Morning Chronicle*, 13 August 1820, BL Place Collection, Set 18
108. George: *Catalogue*, x, pl. 13824
109. Ibid., pl. 13868
110. Strachey and Fulford: *Greville Memoirs*, i, 99
111. Quennell: *Lieven Letters*, 62

Chapter Seventeen
TRIAL, August–November 1820

1. HLRO, LGC, II, 215–18
2. Hansard, 2nd series, iii, 57

3. *The Times*, 18 August 1820
4. Twiss: *Eldon*, ii, 383
5. Maxwell: *Creevey Papers*, i, 307; Smith: *Queen on Trial*, 81
6. BM 1912–3–7–6; Walker: *Regency Portraits*, i, 608–9
7. Hayter: *Descriptive Catalogue*; Walker: *Regency Portraits*, i, 608
8. National Portrait Gallery Registry, reg. pkt 1695 (a–x); Walker: *Regency Portraits*, i, 620–24, 609
9. Wellington: *Wellington and Friends*, 8–9; Maxwell: *Creevey Papers*, i, 310–11
10. *The Times*, 18 August 1820
11. Soane Museum, Soane Notebook, entry 14 August 1820; Maxwell: *Creevey Papers*, i, 306
12. HLRO, LGC, II, 221
13. Ibid., 220
14. Maxwell: *Creevey Papers*, i, 307–8
15. Ibid., 307; Walker: *Regency Portraits*, i, 99
16. Maxwell: *Creevey Papers*, i, 309
17. Ibid., 308
18. Ibid., 309
19. Bamford: *Radical Life*, ii, 29
20. Hansard, 2nd series, ii, 644–5
21. Ibid., 643
22. Ibid., 742–54, 783
23. Ibid., 804; Smith: *Queen on Trial*, 79–80
24. Leveson Gower: *Countess Granville Letters*, i, 161; RA Geo. Box 9/5, 9 August 1820
25. Arnould: *Denman*, i, 165
26. Ibid.
27. RA Geo. Box 13/83, n.d.
28. Strachey and Fulford: *Greville Memoirs*, i, 105
29. Airlie: *Lady Palmerston*, i, 63
30. Hansard, 2nd series, ii, 845–69, 842
31. Ibid., 869
32. Ibid., 895, 905, 920, 931
33. George: *Catalogue*, x, pls. 13808, 13844, 13865
34. Hansard, 2nd series, ii, 910–13
35. Ibid., 934–7; Hyett of Painswick Papers, Gloucestershire Record Office
36. Hansard, 2nd series, ii, 948–53
37. Ibid., 969–72, 1079

38. Ibid., 1167, 1205, 1213
39. Ibid., 1087, 1093, 1100, 1105, 1106, 1239
40. Ibid., 1274–5, 1311–15
41. Ibid., 1331–8
42. Ibid., 1320–30
43. RA Geo. Box 23/57, 9 September 1820, 3 o'clock
44. Aspinall: *Arbuthnot*, 20
45. Cobbett, *History of the Regency*, ii, para. 425
46. Hibbert: *Regent and King*, 161
47. Jennings: *Croker Papers*, i, 177
48. RA Geo. Box 14/61, 5 September 1820
49. Ibid., Box 23/57, 10 July 1820
50. Ibid., Box 11/32c, 29 September 1820
51. Ibid., Box 13/59, bundle 35, 16 October 1820
52. Ibid., Box 23/57, 9 August 1820
53. Ibid., 9 September 1820
54. Ibid., 27 September 1820
55. Ibid., Box 13/81 [September 1820]; Arnould: *Denman*, i, 165–6
56. RA Geo. Box 13/83, Secret Intelligence, passim
57. Ibid., Box 10/2, List of addresses
58. Prothero: *Artisans and Politics*, 140
59. BL Add. Mss. 56541, diary entry 2 October 1820
60. George: *Catalogue*, x, pl. 13903
61. Walker: *Regency Portraits*, i, 99
62. George: *Catalogue*, x, pl. 13895
63. Hawes: *Brougham*, 155
64. Hansard, 2nd series, iii, 112–14
65. Ibid., 114–18
66. Ibid., 119–25
67. Ibid., 125–9
68. Ibid., 130–37, 143–4, 156, 161–2, 166
69. Ibid., 204–5, 209
70. Ibid., 210
71. Smith: *Queen on Trial*, 114, quoting Cobbett Papers, Nuffield College, Oxford
72. Hansard, 2nd series, iii, 212–13
73. RA Geo. Box 23/57, 8 October 1820
74. Hansard, 2nd series, iii, 303–47
75. Ibid., 406, 412

76. Ibid., 363ff., 382ff., 436ff., 446–63
77. Ibid., 522–3
78. RA Geo. Box 23/57, 14 October 1820, 'The newspapers do not give . . .'
79. Hansard, 2nd series, iii, 641–2; Milton, *Paradise Lost*, ii, 666
80. Hawes: *Brougham*, 158
81. Hansard, 2nd series, iii, 607–9, 613
82. Strachey and Fulford: *Greville Memoirs*, i, 109; Hansard, 2nd series, iii, 716ff.
83. Ibid., 975ff., 982ff., 984; RA Geo. Box 23/34, 23 October 1820
84. Ibid., 666
85. Ibid., 990ff.
86. Ibid., 1063, 1087
87. Bamford and Wellington: *Mrs Arbuthnot*, i, 44
88. RA Geo. Box 11/32c, 24 October 1820
89. Hansard, 2nd series, iii, 1184
90. Ibid., 1184
91. Ibid., 1746
92. Ziegler: *Addington*, 390; Arnould: *Denman*, i, 179

Chapter Eighteen
SUDDEN DEATH, November 1820–August 1821

1. George: *Catalogue*, x, p. xxiv; ibid., pl. 14004
2. Maxwell: *Creevey Papers*, i, 341
3. Barham: *Hook*, i, 199
4. RA Geo. Box 23/55, 9 November 1820
5. George: *Catalogue*, x, pl. 13976
6. RA Geo. Box 8/16, Denham report, 16 November 1820
7. Browning: *Leeds Memoranda*, 229
8. Asp/K, ii, 377
9. Ibid., 378
10. Ibid., 380
11. Ibid.
12. Ibid., 386–9
13. Ibid., 377
14. RA Geo. Box 12/45, Queen's Household expenses, June 1820–6 October 1821

15. Bamford and Wellington: *Mrs Arbuthnot*, i, 54; Asp/K, ii, 397
16. *The Times*, 30 November 1820
17. Quennell: *Lieven Letters*, 96
18. Asp/K, ii, 400
19. Maxwell: *Creevey Papers*, i, 341
20. BL Add. Mss 38288, f. 221, 30 November 1820
21. Aspinall: *Politics and the Press*, 29; Barham: *Hook*, i, 203–5
22. George: *Catalogue*, x, pl. 14206
23. Ibid., pl. 14175
24. Ibid., pl. 14196
25. Asp/K, ii, 417
26. RA Geo. Box 23/57, 20 January 1821
27. Asp/K, ii, 406
28. RA Geo. Box 11/32e, 11 November 1821
29. RA Add. 5/10, 3 March 1821
30. Ibid., 5/13, March 1821
31. RA Geo. Box 13/83, 14 March 1821
32. Ibid., 18 March 1821; Asp/K, ii, 423–14
33. RA Geo. Box 13/83, 19 March 1821; Asp/K, ii, 423–4
34. RA Geo. Box 8/13, 29 April 1821; ibid., also 29 April 1821
35. Ibid., 1 May 1821; ibid., 4 May 1821
36. RA Geo. Box 8/13, 5 May 1821
37. Ibid., 5 May 1821
38. Berkeley: *Recollections*, iv, 167
39. Stavordale: *Further Memoirs*, 295
40. RA Geo. Box 8/13, 29 May 1821
41. Ibid., Box 8/15, 12 June 1821, Queen Caroline to Lushington; ibid., Queen's Remonstrance [June 1821]
42. Brougham: *Life and Times*, ii, 420
43. RA Add. 5/1, 15 July 1821; ibid., 5/2, 20 July 1821
44. RA Geo. Box 8/13, 16 July 1821
45. Ibid., also 16 June 1821
46. Richardson: *Disastrous Marriage*, 207–8
47. Fox: *London*, 43
48. Berkeley: *Recollections*, iv, 175
49. Lockhart: *Scott*, vi, 317
50. Arnould: *Denman*, i, 187
51. Maxwell: *Creevey Papers*, ii, 24
52. Hamilton: *Secret History*, ii, 11; Holland: *Recollections*, 146

53. Hamilton: *Secret History*, ii, 11
54. Ibid., 12
55. Arnould: *Denman*, i, 187
56. Ibid., 188
57. Maxwell: *Creevey Papers*, ii, 21
58. Brougham: *Life and Times*, ii, 423
59. RA Geo. 8/14, August [1821], 'From the time . . .'
60. Hamilton: *Secret History*, ii, 13–14, 16
61. Arnould: *Denman*, i, 188; Brougham: *Life and Times*, ii, 424
62. Arnould: *Denman*, i, 192
63. Hamilton: *Secret History*, ii, 17
64. Maxwell: *Creevey Papers*, ii, 21
65. RA Geo. Box 8/14, 11 August 1821, 'Opinion of the cause . . .'
66. Ibid.
67. Letter to author from Professor J. A. H. Wass, Department of Endocrinology, St Bartholomew's Hospital, 28 March 1989
68. Macalpine and Hunter: *George III*, 247–50
69. Letter to author from Professor Wass, 28 March 1989
70. Jennings: *Croker Papers*, i, 200–201

## Chapter Nineteen
### LAID TO REST, August–September 1821

1. Byron: *Poetical Works*, 107
2. Asp/K, ii, 454
3. Langdale: *Mrs Fitzherbert*, 136–8
4. Asp/K, ii, 453–4; Maxwell: *Creevey Papers*, ii, 22
5. Wellington: *Wellington and Friends*, 15
6. Asp/K, ii, 453–4; RA Geo. Box 8/14, codicil, 5 August 1821; ibid., Memorandum, 13 August 1821
7. Ibid., Order of Procession [August 1821]
8. Asp/K, ii, 454–5
9. Ibid., 455
10. RA Geo. Box 8/14, Extract, letter from Colchester [August 1821]
11. Maxwell: *Creevey Papers*, ii, 25; Brougham: *Life and Times*, ii, 428; RA Add. 21/26, Transcript of Mrs Thomas Wilde's Diary
12. Maxwell: *Creevey Papers*, ii, 26

13. Hibbert: *Prince of Wales*, 217
14. RA Geo. Box 13/71, correspondence of 1845–1846; Austin family papers
15. RA Geo. Box 122/57, 30 March 1839; RA 35964-5
16. Borgese: *Perticari*, 143; *Guidaverdi: Guida a Pesaro*, 41
17. RA Add. 21/26, Transcript of Mrs Thomas Wilde's Diary
18. Beerbohm: *Works*, 80

# SOURCES

## MANUSCRIPT

BRITISH

Royal Archives, Windsor Castle
  The papers of George III and George IV
  The private papers of George IV relating to Caroline, Princess of Wales
    and Queen (Geo. Box 8)
  Papers including those of the Milan Commission laid before Parliament
    in 1820 (Geo. Box 9)
  Papers of William Vizard, solicitor, relating to the defence of Queen
    Caroline (Geo. Boxes 10, 11, 12, 13)
  Papers of John Allan Powell, solicitor, relating to the Parliamentary
    proceedings against Queen Caroline (Geo. Box 23)
  The papers of Miss Ann Hayman (Add. 37)
  Copies of the papers of Miss Frances Garth (Add. 21/8)
  Copies of the papers of Anne, Marchioness of Townshend (Add. 21/90)
  Copies of the letters of Queen Caroline to Sir William Gell (Add. 21/
    102, originals deposited in the Derbyshire Record Office)
  Copies of Queen Caroline's Letter-book (Add. 21/122)
  Copies of John, first Lord Eldon's papers (Add. 21/179, originals in the
    possession of Lt-Col Harold E. Scott)
Royal Library, Windsor Castle
British Library, Add. Mss and Place Newspaper Collection
Coutts & Co. Archives
Elizabeth, Duchess of Devonshire Diaries (private collection)
Gloucestershire Record Office, Hyett of Painswick Papers
House of Lords Records Office, Lord Great Chamberlain's Records

National Library of Scotland, Minto Mss
National Portrait Gallery Registry
Scottish Records Office, Hamilton Mss
Soane Museum, Sir John Soane Archives
University College, London, Brougham Mss
Westminster Abbey Muniments
William Austin Papers (private collection)

FOREIGN

House of Brunswick – Wolfenbüttel Papers, Niedersachsisches Staatsarchiv,
    Wolfenbüttel
Archivio di Stato, Milan
Archivio Storico di Commune, Como
Archivio Storico di Commune, Pesaro


PRINTED

*Place of publication is London, unless otherwise stated.*


Acton, Harold, *The Bourbons of Naples, 1734–1825* (1956)
Addams, S. W., *Law, Politics and the Church of England: The Career of Stephen
    Lushington, 1782–1873* (Cambridge, 1992)
Adeane, Jane, ed., *The Early Married Life of Maria Josepha, Lady Stanley of
    Alderley, with extracts from Sir John Stanley's 'Praeterita'* (1899)
Adeane, Jane, ed., *The Girlhood of Maria Josepha Holroyd* [Lady Stanley of
    Alderley] (1897)
Adolphus, J.H., *The Trial of her Majesty, Queen Caroline* (1820)
Airlie, Mabell, Countess of, *Lady Palmerston and Her Times*, 2 vols (1922)
Albemarle, George, Earl of, *Fifty Years of My Life*, 2 vols (1876)
Alison, Sir Archibald, *Lives of Lord Castlereagh and Sir Charles Stewart, the
    2nd and 3rd Marquesses of Londonderry*, 3 vols (Edinburgh, 1861)
Duke of Argyll, ed., *Intimate Society Letters of the Eighteenth Century*, 2 vols
    (1910)
Arnould, Sir Joseph, *Memoir of Thomas First Lord Denman*, 2 vols (1873)
Ashe, Thomas, *The Spirit of the Book; or Memoirs of Caroline Princess of
    Hapsburgh: A Political and Amatory Romance*, 3 vols (1811)
Aspinall, Arthur, *Lord Brougham and the Whig Party* (Manchester, 1927)

Aspinall, Arthur, *Politics and the Press c. 1780–1850* (1949)

Aspinall, Arthur, ed., *The Correspondence of Charles Arbuthnot*, Camden Society Publications, 3rd series, lxv (1941)

Aspinall, Arthur, ed., *The Correspondence of George, Prince of Wales, 1770–1812*, 8 vols (1963–71)

Aspinall, Arthur, ed., *The Diary of Henry Hobhouse, 1820–1827* (1947)

Aspinall, Arthur, ed., *The Later Correspondence of George III*, 5 vols (Cambridge, 1962–70)

Aspinall, Arthur, ed., *The Letters of King George IV, 1812–1830*, 3 vols (Cambridge, 1938)

Aspinall, Arthur, ed., *The Letters of the Princess Charlotte, 1811–1817* (1949)

Atlay, James Beresford, *The Victorian Chancellors*, 2 vols (1906, 1908)

Bamford, Francis, and Duke of Wellington, eds, *The Journal of Mrs Arbuthnot, 1820–1832*, 2 vols (1950)

Bamford, Samuel, *Passages in the Life of a Radical*, 2 vols (1841, 1843)

Barham, Rev. R. H. Dalton, *Life and Remains of Theodore Hook*, 2 vols (1849)

Baron, Abbé, 'A la cour de Brunswick', *La Revue de Paris*, no. 22, 15 November 1906

Barron, Edward, *Memoirs of her Present Majesty, Queen Caroline* (1820)

Beerbohm, Max, *The Works of Max Beerbohm* (1896)

Berkeley, G. C. Grantley, *My Life and Recollections*, 4 vols (1865–6)

Earl of Bessborough, ed., *Georgiana: Extracts from the Correspondence of Georgiana, Duchess of Devonshire* (1955)

Earl of Bessborough, ed., in collaboration with Arthur Aspinall, *Lady Bessborough and Her Family Circle* (1940)

Bickley, Francis, ed., *The Diaries of Sylvester Douglas, Lord Glenbervie*, 2 vols (1928)

Biro, S. S., *The German Policy of Revolutionary France*, 2 vols (1957)

Bladon, F. McKno, ed., *The Diaries of Colonel the Hon. Robert Fulke Greville* (1930)

Borgese, Maria, *Costanza Perticari nei tempi di Vincenzo Monti* (Florence, 1941)

Brougham, Henry, *Contributions to the Edinburgh Review*, 3 vols (1856)

Brougham, Henry, *The Life and Times of Henry Lord Brougham written by himself*, 3 vols (1871)

Broughton, Lord (John Cam Hobhouse), *Recollections of a Long Life*, ed. Lady Dorchester, 2 vols (1909, 1910)

Browning, Oscar, ed., *The Political Memoranda of Francis, fifth Duke of Leeds*, Camden Society Publications, new series, xxxiv (1884)

Buchez, P. J. B., and Roux, P. C., *Histoire parlementaire de la Révolution française*, 40 vols (Paris, 1834–48)

Buckingham and Chandos, Duke of, *Memoirs of the Court of England during the Regency, 1811–1820*, 2 vols (1856)

Buckingham and Chandos, Duke of, *Memoirs of the Court of George IV, 1820–1830*, 2 vols (1859)

Buckingham and Chandos, Duke of, *Memoirs of the Courts and Cabinets of George III*, 4 vols (1853–5)

Bunbury, Sir Henry Edward, *Narratives of some Passages in the Great War with France from 1799 to 1810* (1854)

Bury, Lady Charlotte, *The Court of England under George IV Founded on a Diary*, 2 vols (1896)

Byron, Lord, *Poetical Works of Lord Byron* (Oxford, 1933)

Castle, Egerton, ed., *The Jerningham Letters, 1780–1843, Being excerpts from the correspondence and diaries of . . . Lady Jerningham and of her daughter Lady Bedingfield*, 2 vols (1896)

Cinelli, Carlo, *Carolina di Brunswick* (Pesaro, 1890)

Clarke, M., and Penny, N., eds, *The Arrogant Connoisseur: Richard Payne Knight, 1751–1824* (Manchester, 1982)

Clerici, Graziano Paolo, *A Queen of Indiscretions: The Tragedy of Caroline of Brunswick, Queen of England*, trans. Frederick Chapman (1907)

Cleveland, Primrose, Duchess of, *The Life and Letters of Lady Hester Stanhope* (1914)

Cobbett, William, *History of the Regency and Reign of King George IV*, 2 vols (1834)

Colchester, Charles, Lord, ed., *The Diary and Correspondence of Charles Abbot, Lord Colchester, Speaker of the House of Commons, 1802–1817*, 3 vols (1861)

Cole, G. D. H., *The Life of William Cobbett* (1924)

Cookson, J. E., *Lord Liverpool's Administration, 1815–1822* (Edinburgh, 1975)

Crisp, Mrs, *The Female Captive: a narrative of facts which happened in Barbary in the year 1756, written by herself*, 2 vols (1769)

Crook, J. Mordaunt, and Port, M. H., *The History of the King's Works, 1782–1851* (1973), vi of *The History of the King's Works*, ed. H. M. Colvin, 6 vols (1963–76)

Davies, Catherine, *Eleven Years' Residence in the Family of Murat, King of Naples* (1841) de Bellaigue, Sir Geoffrey, *Carlton House: The Past Glories of George IV's Palace* (1991)

Demont, Louise, *Journal of the Visit of her Majesty the Queen to Tunis, Greece and Palestine*, trans. Edgar Garston (1821)

Derry, Warren, ed., *The Journals and Letters of Fanny Burney (Madame d'Arblay)*, ix, x (Oxford, 1982)

Dolby, Thomas, *Memoirs of T. D. . . . late printer and publisher, written by himself* (1827)

Douglas, David, *Familiar Letters of Sir Walter Scott*, 2 vols (1894)

Draper, Warwick, *Hammersmith: A Study in Town History* (1913, reprinted 1989)

Droysen, Hans, 'Aus den Briefen der Herzogin Charlotte von Braunschweig, 1732–1801', in *Quellen und Forschungen zur Braunschweig*, Geschichte VIII, band 1 (Wolfenbüttel, 1916), 1–219

Duntzer, Heinrich, *Life of Goethe*, trans. T. W. Lyster, 2 vols (1883)

Ehrman, John, *The Younger Pitt: The Reluctant Transition* (1983)

Fairburn, J., *An Inquiry, or Delicate Investigation, into the Conduct of Her Royal Highness the Princess of Wales* (4th edn, 1820)

Fitzgerald, Percy, *The Life of George the Fourth*, 2 vols (1881)

Fitzmaurice, Lord Edmond, *Charles William Ferdinand, Duke of Brunswick* (1901)

Fox, Celina, ed., *London: World City, 1800–1840* (1992)

Frederick the Great, *Mémoires de Frédéric II, Roi de Prusse*, ed. M. M. E. Boutaric and E. Campardon, 2 vols (Paris, 1866)

Fulford, Roger, *The Trial of Queen Caroline* (1967)

G. E. C. [George Edward Cockayne], *The Complete Peerage of . . . the United Kingdom*, reprinted in 6 vols (Gloucester, 1987)

George, M. Dorothy, ed., *Catalogue of Personal and Political Satires, British Museum*, v–xi (1935–54)

Gore-Browne, Robert, *Chancellor Thurlow: The Life and Times of an XVIIIth Century Lawyer* (1953)

Granville, Castalia, Countess, ed., *Lord Granville Leveson Gower: Private Correspondence, 1781 to 1821*, 2 vols (1916)

Gray, Denis, *Spencer Perceval: The Evangelical Prime Minister, 1762–1812* (Manchester, 1963)

Green, Thomas, *Memoirs of her late Royal Highness Charlotte Augusta of Wales* (1818)

Greenwood, Alice, *Lives of the Hanoverian Queens*, 2 vols (1910, 1911)

Greig, James, ed., *The Farington Diary, by Joseph Farington, RA*, 8 vols (1922–8)

*Guida d'Italia del Touring Club Italiano, Roma e Dintorni* (Milan, 1977)

*Guideverdi: Guida a Pesaro*, ed. Glauco Martufi and Umberto Spadoni (Rimini, 1987)

Hamilton, Lady Anne, *Secret History of the Court of England, from the accession of George III to the death of George IV*, 2 vols (1832)

*Hansard's Parliamentary Debates*, 1st series, 41 vols, 1803–20 (1812–20); 2nd series, 25 vols, 1820–30 (1820–30)

Hansard, T. C., *The Parliamentary History of England from the earliest period to the year 1803*, 36 vols, 1066–1803 (1806–20)

Harcourt, L. V., ed., *The Diaries and Correspondence of the Rt. Hon. George Rose*, 2 vols (1860)

Hawes, Frances, *Henry Brougham* (1957)

Hayter, George, *A Descriptive Catalogue of the Great Historical Picture . . . representing the trial of her Majesty Queen Caroline of England* (1823)

Hemlow, Joyce, with Althea Douglas and Patricia Hawkins, eds, *The Journals and Letters of Fanny Burney (Madame d'Arblay)*, xi (Oxford, 1984)

Hibbert, Christopher, *George IV, Prince of Wales, 1762–1811* (Newton Abbot, 1973)

Hibbert, Christopher, *George IV, Regent and King, 1811–1830* (1973)

Holland, Sir Henry, *Recollections of Past Life* (1872)

Holland, Henry Edward, Lord, ed., *Henry Richard, Lord Holland: Memoirs of the Whig Party during my time*, 2 vols (1852–4)

Holme, Thea, *Caroline: A Biography of Caroline of Brunswick* (1979)

Holme, Thea, *Prinny's Daughter* (1976)

Hone, J. Ann, *For the Cause of Truth: Radicalism in London, 1796–1821* (Oxford, 1982)

Hughes, Peter, with Joyce Hemlow, Althea Douglas, and Patricia Hawkins, eds, *The Journals and Letters of Fanny Burney (Madame d'Arblay)*, viii (Oxford, 1980)

Huish, Robert, *Memoirs of . . . Caroline, Queen of Great Britain*, 2 vols (1821)

Hunt, J. H. Leigh, *The Old Court Suburb, or Memorials of Kensington*, ed. Austin Dobson, 2 vols (1902)

Hunt, Tamara L., 'Morality and Monarchy in the Queen Caroline Affair', *Albion*, xxiii/4 (1991), 697–722

Ilchester, Earl of, ed., *Journal of Henry Edward Fox, afterwards last and fourth Lord Holland, 1818–1830* (1923)

Jennings, Louis J., ed., *The Croker Papers: The Correspondence of the late Rt. Hon. John Wilson Croker*, 3 vols (1884)

Johnson, Paul, *The Birth of the Modern: World Society 1815–1830* (1992)

Keppel, Sonia, *The Sovereign Lady: A Life of Elizabeth Vassall, Third Lady Holland, With Her Family* (1974)

Knight, Charles, *Passages of a Working Life, during half a century*, 3 vols (1863–5)

Knight, Cornelia, *Autobiography of Miss Cornelia Knight*, 2 vols (1861)

Langdale, Charles, *Memoirs of Mrs Fitzherbert* (1856)

Laqueur, Thomas W., 'The Queen Caroline Affair: Politics as Art in the Reign of George IV', *Journal of Modern History*, liv (1982), 417–66

Leslie, Shane, *Mrs Fitzherbert: A Life, Chiefly from Unpublished Sources* (1939)

Leslie, Shane, *The Letters of Mrs Fitzherbert and Connected Papers* (1940)

Leveson Gower, F., ed., *Letters of Harriet, Countess Granville, 1810–45*, 2 vols (1894)

Lewis, Michael, ed., *Memoirs of William Henry Dillon, 1780–1839*, Navy Records Society Publications, xciii (1953)

Lewis, Lady Theresa, ed., *Extracts of the Journals and Correspondence of Miss Berry from the year 1783 to 1852*, 3 vols (1865)

Lewis, W. S., ed., *The Yale Edition of Horace Walpole's Correspondence*, 34 vols (Oxford, 1937–65)

Lockhart, J. G., *Life of Sir Walter Scott*, 10 vols (Edinburgh, 1902–3)

Londonderry, Charles, 3rd Marquess of, *Memoirs and Correspondence of Viscount Castlereagh, 2nd Marquess of Londonderry*, 12 vols (1853)

Macalpine, Ida, and Hunter, Richard, *George III and the Mad-Business* (1991)

Malmesbury, 3rd Earl of, ed., *Diaries and Correspondence of James Harris, First Earl of Malmesbury*, 4 vols (1844)

Marchand, Leslie, *Byron: A Biography*, 3 vols (1957)

Marchand, Leslie, ed., *Byron's Letters and Journals*, 12 vols (1973–82)

Martufi, Roberta, *Diletto e Maraviglia: Le ville del colle San Bartolo di Pesaro* (Pesaro, 1991)

Massenbach, Christian Karl von, *Memoiren über meine Verhaltnisse zum preussischen Staat und insbesondere zum Herzoge von Braunschweig*, 2 vols (Amsterdam, 1809)

Maxwell, Sir Herbert, ed., *The Creevey Papers: A Selection from the Correspondence and Diaries of the Late Thomas Creevey, MP*, 2 vols (1903)

May, John and Jennifer, *Commemorative Pottery, 1780–1990: A Guide for Collectors* (1972)

Melville, Lewis, *The Injured Queen: Caroline of Brunswick*, 2 vols (1912)

Melville, Lewis, *The Life and Letters of William Cobbett*, 3 vols (1913)

Melville, Lewis, ed., *The Berry Papers: being the correspondence, hitherto unpublished, of Mary and Agnes Berry, 1763–1852* (1912)

Millar, Oliver, *The Later Georgian Pictures in the Collection of Her Majesty the Queen*, 2 vols (1968)

Minto, Countess of, ed., *Life and Letters of Sir Gilbert Elliot, 1st Earl of Minto*, 3 vols (1874)

Mirabeau, Honoré Gabriel Riquetti, Comte de, *The Secret History of the Court of Berlin*, 2 vols (1895)

Mitchell, Austin, *The Whigs in Opposition, 1815–1830* (Oxford, 1967)

Morrison, Alfred, *The Hamilton and Nelson Papers, collection of autograph letters*, 2nd series, 2 vols (1893–4)

Müller, F. Max, ed., *Memoirs of Baron Stockmar by his son, Baron Ernst von Stockmar*, trans. G. A. Müller, 2 vols (1872)

Mundy, Harriot Georgiana, ed., *The Journal of Mary Frampton, from the year 1779 until the year 1846* (1886)

Musgrave, Clifford, *Royal Pavilion: An Episode in the Romantic* (1959)

New, Chester W., *The Life of Henry Brougham to 1830* (Oxford, 1961)

Nicoullaud, Charles, ed., *Memoirs of the Comtesse de Boigne*, 3 vols (1907–8)

Nightingale, Joseph, *Memoirs of her late Majesty, Queen Caroline*, 3 vols (1821–2)

Oman, Carola, *The Gascoyne Heiress: The Life and Diaries of Frances Mary Gascoyne-Cecil, 1802–39* (1968)

Ompteda, L., ed., *Irrfahrten und Abenteuer eines mittelstaatlichen Diplomaten* (Leipzig, 1894)

Pellew, George, *The Life and Correspondence of the Rt. Hon. Henry Addington, First Viscount Sidmouth*, 3 vols (1847)

Phipps, Edmund, *Memoirs of the political and literary life of Robert Plumer Ward*, 2 vols (1850)

Prothero, I. J., *Artisans and Politics in Early Nineteenth-Century London: John Gast and His Times* (Folkestone, 1979)

*The Queen's Letter to the King, 7 August 1820* (1820)

Quennell, Peter, ed., *The Private Letters of Princess Lieven to Prince Metternich, 1820–1826* (1937)

Richardson, Joanna, *The Disastrous Marriage: A Study of George IV and Caroline of Brunswick* (1960)

Robinson, J. M., *Cardinal Consalvi, 1757–1824* (1987)

Romilly, Sir Samuel, *Memoirs of the Life of Sir Samuel Romilly, written by himself, edited by his sons*, 3 vols (1840)

Romilly, S. H., ed., *Letters to 'Ivy' from John William Ward, 1st Earl of Dudley* (1905)

Russell, Lord John, ed., *Memoirs, Journal and Correspondence of Thomas Moore*, 8 vols (1853–6)

Russell, Lord John, ed., *Memorials and Correspondence of Charles James Fox*, 2 vols (1853)

Schwarze, Walter, *Eleonore von Münster: Eine unbefannte Dichterin aus der Zeit Mosers* (Osnabrück, 1929)

Scott, Sir Walter, *The Poetical Works* (1877)

Sermoneta, Duchess of, *The Locks of Norbury* (1940)

Sichel, Walter, ed., *The Glenbervie Journals* (1910)

Smith, E. A., *Lord Grey, 1764–1845* (Oxford, 1990)

Smith, E. A., *A Queen on Trial: The Affair of Queen Caroline* (Stroud, 1993)

Somerset, Anne, *Ladies-in-Waiting: From the Tudors to the Present Day* (1984)

Spalletti, Gian Battista, ed., *Souvenirs d'enfance d'une fille de Joachim Murat, la Princesse Louise Murat, Comtesse Rasponi, 1805–1815* (Paris, 1929)

Stanhope, Earl, *Life of the Rt. Hon. William Pitt*, 3 vols (1861)

Stanhope, Lady Hester, *Memoirs of Lady Hester Stanhope, as related by herself in conversations with her physician*, 3 vols (1845)

Stapleton, Augustus Granville, *George Canning and His Times* (1859)

Stavordale, Lord, ed., *Henry Lord Holland: Further Memoirs of the Whig Party, 1807–1821, with some miscellaneous reminiscences* (1905)

Stevenson, John, 'The Queen Caroline Affair', in John Stevenson, ed., *London in the Age of Reform* (1977)

Stewart, Robert, *Henry Brougham: His Public Career, 1778–1868* (1985)

Strachey, Lytton, and Fulford, Roger, eds, *The Greville Memoirs, 1814–1860*, 8 vols (1938)

Stuart, D. M., *The Daughters of George III* (1939)

Swinnerton, Frank, *Conversations of James Northcote ... by William Hazlitt* (1949)

Tooke, John Horne, *A Letter to a Friend on the Marriage of His Royal Highness the Prince of Wales* (1787)

Trench, Richard Chenevix, ed., *Remains of the Late Mrs Richard Trench* (1862)

Trevelyan, G. M., *Lord Grey of the Reform Bill, being the Life of Charles, Second Earl Grey* (1920)

Twiss, Horace, *The Public and Private Life of Lord Chancellor Eldon*, 3 vols (1844)

Walker, Richard, *The Eighteenth and Early Nineteenth Century Miniatures in the Collection of Her Majesty the Queen* (Cambridge, 1992)

Walker, Richard, *Regency Portraits, National Portrait Gallery*, 2 vols (1985)

Webster, Sir Charles, *The Foreign Policy of Castlereagh, 1815–22*, 2 vols (1934)
    Weigall, Lady Rose, *A Brief Memoir of Princess Charlotte of Wales* (1874)
Weil, M.-H., *Joachim Murat, Roi de Naples: La dernière année de la règne (Mai 1814–Mai 1815)*, 5 vols (Paris, 1909–10)
Wellington, 2nd Duke of, ed., *Despatches, Correspondence, and Memoranda . . . of Arthur, Duke of Wellington* [1819–31], 8 vols (1867–80)
Wellington, 2nd Duke of, ed., *Supplementary Despatches, Correspondence, and Memoranda . . . of Arthur, Duke of Wellington* [1797–1819], 15 vols (1858–65)
Wellington, 7th Duke of, ed., *Wellington and His Friends: Letters of the First Duke of Wellington* (1965)
Wheatley, H. B., ed., *The historical and posthumous memoirs of Sir Nathaniel William Wraxall, 1772–1784*, 5 vols (1884)
White, Newman Ivey, *Shelley*, 2 vols (1947)
White, Terence de Vere, 'A Lost Correspondence: The Letters of Peter, Marquess of Sligo, to Lord Lowther', *Twentieth Century*, clxiii (1958)
Whitley, W. T., *Artists and Their Friends in England, 1700–99*, 2 vols (1928)
Wilberforce, Robert Isaac and Samuel, *The Life of William Wilberforce . . . with extracts from his diaries, correspondence*, 5 vols (1838)
Wilkins, W. H., *Mrs Fitzherbert and George IV*, 2 vols (1905)
Yonge, Charles Duke, *The Life and Administration of Robert Banks, 2nd Earl of Liverpool . . . Compiled from original documents*, 3 vols (1868)
Ziegler, Philip, *Addington: A Life of Henry Addington, First Viscount Sidmouth* (New York, 1965)

# INDEX

A NOTE ON THE TYPE

This book was set in Janson, a typeface long thought to have
been made by the Dutchman Anton Janson, who was a practic-
ing typefounder in Leipzig during the years 1668–1687. However, it has been conclusively demonstrated that these types are
actually the work of Nicholas Kis (1650–1702), a Hungarian,
who most probably learned his trade from the master Dutch
typefounder Dirk Voskens. The type is an excellent example of
the influential and sturdy Dutch types that prevailed in England
up to the time William Caslon (1692–1766) developed his own
incomparable designs from them.

Composed in Great Britain
Printed and bound by Haddon Craftsmen,
Scranton, Pennsylvania.